RUSSIAN fuTURISM: A HISTORY

Published and Forthcoming in the Russian History and Culture Series

Russian Futurism: A History
Vladimir Markov

Words in Revolution: Russian Futurist Manifestoes 1912-1928
Anna Lawton and Herbert Eagle, eds., trs
(Originally published by Cornell University Press as *Russian Futurism through Its Manifestoes 1912-1928*, this collection made available for the first time in English the writings of the Russian Futurists, which are discussed in Markov's *Russian Futurism: A History.*)

The Inner Adversary: Struggle Against Philistinism as the Moral Mission of the Russian Intelligentsia
Timo Vihavainen

Imaging Russia 2000: Film and Facts
Anna Lawton (CHOICE Outstanding Academic Title 2005)

Before the Fall: Soviet Cinema in The Gorbachev Years
Anna Lawton

Red Attack, White Resistance: Civil War in South Russia 1918
Peter Kenez

Red Advance, White Defeat: Civil War in South Russia 1919 - 1920
Peter Kenez

Published and Forthcoming in the Eastern and Central Europe Series
Series Editor: T. Mills Kelly

Slavic Thinkers or the Creation of Polities: Intellectual History and Political Thought in Central Europe and the Balkans
Josette Baers

Aspects of Balkan Culture: Social, Political, and Literary Perspectives
Jelena Milojković-Djurić

SCARITH Books (fiction), an imprint of New Academia Publishing

On the Way to Red Square
Julieta Almeida Rodrigues

RUSSIAN FUTURISM:
A HISTORY

BY VLADIMIR MARKOV

NEW ACADEMIA PUBLISHING | Washington, DC

New Academia Publishing, 2006
University of California Press, 1968

Designed by David Comstock

Printed in the United States of America

Library of Congress Control Number: 2006921872
ISBN 0-9777908-0-0 paperback (alk. paper)

New AcademiaPublishing, LLC
P.O. Box 27420, Washington, DC 20038-7420
www.newacademia.com - info@newacademia.com

TO YDIA

PREFACE

This is the first history of Russian futurism in any language, though I know of at least five persons—scholars, critics, futurist poets—who have undertaken similar projects at different times.[1] Two or three such histories may exist in state archives or in private desk drawers in Russia, but the possibility of their publication is still very remote, and will remain so for several years. Despite the fact that the poets and artists of the Russian avant-garde were more enthusiastic in welcoming the Communist Revolution and more willing to serve it and the young Soviet state than any other group, their aesthetics and most of their poetic practices have nearly always been officially rejected in

[1] In March, 1918, Aleksej Kručenyx gave a lecture entitled "Istorija russkogo futurizma" at the nightclub "Fantastičeskij kabačok" in Tiflis. He also wrote "Žizn' i smert' Lefa" in free verse (see his *Govorjaščee kino* [Moscow, 1928], pp. 51–62), which is actually the entire history of the "Hylaea" group in a nutshell. There is evidence that Kamenskij was writing a history of futurism, which remained among his unpublished MSS. The scholars V. Trenin, N. Xardžiev, and T. Gric planned a similar project, plus three monographs on individual futurists (see *Krasnaja Strela*, p. 3).

Russian Futurism was the pioneer of this avant-garde, and it still occupies a place of honor in the Soviet "rogues' gallery." This colorful, complex, and influential movement was systematically denigrated and belittled, considered "a harmful influence" or "a bourgeois error," and, since approximately 1930, thought unworthy of any serious consideration.

Such a situation led, of course, to predictable results, the worst being a distressing ignorance of what Russian futurism was, even among those wanting an accurate picture.[2] Specialists in Russian literature have, as a rule, a one-sided idea of what really happened, who belonged to the movement, what they wanted, and what they achieved. The very word "futurism" is often used incorrectly, as are other terms connected with it, such as *zaum*. In short, this book had to be written.

Paradoxically, this first history of Russian futurism is written in English, although so much of its poetry is not only untranslated, but untranslatable as well, and is still considered incomprehensible by many Russians. Hence, the dearth of poetry quotations in this book. Nevertheless, I wrote it not only for those who study Russian literature and those who know something about it, but also with an eye toward those who want to enlarge their picture of the European avant-garde, but lack fundamentals in the Russian area. It was a hard thing to do, because futurism is only a part of a larger and equally neglected literary and cultural context of contemporary Russia, and I could not write "a famous leader of Russian symbolists, who . . ." each time that I mention the name of, for instance, Valery Bryusov. So I hope

---

[2] An example from the preface to the recent edition of V. Kamenskij's prose (*Leto na Kamenke* [Perm', 1961], p. 12) will suffice. The author, S. Ginc, writes that the first *Sadok sudej* "began to overthrow literary traditions and began to announce futurist slogans," thus proving that he has never seen *Sadok sudej*. He further credits Kamenskij with organizing the cubo-futurist group, which published *Sadok sudej*, not knowing that both issues of *Sadok sudej* had appeared before the term "cubo-futurism" was in existence. Ginc also calls the first edition of Kamenskij's novel *Stepan* (not *Sten'ka*, as it really is) *Razin*.

The general knowledge of the history of modern literature fares no better in the Soviet Union nowadays. On the pages of *Voprosy Literatury*, I have come across statements that Zinaida Gippius was an Acmeist and that the imagists were a prerevolutionary group.

that anyone who has difficulties with the Who's Who of modern Russia will read a few pages from the standard English-language works on Russian literature by Mirsky or Slonim, or will resort to the well-known dictionary by Harkins.

This book is both ambitious and limited in its aims. I had the unique opportunity to acquaint myself with more than 90 percent of everything (in the originals, or in microfilm or xerox copies) that the Russian futurists published, and with very much of what was written about them. (The titles of unobtainable works are followed by an asterisk in the text.) I wanted to include every significant fact and made it a point to discuss, even if briefly, every book or important article by a futurist, or by a contemporary, on the subject of futurism. Even imitations by cranks are not neglected, because they belong to this history no less than do masterpieces. I wanted to describe Russian futurism as exhaustively as possible, so that later both my colleagues and I could begin to speak about what this movement really means. Herein lies the limitation: I have tried to avoid analyses, definitions, and general judgments. This account is more or less a chronological accumulation of facts, mostly dealing with books, so my approach resembles taking books from a shelf, one after another, and trying to tell what they are about. I feel (and here I might be wrong) that such a stringing together of facts is preferable to focusing on and discussing, one at a time, important aspects of Russian futurism. People and groups are presented in the process of their invisible growth and/or development, so that the reader who has finally waded through feels that he is enveloped by, and has lived through, the whole movement, rather than that he has picked up a few anecdotes and catchy definitions after a perfunctory leafing through a book.[3] Another reason for such an excess of description is the fact that most of the books described will remain unavailable or difficult to obtain for a long time.

Because this approach could easily result in a chronological annotated bibliography, I have not refrained from critical judgments on individual achievements and have not hesitated to present occasional portraits of futurist poets. In short, I have tried to balance bibliography

---

[3] An example of the opposite method is the book on futurism by Ja. E. Šapirštejn-Lers (*Obščestvennyj smysl russkogo literaturnogo futurizma* [Moscow, 1922], which approaches the movement in an a priori way with fantastic and sometimes ridiculous results.

with criticism and biography. This procedure does not contradict the method of taking book after book from a shelf, and it may add subjective unity to a narrative that tends toward amorphousness and repetition, a narrative that cuts poets into pieces and spreads them throughout the book.

On the whole, this history does not go beyond the Revolution of 1917, for the reason (a valid one, I hope) that futurism does have a beginning, and an end of sorts, in such a framework. Besides, after the Revolution the Russian avant-garde becomes more dispersed (though not less rich), with a few veterans continuing to consider themselves futurists, and the rest ostensibly fighting futurism though at the same time shamelessly borrowing from it.

I am only too painfully aware of other kinds of incompleteness. I did not use archival, unpublished materials, nor did I use all contemporary newspapers and magazines. Still, a point in my favor is that perhaps 85 percent of the material presented in this volume is unknown to the majority of students of Russian literature. It could be their first acquaintance with, to name only a few items, Centrifuge, the Mezzanine of Poetry, the history of ego-futurism, "41°," or the poetry of Livshits, Bobrov, and the prerevolutionary Shershenevich.

Even as a description, this study is only the first step; a discussion of postrevolutionary developments should be the second step. Simultaneously the role of Russian futurism in the larger context of Russian—and European—modernism should be clarified. It goes without saying that a comprehensive anthology of Russian futurist poetry, prose, and literary theory should be compiled. I intend to accomplish at least a part of this task. Only after all these studies have been written can one start meditating about the nature and meaning of Russian futurism.

A few more points should be made. Beginning with chapter 5, and particularly in chapter 7, the reader says good-bye to the major futurist poets one by one, as they fade out of the movement or as the movement itself reaches a full stop. This is done in the form of individual survey-like interpolated essays which conclude with "epilogues" describing the poets' postrevolutionary work. There is a conscious imbalance in assigning such epilogues. Poets whose development after 1917 has been sufficiently studied (Mayakovsky, Khlebnikov, Aseyev) get comparatively brief epilogues; those who received less attention get a more detailed discussion. Khlebnikov probably suffers most of all (despite the fact that I consider him the greatest futurist poet of Russia and perhaps one of only two or three of the greatest avant-garde poets of the world), but I have described in detail his major narrative poems in my *The Longer Poems of Velimir Khlebnikov* (in English), which also contains his biography and a short survey of the rest of his work.

I have attempted to translate nearly all neologistic titles into newly coined, though not necessarily palatable, English. Clumsy or obscure English in quotations often reflects the original, and to make futurist writings sound uniformly readable in English would be a distortion. All titles are cited in the original Russian the first time (with a translation or explanation following in parentheses); thereafter, they are usually cited in translation. Long titles are often shortened when repeated (e.g., *A Slap* instead of *A Slap in the Face of Public Taste*).

The spelling of Russian names and titles in this volume is based on a schizophrenic principle: in the text, they are presented in an established form (e.g., Mayakovsky), or in such a way that they can be pronounced with reasonable accuracy. In the notes and the bibliography, on the other hand, I have employed the accepted scholarly transliteration. The index uses both methods. My reasons for this duality are twofold:

1. The book will probably be read by those who are interested in the subject, and not exclusively by Slavists. It would annoy non-Slavists to have to study a table of conversion of Cyrillic letters, and then to accept names like "Majakovskij." An American friend once complained to me that he has known the wonderful writer, Chekhov, all his life, only to learn finally, to his dismay, that the writer is "Sexov" (Čexov, of course). What especially irritates some readers is to see *j* when they expect *y*, which, in an English book, tempts them to pronounce the letter as in "John," tables or no tables. I must confess that the prospect of seeing, in the text of this book, names like "Xlebnikov" (instead of "Khlebnikov") dismays me, no matter how aware I am of the traps and pitfalls of not using the scholarly transliteration.

2. Notes (which contain quotations in Russian) and bibliography require the utmost precision. Nonspecialists seldom read either.

V. M.

INTRODUCTION to the 2006 edition

Ronald Vroon

It is difficult for us in the first decade of the twenty-first century to appreciate the impact Vladimir Markov's Russian Futurism: a History produced when it appeared in 1968. I discovered the book as a twenty-year-old undergraduate who had just taken up Russian studies at the University of Michigan. It would have been a serendipitous find in the present decade, dominated as it is by borders, barns and nobles, but the 1960s were a more auspicious time, when such exotica frequently found their way onto the shelves of unchained bookstores. A score of these encircled the university campus. The volume happened to be stocked by Centicore Books, a magnet for young poets and intellectuals on South University Avenue. Though it was obviously an academic work, what immediately caught my eye were the typographical oddities of the title page and chapter headings, along with the rich illustrations—a thick, thirty-two page signature in dead center with black-and-white pictures of poets, paintings, and pages from Futurist publications—printed on what looked like butcher-block paper. Only after reading through the book did I come to appreciate how its design paid tribute to the avant-garde productions it described. But even without such knowledge, who could help but be intrigued by such curiosities as the Crematorium of Common Sense or Vasilii Kamenskii's ferroconcrete "Constantinopole"? The book, priced at twelve dollars, was well beyond the means of an impecunious undergraduate, but it nonetheless found its way on to my shelves. It inspired me not only to continue my pursuit of Russian studies, but to focus on Futurism as my first field of research. I suspect that the book had a forceful impact on the intellectual lives of many other young scholars as well.

The significance of Markov's study stands out in high relief against the background of the oversimplified and politically correct treatments of Futurism that had dominated up to that time. As early as 1925 the Marxist critic Vasilii L'vov-Rogachevskii, writing in the first Soviet literary ency-clopedia (1925), managed to reduce the complex phenomenon of Russian Futurism to two competing movements, Ego-futurism and Cubo-futurism (represented respectively, by the "chocolaty" Severianin and the "rowdy" Maiakovskii). While admitting that it had "played a positive role in Russia by foregrounding the dynamics and rhythms of the contemporary world in the course of emphasizing it characteristic urbanistic traits," he concluded that "the excesses of the transrationalists, which are evidence of the disintegration of the personality and the disintegration of the word as a means of commu-nication, will be rejected by a literature closely bound up with the collective." L'vov-Rogachevskii's prediction was enforced, not merely reinforced, by the Soviet Academy of Science's ten-volume *History of Russian Literature* (1941-1956), which put Symbolism, Acmeism, and Futurism in one basket labeled "The Poetry of Bourgeois Decadence." It accused Futurism of attempting not only to discredit the finest traditions of Russian culture, but of adopting an anti-populist position and a nihilist attitude toward language. As a con-sequence, concludes the Academy history with a citation from Communist Party Central Committee Secretary Andrei Zhdanov, "this and other such fashionable movements have sunk into oblivion together with those classes whose ideology they reflected." Twenty years later Futurism and its fellow "bourgeois" movements were fished out of Lethe by the *Short Literary Ency-clopedia*, which finally acknowledged that there were many futurisms, some of which (Cubo-futurism in particular) might be redeemable by virtue of their "anti-bourgeois cast." For the first time Markov's *History* was mentioned as a primary reference, and a short parenthetical note ("Includes bibliography") hinted that this was a fundamental study.

Access to it was another matter. Andrei Krusanov, one of the principal inheritors of Markov's mantel, notes in his review of the Russian translation of the *History* (St. Petersburg, 2000) that "for 1968 the work was, without question, an event, especially in the USSR, where Futurism was mentioned at the time only in connection with Maiakovskii's early work. Markov's study exploded the whole scrupulously edited and varnished history of literature. Not surprisingly, the American edition of the book was immediately secreted away in special library repositories, where it remained until the beginning of perestroika, accessible only to the most persistent specialists" (*Novaia russkaia kniga*, № 6, 2000). And even these specialists were long obligated by Soviet censorship to refrain from citing the work in scholarly publications, though it was patently obvious that it was a primary reference.

Initial reviews of Markov's *History* in the West are also revealing as an index both of the book's significance and the state of field that prevailed at the time, particularly with respect to our understanding of Russian modernism. Most reviewers take their principle cue from Markov's preface, in which he notes straightforwardly that the book is "the first history of Russian futurism in any language." This makes its publication "an event in the world of Slavic scholarship" (Xenia Gasiorowska writing in the *Slavic and East European Journal*, 14, № 1, Spring 1970) and a "most impressive achievement" (Christopher Barnes in *Soviet Studies*, 22, № 1, July 1970). Such praise is commonplace. More striking is the fact that reviews of the book uniformly assess the scope and historical accuracy of the contents based principally on what Markov himself has written. His book thus takes on, for its time, the same self-sufficiency (*samovitost'*) that is a hallmark of so many texts it surveys, for there are no serious antecedent texts with which one can compare the work.

The very pioneering status of his history led Markov to adopt a critical approach that actively avoided, in his own words, "analyses, definitions and general judgments." He chose instead to guide his readers through an extraordinary virtual library of rare books, broadsheets, articles, and newspaper clippings arranged chronologically around the principal characters and coteries of the Futurist movement. In so doing he was clearly following Pimen's exhortation in Pushkin's *Boris Godunov* as set forth in one of the book's epigrams: "Opisyvai, ne mudrstvuia lukavo."

This approach was itself something of a novelty in a decade when ideology deeply colored scholarship on both sides of the iron curtain, and those who resisted the politicization of discourse did so mostly behind the walls of New Criticism and structuralism. And Markov's methodology had its admirers. Christopher Barnes, in the aforementioned review, notes that "questions of literary excellence or importance or talent are for once happily ignored and the reader is treated to a thoroughgoing discussion not only of the main Futurist almanacs and works by individual Futurists but also of the movement's attendant critical literature and various contemporary Futurist hoaxes." But the approach had its critics as well. In his review (*Modern Philology*, 69, № 4, May 1972) Edward Wasiolek disparages Markov's offer to serve as a guide but not an interpreter, insisting that "the vantage point of more than half a century should permit us to analyze, define and judge, as well as to record" and concluding that Markov's study will prove enlightening only to one who is "very well-acquainted with the Futurist movement" and has "worked out for himself the shape and direction of the movement." Such a point of view was understandable coming from a Dostoevsky scholar who could build his critical edifices on a vast foundation of existing textual and critical data. The problem with Futurism was that the vantage point of even half a century would carry no benefit in the absence of a coherent body of information that could be targeted for analysis. The fact is that most of the empirical data concerning the movement was unknown to both Russian and Western readers prior to the publication of Markov's book, and for many years thereafter remained accessible only in the form of his detailed summaries and descriptions. Markov's refusal to be selective and pass over in silence those events, persons, or works he himself might have deemed "unessential" or lacking in merit, is less a tribute to his scholarly modesty than his perspicacity. No approach could have been more felicitous in encouraging further scholarship on Futurism, as the flood of works that followed amply demonstrates.

Yet one must not underestimate the extent to which Markov goes beyond both bibliography and biography. For one thing, Markov is "too discriminating a critic not to pass specific judgments," Helen Muchnic notes in her critique (*The Russian Review*, 28, № 3, July 1969) and these are interspersed at regular intervals throughout the book. Their acuity has been born out in subsequent studies. David and Nikolai Burliuk may have played a major organizational role in the movement, but few would question that their works are, as Markov notes, those of amateurs, "not strong enough to appear radical, and lacking completely in poetic maturity or vitality." By the same token few would question Markov's assertion that "Guro is probably the most neglected among the early Russian Futurists, a fate that is undeserved because she is one of the very original and talented Russian writers." Indeed, the only "error" here is the tense of the opening verb "to be": Guro is among those Futurists who have enjoyed a significant renaissance in the last two decades, due in large measure, one suspects, to the loving attention she receives in Markov's *History*.

But there are other ways in which the book reaches higher than the goals of compilation and criticism. The book abounds in scholarly discoveries: the complex stages of impressionism, primitivism, and "logism" that characterize the evolution of Cubo-futurism, the importance of Shershenevich in his pre-imagist guise, the complex aesthetics of Centrifuge, and many, many more. Equally important, Markov's work shaped our perceptions of the movement at a time when it was approachable only in terms of the fragmentary and highly subjective accounts of a few representatives (chiefly Alexei Kruchenykh, Vasilii Kamenskii, and Benedikt Livshits). To write a history compelled him to identify origins, pinpoint literary antecedents, single out the principle players, trace the evolution and devolution of groups and their interaction, define apogees and perigees for both individual groups and the movement as a whole, and at least tentatively define its chronological and geographic boundaries. Markov's most significant achievement is, ultimately, the compelling emplotment of an extraordinary mass of historical data, the transformation of disparate chronicles into a coherent history, and in so doing he has left his stamp on all subsequent scholarship.

Since the book's appearance in 1968 a very substantial body of literature has arisen either building on or buttressing the foundations laid by Markov work. Perhaps the single most important development has been the intensive study of Futurism as a movement that encompassed various art forms, including painting, music, cinema, and architecture, as well as poetry and prose. It is now clear that these various artistic manifestations of the avant-garde are so intimately interconnected that the study of one necessarily implicates the other—a phenomenon acknowledged but mostly ignored in Markov's study, which focuses almost exclusively on Futurism as a literary movement. One of the ironies of literary history is that substantial intermedial studies were among the first to be undertaken—by Nikolai Khardzhiev, Teodor Grits and Vladimir Trenin—years before Markov's, but could not be published for political reasons until the 1970s and later. Their work was taken up by numerous scholars, both Western (among them John Bowlt, Jean-Claude Marcadé and Charlotte Douglas) and Russian (Nina Gur'ianova, Irina Sakhno, Evgenii Koftun, Andrei Krusanov and many others). The contributions of Krusanov and Sakhno stand in particularly interesting contrast to Markov book. The former's three-volume *Russkii avangard: 1907-1932 (Istoricheskii obzor)*, a work still in progress (the first volume appeared in 1996 and the second, consisting of two book-length parts, in 2003), comes much closer to being the sort of journalistic history that Wasiolek denigrates, presenting a season by season chronology of the social life rather than the productions of the artistic and literary avant-garde, replete with accounts of exhibitions, public disputes, reviews and press notices. Sakhno's *Russkii avangard: Zhivopisnaia teoriia i poeticheskaia praktika*, in contrast, explores the multifarious ways in which painting and poetry interface in the avant-garde, moving thereby into that area of "analyses, definitions and general judgments" eschewed by Markov.

Special mention should be made of those studies that focus on the Futurist book itself. Markov frequently mentions the illustrations that adorn these collections as well as their graphic peculiarities, but the true significance of the artistic partnership between artists and writers is now evident thanks to the work of Susan Compton (*The World Backwards: Russian Futurist Books, 1912-1916*), Gerald Janecek (*The Look of Russian Literature: Avant-Garde Visual Experiments, 1900-1930*), Evgenii Kovtunov (*Russkaia futuristcheskaia kniga*), and Vladimir Poliakov (*Knigi russkogo kubo-futurizma*), among others.

A second significant development in the study of Futurism is an examination of its fate during and after the Revolution and Civil War. Although Markov touches on these years in his capsule epilogues to the lives of the major Futurists, the movement's evolution after 1917, he asserts, is "sufficiently peculiar to deserve another book, or perhaps a series of essays." Just how deserving is best exemplified by Krusanov's aforementioned study, which devotes an eight-hundred page volume to the brief period between 1917 and 1921 in the leading literary centers of Moscow and Petersburg. Here he follows thematically, though not methodologically, in the footsteps of such Western scholars as Bengt Jangfeldt (*Majakovskij and Futurism 1917-1921*), Gert Wilbert (*Entstehung und Entwicklung des Programms der "linken" Kunst und der "Linken Front der Künste" (LEF) 1917-1925*), and Halina Stephan (*"Lef" and the Left Front of the Arts*).

Numerous studies have also extended our knowledge of the geographical boundaries of Futurism. Markov touches only superficially on the movement's appearance and development in the provinces. Krusanov devotes six hundred pages to this topic, covering Ukraine, Belarus, the Russian Far East, the Caucasus, the Crimea, and the Urals as well as central, northern and southern Russia, covering only the period of the Revolution and Civil War. Oleh Ilnytzkyj's *Ukrainian Futurism: 1914-1930: A Historical and Critical Study* is a major contribution to our understanding of the avant-garde outside Petersburg and Moscow, as are the monographs on Russian Futurism in Georgia by Tat'iana Nikol'skaia, Rosemary Ziegler and Marzio Marzaduri.

Studies of individual Futurists have also proliferated. At the time Markov wrote his book only the chief figures—Maiakovskii, Pasternak, Khlebnikov—had been singled out for study in major monographs, and the author of one of them was Markov himself (*The Longer Poems of Velimir Xlebnikov*). Since then the number of works devoted to these giants of the movement has grown precipitously (Khlebnikov and Pasternak have been targeted with particular freqeuency), but other figures have also earned book-length studies, among them Igor' Severianin (Mikhail Shapovalov, Lenie Lauwers), Alexei Kruchenykh (Sergei Sukhoparov) Vasilisk Gnedov (Crispin Brooks), Vadim Shershenevich (Anna Lawton), Elena Guro (Kjeld Jensen, Anna Ljunggren,

Alla Povelikhina), and others. More and more primary texts by these and other writers have also appeared—by Nikolai Kul'bin, Lev Zak, Benedikt Livshits, Vasilii Kamenskii, Il'ia Zdanevich, Igor' Terent'ev, David and Nikolai Bur-liuk, Sergei Bobrov and Nikolai Aseev, to name only the most prominent, as well as many collections of documents associated with the various Futur-ist and neo-Futurist subgroups. Among the most important are collections of manifestoes, treatises and tracts that supplement Markov's path-breaking anthology, *Manifesty i programmy russkikh futuristov* (Munich, 1967), published only a year before his *History*. They include, first and foremost, Konstantin Kuz'minskii's two-volume *Zabytyi avangard—Rossiia, pervaia tret' XX stoletiia*, and also the first English anthology of the manifestos and other theoretical writings of the Futurists, Herbert Eagle and Anna Lawton's *Russian Futurism through its Manifestos* (1988), now reprinted as *Words in Revolution* (2005).

The explosion of new materials—and we have barely skimmed the sur-face here—raises the inevitable questions: has Markov's *History* been super-seded, and if so, what motivates its republication? Readers who are familiar with the literature on Futurism that has emerged over the past four decades have rightly pointed out various lacunae and errors in Markov's *History* (many of these are corrected in the Russian translation of the book, but regrettably many new errors are introduced, some of which are catalogued in Krusanov's review of the translation). Rather than rendering Markov's study obsolete, however, they have, in a sense, relegated it to the status of a textbook, a work students might begin with in order to get a broad picture of the movement in its formative years. Correctives and corrections can come later, in more spe-cialized studies. Indeed, one hopes that a new annotated Russian translation might one day appear that will undertake the requisite emendations, adjusting or filling in missing dates and footnoting what has become genuinely obso-lescent. But beyond its obvious utility as an introduction to the subject for both English- and Russian-speaking audiences, the book is a landmark in the intellectual history of critical discourse on the Russian avant-garde, and that alone justifies making it available to a new generation of scholars.

Ronald Vroon, 2006

Ronal Vroon is Professor of Slavic Languages and Literatures, University of Cali-fornia, Los Angeles.

ONTENTS

Opisyvai ne mudrstvuya lukavo.
[Give me the facts, ma'am.]
·—**Pushkin**

*uturism as a united, well-defined
movement did not exist in Russia
before the October Revolution.
—Mayakovsky*

would say that there was no point at which the
term **"futurism"** really characterized our movement.
—Livshits

1 IMPRESSIONISM

This book could perhaps begin like a traditional Russian novel in the manner of Turgenev or Goncharov: "On such and such an autumnal day of 1908, about ten in the morning, a tall blond youth in a university student's uniform timidly opened the door to the office of the managing editor of the short-lived Petersburg magazine *Vesna*, which printed anything written by anybody. The name of the youth was Victor Khlebnikov; that of the editor, Vasily Kamensky. Kamensky was a young man about twenty-four, dressed in . . ." This meeting *was* the first one to take place between the poets later associated with futurism. Moreover, it resulted in the first publication by Khlebnikov of a piece of writing which even then could have passed as a "futurist" work, had the word existed [1] (and had anyone paid attention to the work).

But to begin the book in this manner would

1

be arbitrary. The history of Russian futurism has more complex beginnings, though to pinpoint them would be impossible. It has several sources, and at least two of these sources must be mentioned briefly before the tangible history begins to unfold. One source is the formidable phenomenon of Russian symbolism (or "decadence"), a fascinating movement in Russian poetry which began in the 1890's and changed the literary climate of Russia beyond recognition. It dealt a mortal blow to the already disintegrating realism, turned Russia's face toward Europe, where new ideas had been rampant for some time, and made poets form-conscious again after decades of stagnation. Even more important was the fact that symbolism produced many important poets, such as Valery Bryusov, Constantine Balmont, Zinaida Hippius, Fyodor Sologub, Innokenty Annensky, Vyacheslav Ivanov, Alexander Blok, Andrei Biely, and Mikhail Kuzmin, whose names appear, time and again, on the pages of this book. It was a magnificent spectacle. A handful of erudite and difficult poets, writing for the few, made a complete reappraisal of aesthetic values. They became a dominant and victorious force in the country where the reading audience since the 1840's had been led by politically minded intellectuals, who used literature only as illustration for their verbose and monotonous, though no doubt well-intentioned, social criticism, and who often had little use for poetry.

Those who were to call themselves futurists could not withstand the impact of their symbolist "fathers";[2] individual futurists and whole futurist groups made their debuts as imitators of symbolism or as neo-symbolists (or neodecadents). Several of them were encouraged or even sponsored by senior symbolists.[3] But the literary situation was transformed by the sudden end of symbolism as a movement. Symbolism became entangled in the complexities of its own theory, spent itself in fratricidal struggles, gave birth to second-rate literature which caricatured symbolist ideals, and, most important, lost its feeling of the limits of art. All this brought about a crisis in 1909–10, after which symbolism ceased to exist as a literary school, with each of its participants going his own way.[4]

The other main source of Russian literary futurism was doubtless contemporary Russian avant-garde painting.[5] The ideas of French impressionism and postimpressionism, especially of cubism, engendered many and varied groups in Moscow and St. Petersburg, which made alliances and quarreled so often that to follow the twists and turns of their relations is the despair of a historian. Futurists took part in the painters' public discussions and polemics, made and broke alliances with them; some of the painters even tried to influence literature. "An artist of the word always has the ability to paint," [6] said Nikolai Kulbin, a leader of the Russian avant-garde in the second decade of the twentieth century. Futurists, early and late, present a good illustration of this statement. The reputation of two of them (David Burliuk and Léon Zack) is much better established in painting than in poetry. Many futurists were professional artists (Guro, Mayakovsky, Kruchenykh, Bobrov); practically all the others could and did paint or draw.[7] Some of the important terminology used by futurists in their literary polemics was borrowed from painting (*sdvig, faktura*), and futurists consistently and frequently tried to add the visual element to their poetry, using different typefaces, introducing offbeat illustrations, employing the author's handwriting. More important, however, were the attempts of some of them to apply the principles of painting to poetry (Khlebnikov,[8] Mayakovsky, Livshits). For one of them modern painting was "not only a new vision of the world in all its sensuous magnificence and staggering variety . . . , it was also a new philosophy of art, a heroic aesthetics, which shattered all established canons and opened . . . breathtaking perspectives." [9]

In addition to the symbolist origin of Russian futurism and its symbiosis with avant-garde painting, one could possibly point to a connection between western European poetry and Russian futurism,[10] or tie the latter to the past of Russian literature (which would have made some of the futurists squirm).[11] These are, however, relatively unimportant. The major element to be considered in this preliminary discussion is impressionism. Some futurist poets began their artistic careers as impressionist artists;[12] what is more important, many of them at first preferred to apply the term "impressionist" to literary production as well.

There is nothing particularly unclear about impressionism as a movement in art, but in literature it is still vague and has been little investigated. Basically, it is "as I see it at the given moment," but one can easily imagine two different and almost mutually exclusive roads leading from this simple starting point. One of them would be the desire to present a moment of external reality with the utmost objectivity—and this is exactly how it was in French painting, especially with that "classical" impressionist, Claude Monet ("Just an eye, but what an eye!" exclaimed Cézanne). There is, however, another road going in the opposite direction. If one stresses "I" rather than "see" in "as I see it," objectivity is in danger. It is this subjective emphasis that usually characterizes impressionism in literature. Of course, one can find in literary impressionism features that it shares with its namesake in art, such as vaguer outlines, broad strokes (notice that in a literary context these words become too metaphorical to be used successfully), the "accidental" in the foreground, and so on;[13] but it is only a similarity of secondary aspects. Other aspects, on the contrary, may not be similar at all. For instance, it is generally recognized that impressionism in literature concentrates on details, whether expressive of the whole or not, whereas in painting the stress is on the whole. Basically, impressionism in painting is an attempt to present nature in the open, to show the real color of light and shadow, to paint such things as the density of air. In literature (as far as Russia is concerned), more often than not, impressionism can be equated with lyrical realism, which may have carried in itself the seeds of destruction of the usual realistic method, as some critics suggest, and thus have been one of the predecessors of symbolism in Russia. The word "impressionism" began to be used in Russian literary criticism long before it became a fact in Russian art. Chekhov, Garshin, Fet, Fofanov, and Lokhvitskaya have been mentioned as Russian impressionists. It is not my aim to investigate what these poets and writers have in common (although one may suggest that at least one of the ancestors of lyric realism in Russia was Turgenev). What interests us is the fact that impressionism not only preceded Russian symbolism, but also accompanied it and became one of its facets, almost an ingredient. Thus V. Bryusov, in 1906, saw in Russian literature "symbolism, impressionism, and decadence," in that order, and he considered Constantine Balmont, another prominent symbolist poet, "as much an impressionist as Verlaine." [14] But impressionism was not always identified with the symbolist movement. Its central figure, Boris Zaitsev, definitely stood apart from symbolism in his continuation of the Turgenev tradition.

The early futurists did not side with Zaitsev.[15] They formed, however, a definitely impressionist group at first, in which the quiet Guro and the loud Kamensky fit the word better than anyone else, no matter how one interprets it. But the word has been applied to other futurists (Khlebnikov[16]), sometimes even with a derogatory meaning (Mayakovsky[17]). There was an actual struggle within futurism to get rid of impressionist elements; there was even a futurist periodical (the *Enchanted Wanderer;* see chap. 3) which can be described as impressionist in outlook.

Among the figures who stood close to futurism and the futurists in the Russian artistic world of the second decade of the twentieth century were the colorful theatrical director-playwright-theoretician-historian, Nikolai Evreinov (1879–1953), and Nikolai Kulbin. Both were leading men in neoimpressionist circles, and Kulbin deserves our special attention. Without ever belonging to a specific futurist group, Kulbin identified himself so closely with the avant-garde movement of his time that one contemporary later credited him with being a genuine futurist who gave expression to their program long before there was a futurist group.[18]

Dr. Nikolai Ivanovich Kulbin (1868–1917) was the least likely person to be found among the Bohemian modernists. A professor at the Military Academy, a physician for the General Staff, and a Right State Councillor (the civilian rank that corresponded to a major general in the military service), he was also an artist, a fanatical sponsor of avant-garde causes, organizer of many modernist art exhibitions (among them, "Impressionists," "Triangle," "Stephanos"), and an indefatigable propagandist of new ideals in art, mainly through his lectures. His own efforts in painting were rather eclectic and betrayed some influence of cubism, Gauguin, and Russian icons. Kulbin preached a "free art" and called himself an impressionist and "intuitivist," but he should rather be described as the avant-garde's eclectic individualist. His impressionism was probably the most subjective of all Russian varieties of this movement. His main tenet was: "Except its own feelings, the self does not know anything, and, while projecting these feelings, it creates its own world." [19] Vasily Kamensky recalls in his memoirs how Kulbin explained to the audience at an exhibition: "We are impressionists, we give our impressions on the canvas. . . . Everything is relative in the world; even the sun is seen by some as being golden, by others, gray, by still others, pink, and by some, colorless." [20] The famous formalist critic Victor Shklovsky later called him "the man who built his art on chance," [21] and another critic saw in Kulbin's idea "a kulbination" after which there is no way to go.[22] Kulbin was generally respected and even loved by those who surrounded him, perhaps because he considered everybody a genius. The futurists also appreciated Kulbin's ability to announce the highlights of their lectures on posters in so effective a way that a full house was guaranteed. In 1912 Kulbin was honored with a book,[23] which, in addition to some biographical data and a list of his paintings, with reproductions of some of them, contains appreciations of his art in three short essays by the painter Sergei Sudeikin, by Nikolai Evreinov, and by Sergei Gorodetsky, a poet who was then popular (and who also printed in the book a poem to Kulbin). Livshits, who also wrote a poem, an acrostic, to Kulbin, did not think very highly of him as a theoretician and called his aesthetics "a salad of Bergson, Ramsay, and Picasso." [24] The outsiders considered Kulbin "confused and strange," [25] and the poet George Ivanov, who, upon his entrance into literature, considered himself, briefly, a futurist, left in his fascinating, though unreliable, book of memoirs a caricature portrayal of Kulbin as a complete madman.[26]

It was in Kulbin's *Studiya impressionistov* ("The Studio of Impressionists") that some leading futurists made their first noticeable appearance. This book was published in St. Petersburg in February, 1910, about two months before *Sadok sudei* ("A Trap for Judges"), and so can be considered a kind of prologue to the history of Russian futurism. The volume opens with an article by the editor himself entitled "Svobodnoe iskusstvo kak osnova zhizni" ("Free Art as the Basis of Life"). In this essay Kulbin emphasizes the importance of dissonance, which for him is the manifestation of life, and finds examples of it in Sophocles, *The Igor Tale,* and *Hamlet.* He does not reject or deny harmony, even the absolute harmony, which is death. Death is life resting, not life absent, says Kulbin, and he concludes: "There is no No [*Neta net*]." Further, Kulbin speaks about the necessity of having a "theory of art" to help creative people and he even tries, rather confusingly, to draft such a theory, seeing the sources of art in nature and in the psychology of the artist (for whom art is revelation). Kulbin's essay, clear and rather coherent at first but becoming progressively more rambling and chaotic, turns at last to music and points out specific ways to achieve novelty in it: quarter-tone music, "colored" music, and the "abolishment of staves." The rest of the book consists mostly of amateurish poetry written by completely unknown men and women, chiefly in the symbolist tradition, sometimes displaying a certain naïve experimentalism (e.g., a poem that plays on the past tense forms). There are also essays with themes ranging from the Javanese puppet theater to painting in music, and a "monodrama" (described by the author as "the most perfect form of drama") by Nikolai Evreinov. Entitled "Predstavlenie lyubvi" ("The Performance of Love"), it was obviously intended as the *pièce de résistance*. Finally, there are five short poems signed with names that later became well known or famous in the history of Russian futurism. The two pieces by David Burliuk are incoherent and disappointingly symbolist in sound. Only one poem by David's brother Nikolai was included in the volume. It sounds as symbolist as the two by David, but displays at least some feeling for language, if not for style. Two poems by the then unknown Velimir Khlebnikov are the real highlight of the book. One of them, "Byli napolneny zvukom trushchoby" ("The Thickets Were Filled with Sounds"), shows a complete mastery of primitivist technique; the other, "Incantation by Laughter," has remained Khlebnikov's most famous poem even to this day, often obscuring many of his other more outstanding achievements. It is a poetic exploration of the possibilities of morphological derivations inherent in the Russian language, based on adding various prefixes and suffixes to the Russian root *smekh-* ("laugh"). The result can only be suggested in English as I try to do in the following translation, which does not aim at complete fidelity in rendering the meaning, but rather demonstrates the principle while trying to keep the metrical scheme of the original:

O you laughniks, laugh it out!
O you laughniks, laugh it forth!
You who laugh it up and down,
Laugh along so laughily,
  Laugh it off belaughingly!
Laughters of the laughing laughniks, overlaugh the laughathons!
Laughiness of the laughish laughers, counterlaugh the Laughdom's laughs!
  Laughio! Laughio!
  Dislaugh, relaugh, laughlets, laughlets,
    Laughulets, laughulets.

O you laughniks, laugh it out!
O you laughniks, laugh it forth!

The poem was, of course, ridiculed in numerous reviews and articles, especially later, when Mayakovsky began to recite it regularly
during his public readings; but some critics were enchanted. Kornei
Chukovsky was one of them, exclaiming, after quoting the poem *in
toto*: "What bounty and what sweet spell there are in our Slavic
idiom!" [27] For Chukovsky, the appearance of the "Incantation by
Laughter" meant the beginning of futurism in Russia. It is a curious
fact that, of the thousands of words created by Khlebnikov, only
smekhach, which could be translated as "laughnik," ever became a part
of spoken Russian; it even became the title of a short-lived satirical
Soviet magazine in the 1920's.

The real appearance of Russian futurists as a group was their publication of the "almanac" (as Russians call nonperiodic literary miscellanies) entitled *Sadok sudei*. It appeared in the second half of April
in 1910, a year after the birth of Italian futurism. The fact of Italian
futurism's prior existence was obviously unpleasant to the Russians
when they later applied the term "futurism" to their own work and
began to publicize their independence from the Italians. On occasion,
they even tried to prove their priority. The name of the book was
Khlebnikov's invention, and one could tell it from the richness of
sound: the identity of consonants is juxtaposed to the change in
vowels which almost suggests Khlebnikov's theories about "internal
declension." The meaning of the title, however, is slightly obscure
and ambiguous, which is also characteristic of Khlebnikov. As it
stands, it may be translated as "A Trap for Judges," meaning that the
traditional critics are sure to misjudge the appearance of new literature, lacking criteria by which to evaluate it; but another translation,
"A Hatchery of Judges," is also possible, and then the book becomes
a cradle containing new judges of Russian literature, the judges being
the participants themselves in this instance. Given this double meaning, which is further obscured grammatically, it is no wonder that
even a fellow futurist, Victor Shklovsky, later found the title "slightly
puzzling." [28] It is interesting that a leading writer of the time, Alexei
Remizov, who was personally close to some of the participants, suggested to them another title, "Pesyegolovtsy s edinym okom" ("The

Dogheaded Men with a Single Eye"), which brings to mind the dreaded *oprichniki* who were used by Ivan the Terrible in his fight against the Russian aristocracy. All these details show that the book was really meant to be "a shocker" and that the *Sadok* people wanted "to throw a bombshell into the joyless, provincial street of the generally joyless existence," as Kamensky later admitted.[29] Kamensky was one of the editors of *Sadok sudei,* and the book was prepared in his apartment in St. Petersburg in an atmosphere of youthful exuberance and fun.

The appearance of this first publication has a prehistory that leads as far back as 1908 (the year, incidentally, of the origin of cubism in France), when David Burliuk, already a veteran of several modernist art exhibitions with a few alliances and a few splits on his record, came to St. Petersburg and met first Kulbin and then Kamensky. Kamensky, who already had met Khlebnikov by that time, became acquainted with the Kulbin art group, which included Elena Guro and her husband, Mikhail Matyushin. This group, which at that time bore the name "Triangle," eventually made an alliance with the tautological "Venok Stefanos" ("The Wreath Stephanos") to which David Burliuk and his brother Vladimir belonged (and which was a fragment remaining after a split in another artistic group exhibiting in Moscow under the simpler name of "Stephanos"). The result of the new alliance in St. Petersburg was another exhibition in February, 1910, held at the time *The Studio of Impressionists* appeared and *Sadok sudei* was being prepared.

Among the main participants in *Sadok sudei* was David Davidovich Burliuk[30] (1882–1967), an artist and a poet. He was the man without whom there probably would have been no Russian futurism. A genius of organization, he inspired the others to action, made important decisions, and found new poetic forces at the crucial moments in the history of futurism. He was responsible for the publication of such landmarks of futurism as both volumes of *Sadok sudei* ("A Trap for Judges"), *Poshchëchina obshchestvennomu vkusu* ("A Slap in the Face of Public Taste"), *Dokhlaya luna* ("The Croaked Moon"), *Moloko kobylits* ("The Milk of Mares"), and *Pervyi Zhurnal Russkikh Futuristov* ("The First Journal of Russian Futurists"). He was the publisher of early books by Khlebnikov, Mayakovsky, and Livshits. To some futurists, he was also a mentor, especially to Kamensky and

Mayakovsky. He was born on a farm called Semirotovshchina near Kharkov[31] in a patriarchal family of a farming merchant who later became a manager of large estates in the south of Russia. He began to write poetry when he was fifteen, making his literary debut in a Kherson paper, *Yug*, and started writing verses regularly in 1902. His first opus was printed by him "for history" much later,[32] when he was living in the United States. It is a dreadful and dreary imitation of run-of-the-mill poetry of the 1880's, which was dreadful and dreary in its own right. In painting, Burliuk's background was much more substantial.[33] After 1898, he studied almost continuously both in Russia (Kazan, Odessa, later Moscow) and abroad (Munich, Paris). He also exhibited indefatigably in Kiev, Moscow, and St. Petersburg with artists whose names now read like a history of twentieth-century Russian painting. In 1911 Burliuk entered the history of European modern art by becoming a part of "Der blaue Reiter" and later of "Der Sturm." Equipped with such a background, this energetic man, a born fighter, was determined to leave his mark in literature, too.

David had two brothers, and both took part in the movement. Vladimir (1888–1917), a healthy, good-natured giant, never wrote poetry, but he illustrated some of the futurist editions. Nikolai (1890–1920), on the other hand, wrote poems and prose. Livshits describes him as "shy, genuine, having his own original world, which, however, could not be expressed in his rickety verse." [34]

Vasily Vasilyevich Kamensky (1884–1961), before he joined the *Sadok sudei* group, had a varied and colorful life which he described in detail in five autobiographies. Born into the family of a foreman at a gold mine in the Urals, he became an orphan early and spent his childhood in his uncle's house in Perm, on the river Kama, where he later worked as a bookkeeper in the railroad office. He was twice in Turkey (1902, 1906) and once in Iran (1906) for brief visits, and was impressed by the fairy-tale splashes of color that characterized both countries. In further flight from his drab provincial existence, Kamensky became a member of a traveling actors' company. Anton Chekhov himself came once to see a performance when they played in Yalta, but later Vsevolod Meyerhold, then a young and unknown director, persuaded Kamensky to give up the stage. In 1905, Kamensky took an active part in the revolution as a member of the Socialist-Revolutionary party in Perm and was jailed after the revolution failed.

Then he moved to St. Petersburg to study agronomy at the university extension. His occupations at this time ranged from lecturing on sex problems to restoring ancient icons.

It was in St. Petersburg, in 1908, that Kamensky, whose literary activities prior to this time were limited to writing topical articles and "civic" verse for the local paper in Perm, became a contributor to, and soon the managing editor of, *Vesna* ("Spring"),[35] published by N. G. Shebuyev, whose policy was to print everything submitted. Printing poetry and fiction in the newspapers was not unprofitable, so Kamensky had a chance to meet some of the best-known literary figures of the time (Leonid Andreyev, Alexander Blok, Fyodor Sologub, Alexander Kuprin). He also launched new talents; among those who later made a name in Russian literature were Victor Shklovsky, Mikhail Prishvin, Demian Bedny, and Nikolai Aseyev, who made their literary debuts in *Vesna*. But Kamensky's greatest discovery was Velimir Khlebnikov. This morbidly shy student appeared one day at the newspaper office, put a copybook into Kamensky's hands, and then immediately fled. Kamensky found some mathematical formulas on the first page, the beginning lines of unfinished poems on the second, and on the third page some prose under the title "Iskushenie greshnika" ("A Sinner's Temptation"), which was written over another, crossed-out title, "Muchoba vo vzorakh" ("Sufferhood in the Glances"). There was no sinner and no temptation in this work, no beginning and no end. It consisted of incoherent, but strangely beautiful visions of the type critics twenty years later could call surrealistic. The strangeness was further intensified by a large number of whimsical neologisms. Kamensky printed it; no one noticed it. But only much later did he begin to credit himself with "a discovery of the first genius" [36] (Mayakovsky, the second genius, was discovered three years later by David Burliuk). In his memoirs written before the 1930's, Kamensky hardly noted Khlebnikov. By the time of *Sadok sudei*, Kamensky was already a part of the artistic life of the capital. He studied painting under David Burliuk, was a friend of Nikolai Evreinov, and was married to a wealthy woman; but he felt he had to prove himself in his own and in others' eyes, so he worked on a novel.

Victor Vladimirovich Khlebnikov, who later adopted the name of Velimir given to him in a literary salon, was born in 1885 into an ornithologist's family in a village near Astrakhan. His parents lived briefly in Volhynia, then returned to the Volga region, to Simbirsk, and finally made their home in Astrakhan. Khlebnikov's consuming passion was mathematics which he studied at the University of Kazan; however, he later switched to biology. When in 1904 this shy youth visited Moscow for the first time, he wrote a letter to his family[37] in which nothing augured a futurist: he was impressed, most of all, by recent architecture in the so-called pseudo-Russian style, by realistic paintings of V. Vereshchagin, which were nothing but war reportage, and by Canova's sculpture. The same year, however, the same youth was deeply shaken by the sinking of the Russian fleet at Tsushima and made a pledge, which he carved into the bark of a tree, to discover the mathematical laws of history. Khlebnikov did not escape the favorite occupation of the students of that time, the antigovernment political activities. He participated in a demonstration, was jailed for a month, and, after that, lost all taste for politics.

Little is known of Khlebnikov's early writings, which he is said to have sent to Maxim Gorky for suggestions; the few fragments in prose which have been preserved, dating from 1903 or 1904, are imitations of Russian folklore. Works of as early as 1905 betray the influence of the Russian symbolists. While resting in Crimea after his unfortunate jail experience, Khlebnikov met Vyacheslav Ivanov, the influential and erudite leader of symbolism in its last phase, who took a liking to the young man. In 1908 Khlebnikov transferred from Kazan to St. Petersburg, and gave up biology to pursue Slavic studies. But there was little time for studies: he was introduced into literary circles, probably by Vyacheslav Ivanov himself, and began to come to the meetings of the Academy of Verse and to Ivanov's famous Wednesday literary gatherings. The Academy of Verse, in which Vyacheslav Ivanov, Nikolai Gumilev, and Mikhail Kuzmin, another of Khlebnikov's sponsors, were the leaders, stood above literary groups. Poets of different ages and reputations recited their poetry there and submitted it to the professional criticism of their colleagues. The gatherings took place once a month at Ivanov's, but in October, 1909, they moved to the publishing offices of the influential art journal *Apollon*. At first Khlebnikov was filled with great expectations. In October, 1909, he wrote in a letter: "Someone said there are lines of genius in my poetry." [38] One of his works, probably "Zverinets" ("Zoo"), was to be printed in *Apollon;* however, it was not, and in February, 1910,

Khlebnikov broke with the Academy of Verse. A bitterness against such circles is strongly felt in some of his works of this time ("Markiza Dezes," for instance). But was there ever any chance of Khlebnikov's becoming an *Apollon* poet? His obsession with Slavic themes, especially his interest in the Slavic prehistoric past and mythology, was no obstacle: such themes were still in high fashion after the success of books by Sergei Gorodetsky and Alexei Remizov. Some symbolists could even approve Khlebnikov's fierce nationalism and anti-Westernism. But he himself obviously did not realize at the time that he was already a mature poet, possessed of a highly original poetic system that could not fit the established canons of symbolism and satisfied even less the aesthetics of *Apollon*, which in a few years was to become the center of the activities of the Russian neoclassicists who called themselves Acmeists.

From the point of view of Sergei Makovsky, the editor of *Apollon*, Khlebnikov's poetry must have seemed not even gibberish, but simply trash, with perhaps a few decent lines in it. Makovsky, throughout his life, could not accept Blok's poetry because it was based on catachrestic imagery.[39] How could he accept Khlebnikov's poetry, a poetry where everything was slightly "dislocated"? The familiar meters were not destroyed but made impure and imperfect by mixing. The words were used not quite correctly; in fact, the famous motto of "the best words in the best order" was abolished and replaced by the principle of "the wrong word" so that clichés looked new and fresh and additional meanings were created. Fragment seemed to be the favorite genre, and bigger structures were created by sheer addition, "stringing" those fragments without any attempt at traditional composition. In diction there was much mixing, too, and lines that sounded conventionally poetic were freely intermingled with "prosaic" conversational passages. Rhyme was overrich, moving dangerously close to homonym rhyme; sometimes compound rhyme appeared, which in the past had been used almost exclusively in humorous poetry. There was much too much verbal experiment: Khlebnikov placed a word inside another word, wrote palindromic verse, even used palindromic rhyme, and constructed poems entirely of words built upon a single root. But most of all, there was too much neologism. This was an attempt to create that "all-Slavic language" about which Khlebnikov wrote to Vyacheslav Ivanov in one of his letters, and whose "sprouts" were supposed "to grow through the thickness of modern Russian." [40] Actually it was a producing of any part of speech from any existing root. Livshits later described his feelings when he first read Khlebnikov's neologistic poetry at the Burliuks' house: "I saw before me language become alive. The breath of the original word seared my face; . . . the jungles of Dahl [the compiler of the famous dictionary of the Russian language, which contains many words not in general use] became familiar and cozy. . . . The baring of roots was . . . a real mythmaking, an awakening of meanings dormant in the word, as well as the birth of new ones." Further, Livshits spoke about "the vague, amorphous substance of a word not yet filled with a meaning" in Khlebnikov's poetry and concluded that Khlebnikov "enlarged the capabilities of words to limits that formerly were not thought possible." [41]

Elena Guro was the pen name of Eleonora Genrikhovna von Notenberg (1877–1913), who seems in many respects to be a stranger among the early futurists. The only woman among the men, most of whom tried to be as masculine, loud, and colorful as possible both in their verse and in their lives, she was a quiet, introverted person who shunned people and was preoccupied with soft nuances in her work. Even the fact that she was born in St. Petersburg into a general's family (some say that she was an illegitimate daughter of the Emperor) sets her apart from her fellow futurists with their provincial and often plebeian backgrounds. Guro was a professional painter who, after graduating from the School of the Society for the Encouragement of the Arts, worked under such famous artists as Tsionglinsky, Bakst, and Dobuzhinsky, but she also had her own studio. She lived on a government pension and had an estate in Finland, where she died of tuberculosis after suffering for many years from pernicious anemia and neuritis of the heart. She knew French poetry well, and her work betrays an interest in German and Scandinavian literature. Among her favorite authors were Verhaeren, Vielé-Griffin, Alexander Blok, Ivan Konevskoi, Andrei Biely (with emphasis on his "symphonies"), and Remizov.

Guro is probably the most neglected among the early Russian futurists, a fate that is undeserved because she is one of the very original and talented Russian writers. She made her literary debut with a story, "Rannyaya vesna" ("Early Spring"), printed in 1905 in the inconspicuous *Sbornik molodykh pisatelei* ("An Anthology of New Writers"). She published some of her work in five of the futurist miscellanies. That published in *Troe* ("The Three") appeared posthumously, as did the last of her three published books. The announced *Bednyi rytsar* ("The Poor Knight") never materialized, although as late as 1917 Mayakovsky tried to persuade Maxim Gorky to publish it.

When *Sadok sudei* was being prepared, Guro was already the author of *Sharmanka* ("The Hurdy-Gurdy"), which appeared in February of 1909 and attracted no attention at all, though Guro showed herself in it as a mature and interesting writer. Most illustrations in the book are by Guro herself. Although the influence of symbolism is unmistakable in the prose, poetry, and especially the dramas printed in the book, Guro stands here on her own two feet as probably the most representative of all Russian impressionists. Guro's impressionism is particularly noticeable in the first part of the book, which contains eight examples of her prose. "Pered vesnoi" ("Before Spring"), for instance, is an impressionistic description of St. Petersburg first during the day, then at dusk, by a person who is drawn outside, unable to stay inside four walls, and who, at the end of the story, comes back home and falls asleep on the bed in street clothes, exhausted. Nothing happens in the story. There are hurried descriptions of passersby and memories of Nice; the narrator gives alms to a beggar, enters a florist's shop, imagines the ideal life of the shop owners (here Guro is on the verge of the stream-of-consciousness technique). The real content of the story is those "light thoughts, which touch everything lightly," brief, ephemeral states of mind the narrator experiences while walking around the city. Guro frequently resorts to short or single-word sentences to suggest those "light touches," as in the following brief excerpt: "Chisto umytaya. Syro. Veterok . . . —I svetlaya" ("Am washed clean. It's damp. A breeze . . . —And transfigured"). There are two more pieces that can be termed urbanistic, fragments of impressions of the same city, mostly at night, often disconnected and intermingled with passages in which the author tries to imagine what is going on in the minds of the people she meets or in the rooms behind the lighted windows, or what is going to happen to some of the passersby. Sometimes there are suggestions of a plot (as in "Tak zhizn idet" ["Thus Life Goes"] where the impressions of the city and the feelings of pain are those of Nelka, a man-crazy teenager, mistreated by her stepfather), but the story never materializes. Occasionally there is out-right symbolism, as in the appearance of a mysterious king amidst the city crowds in "Pesni goroda" ("Songs of the City").

Guro not only poeticizes the city, but she worships nature, as can be seen in her stories with a country background (it is invariably the Finnish *dacha* areas with pine trees and coastal landscapes). She almost equates nature with poetry: "Take a lump of black earth, dilute it with water from a rain barrel or from a ditch, and you will get excellent poetry." Nature is often anthropomorphic, as in the creative efforts of trees and stones in "Da budet" ("Fiat"); but, on the other hand, mankind is sometimes decivilized as in the same story, where modern life is presented as the eternal life of prehistoric people. In her attempt to animate the whole universe, Guro frequently makes inanimate things alive. In her prose, "chairbacks smile," "the dark day stoops and almost hides its head in its shoulders," armchairs and chests not only "gaily . . . look into your eyes," but are intimately tied with Fate. In her efforts to achieve freshness and closeness to nature, Guro is particularly attracted to the theme of childhood. Often things are presented as perceived or imagined by a child. In the prose miniature, "Domashnie" ("Home Creatures"), when there is rain outside, a child receives visits from all kinds of vague, fantastic creatures. Children are able not only to see things as if for the first time, but to hear words in their original freshness. In one story, the girls, having arrived at a newly bought estate, listen to the adults' conversations about a brick factory and about the delivery of the coal tar, and "both the novelty and the uplift from those new, fresh, raw, and hard words not worn by usage were communicated to them." One could see here futurism with its efforts to renovate words, but that would be an anachronism in a book published at the very beginning of 1909. Impressionism would be the correct word here, too, and any reader of Russian literature would probably find this passage reminiscent of Chekhov's "The Peasants" in which the women are touched to tears by incomprehensible words in the Gospel.

Guro's poetry is less successful and less original, on the whole, than her prose. The more metrical her verse, the less at ease she seems to feel; in this early book, she is already attracted by accentual verse and sometimes comes close to free verse. A certain predilection for Germanic themes (Walter von der Vogelweide, Wolfram at the coffin of

Elisabeth) can be noted. Her lyric, often strongly rhythmic prose, on the other hand, shows maturity and a sure hand. Fragmentary composition is sometimes emphasized by separating portions of her "stories" from each other by dots. Guro also uses more original visual devices both for separating fragments of prose and for creating a mood: tiny drawings of leaves, fir trees, stars, or just plain circles with dots in the middle—all these placed between the lines or in the margin.

Probably the best prose in *Sharmanka* is "Poryv" ("An Impulse"), a story of the meeting of, and the subsequent friendship between, two women, both writers, living in the country, one of them having heart trouble. Here again there is impressionism in the way and in the order in which the story is told. At the beginning, we do not know who the characters are or exactly what is going on. Only gradually, mostly through pieces of conversation, are the relationships and situations clarified. At what would be the end, the author refuses to "terminate the tale" and leaves the whole thing up in the air. The influence of symbolism, especially of Biely, is clearly seen in the story's being told on several planes, with "eternity looking through the fir tree" and the women appearing, in a metaphysical glimpse, as "two rays of light getting hooked to each other among worlds." In addition to "Prose," "Trifles," and "Poems," there is a portion of *Sharmanka* entitled "Plays" containing two lyric dramas, "Nishchii Arlekin" ("The Indigent Harlequin") and "V zakrytoi chashe" ("In a Closed Chalice"), both well done, though completely in the tradition of Alexander Blok.

Most of Guro's next book, *Osennii son* ("The Autumnal Dream"), published in 1912, is a play with the same title. It is dedicated to the memory of Guro's son who died as a child and whom she continued to think of as alive, so much so that she bought toys for him and made drawings of him as she imagined he would have looked at various stages in later life. In the drawings in *Osennii son*, he is a lanky youth of about eighteen with a dreamy, aristocratic face. The hero of the play is Baron Wilhelm Kranz, a pathetic dreamer, mocked by vulgar and prosaic people and consciously presented as another embodiment of Don Quixote, as well as an imaginary portrait of Guro's son. At the end of the play, Guro presents a rather obvious moral of the temporary victory of prosaic vulgarity over romantic idealism, though the latter is assured an eternal life. The play is followed in the book by a few pieces of Guro's typically lyric prose, as well as two poems written in free verse. One of the prose fragments, without a title, has surrealistic features: it is a description of a horselike creature with a horse name (Bulanka) who is clothed and speaks like a human being, and is attacked by *koromysla* ("yokes to carry pails with water").

Guro's third book, the posthumously published *Nebesnye verblyuzhata* ("The Baby Camels of the Sky"), appeared in 1914 when Russian futurism had already reached the peak of its development. This book, with the letters of its title sprouting leaves and with two photographs of the author and many illustrations between its covers, is Guro's most typical work, and probably her best. It contains only lyric prose miniatures and several poems, mostly written in free verse; here they are not assigned to different parts of the book, as they were in *Sharmanka*, but are freely mixed so that the boundary between prose and verse is obliterated. The fragmentary character of the work is further enhanced in that titled and untitled pieces are printed in such a way that it is often difficult to determine whether a given fragment is independent or is the sequel to the one before it. We find here the familiar themes and motifs such as trees, spring, silence, earth, nature in general, faithfulness to one's youth and one's dreams, the awkward shyness of chuldren and poets, objects with a soul, Don Quixote, and the like. Despite a certain unevenness, one finds in the book a more mature and sure hand, as well as much of that engaging purity of spirit characteristic of Guro. The first piece, "Gazetnoe obyavlenie" ("A Newspaper Ad"), is the keynote of the book with its combination of childish fantasy and serious overtones: it is about capturing "the baby camels in the sky," good-natured and clumsy spirits who are shorn of their fluff (from which shirts are made) and then released. Fantasies and lyric sketches of real life are freely interspersed in the book with moralistic admonitions. The final piece, entitled "Obeshchaite!" ("Promise!"), admonishes people not to betray their dreams and what their works represent, and was recited at Guro's funeral. In the book Guro pays tribute to the futurist predilection for neologism, though she has included very few of them; the most successful ones are created in the manner of the language of children.

Elena Guro may present a stumbling block for those who try to create a unified picture of Russian futurism. At first glance she does not look like a futurist, and some critics have been on record against her being so classified.[42] Difficulties arise if one considers her against the background of later futurism. She lacks the iconoclastic spirit and the loudness usually associated with the movement; nor can one find in her work much verbal experiment. One may also remember that she did not sign the first important manifesto in *A Slap,* rarely participated in futurist public appearances, and refused to print her work in the second volume of *Sadok sudei* if it carried the name of "Hylaea," accepted by 1912 by practically all the rest of the futurists as the designation for their literary group. Sometimes she almost seems to belong to futurism because of her bitterness at not having been accepted by the "ruling" literary circles of symbolism: she occasionally betrays this feeling, as, for instance, in the words about her "poems no one wants to print" in *The Baby Camels in the Sky.* If, however, one accepts the idea that impressionism played an important part in the early stages of futurism, Guro easily takes her legitimate place in it. For example, her urbanism is impressionistic, rather than "classically" futuristic as found in Marinetti, Mayakovsky, and Shershenevich; this may explain the paradoxical fact that urbanism coexists with her worship of nature. One should also remember that the whole picture of Russian futurism was never smooth and clear. Some of Guro's "unfuturistic" features are shared with Khlebnikov, who also was an introvert and not much of a fighter. (One may add Guro's similarity to Khlebnikov in her fragmentary structure, in her attraction to a primeval freshness, and in her preoccupation with children's language.) But there are enough details that link Guro with the usual image of futurism. Critics (Aseyev, Khardzhiev) were right when they saw in Guro's poem "Gorod" ("City"), published in *Rykayushchii Parnas* ("Roaring Parnassus"), many qualities connecting her with Mayakovsky.[43] She also made a minor contribution to what is generally considered futurism's most radical creation—*zaum,* the so-called transrational language—but she did it inconspicuously, subtly, and with feminine gentleness. In her poem "Finlandia," published in *The Three,* the trees *shuyat* (a word invented by Guro) rather than *shumyat* (the usual Russian word to describe the sound of trees in wind). Alexei Kruchenykh, the futurist extremist and the most ardent champion and propagandist of *zaum,* admired this innovation and wrote that coniferous trees precisely *shuyat,* whereas deciduous ones *shumyat.*[44] Another futurist, Sergei Bobrov, saw in the same poem an imitation of the sounds of the Finnish language,[45] and much of the Russian *zaum* was later written to imitate the sound of foreign tongues. For Kruchenykh, Guro's work was to be an example of one of the basic qualities of futurist literature, its being written for "momentary reading" or immediate comprehension (*chtoby smotrelos v mgnovenie oka*).[46] Her attempts to illustrate her works in an original way are also similar to those of Kruchenykh and other acknowledged futurists.

It seems, however, that Guro's real stature and literary importance will be established only when she is discussed in the entire context of Russian impressionism, which is not my intention here. It is not an accident that her strongest influence is felt in Vasily Kamensky's most impressionistic book, *Zemlyanka* ("The Mud Hut"), published in 1910. The sources of Guro's impressionism, it can be suggested here, may be partly of foreign origin, but such a proposal requires careful and detailed scrutiny. It was only natural to borrow from German-Austrian literature in which impressionism had its clearest manifestation. For instance, literary miniatures, sketches, notes, pieces of dialogue, occasionally with an admixture of free verse poems, can be found in the work of the Austrian impressionist Peter Altenberg (particularly in his *Was mir der Tag zuträgt* [1901]), who, to be sure, differs from Guro in his hedonistic world outlook. But it is not hard to hear in Guro's tone echoes of some of the impressionistic works of Rainer Maria Rilke, especially in his *Aufzeichnungen des Malte Laurids Brigge*; it is in Rilke, too, that one finds Guro-like objects with a soul. Guro's sources, however, are much more complex. For example, her free verse may owe something to that of Vielé-Griffin, and her prose miniatures, to Remizov (*Posolon*). The anonymous writer in the third issue of *Soyuz molodezhi* ("Union of Youth") tried to connect Guro with the contemporary painting of Artur von Wiesen;[47] and Soviet scholars very convincingly saw musical composition and a system of leitmotivs in her prose, reminding the reader that Debussy, Scriabian, and Liadov were her favorite composers.[48]

Some futurists respected Guro and tried to promote her reputation during her lifetime and after her death. Others were more restrained in their evaluation and called her work a "mixture of Maeterlinck and [Francis] Jammes made with Russian starch jelly [*kisel*]" and spoke about "the quiet melopeia of her words drained of blood, with which Guro tried to translate her astral shimmer into spoken

Russian." [49] Guro never attracted much attention on the outside, and critics began mentioning her *Sharmanka* only four years after it was published. It is interesting to note, however, that Alexander Blok himself entered in his diary on March 25, 1913: "Guro deserves attention." Soon after Guro was buried in a country cemetery near her *dacha* in Finland, her husband observed some unknown young people reading from her work near her grave. He became understandably touched and placed a bench there with a built-in shelf for Guro's books. It is not known whether such readings continued, but more than once Guro became the object of minor cults. The most extensive cult manifested itself on the pages of the periodical *Ocharovannyi strannik* ("The Enchanted Wanderer"), where appeared some of her poetry, both new and reprinted, and an essay about her as well. [50] Poetry was published in her memory, for example, that written by Samuil Vermel, Innokenty Oksenov, and others.

Elena Guro strongly influenced the little-known poetess Ada Vladimirova; another poetess, Maria Shkapskaya, who was known in the 1920's, chose a line from Guro's play for the title of one of her verse collections (*Baraban strogogo gospodina* ["The Drum of the Strict Master"]). Guro's influence on Boris Pilnyak and Poletayev has, however, been exaggerated. [51] As late as 1935 N. Bukharin quoted from Guro's poem in his famous speech at the First Congress of Soviet Writers, but he did not identify the author. The many-volumed *Literaturnaya Entsiklopedia,* published at that time, ignored Guro completely. The best student of futurism among Soviet scholars, N. Khardzhiev, tried to save her from oblivion several times. In 1938 he called her a "remarkable craftsman" and an innovator in prose. He also focused attention on similarities between the works of Mayakovsky and those of Guro in 1958. [52] It may well be that in Guro's conscious effort to obliterate the difference between prose and verse lie her main historical importance and the guarantee of eventual discovery and appreciation. In her unpublished diary she left a note: "Free rhythms. Prose into verse, verse into prose. Prose that is almost verse." [53] As a pioneer in this area, Guro deserves as much attention as Andrei Biely with his attempts to "versify" his prose. But Guro is bound to attract the attention of critics and scholars also as an impressionist (or an "intimist," as she was sometimes called) when the problem of the analysis of Russian impressionism faces literary scholarship, as it inevitably must. Someday her free verse will also become an object of study. Nor should the name of Guro be omitted in any survey of the theme of childhood in Russian literature.

One of the editors of *Sadok sudei* was Mikhail Vasilyevich Matyushin (1861–1934), Guro's husband. Matyushin was an artist, a musician, and a composer interested in quarter-tone music. He played first violin in the St. Petersburg Philharmonic and was the publisher of the second *Sadok sudei, Roaring Parnassus,* and *The Three,* as well as of some books by individual futurists (Guro, Khlebnikov), usually under the imprint "Zhuravl" ("the Crane"), some of which he illustrated. He wrote articles about color and translated into Russian *Du cubisme* by Gleizes and Metzinger. Matyushin showed a pioneering interest in the forms of driftwood.

Such were the main forces of early Russian futurism as displayed on the pages of *Sadok sudei,* a book of rather small format with a light-gray cover on which there were red spots and a stripe with the title pasted on it. The paper chosen for the book was wallpaper, so that the text was printed only on the reverse side, which formed the recto pages; the verso pages remained blank and unnumbered. The items were printed without spacing so that sometimes it is difficult to decide whether one is a new poem or a continuation of the old one. On the margins there is, however, some identification of the works, usually in the form of numbered opera (probably the idea of David Burliuk who did that sort of thing in most of his own work throughout his lifetime). There are nine drawings by Vladimir Burliuk in the book, most of them the portraits of contributors. The letters "yat" and "hard sign" were not used. Using wallpaper entailed some difficulties: for instance, the printers continually had to wash chalk off plates and type. As David Burliuk later said, "Our whim caused much profanity in the print shop." [54] Three hundred copies were printed (some sources say there were 480), but as the bill for printing was never paid, all but 20 copies taken by Kamensky remained in the warehouse and later disappeared, which makes this edition quite a bibliographic rarity.[55]

Twelve poems by Vasily Kamensky open the book; most of them, with insignificant changes and additions, were later included in his novel, *The Mud Hut.* These are, for the most part, poems about enjoyment of life and nature. Kamensky's Neo-Rousseauism has its clearest expression in the poem "Rostan'" ("Crossroads") where the poet seems to divide mankind into those who wash with a towel over their shoulders and those who just roll in the dewy grass. Some poems are loud and exuberant, glorifying sun and day, full of exclamations, but most are detailedly descriptive. For instance, in one poem a man lying in tall grass describes countryside sounds, while in another the poet watches fish in water while he himself is lying on the edge of a raft. Kamensky knows nature, but as he lacks means to present it, he frequently resorts to direct expression of his feelings. Imagery is rare and undeveloped. He writes mostly in a rather primitive free verse, but traditional metrical versification can be found, too. There is occasional rhyme. Khlebnikov's influence can be seen in a rather mild and shy use of neologism (*zhurcheek churlit, grustochki*); one poem even carries a dedication to Khlebnikov. The most "futurist" poem is "Na vysokoi gorke" ("On a Tall Hill") where there is some coarseness of diction and one line ends with a preposition. The critics did not fail to single this poem out for mockery.[56] In contrast with the gaiety of the rest, there is "Skuka staroi devy" ("Old Maid's Boredom") with its rainy background and the howling verbal leitmotiv "Suka skuka." On the whole, there is much freshness in Kamensky's poetry, but little know-how or taste.

Freshness is also the word that comes to mind when a reader looks through the six specimens of Guro's verse and prose. Though some of them reveal too much symbolist influence, one can also find some of her individual traits, such as her preoccupation with the atmosphere of childhood. Those of Guro's poems contained in *Sadok sudei* are not among her best, with the possible exception of "Kamushki" ("Pebbles"), a charming piece containing animation of objects and infantilistic neologisms.

Khlebnikov's contributions to *Sadok sudei*, as could be expected, stand head and shoulders above the rest, though the selection could be called not typical enough. Here is found his excellent "Zverinets" ("Zoo"), written in a Whitmanesque style, and one-half of "Zhuravl" ("The Crane"), in which a gigantic bird made out of inanimate objects terrorizes mankind. The most interesting work is "Markiza Dezes" ("Marquise Desaix"), a strangely beautiful drama in verse whose

conversational character is said to be based on the style of the nineteenth-century classical poet, Alexander Griboyedov.[57] It reminds one
a little of Alexander Blok's dramas, too, in its mixture of vulgar reality
and romantic poetry at an art exhibition, which is clearly a satire on
exhibitions sponsored by *Apollon* (the editor, Sergei Makovsky, even
appears in person). Satire is mixed, however, with surrealistic fantasy.
Pictures come out of their frames and speak, Raphael appears in person after someone asks for St. Raphael wine, and the protagonists, a
marquise and her escort, are, at the end, transformed into two naked
statues, whereas animals (from her furs) come alive. There is a
curious pun rhyme often used in this play, which seems to predestine
the next line and is connected with the motif of the mysticism of
similarly sounding words. After its publication in *Sadok sudei*, Khlebnikov shortened and slightly changed his "Markiza Dezes."

There is nothing to praise in the eighteen poems by Nikolai Burliuk,
who reveals himself here a third-rate poet of the symbolist school.
These are clearly an amateur's works, showing little feeling for
language or originality, though N. Burliuk tries clumsily to mix different styles. In this he reminds one of Khlebnikov, with the difference
that Khlebnikov achieves a certain poetic effect, whereas N. Burliuk
drowns in a chaotic mélange.

Practically all this criticism can be repeated in describing the nineteen poems by David Burliuk. These poems rarely succeed in making
their point in content or technique, though one can notice a certain
predilection for the theme of violence. There are at least four suicides
in them: two die by jumping from windows, one by throwing himself
under the train, and one by poisoning himself. Livshits saw in them
"heavy archaism and incompleteness of form," [58] and he liked it. Now,
more than fifty years later, Burliuk's style seems very flimsy and tame,
not strong enough to appear radical, and lacking completely in poetic
maturity or vitality. For the most part, it sounds like traditional,
"beautiful" verse (which the poet obviously did not want to achieve)
ineptly handled to the point of being ridiculous. The worst thing is
that all of it is terribly boring and cliché-ridden. Such "innovations"
as the lack of commas or infrequent and shy asyndeton (i.e., omission
of prepositions, which will later become one of Burliuk's trademarks)
do not save anything. Twenty years later Burliuk printed all nineteen

poems again in one of his American collections,[59] changing them radically and adding many devices he developed in his subsequent poetry, but, curiously enough, he punctuated these later versions.

Among the contributors to *Sadok sudei,* there are three minor figures, two of them appearing for the first and the last time in futurist editions. E. Nizen is Ekaterina, Elena Guro's sister (which makes *Sadok sudei* almost a two-family enterprise, with Matyushin and the three brothers Burliuk also there). Nothing is known about her, except the fact that she was once exiled to Vyatka for socialist-democratic activities. In *Sadok sudei* were printed two of her prose sketches, betraying her sister's influence, but interesting and quite competent, combining impressionism with such images of symbolist poetry as hunchbacks and dwarfs. The first work, "Detskii rai" ("Children's Paradise"), is a description of a playground at a summer resort based on what the formalist critics later would call *ostranenie* ("making strange"): children are consistently called "little animals," their mothers, "the mauve ones." The other piece, "Prazdnik" ("Holiday"), introduces the reader into the thoughts and feelings of a boy (who looks out the window and then falls asleep), as well as those of the passersby on the street.

S. Myasoyedov contributed a fascinating prose piece about people on a train going to the puzzling land of Bleyana, in which he breaks off his description just before the border crossing. Myasoyedov was a teacher of mathematics who in his childhood spoke an invented language with his brothers. Nothing else is known about him. Later, in 1911, Khlebnikov inquired in one of his letters whether Myasoyedov was still writing, adding "he could create great and beautiful things." [60]

Finally, there is one poem, in a symbolist, "musical" style, written by A. M. Gei, who is the only participant not honored with a portrait drawing by Vladimir Burliuk. Gei is Alexander Mitrofanovich Gorodetsky (1886–1914), a brother of the well-known poet, Sergei Gorodetsky.[61]

David Burliuk and Kamensky were always to consider *Sadok sudei* the beginning of Russian futurism and to recall it with tenderness and enthusiasm; but now, retrospectively, it hardly seems a great event or a success. In 1910 Innokenty Annensky's best book, *Kiparisovyi larets* ("The Cypress Chest"), was published; Valery Bryusov summed up

his most influential period in *Vse napevy* ("All Melodies"); Andrei
Biely proved to be a first-rank novelist in his *Serebryanyi golub* ("The
Silver Dove") and made a sizable contribution to the aesthetics of
symbolism with his collection of articles *Simvolizm;* and Nikolai
Gumilev made his real entrance into Russian poetry with *Zhemchuga*
("Pearls"). Against such competition, *Sadok sudei,* with its uneven,
not very representative, and often amateurish selection of works, seems
relatively insignificant. Its radicalism can hardly be felt now, unless
one considers printing on wallpaper a revolution; and those outmoded
letters omitted by its contributors were dropped from the Russian
alphabet officially a few years after 1910 anyway, not as the result of
the influence of *Sadok sudei* (and, besides, the *Sadok* people were
not the first to omit them).[62] In addition, the book contained no manifesto or program article, which might have clarified the aesthetic position of the *Sadok* people a little, though it could not have redeemed
the volume's general lack of artistic distinction.

Sadok sudei* was noticed, but hardly accepted, by two leading critics
of the day. Valery Bryusov thought the book was "beyond the limits
of literature" and "full of boyish pranks in bad taste." He saw some
good imagery in the poems of Kamensky and N. Burliuk, but added
that it was "not easy to find felicitous verses in the endless inarticulateness [*nelepitsa*] of poems and stories." [63] On the other hand, Nikolai
Gumilev, in his review, called the majority of the authors "beyond
help," singling out as "true innovators" (*podlinno derzayut*) only
Kamensky and Khlebnikov. He praised Kamensky's "numerous[?]
neologisms," and called Khlebnikov "a visionary" whose works remind
one of "a record of a dream." [64]

Nevertheless, in *Sadok sudei* several poets gathered as a group
which, with only a few changes and additions, was reassembled about
two years later when Russian futurism really started moving. Thus,
one could agree with Burliuk and Kamensky that the beginning of
Russian futurism dates from 1909 (more precisely, the end of 1909
when they began to work on the book). Even if one accepts this early
date, Italian futurism remains almost a year older, despite all the later
efforts of some of the Russians to prove their seniority. However, it is
true that in its origins the Russian group was quite independent of the
Italians. In 1909 not one of the *Sadok* people had even heard of

futurism; no one could dream that three years later they would call themselves futurists.

It is worth noting that there was no agreement among the futurists later as to the significance of *Sadok sudei*. Kruchenykh and Mayakovsky dated futurism from 1912 (significantly, Mayakovsky called *Sadok sudei* futurism's "first impressionistic flare-up").[65] Livshits dated it from 1911. But Burliuk and Kamensky stubbornly continued to consider the book "a bombshell," "the dawn of a new epoch," and the like, and saw in it "the destruction of syntax,"[66] being obviously unclear as to precisely what syntax meant. Kamensky not only insisted later that in *Sadok sudei* he and his cohorts "made poetry and prose of new form, invented by ourselves,"[67] but tried to convince the reader, and probably himself, that the book was one of the greatest literary sensations of history, that it was met by the press with screams and howls, but was accepted by youth. How could youth accept a book that was not even on sale? (The authors were unable to raise the money to pay the printing bill, so all but twenty of some three to four hundred copies were held in a printshop warehouse.)

Before the discussion of this earliest phase of Russian futurism is finished, one more thing must be mentioned. Practically all histories of Russian literature mention the fact that the futurists called themselves *budetlyane*. *Budetlyane* is a plural form of the word *budetlyanin*, coined by Khlebnikov, which means "a man of the future." Thus, Russian futurists did call themselves "futurists," in a way, before they accepted the name of *futuristy*. But this seems to have been just a private verbal invention of Khlebnikov's, used only now and then by the others. They never called themselves *budetlyane* officially as a group. Kamensky mentions vaguely in his memoirs that Khlebnikov wanted to make "propaganda about the coming of *budetlyane*."[68] Khlebnikov obviously was serious about this. As early as 1910 he wrote in a letter: "We are a new breed of people-rays." In 1912, when everyone else was using the name "Hylaea" for this group, he insisted that *"Budetlyane* must move toward the East, where the future of Russia lies." In 1913, however, when the organization of a futurist theater was being discussed, "Budetlyanin" was proposed as its name. Khlebnikov still used the word in 1914 in a letter.[69] And even after the Revolution, Kruchenykh used this name when referring

" Будетлянин "

to himself. The most curious thing is that, shortly after Khlebnikov died in 1922, the author of an article about his work insisted that "*Budetlyanstvo* and futurism are two different things. Futurism rejects tradition, whereas *budetlyanstvo* is a creation of new things, grown on the magnificent traditions of Russian antiquity." [70]

```
222222
22222222
2222  2222
2222  2222
2222  2222
      2222
     2222
    2222
   2222
  2222
 2222
222222222
222222222
```
HYLAEA

In November, 1910,[1] Vasily Kamensky
published a book entitled *Zemlyanka* ("The
Mud Hut"). It is a romantic story with some
autobiographical elements. Philip, a provincial
turned fashionable writer now living in the
capital, is a naïvely glamorized self-portrait of
Kamensky down to the red shirt he wears,
which Kamensky tried to use as a trademark.
Philip's love affair with the beautiful Marina
is on the rocks, and he is on the verge of
committing suicide, but is distracted by the
rising sun and the singing birds and decides
to leave Marina for nine years to test her
and his own love. He goes to live in the country,
in a forest on the bank of a river, in a mud
hut abandoned by some hunter, in the company
of a peasant boy, a dog, and a thrush. Tortured
thoughts of Marina are soon replaced by his
communication with the vision of the fairy-
tale-like Maika; but, finally, Philip meets a

peasant girl, Mariika, with whom he finds paradisaic happiness through marriage.

The Mud Hut is an antiurbanistic work, and the first chapters are devoted to depicting the city as the reign of death. The protagonist abandons the tragic chaos of city life and returns to mother earth. In fact, for the author, the novel was an ambitious undertaking, something terribly significant, a kind of *Divine Comedy* with the hero going through the hell of city life, then cleansing himself in solitary communion with nature, and, at the end, entering the paradise of peasant life. The peasant, according to Kamensky, partakes of the "enormous mysteries of earth," which the author refuses to reveal to anyone. At the end of the novel, he does reveal, however, that he follows Leo Tolstoy. Tolstoy is mentioned by name and praised for his ability to write "in plain Russian so that one can understand him" while the rest of the Russian literati are dismissed as "Russian foreigners."

The best pages in *The Mud Hut* are those on which Kamensky describes nature. "Describes" is not the right word, because this lyric novel is an exuberant paean to nature, which it extols as the force making a wise child of a man. In all fairness, one should add, however, that though Kamensky is certainly familiar with and fond of nature as it is found in his beloved Perm region, his observations concerning it are inaccurate: in his novel, for instance, buttercups, bluebells, and cornflowers grow at the same time. The lyric quality of the nature chapters is further intensified by the free verse poetry that often interrupts the emotional prose in which the work is written. Many of the *Mud Hut* poems were published earlier in *Sadok sudei*. Kamensky later attached much importance to the fact that he intermingled prose with poetry in his novel. He called *The Mud Hut* "a new kind of novel" [2] and was inclined to consider this intermingling a futurist device. Though some originality could be claimed in the employment of this device when seen within the context of Russian literature,[3] its use did not constitute futurism. Kamensky's later claim that he had achieved a *sdvig* ("dislocation, shift") through this intermingling of prose and poetry can hardly be recognized, because poetry does not actually interrupt prose in his work, thus producing a dissonant effect, but rather enhances the lyricism that fills the prose throughout the novel. Otherwise, the mixture of monologue and third-person narrative, the frequent exclamations, and the fragmentary composition of the work add further to the impressionistic effect. Actually, Kamensky's originality is somewhat diminished by the fact that Guro used the same device in a less obtrusive and more subtle way. Kamensky appears as a pupil of Guro also in the frequent use of one-word sentences and in his admonitions to preserve the child in oneself. He also borrows from E. Nizen (the scene with children playing in a city garden has much in common with her "Children's Paradise") and from Khlebnikov (some poems are obviously patterned on the latter's "Zoo"; reproducing birdcalls comes from Khlebnikov, too).

As a whole, to put it mildly, *The Mud Hut* is hardly a masterpiece. It needs much cutting, its diction is often banal, and it shows that Kamensky's taste was always his weak point. When Philip is in distress after Marina has left him, and the homeless dogs in the streets come and sniff with sympathy at his tears dropping to the sidewalk, it is too much. The childish exuberance of the hero's communion with nature can also be too much, as when he, overcome by the child awakening in him, jumps fully clothed into the river from a steep bank, holding the burning tree trunk pulled out of a bonfire. Nevertheless, the novel occupies an important place in this history because (1) it is another example of the impressionist beginnings of Russian futurism; (2) it is the first major work published by a leading futurist; and (3) it is the first extensive presentation of Kamensky's favorite subject, nature in Russia, especially that aspect of it associated with hunting and fishing. It is also interesting that while Kamensky is here an impressionist in technique, this work could be labeled primitivist in ideology because of his preaching a return to nature; and primitivism was to be the next preoccupation of the Russian futurists. Kamensky wrote *The Mud Hut* surrounded by the best comforts of civilized life, having just married a very wealthy woman (who, unfortunately, was soon to go bankrupt). This wife (the first of many for Kamensky) did not like the novel. When clippings of negative reviews began to arrive, Kamensky's authority in the family dropped drastically, and he left literature in disillusionment. To regain his self-respect, he decided to enter aviation, another dangerous occupation and one that was then in its infancy in Russia. After training in Europe, he bought an airplane in France and soon became a famous pioneer pilot in Russia, until his airplane crashed in Poland before a festive audience during one of his demonstration flights. Kamensky survived, but gave up aviation, and, having purchased a farm near Perm, went there to practice what he had preached before in *The Mud Hut.* Until 1913 he was outside literature; and if it had not been for David Burliuk, he might never have reentered it.

David Burliuk, in the meantime, was as active as ever. He studied art in Moscow.[4] He participated not only in Kulbin's "Triangle" exhibition, but also in another St. Petersburg modernist artists' exhibition, the "Union of Youth," both at the beginning of 1910. In the summer, he went to spend his vacation with his family in the south of Russia, and he took along two guests, Velimir Khlebnikov and the artist Mikhail Larionov. That winter Burliuk participated in the first exhibition of the most important group of the Russian artistic avant-garde, "Bubnovyi valet" ("Jack of Diamonds"). He did not neglect his friend, Vasily Kamensky, for he disturbed the latter's rural solitude with boisterous letters, inviting him to come back at once and rejoin the movement. Soon, Burliuk made perhaps the greatest discovery in the history of futurism. While studying at the Academy of Painting, Sculpture, and Architecture in Moscow, in September, 1911, he met another student, a poorly dressed young giant, unkempt and unwashed, with penetrating eyes and a deep bass voice—Vladimir Mayakovsky. About a year after this meeting, Mayakovsky read Burliuk a short poem. "You're a genius," declared Burliuk, and he began to introduce him to people as a genius of Russian poetry. At about the same time, Alexei Kruchenykh, Burliuk's acquaintance of several years who was to become one of the most colorful figures of Russian futurism, joined the movement.

In December, 1911, when David Burliuk, on his way to his father's place to spend his Christmas vacation, stopped in Kiev, a fellow artist, Alexandra Exter,[5] introduced him to Benedict Constantinovich Livshits (1887–1939), a twenty-four-year-old student of law and son of a wealthy merchant. Livshits was the last addition to Russian futurism. The group soon became very exclusive and accepted no new members, though they did ally themselves on occasion with other groups and individuals. Burliuk evidently saw in Livshits, a well-read young man and an admirer of Corbière and Rimbaud, the potential theoretician of the group. Livshits had been at that time a contributor to *Apollon* and the author of one book of verse, *Fleita Marsiya* ("The

Flute of Marsyas"), published in 1911 and reviewed rather favorably by the influential Bryusov. More than twenty years after this meeting, Livshits wrote a book of memoirs, *Polutoraglazyi strelets* ("The One-and-a-half-eyed Archer"), which, though it covered a span of only three years, still remains not only the best source on the history of Russian futurism, but also one of the best among Russian memoirs, deserving translation into other languages. In late 1911, however, Livshits, a constant searcher, considered his first book a thing of the past and was looking for new ways in poetry. Symbolism, in his opinion, had led the poetic word into a blind alley. The new ways seemed to be opening up for him in modern painting, whose discoveries needed only translation into the verbal medium. With the zeal of a recent convert, Livshits wanted a complete break with the past, and he saw a duplicity in Vladimir Burliuk's painting still lifes in the Dutch manner at school while experimenting with cubism at home. But the healthy and energetic Burliuks looked like valuable cofighters for the new aesthetics because they had strong fists, both literally and metaphorically; thus, Livshits so readily followed David Burliuk after the latter's unexpected invitation to spend the vacation with him at Chernyanka.

Chernyanka was a place in the area of the former Tavrida (Taurida) Government not far from the city of Kherson and the Black Sea coast, and from there the Burliuks' father managed the huge estate belonging to Count Mordvinov. The senior David Burliuk lived there in patriarchal simplicity and abundance, surrounded by a big family (three sons and three daughters) and enormous expanses of the steppes on which uncountable herds of sheep and pigs were grazing. For Livshits, there was something Homeric in this way of life. Prehistory looked at him not only from the meandering ornamental patterns on the houses and from the Scythian arrows found in numerous mounds, but also from the simplicity of their eating, hunting, and courtship habits. In short, it was the Hylaea ("Gileya" in Russian),[6] the name used by the ancient Greeks for this area, mentioned four times by Herodotus, and familiar to all these future futurists from their school lessons in classical history as the setting of some of the deeds of Hercules. "Hylaea, the ancient Hylaea, trod upon by our feet, took the meaning of a symbol and had to become a banner." To Livshits, it meant a new and fresh vision of the world, so indispensable for the new art they were going to create, and it was full of "animalistic power." "The world lies before you, wherever your eye can reach, in utter nakedness. . . . Grab it, tear it, bite into it, crumple it, recreate it—it belongs to you, all of it," he wrote.[7]

The brothers Burliuk were very busy during that vacation. They had just discovered Picasso and cubism, and were trying to assimilate the discovery in time for the next "Jack of Diamonds" exhibition, which was to take place in Moscow in a month. But all the methods they used—multiple perspective, flatness of portrayal, dislocation of planes, unusual coloring, even throwing the freshly painted canvas into the mud and, after this, painting it over again to make the surface "less quiet"—served, for Livshits, a single purpose, that of "the renovated vision of the world."[8] Livshits' failure at painting did not prevent his applying to poetry the methods he learned from the painters. He called his prose work "Lyudi v peizazhe" ("People in a Landscape") "100 percent cubism transferred to the area of organized speech."[9] In addition to technical problems, some ideological contours began to take shape for Livshits at that early time, the shape of Hylaean nationalism: atavistic layers, "diluvial" rhythms, flooded by the blinding light of prehistory, moving toward the West, and, ahead of all these, the wildly galloping Scythian warrior, the one-and-a-half-eyed archer. Livshits was deeply shaken by his acquaintance with Khlebnikov's manuscripts, left by the poet in Chernyanka after his sojourn there a year before, because of his own ideological outlook and because in them he found that amorphous, antediluvial verbal mass. But, of course, Livshits exaggerated in his newly acquired Hylaean enthusiasm, and he underestimated the strong rationalistic element in the work of Khlebnikov, who was an engineer of the word, too.

Thus the three brothers Burliuk and Benedict Livshits founded the group "Hylaea." The name was used for more than two years before they began to call themselves futurists. It went without saying that Khlebnikov was one of them. Shortly thereafter, Mayakovsky and Kruchenykh were to join the group. Livshits did not care very much for the name "Hylaea," which, he thought, sounded too "languorous" and was the result of their "being stuffed with high school classical reminiscences and yielding to the temptation of the mythology that surrounded them"[10] at Chernyanka. He would have preferred the meaningless, but strong and energetic-sounding, word, *chukuryùk*, invented by Vladimir Burliuk for one of his pictures.

The Burliuks were going to Moscow to impress their colleagues with the newly found cubism; but, poetically speaking, Hylaea did not mean cubism at all (cubism began to be felt in Russian futurist poetry later), but primitivism. Russian primitivism was broad in its extent and complex in its sources. It included not only painting and poetry, but music as well (the best example is Stravinsky's *Rite of Spring*). Its beginnings were, in one sense, connected with the symbolists' wide interest in Slavic mythology, as well as with the theme of the human beast in the Russian prose of the period (Leonid Andreyev, Artsybashev). In a more specific sense, however, Russian primitivism began in December, 1909, with the third exhibition of the Golden Fleece, which boasted not only examples of the fauvist line and the abstract use of color, but also specimens of folk art, such as lace, popular lithographs (*lubok*), icons, and even ornamented cookies. Soon after that, Kulbin wrote about "the art of children and prehistoric men" [11] in the same context with manifestations of beauty in nature (flowers, crystals). Even the conservative *Apollon* showed interest in children's drawings (the article by Bakst in no. 3, 1909).

The three outstanding figures of primitivism in Russian art are David Burliuk, Natalya Goncharova, and Mikhail Larionov. Burliuk's primitivistic art (unfortunately, still little studied and insufficiently appreciated) is of complex origin, being not only an outgrowth of his interest in ancient Scythian sculpture (*kamennye baby* of the southern Russian steppes, which more than once appear in Khlebnikov's poetry) and in contemporary signboards (Burliuk had a large collection of such signboards), but also based on his study of Polynesian and old Mexican art. Goncharova was strongly influenced by icons, *lubok*, and folk ornament; and Larionov added infantilist features to his primitivism (as did Khlebnikov), which contained elements of parody (also to be found in Khlebnikov) and eroticism (and in this Larionov resembles Kruchenykh). This primitivistic art was created in close personal cooperation as Larionov and Goncharova were husband and wife, and Burliuk was their close friend from 1907 until 1911. Larionov was probably the artist whose work had the greatest influence on the primitivistic poetry of the Russian futurists, especially on that of

Khlebnikov and Kruchenykh. There is much truth in Camilla Gray's words that the futurist poets took from Larionov "the use of 'irreverent-irrelevant' associations, the imitation of children's art, and the adaptation of folk-art imagery and motifs." [12] As mentioned above, both Larionov and Khlebnikov were Burliuk's guests at Chernyanka in the summer of 1910, and it is a great pity that we do not know any details of this sojourn, which might have been the real prologue to Hylaea. At any rate, in some of Khlebnikov's poetry, one can find imitation of such specific devices of painting as *protekayushchaya raskraska* ("color extending beyond the outline").

There were three main areas that attracted Russian futurist poets in their efforts to create primitivism. Childhood was one of them, and here primitivist futurism overlaps with its own impressionist stage, for example, when the inner processes in a child's life drew Guro's attention. Guro also preached (as did Kamensky) the preservation of the childlike in man. Now, in the Hylaean period, Khlebnikov used infantilism as an artistic method, and later he tried to build some of his poems on a child's vocabulary. Both Khlebnikov and Kruchenykh were interested in poetry and prose written by children and made efforts to publish it. Kamensky collected children's drawings. Another area that interested these futurist writers of primitivistic poetry was prehistory. Khlebnikov placed the action of some of his longer poems in an imaginary "Slavic Stone Age," and some of his short poetic sketches may remind the reader of drawings on cave walls. Finally, both Khlebnikov and Kruchenykh were preoccupied with certain kinds of Russian folklore. It is, however, not the "respectable" imitation of, or use of motifs from, folk epics, lyrical songs, and fairy tales which is so widespread in Russian literature. It is, instead, an interest in the naïve and "illiterate" imitation and distortion of literature, especially of romantic poetry, in numerous songs, ballads, and poems which seldom attracted the attention of scholars, who to this day tend to dismiss them as having no artistic merit.

The greatest achievements of Russian poetic primitivism are, undoubtedly, some of the longer poems by Khlebnikov. In 1911 he wrote "The Forest Maiden" and "I and E"; in 1912 appeared *A Game in Hell* (which he wrote with Kruchenykh), "The End of Atlantis," "A Vila and a Wood Goblin," and "A Shaman and Venus." After the Revolution, Khlebnikov was to continue his primitivism in "The Sylvan Sadness" and, partly, in *Ladomir*, "Poet," and "Razin's Boat." [13] The combination of naïveté and of a special kind of freshness with technical clumsiness, which is characteristic of any primitivist art, is achieved by Khlebnikov through the use of a system of artistic devices in which absurdity of situation or imagery in one poem may be followed by naïve and unaccountable omissions or anticipations of events in another one, as well as by deliberate inarticulateness in relating these events. All this is presented against a highly involved lexical and metrical background, where many kinds of irregularities are used in a virtuoso way. After Khlebnikov, only the Soviet poet Nikolai Zabolotsky (1903–1958) was able to reproduce primitivistic absurdity with such consummate skill.

The Hylaea group made its appearance only at the end of 1912 with *A Slap in the Face of Public Taste*; but for many months before its publication, leading futurists actively participated in discussions of modern art, which accompanied the exhibitions sponsored by the main groups of avant-garde painters. These discussions, often resulting in public scandals, created the atmosphere in which literary futurism was to thrive for many years. In order to understand this situation, a very short survey of Russian avant-garde art is needed, though it may repeat a few facts previously mentioned.

On December 20, 1907, a group of artists, most of whom were destined to play important roles in the history of Russian avant-garde art, opened an exhibition in Moscow under the name "Stephanos." In addition to the artists from the Blue Rose, an impressionist group that tended toward lyric mysticism, the following exhibited their work in it: David and Vladimir Burliuk, as well as their sister Lyudmila, Larionov, Goncharova, Lentulov, Yakulov, Sapunov, and Sudeikin. After a split, the Burliuks and Lentulov organized in St. Petersburg, in 1908, another exhibition under the tautological name of "Venok Stephanos" ("The Wreath Stephanos"), whereas Larionov remained in alliance with the Blue Rose and was instrumental in organizing, under the auspices of the magazine *Golden Fleece* and its millionaire founder and sponsor N. Ryabushinsky, two consecutive exhibitions, in 1908 and 1909, in which paintings by Cézanne, Van Gogh, Gauguin, Matisse, Rouault, and Braque were shown. In November, 1908, David Burliuk and Alexandra Exter were responsible for the exhibition in Kiev, "Zveno" ("Link"), which had little success. In

1909 David Burliuk allied his Wreath Stephanos to Kulbin's impressionist Triangle, which resulted the following year in a joint exhibition in St. Petersburg under the latter name. Incidentally, it was during this exhibition that *The Studio of Impressionists* appeared (as planned) and *Sadok sudei* was prepared. A year before, in 1908, Kulbin, also in St. Petersburg, organized "The Exhibition of Modern Art," which some sources also call "The Impressionists" (and which included, among others, some paintings by a blind artist). A much more profound influence, however, was exercised by the exhibitions in Odessa, Kiev, and St. Petersburg of the "Salon" of V. Izdebsky, which opened in October, 1909, and, together with the works of Larionov, Lentulov, Matyushin, and Exter, and children's drawings, showed paintings by Braque, Matisse, and other famous European postimpressionists. It was this exhibition that made so deep and lasting an impression on the young Kievan poet, Benedict Livshits.[14] A little later, some Russian avant-garde artists (including David and Vladimir Burliuk, Larionov, and Goncharova) showed their work abroad at the exhibitions of "Der blaue Reiter" and "Der Sturm."

It was during this complex and rich period that Russian painting assimilated and went beyond Western impressionism, and, on the basis of European postimpressionist trends in the arts, the original Russian contribution began to take shape. It is mostly connected with the activities of the Bubnovyi valet ("Jack of Diamonds"), a small group that soon became an influential organization, dominating Russian artistic life for several years. Its first exhibition took place in December, 1910, in Moscow, and included the works of Larionov, Goncharova, the Burliuks, Exter, Kandinsky, A. Lentulov, Konchalovsky, Ilya Mashkov, Robert Falk, and Tatlin. By the time the Hylaea group was organized, the members of Jack of Diamonds were getting ready for their second exhibition, which opened in Moscow on January 25, 1912.

In addition to the exhibition, it was decided to have lectures with discussions about modern art. Such a thing had been done before in St. Petersburg by another avant-garde group, the Union of Youth. Despite the participation of David Burliuk, this earlier lecture-discussion had passed without incident and was conducted on an almost academic note; however, at the first and historic debate of Jack of Diamonds, which took place in Moscow on February 12 in the overfilled auditorium of the Polytechnical Museum, Burliuk shocked the audience. In his lecture about cubism, he declared that the subject of painting did not matter and that Raphael and Velázquez were philistines and photographers. The audience was entertained much more, however, by Goncharova, who appeared on the stage with an unscheduled attack on Jack of Diamonds and an announcement about the coming exhibition of a new avant-garde group under the name of Oslinyi khvost ("Donkey's Tail"). The evening ended in an uproar.

There was no disturbance during the second Jack of Diamonds debate, held two weeks later without representatives of Donkey's Tail. This time Burliuk spoke on "Evolution of Beauty and Art." He insisted that the life-span of any truth in the arts is twenty-five years and, therefore, that any concept of beauty is relative and temporary. Art for Burliuk was not a copy of life, but its distortion, and he posited three artistic principles, which he called disharmony, dissymmetry, and disconstruction. The interesting fact is that Burliuk, during this lecture, mentioned Italian futurism for the first time publicly. Though at that time he knew next to nothing about Italian futurism, having not even seen a single reproduction of paintings by Italian futurists, he accused it of sacrificing the principles of the arts in favor of literature. Donkey's Tail, on the other hand, was in favor of Italian futurism, though in the work of Goncharova, Malevich, and others it never developed into an artistic *Weltanschauung,* remaining just an episode.

Donkey's Tail began to take shape before the open break of its members with members of the Jack of Diamonds group in January, 1912, for Larionov's idea to organize the group goes back to the beginning of 1911. The group, which included also Malevich, Tatlin, Von Wiesen, Ledentu, and Marc Chagall, took issue with Jack of Diamonds' "conservatism" and predilection for theorizing, insisting that subject matter was of great importance in painting and stressing its own ties with Russian primitive folk art, as well as with Oriental art. Members of the group were also against Burliuk's fighting the past and did not see anything new in cubism (cubism could be found in Russian dolls and in ancient Scythian sculptures, they said). There was also much that was personal in this break between the essentially similar founders of Russian primitivism, Goncharova and Larionov on the one side, and David Burliuk on the other. Their friendship had come to an end by 1913, and was never renewed.

In comparison with the tension and militancy displayed in artistic circles during this time, peace and tolerance were characteristic of the literary activities of the future futurists (a clumsy, but practically unavoidable expression). At the beginning of 1912 Benedict Livshits continued to contribute to *Apollon*, Nikolai Burliuk had plans to enter the Guild of Poets, which was the cradle of Russian Acmeism, and both saw in such actions no conflict with their membership in Hylaea. Preparations for new action were under way, even though during the rest of 1912 Hylaean activities in literature seemed to be in the doldrums, with Livshits having to join the army for one year, David Burliuk traveling in Europe in the summer, and Kamensky enjoying nature at his farm in the distant Urals. There was, however, some activity. Nikolai Burliuk was entrusted by his brother, David, with editorial duties, and he collected material for future joint publications quietly and efficiently. He found a common language with the demanding Livshits, who was less and less satisfied with David because of the latter's tendency to compromise and his utter unconcern with theoretical consistency.

Upon his return from Europe, David Burliuk found time to help Khlebnikov publish his first work in an individual edition—the pamphlet *Uchitel i uchenik* ("A Teacher and a Pupil"), published in Kherson with Burliuk's money. In this booklet, Khlebnikov uses dialogue as a vehicle for theorizing on the problem of "internal declension," and criticizes leading Russian symbolist writers for being preoccupied with death and violence while being far from the roots of Russian folk poetry. It was also the first presentation of Khlebnikov's attempts to find the mathematical foundations of history, which enabled him to make a strangely correct prediction about a collapse of "some empire" in 1917. No matter what one thinks about the scientific value of Khlebnikov's formulas, this preoccupation makes him practically the only real "futurist" among his friends, who rather deserve the name of "presentists."

David Burliuk had plans to publish a book, financed by Jack of Diamonds, in which both the artists and the Hylaean poets would participate. The book was in preparation throughout 1912, but did not materialize because Jack of Diamonds did not like the fact that Khlebnikov and Kruchenykh began publication of several books with illustrations by their archenemies, Goncharova and Larionov, as well as by other artists from the Donkey's Tail group. This disagreement led the Hylaeans to break with Jack of Diamonds and search for other publishers. These publishers were finally found by David Burliuk in George Kuzmin, a pilot, and Sergei Dolinsky, a composer; and *A Slap in the Face of Public Taste* was the result.

Before *A Slap in the Face of Public Taste* was published, there appeared three little books by Kruchenykh (two of them written in collaboration with Khlebnikov): *Igra v adu* ("A Game in Hell"), *Starinnaya lyubov* ("Old-Time Love"), and *Mirskontsa* ("Worldbackwards"). Alexei Eliseyevich Kruchenykh, born in 1886 to a peasant family near Kherson, was a high school art teacher when he met the Burliuks in 1907. He helped David Burliuk organize some of his exhibitions and exhibited impressionist canvases himself. Soon he moved to Moscow and, having abandoned painting for literature, became one of the most controversial of Russian futurists and probably the most radical innovator among them. He called himself "the wildest one." [15] These three books by Kruchenykh aimed at a creation of primitivistic poetry, but in some of them he went much further than that in his technique. No less important was the outward appearance of these books: they were illustrated by some of the most radical artists of the day (mostly by Goncharova and Larionov), and the texts were either written by hand and then mimeographed, or printed as if by hand in stamped letters of unequal size. All kinds of misprints or errors, as well as deletions or corrections, abounded in them. It was obviously meant to be a complete break with the tradition of symbolist deluxe editions. The illustrations were either primitivist in the manner of folk art, or imitative of children's drawings, but some of them could be termed nonobjective.

Igra v adu ("A Game in Hell") appeared in August, 1912, with sixteen illustrations by Goncharova, and was printed by hand in characters resembling Old Church Slavonic letters. This long poem about a card game going on between devils and sinners in hell was begun by Kruchenykh in the style of a folk lithograph (*lubok*), as he himself admitted.[16] Then Khlebnikov added his own stanzas and lines, with the result that the text became even more disorganized. Both Khlebnikov and Kruchenykh added to, and changed parts of, the poem after it was published. In the resulting new form, the poem was published again at the end of 1913, in a new edition, illustrated this time by Olga Rozanova and Kazimir Malevich.

Simultaneously with *A Game in Hell* (or perhaps even prior to it), there appeared another primitivist book, this time authored by Kruchenykh alone, under the title *Starinnaya lyubov* ("Old-Time Love"). Most of its illustrations, by Larionov, were in the style we now would probably call abstract expressionist. The poems were printed by hand with deliberate misprints and omissions of commas and periods, but exclamation marks were used. There were seven poems altogether, written in different manners. The first one, for instance, may be slightly parodic of the love poetry written by provincials. To the clichés and melancholy languor of nineteenth-century romantic poetry are sometimes added stylistic dissonances or nonaesthetic details (e.g., pus, vomit). Two poems form a cycle entitled "Natasha's Letters to Herzen," and are straightforward imitations of the romantic poetry of the past without any persiflage.[17] Later, in 1913, Kruchenykh added to this book a few poems and stanzas by Khlebnikov and himself, illustrating it himself in collaboration with Rozanova and Kulbin, who drew Kruchenykh's portrait for this edition. Kruchenykh also provided dedications to two poems previously not dedicated to anyone and published the entire book under the new title, *Bukh lesinnyi* ("A Forestly Rapid"). This habit of reprinting old writings in new contexts and under new titles was to become Kruchenykh's favorite method. In the same year there appeared a book whose title was a combination of both old ones, *Old-Time Love–A Forestly Rapid*. This version was built around the old material, again with addition of some new poems by both Khlebnikov and Kruchenykh.[18]

Much more experimental was the third of the three books, *Mirskontsa* ("Worldbackwards"), published by Kruchenykh in 1912 and illustrated by Larionov, Goncharova, Tatlin, and I. Rogovin in a semiabstract or primitivist manner. Outside, a polyfoil green leaf is pasted on each side of the book's yellow cover, and inside, the texts are printed only on odd pages, some in handwriting, others as if individual rubber stamps of various sizes had been used for each letter. Lapses and errors reign supreme in this book, with wrong word transfers, incorrect spelling, spaces of varying length between words, capital letters inside words, and repetitions of some texts (sometimes printed upside down). Many but not all of the letters in one poem by Khlebnikov are printed in mirror image form. Khlebnikov is represented in the book by a haphazard selection of poems, excerpts from longer works, and impromptu material. Kruchenykh's work, to which most of the book is devoted, reveals new qualities. In addition to the rather solemn introductory poem written in traditional iambic tetrameter, there are verses that imitate the spoken idiom and are full of crude energy in their short, uneven lines. In their content, they are mostly strings of images without much connection (in one poem, such an image string is motivated by a dream). Most interesting in the book are the attempts to write a new kind of prose. For instance, there are twenty pages of text printed without punctuation, with sentences overlapping and blending, under the title "A Voyage across the Whole World," which does describe some kind of travel despite the inclusion of much irrelevant material and seems to be an exercise in automatic writing.

These three books were followed by three more by Kruchenykh at the very beginning of 1913, also published by Kuzmin and Dolinsky. *Poluzhivoi* ("Half Alive") is another book of primitivist verse, illustrated by Larionov. This poem is rather obscure and in it predominate images of war and violence culminating in the picture of a vampire sucking the blood of dead and wounded warriors on a battlefield. Analysis of the diction and metrics of the poem reveals a conscious imitation of the primitivistic style of Khlebnikov even to the smallest detail—and Khlebnikov actually "retouched" this book as he did the next one and others that followed. Another book, *Pustynniki* ("Hermits"), contains two long poems, the second being "Pustynnica" ("A Hermit Woman"). It begins as an imitation of *dukhovnye stikhi* ("religious folk poetry") about life in a hermitage, but develops into an almost surrealistic succession of images, which depict not only the life of the holy men, but their conscious and suppressed desires. The main theme is usually quite clear, but it is in the development and in the details that Kruchenykh resorts to absurdity and alogism. A closer scrutiny of "A Hermit Woman" is imperative in any study of Russian primitivism because this poem points, in some passages, as far into the future as the poetry of Nikolai Zabolotsky, written in the 1920's. Kruchenykh's familiar tendency to shock his audience manifests itself here in the emphasis he places on erotic scenes, as well as in the pictures he paints of holy men and women as anything but holy, which, in 1913, seemed blasphemous. Both eroticism and blasphemy are shown in excellent illustrations by Goncharova, in which she reflects the strong influence of Russian icon painting. *Pomada* ("Pomade"), published in January, 1913, is a very small book, containing less than a dozen poems, three of them, with tricky compound rhymes, written, as Kruchenykh notes on the last page, together with E. Lunev.[19] *Pomade* was illustrated by Larionov not only in a primitivistic style (as, for example, the drawing on the cover which shows a diminutive barber suspended in the air and rubbing pomade into the hair of a big head underneath), but in his new, "rayonist" manner. The book's value in reference to the history of futurism lies mainly in the fact that it opens with three tiny poems written, as the author says in a very short introduction, "in my own language differing from the oth[ers]: its words do not have a definite meaning." In short, here Kruchenykh introduced what later was to become known as *zaum*, the so-called transrational language, of which he would become one of the main practicians and theoreticians. Later the first of these three poems became particularly familiar to many because the author announced in a subsequent booklet that it was more Russian than all the poetry of Pushkin. After this announcement dozens of critics began to quote it or refer to it, often distorting it. The poem begins with energetic monosyllabics, some of which slightly resemble Russian or Ukrainian words, followed by a three-syllable word of shaggy appearance. The next word looks like a fragment of some word, and the two final lines are occupied with syllables and just plain letters, respectively, the poem ending on a queer, non-Russian–sounding syllable:

> dyr   bul   shchyl
> ubeshshchur
> skum
> vy   so   bu
> r   l   èz[20]

Thus, in his first publishing ventures, Kruchenykh added his own note to Russian primitivism; created, mainly with the artists Goncharova and Larionov, the classic form of a futurist publication; and inaugurated the most extreme of all futurist achievements, *zaum*. Credit is overdue to this fascinating writer, who never in his life achieved anything but cheap notoriety. Even his own colleagues tended to dismiss him as the man who "brought to absurdity some of our extreme tenets by his flippant extremism." [21]

When *Half Alive, Hermits,* and *Pomade* appeared, the most famous joint publication of the Hylaean poets, *A Slap in the Face of Public Taste,* had already been published. After the Jack of Diamonds refused to finance this publication, Burliuk found backers in Kuzmin and Dolinsky, guaranteeing them the gratitude of posterity for their part in his publishing venture. *A Slap* was printed on gray and brown wrapping paper, and the cover was of coarse sackcloth, later described by reviewers as being the color of "a fainted louse." [22] Otherwise, there was nothing shocking about the book, the texts being printed in large, clear print, with no illustrations accompanying them. Strangely enough, there was no mention of Hylaea anywhere in the book. The opening piece, also entitled "A Slap in the Face of Public Taste," was the first and most famous manifesto of the group. It was signed by only four of the seven contributors, and one of the signatories, Khlebnikov, did not participate in its writing. Livshits and Nikolai Burliuk were not in Moscow, so their signatures were not there. Livshits makes it clear that he would not have signed it anyway, and his refusal was based on grounds other than that, as a soldier, he could not afford at that time to take part in controversial enterprises. Even Livshits was unable to determine (as set forth in his memoirs) who was the actual author of the manifesto, but he recognized in it one of his own phrases used in a conversation with Mayakovsky. "A Slap" was probably written by David Burliuk, Kruchenykh, and Mayakovsky[23] together in November or December, 1912, in the Romanovka Hotel in Moscow, where they spent their evenings. The recently married Burliuk lived there with his wife, a student of music, because there one could practice voice or instruments from 9 A.M. to 11 P.M. (and so the hotel was full of students from the Conservatory). Here is the complete text of the manifesto:

To the readers of our New First Unexpected

Only *we are the face of our Time.* The horn of time trumpets through us in the art of the word.

The past is crowded. The Academy and Pushkin are more incomprehensible than hieroglyphics.

Throw Pushkin, Dostoyevsky, Tolstoy, *et al., et al.,* overboard from the Ship of Modernity.

He who does not forget his *first* love will not recognize his last.

But who is so gullible as to direct his last love toward the perfumed lechery of a Balmont? Does it reflect the virile soul of today?

Who is so cowardly as to be afraid to strip the warrior Bryusov of the paper armor he wears over his black tuxedo? Is the dawn of an undiscovered beauty seen there?

Wash your hands, you who touched the filthy slime of the books written by all those innumerable Leonid Andreyevs.

All those Maxim Gorkys, Kuprins, Bloks, Sologubs, Remizovs, Averchenkos, Chernyis, Kuzmins, Bunins, etc., etc. need only a *dacha* on a river. Tailors are rewarded by destiny in this way.

We look at their nothingness from the heights of skyscrapers! . . .

We decree that the poets' *rights* be honored:

1) to enlarge vocabulary in its *scope* with arbitrary and derivative words (creation of new words).

2) to feel an insurmountable hatred for the language existing before them.

3) to push aside in horror from our proud brow the wreath of dirt-cheap fame, which you have fashioned from bathhouse *venik*'s ["swishes"].

4) to stand on the solid block of the word "we" amid the sea of boos and indignation.

And if *for the time being* even our lines are still marked with dirty stigmas of your "common sense" and "good taste," there tremble on them *for the first time* the summer lightnings of the New-Coming Beauty of the Self-sufficient (self-centered) Word.

Moscow, 1912, December	D. Burliuk, Alexander Kruchenykh[24]
	V. Mayakovsky, Victor Khlebnikov

As a polemical work, the manifesto was effective. The attacks on the popular writers of the day drew the attention of literary circles and of the press, though it does not seem that any of the victims felt offended. The appeal to discard the classics created an even greater sensation, and it has never been forgotten. Both points were purely tactical and did not express the real ideas of the writers. Most of them were far from actually rejecting Pushkin, and they were on good terms with some of the attacked contemporaries. And when in 1915

Maxim Gorky publicly endorsed some of the leading futurists (see chap. 7), the attitude shown by them was that of almost servile gratitude rather than of "pushing aside with horror." Strictly speaking, only Kruchenykh, in the overwhelming majority of his subsequent works, lived up to the declaration of "hatred for the language existing before them," as well as to the professed rejection of common sense and good taste. On the other hand, the promise to stand on the solid block of the word "we" (if one is to understand it as the intention to stick together as fellow futurists) has been, on the whole, kept even during times of adversity. As far as the positive program of the manifesto is concerned, it is vague and insufficient, betraying the fact that the writers were unsure of their purpose. Creation of new words was not enough for aesthetic foundations of a movement; moreover, only Khlebnikov actually practiced it to some extent (not to speak of Igor-Severyanin who was not a Hylaean). The mention of the "self-centered word" (which also could be translated as "autotelic") was unfortunately only a mention.

The rest of *A Slap* was a letdown in the sense that it contained no "skyscrapers," some of the works being as passé as they could be, as far as subject matter was concerned. But, unlike *Sadok sudei*, the quality of the material presented was consistently good. The book begins with, and gives the largest amount of space to, Khlebnikov. Eight of his short poems are printed (under a wrong heading), and most of them are veritable gems, especially the semiabstract "Bobeobi," perfect in its sound painting. Among more sizable works, one should single out "Devii-bog" ("The Maidens' God"), a dramatic work set in pagan Russia. In this play, which is marked by anachronisms, different levels of action are mixed. Then there are "I and E," Khlebnikov's primitivistic masterpiece, and "Pamyatnik" ("The Monument"), perhaps artistically the most successful expression of his nationalism. "Pesn miryazya" ("The Song of the Peacer") should be mentioned, too, as Khlebnikov's most typical piece of neologistic prose.

Benedict Livshits is represented in *A Slap* by six poems printed in his second collection of verse, *Volchye solntse* ("The Sun of the Wolves"). They are full of allusions, exquisite artificiality, and restrained beauty, some of them resembling Rimbaud's works. After reading Khlebnikov, one cannot help noticing Livshits' non-Russian sound (this was also one of the characteristic features of much Russian symbolist poetry). The most arresting piece by Livshits is his "People in a Landscape," whose title was taken by the poet from one of Léger's paintings. Consisting of three short chapters written in prose, its aim is "a cubist shaping of the verbal mass," [25] and it represents an attempt to create a much more sophisticated futurist prose than that exemplified by Kruchenykh's *Worldbackwards*. Typical of Livshits are the lack of predicates, unusual use of adverbs and prepositions, and words placed together in an alogical way.

Nikolai Burliuk showed himself in *A Slap* exclusively as a prose writer. There is a pleasant strangeness (as well as some influence of Khlebnikov and Guro) in his three pieces, but they are neither cubistic nor primitivistic, but rather impressionistic. In "Smert legkomyslennogo molodogo cheloveka" ("Death of a Frivolous Young Man"), the hero takes poison and dies; but, after crossing Lethe with Charon, he finds that Hades has been abolished. "Tishina Ellady" ("The Stillness of Hellas") is a piece of lyric prose describing the Black Sea region (i.e., Hylaea). Autobiographical elements can be seen in the description of a childhood on a country estate in "Solnechnyi dom" ("A Sunny House"), which develops into a fantasy about the mysterious forces that conquer one room of the house after another. David Burliuk's several poems united under the title "Sadovnik" ("The Gardener") show a firmer hand and the same old inability to make his points clearly.

Vasily Kandinsky's participation in *A Slap* adds special interest to this book, although the futurists themselves later described it as an accident.[26] His four little sketches in prose are the Russian originals of some of his writings published in Munich in German under the title *Klänge*. They are written in an impressionistic manner and show Kandinsky, at that time, at least, a better prose writer than Nikolai Burliuk, even if Livshits called the latter's prose in *A Slap* "delightful."

Kruchenykh made his debut as a member of the group with an interesting primitivist poem, written in a kind of trochee which later gives way to rhymed prose, with a suggestion of a plot involving an officer and the redheaded Polya. The poem is printed without punctuation or capital letters, and contains words incorrectly stressed (*glázami*) which is one of Kruchenykh's trademarks. At the end there is the author's note to the effect that the events in the poem are not related in their chronological sequence, but in the order 3–1–2.

Another debut proved later to be of the greatest historical importance because the name of the poet was Vladimir Mayakovsky. His two short poems, "Noch" ("Night") and "Utro" ("Morning"), with their colorful urbanism and anthropomorphism, are a strange and dissonant note in this rather peaceful book, for Mayakovsky's thunderous voice can already be heard in them. Their dynamism reminds one of Italian futurism, rather than, to quote Khlebnikov, the "pure Slavic element in its golden, linden tree quality." [27]

A Slap concludes with four essays. The first two, wrongly attributed to Nikolai Burliuk, are actually by David. "Kubizm," written in a deliberately disorganized fashion, with capital letters in the wrong places, contains both long-winded, impressionistic passages, which remind one of the worst excesses of symbolist criticism, and excellent professional observations. Painting, says Burliuk, has become an art only in the twentieth century, because it is now an aim in itself. Earlier painting knew only line and color; the new painting has discovered surface and texture. Cézanne is declared the father of cubism, and cubism is defined as "understanding of everything we see only as a series of certain cuts through various flat surfaces." He also speaks of "free drawing" and sees the best examples of it in children's drawings, as well as in Kandinsky and Larionov; in poetry, its equivalent is free verse, the best example of which Burliuk finds in Khlebnikov. In both articles, Burliuk uses generously the terms *sdvig* ("shift, dislocation") and *faktura* ("texture"), which were to become also the favorite words of futurist literary criticism. The second article, "Faktura," is written in fanciful, lyric prose which alternates with dry and specific outlines. In content it ranges from attacks on traditional art criticism (with the artist and art historian Alexander Benois serving as Burliuk's usual whipping boy) to a highly detailed classification of picture surfaces, and subtle observations about the textures of paintings by Monet, Cézanne, and some Russian contemporaries. Khlebnikov's "Obrazchik slovonovshestv v yazyke" ("A Sample of Neologisms") demonstrates the first premise of the manifesto. *A Slap* concludes with Khlebnikov's earlier prediction of the fall of an empire in 1917. This prediction had so impressed Burliuk that he placed it at the end of the book in the form of a simple list of names and dates.[28]

(Perhaps to confound future bibliographers, the Hylaeans, in February, 1913, published in Moscow a leaflet also entitled *A Slap in the*

Face of Public Taste. It echoes the main tenets of the miscellany manifesto, but, on the whole, differs widely from its famous predecessor. In
the leaflet the authors castigate the leaders of Russian literature for
not having recognized Khlebnikov as a genius in 1908 (*sic*), after the
publication of *Sadok sudei.* They attack the leading journalists of the
day, who mistook the Hylaeans for "decadents," and describe the group
around Khlebnikov as people who are united in their rejection of the
word as a means and their glorification of the self-sufficient word,
though each goes his own artistic or literary way. Instead of signatures,
the leaflet, which also contained some poetry by Mayakovsky, ends
with a photograph of Mayakovsky, Khlebnikov, David and Nikolai
Burliuk, and both publishers of the Hylaeans, Kuzmin and Dolinsky.)

Simultaneously with *A Slap,* Burliuk started collecting material
for another joint publication to be printed in St. Petersburg by Guro
and Matyushin. To emphasize continuity in the development of the
movement, it was decided to call the book *Sadok sudei II,* but the
name of the group, as in the first *Sadok sudei,* was not identified, because Guro was against using the word "Hylaea." With her northern
background (Finland and St. Petersburg), she was not impressed by
the classical connotations of that southern Russian area. The book appeared in February, 1913, with a cover only slightly reminiscent of the
wallpaper on which the first volume had been printed. It was illustrated
not only by Guro and Matyushin themselves and by Vladimir and
David Burliuk, but also by Larionov and Goncharova who, despite
their break with the group, participated in a Hylaean venture, but for
the last time. Myasoyedov and Gei, two minor participants in the
first *Sadok sudei,* were not among the contributors this time; and particularly conspicuous was the absence of one of the group's "stars,"
Vasily Kamensky, who, still bitter about the failure of his first novel,
The Mud Hut, was nursing his wounds in the seclusion of his farm.

The most important single piece in *Sadok sudei II* is its untitled
manifesto which opens the book, as in *A Slap.* Although it never
received as much publicity as the latter, it is in a way more interesting
because it tries, for the first time, to provide the movement with a
specific and detailed constructive program. Yet, it lacks the unity and
thrust of the manifesto that opened *A Slap.* On the whole, it is also
too diffuse, being an eclectic combination of the favorite ideas of individual group members, rather than an attempt to set forth basic tenets

common to them all. It is also confusing, not only because of the clumsy use of scholastic terminology, which in 1913 was rudimentary, but also because of the wrong claims and contradictory statements that characterize it. At the beginning of the manifesto, which, surprisingly, does not contain any attacks on literary enemies, there is the rather high-handed declaration that all the principles outlined there had been fully expressed in the first *Sadok sudei*, which the authors must have known to be false because the first *Sadok sudei* was a very shy and inept attempt to create a "new art." The formative stage is said to be past, and what was born in 1908 (*sic*) is now open to development by "those who have no new tasks." Thus the manifesto's authors strike the pose of adults far ahead of the children who come behind and are still busy repeating the discoveries of their predecessors, though they never make clear what new tasks lie ahead. From the rest of the manifesto, which enumerates in detail the achievements of the group, it becomes clear that theory is once again marching ahead of practice. One obscure statement in the introductory part deserves special attention. It speaks rather inarticulately about "having given a start" (*vydvinuv*) to the "formerly notorious" (*ranee preslovutykh*) and wealthy futurists. The reference is to the St. Petersburg group of ego-futurists, who at exactly this time clearly turned to verbal experimentation and thus became rivals of the Hylaeans (see chap. 3). It is amusing to see that someone else is called "futurist" by people who were themselves to become (for everyone else) *the* Russian futurists. The "new principles of creation," which occupy the rest of the manifesto, are enumerated and discussed briefly below.

1. "We have ceased to look at word formation and word pronunciation according to grammar rules, beginning to see in letters only the determinants of speech. We have shaken syntax loose." The author of these words was Khlebnikov. Despite some confusing parts (e.g., mixing pronunciation and grammar) and questionable terminology ("letters"), which may make modern linguists wince, this is a reasonably accurate statement of what Khlebnikov himself tried to or did accomplish; Livshits, who made his own effort to "shake syntax loose" in *A Slap*, was in complete agreement.

2. "We have begun *to attach meaning to words according to their graphic and phonic characteristics*" seemed like a good program for any consistent futurism.

3. "The role of prefixes and suffixes has become clear to us" is another statement that Khlebnikov could have made about himself.

4. "In the name of the freedom of personal chance [*svoboda lichnogo sluchaya*], we reject orthography." This principle was fully demonstrated by Kruchenykh in his mimeographed publications.

5. "We characterize nouns not only by adjectives (as was chiefly done before us), but also by other parts of speech, as well as by individual letters and numbers:

a) considering corrections [*pomarki*] and the vignettes of creative expectation inseparable parts of a work,

b) deeming that the handwriting is an ingredient [*sostavlyayushchaya*] of a poetic impulse,

c) therefore, we have printed in Moscow 'self-written' books (of autographs)." This lengthy paragraph obviously refers to Kruchenykh's publications.[29]

6. "We have abolished punctuation, which for the first time brings the role of the verbal mass consciously to the fore." Livshits liked this one, and it is certainly a fascinating explanation of what the Hylaeans actually did, but they were never consistent in such efforts, nor was the whole idea so new.

7. "We think of vowels as space and time (the character of direction); consonants are color, sound, smell." Only a few years later David Burliuk expressed the same ideas in a poem. Khlebnikov's experiments with consonants were contained in "Bobeobi," printed in *A Slap*.

8. "We have smashed rhythms. Khlebnikov brought the poetic cadence [*razmer*] of the living conversational word. We have ceased to look for meters in textbooks; every new turn of movement gives birth to a new and free rhythm for a poet." Khlebnikov did introduce conversational rhythms, but so did his symbolist teacher, Mikhail Kuzmin. Besides, Khlebnikov's main efforts were concentrated on something else, namely, on mixing identifiable meters in adjacent lines or within a line. Only after the Revolution did he begin to practice free verse consistently. The Mayakovsky revolution in Russian metrics also was to come later. Burliuk could never really break with the "textbook meters"; Livshits never even tried.

9. "The front rhyme (David Burliuk), the middle and reversed rhymes (Mayakovsky) have been worked out by us." "Worked out" is a cautious term, and the authors probably were afraid of claiming the

invention of these kinds of rhyme because many of them were used before by the symbolists.

10. "The poet's justification is in the richness of his vocabulary." This statement refers not only to Khlebnikov's neologisms, but to the futurists' general tendency to introduce regional and unusual words in their writings.

11. "We consider the word a creator of myth; the word, when dying, gives birth to a myth and vice versa." This point, hardly original, was proposed by Nikolai Burliuk, who was seconded by Livshits. Livshits realized that the statement smacked of Potebnya's philological theories, but thought it necessary "to tie a scholarly theory, directed toward the sources of human existence, to the artistic practice of today." [30]

12. "We are obsessed with new themes: futility, meaninglessness, and the mystery of a power-hungry mediocrity were glorified by us." This point by Kruchenykh was particularly resented by Livshits.

13. "We despise fame; we experience feelings that did not exist before us." Though Livshits attributes this point to Kruchenykh, it is actually a repetition of what was said before in the manifesto, "A Slap." The document ends with the words, "We are new people of new life"; and there follow the signatures of D. Burliuk, Guro, N. Burliuk, Mayakovsky, Nizen, Khlebnikov, Livshits, and Kruchenykh.

Though Livshits signed the manifesto, he did not like its confusion and heterogeneity, for which he blamed David Burliuk. But it was inevitable, for each of the members was already beginning to acquire his own poetic technique, whose details might not have been shared by the rest. For this reason, the Hylaeans dropped all aesthetic subtleties in the next joint manifesto (in *Roaring Parnassus*) and concentrated on offending the rest of contemporary literature, a familiar method used with great success in *A Slap*.

Other than the manifesto, there was little that was new in *Sadok sudei II*. Livshits, disillusioned by the manifesto, gave for the book only a few poems, which were written soon after his first book of verse and which he himself considered "academic." Khlebnikov, as usual, was the main attraction with his two longer poems, both written in a primitivistic manner. "The End of Atlantis" was somber and restrained, almost classical in its texture, whereas "A Shaman and Venus" was built on absurdity and travesty. There was also a delightful exercise in infantilistic romanticism in "Maria Vetsera," a poem about the famous

Mayerling tragedy; "Krymskoe" ("Crimean"), a free verse poem written as an exercise in intricate rhymes, mostly homonymic; a few exercises in neologism, similar to the laughter poem, and a short poem-
palindrome, Khlebnikov's first attempt to appropriate the technique he
would perfect in 1920 to produce his 408-line palindromic masterpiece, "Razin." The short essay, "O brodnikakh" ("On Roamers"),
which followed was a historical sketch about ancient Slavs containing
some etymological ideas. Contrary to the identification in the book, it
was not by David Burliuk, but also by Khlebnikov. The old-fashioned
diction, melody, and metrics of the fourteen poems, however, indicate
they are indisputably the work of David Burliuk; but this time Burliuk tried very hard to appear as radical and experimental in other
aspects of his verse as possible. In "Opus 29" (Burliuk continued
here, as elsewhere, the count of his poems in this way, beginning with
the first *Sadok sudei*), for instance, he not only uses the sound "s" in
abundance, but tells the reader about it in a footnote. He also introduced the device of printing a few words in a poem in a larger print
size, explaining this in another footnote as "leading words" (*leitslova*).
But such devices were only a later touching-up of poems written mostly
between 1908 and 1910, which explains why some of them are clearly
impressionistic (e.g., "Opus 29" and "Opus 33"). Two later poems,
however, show Burliuk's experiment of stringing words in an alogical
manner,[31] similar to what Kruchenykh did a few pages later and, in
a much subtler way, to what Livshits tried in his "People in a Landscape." Here, as an example, is Burliuk's "Opus 38," written in 1912:

> Temnyi zloba golovatyi
> Sero glazoe pila
> Utomlennyi rodila
> Zvezd zhelatelnoe laty

As to Nikolai Burliuk, he continued here to develop further his
impressionistic manner in the two prose miniatures, "Sbezhavshie
muzy" ("The Muses Who Fled"), about the Muses who vanished from
a picture, and his first real artistic achievement, "Polunochnyi ogon"
("Midnight Fire"). In this story the protagonist arrives home and finds
a letter with an oak leaf enclosed. During the night he is awakened
by a noise in the shower and discovers there a young stranger with

closed eyes. Fire approaches the youth and, through water, devours him, while he is transformed into an oak leaf. Less original and still very much in the symbolist tradition are several poems by Nikolai Burliuk, but they are appealing in their quiet modesty. Nikolai Burliuk was probably the only group member who entered neither the area of primitivism nor that of verbal experimentation, but stuck to his impressionism. On the other hand, Kruchenykh seems in *Sadok sudei II* to have adopted completely the new, abstract or semiabstract manner. His poems, printed under the general title "Myatezh v snegu" ("Rebellion in Snow") and subtitled "Words with Someone Else's Bellies," begin with four and a half lines of words, invented, distorted, or, sometimes, taken from the existing Russian lexicon, all printed without punctuation (except a comma after the first word).[32] The next poem is vertical in that nearly every word occupies a separate line, there being almost no logical connection between them. In one poem, several lines end in capital vowel letters which are not parts of words. Much of *Sadok sudei II*'s space is given to Guro's prose which, after her death, was to become part of her *The Baby Camels of the Sky.* Her sister, E. Nizen, is represented by one prose work, "Pyatna" ("Spots"), built on a stream-of-consciousness technique. A curious finale to the book are the two poems written by a thirteen-year-old girl, Militsa, from the Ukraine. Khlebnikov virtually forced the editors to print these and even withdrew one of his own poems to give space to the girl. These examples of authentic primitivism must have appealed to him, but even dearer to his nationalistic heart must have been the beginning of the first of the poems:

> I want to die,
> And in Russian soil
> They will bury me.
> I'll never study French,
> I won't look into a German book.

In March, 1913, the Hylaeans again appeared in print as a group, scarcely giving their reading audience time for a breather. This time they appeared as an autonomous section of the group of the St. Petersburg avant-garde known as the Union of Youth.[33] Formed at the beginning of 1910, this group had held its first exhibition in March of that year. Sponsored by a wealthy patron of the arts, L. Zhever-zheyev, the group had a less pronounced artistic profile than either Donkey's Tail or Jack of Diamonds. Nor could it boast the same consistency of achievement. Among the Union of Youth, only Olga Rozanova and Pavel Filonov could be considered first-rate artists. Nevertheless, they fought for the ideals of the "new art," however vaguely understood. They popularized the recent trends of art in western Europe and tried to go beyond European borders and discover new areas in Oriental and African art. David Burliuk was in touch with them from the very beginning, participating in their exhibitions and public lectures. The alliance that he engineered between the Union of Youth and his Hylaea lasted until December, 1913, soon after which the Union of Youth dissolved.

In 1912, the Union of Youth began to publish a magazine, *Soyuz molodezhi* ("Union of Youth"), which printed not only articles on art, but also translations of Chinese poetry. In its second issue, two manifestos of the Italian futurist artists were printed. The Hylaeans found a place in the publication's third issue, and their mention on the title page marked the first time they publicly called themselves "Hylaea." The preface to this third issue announced the creation of an autonomous section, "Hylaea," within the Union of Youth and stated that the time had come for a union of artists and poets in general. The poetry of the Hylaeans was referred to as that of the most essential and perceptive poets. There was also an enumeration of rather vague points uniting the two organizations: (1) the definition of the philosophically beautiful; (2) the establishment of a difference between the creator and the cospectator [*soglyadatai*]; and (3) the fight against automatism and temporality [*mekhanistichnost i vremennost*]. These first three points were followed by three points "which unite as well as separate": (1) the extension of the evaluation of the beautiful beyond the limits of consciousness (the principle of relativity); (2) the acceptance of the theory of knowledge as a criterion; and (3) the unity of the so-called material.

The third issue of *Union of Youth* was divided into two parts, and the first part was devoted to essays on the arts. Among these, the following are of interest: Avgust Ballyer's polemics with *Apollon* entitled "Apollon budnichnyi i Apollon chernyavyi" ("The Everyday Apollo and the Negritudinous Apollo"); "Osnovy novogo tvorchestva"

("The Foundations of the New Art") by O. Rozanova; and M. V. Matyushin's synopsis of *Du cubisme* by Gleizes and Metzinger intermingled with long quotations from Peter Ouspensky's *Tertium Organum*. Two Hylaeans also contributed essays. Nikolai Burliuk wrote the essay "Vladimir Davidovich Burliuk," in which he mentions his brother's name only once—in the last paragraph—devoting the rest of his work to a discussion of Vladimir's aesthetics. Khlebnikov is represented here by a shortened version of his *Teacher and Pupil*, published earlier in book form, and by another dialogue, "Razgovor dvukh osob" ("A Conversation between Two Personages"), which attacks Immanuel Kant and tries to demonstrate the relationships between word and number. The second part of the magazine contains the verse of the Hylaean poets. David Burliuk is represented by two poems; his brother Nikolai, by six, most of which are among his best (see especially "Πάντα ῥεῖ" and "Babochki v kolodtse" ["Butterflies in a Well"]); and Livshits, by three. Among Kruchenykh's four poems, two deserve attention. "Tyanut konei" ("Horses Are Pulled") is essentially a typographical poem with most letters being uppercase; there are some curious anticipations of e.e. cummings' devices as, for example, in printing the word *zazhatyi* ("clamped") as zAZHAtyi. The second poem, which describes the pleasure of lying on the ground next to a pig, was to become a favorite source of quotations for critics of futurism. Guro printed only one short, impressionistic sketch, "Shchebet vesennikh" ("Chirping of Springtime [creatures]"), and Khlebnikov is represented as a poet by his magnificent tour de force, "Voina smert" ("The War, the Death"), his only long poem built on neologisms.

Also in March, 1913, Kuzmin and Dolinsky published another futurist miscellany, *Trebnik troikh* ("The Missal of the Three"). The title is a triumph of alliteration over meaning, because there are four participants in this book, even if one does not count its illustrators, Vladimir and Nadezhda Burliuk and V. Tatlin. These four are Khlebnikov, Mayakovsky, and David and Nikolai Burliuk, with Mayakovsky and David Burliuk contributing illustrations as well as poems. The appearance of the book is rather conservative with the title printed on a white label pasted on the gray cover and each poem printed on a separate page in clear print. There are portraits of Khlebnikov, Mayakovsky, and all Burliuks, including Vladimir. *The Missal of the Three* differs from all previous futurist joint publications in that it contains neither articles nor prose. Its aim is to present pure poetic achievement, and in this it succeeds. In previous publications, Khlebnikov was usually represented by his longer works; here for the first time he could be seen as a master of the miniature fragment, and there are twenty-five of these in *The Missal*. Later, scholarly editors had difficulties in deciding which of these were finished products and which were just sketches for future works, and they accused the first publisher, David Burliuk, and one another of confusing these two categories. In the Soviet five-volume edition of Khlebnikov's works, some of the best poems were, therefore, relegated to the back of a volume. It is true that Burliuk, to put it mildly, was not very scholarly when he published Khlebnikov at this or any other time. Nevertheless, the selection in *The Missal* is very good, and the majority of the poems are gems, so that one suspects that, for once, Burliuk acted with the author's consent. Furthermore, scholars have always maintained that it is hard to draw a line between Khlebnikov's finished and unfinished works; and more than once the author himself incorporated an earlier, finished poem into a later, longer and more complex work. Most of Khlebnikov's poems in *The Missal* are built on, or contain, neologisms, and many are perfect in what can be paradoxically described as their transparent obscurity. Even some of the mere enumerations of neologisms printed one under another are successful poems. Especially ingenious is a list of the names of dramatis personae from some imaginary Russian tragedy (which could have been written by Sumarokov, for example): Negava, Sluzhava, Belynya, Bystrets, Umnets, Vlad, Sladyka. Here the names express the qualities or positions of the characters in a true eighteenth-century manner, and one even begins to distinguish the vague outline of the plot behind them.

As to Mayakovsky, his urbanist cubism was never better presented than in *The Missal*. Later he made changes in some of these poems, but not all of them were improvements. For instance, his well-known "Iz ulitsy v ulitsu" ("From One Street to Another"), as printed here,[34] reads like a succession of five shorter poems, and I think some readers would prefer it in this form. It is also interesting to note that in this early version of the poem, which later received the title "Vyveskam" ("To the Signboards"), there is a first example of compound rhyme, which later became Mayakovsky's trademark (*parche ven: kharche-ven*).

The most fascinating thing about *The Missal* is that the poetry of Nikolai and David Burliuk which it contains is practically on the same level as that of their colleagues. Nikolai Burliuk shows in his fifteen poems (some of them reprints) that he has grown into a mature minor poet with varied artistic devices, which only maliciously could be described as eclecticism. To look in his work for the familiar "futurist" features, such as loud tone, coarse imagery, and radical verbal experiment, would lead to disappointment. Often he reminds one of Khlebnikov, especially in his short, four-line sketches, but he does not use neologisms. He may mix archaisms and poeticisms with "low" diction (*K lanitam klonitsya koryavyi palets*), but he never stresses this device. In fact, he sometimes seems an Acmeist with occasional eccentricities; and one is almost tempted to call him an Acmeist among futurists who would prefer to appear as a futurist among Acmeists. Actually, though, he belongs to no party, and it is no accident that in one of these poems he mentions the "soul of a dissenter" (*dusha inovertsa*). He is a quiet and independent soul who goes his own way. It is easy to imagine the following little poem in the hands of another futurist (or a postrevolutionary imagist): it would be defiant and involved. Nikolai Burliuk makes it almost classical:

> Nad stepyu krysh
> I stadom trub
> Plyvet luny
> Sozhzhennyi trup
>
> (Over the steppe of roofs
> And the herd of stacks
> There floats
> the burnt cadaver of the moon)

It is also necessary to note the beginning of the futurists' shift toward the Orient in his first poem, which ends with the words:

> Vo mne ariitsa golos smolk
> Ya vizhu minarety Kryma
>
> (The Aryan's voice is silent in me
> I see the minarets of Crimea)

Much more amazing is the selection that David Burliuk printed in

The Missal. Nothing in his previous publications (or his later ones, for that matter) prepares us for the consistently high quality displayed in this book. David Burliuk is often a provincial who can hardly camouflage his old-fashioned poetic culture with superdaring "innovations," who drowns in the banal while trying to be original; an artist who clumsily applies the devices of his painting to verse without noticing that this transferal does not save the situation; a versifier who thinks that a cerebral rhyme he has just invented or a shocking image suffices to make his poem avant-garde. But in *The Missal* Burliuk, for once, succeeds both rhythmically and stylistically. There is an energetic stubbornness in many of his poems here, but even the autumnal ones are full of convincing strangeness. There is not a single superfluous word in his slightly primitivistic "Zakat malyar shirokoi kistyu"; the four-line "Veshchatel' tainogo soyuza" is worthy of a Khlebnikov; and his little poem about "that flea of the swamps, the frog," is excellent. None of the strain often noted in Burliuk's work is present in his exercise in rhymed beginnings of lines or in other rhyming tours de force. Only four of the sixteen poems fall short of this suprising level of poetic achievement.

If in *A Slap* the Russian futurists suddenly and violently attacked the present and the past of Russian literature, if in *Sadok sudei II* they made a claim at being the possessors of a new aesthetics and in *Union of Youth* they demonstrated that they had allies in Russian art, in *The Missal* they showed they could create first-rate poetry of consistently high quality.

3 EGO-FUTURISM & THE MEZZANINE OF POETRY

It has become customary to disregard Russian ego-futurism as an ephemeral and insignificant movement that can boast of little poetically and scarcely deserves to be called futurism;[1] but this judgment is only half true, and the actual picture is much more complex. Unfortunately, the ego-futurists' publications, except for the works of their initial leader, Igor-Severyanin, are practically unavailable, and for this reason scholars are seldom able to realize the historical importance of the movement or to trace its actual development. Ego-futurist ties with the tradition of earlier Russian modernism are clearer than those of the Hylaea poets. The connections of ego-futurism with European literature and with other Russian futurist groups place the whole history of Russian futurism in a new perspective. The very fact that the ego-futurists brought the word "futurism" to Russian literature was full of consequences: the Hylaeans accepted it, too, and both Hylaeans and ego-futurists had to live up to their name, which modified and, one may add, clarified their initial aesthetics. Historically, it is also important to remember that for contemporaries futurism meant, for a considerable time, ego-futurism, and the Hylaeans, more than once and much to their displeasure, were called "ego-futurists" by critics. The majority of provincial imitations of the eventually fashionable futurism were written in the ego-futurist vein.

Ego-futurism was the creation of Igor Vasilyevich Lotarev (1887–1942), who published his poetry under the name of Igor-Severyanin.[2] Severyanin was born into a noble family: his father was an officer and his mother, a distant relative of the famous nineteenth-century poet, Afanasy Fet. He began writing poetry while quite young, and, as early as 1904, published his verse in pamphlet form in St. Petersburg. Severyanin began his career as a poet with patriotic verse inspired by the Russo-Japanese War and slowly progressed through various imitative stages, being greatly influenced by the work of Constantine M. Fofanov (1862–1911) and Mirra Lokhvitskaya (1869–1905), two neoromantic poets who were also often labeled impressionists. Later he met Fofanov personally and became a friend of his son's. (Fofanov's son shared with his father the first name Constantine, but wrote under the assumed surname Olimpov.) The poetry of Fofanov and Lokhvitskaya, uneven but not without old-fashioned charm, remained an ideal for Severyanin throughout his life. He commemorated in verse the anniversaries of their deaths almost every year, and once even declared that he considered Lokhvitskaya superior to Dante, Byron, and Pushkin.[3] The impact these two poets had on Severyanin was reflected in the titles of the latter's booklets (whose number had reached twenty-five by 1909), such as *A sad vesnoi blagoukhaet* ("And the Garden Is Fragrant with Spring). Toward the end of 1909, however, another feature appears in both Severyanin's titles and his poems themselves: foreign-sounding words of certain intellectual or social glamour. In 1909 he published *Intuitivnye kraski* ("Intuitive Colors"), whose title anticipated one aspect of the coming ego-futurist aesthetics. In 1910 it was *Kolye printsessy* ("The Princess' Necklace); and at the beginning of 1911, his *Elektricheskie stikhi* ("Electrical Poems") appeared. Bearing a title already suggesting futurism,[4] this volume contained the amusing "V limuzine" ("In a Limousine") and the tour de force, "Kvadrat kvadratov" ("The Square of Squares"), in which all stanzas following the first one employ the same words in all respective lines, only in a different word order. It was after this "brochure" (as he called his booklets) that Severyanin was finally noticed by influential critics (M. Voloshin, V. Bryusov, N. Gumilev),[5] but no more than that.

The first really Severyaninesque "brochure" was *Ruchyi v liliyakh* ("Brooks Full of Lilies"), which appeared in the summer of 1911 and was subtitled "Poesas." Afterward, not only Severyanin, but most of his fellow ego-futurists and imitators were to use this rather mannered word to denote simply "poems." [6] One can find in this booklet not only Severyanin's adoration of Fofanov and Lokhvitskaya, and his preoccupation with neologisms, many of which are built on French words or roots, but also his tendency to introduce, revive, or transplant (drawing mostly on the field of music) various genres of lyric poetry, based on mood, theme, or structure. Here one can find an epithalamion, a prelude, a brindisi, a polonaise, a rondel, and what he calls "quinzels." There is also one "intuitta." Some of the poems included in *Brooks Full of Lilies* are among Severyanin's best and later became famous, especially "Fioletovyi trans" ("A Purple Trance"), "Kenzeli" ("Quinzels"), and "Karetka kurtizanki" ("The Calèche of a Courtesan"), depicting the slightly ridiculous never-never land of Severyanin's poetic dreams, populated by fragrant demimondaines, habitués of fashionable restaurants, limousine passengers, and exotic captains. This world combines Bohemianism and aristocratic manners, gentility and adventure; its inhabitants are gifted, refined, and terribly "modern." The historical importance of this little book was not only in its anticipation of Severyanin's celebrated *Gromokipyashchii kubok* ("Goblet Seething with Thunders"), in which all these poems were to be reprinted, but also in the subtitle of the poem, "Ryadovye lyudi" ("Ordinary People"), where the poet said: "Calmly, sadly, radiantly, and sternly I despise the people who are talentless, backward, flat, and darkly stubborn." The subtitle read "From the Cycle 'Ego-Futurism,'" and thus it was the first use of the word "futurism" in a Russian context.[7]

Brooks Full of Lilies also contained a poem entitled "Poezoantrakt"

("Poesoentracte"), which describes a utopian academy of poetry in a marble castle by a lake, with young poets and poetesses composing inspired ghazels and rhapsodies, reposing on velvety sofas, drinking wine, and sniffing lilies. In the last line, Severyanin calls himself the rector of this academy. The poem is dated March, 1911. At that time the academy was probably nothing but Severyanin's daydream, but in a few months there was already a group of four poets who called themselves both "the Ego-group" and "the rectorate of the Academy of Poetry."

The group was formed in October, 1911, and soon produced a manifesto. But even before this manifesto, in November, 1911, Severyanin proclaimed his ego-futurism single-handedly in a brochure (the thirty-second such publication) entitled *Prolog Ego-Futurizm*, where, in four-foot iambics, he once more put Lokhivtskaya and Fofanov upon a pedestal, declared contemporary poetry a desert, and suggested that Pushkin was old-fashioned ("For us, Pushkin has become a Derzhavin"). He asserted that the new age of dirigibles required new, original verse with assonances replacing traditional rhyme and with "every word a surprise." The new poet's arrival is imminent, he continued, and he "will transform all Muses of the past into his odalisques" and create poetry not based on reason. Severyanin also glorified his own verse, claiming the ability "to get a direct knowledge of what is unclear on earth" (*Ya neposredstvenno sumeyu / Poznat' neyasnoe zemli*), which was his first attempt to formulate the intuitivist foundation for his aesthetics. In a burst of impartiality, he exclaimed: "No requiem for savagery, but no hymn to culture either." The rest of the poem stated, rather prematurely, that he, Severyanin, was famous throughout Russia. In short, it was perhaps the first futurist display of the "immodesty formulas." [8] *Prolog Ego-Futurizm* was also the first ego-futurist publication of the newly organized publishing enterprise "Ego."

The Ego-group began its real activities in January, 1912, with the announcement,[9] in a leaflet, of the Academy of Poetry's "program," later usually referred to in a rather Mosaic manner as "The Tables." The creators of "The Tables" did not waste words while writing them, so theirs is probably the most laconic manifesto in Russian literature. The complete translation of the text follows:

(Universal Futurism)
19 Ego 12
Predecessors:
K. M. Fofanov and Mirra Lokhvitskaya

The Tables

I.   Glorification of Egoism:
    1. Unit = Egoism.
    2. Deity = unit.
    3. Man = fraction of God.
    4. Birth = separation (*otdroblenie*) from Eternity.
    5. Life = fraction outside Eternity.
    6. Death = fraction's return to unity (*vozdroblenie*).
    7. Man = Egoist.
II. Intuition. Theosophy.
III. Thought reaching madness: madness is individual.
IV. Prism of style = reconstruction of the spectrum of thought.
V.   Soul = Truth.
The Rectorate: Igor-Severyanin, Constantine Olimpov (C. C. Fofanov),
    George Ivanov, Graal-Arelsky.

It is hardly necessary to plunge into the writings of Blavatskaya, Stirner, or, for that matter, Bergson, to appreciate these solemn pseudo-profundities. The last two signatories, being only shy beginners in poetry, were hardly anything more than signatories; but as far as Severyanin himself was concerned, "The Tables" were a far cry from the "calèches of courtesans" of his earlier poems. Actually, they are a proclamation of limitless individualism; but, as Bryusov correctly wrote upon reading "The Tables," in all this there was hardly "a new word" [10] (politely, he did not call the manifesto what it really was: a caricature of early Russian decadence). At any rate, the ego-futurists thought they had everything necessary for a self-respecting literary movement: an ideology "more profound" than that of the symbolists, their literary bombshell in *Prolog Ego-Futurizm*, and their own "*maître* of the intuitive school." [11] Severyanin, who was poorly educated and not even well read, hardly fitted this role; but self-doubt was never one of his virtues, so he obviously enjoyed the masquerade. In 1912 he wrote ideological poetry; but, since censorship would not permit it to be printed, he did not publish it until 1923. When it appeared then in *Mirreliya*,[12] he was an *émigré* and few people could remember what ego-futurism had been. Here is one of these poems:

POESA OF TRUTH

In nothing is nothing. And suddenly Something out of nothing.
    And this is God!
He did not render an account in this self-creation—
    To whom could He?
He had a wish to create Himself and He did,
    Right in Himself.
He is an Egoist. And this is as simple
    As the fragrance of flowers.
God created the world, but the people never learned
    How the world was created.
And it is poetical for us to dream about a miracle,
    And God is a Poet!
And all people are God's likenesses:
    We are fractions of God.
And if we are subject to eternal evil,
    Let's not be sad about it:
The fallen angel was not destroyed by God,
    Not killed.
He is in woman, in a frenzied mustang,
    He is everywhere.
So God wills. His dreams are pure,
    His eyes are beaming.
Nature, God, and people are egoists:
    I am Egoist!

George Ivanov and Graal-Arelsky were brief visitors in the ego-futurist movement. Ivanov's first book, *Otplytie na o. Tsiteru* ("The Embarkation for Cythera"), was published in 1912 by Ego. It bore the subtitle "Poesas" in true ego-futuristic fashion, but contained little that could be considered ego-futuristic. There were, to be sure, one neologism (*obrámennye*), one epistle to Severyanin, a few triolets (and these, after all, were written in Russian poetry not only by Severyanin), and two lines expressing the desire to embrace both monk and blasphemer (a faint echo of the ego-futuristic combining of extremes). Otherwise, the book betrayed the typical eclecticism of most poetic debuts of that time and the influence of Kuzmin and Blok. The last poem in the book, significantly, could be mistaken for a poem by Gumilev, and indeed, Gumilev later became Ivanov's friend and mentor. Nothing in *The Embarkation for Cythera* augured the Ivanov of later years, who, in the opinion of some, developed into the greatest poet of the Russian emigration; but for a beginner, there was an unusual display of technique. His rhymes are exquisite. He is not afraid of attempting ghazels and sonnets, or of playing with accentual verse; but his cupids and Chloes, as well as the adolescent melancholy and affected aestheticism of his poems, soon wear thin. The book was favorably received: Bryusov found it unoriginal, but promising; and Gumilev described Ivanov's verse as "precipitous[?] and refined." [13] Ivanov himself reprinted in later collections some of this early poetry in new versions, and he used the same title for one of his later books. He described his ego-futurist episode mockingly in his memoirs, *Petersburg Winters*.

Graal-Arelsky (1889———), an astronomer, had in real life the much more prosaic name ("Graal" = the Grail) of Stepan Stepanovich Petrov. As early as 1911 he published privately a book of verse entitled *Goluboi azhur* ("Blue Ajouré"), which was full of imitations of Balmont and Bryusov. Later poems show the distinct imprint of Severyanin. His is mostly an oleographic poetry with slave women, Egyptian priests, satanists burned at stakes, and monks passionately kissing the lips of madonnas. Arelsky, together with George Ivanov, paid a visit to Alexander Blok, who noted Arelsky's "unpleasant face," but later came to the observatory to discuss stars with him. Blok even wrote Arelsky a letter, in which he praised *Blue Ajouré* for its portrayal of the stars, but expressed his dislike for the author's pen name and the title of his book.[14] Gumilev praised the book for its good taste and versification,[15] but preferred to overlook absurd stylistic blunders (e.g., *akkordy sozvuchii*). After both Ivanov and Arelsky left ego-futurism and joined the Acmeist Guild of Poets, the latter published there in 1913 another book, *Leteiskii breg* ("The Bank of Lethe"), in which there were no new developments, though his verse improved. Afterward, the name Arelsky appeared several times in magazines, futurist and nonfuturist,[16] and in 1925 he published a book of science fiction under the title *Povesti o Marse* ("Tales from Mars"), consisting of three separate but interconnected stories, the last of which ends with a successful revolution of Martian workingmen against their capitalist oppressors.

Ego-futurism would hardly have been noticed had not Ivan Ignatyev joined its ranks. Ivan Vasilyevich Ignatyev (1882–1914) welcomed Severyanin and his *Prolog Ego-Futurizm* in the newspaper *Nizhegorodets,* published by a relative of his for businessmen who participated in the famous Nizhni-Novgorod annual fair. Before he met the ego-futurists, Ignatyev was writing, among other things, literary and theatrical criticism for more than a dozen newspapers and magazines. In 1912 some of his work from this pre–ego-futurist period was published by him in a book *Okolo teatra* ("Around the Theater"), which consisted of stories reminiscent of the early Chekhov, humorous sketches, parodies, and often pretentious poetry. Judging by his announcement in this book, he planned many more books "around the theater": poetry for recitation, an operetta, and a play.

Ignatyev had some money and was a good organizer. He played in ego-futurism approximately the same role that David Burliuk played in the Hylaean group. His activities began with publishing two issues of the newspaper *Peterburgskii Glashatai* ("Petersburg Herald"), one on February 12, 1912, and another on March 11, 1912. The paper chiefly consisted of essays on art (mostly theater) and reviews of books and theatrical performances, almost exclusively written by Ignatyev under numerous pseudonyms and under his real name, Kazansky. Despite the author's generous use of neologisms built on French roots, most of these columns were in the worst traditions of the cheap pre-revolutionary press.[17] There was also poetry, in noticeable quantity, by all signatories of "The Tables" and by the publisher himself. The only new name was that of Ivan Lukash, who wrote poetry under the name of Oredezh and later became an *émigré* novelist. Lukash's poetry was an imitation of Walt Whitman with curious anticipations of Mayakovsky; he was preparing a book of poetry, *Tsvety yadovitye* ("Flowers Poisonous"). If one ignores the bulk of the printed material (i.e., Ignatyev's pretentious and vague meditations on Beauty in close proximity with vulgar attacks on various personalities), one can still glean a few interesting details from the *Petersburg Herald.* For example, there is a sentence about "the new impulse of the future" which is Speed, betraying some acquaintance with Marinetti, and an announcement of the forthcoming paper, "Futura." The second issue of the *Petersburg Herald* opened with an article under the promising title "Futuristy i futurizm" ("Futurists and Futurism"), which, however, is nothing but an immoderate glorification of Severyanin as "the father of Russian ego-poetry and the core of native futurism," "the winged Colossus," "the Chosen One marked by God," and "our high priest." The essay does not, however, give any clue as to what futurism means to Ignatyev, but it does announce "the victorious procession, begun [*onachalennoe*] by the *sociétaires* of the rectorate of the Academy of Ego-Poetry." Ignatyev later admitted that the newspaper was "timid and indefinite," but claimed that its appearance found an echo in cities throughout the whole of Russia, including Vladivostok, Kostroma, and Rybinsk.[18] In November he resumed publication of the paper with the comment that ego-futurism would not be discussed in it and had to be found in the almanacs. But the paper seems to have been discontinued after the fourth issue.

The Ego publishing enterprise continued its activities, bringing out Constantine Olimpov's *Aeroplannye poezy* ("Airplane Poesas")* in 1912.[19] Severyanin went on publishing his brochures and planned a three-volume edition of his verse. A miscellany, *Ego*, was being planned with the participation of Severyanin, Arelsky, Olimpov, and Ivan Lukash. Ego-futurists also printed their articles in *Nizhegorodets* in strange proximity to stock market charts and other commercial and financial items. Ignatyev even tried to organize in Nizhni-Novgorod an ego-futurist group and to publish there a joint miscellany entitled "I." [20] Simultaneously, Ignatyev arranged several banquets under the auspices of the *Petersburg Herald*, which would begin as aesthetic gatherings of half-baked Oscar Wildes, but would often end in general drunkenness with guests leaving the party with their heads partly shaved. This social aspect of ego-futurism was an important part of its snobbish attraction, especially in the provinces. In the *Petersburg Herald*, there were items to the effect that in view of the large number[21] of visitors to the newspaper office they should first register with the "majordomo." These visitors were required to appear in tails from 10:00 until 11:30 A.M. In the almanacs, one can come across such announcements ("annoncettes") as that Olimpov was leaving for Arbonier,[22] or that he wears collars "Toreador," or that Severyanin would spend the summer in Pyatigorye, preparing his "Elegant Models" for "estampage" in the spring. Then Severyanin would send a letter to the editor and say that he had changed his mind and would go to the estate of Princess Obolensky instead. It was particularly well expressed in the program drawn up for their poesa concert planned for spring, 1912, in the suburbs of St. Petersburg, but never held:

EGO

Estate Ivanovka

Station Pudost, Baltic railroad, Gatchino Mill.
In the park surrounding the Hunting Palace of Paul I, on the Estrade near the marble urns, in the prelude of May, 1912—
The first Spring Concert of Universal Futurism, organized under the Direction of the Newspaper, *Petersburg Herald.*

Coperformers:

Igor-Severyanin, I. V. Ignatyev, Constantine Olimpov, I. S. Lukash.
The beginning is precisely at midnight.
In the park, there will be lilac illumination. Aeolian bells. Invisible ocarinas and pipes. Pavilions of Seclusion, of Ego-books, of Milk and Black Bread. Chalet of Cupid.
Buffet at the eastern veranda of the Palace next to the Estrade. Wines from Prince Yusupoff's gardens; liqueur Crème de Violettes from the Cusenier firm. Gatchino pink trout; umbers. Bonbons-Violettes from Gourmet. Tea from petals of fleur d'orange. Gondolas to cross the river Makhalitta: "La Princesse Lointaine" and "À la vie."
Access [*vshag*] by invitation *vergettes*[23] only.
Return train at 5 A.M.
The day of the Concert will be announced in all publications of the capital.
The Newspaper Director
I. V. Ignatyev

Abandoning the poesa concert and the unprofitable paper, Ignatyev began to publish miscellanies (*almanakhi*), using the name of the paper as that of the publishing enterprise. The first of these miscellanies, the four-page *Oranzhevaya Urna* ("The Orange Urn"), was published in 1912 and dedicated to the memory of Fofanov. Fofanov was glorified in the poems by Severyanin and Dimitri Kryuchkov and in the article "Tsarstvennyi solovei" ("A Regal Nightingale"), written by Fofanov's son, Olimpov. There was also the poem "Ya slavlyu" ("I Glorify"), written by Ivan Oredezh (I. Lukash), again in imitation of Walt Whitman.[24] The main interest was, however, in the participation of Valery Bryusov, whom ego-futurists managed to attract as a contributor. He provided them with two poems. One of these sounded like Severyanin, while the other was mildly ego-futuristic, with its single neologism, one foreign word, and the metaphor of "the airport of the sky." Very pretentious was Ignatyev's "Miniatyura," which, in rhythmic prose with numerous words beginning with capital letters, described the suicide of a widower. There were two articles on ego-theory. One of them, "Egoizm," written by Peter Mikhailovich Fofanov (probably the poet's brother), asserted that all life is based on egoism, though it clearly comes to the fore only in art and business. He appealed for recognition of this fact, which would lead to a truer altruism than the one now preached in society. Graal-Arelsky was the author of "Ego-poeziya v poezii" ("Ego-Poetry in Poetry"), which repeated some of the ideas of Peter Fofanov and, after surveying human history from ancient Egypt to Christ, proclaimed that "the aim of ego-poetry is the glorification of egoism as the sole true and vital intuition." Arelsky also affirmed the existence of a Beauty that is beyond morality and consists of harmony and dissonance, and, toward the end, called for a merging with Nature. Neither essay can be considered a masterpiece of prose.

The Orange Urn was followed in the same year by *Steklyannye Tsepi* ("Glass Chains"), another slim almanac, containing poetry by Severyanin and Leonid Afanasyev (the latter never became an active member of the group), prose by Ignatyev, and some "intuitivist" reviews. Of more historical importance was the third miscellany, entitled *Orly nad propastyu* ("Eagles over the Abyss"), which appeared in the fall of 1912, this time growing to six large pages. Among the famous guest contributors were Bryusov, whose acrostic sonnet addressed to Severyanin was included, and another great figure of Russian symbolism, Fyodor Sologub, who by that time had become, surprisingly, a great admirer of Severyanin's poetry.[25] Severyanin himself printed in this book his famous "Morozhenoe iz sireni" ("Ice Cream Made with Lilacs"). The lesser names occupied the last page, and among them one may note the not very gifted Pavel Kokorin (see chap. 5) and Pavel Dmitrievich Shirokov (1893–1963).

Shirokov became one of the ego-futurist inner circle and a close friend of Ignatyev, who had published Shirokov's first book of poetry,

Rozy v vine ("Roses in Wine"), a few months before.[26] Even the title of this eight-page collection betrays Severyanin's influence, and in much of his poetry Shirokov remained little more than an imitator. Most of his poems contain neologisms and French words; in the manner of Severyanin, he calls his poems triolets, virelays, romances, and the like. Usually they reproduce ego-futurist salon-like motifs (the desire to be a marquis, images of Pierrot). There are also echoes of Lokhvitskaya, and Shirokov follows Fofanov into the land of beautiful princesses. In some of his poems, however, Shirokov is trying to be "futurist" (i.e., to present aspects of modern urban life). Thus one of his triolets is about an airplane, and his sonnet describes meeting a woman on a streetcar (*tram*). In the final poem, "Tsvety bezvolya" ("Flowers of Will-lessness"), Shirokov pays tribute to ego-futurist ideology by remarking that "the meaning of *vozdroblenie* ["fraction's return to unity"; see p. 65, "The Tables"] is dear and clear to him." *Roses in Wine* was followed in January, 1913, by a much less successful and, strangely enough, less futuristic book, which, nevertheless, had a much more avant-garde title, *V i vne* ("Inside and Outside"). This book, published during the time ego futurism turned toward more radical verbal experimentation, is disappointing not only because the Fofanov-Lokhvitskaya, ladies' journal motifs (lilies, princess in a forest, Columbines), are intensified in it, but also because it is characterized by slipshod versification and incorrect word usage. There is, however, an attempt at urbanism in one poem (rather inconsistent, since it ends with an admonition to leave the city if one is fed up with it), and in the last poem, "Itog" ("Sum Total"), Shirokov makes some manifesto-like gestures, denouncing the critics of ego-futurism and extolling modern times which are full of progress everywhere except in poetry. His own book is a good illustration of the latter point.

Poetry printed in *Eagles over the Abyss* is not as interesting as Ignatyev's survey of ego-futurist activities and theories. It is entitled "Pervyi god ego-futurizma" ("The First Year of Ego-Futurism"); and, while it is easy to mock the attempt to write one's own history after barely a year of existence, a scholar can only be grateful, because no one else tried to write such a history afterward and there are few mentions of ego-futurists in memoirs. (An exception is Severyanin's *Kolokola sobora chuvstv* ["The Bells of the Cathedral of Feelings," 1925], a "novel in verse," in the time-honored tradition of Pushkin's *Eugene Onegin*, which speaks mostly of the period after the poet had abandoned the ego-futurist group.) Ignatyev, in his survey, writes in detail about the events already mentioned in this chapter, but also indulges in polemics with critics. He cites the text of the "Doctrines of Universal Ego-Futurism," printed as a leaflet by Ego in September, 1912. The doctrines are (1) recognition of Ego-God (union of two contrasts); (2) finding [obret] of universal soul (all-justification); (3) extolling Egoism as one's individual essence; and (4) limitlessness of artistic [iskusstvovye] and spiritual searchings [izyskaniya].

After defending ego-futurism against possible accusations of a lack of originality ("ego-futurism is the quintessence of all schools"), Ignatyev says that "the aim of every ego-futurist is self-affirmation in the future" and that the basis of ego-futurism is intuition. Toward the end of his survey, he also attacks "the Guild of Poets, which had just accepted two ego-futurist renegades, Arelsky and G. Ivanov, and says, "For the impotents of soul and verse, there is the 'Guild of Poets,' where cowards and freaks of modernism find shelter." It is also necessary to note Ignatyev's casual mention of Marinetti and Italian futurism. At the beginning of his article, he regrets that the "universal ego-futurism" that has grown on Russian territory is constantly confused with the three-year-old "Italo-French futurism." At the end, while accusing the Guild of Poets of having no soul, he adds, "just like the foreign futurists who deathified [osmertivshie] the pronoun 'I' and who do not know all-justification [see the "Doctrines," item 2]."

While Ignatyev was stating the case for Russian ego-futurism in such strong terms, the movement was struggling through its first serious crisis, which almost brought it to an end. In October many St. Petersburg newspapers received a protest leaflet written by Constantine Olimpov, who reminded the editors that he was the coauthor of "The Tables" and the inventor of the imprint of the Ego publishing enterprise (which consisted of the word "Ego," written, in Latin letters, inside a triangle) and practically accused Severyanin of plagiarism. The ideas expressed in the "Doctrines," Olimpov insisted, were taken from his interview about ego-futurism published in an obscure local paper. Severyanin answered this claim with his letter to the editor in which he simultaneously called Olimpov a slanderer and generously forgave him. "I consider my ego-futurist mission completed," he continued; "I wish to be alone to consider myself just a poet and am sunnily glad about it. My intuitive school, Universal Ego-Futurism, is the way to self-affirmation. In this sense, it is immortal. But my own ego-futurism exists no more: I have already affirmed myself." This announcement meant Severyanin's break with the group, whose support he no longer needed since he was rapidly becoming a celebrity. Olimpov answered with another letter, entitled "Declaration," which reiterated his plagiarism charges. Severyanin made his break with ego-futurism final when he wrote a letter to the editor of the popular *Birzhevye Vedomosti* and when he published, in November, 1912, his last brochure (no. 35), *Epilog Ego-Futurizm*. This well-known poem begins with the line "I, Igor-Severyanin, a genius," then proceeds to describe the history of the ego-futurist movement in a nutshell. The poet does not try to hide his conviction that he was the only real poet in the group, calls Olimpov a Judas, and, in the last part, hints at a change in his orientation: "being attracted by the primitive," he is going to the country. Thus Severyanin sealed his break with a rejection of ego-futurist urbanism, and thus ended the first phase of Russian ego-futurism, in which Severyanin had been the leading figure. The movement continued to exist, change, and develop under the leadership of Ignatyev; therefore, the customary total identification of the entire ego-futurist movement with Severyanin is far from being historically correct.

In the critical moment of Severyanin's "resignation," Ignatyev gave a new formulation to the group's ideology and energetically continued publishing: in 1913 he issued six almanacs, at least as many books of poems by individual poets, and one theoretical pamphlet. He tirelessly, though not very coherently, explained the essence of ego-futurism in articles and books, made connections with some Moscow futurists, and began polemics with the Hylaeans, who at this time were assaulting contemporary literature with one published volume after another. Without breaking with the "intuitive" ego-philosophy of the earlier stage, Ignatyev, in his theoretical statements, his poetry, and his editorial practice, began to emphasize and single out verbal experiment, thus coming close to the ideas of his enemies, the Hylaeans. As successor to Severyanin's "intuitive school of Universal Ego-Futurism," Ignatyev established the "intuitive association" which published in January, 1913, a "charter" (*gramota*) with the following text:

I. Ego-Futurism = The incessant striving of every Egoist for the achievement of the possibilities of the Future in the Present.

II. Egoism = Individualization, awareness, worship, and praise of the I.

III. Man = Essence.

Deity = Shadow of Man in the mirror of the Universe.

God = Nature.

Nature = Hypnosis.

Egoist = An Intuitionist.

Intuitionist = A Medium.

IV. Creation of Rhythm and Word.

Areopagus: Ivan Ignatyev
Pavel Shirokov
Vasilisk Gnedov
Dmitri Kryuchkov

One easily notices that not a single "Areopagite" belonged to the "Rectorate" that signed "The Tables." Even the name of Olimpov is missing.

Constantine Olimpov (Constantine Constantinovich Fofanov; 1880–1940) never broke with the Ignatyev group (though he remained aloof for a few months), and even published in 1913 his most notable book under the imprint of the Petersburg Herald. It was *Zhonglery-nervy* ("Nerves, the Jugglers"), which almost simultaneously appeared in its entirety in the seventh ego-futurist almanac, *Vsegdai* ("The Alwayser"). The first page of the book carries a typically Olimpovian quasi-cabalistic chart:

Airplane Poems

Nerve Center I [*nervnik*]   Window of Europe

△ Ego

Blood I   1912, Spring

The origin of the river
Universal Ego-Futurism

Immediately below, Olimpov goes on to explain the origin of the term "universal ego-futurism" as follows: "Immortality in Eternity plus 'Alter Ego' of Fofanov plus Futurism and—as a generalization—'Universal Ego-Futurism.'" Below this is found a poem by Olimpov's fa-

ther, C. M. Fofanov, addressed to his son, in which the son is praised
for combining in himself a scholar and a poet. The rest of the book is
occupied by seven short poems. Judging by the statements of those
who knew Olimpov and by much of his poetry, he was a madman.[27]
As a poet, though, he was not devoid of talent, and a scholar will
appreciate in his work what probably is the most successful merger
of ego-futurist mysticism and poetics. In fact, he may be the most
typical ego-futurist poet. In his poetry, Olimpov expresses a desire for
madness, proclaims himself a genius, worships Fofanov and Lokhvitskaya, and glorifies aviation (e.g., the poem "Shmeli" ["Bumble-
bees"]). His diction is characterized, as is that of Severyanin and Shirokov, by a wide use of neologisms and foreign words; his metrics include
both the old-fashioned anapests of the 1880's and some metric forms
made popular by Severyanin; and he moderately experiments with
dissonant rhyme. In "Troika v troike" ("A Three in a Three") he
accumulates words with the root *kolokol-* ("bell") and plays on different meanings of the word *troika,* so that the final result has a remote
resemblance to Khlebnikov's laughter poem. In "Amuret" ("Amou-
rette") Olimpov imitates the salon manner of Severyanin, and in
"Esquise" he is altogether nonfuturist. When he ceases to imitate and
speaks with his own voice, his work becomes nothing but a chaotic
verbal conglomeration echoing his occult erudition, as in these words
from "Interlyudiya" ("Interlude"):

> Empirei—emblema feurgii,
> Siluet sabeizma fetisha.
> V rodnike vdokhnovennykh val'purgii
> Ishchet lunnoe serdtse finisha.

> (The empyreans are the emblem of theurgies,
> A silouette of the Sabaism of a fetish.
> In a spring of inspired walpurgies
> The lunar heart looks a goal line.)

After 1913 Olimpov began to publish, one after another, books[28]
marked by his growing *mania grandiosa* and full of cosmic visions,
hyperbole, self-glorification, and capital letters. An example of these
books is *Fenomenalnaya genialnaya poema Teoman velikogo mirovogo
poeta Konstantina Olimpova* ("The Phenomenal Poem of Genius

Called Theoman by the Great World Poet Constantine Olimpov"),
in which the entire evolution of life in the universe is presented as
striving for the ideal, which is, of course, Olimpov. The poem was
published in 1915 and promptly confiscated, probably because of the
poet's self-identification with God. Though it is too long and its grandiose manner is often annoying, one can find in it magnificent lines,
especially where Olimpov tries to assimilate the language of science
into poetry. Finally, the poem develops into an ode to himself, which
sounds very much like Russian eighteenth-century odes. It is possible
to view *Theoman* as an amplification of ego-futurism; but the last
vestiges of ego-futurist influence have faded by 1922, as can be seen
in Olimpov's poem *Tretye Rozhdestvo velikogo mirovogo poeta tita-
nizma sotsialnoi revolyutsii Konstantina Olimpova, Roditelya Miroz-
daniya* ("The Third Nativity of the Great World Poet of the Titan-
ism of the Social Revolution, Constantine Olimpov, the Parent of the
Universe"), published in that year and perhaps his last published
work. This is both a paean to destruction and a crazy, belated attempt
to sell the Soviet government, which then for a short time tolerated
avant-garde art, a new kind of futurism, the "Universal Ego-Olimpism,
the Futurism of Communism." Here Olimpov declares himself a
"proletarian, wandering in beggar's clothes," and shouts hurrahs to
the Seventh of November and to the International. "Down with
Christ! Long live robbery," he exclaims in a possible response to
Alexander Blok's *The Twelve* (where Christ precedes the marauding
revolutionary patrol in the streets of Petrograd). In the same year
Olimpov, surrounded by completely unknown poets, organized a
group, *Koltso poetov* ("A Ring of Poets"), named after C. M. Fofanov. They published a request for memoirs about, and unpublished
works of, Olimpov's father and planned a joint publication which
did not materialize.[29] Shortly afterward, Olimpov's name disappeared
from literature.

Ignatyev himself saw the beginning of a new phase in ego-futurism
in its fourth almanac, *Dary Adonisu* ("Gifts to Adonis"), published
at the beginning of 1913, and subtitled "Publication of the Ego-Futurist Association IV." The usual crowded format employing two-
column pages is gone, and each poem begins on a separate new page.
There is no criticism in the book, only poetry and prose, which was
probably planned as a demonstration of the movement's ability to sur-

vive any crisis. The book begins with a five-page "ego-prose" piece dated Rostov-on-Don, 1911, and written by Vasilisk Gnedov, a new futurist genius discovered by Ignatyev. This piece, entitled "Zigzag pryamoi sred'mirnyi" ("The Straight World-Piercing Zigzag") is written in semirhythmic, lyric, remotely Nietzschean prose with many capital letters, some neologisms, and special punctuation. It boldly but without much result tries to be "metaphysical" and to portray the situation of the "ego in the universe." All remaining Areopagites are represented by poetry that is not very distinguished. The volume is further watered down by guest contributors, of whom only one deserves mention, Vadim Shershenevich from Moscow, who was to play a notable role in the history of Russian futurism. The puzzling final "poem of pauses," "Gurebka Proklenushkov,"[30] signed by the enigmatic Josephine Gante d'Orsaille, was obviously meant as a hoax, probably inspired by the famous Cherubina de Gabriac hoax in *Apollon* in 1909.[31] *Gifts to Adonis* closes with a photograph of the Areopagus (Ignatyev wearing a top hat sits; the other three solemnly stand behind him). It was announced that Marinetti would participate in the next almanac, but he did not.

A real change in ego-futurist orientation became noticeable in the group's fifth miscellany, *Zasakhare kry*. The title was meant both to shock and to demonstrate verbal experiment: it consists of the first halves of *zasakharennaya krysa,* which means "a candied rat," a title scarcely in harmony with the romantically languorous lady drawn by Léon Zack on the cover.[32] The central work in the book is an ambitious, though poorly written, critical essay by Ignatyev, "Ego-Futurism," in which he attempts a new formulation of the movement's philosophy. Civilization is declared a mortal enemy of self, erasing its immortal element. Those who recognized this truth make an impressive list: Buddha, Jean Jacques Rousseau, Nietzsche, Herzen, Maxim Gorky, Ibsen, Evgeny Solovyev (Andreevich), Fichte, Tolstoy. Finally, Ignatyev comes to the conclusion that, as Christianity was a religion of slaves, directed against Roman civilization, and socialism is a religion of labor, so egoism is a religion of "spiritual serfs," slaves of civilization and the city. The fact that here he undermines urbanism, an important aspect of ego-futurist aesthetics, does not dismay Ignatyev and he goes on with incoherent, but sublime-sounding words until he concludes by offering yet another historical survey of ego-futurism, which this time includes the whole story of Severyanin's break with the group. Ignatyev accuses Severyanin of self-glorification, inconsistencies, and contributing to the movement nothing but the word "ego-futurism," and asserts that its meaning was never clear to him. The role of Severyanin in the history of ego-futurism is not denied, but reduced to that of Newton's apple in physics.

Verse is represented in *Zasakhare kry* by Shirokov's rather inept attempt at writing ideological poetry and Shershenevich's mannered aestheticism with its Pierrots and Columbines; but the most radical works are those presented by Vasilisk (Vasily Ivanovich) Gnedov (1890———), this Khlebnikov of ego-futurism. His trademark is folksy neologism, and he tends to shock the reader with coarse or unpleasant words and images. Though his poems are filled to overflowing with coined words that are often indecipherable, the general background of his poetry can be easily recognized—it is nature, and, in contradistinction to the other ego-futurists, this makes Gnedov sometimes sound like Vasily Kamensky. Since his predilection for *épater les bourgeois* also makes him similar to Kruchenykh, many critics wondered why this poet joined the ego-futurists and not the Hylaeans in the first place. Livshits says in his memoirs that Gnedov was actually considered for membership in Hylaea, but had to leave for the south for reasons of health.[33] In addition to three poems, Gnedov also printed in *Zasakhare kry* a piece of futurist prose, which is strongly rhythmic and is built on neologisms and exclamations.

By the time *Zasakhare kry* appeared, Gnedov was already the author of two books of verse, both published in 1913 by Ignatyev's Petersburg Herald publishing enterprise. In *Gostinets sentimentam* ("A Treat for the Sentiments"), there is a familiar display of rustic neologisms and primitivistic shouts; however, in the overlong "Skachek Toski—Pobeda Ogne-Lavy" ("A Jump of Longing—A Victory of Fire-Lava"), which is almost devoid of neologisms and full of words beginning with a capital letter, Gnedov parades again as a half-baked Nietzschean, indulging in symbolism of the worst kind. When he subtitles some of his poetry with *rapsoda* or *eskizev*, the clumsy attaching of Russian suffixes or endings to foreign roots and words looks almost like a parody of the favorite devices of his fellow ego-futurists.

Much more radical in conception was Gnedov's second book, *Smert iskusstvu* ("Death to Art"), with a preface in which Ignatyev prophesied the extinction of the word in the future and its replacement by a highly organized intuition. Of fifteen poems by Gnedov, nine are one-line poems, most of them consisting of neologisms. One poem (no. 6) uses seemingly meaningless syllables; another (no. 9) simply repeats a word (or a name?) three times; two poems, though bearing neologistic titles, use known Russian words. Of the rest, two consist of one neologistic word each, and two of just one letter each. Finally, page 8, which is also the back cover of the book, has only the title of poem number 15, "Poema Kontsa" ("Poem of the End"). The intended effect is spoiled, however, by the fact that the stamp of the printshop, with the address and the year of publication, is down below on the same page. This poem made Gnedov a celebrity, and, at public appearances, he was often asked to recite it. A memoirist described such a recitation as follows: "[This poem] had no words and consisted only of one gesture, the arm being quickly raised in front of the hair, then sharply dropped, and then moved to the right." Ignatyev, in his preface to *Death to Art*, gives a different description: "He read [this poem] with a rhythmic movement. The hand was drawing a line: from left to right and vice versa (the second one canceled the first, as plus and minus result in minus). 'Poem of the End' is actually 'Poem of Nothing,' a zero, as it is drawn graphically." [34]

This preface by Ignatyev is interesting in itself for its style, tone, and content. All that he had written before is a paragon of modesty in comparison with this exercise in prophecy, crowded with capital letters and neologisms. Ignatyev's point is that art is in agony, and one sign of this is the excessive refinement of the word and the variety of languages at man's disposal. The word, however, is needed only by people living collectively; but when everyone is transformed into an "individualized ego-self" there will be no need of words and the lost paradise of the past, when Man spoke only with God, will exist once again. The preface also contains attacks on "way-out frontlings" (*peredunchiki*) of our literature, who use "individual words, syllables, and letters." Ignatyev obviously means the Hylaeans, Kruchenykh in particular, who, he obviously feels, had become dangerous rivals. He tries to discredit them by calling them "our imitators," who aim only at shocking the audience and destroy without constructing. "It is about time for them to know," he continues, "that every letter has not only sound and color, but taste as well, and also weight, surface that can be felt, extension, and its own meaning which is closely tied to the rest of the letters. For example, how much one can express by only one disyllabic word, 'vesna' ["spring"]. There is a sunny quality in 's,' the letter 'a' expresses a joy after achieving something long awaited, etc."

Gnedov appeared once, in 1914, in a joint publication with Shirokov, the slim *Kniga velikikh* ("Book of the Great"). It contained only his "Poema nachala" ("A Poem of the Beginning"), a rather lyric work, containing no neologisms. This technically most traditional poem by Gnedov is perhaps his best one. On the other hand, Shirokov showed in this book a desire to write in a new manner. He abandoned his usual salon pieces with Frenchified words and his saccharine fairy-tale pictures, and devoted one poem, "Da zdravstvuet reklama" ("Long Live Publicity"), to self-aggrandizement, while writing about houses, street lights, crowds, and prostitutes in accentual verse in another, the urbanistic "Shopot stalnykh trub" ("The Whisper of the Steel Stacks"). In "Boi" ("The Battle") he wrote about war in an expressionistic manner slightly reminiscent of Mayakovsky, and in the three remaining poems he did what Mayakovsky never did in his prerevolutionary poetry, namely, wrote about the life, work, and rebellious intentions of Russian workingmen (all in very old-fashioned verse). Both Gnedov and Shirokov later participated in publications of the Moscow futurists (of both the Mezzanine of Poetry and Centrifuge) but never published any books.[35] Shirokov soon disappeared from literature and is now forgotten.[36] Gnedov was around for some time, attracting the attention of memoirists as a personality rather than as a poet. He was one of the "presidents" in the Society of Presidents of the Globe, later organized by Khlebnikov.[37]

Ignatyev continued publication of almanacs with arresting titles such as *Bei* ("Strike!"). This title is printed in large letters on the almanac cover, but the effect is unexpectedly softened with the continuation of the sentence on page 1, in small print, "no vyslushai" ("but hear me"), so that it becomes a quotation from Themistocles. The book opens with Ignatyev's photograph, and Ignatyev is the featured poet of the edition with five works, in each of which he tried to reach extremes. "Onan," with almost every word printed as a separate line, acquired some notoriety; very ambitious also was "Tretii vkhod" ("Third Entrance"), whose printed text is interspersed with notes of music and angular symbols. A footnote states that this "melo-letera-grapha" combines word, color, melody, and movement. Probably the most successful piece is Ignatyev's attempt to write futurist prose. Entitled "Sledom za . . ." ("Following the . . ."), it is a stream-of-consciousness fragment in which each sentence, rather than ending, becomes another, with punctuation either lacking or present where not expected, but each mark is used at least once. Besides regular Russian print, Church Slavonic, Latin, and German Gothic letters were used. In translation, with typographic details omitted, it might sound like this:

FOLLOWING THE . . .

. . . heart has a cold Wait *I'll* show you. would like the bill Is falling As in elevator go or no. I want. To give myself. To Dominic; You write and write, and they don't pay Say, what a creep works for both sides Turn on electricity—"Yours Truly" doesn't think, known to me he repudi good breeding will always chévalier!!! Cavalier Ca ma'am be please four hundred Schopenhauer in shagreen forty-four twenty nine Twenty ten twenty eleven twen . . . Cavalier Cav enough? Keep the change. . . .

There was only one essay in the book, "Simvolicheskaya simfoniya" ("Symbolic Symphony"), in which the author, Vsevolod Svetlanov, spoke about a synthesis of light and sound and gave the table of correspondences between musical tones and colors. Besides Ignatyev only two poets were represented in *Strike!*: Shershenevich, with two salon poems, and Kryuchkov. Dmitri Alexandrovich Kryuchkov (1887–?), the fourth Areopagite, had been associated with ego-futurism since the publication of its first almanac, *The Orange Urn*, and displayed fewer avant-garde features than any of his colleagues.[38] His main occupation seems to have been journalism. There is a smoothness, a lilt, and sometimes a kind of energy in his rather conventional verse. Only seldom does he resort to neologisms; otherwise one hears in his lines echoes of many symbolist poets, such as Balmont, Sologub, and Blok. Two characteristics that particularly set him apart from the rest of the ego-futurists are his preoccupation with landscape and his constant religious themes. In his first book of verse, *Padun nemolchnyi* ("The Incessant Faller"), perhaps only the title, with its neologism, suggests futurism. Otherwise, it is poetry of moods and landscapes, often with religious overtones. One poem, "Chitaya Zhamma" ("Reading Jammes"), suggests that Kryuchkov probably had the ambition of becoming the Russian Francis Jammes. A year later, in 1914, Kryuchkov published another book, *Tsvety ledyanye* ("Icy Flowers"), which developed the same themes, the only difference being the exclusive use of winter landscapes. This book was published by the *Enchanted Wanderer* (his first book had been published by the Petersburg Herald), a futurist periodical to which Kryuchkov contributed not only poetry, but his impressionistic criticism as well.

The seventh ego-futurist almanac came out under the outlandish, neologistic title, *Vsegdai* ("The Alwayser") built on the Russian word *vsegda* ("always"). It was much bigger than the previous miscellanies, which were at first four- or six-page publications and later grew to sixteen pages. *The Alwayser* opened with Ignatyev's first full-scale attack on the Hylaeans in the article, "An Ego-Futurist about Futurists," printed under another pseudonym, Ivei. He accused the Moscow futurists of being indistinguishable from the first Russian decadents and impressionists and found too many inconsistencies in their theory and poetic practice. In addition to the familiar poetic exercises of Ignatyev himself, Olimpov, and Kryuchkov, one finds in *The Alwayser* some new names. Rurik Ivnev, the future imagist, printed here one impressionistic poem anticipating the favorite themes of his later poetry (suffering, death, sin). Pavel Korotov, a poet from Kharkov, not only contributed a poem, but also an "intuitive" essay in sixteen lines defending the idea of an ego-theater (i.e., the theater of one actor in four walls) against the unnecessarily complicated conventional theater. New quality is noticeable in several poems by Shershenevich printed in this book. He clearly begins here to develop his own brand of futurism, which exhibits an Italian orientation mixed with the influence of the *poètes maudits*. He experiments with dissonant rhyme. The book ends with an anonymous essay (later evidence shows that it was written by Ignatyev himself), "O novoi rifme" ("About New Rhyme"), in which many types of rhymes in use before are enumerated with examples. Ignatyev's forthcoming book of poetry is mentioned as introducing a new type of "vowel" and "consonant" rhyme, which seems to be based on the identity or phonetic similarity of the last phoneme of a word.

Ignatyev did not contribute anything to the next almanac, which also appeared in 1913, under the title *Nebokopy* ("The Sky Diggers"), but he opened it with another of his photographs. This time he entrusted others with the literary polemics. Anastasiya Chebotarevskaya, Sologub's wife, unexpectedly turned up here in a futurist publication with her "Zelenyi bum" ("A Green Boom"), a rather mild criticism of the Hylaeans (among whom she really liked only Livshits). Her conclusion was that the Hylaeans were not original, having borrowed much from "the more modest and more talented ego-futurists," but were to be welcomed as fighters against academicism and vulgarity. Curiously enough, it was Chebotarevskaya, a nonfuturist, who preached here a united front of all futurists. The other critical essay, "Modernizirovannyi Adam" ("A Modernized Adam"), was an attack on Acmeism written by Victor Khovin, who never became a part of the Ignatyev group, but continued ego-futurism in a new shape after the original group had disintegrated. The Acmeists' fight against symbolism was, for Khovin, a dishonest attempt of poorly educated people to distort the ideas of their enemy. Their poetry was judged as unoriginal and second-rate, and *Apollon* was criticized for taking the Acmeists under its wing. There was also an interesting letter to the editor by Shershenevich exposing the "illiteracy" of A. Redko, a critic from the liberal magazine *Russkoe Bogatstvo*. Redko had confused the Hylaeans and ego-futurists in one of his articles, which seemed an unpardonable sin to Shershenevich, because, he said, Kruchenykh, Khlebnikov, and the Union of Youth were "the worst enemies of ego-futurism" and their work was "illiterate daubing" (*bezgramotnaya maznya*). Shershenevich also noted that, contrary to Redko, *zaum* was never invented or used by the ego-futurists, to which the publisher, Ignatyev, made a correcting footnote, claiming that the Hylaeans did borrow *zaum* from the ego-futurists, but presented it "in a different sauce," as they did with many other ideas.

Vasilisk Gnedov monopolized the poetry pages of *The Sky Diggers*; in fact, his poetry opened and ended the book. The main device used by him in these poems was placing the two Russian characters, hard sign and soft sign (in both existing words and ones he coined), after vowels, thus rendering the words unpronounceable. He also printed some words without spaces between them, while blending them with meaningless syllables, and continued his irrelevant use of capital letters. The dates under the poems are deliberately absurd, for example: "second year after my death," or "1915" (i.e., two years later), or even "A.D. 2549" and "A.D. 38687." Here is one short poem entitled "Segodnya" ("Today") (the apostrophe is used for the soft sign and quotation marks for the hard sign):

> Nebokopytoprivol'ya'
> luzhapri"bet'moryakakh
> babushkakulikazelen
> nashi'gorokhishutakh

One of Gnedov's works was in prose and used spaces between words, but it was an illogical mélange of meaningful and meaningless words with an admixture of existing words typographically distorted in various ways. There was also a piece entitled "Pervovelikodrama" ("First-greatdrama"), which actually did not contain any suggestion of dramatic form, being written exactly like most of Gnedov's poems in *The Sky Diggers* (i.e., without spaces between words and using typographical incongruities). It ended (and this is Gnedov's favorite device) with two perfectly understandable lines *pour épater les bourgeois*: "is performed without any help from mediocre Stanislavskys *et al.*" At the end of the book, there was Gnedov's poem "Ognyanna svitka" ("A Fiery Coat"), which called itself, somewhere in the middle, "the first ego-futurist song in Ukrainian," and tried to imitate, without much consistency or knowledge, the sound and spelling of the Ukrainian language and attacked some of the Ukrainian greats. Toward the end, Gnedov switched over to his variety of Russian and ended his poem with the statement: "Shakespeare and Byron together used 80,000 words—the genius poet of the future, Vasilisk Gnedov, uses every minute 80,000,000,001 squared words."

The ninth (and last) joint appearance of the St. Petersburg ego-futurists was the almanac *Razvorochennye cherepa* ("Shattered Skulls"), likewise published in 1913. It had on its cover a drawing by the famous artist, Ilya Repin, of Constantine Olimpov reading his poetry. Almost all ego-futurist poets were represented in this final publication: Gnedov, Ivnev (with very unfuturist poems), Kryuch-kov, and Olimpov. Ignatyev printed here his most radical poems, such as "Opus —45," which was a treelike, vertical and horizontal interlacing of words. At the end, Ignatyev informed the reader that the most daring experiment of all, his "Lazorevyi logarifm" ("Azure Logarithm"), could not be reproduced in the book because of the "technical impotence" of contemporary typographical technology. There was in *Shattered Skulls* an essay, "Muzyka slov" ("Music of Words") by Vsevolod Svetlanov, subtitled "Linguistic Sketches," which dealt in fantastic word etymologies. Svetlanov saw in *chelovek* ("man") "chelo, ukrashennoe vekami" ("a forehead adorned with eyelids"); related the Latin *vita* to the Russian *vitat'* (one of whose meanings is "to inhabit"); connected the Russian words *grudi* ("breasts"), *ud* ("member"), *udit'* ("to fish"), and *gruda* ("heap"); found inside the word *krasota* ("beauty") not only *krasnyi* ("red"), but also *soty* ("honeycomb"), *rasa* ("race"), and even *o ty* ("O you"). But the most significant feature of the publication was the participation of Sergei Bobrov, the future leader of the Moscow futurist group *Tsentrifuga* ("Centrifuge"). Bobrov's contribution consisted not only of poetry (largely in the symbolist tradition), but also of a critical essay "Chuzhoi golos" ("Somebody Else's Voice"), which contained all the main features of his future criticism: deliberate demonstration of his erudition, glittering aphorisms, and viciously destructive criticism of enemies. In his attacks on the Hylaeans, he found some value, though no originality, in Khlebnikov and Mayakovsky, but uncompromisingly declared that all the rest, especially Kruchenykh and Burliuk, were beyond the limits of art and should be considered forgers. In his final verdict, Bobrov anticipated the later Soviet condemnation of futurism as decadent bourgeois literature when he wrote: "The Russian reader used to be preoccupied with revolution, then with sex, wrestling, football, Verbitskaya.[39] . . . Now he simply cannot find anything to do, so, to amuse his bored stomach, the 'art' of *budetlyane* comes."

In the fall of 1913, Ignatyev published his most ambitious attempt to explain and outline his movement. It was his treatise *Ego-Futurism*, printed on sixteen elongated pages of a pamphlet. As usual, it contained details on the history of the movement, most of which were not new. What was new was an effort to minimize the historical role of Severyanin (for whom, Ignatyev says, "the doors of ego-futurism are closed forever"). Ignatyev even suggested that the first phase of the movement be considered not ego-futurism but "ego-Severyaninism," from which the movement took only unimportant things. The present phase, it was stated, was something completely new, based on the idea of fight, whereas Severyanin's foundation was "all-justification." Compared with other theoretical writings of Ignatyev, there was little emphasis here on the philosophical tenets, but rather a strong tendency to demonstrate a specific contribution of ego-futurism to the enrichment of poetic technique. Ego-futurism was credited with such innovations as movement of a theme in prose, as illustrated by Ignatyev's "Following the . . ."; and Gnedov, "the great master of ego-futurist prose," was cited as one who represented "the ignoring of theme in prose." Ego-futurism was also credited with the renovating of or the ignoring of verse meter and with new ventures in rhyme. The other three achievements, which were named but not exemplified, were "ego-prism," "contemporaneity," and "mechanical quality." The first one is the old ego-futurist tenet of individualism as reflected in the personal style of a poet; the second refers to the contemporary urbanist themes in the works of ego-futurists; and the third probably means their attempts to write in illogical sequences of words similar to later surrealist practice of "automatic writing." There are many interesting statements in Ignatyev's essay, which is, as usual, chaotic and full of contradictions of what he said in his previous writings or even in this very work. He says, for instance, that the Severyanin phase was a product of foreign influences, not, though, as was customary to say, of Italian and French futurism, but rather of Whitman and Verhaeren. In addition, Ignatyev wrote that "ego-futurism did not deny its connections with symbolism," that "there is more 'ego' in it than 'futurism,'" and that there are two kinds of ego-futurists, some trying to 'unify the fraction' " (see "The Tables"), others stenographing speech. Only Gnedov, and partly Ignatyev himself, could be considered "stenographers of speech," but anyone could qualify as a "fraction unifier," so even Kryuchkov and Ivnev could be legitimately considered true ego-futurists. The essay ended with the image of "an intuitive tragic poet who faces self-immolation in the name of Ego."

Ignatyev's next book, *Eshafot ego-futury* ("The Scaffold of the Ego-Futura," or "The Scaffold: Ego-Futuras") appeared in 1914 and, for the most part, consisted of poems previously published in his nine almanacs that bore the Petersburg Herald imprint. They can be roughly divided into obscure metaphysical poems, which develop some of the tenets of ego-futurism, and verbal experiments. Their only virtue is brevity; otherwise they are almost painful reading, so clearly do they show Ignatyev's pretentiousness and utter lack of poetic talent. The experimental poems, which are never completely devoid of ideology, are more interesting in their intent than in their execution. Ignatyev was not destined to see this first collection of his poems. On January 20, 1914, the second day after his wedding, he attacked his wife with a razor, and when she managed to escape, slashed his own throat. Bobrov and Shershenevich, the leaders of two different Moscow futurist groups, always mentioned him with respect; the Hylaeans never attacked him personally, and a fragment by Khlebnikov has been preserved in which Ignatyev's suicide is used as an image.[40]

With Ignatyev's death, his group disintegrated, though some of them continued to collaborate in Moscow futurist publications. Soon their names were forgotten, and gradually critics began to identify Russian futurism with the Hylaeans alone. Although ego-futurists partly deserved this oblivion because they never produced anything artistically successful, it is difficult to deny them historical importance. Without this group, the picture of Russian prerevolutionary literary life and struggles is one-sided. Distortion is the usual result of such ignoring of a whole group in literary history. Thus, it is customary now to identify ego-futurism with Severyanin, which is an excellent example of a dangerous half-truth. It is true that Severyanin continued to influence the work of some ego-futurists and of the poets who were close to them (Shirokov, Shershenevich), but this problem still needs investigation: often what seems a personal influence, is, at least in part, a manner accepted by the group as a whole. Moreover, such active poets of ego-futurism as Ignatyev and Gnedov did not make any use at all of what is considered the Severyanin manner.

It is difficult to sum up ego-futurism. Certain things cannot be elucidated partly because, in contradistinction to the Hylaea group, there is a lack of memoirs about the movement. Besides, its main components—the urbanist theme, the philosophy of extreme individualism, and poetic experiment—do not easily add up to a whole. As early as 1912 Valery Bryusov wrote that the ego-futurists wanted to give expression to the soul of contemporary man, who was a big-city dweller.[41] It is well known that Bryusov himself was probably the first real urbanist in Russian poetry and that he took this theme from Verhaeren. Alexander Blok made use of this theme, too, following Bryusov. In the work of the Hylaean poets, the city theme was not dominant (though one can discover it even in Khlebnikov). Only Guro developed it extensively, and later, Mayakovsky made full use of it. With the ego-futurists, urbanism immediately took on a salon coloring: they wrote about the city of drawing rooms, rather than of streets. For this reason, they were fond of the French language, in contrast with the Hylaeans who went to the sources of the Russian language. And it was not original, for much of this atmosphere came from the poetry of Kuzmin, who was for some time considered the leader of the Russian aesthetes. Ignatyev was never capable of creating any kind of theoretical foundation for this urbanism. In his *Ego-Futurism* he became entangled in contradictions, asserting in one place that contemporaneousness was one of ego-futurism's virtues, and, in another place, that the city was important for the movement not because it was contemporary and modern, but because it was independent of nature (thus, unwittingly, disqualifying such poets as Kryuchkov). Ignatyev obviously forgot here that only a few months earlier he had complained that modern civilization took man away from nature, and therefore away from God. Devoid of an aesthetic foundation, ego-futurist urbanism became a mannerism.

Unlike the Hylaeans, ego-futurists attached much importance to metaphysical questions, and the first part of their name forced them to do so. For them, their movement could be described as discovering and revealing oneself by creating poetry, and thus it was easy for Severyanin to vulgarize it by finally declaring that, since he had established his poetic reputation and thus affirmed his ego, he did not need the movement any further. All other manifestations, including the ego-futurists' grandiloquent pronouncements about God, ego, and the universe, were nothing more than external trappings dedicated to a childish desire to be more "profound" than the symbolists and to a naïve belief that one could build a philosophical system after reading a few popularizing books. Anyone who looks into *Opyt filosofii russkoi literatury* ("Essay in a Philosophy of Russian Literature") by Andreevich (Evgeny Solovyev) will find that Ignatyev took most of his ideas from this author. Extreme eclecticism and a tendency to broaden everything extensively resulted in the creation of so flexible a foundation that anyone could enter the movement and consider himself a futurist. Several critics (Chukovsky and Shershenevich, for example) noted that Gnedov should have been a Hylaean, rather than an ego-

futurist, and one of them (Tasteven) actually considered him a
Hylaean.[42] On the other hand, one could imagine Livshits as an ego-
futurist, and he would have made a much better leader of the movement than either Severyanin or Ignatyev; however, Livshits had little
patience with ego-futurist philosophy: ". . . their theories make little
sense. Try as one may, one cannot find in them a single clear, developed idea." He saw in these theories "helplessness and a mechanical
combination of haphazardly collected ideas [ideiki] or, perhaps,
merely fashionable words. . . . Even with the utmost attention," he
continued, "one cannot understand what it is that they want, after
all, and with whom and in the name of what they want to fight."
Livshits blamed the ego-futurists for the pejorative character attached
to the word "futurism," which they were the first to use, thus making
the Hylaeans reluctant to accept the term for themselves. But Livshits
admits that, even without Severyanin, there were capable (ne-
bezdarnye) poets among the ego-futurists,[43] whereas most critics, while
singling out Severyanin, considered all his colleagues hopelessly devoid of talent. On the other hand, many critics, while examining the
spiritual foundations of ego-futurism, which may be roughly described
as intuitivist individualism moving towards anarchism, saw its amateurish and derivative character and often refused its members the right to
call themselves futurists. Chukovsky, for instance, could not find "a
single futurist comma" in Severyanin's poems, and Professor Bagrii
accused the group of "camouflaging themselves with the name of futurism."[44] Such strong criticism and intimations of "excommunication"
are hardly deserved. The phenomenon of ego-futurism simply proves
that Russian futurism was more complex than is generally assumed; by
its very existence it challenges critics to broaden their concept of futurism to include rather than exclude it.

The most convincing basis for claim of the ego-futurists to the name
"futurists" is their desire to enrich the area of Russian poetics by radical
means. They sought to do so through the creation of neologism, the
broadening of Russian rhyme, typographic experimentation, and approaches to alogism in putting words together. It is not difficult to see
that in all these efforts they parallel the Hylaeans. Being the only Russian futurist group seriously preoccupied with ideology and metaphysics, the ego-futurists came to realize, in the end, the importance
of concentrating on poetics.

Actually, in the history of all futurist groups in Russia, one can observe the tremendous role of the very word "futurism." Some rejected the name at first, others used it from the very beginning. Practically all claimed independence from the Italians, afraid of being considered imitative. But slowly the implications of both the meaning of the word and of its western European history dawned on them in different ways. Thus there is the fascinating spectacle of various individual futurists at different stages in their development trying to live up to the name, depending on how they interpreted its meaning. The fact that "futurism" could mean so many things explains why Shirokov went over from the urbanism of salons to the urbanism of streets, Shershenevich seriously studied Marinetti, Kamensky switched from rustic impressionism to composing "ferro-concrete poems" (see chap. 5), and Burliuk, much later in the United States, began to write his "entelechial" verse (see chap. 7), perhaps realizing too late that much of what he had done in Russia was not sufficiently futuristic.

The Hylaeans were historically luckier than the ego-futurists, and there was more solidarity among them and more talent; but there is no reason for forgetting ego-futurism. After all, for many contemporaries they were *the* futurists when futurism was the center of literary discussions (i.e., in 1913 and 1914). The influence of ego-futurism was more lasting than is generally thought, as can be seen, for example, in *Kiosk nezhnosti* ("Kiosk of Tenderness") by Sergei Alymov, published in Kharbin in 1920, or in the almanac *Via sacra*, which appeared, with Severyanin participating, in 1922 in Dorpat, Estonia. (In the latter, ego-futurism was intertwined with the then fashionable imagism.) And as late as 1937, David Burliuk used for one of his poems the ego-futuristic title, "Poesa." [45]

When in November, 1912, Igor-Severyanin made his final break with the group organized by him only a year before, the reading audience did not cease to consider him a futurist and neither did he. Moreover, there was no basic change in his style until approximately the 1930's when he was living in Estonia as an *émigré*. His *Goblet Seething with Thunders,* published in 1913 by the symbolist publishing house "Grif" in Moscow, was an enormous success. Fyodor Sologub himself wrote an enthusiastic preface to the book and soon took Severyanin with him on a recital tour. Severyanin "recited" his poetry by singing it to one or two melodies from Ambroise Thomas operas, while holding a white lily in his hand. Soon his popularity became equal to that of a movie star, and probably no other Russian poet's books sold so well as Severyanin's during his lifetime. For example, *Goblet Seething with Thunders* went through seven editions. Two years after this success, the first volume of a six-volume edition of his works was published.

Severyanin's success is not so difficult to explain, even if now one cannot suppress a smile while reading his works. First of all, his themes gave his wide audience excellent material for their daydreams because they combined exoticism, *haut monde* pictures, and modernity. It did not matter that all three ingredients were phony, because Severyanin had never traveled abroad (as, e.g., Balmont did), knew only the "high society" of cheap novels and operettas, and spoke about airplanes and dirigibles merely to keep up his futurist reputation. But in his poetry he was a gourmet and a dandy, had many easy affairs, and received letters in perfumed envelopes. He also poured champagne into a lily, and in his verses, his heroines yielded on rugs made of lilies of the valley. His poems teemed with flowers, fruit, wines, and liqueurs. He said that he had "a refinedly cruel soul" and preached that "sin is sinless"; in short, he was so contemporary in his amoralism that he was irresistible, especially to the ladies. All this was silly and often cheap and easy to parody, but it was also garishly colorful and full of contrasts, and, like a good tenor, Severyanin was capable of producing a high C on demand and without much strain. In addition, he proclaimed himself a futurist, and futurism was becoming the talk of the day and was apparently the wave of the future. Moreover, this futurism, or whatever it was, charmingly coexisted with good old poetic romanticism. Faced with this popular success, which was further strengthened by favorable acceptance of Severyanin by such arbiters of good taste as Bryusov and Sologub, the newspaper critics, who at first ridiculed Severyanin, began to admire some of his qualities. No one even dared to doubt his talent, though practically everybody found something to critize in his work. Khodasevich called him "a poet by God's grace"; Chukovsky wrote that Severyanin's verse "carries one away like a river." Only Zinaida Hippius called him "Bryusov's ape" and refused to be taken in.[46]

But Severyanin's is not merely a story of a popular success; he deserves serious study. Though he was almost too ready to entitle, or subtitle, his poems nocturnes, poemettes, "heroises," mignonettes, and even "asso-sonnets," this propensity to classify requires further investigation as a highly interesting attempt to emphasize genres when genres were already presumed dead. No less deserving of attention are Severyanin's metrics. Contemporaries found his verse "magnetic, magic, intoxicating, thrilling, and delicious," [47] and much of his secret lies in his handling of caesura in his prolonged lines and in his occasional use of different meters in the two halves of one verse. A study of Severyanin's rhyme is no less imperative. He was probably the first poet to use compound rhyme nonhumorously, though he may share this honor with Khlebnikov. At any rate, those who now write about Mayakovsky's rhyme and fail to mention Severyanin distort the picture. Severyanin was fond of other unusual kinds of rhyme (and rhyming), especially the dissonant (*kedr:eskadr:bodr:mudr:vydr*) and the heterosyllabic.

If Khlebnikov, through his neologisms, tried to explore the inner life of the word (as well as to rid the Russian language of foreign borrowings), Severyanin used his neologisms for color and surprise. His favorite procedures were the forming of new verbs and participles from noun roots (*okaloshit', otransen*) and the building of compound nouns (*ozerzamok, sladkolëd,* etc.), which are identical with David Burliuk's "compact words." Neologism for many readers was a primary feature of futurism, and even for the futurists themselves the first concrete task was to enrich the existing language with as many newly coined words as possible. Severyanin's originality lies in his mixing of neologism with foreign words, and in this he deeply influenced many of his fellow ego-futurists. French had been the language of the Russian aristocracy for many decades, and Severyanin clearly strove to make his verse as genteel as possible through the use of French words and formations. French proper names had a hypnotic attraction for him, so he used such names as Berlioz and Rimbaud obviously because of their sound, displaying scarcely any acquaintance with the work of either. Sometimes he distorted French words unmercifully to make them sound even more "beautiful" (or perhaps more French, in his opinion). Thus, judged not only by his Russian spelling, but also by his rhyme, he pronounced "chauffeur" as if it were "chauffaire," and even formed new Russian words in this manner (*grezer* from *greza*, "a dream"). This practice made one journalist say mockingly that he did not understand Severyanin's poetry because it was written in Rumanian.[48] It is when Severyanin is inebriated with foreign words and names that he sometimes betrays his lack of education, for example, by making Greek hetaeras look from the loges of the parterre. He invents the strange *koktebli* (an unconscious contamination of "cocktail" with Koktebel, a place in Crimea), which seem to be some kind of songs. But he also can make a line of Russian verse burst with barbarisms and still be poetically convincing, as in "Garson, s'improvizirui blestyashchii faiv-o-klök" ("Garçon, improvise a brilliant five-o'clock [tea]").

Historically, Severyanin's short alliance with the ego-futurists' "worst enemies" should be noted. Kulbin persuaded the Hylaeans to enter into this alliance, and soon Mayakovsky had to compete with Severyanin's success with the women present at their joint public poetry readings. At the beginning of 1914 Severyanin toured the Crimea with David Burliuk and Mayakovsky in poetry recitals organized by his admirer and imitator, Vadim Bayan (Sidorov), who lived in Simferopol. Before the third recital, Severyanin quarreled with Mayakovsky because of money and refused to continue the tour; in Odessa he gave an interview in which he declared that there were no points in common between ego-futurism and the cubo-futurists (as the Hylaeans had come to be called by that time). After that he wrote two anti-Hylaean poems, one of which ("Poeza istrebleniya" ["Poesa of Destruction"]) was especially violent in its attack. In it he condemned the Hylaeans for mocking all that was sacred, called them pseudoinnovators, and said that, instead of throwing Lermontov (*sic*) overboard from the ship of modernity, one should exile the Burliuks to the island of Sakhalin, the penal colony of the czarist government. Later, when living abroad, he published (in *Menestrel*, Berlin, 1921) "Poema dopolneniya" ("Poem of Amplification"), in which he accused Burliuk and his friends of contributing to the Russian Revolution. Later, however, in *Bells of the Cathedral of Feelings* he described the Crimean tour with mild and good-natured amusement. Severyanin's short-lived alliance with the Hylaeans also found expression in his contributing one poem to their *Milk of Mares* and three to *Roaring Parnassus*; in the latter he also signed a manifesto (see chap. 4). Despite this break with the Hylaeans, Severyanin continued to be on good terms with Vasily Kamensky.

No other book by Severyanin ever equaled the success of his *Goblet*. Slowly, his audience dwindled, perhaps disappointed in the poet's failure to grow and change poetically. All the rest of his prerevolutionary books were repetitions of the first. Yet *Zlatolira* ("Goldilyre," 1914) went through five editions, even though Ignatyev sarcastically remarked: "We are afraid that Severyanin's goblet has been emptied." [49] Even less interesting was *Ananasy v shampanskom* ("Pineapples in Champagne," 1915), which, moreover, included much of Severyanin's early poetry, going back as far as 1903. *Victoria regia*, published in the same year, showed at least some variety, because it contained his poetry connected with the war. His anti-German poems were crude, but the controversial poems in which he defended himself against accusations of leading a safe life far from the front lines were not devoid of interest. His worst book of all was *Poesoentracte* (1915), which consisted of nothing but earlier, immature poems that could find no place in *Pineapples in Champagne*. These poems reveal, however, how close Severyanin was to the Russian poetry of the second half of the nineteenth century. In addition to these other works, there was, in 1916, the dull *Tost bezotvetnyi* ("A Toast without Response"). Severyanin also participated in joint publications with little-known poets like Massainov, Tolmachev, and A. Vinogradov (*Ostrova ocharovanii* ["Islands of Enchantment"], 1917; *Mimozy lna* ["Mimosa of Flax"], 1916; *Vintik* ["Little Screw"], 1915).

Interest in Severyanin continued, however, judging by the publication in 1916 of a book, *Kritika o tvorchestve Severyanina* ("Criticism of Severyanin's Work"). The book opens with autobiographical data; then Bryusov, in an essay, repeats that Severyanin is a true poet, but adds a chapter about his shortcomings, such as lack of taste and education and an inability to think. Next, Sergei Bobrov supplies a thorough survey of the criticism of Severyanin's work, followed by numerous examples. An article by Professor Roman Brandt about Severyanin's poetic language closes the book.

In 1919 Severyanin emigrated to Estonia, where he was held in esteem by Estonian poets (he published several books of translations from Estonian).[50] In addition to two books of selections from previously published poetry,[51] he published twelve books of poems,[52] and several more remained in manuscript form. Severyanin often traveled and read his poetry wherever he could find Russians in Europe to listen to it, but lack of the kind of appreciation he was accustomed to during the time of his fame made him bitter, and he accused his compatriots in some of his verse of inability to understand fine things. Most of his poetry published abroad is characterized by familiar Severyaninisms and by a constant deterioration in quality—and the poet had the deplorable habit of publishing even his most atrocious lines. Toward the end, however, he almost got rid of his neologistic and barbaristic mannerisms, and began to write in a traditional, neoclassical vein. Some of his best *émigré* poetry was written in this manner, and most of this best can be found in *Klassicheskie rozy* ("Classical Roses"), published in 1931 in Belgrade. Perhaps Severyanin's most interesting book of this time was *Medalyony* ("Medallions"; 1934), consisting of nearly a hundred sonnets about, or addressing, a variety of famous persons from Beethoven to Jules Verne and from Pasternak to himself. When the Soviets occupied Estonia in 1940, Severyanin began to publish in Soviet magazines. He was asked to write a poem about Stalin, but claimed he was ill. When the Germans started their war against Russia, Severyanin was desperate and telegraphed the Soviet government about evacuation. He died on December 20, 1941, during the German occupation.[53]

It is possible to speak of a third period in the history of ego-futurism, a period connected with the *Enchanted Wanderer,* a magazine first published while Ignatyev was still alive, in the fall of 1913. Begun as a monthly, it soon became a quarterly. The last issue (no. 10) appeared at the beginning of 1916. Starting with number 5, the magazine began to designate itself officially on its cover as ego-futurist. The importance of the *Enchanted Wanderer* lies in its stressing that ego-futurism was a continuation of the decadent movement started at the beginning of the century and in its crusading for a return to the ideals of that movement. The editor of this periodical was Victor Romanovich Khovin, who once wrote an essay for Ignatyev's *Sky Diggers.* The first issue had the subtitle, "Kritik-intuit" ("Critic-Intuitionist") and contained only critical essays and reviews, but Khovin began to print poetry in the second issue, and changed the subtitle to "An Almanac of Intuitivist Criticism and Poetry." Despite his verbose and sometimes mannered style, Khovin was an able and serious critic who was convinced that, after the initial flowering of Russian decadent poetry, there came a period of stagnation and popularization, and he made a futile attempt to refresh the atmosphere, while fighting the symbolists, the Marxists, and the "New Christianity" of Merezhkovsky.

The other leading figure associated with the *Enchanted Wanderer* was the former Areopagite of ego-futurism, Dimitri Kryuchkov, who, in addition to poetry, published criticism, often under the pseudonym of Keleinik. Among his articles, one should note the one about Innokenty Annensky as a critic, that about Francis Jammes, and Kryuchkov's attack on Maxim Gorky in the magazine's first issue after Gorky had made his assault on the production of the stage adaptation of Dostoyevsky's *The Possessed* in the Moscow Art Theater. Kryuchkov declared Gorky's criticism amounted to "an open war against art and religion" and said that "the soul of the Russian people was a closed book" to Gorky. In 1915 Khovin and Kryuchkov were joined by the young critic Boris Gusman. Anastasiya Chebotarevskaya, Sologub's wife, was also associated with the magazine.

The cornerstone of the magazine's program was a return to the ideals of Russian decadence, which included pure art, unlimited freedom of creation, and spiritual search. Extreme individualism and separation from the world were considered the basic prerequisites of true decadence. Thus, on the pages of the *Enchanted Wanderer,* one could come across not only Fyodor Sologub, but also Zinaida Hippius—both leading figures of the so-called early Russian decadent movement.[54] Fofanov was for Victor Khovin also a decadent. "Decadence is a golden gate leading into the mysterious world of the poet's free wanderings on the exhausting, but joyful, ways of realizing one's creative self," wrote Khovin (*Enchanted Wanderer,* no. 1). The ideal decadent for him was Oscar Wilde, who was honored in two articles (in nos. 1 and 9) and whom he considered to be "a genius of intuitivism." Oscar Wilde, incidentally, was deemed to be a critic of genius, rather than a poet (even *The Picture of Dorian Gray* was called a critical work). The quotation from Wilde about lie for lie's sake, whose highest form is art, adorned every issue of the magazine as a motto. Earlier decadent ideals were, to Khovin's mind, betrayed by Balmont's and Bryusov's having turned "academic," by Merezhkovsky's embracing the public (*obshchestvennost*) on his way to the New Christianity, and the symbolists' coming dangerously close to actuality and dogmatism.

Though the *Enchanted Wanderer* considered Russian symbolism the most important movement of modern times, the recent developments in it, under the leadership of Vyacheslav Ivanov and Andrei Biely, were, for Khovin, an abandonment of that most sacred thing, the intuition, and a submission to rationality and schematism. He asked, in the third issue: "Have we gone through the temptations of decadence in vain, in order now, from stormy, violet-colored worlds and from the inner world of a restless individuality, to come again to a school-like dogma?" The only solution for Khovin was a return to the spiritual underground in order to purify the ideals of decadence. Such an underground was ego-futurism.

Though Khovin had little use for Gnedov's verbal experiments or the shocking titles of some of the ego-futurist almanacs, he welcomed even this as a way to disturb the stagnant swamp of contemporary literature. "Ego-futurism alone is loyal to Russian decadence in its faithfulness to art and to creative freedom," wrote Khovin in the third issue of the *Enchanted Wanderer*. That same issue carried a whole page devoted to mourning Ignatyev's death. Khovin's attitude toward the members of Shershenevich's futurist group in Moscow, which called itself *Mezonin poezii* ("The Mezzanine of Poetry"), was favorable, though he deplored their lack of spirituality and called them "flippant clowns of modernity with a tragic twist to their lips" (*Enchanted Wanderer*, no. 2). Khovin was, however, against the Hylaeans, though he had a high opinion of Mayakovsky as a poet. They were, for him, "insolent Muscovites," who were not only preoccupied with loud eccentricities, but were also too theoretical. Khovin accepted the "vandalistic" character of contemporary futurism only with difficulty, but he dreamed of the coming futurism, which would be constructive, and he divided the futurists into the false ones, who were too busy destroying the past, and the genuine ones, who were accepting "the marvelous future." The task of the day for him was not creating schools and theories, but being in opposition to the prevalent literature. For him, Marinetti was a real futurist and rebel, whereas the Russian futurists were too fond of applause and preferred teasing to a real war.

Khovin organized the *Enchanted Wanderer* public discussions and even thought of opening his own literary cabaret. In the magazine, he tried to produce the impression of a movement rather than of a small sectarian group. The poetic stars were Kryuchkov and Severyanin.

Kryuchkov continued to publish his smooth, but hardly original, poetry, in which one can find echoes of all previous twentieth-century poetry from Balmont to Severyanin. Interesting is his poem to Trediakovsky (*Enchanted Wanderer*, no. 4), the poet of the eighteenth century, in which Kryuchkov refuses to consider as poets those who mock Trediakovsky.

In his critical essays, Kryuchkov praised Severyanin, whose career, "changeable as city noise, is, like a demimondaine's whims, . . . intoxicated by the liqueur of modernity" (no. 1). Beginning with the second issue, Severyanin's poetry was printed in the magazine regularly almost to the very end. From Moscow, Ivnev and the ubiquitous Shershenevich sent their verses; but the most arresting fact was the printing of works by Khlebnikov, Kamensky, and Guro, which was not a maneuver to split the Hylaeans, but rather another effort on the part of Khovin to broaden his concept of futurism. Moreover, Khlebnikov and Kamensky became contributors in 1915, by which time their Moscow group had practically ceased to exist. Kamensky was honored with a critical essay written by Boris Gusman, in which the "wise naïveté of his soul" was praised (no. 8). Nikolai Evreinov, the famous theatrical figure of the period, was often given opportunity to criticize the commercial theater and to propagandize his "theater for oneself" in the *Enchanted Wanderer*. One can find on its pages the names of such little-known poets as Mikhail Struve, Mikhail Kozyrev, Alexander Tolmachev, and Alexei Massainov, as well as those of several woman poets (Princess Shakhnazarova, V. Solntseva, Vera Werther[55]), among whom the most talented was Ada Vladimirova,[56] the poetess of the Guro school.

Khovin tried to establish "intuitivist criticism," which was to be irrationalist, nonpopularizing, and alien to systems and blueprints. For him this was a return to the "idle dreams" of the decadents. But it was also a return to the impressionism of early futurism. That is why Innokenty Annensky, one of the most impressionistic of Russian critics, was so much praised on the pages of the magazine ("Annensky does not analyze, he does not evaluate, he gives himself to the work," *Enchanted Wanderer*, no. 3). For Khovin, a critic "depicts his own self" in his criticism, and his enemies were the history of literature and scholarly criticism. In the works discussed, changeability and a two-faced quality were particularly appreciated as signs of individualism (for example, hedonism and apologia of suffering in Oscar Wilde). For this reason, Kamensky and Guro, the most impressionistic of Russian futurists, were readily accepted by Khovin. There was a genuine cult of Guro, who was extolled as an ideal poet in two issues of the *Enchanted Wanderer* (nos. 5 and 10).

Toward the end Khovin changed and moved further to the left. In the final issue of the *Enchanted Wanderer,* there were many signs of this turn. In an open letter Khovin admitted his break with Severyanin, who was now branded a nonfuturist, and his work after *Goblet* was declared "a tasteless, cowardly act of a man thirsty for success." The word "ego-futurist" was removed from the magazine cover, and even the quotation from Oscar Wilde disappeared. Suddenly, Khovin began to defend Khlebnikov, and even Kruchenykh, from his intuitivist position. Not only were Khlebnikov's poetry and an article printed, but his theories about the mathematical foundations of history were praised by M. Kozyrev in a short essay. Khovin now preferred Mayakovsky to Sologub and, while discussing symbolism, he respectfully quoted, of all people, Kruchenykh. Finally, in the anonymous article "Dinamitu, gospoda, dinamitu" ("Let's Have Dynamite, Gentlemen"), he confessed the failure of the *Enchanted Wanderer,* which "had in vain tried to open with a new key the old valise of Russian decadence."

After the Revolution of 1917, Khovin continued the *Enchanted Wanderer* but only as a publishing enterprise. In 1918 he published a pamphlet, *Segodnyashnemu dnyu* ("For Today"), in which the primary futurist task, that of the destruction of the cultural past, was declared accomplished. But he condemned Mayakovsky and his friends for placing their talent at the disposal of the new master, communism, when true futurism's task was a rebellion against all masters. He accused Mayakovsky of servility and refused to accept the new ideals of proletarian art, ending his book with his old words, "Let's have some dynamite, gentlemen." Strangely enough, Khovin was evidently not arrested immediately after that, because his new magazine, *Knizhnyi Ugol* ("Book Corner"),[57] which had among its contributors Vasily Rozanov and Boris Eichenbaum, appeared once more in 1919 (there were six issues). Then there was a two-and-a-half-year pause, after which Khovin briefly resumed publication with issue number 7 in November, 1921. After this, however, the name of Khovin disappeared.

If the *Enchanted Wanderer* was a more or less direct continuation of St. Petersburg ego-futurism, the Mezzanine of Poetry was an independent futurist group in Moscow, which was in alliance with ego-futurists and only occasionally termed itself ego-futurist. It was organized in the summer of 1913 by Vadim Shershenevich, a frequent guest in Ignatyev's almanacs, and by the artist, Léon Zack, who published poetry under the name of Khrisanf. Together they issued three miscellanies. The first of them, *Vernissazh* ("Vernissage"), appeared in September and was printed, like all Mezzanine publications, on unnumbered pages. It opened with the "anonymous" (composed by Khrisanf) "Overture" written as an informal, affected chat inviting a lady to the opening of the Mezzanine of Poetry and to the exquisite, though not filling, dinner. The members of the group are presented as inhabitants of an apartment, where also the Most Charming One (Poetry) lives. She is, however, inaccessible, and no one has ever entered her bedroom, though they have given her roses and compliments and have picked up her handkerchief for her when she has dropped it. Being allowed to serve her in this way has kept the Mezzanine poets enamored. Otherwise these poets are described as friendly, slightly crazy, and preferring that which is close by to that which is remote. This veiled polemic with symbolism is continued with the assertion that one should not write about castles if one sees only a bakery through the window, and one should compare sadness to a penknife rather than to an ocean, because what one really knows is one's room.

Ten poets are represented in *Vernissage,* some of them completely unknown, like K. Chaikin, N. Benediktova, and Alexei Sidorov, the latter also belonging to the Lirika group (see chap. 6). It is interesting to note that Boris Lavrenev, the future Soviet novelist, began in this miscellany as a futurist poet managing to combine bits of Blok, Severyanin, Shershenevich, and Mayakovsky in his exaggeratedly foppish verse.[58] After having honored the St. Petersburg ego-futurists with his contribution, Valery Bryusov did the same for the Mezzanine of Poetry, giving them one poem whose imagery is based on a soccer game. The leaders, Shershenevich and Khrisanf, each contributed four rather mannered poems with unusual rhymes. Two poems by Rurik Ivnev, which were filled with self-pity, were also published; and Pavel Shirokov, the guest star from St. Petersburg, tried to be as urbanist as possible in his two poems. The book contained one critical essay written by Khrisanf (signed "M. Rossiyansky") entitled "Perchatka kubo-futuristam" ("A Gauntlet Thrown Down before the Cubo-Futurists"), which was actually a polemic against Hylaeans, who at that time were generally known as cubo-futurists. Khrisanf chiefly criticized here the consequences of the Hylaean contention that poetry was nothing but the art of combining words, the word being a value in itself. He argued that the Hylaeans reduced their theories to absurdity by ignoring aspects of the word other than its sound. As a result, he said, they created sound combinations and not words, thus missing their target, the very "word as such." Poetry, in this way, comes to nothing, Khrisanf continued, and he likened Kruchenykh's effort to write in his own language to a pianist's playing a mute keyboard. He concluded by asserting that destruction of content was not a broadening, but a narrowing of the field of poetry, and that the Hylaeans were annihilating the old ways of creating poetry without discovering any new ones. "They are ignorant of logics, they do not know the nature of the medium of poetry, and, throwing overboard the old pilots, they themselves are ignorant of navigating by the stars, while they also do not know the function and mechanism of a compass." [59]

The central figure of the Mezzanine of Poetry, Vadim Gabrielevich Shershenevich (1893–1942), now chiefly known for his role in the postrevolutionary Russian movement of imagism (or "imaginism," as it is called in Russian), deserves more attention than he is usually given. One of the most active Russian futurists from 1913 to 1916, he was a controversial but fascinating figure, prolific and peripatetic (he made and broke more literary alliances than any other Russian futurist), who assimilated all the basic traits of Russian modernism and appeared as poet, prose writer, dramatist, critic, theoretician, group leader, and translator. The son of a well-known professor of law in Moscow, Shershenevich published his first book, *Vesennie protalinki* ("Patches of Earth Free of Snow"), in 1911. A beginner's book, it was imitative and adolescently romantic, a mixture of Fofanov and the Balmont of *The Burning Buildings*. It displayed some interest in German-language literature (imitations of Heine, epigraphs from Peter Altenberg), and attracted the critical attention of Gumilev, who praised the author's good taste while deploring his lack of originality.[60] Evidently Shershenevich was later ashamed of Balmont's influence and once even omitted the book from a list of his publications, which he was so fond of printing on the final pages of his subsequent books. And he never tired of attacking Balmont, alone among the symbolists, for being a pseudoinnovator. His next book, while being even more eclectic in style, was more mature in technique. *Carmina* (Moscow, 1913) shows the young poet learning not only from many contemporaries, but from such poets of the past as Pushkin and Nikolai Yazykov (1803–1846), "an excellent, though unfortunately little-known poet," as Shershenevich wrote in his notes. The first part of the book was dedicated to Alexander Blok, and it was full of poetry of wine and snow; but another part had a dedication to Mikhail Kuzmin, the leader of the Russian poetic dandies, and to be sure, one finds in it clavichords, sofas, pastorals, masquerades, Pierrots, and Harlequins. There is also an entire section of poems with Russian fairy-tale motifs, which betrays an acquaintance with the famous collection of Afanasyev. In the translation section, which is dedicated to Gumilev, German poetry still predominates (Heine, Rilke, Dehmel, Liliencron, Verlaine), but the overall tone is classical rather than romantic, being characterized by the clear-cut composition of the poems, precise traditional meters, and even use of the ancient, classical, elegiac distich. In one poem Shershenevich says:

> Ya perelyu glukhuyu grust'
> V otchetlivye pesnopenya
>
> (I shall recast my vague sadness
> Into precise songs)

Epigraphs remained a favorite device, and in *Carmina* one could find among the sources seven Russians (including Shershenevich himself) and one Italian poet (quoted in the original). Notes to the book not only justified such orthographic and prosodic idiosyncrasies as *kchemu* (written together) or the word *korabl* used as a trisyllabic, but also pedantically informed the reader when the author had borrowed a rhyme from a fellow poet. Gumilev, whose review was even more favorable than before,[61] was, however, mistaken when he thought (not without reason) that he was encouraging a potential Acmeist.

Carmina was only a summing up of the early apprenticeship, and when it came out it was an anachronism, because Shershenevich simultaneously published, with the Petersburg Herald, his third book, the slim *Romanticheskaya pudra* ("Romantic Face Powder"),[62] a typical example of ego-futurist salon aestheticism. Although Shershenevich entitled the opening poem "L'Art poétique," it contained only an invitation to treat poems (*poezy* in Russian, to be sure) as if they were ladies of the *haut monde*. The last poem of the book, "Segodnya" ("Today"), was manifesto-like in its contempt for academicism, proclaiming the poet's madness and the appeal to burn the past in the fire of the present; but the effect was softened by its being addressed to a lady. In between, there was more of the atmosphere of the perfumed boudoir than of a rebellion, and "modern" imagery (love likened to electricity, a heart melting like ice cream, the moon compared to absinthe, buttercups wearing a makeup of dew) was entirely in this vein, so that even Cleopatra had "a rendezvous" with Antony.

Shershenevich, like a good convert to ego-futurism, dutifully borrowed epigraphs from Lokhvitskaya and, like Severyanin, wrote triolets and "esquisettes," but his imitation of Severyanin was certainly exaggerated by the critics, and he was right when, in his defense, he invited them to compare his lines closely with those of Severyanin.[63] His not having copied Severyanin as closely as his critics charged does not make Shershenevich a very original poet, but he is a complex one in his leterary backgroud and affiliations, borrowing directly from European poetry, an area Severyanin knew only by hearsay. Much of the imagery in *Romantic Face Powder* was taken directly from the *poètes maudits* (the moon like a disintegrating skull; the sky which is heavier than the eyelashes of a dead woman), and, on the whole, this book marked for the author the shift from Heine and Rilke to the French poets. On the very first page there was a quotation from Huysmans, followed by epigraphs from Musset, Rimbaud, and Laforgue. The book had a rather coquettish preface, addressed to Ignatyev and anticipating the readers' neglect and the critics' abuse with which the book would be met, while confessing that the poet was sorry he had written these poems "instead of frequenting the *café chantants* with their confetti of kisses and paper streamers of caresses."

When Shershenevich's next book of poetry, *Ekstravagantnye flakony* ("The Extravagant Scent Bottles") appeared in the fall of 1913, he was already a leader of the Mezzanine of Poetry and felt obliged to offer a good example of what real futurist poetry should be. In this endeavor he was like a skillful stage director showing his actors how a scene should be played, though no true actor himself. Almost every poem in the book consistently demonstrated a solution to some technical problem. Shershenevich's historical importance lies in the fact that he was the first, and probably the only, Russian futurist who acknowledged Marinetti's futurism as the starting point and tried to create a Russian version along the same lines. A critic once called him "the first who has actually read Marinetti." [64] Within a year he published a translation of Marinetti's main manifestos into Russian, which was later followed by two translations of Marinetti's works. Although in the poems of *The Extravagant Scent Bottles* his earlier snobbish affection can be found, for example, in the *vin des Graves* being poured into a feminine slipper, there is also an invitation to the beloved to go and see a bonfire of books. Shershenevich has become now consciously urbanist and in a new way: he sings of the noise of boulevards, of the roar of automobiles, of street lights and skyscrapers. In one poem, a crowd and buildings persecute a woman; in another, a woman strangles her infant child out of boredom and then phones her husband; in still another, a youth screams hysterically in a café and, after a prostitute comes and kisses him, transforms himself into a satyr and pierces her with his horns; in a movie theater, the poet makes a special effort and begins to see the image upside down.

Shershenevich's main experiments are concentrated in the area of rhyme. In poem after poem he tries different kinds of new, or at least nontraditional, rhyme. There are various types of inexact rhymes (*krichá–plechám, vualétku–prospéktu, skúchno–túchi*), compound rhymes (*davnó ona-klóuna*), heterosyllabic rhymes (*púnsha-yúno-sha, dúshu-slúshayu*), enjambment rhymes (*fiálki–ustál ki- / váya*), and even heterotonic rhymes (*nóvoi–safyánovoi*). Usually an entire poem is devoted to one specific type of rhyme. In one of the poems Shershenevich wrote about his own verse: "For other poets, rhymes enter into legitimate matrimony; in my poetry, they go to bed for one night only." Metrically, he experimented here with various kinds of accentual verse, often chaotic on first appearance, but actually carefully organized; lexically, he continued to fill the lines with neologisms and foreign words; and in imagery, he tried *épater-les-bourgeois* tropes like "the sky opened like a woman's bodice, revealing the breasts of the clouds." Shershenevich was often attacked by critics as a poetaster, devoid of talent;[65] in fact, next to Kruchenykh, he may be considered one of the most abused Russian poets of this century (which explains the title of his 1916 book of criticism, *Zelenaya ulitsa,* which may be translated as "Running the Gauntlet"). Such criticism was utterly unfair. Shershenevich may have lacked a true lyric gift, but he was a clever and smooth versifier who tried to enrich the Russian poetic palette with new means and did it with more sense and consistency than many others. His "rebellious" lines and coarse images are nothing but the play of an aesthete, but the very combination of Severyanin and Mayakovsky in his urbanist verse was no small achievement, though it may lack the glamour of originality.

To round out his image as a futurist leader,[66] Shershenevich also had to appear as a critic and a theoretician, and he did it in 1913 in the book *Futurizm bez maski* ("Futurism without a Mask"). It is a rather well-written book (or perhaps it seems so after the rambling writings of Ignatyev and David Burliuk), displaying clarity and good taste, though hardly showing the author as a profound and original mind; but he was aware of these limitations when he subtitled the book *kompilyativnaya introduktsiya.* His aim, as he says in the first lines, is to explain to the confused public what futurism is. He begins by establishing novelty as the basic quality of real poetry: only the new excites, and this is likened to a car that runs into a group of gaping bystanders and drives away, perhaps leaving someone injured. According to Shershenevich, the fortress of Russian literature was at that time occupied by the symbolists, who had received the keys from the vanquished realists. The symbolists, though rebels in the past, had turned academic and forgotten that poetry is alive only in a fight.[67] But already "an army in the uniforms of clowns and jesters, turning somersaults and shouting absurd *boutades,* is rushing from Italy," and this is futurism. Comparing this new phenomenon with the older movements, Shershenevich says that while realism sacrifices form to content and symbolism blends both, futurism proclaims form superior to content. The most important innovator is, for him, Marinetti, who introduced the new beauty of speed and taught how to catch the rhythm of modern life. According to Shershenevich, however, Marinetti's invitation to burn the museums should not be taken literally. He also finds that the Italian futurists failed to provide a new form for the new content; moreover, Marinetti's own poetry is found to be boring, tasteless, and imitative. Marinetti discovered only one aspect of an important process, our "dissolving" in the city, but not our further "re-creation." The latter seems to be one of Shershenevich's favorite ideas, and it later helped him to include in futurism even such poets as Rurik Ivnev. Among the specific poetic means and procedures of futurism, he considers ametrical verse (which he calls "rhythmical"), unexpected rhyme, neologism, and colloquial diction. Shershenevich denies the Hylaeans the right to call themselves futurists and criticizes the alleged inconsistencies in their theory and practice; closer to futurism is the Petersburg Ego-group (he lists his own name among theirs), but even Severyanin, whom he rates highly as a poet, does not qualify as a real futurist. In his conclusion, Shershenevich expresses the hope that, after the dust of destruction settles, the poets will turn their efforts toward constructive tasks. Though rather simplified and too schematic and with a tendency to skip over things the author cannot easily solve, it was, nevertheless, the first full-scale book about futurism by a futurist. It gave a clear picture of futurism as understood by the Mezzanine of Poetry: moderate, civilized, based on "good taste," without manifestos, but not shunning theory, Western in orientation, avoiding extremes, and tolerant of the past. In a typical sentence, Shershenevich said in one of his later books: "Every innovation is only a development of a stroke used by a predecessor." [68]

Although the Mezzanine of Poetry was the shortest-lived futurist group, lasting for only about half a year, it included some poets whose work merits discussion from other than merely a historical viewpoint, in contrast with most of the Petersburg ego-futurists. The other leader of the group was the artist Lev Vasilyevich Zak (Léon Zack), who wrote poetry under the name of Khrisanf and criticism under the name of Rossiyansky. He was born in 1892 in Nizhni Novgorod (now Gorky) and studied literature at the University of Moscow. His book *Pirotekhnicheskie improvizatsii* ("Pyrotechnical Improvisations") was announced, but never appeared, so one can judge him only on the basis of a few poems published in the three almanacs of the Mezzanine of Poetry, often marked "Paris." Khrisanf was potentially an important poetic phenomenon; and had he devoted more time to poetry than to painting, he would have had a profound effect on Russian futurism. His preoccupation with verbal texture was unique in his group because the other poets of that group had never been very radical in this respect. His poetry, filled with images of violence and death, is built on intricate rhyme; but, unlike Shershenevich, Khrisanf mixed all kinds of it in one poem: compound, heterosyllabic, heterotonic, homonymic, truncated, and many others. Here are examples: *kandelyábrom–táborom, mímo–gromí moi, trub–trup, né bylo–péplom, k chemú–chumú, ústrits–lyústre, vinaigre–negr, elektríchestvo–Beatríche, vózglasam–slëz glazám, lézviyam–trézvyi em, vvys' litsóm–víselitsam, zá ruki–árki, rukámi–kámera, veroyátno–yád ono, dévushki–nadév uzh, mórfiya–mërtvye, odinákovo–privedená k vam, úmer–yúmor, rádius–ráduisya.* As can be seen from this list, no discussion of Mayakovsky's rhyme is complete without taking into consideration not only Khlebnikov, but also Khrisanf.[69] What makes Khrisanf's style still closer to that of Khlebnikov is his tendency toward paronomasia or homonymy in general, so that occasionally his lines are on their way to becoming "nothing but rhyme." Here is the beginning of one of his poems, which demonstrates this point:

Skorbyu	With my grief
Ya skoro ubyu	I will soon kill
Adovy kavalkady.	The cavalcades of hell.
V trupakh tropy.	The paths are full of corpses.
Tropicheskaya truba,	A tropical trumpet
Skorb moya! Bayron	Is my grief! Byron
Pered neyu bednee gorba,	Is poorer than a hunchback
	in comparison,
V mantii gaer on.	He is a buffoon in a robe.
Karlik i arlekin	A midget and Harlequin
Dyavola i lovelasa	Of the devil and Casanova
K viselitsam	To gallows,
Vvys litsom	And face up,
Chelovecheskuyu rasu!	The human race!
Toshno dushe. Potushu,	Soul is disgusted. I, an unlamented
Neoplakivaemyi palach,	executioner, will put out
Plamena, i plakaty, i plach—	Flames, and posters, and the cry—
Konchena gonchaya.	Finished is the race.

Rurik Ivnev (the pseudonym of Mikhail Alexandrovich Kovalev) was born into a military family in Tiflis in 1893, and was another of Shershenevich's friends not devoid of talent. Ivnev had some reputation in poetic circles before the Revolution; then after the Revolution he joined the imagists (also led by Shershenevich). Until very recently his name was little remembered. In the poems of his only book published by the Mezzanine of Poetry, *Plamya pyshet* ("The Flame Is Raging"), he appeared as an impressionist who captures the minute movements of his sick soul or the details of his surroundings. These surroundings are not necessarily urban. In fact, Ivnev was the only Mezzanine poet who was genuinely interested in landscape (especially Volga wharfs). Ivnev's poetic genealogy includes Alexander Blok and Mikhail Kuzmin. He is also one of the rare Russian male poets who resemble Akhmatova. Nevertheless, Ivnev had his own distinct poetic voice and his own themes. These words from *The Flame Is Raging* might well be used to describe the whole of his writings:

> Ya v dushe svoei, kak v zemle izrytoi,
> Koposhus rukami izmuchennymi
>
> (I am rummaging with my hands in my soul
> As if in dug-up soil)

Suffering, his own or that of other people, morbidly attracts Ivnev (see, for instance, the description of a coachman's mutilated body in "Gibel kuchera" ["A Coachman's Death"]). Ivnev's rhythms of spoken language which result in accentual verse (the so-called *dolnik*) and lines of unequal length should attract the attention of any student of Russian verse, but his occasional unusual rhymes and neologisms seem to be a dutiful tribute to his reputation as a futurist. Ivnev does not display any genuine interest in verbal experimentation.

In 1913, Ivnev published in Moscow the first "leaf" (actually a small collection of verse) of his *Samosozhzhenie* ("Self-Immolation"), probably his most typical work. It is poetry of self-pity and nervous disgust with oneself, alternating with prayerlike poems expressing the hope of the final purification of his soul. Ivnev is often attracted by the theme of Holy Russia and its shrines, but the predominant motif remains "Why am I so bad, O Lord?" The second "leaf" was published in 1914 in St. Petersburg by the Petersburg Herald publishing enterprise, the third one in 1916, by the *Enchanted Wanderer*, after which Ivnev added many poems from his other publications to those contained in the three leaves and published them in Petrograd in 1917 in one book under the same title (see chap. 6).

More promise was shown by another poet of the group, once described as Shershenevich's alter ego,[70] Constantine Aristarkhovich Bolshakov (1895–1940), who entered literature with a very immature, though weighty book, *Mozaika* ("Mosaics"), in 1911. His prose and drama were here entirely in the decadent tradition, and the sources for his poetry could be traced even further back, to the romantic poetry of the nineteenth century. The prevalent influence, however, was, as in Shershenevich's first book, Balmont.[71] Bolshakov's second book was also published in Moscow, probably in the fall of 1913 (though the poem was written more than a year earlier), and illustrated by Goncharova and Larionov in their rayonist manner. The text is handwritten as in Kruchenykh's publications. In it the young poet definitely chose futurism, though his idea of this movement was very much along decadent lines. The book, *Le futur*, contained one long poem, written in a kind of free verse, in which the main episode dealt with the appearance of a naked woman in a modern city, arousing "the ancient Adam" in the city's crowd of males. The next day the streets are strewn with the bodies of men who have obviously died of exhaustion, but the poem ends on the optimistic note that from them, in time, a new world will be born. There is some predilection for geometric forms in the poem (the triangular sunset at the beginning, to which the woman's body is later likened). The book was confiscated by the police.

The Mezzanine of Poetry published Bolshakov's third book of poetry, *Serdtse v perchatke* ("A Heart Wearing a Glove"), in 1913. The cover, abstract in its design, was the work of Goncharova. Here Bolshakov showed definite poetic maturity. In his themes he did not avoid the customary ego-futurist effete drawing-room and boudoir poetry, complete with powder boxes, rugs, and scent bottles, of the sort found in Severyanin and Shershenevich; but there are airplanes and city streets in it, too, and they are more specifically the streets of Moscow than those in Shershenevich's poetry. Unlike Severyanin's poetry, however, that of Bolshakov is truly refined and complex. Its direct connection with modern French poetry was emphasized by the epigraph from Laforgue, explaining, by the way, the title (*Et celles dont le coeur gante six et demi).* And unlike the poetry of the well-read Shershenevich, Bolshakov's is much more genuinely sophisticated, though it may coincide with the former's in purely external devices. Bolshakov, for example, also uses neologisms, often abandons traditional meters for accentual verse, and, like other Mezzanine poets, experiments with offbeat kinds of rhyme (*dushí–tishíný, prinósyat-bóisya, skúchen–slúshai*), which more often approximate pure assonance than in the verse of his colleagues. But his true originality lies elsewhere. First of all, his is a special kind of musicality, based on repetition of a phrase, an image, a word, or a root. Sometimes this brings about tautological effects (which are not unlike Khlebnikov's) as in his "Svyatoe remeslo" ("The Sacred Craft"). Repetition of an image may be accompanied by a change of plane (sidewalk of streets–sidewalk of the heart); and that of a sound may result in alliteration and other consonantal effects. Second, there are semantic gaps with ensuing obscurity, which is not typical of the work of other Mezzanine poets with their almost Gallic predilection for clarity. Bolshakov resorts sometimes to grammatical incongruities and in this comes close to Benedict Livshits. Finally, there is Bolshakov's very individual imagery, which, despite traditional ingredients, prefers nontraditional combinations (e.g., "the roses of the eyes") and contrasts. One can come across deliberate antiaestheticism ("my face is whipped with the sweat of the stockings"), macabre grotesque (in "Polnoch" ["Midnight"]), or cosmic hyperbole ("I hung my coat on the moon"). In "Fabrika" ("Factory"), Bolshakov deliberately mixes "the aesthetic" and "the nonaesthetic," combining factory stacks and a woman's eyelashes, Medicis and expectoration. The most arresting poem in the book is "Gorodskaya vesna" ("A City Spring") in which meaningful words often ungrammatically join words invented for the sake of sound. It is perhaps the only example of "transrational" language in the work of the Mezzanine poets, and it is quite different from Kruchenykh's earlier attempts in the same direction. Whereas Kruchenykh reveled in barbaric, often Slavic-sounding, monosyllabics, Bolshakov aimed at a re-creation of a language with Romance connotations in the very first line: "Esmerami verdomi truverit vesna."

Still another interesting poet was Sergei Mikhailovich Tretyakov (1892–1939), who spent his childhood in Latvia and, in the first outpourings of his Muse, was, like Khlebnikov and Severyanin, inspired by the Russo-Japanese War. He also wrote old-fashioned civic-minded poetry and imitated the symbolists. During his university days in Moscow, he was introduced to Shershenevich through Boris Lavrenev, and in 1913 became a futurist. His first poems appeared in Mezzanine publications, but his book *Gamma-luchi* ("Gamma-Rays"), though announced, was never published. The bulk of his prerevolutionary poetry, together with later work, was published in 1919 in *Zheleznaya pauza* ("The Iron Pause") in Vladivostok. All the poems in that book were dated, and so can be conveniently discussed here. In 1913 Tretyakov wrote urbanistic poetry, which, in true Mezzanine fashion, showed the modern city both from outside and inside. In one poem, the poet feels a gay desire to approach a female passerby; in another, an automobile ride to the beach is described in all its futurist beauty of speed; in a poem filled with images of steel, factories, railroads, and construction, a paean to the strong is sung and new music is heard in the clanking of metal.[72] Despite some attempts to introduce futurist imagery (the poet pushes back the street with his feet while remaining motionless himself), Tretyakov's technique is essentially impressionistic, relying on individual brush strokes to convey an image of the whole.

The "inside" urbanist poetry of Tretyakov differs from that of his colleagues in that it is seldom effete or salon-like. It is a true poetry of the interior, concentrating on little objects in a city apartment, while the city outside the walls is not forgotten and sometimes momentarily introduced as an impressionistic detail. One of these poems describes an Oriental figurine standing on a shelf; then there are poems about scissors, a fan, a matchbox, and a rug. "Press-byuvar" ("A Blotter"), moving as it does from association to association, is one such poem:

> Kachalka iznezhennoi damy.
> Podoshva stikhi otdavila.
> I vse naoborot.
> Kha, kha! Kachnulsya nalevo-napravo.
> Ne pyanyi li mayatnik trezvykh chasov?
>
> (A rocking chair of a pampered lady.
> A sole has stepped on my poetry.
> And everything is in reverse.

Ha, Ha! It rocks to the left, to the right.
Is it not a drunken pendulum of a sober clock?)

Tretyakov is little interested in rhyme and even less interested in neologism, but metrically he is eclectic in the extreme and uses not only accentual verse, but the most radical forms of free verse side by side with traditional Alexandrines. Metaphor attracts him, too, and the whole poem "Portret" ("A Portrait") is built on tropes such as "trefoil of lace," "spout of arms," "blacksoil of dress," "colon of eyes," and "a shot of blue water on the forest outskirts of buried ears." Occasionally there are graphic devices, and the poem "Veyer" ("Fan") first unfolds and then folds in the way it is printed. There is some influence of Russian folklore in Tretyakov's poetry: one poem imitates children's counting rhymes, another includes an image from a Russian riddle. By the end of 1914 Tretyakov was writing about the war in the manner of Mayakovsky; and after the Revolution he became one of the very active members of, first, the Far Eastern futurist group, *Tvorchestvo* ("Creativity"), and later, of the Lef group led by Mayakovsky. He was arrested and died in a Communist purge.[73]

After *Vernissage*, only two more Mezzanine almanacs appeared. In October, 1913, it was *Pir vo vremya chumy* ("A Feast during the Plague"), alluding, of course, to the title of Pushkin's famous "little tragedy," which was also echoed in the opening poem by Khrisanf. In addition to Khrisanf, there are, as expected, poems by Shershenevich, one of which is a twelve-line rhymed tour de force in the form of a square, with an equal number of letters in each line, and, in the middle, two crossing lines and one vertical line reading "To Valery Bryusov from the author." There are not only poems by Tretyakov, Ivnev, and Shirokov, but also by Severyanin, Graal-Arelsky, Peter Pogodin, and Nadezhda Lvova, the poetess who played an important part in Bryusov's life. Here she tries to write in the Mezzanine manner, imitating Shershenevich and Khrisanf and rhyming *resnítsy–litsóm, nado–vzglyádami,* and even *oknó–on.* The book ends with two critical essays. The first one is Shershenevich's attack on Kruchenykh (signed L'abbé Fanferluche) and an appeal for a "decent futurism" entitled "Poeticheskaya podtasovka" ("Poetic Double-Dealing"). Shershenevich's wrath was aroused after the Hylaeans began to call themselves "futurists," and even "the only futurists in the world" (see chap. 5); and he accused them of appearing under false pretenses, but diplomatically assaulted only Kruchenykh personally. The second piece is a lengthy "Moment philosophique" by M. Rossiyansky (i.e., Khrisanf), which is a rare example in Russian literature of a true literary essay, as written in the West. The basis of this essay is a polemic with positivism and the defense of intuitivist and irrationalist values, developing occasionally into literary criticism (e.g., an analysis of Khrisanf's own poetry). An attempt is made to establish a new type of causality of form, rather than of content. In the list of the participants printed at the end of the book, one finds the names of a few important poets who actually never participated, but were obviously considering such participation. Among these are Fyodor Sologub, who, as observed, was no less favorably disposed toward the ego-futurists than was Bryusov. Also on the list are Vladislav Khodasevich and Vladimir Mayakovsky, the latter clearly being wooed by both Shershenevich and Bolshakov in their efforts to split the Hylaeans. The Hylaeans, on the other hand, made similar overtures to Bolshakov and even announced him as a participant in one of their public recitals. Bolshakov, who was probably not entirely without blame, hastened to whitewash himself in an open letter to the editor of the next Mezzanine almanac, in which he wrote that he never belonged or intended to belong to the Hylaea group. Nevertheless, both Bolshakov and Shershenevich joined the Hylaeans a short time later, and still later Bolshakov became a member of another futurist group organized in Moscow, the Centrifuge, and even attacked Shershenevich on the pages of its publications.

The next and last Mezzanine almanac was a double issue (III–IV, for November–December, 1913). Fourteen poets are represented in it, which makes it quite an impressive display, though, ironically enough, it appeared only shortly before the Mezzanine's demise. This last issue was titled *Krematorii zdravomysliya* ("The Crematorium of Common Sense"), and the only new names in it (in addition to that of Bolshakov who, thus, joined the group formally at its very end) are those of a few woman poets. Among them there is a mysterious Nelli, presented here as a poetess from the Caucasus. Her name and appearance are obviously connected with Bryusov's mystification of the same year, published under the title *Stikhi Nelli* ("Nelly's Poems"). Whether Bryusov wrote all these poems or collaborated with N. Lvova, here is unmistakable proof that the flirtation of the former leader of the Russian symbolists with ego-futurism was more serious than is usually assumed. Otherwise, *The Crematorium of Common Sense* is interesting as a concerted effort of both leaders of the group to create futurist prose. Shershenevich printed in this almanac two excerpts from his projected novel "Introduktsiya samoubiitsy" ("Prelude to a Suicide"). The novel, it seems, was never continued. The excerpts depict life in a future of skyscrapers and technology, and remind one of both science fiction and some of the similar attempts by Khlebnikov. Shershenevich writes his prose in a simple and lucid style, but fills it with rather deliberate imagery. In the first excerpt, his imagery mixes meteorology and gastronomy; in the second, there is something that can be called an objectization of mental processes and exteriorization of internal things: the author takes off his thoughts and wipes off his brain, his heart itches, he holds memories in his hands. The city, on the other hand, is anthropomorphized. The first excerpt begins: "The aero was small. The poet, as was his custom, spoke banal news and took out of his brain little green worms. A demimondaine was putting makeup on her soul with a gay pencil. I put pince-nez on my heart and began to examine the aerial prostitutes."

Another example of prose is Khrisanf's story "Knyazhna Karakatitseva" ("Princess Cuttlefish"). It is written in a completely different manner from Shershenevich's: in long sentences, with emotional, even hysterical inflections. Khrisanf's urbanism here is hyperbolic, almost surrealistic, and he mixes different planes. The story begins with a description of a disgusting old woman, who, with the coming of night, strews from her left pocket "electric machines, gouty sighs, old people's homes, malice wearing widow's weeds, gossipy blood-spitting, cutlets, and dentures" on the city. The old woman is in love with the baritone N. N. and watches him every night through the window from the seventeenth step of the ladder she carries in her pocket, while dripping her despair into a shoeshine can. At the end of the story, she falls from the ladder and is lying dead in front of the house just as the author passes by with his beloved, Arzarumochka, tickling her ears and armpits. He covers the street and the dead woman with his handkerchief to prevent the girl from seeing the ugly spectacle and they continue their walk.

The next item is Shershenevich's "An Open Letter to M. Rossiyansky," in which he tries to approach prose theoretically. After establishing four aspects of the word—scent, sound, sense, and image—he asserts that, in contrast with poetry, Russian prose has not developed recently. In Shershenevich's opinion, artistic prose should be based on the image (which is intuitive) rather than on meaning (which is intellectual). "Prose must be a combination of words-images, as poetry is of words-scents. In prose we deal with the word's face, whereas in poetry, it is the word's face's face."

The Crematorium of Common Sense also contains Shershenevich's attack on Balmont ("Vulgarity on a Pedestal") and Rossiyansky's little sketches on poetic themes under the title "From the Tear-off Calendar of Celebrities," in which, toward the end, the author tries to define the differences among the main literary movements of the day in vignette-like soliloquies. The Realist says: Dig deeper, get those stones, as many stones as possible; you may wash them and let them shine. The Symbolist says: Dig deeper, but do it wearing a chiton. Get that philosopher's stone from the depths, polish it, and then the sky will reflect in it—this is the main thing. And the Futurist says: Dig deeper, look for whatever you like: stones, unrequited love, or gold, but do not make any superfluous movements. It does not matter what you find; I am only looking at your movements. Rossiyansky's (i.e., Khrisanf's, i.e., Léon Zack's) formulation was probably the most concise statement of Mezzanine aesthetics.

The Mezzanine's next publication, *Yanvarskie futurnalii* ("January Futurnalias"), never appeared, and after three almanacs and three books of verse (by Shershenevich, Ivnev, and Bolshakov), the group ended its activities. Its members eventually joined other futurist groups, or, like Khrisanf, abandoned literature altogether.

4 CUBO-
4 4 FUTURIS
4 4 4 M
4 4
4 4
44444444444
4
4

In 1913 members of the Hylaea group became
known as "cubo-futurists"; however, the designation "Hylaea" was not abandoned. It continued
to appear on the covers of futurist publications,
sometimes together with the new name,
"futurists." (The "futurist" part of the new name
was used before the "cubo" one was added.)
According to a newspaper report[1] about the
second Jack of Diamonds public discussion
(February 24, 1913), Mayakovsky called himself
a futurist there. The same word was used by
him in his lecture on March 24 in St. Petersburg
at a discussion sponsored by the Union of Youth.[2]
At the end of 1914, however, the same
Mayakovsky wrote in a newspaper article:
"Newspapers gave us the name [*okrestili*] of
futurists." [3] David Burliuk made a similar statement in his unpublished memoirs.[4] Livshits,
who in October, 1913, had just been discharged
from the army, did not like the fact that he

unexpectedly found himself a member of a futurist group after the
word "futurist" had been used by him and his friends for at least half
a year in a derogatory manner. More than that, he discovered that his
friends now denied any other group the right to call itself by this name.
David Burliuk and Mayakovsky took it upon themselves (it would
seem) to accept the name, used indiscriminately by the newspapers,
for practical reasons, and then presented the rest of the group with
the accomplished fact. Their primary reason for doing so appears to
have been that in the eyes of the audience any avant-garde art came
to be associated with futurism, and accepting the label was a sure way
of achieving hegemony in this field. A voice in this matter may be
ascribed to the influential Valery Bryusov, who in March, 1913, divided Russian "futurists" (he used quotation marks in his article)[5]
into the Moscow group and the St. Petersburg group, meaning Hylaea
and ego-futurists, respectively.[6] "Picking up the already popular label,"
continues Livshits in his memoirs, "Burliuk was moved by definite
practical calculations, and his expectations were rewarded: the scope
of the word fitted the growing movement perfectly, and the rest did
not bother Burliuk, who never took the problems of terminology seriously."[7] It can easily be understood, too, why Mayakovsky played a
part in the acceptance of the term: he was the only real urbanist in
the group and probably felt uncomfortable in the rural-oriented primitivism of Hylaea. Being a purist, Livshits never liked this "illegitimate" term that did not express the essence of the movement at all.[8]

It is even more difficult to discover when the prefix "cubo" was
attached to "futurism." Some scholars think the Hylaeans did it themselves so as not to be confused with the ego-futurists or the Italian
futurists. Others credit the press with adding "cubo" to the name of
the Moscow futurists because of the connection between cubist painting and Moscow futurist ideas.[9] It is true that both Burliuks were at
that time going through a cubist phase in their painting, and the
Hylaeans as a group were allies of the largely cubist Union of Youth.
There was much discussion of cubism in Russia in 1913: the book
Printsipy kubizma ("Principles of Cubism," Moscow) by Alexander
Shevchenko, a member of the Donkey's Tail group, appeared (he was
also the author of *Neoprimitivizm*, published the same year); and
there were two translations into Russian of Gleizes and Metzinger's
Du cubisme, one by E. Nizen published in St. Petersburg, and an-

other published in Moscow. Shershenevich remarks in his book, "In one lecture, they were called 'cubo-futurists,' and the name stuck." [10] This lecture was probably the one given by Kornei Chukovsky; it was published as an essay in December, 1913,[11] and after that the word had an active life in articles and books. As early as March, 1913, however, Mayakovsky spoke in his lecture about "cubism in the word." [12]

Dokhlaya luna ("The Croaked Moon") was the first collection in which the group officially assumed the name "futurists." The name of the book was probably chosen by David Burliuk, who, by that time, had begun to mix the "low" and the traditionally poetic frequently in his imagery and diction, imitating in this the *poètes maudits* of France, and later developed this practice into his own trademark. The full title on the cover was *Futuristy. "Gileya." Dokhlaya luna*, followed by the enumeration of the names of all the participants. This time all members of the group participated except Guro, who died on May 6 and who would not have appeared as a "Hylaean" anyway. The book was marked "Fall, 1913, Moscow," but was printed in Kakhovka, a small southern town not far from the estate where the Burliuk family lived, and actually appeared in August. The title page repeated the cover with one difference: the book was called "the miscellany of the only futurists of the world! the poets of 'Hylaea.' " This Hylaean claim of exclusiveness naturally aroused the indignation of other futurist groups.[13]

The main item of interest in *Dokhlaya luna* is the essay by Benedict Livshits, "Osvobozhdenie slova" ("Liberation of the Word"), his first and last opportunity to appear as a theoretician of the group. He began to write the article while still in the army and wanted both to sum up in it his personal ideas about the essence of art and to outline a program for the movement. After the customary argument against critics, Livshits carefully differentiated between his movement and Russian symbolism, the latter being preoccupied with "purely ideological values" and using words because they express certain ideas. Ego-futurism and the sprouting Acmeism are dismissed by Livshits as "ephemeral and hollow." Then the theoretical part begins. Any movement must start with a proclamation of creative freedom, says Livshits; but he doubts that the criteria of creativity should or could be found as long as one remains in the sphere of the relationships between the world and the poet's creative consciousness. Any poet seeks and finds a pretext for creation in the surrounding world; and his choice, no matter how free it seems to him, is conditioned by the subconscious. But there is freedom as soon as one moves those criteria to the area of the autonomous word. "Here our poetry is free, and, for the first time, we do not care whether it is realistic, naturalistic, or fantastic; except for its starting point, it does not place itself in any relationships with the world and does not coordinate itself with it; all other crossing points of this poetry with the world are a priori accidental." Thus poetry joins the company of music, free from time immemorial, and of the then recently liberated painting, and it could have been free long ago "from the sad necessity of expressing the logical connection of ideas" if people used something other than words for communication. Here Livshits hastens to add that he does not mean a rejection of all objective criteria. In his choice, the poet is influenced "by plastic affinity of verbal expressions, by their plastic valence, by verbal texture, by rhythmic problems and musical orchestration, and by the general requirements of pictorial and musical structure." Being aware that some of these elements have been taken into consideration by others, Livshits nevertheless asserts that only his group has given them an exclusive character. He also insists that his own and his friends' poetry abolishes the traditional division into the epic, the lyric, and the dramatic. Toward the end, Livshits admits that all these principles have not yet found a complete realization in the work of Hylaeans, but adds that this work is not merely writing in neologisms, either. The most valuable point of the new movement for him is a new view of poetry, in which Pushkin and Tolstoy actually lose a part of their spell and begin to look illegitimate. He disagrees with Bryusov who, in his analysis of the Russian futurist movement,[14] had tried to catch its essence in rhyme, in deviations from traditional syntax, and so on. For Livshits, all these concrete devices were temporary means for a transition to new poetry, and might be discarded the next day. Thus Livshits made a careful and honest effort to delineate a new concept of poetry, which was to be dynamic and directed toward a complete autonomy of the word. He took care not to be distracted by specifics; but in doing so, he spoke over the heads of his fellow futurists, who needed concrete slogans more than solid aesthetic foundations.

The rest of *The Croaked Moon* is occupied by poetry. Livshits himself contributed three poems, which are among his best and in which

he tried to apply the principles of the newly liberated paintii
poetry, especially in "Teplo" ("Warmth"). Kruchenykh is represe ____
by only two poems, one of which was the first attempt in Russian
poetry to write in vowels only:

HEIGHTS
(universal language)

e u yu
i a o
o a
o a e e i e ya
o a
e u i e i
i e e
i i y i e i i y

(In the original, "yu" and "ya" are, of course, represented by only one
vowel-letter each.) Incidentally, what actually stands behind these
vowels is the Russian text of the prayer "Credo."

Mayakovsky's contribution consisted of the most representative selection of his early poetry: five poems plus a four-poem cycle "Ya"
("Me"). The latter appeared two months later as an individual pamphlet made from a handwritten mimeograph stencil and illustrated
by two artists. Mayakovsky's is a poetry of metaphor and hyperbole,
rather than of neologism, and he employs urbanistic imagery or
themes throughout. In fact, nowhere does Mayakovsky stand as close
to Italian futurist painting as he does in these few poems. They are
characteristically strong and loud, but at the same time hysterical,
and they express a deep loneliness. There is a primitivist eroticism in
some of the poems ("Lyubov" ["Love"]); and one of them, "Po ekham
goroda" ("Along the Echoes of the City"), is an interesting poetic
typology of city sounds, which has been traced by one scholar to the
manifesto of Russolo.[15] There is also the familiar anthropomorphism
of Mayakovsky: his kissing the balding head of the earth, or midnight's feeling the poet with moist fingers. The moon is the poet's
wife, and she is riding in a city carriage. The poem continues with a
series of urbanistic images; the poet's own soul is transformed into a
cityscape ("On the pavement of my trampled soul"). All these poems
were printed mostly without commas, as fragments of lines placed one

under another, and with arresting rhymes, often of compound structure, which sometimes echoed one another from a distance, sometimes
clashed with one another within a short line fragment. Mayakovsky
broke words in two, used mirror devices (*lezem zemle*), and took great
care to emphasize such effects by visual means as well. (In later editions he abandoned some of these typographical tricks and trusted his
reader to find his verbal tours de force for himself.)

Many aspects of Khlebnikov's art were displayed in *The Croaked
Moon*. Among his shorter poems here are "Semero" ("The Seven"),
a manly ballad about Hylaea which echoes Alexei K. Tolstoy's poetry;
the exuberant "Chernyi lyubir" ("The Black Loveling"); "Chisla"
("Numbers"), in which the poet's preoccupation with numbers is
combined with his interest in prehistoric times; "Tak kak moshch mila
negushchestv," one of Livshits' favorites, uniting complex imagery with
most whimsical neologisms; and "Ya nakhozhu . . ." ("I Find . . ."),
an exercise in compound and heterotonic rhyme. There were also four
pages of derivations from the root *lyub-* ("love") under the title
"Lyubkho." Among Khlebnikov's longer poetic works in the book are
"Lyubovnik Yunony" ("Juno's Lover"), a primitivist work based on
deliberate anachronism, and "Vnuchka Malushi" ("Malusha's Granddaughter"), which nostalgically juxtaposed the pagan Russia of the
tenth century with that of modern times. One of Khlebnikov's longer
works included in *The Croaked Moon* was a drama written in prose
and entitled "Mrs. Le Nine" ("Gospozha Lenin"), in which Khlebnikov admittedly tried to use "the smallest elements of art." [16] The scenes
for the two short acts are the heroine's house and the psychiatric ward;
but the heroine herself is fragmented into a number of senses and
emotions, and we hear only what the voices of her sight, hearing, reason, memory, logic, will, fear, attention, and so on, speak.

The larger part of *The Croaked Moon* is occupied by the writings
of the Burliuk family. Nikolai Burliuk contributed only a few poems,
written in his usual individual, impressionistic manner, often combining descriptions of nature with an inobtrusive lyricism. "Babochki
v kolodtse" ("Butterflies in the Well") is perhaps the most noteworthy
of these.[17] More interesting are his six prose miniatures, which are
mostly impressionist sketches of human loneliness. The "Hylaean"
background of some of these contrasts with the St. Petersburg background of others. One of the best among them is "Glukhonemaya"

("The Deaf-Mute Woman"), which begins with a description of dust carried by the wind, which penetrates into the house, and of a peasant girl with a splinter in her foot. The author is haunted by two rhymed lines about his deaf-mute soul.[18] At the end he learns that the girl is deaf-mute, too. Another story, "Artemida bez sobak" ("Artemis without Her Dogs"), describes the author's night walk along the streets of St. Petersburg in the company of a strange woman. Then he admits that there was no woman. The next morning, he reads in the paper that a naked madwoman was arrested the night before exactly where he walked.

David Burliuk, who with his brother Vladimir illustrated the book, decided to give the reader a proper exposure to his poetry and published in *The Crooked Moon* thirty of his own poems. They are presented, as usual, with opus numbers, but these numbers are not printed in order. (Throughout the book, different typefaces are alternated with one another.) Perhaps the best among these poems is Burliuk's celebrated hymn to voraciousness, which begins with the words "Kazhdyi molod, molod, molod / V zhivote chertovskii golod" ("Everybody is young, young, young / In the stomach there is one hell of a hunger"), then invites the reader to eat anything: stones; grasses; sweet, bitter, and poisonous things; emptiness; depth and height; birds; beasts; monsters; fish; wind; clay; salt; and water ripples. There is a certain dullness in such primitivistic exuberance, and the outlines of Rimbaud's poem "Fêtes de la faim," which Burliuk had imitated, are hardly recognizable. Incidentally, Burliuk entitled it "i.A.R.," which can only mean "iz Artura Rembo" ("from Arthur Rimbaud"). The rest of Burliuk's poetry is, for the most part, thematically in sharp contrast with the life affirmation expressed in this poem. Motifs of autumn, poverty, despair, illness, death, jail, and fatigue predominate in the verse of this man, who was, in reality, bursting with energy. Even more astonishing is the fact that Burliuk's poetry remains basically very old-fashioned despite his great effort to cover it with a "futurist" veneer. He tries to create this veneer in many different ways, for example, with his antiaesthetic themes, motifs, and images, borrowed directly from the French *poètes maudits,* such as calling the sky a cadaver; stars, worms; and the sunset, a scoundrel. Technically, he employs many devices, both typographical (italics, quotation marks, brackets) and syntactical (a rather shy omission of prepositions). When he uses metaphoric periphrases, he hastens to explain to the reader in a footnote that, for example, "to pour yellow wine into the blue bottle" actually means moonlight and sky. Some poems deliberately exclude certain sounds, a fact announced by such titles as "Without *R*" or "Without *R* and *S*." Some attention could be given to Burliuk's alogism (which is so easily confused with pointlessness) and to his chains of images apparently moved by rhyme alone, to his persistent use of a certain amount of archaic diction and to his romantic grotesques, but essentially his is an eclectic poetry whose creator often tilts with aesthetic windmills. Like Khlebnikov and Mayakovsky, Burliuk often experiments with rhyme, especially with a punning rhyme (for example a two-syllable word rhyming with two monosyllabics which happen to be its components).

At approximately the same time, David Burliuk published in Kherson (though it was marked Moscow on the cover) a little pamphlet (illustrated by Vladimir Burliuk) containing a few poems by Khlebnikov, his brother Nikolai, and himself. Both in title and in selection, the book continued Burliuk's antiaesthetic line so clearly emphasized in *The Croaked Moon*. The booklet was called *Zatychka*, which means "a stopper," but is not exactly a nice word in Russian. In Burliuk's own four poems, the familiar "shocking" imagery predominates (e.g., "the armpits of spring," in "syphilitic dust," etc.). He also omits commas and prepositions, violates meters, and again explains his metaphors in the footnotes. Even David's gentle brother, Nikolai, tries to insert a few "rude" details into his essentially well-mannered poetry (there are three poems of his in this book). Khlebnikov, in addition to his two-page-long verse satire on the St. Petersburg *Apollon* circle, is represented by two very short poems which are perhaps his most Burliukian works, with images like "earth is a pimple somewhere on the cheek of the universe" or "eternity is my chamber pot." The publication of these poems made Khlebnikov very unhappy, and he protested against it.[19] Khlebnikov was seldom aggressive in his poetry, and he dreamed of "a book transparent like a drop of water." He once wrote in a letter about the paintings of the Burliuks: "In their painting, the artistic element is often sacrificed to intellectual invention and partly torn to pieces like a gazelle by a lynx." [20] In *Zatychka*, Burliuk also generously used different typographical prints, singling out by large letters words that he considered "leading words" (*leit-*

slova) not only in his own verse, but also in the poetry of his collaborators.

At the beginning of September, 1913, another futurist collection appeared. It was *Troe* ("The Three"), published by Matyushin and with the cover and illustrations by Kazimir Malevich. The "three" were Khlebnikov, Guro, and Kruchenykh. No short poems by Khlebnikov were included. One of Khlebnikov's poems published in *The Three* satirized Severyanin; another was his magnificent "Khadzhi-Tarkhan," the poetic history and geography of his native city of Astrakhan. The two stories he contributed, written in austere and limpid prose, show the author's masterful handling of this medium. That Khlebnikov, surprisingly, appears here as a disciple of Pushkin's is especially noticeable in "Okhotnik Usa-Gali" ("The Hunter Usa-Gali"), which, in its admiring description of a primitive man, has more than one point in common with Pushkin's "Kirdzhali." The second piece, "Nikolai," is also about a hunter who shunned civilization. Nikolai was "free from the iron laws of life," but he was also, ironically, a man of nature whose work was to destroy nature. The story, though simple in style, is very complex in composition; it is both clear "like a drop of water" and full of dark corners and premonitions of death, concluding with the hero's terrible end. "Nikolai" deserves to be included in any good anthology of Russian twentieth-century prose.

The Three was dedicated to the memory of Guro. Matyushin, in his unsigned preface to the book, speaks lovingly of his late wife, who, he says, was the actual planner of the book. He is certain that she died at the very threshold of "the spring" (i.e., the triumph of the new art). "The days are not far," he writes, "when the conquered phantoms of three-dimensional space, of the illusory, drop-shaped time, and of the cowardly causality . . . will reveal before everybody what they really have been all the time—the annoying bars of a cage in which the human spirit is imprisoned." Matyushin prophesies "a new, marvelous world, where even the objects will be resurrected." He also tries to place Guro within the context of Russian futurism in this way: Some fight for this new world; others live in it. Guro was too gentle to break things, to rebel against the past. She was little hampered by the old forms, but in the assault of the "new" ones she recognized kindred souls. Those who think that her ties with them are based on misunderstanding, misunderstand both her and the futurists. Matyushin ends by describing Guro as "an extraordinary phenomenon" and the symbol of the arrival of new times. Guro's works in this book include, as usual, both prose and poetry, and most of them were to find places later in her posthumous *Baby Camels of the Sky*. In *The Three*, Matyushin tried to include his wife's most ebullient miniatures, full of expectation of spring (and thus in tune with his preface); but, despite his efforts, she appears here as a full-fledged impressionist, even when she follows the way of pure sound (and then she occasionally sounds like Marina Tsvetayeva). Moreover, one finds the familiar Finnish landscape, the preoccupation with children and animals, and the defense of dreamers and eccentrics. In the piece tantalizingly entitled "Picasso's Violin," Picasso receives a turn-of-the-century, decadent treatment. The most avant-garde of all Guro's works (and the one not included in the posthumous book) is the poem "Finlyandiya" ("Finland"), about the rustling of pine trees.

The third participant was Kruchenykh, whom one would scarcely expect to find in the company of Guro; but there were strange inner alliances and subgroups within Hylaea, and Kruchenykh seems to have been more welcome in Guro's circle than either Mayakovsky or the Burliuks. Kruchenykh's contributions are mostly his exercises in alogism, the most noteworthy among them being his abstract prose, "Iz Sakhary v Ameriku" ("From Sahara to America"), which at times goes over into free verse and, lexically, is a whimsical mélange of modern Russian words, archaisms, compound words, words with letters omitted, Ukrainian words, and invented words. Most interesting, however, among Kruchenykh's contributions to *The Three* is his article "Novye puti slova" ("The New Ways of the Word") in which he attempts to be the group's theoretician. This article is the predecessor of numerous pamphlets by Kruchenykh in which he preached the pure art of the antiaesthetic word, assailed the literary past and his contemporaries more consistently and more specifically than any of his colleagues, and managed to *épater les bourgeois* perhaps more effectively than anyone.

Kruchenykh begins "The New Ways of the Word" with attacks on critics. He accuses them of neglecting the problems of the word and calls them parasites, vampires, and gravediggers. "There was no verbal art before us," he continues, "but everything was done to stifle the primeval feeling for one's native tongue." The preceding literature is dismissed by Kruchenykh as slavish attempts to re-create one's own way of life, philosophy, and psychology, or as rhymes for domestic use. Language has become a eunuch. Verbal art has been steadily deteriorating since the writing of the folk epics and *The Igor Tale*, and has reached its lowest point in Pushkin. Then begins Kruchenykh's positive program. A proof that the word has been in chains is its subordination to meaning. The futurists have discovered this shortcoming and have devised a free language, transrational (*zaymnyi*) and universal. Whereas artists of the past went through the idea to the word, futurists go through the word to direct knowledge. In addition to the existing sensation, notion, and concept, the fourth unit, "highest intuition," is being formed.[21] The word carries not only an idea, but also the transrational, which Kruchenykh specifies parenthetically as "irrational parts, mystical and aesthetic." The word is broader than its meaning (this statement later became Kruchenykh's favorite slogan). As an example, he compares the word *gladiatory* ("gladiators") with the Russian neologism *mechari* ("swordsmen"): the idea, he says, is the same; but the former is lusterless, gray, and foreign in comparison with the latter. On the other hand, *mechari* and *smekhiri* (another neologism, meaning "laughing ones," used by Khlebnikov in one of his poems) have more in common, though they mean different things. Sound makes the word alive.

Kruchenykh recalls the famous poetic confessions of the celebrated nineteenth-century Russian poets Fet ("O, if the soul could express itself without words") and Tyutchev ("A thought, once expressed, becomes a lie"). He regards these quotations as admissions by earlier poets of their failure—a failure that is the direct result of their never having mastered the medium of the word. But Kruchenykh does find in the Russian past some people who used the "new word" and thus were precursors of the futurists (Kruchenykh hastens to add, however, "we are not their imitators"). These were the religious dissenters who spoke the "meaningless" language of the Holy Ghost.[22] To depict the new and the future, one needs new words and their new combinations. Kruchenykh has nothing but scorn for contemporary writers (he obviously means such authors as Leonid Andreyev) who speak about the meaninglessness of life in a meaningful language. As new artists discovered that movement creates convexity and vice versa, or that incorrect perspective creates the fourth dimension, so the futurists (he does not yet use this word, but prefers instead the neologism *bayachi* ["speakers"] from the dialectal *bayat'* ["to speak, to tell"]) have discovered that incorrect structure of sentences brings about movement and the new perception of the world. For this reason, the futurists shattered grammar and syntax. "One should write in a new way, and the more disorder we bring to the composition of sentences, the better." The symbolists are afraid of not being understood, but the futurists are glad when a reading of their work results in confusion.

Then Kruchenykh undertakes a typology of poetic irregularities, which he divides into grammatical and semantic. The examples of the former are lack of agreement in gender, number, case, and tense; omission of components; arbitrary word-coining; phonetic surprise; and unexpected word formations. The latter is demonstrated in the development of action and in unexpected similes. Kruchenykh adds that the list is incomplete, and irregularities can also occur in rhyme, meter, graphic aspects, color, and word placement.

Kruchenykh next directs his attention to the importance of dissonance and "primitive coarseness" in art and to the influence of African art. Man now stands in the center of the world, not behind a screen as in the philosophy of Plato and Kant.[23] We now see things on both sides; the irrational (transrational) is as directly given us as the rational. For this reason futurist poetry should be joyful, in contrast with symbolist poetry, which is lacking in joy because, for its authors, the truth is always concealed somewhere. Kruchenykh announces as a slogan "subjective objectivity," which allows one to cut through objects, to see through the word, to follow the word in reverse. "One can read a word backward, and then one gets a deeper meaning."

Toward the end, Kruchenykh indulges in some polemics with the Italian futurists, whose devices seem to him childish ("their endless ra-ta-ta ra-ta-ta"), and he compares them mockingly with Maeterlinck who, Kruchenykh says, thought that "the door" repeated one hundred times equaled revelation. The most unexpected aspect of his criticism of the Italians is the passage where he accuses them of coarseness, cynicism, and impudence, the very qualities that the Russian futurists (and Kruchenykh especially) were to demonstrate in abundance throughout the history of their movement. Here, however, Kruchenykh says with a deadpan expression: "We are serious and solemn,

and not coarsely destructive; we have a high respect for our motherland." The article ends with attacks on symbolists, ego-futurists, and
realists. It is followed by "Notes on Art," also by Kruchenykh, which
consists of a series of brief remarks about literature and attacks on
different writers and artists. Here is one entry: "I hate long works
and big books. . . . Let a book be small, but contain no lie—everything the writer's own, to the last ink blot."

Despite the fact that Kruchenykh was never an equal of Livshits',
either in talent or in education, his "The New Ways of the Word"
in *The Three* was an important landmark in the history of futurism.
It was "classical" futurism: the main tenets of the movement were
brought in it to their logical conclusion, and it was specific and detailed. With the courage of a semieducated man, Kruchenykh had
taken the bull by the horns and given the futurist concept of word-
oriented poetry its most consistent theoretical basis. Among his colleagues, he was the most persistent negator of literature of the past.
Finally, it was perhaps here that the word *zaumnoe* ("transrational")
was uttered for the first time. The idea of transrational poetry, though
it has been differently understood by various critics and by the futurists
themselves, was one of the most original parts of the futurist creed and
later gave rise to a whole group of poets ("41°" in 1918 and 1919).

Also in 1913 there appeared in Moscow the fifteen-page pamphlet
written by Khlebnikov and Kruchenykh, *Slovo kak takovoe* ("The
Word as Such").[24] It must have appeared some time in September,
and unlike Kruchenykh's earlier editions, was printed in the usual
typographical way; it was illustrated by Malevich and Olga Rozanova.
The Word as Such is a mixture of manifesto and verse. Theories are
proclaimed and then demonstrated in poetic practice by examples from
the work of individual futurists, sometimes with detailed analysis.
From time to time there are also poems, some of them probably the
joint work of the two poets.[25] The book begins with a proclamation
of two contrasting principles of true futurist poetry:

1. As if it were written and read [*smotrelos'*] in the twinkling of an eye!
(singing, splash, dance, throwing down of clumsy structures, forgetting,
unlearning). [Those using this approach are Khlebnikov, Kruchenykh, and
Guro.]
2. As if it were written with difficulty [*tugo*] and read with difficulty,
more uncomfortable than blacked boots or a truck in a drawing room. [This

time the representatives are David Burliuk, Mayakovsky, Nikolai Burliuk, and Livshits.]

Both methods are considered equally valuable ("What is more valuable, wind or stone? Both are priceless"). In elaboration, the authors write about the importance of one "clearly pronounced consonant" to be repeated many times in a poem. This rough orchestration is contrasted with the bloodless consonantism of the poetry before futurism which is parodied as nothing but "pa-pa-pa pee-pee-pee tee-tee-tee" and is compared to milk and fruit jelly. Kruchenykh's notorious "Dyr bul shchyl" is inserted here and declared "more Russian than all Pushkin's poetry." The past, it is continued, required from language such qualities as clarity, purity, honesty, and pleasure; but these requirements fit a woman, rather than language. This implied accusation of effeminacy leveled against all previous poetry from Pushkin to the symbolists was to be repeated later many times by the Russian futurists; and in this repeated accusation, of course, they echoed their Italian counterparts. "Language should first of all be a language; and if it is to remind one of anything, let it remind us of a saw or a poisoned arrow of a savage." In this comparison, the voice of Khlebnikov is heard. The preceding literature is blamed for devoting too much time to the human soul, neglecting "the word as such," and for a preoccupation with finish and polish, whereas true poets "should write on their books: after reading, tear it up." If in *The Three* Kruchenykh defined "transrational" as "irrational," here he changes his definition, shifting the emphasis to the technical aspects: "The futurist poets [*budetlyanskie rechetvortsy*] . . . [like to use] chopped words, half-words, and their whimsical, intricate combinations (transrational language)."

Somewhat earlier, during the summer of 1913, Kruchenykh published the leaflet, *Deklaratsiya slova kak takovogo,** [26] which was even more explicit than his previous writings concerning the formulation of a "transrational language." The paragraphs of this leaflet were numbered deliberately in a haphazard way, beginning with point 4 and placing point 1 fifth. A shortened version of its text is given here:

DECLARATION OF THE WORD AS SUCH

4. Thought and speech cannot catch up with the emotional experience of someone inspired; therefore, the artist is free to express himself not

only in a common language (concepts), but also in a private one (a creator is individual), as well as in a language that does not have a definite meaning (is not frozen), that is *transrational*. A common language is binding; a free one allows more complete expression. . . .

5. Words die, the world stays young forever. An artist has seen the world in a new way, and, like Adam, he gives his own names to everything. A lily is beautiful, but the word "lily" is soiled with fingers and raped. For this reason I call a lily "euy" [pronounced in Russian approximately "ehooee"], and the original purity is reestablished.

2. Consonants create a national everyday atmosphere; vowels, on the contrary, a universal language. . . .

3. A verse presents, unconsciously, a number of series of vowels and consonants. These series are untouchable. It is better to substitute for a word one similar in sound, rather than one similar in idea. . . .

1. New verbal form creates a new content, and not vice versa.

6. Introducing new words, I bring a new content, where everything begins to slide (shift). . . .

7. In art there can be unresolved dissonances—"something unpleasant for the ear"—because there is a dissonance in our soul, which resolves the former [i.e., the unresolved dissonances in the art]. . . .

8. All this does not narrow the art, but rather adds new areas to it.

Kruchenykh sent Khlebnikov a copy of this leaflet in August, 1913, and received a favorable answer: "I agree that the series *aio, eee,* has a certain meaning and content and that in clever hands it could become the basis for a universal language. *Euy* fits a flower. The rapid change of sounds reproduces tight petals of a curved flower." [27] There is, however, something patronizing in Khlebnikov's approving nod. He was preoccupied in 1913 with the creation of his own "transrational" language, an elaborate system by means of which he tried to distill pure meaning from every single consonant of the language. The final results of his effort were to be published only after the Revolution. Kruchenykh's experiments must have looked like the primitive play of an inexperienced apprentice to Khlebnikov; and, in comparison with the highly varied and profound work of the latter, they were. But it was Kruchenykh who was largely identified with, and who popularized, the idea of *zaum* as the language of new poetry in which new meanings are created out of the pure sound of the word. Despite all contradictions and occasional vulgarizations, he achieved a directness in his message which few of his fellow futurists were able to rival.

be fruitfully investigated at this point because doing so
̣e not only a more detailed presentation of Khlebnikov's
subject (treated in part in chap. 7) but also an analysis
ies of the postrevolutionary futurist group "41°."

The year 1913 was the *annus mirabilis* of Russian futurism. Its
poetry began to show genuine quality and variety, joint publications
followed one another in rapid succession, and several books by individual authors were prepared for publication, though most of them
did not appear in print until 1914. The first productions of futurist
dramas occurred at the end of 1913. The press wrote about futurism
practically every day, and the movement was seriously thought of as
heir to the aging symbolism. Finally, the numerous public appearances
of Russian futurists in Moscow, St. Petersburg, and provincial cities
aroused the interest of the reading audience, were reported by the
newspapers with relish, and gave rise to imitations and hoaxes. Most
of these public appearances were organized by David Burliuk, who
shrewdly understood that theory and poetic practice alone would not
attract enough attention. The value of such appearances was realized
after participation in the discussions organized by the Jack of Diamonds
and Union of Youth groups, which have already been described. In
the latter, even Khlebnikov took a passive part, sitting on the stage,
standing up and bowing when his poems were recited by Mayakovsky,
or when Burliuk, in a lecture, called him a genius. When one of the
most popular symbolists, Constantine Balmont, returned to Russia
after a seven-year exile, Mayakovsky met him at the station as a member of the delegation that welcomed the poet home, and spoke, two
days later, when Balmont was honored by the Society for Free Aesthetics. Both times Mayakovsky did his best to be disrespectful, and
the press dutifully reported the incidents. But such glancing blows
as these were not enough; and, after the summer season, futurists decided to begin their frontal attack. David Burliuk finally persuaded
Vasily Kamensky to come back from his rural retirement and join
them, a particularly shrewd move because Kamensky was a famous
pilot, one who could show his credentials to any city authorities, who
were likely to regard the futurists as potential troublemakers. Moreover, flying was in character with, and added respectability to, futurism.

Kamensky did not participate, however, in the first independent public joint appearance of Russian futurists in Moscow on October 13, in the hall of the Society of Art Lovers. The posters announcing this event were printed on toilet paper, and they described it as "the first recital of speech creators [rechetvortsy] [28] in Russia" with lectures by Mayakovsky (entitled "Perchatka" ["Gauntlet"]) and David Burliuk ("Doiteli iznurennykh zhab" ["The Milkers of Exhausted Toads"]). The other members of Hylaea were scheduled to participate. At first the Moscow police banned the recital, but finally they allowed it. Several days before the appearance, David Burliuk gathered at his apartment all Hylaeans who happened to be in Moscow and announced a long-range strategy for the group, including his plans for a series of publicity stunts before the recital. The first of eleven conditions committed everyone to convene three days later at noon on Kuznetsky, the main street of Moscow, and walk with painted faces among the crowds, reciting futurist poetry, which they did. Even the introverted and shy Livshits paraded with an outlandish necktie and handkerchief. The one who enjoyed this "maskers' parade" most was Mayakovsky, a born actor, who soon displayed excellent stage presence as well as the art of repartee. He paraded along Kuznetsky in a new yellow blouse, made by his mother, with a wooden spoon in the buttonhole (like the others), and read his own poetry in a pleasant, velvety bass voice. The passersby were naturally curious; some of them followed the futurists and spoke to them. One little girl gave Mayakovsky an orange, which he began to eat. The crowd, astonished, whispered, "He's eating, he's eating."

The Hylaeans took five such publicity strolls before the announced recital. The tickets were sold out within an hour of the time they went on sale; and the recital was a tremendous success, despite the fact that it did not proceed according to the poster: Khlebnikov was not in Moscow, and, as David Burliuk could not come, he asked his brother, Nikolai, to read the text of his lecture. But those in the audience were, nevertheless, delighted, and applauded even when Mayakovsky insulted them or when Kruchenykh shouted that he wanted to be hissed off the stage. The conscientious Livshits, who recited futurist poetry, saw, to his amazement, that the enigmatic points of Mayakovsky's lecture as announced on the posters were only a publicity stunt and that, in fact, the whole lecture was nothing but "gay nonsense." Mayakovsky spoke about the ancient Egyptians and Greeks who used to stroke cats and thus produce electricity, about drainpipes playing a berceuse, and so on—all of which was supposed to be an apologia of urbanism. The audience accepted everything, even Kruchenykh's spilling a glass of hot tea on the first row of the orchestra seats. Soon afterward, on October 19, Mayakovsky read his poetry at the opening of a futurist cabaret, the Pink Lantern. The reading ended in a scandal: his poem "Nate" ("Take This!") was calculated to offend the audience.

In the meantime, the well-known critic Kornei Chukovsky began to lecture about futurism, both in St. Petersburg and in Moscow. Sometimes the futurists debated with him in public discussions after his lectures. Once the police allowed the lecture, but forbade recitation of futurist poetry after it. In November, David Burliuk finally gave lectures in both Russian capitals. He varied the title of his lecture (in St. Petersburg it was provocatively called "Pushkin and Khlebnikov"), but the content was actually the same: attacks on the critics, on the past and present of Russian literature, and on "pseudofuturists" (which meant ego-futurists and the Mezzanine of Poetry, as well as Marinetti), plus some recitation of the Hylaean verse. As Livshits reports in his memoirs, the subjects to be covered in such lectures, as announced on the posters, did not put the lecturers under any obligation: they always improvised and preferred arguing with the audience to actually delivering a speech.

On November 11 there was another well-publicized futurist recital in the Polytechnic Museum in Moscow. Mayakovsky, again wearing the yellow blouse that became his trademark, spoke in his lecture about urbanism and the artistic achievements of individual futurists. David Burliuk, wearing a frock coat with the collar trimmed with multicolored rags, a yellow vest with silver buttons, and a top hat, had a little dog with its tail up painted on his cheek ("the symbol of my sharp poetic sense of smell," he explained). He spoke about the new art, the meaning of line, color, and texture, and about cubism. Kamensky delivered a lecture under the appropriate title "Airplanes and Futurist Poetry." He wore a cocoa-colored suit trimmed with golden brocade, which he had purchased in Paris. There was an airplane painted on his forehead ("the symbol of universal dynamism," he said). Kamensky later described this recital in his memoirs. The issue of the connection with the futurism of Marinetti was raised, and it was declared that the seniority belonged to the Russians, because Khlebnikov began to publish futurist works in 1908, whereas Italian futurism did not become known in Russia until 1910. The latter statement was incorrect: a Russian paper carried a story about Marinetti's first manifesto of February 20, 1909, no later than March 8 of that same year. It is true, however, that Khlebnikov's first publication was in the fall of 1908 (he began to write even earlier), but it may be argued that neologistic prose and poetry are not necessarily futurist. Khlebnikov himself took part in this recital; this time he tried to read his verse, but no one could hear him.

The evening in the Polytechnic Museum was actually a dress rehearsal for the first futurist tour across Russia.[29] Planned in November, 1913, this tour was organized by David Burliuk. The three participants (Burliuk, Mayakovsky, and Kamensky) visited seventeen cities (though they themselves claimed a much larger number, sometimes as many as twenty-nine). The aim of the tour was to propagandize their movement. Mayakovsky's lecture, as in Moscow, was entitled "The Achievements of Futurism." In it, he accused the critics of futurism of following an "unscientific" approach and declared that the poetry of futurism was the poetry of the modern city. He said that the modern city had enriched the human soul with new emotions and impressions, unknown to the poets of the past. All the world was becoming one huge city and nature would soon be obsolete, which would make the poetry of nature obsolete, too. The rhythm of modern life was different from that of the past: it was fast and feverish. Poetry needed to be in step with this new life. The word, however, should not describe, but rather express, things by itself. It is not merely a sign, a symbol: it has color, soul, and scent; it is a living organism. Mayakovsky's lecture contained attacks on the symbolists, Balmont and Bryusov in particular. He also acquainted the public with the poetry of his fellow futurists. David Burliuk, in his lecture "Cubism and Futurism," tried to establish the genealogy of these two movements in the arts and demonstrated with slides the paintings of Cézanne, Van Gogh, and the French impressionists. If Mayakovsky made fun of Balmont, Burliuk tried to discredit Raphael and to point out the photographic nature of his work. He also explained the essence of cubism. Kamensky repeated his Moscow lecture only at the end of the tour. Prior to that he read "Our Answer to the Laughniks"

nash otvet"), an attempt to add respectability to fu-
refute the mocking critics, who continued to write
was nothing but a clever way to earn money, based on
and curiosity of the public. Kamensky insisted on three
futurism: intuition, individual freedom, and abstraction.
He also emphasized the essentially gay quality of futurist poetry and
coined the slogan, "Poetry is the nuptials of words [*brakosochetanie
slov*]," which he never tired of repeating in his numerous public appearances up to the Revolution and even after it. As usual, Mayakovsky wore his yellow blouse, and the others painted their faces. Authorities kept a watchful eye on the three, sometimes surrounding the
theaters with mounted police and even placing their men in the aisles
inside. A few performances were canceled because permission by the
local police chief was not given.

The first stop on the tour was Kharkov, and the evening (December
14) was a success. It was there, by the way, that the veteran futurists
met Grigory Petnikov, who soon became an interesting minor poet of
futurism and a disciple of Khlebnikov's. After a break in their sched-
ule, they continued the tour, temporarily without Kamensky, through
the cities of the Crimea: Simferopol on January 7, Sevastopol on January 9, and Kerch on January 13. Igor-Severyanin joined them in the
Crimea; but, as noted above, he quarreled with Burliuk and Mayakovsky, and in Kerch the two cubo-futurists had to appear before
a half-empty theater whose hissing audience had come to hear the
much more popular Severyanin. It should be noted that Mayakovsky
added another point to his lecture after Severyanin became part of the
tour: "As long as David Burliuk exists, heavy steel monsters are more
necessary than *Eugene Onegin;* and [since there is Severyanin] *crème
de violettes* is more profound than Dostoevsky." [30] Even after their
split, Mayakovsky continued to recite Severyanin's (and Shershenevich's) poetry on the tour because he considered it a true poetry of the
big city. Kamensky rejoined Mayakovsky and Burliuk when they
reached Odessa, where they gave two recitals. A lady who sold tickets
allowed them to paint things on her cheeks and to color her nose gold.
Despite the participation of the well-known provincial critic Peter
Pilsky, who, though not a futurist, defended the futurists in his lecture and said that there was a profound truth in the movement, the

audience was not very friendly and resented the lecturers' attacks on their favorite symbolist writers.

After these two performances (January 16 and 19), the trio went to Kishinev (January 21), where they hired fifty little boys to run through the city and shout, "The futurists have come!" The boys, however, distorted the unfamiliar word and shouted instead, "The soccer players have come" (in Russian, changing *futuristy* into *futbolisty*). In addition, the local goats ate the futurist posters, which had been put up with the same flour paste used for making bread.

There followed the recitals in Nikolayev (January 24), where police demanded from the visitors a pledge not to mention politics and classical writers, and in Kiev (January 28), where Mayakovsky unwittingly insulted the Governor, and the trio had to make a hasty escape from the theater to avoid arrest.[31] Then, after a brief return to Moscow (just before Marinetti's final lectures there), they gave a rather successful recital in Minsk (without Kamensky, who was ill) and returned again to Moscow in time to take part in various anti-Marinetti activities. The lectures in Kazan were on February 20, but the planned evenings in Grodno and Belostok were not allowed because the Governor of Grodno inquired in Moscow about the lecturers and received information about Mayakovsky's earlier police record.[32] Another appearance, in Poltava, did not take place because city authorities got wind of Burliuk's and Mayakovsky's expulsion from art school. This expulsion took place February 21 and resulted from their failure to comply with a rule forbidding students to deliver lectures or participate in public discussions.

Even after these reverses, there were still several more recitals in different parts of Russia: Penza on March 3, Samara on March 8,[33] Rostov-on-Don on March 17, and Saratov on March 19. Most of them were financial failures, and the futurists often appeared before nearly empty houses. More successful were the recitals in the Caucasus: in Tiflis on March 27 and in Baku on March 29. These marked the end of the tour. The Georgians in Tiflis were particularly (and traditionally) hospitable, and they were so charmed by Mayakovsky's saying a few introductory words in their own language that they were ready to accept all the tenets of futurism. "One could agree with many of his [Mayakovsky's] statements about the evolution in the arts,"[34]

.omment in the local newspaper. Otherwise, these final ap-
.es differed little from the others. Memoirists describe the fu-
making preperformance publicity strolls through town with
paint.d faces and wearing strange, colorful costumes. Burliuk, for
instance, in addition to a gilded nose, a raspberry coat, a powdered
face, and a woman's lorgnette, had the inscription "I'm Burliuk" on
his forehead. All three had radishes in their buttonholes. Street
urchins would shout, "Are these Americans?" During the recitals,
futurists invariably drank tea and, encouraged by Kruchenykh's example, spilled it into the audience. Burliuk, who usually presided over
the discussions after the lectures, established order by ringing a church
bell. A grand piano was usually hanging upside down over the heads
of the performers. Sometimes they tried to vary their recitation by each
reading his own verse simultaneously with the others, thus anticipating Dada.

Kamensky, reminiscing about this tour five years later, called it "a
triumphant march of the three Poets-Prophets-Futurists, whose sun-
emanating Will, in an aura of gay youth, rose upward as an anarchistic
banner of modernity and established the Rebellion of Spirit in tens
of thousands of hearts." [35] Much later, Kruchenykh, speaking not
about this particular tour but about public appearances of futurists
in this period in general, wrote: "We held our banner high, had fine
fracases, shouted loudly, and were paid handsomely, up to fifty rubles
an hour." [36] The big tour, however, proved in the end a rather qualified success, marred as it was by financial losses, too much police attention, and sometimes a lack of interest on the part of the towns-
people or the press. When in April Mayakovsky went alone to Kaluga
for two lectures, the second one attracted only about two dozen people.
But the poets accomplished their main objective—making themselves
known throughout Russia.

There was no doubt about the futurists' success in St. Petersburg
and Moscow. Everyone talked about futurism in the fall of 1913 and
the winter of 1913–14. The futurists were lionized in literary circles.
They suddenly became the center of attention in the famous café for
poets and artists Brodyachaya sobaka ("The Stray Dog"). Summing
up Russian poetry from April, 1913, to April, 1914, Valery Bryusov
wrote:

The past year will remain memorable in Russian poetry chiefly because of the arguments about futurism. In the capitals and in provincial cities, there were public recitals of futurist works and discussions about futurism before filled houses. Futurist dramatic performances were sold out. Thin and not-so-thin miscellanies of futurist verse and prose (approximately forty of them were published during the year) always found critics, readers, and buyers. There were several futurist periodicals. . . . Futurists were mocked and called all kinds of names, but, nevertheless, they were read, listened to, and watched in theaters; and even the cinema, this true reflection of our "today," considered it its duty to touch on futurism and futurists as the news of the day.[37]

There were even rumors that the visiting Isadora Duncan was going to dance to futurist verse.[38]

Though the futurists were active in both capitals, their real headquarters was in St. Petersburg. Even during the summer months, when practically all artists and poets went to the country, they stayed near St. Petersburg, in a Finnish *dacha* area called Kuokkala. Matyushin and Kulbin had their *dacha's* there; soon they were joined by the avant-garde painter Ivan Albertovich Pugni (1894–1956) and his wife (his apartment in the city became a futurist salon). Also among the Kuokkala summer inhabitants were N. Evreinov and K. Chukovsky, who were always friendly toward futurists.

Relations with other literary groups were at first relatively friendly, at least on the personal level. Despite the fact that the leader of the Acmeists, Nikolai Gumilev, once described futurists as "the hyenas following the dying lion of symbolism," [39] he and his fellow Acmeists were at first at peace with futurism. This temporary harmony between Acmeists and futurists could be explained by certain coincidences in their aesthetic creeds: the Acmeists, who spoke much about a return to Adam, could not help favoring futurism's primitivist phase. An Acmeist such as Vladimir Narbut could even be described as an Acmeist futurist, because of his emphasis on antiaesthetic elements and his desire to shock the reader with the strange physical appearance of his books. Moreover, Kulbin welcomed Acmeism when it first sprang up, "in confused and strange expressions," [40] as *Apollon* put it. Nikolai Burliuk was personally close to Acmeist circles. There was an interesting review of *Sadok sudei II* in the Acmeist magazine *Giperborei*

("The Hyperborean," V, February, 1913), written probably by Gumilev himself (signed N. G.). In this review, Khlebnikov and Nikolai Burliuk were singled out as noteworthy and strong writers; Mayakovsky was credited with many ego-futurist traits (possibly because of the predominance of urbanism in his work, a quality that his contemporaries associated more with ego-futurism than with Hylaea); and only Livshits was scolded for the "cheap prettiness" of his verse (he was the only Hylaean who could easily have become an Acmeist). The group as a whole was welcomed for "indubitable revolutionary attitudes toward the word" and "the efforts to return to the word its lost freshness." It was the manifesto in *Rykayushchii Parnas* ("Roaring Parnassus"), with its insulting remarks, which made Gumilev an enemy of futurism.

There were individual men of art who came close to futurism during this time. Hylaea even considered accepting new members. Vasilisk Gnedov was so considered, but he became ill and had to leave for the south. Livshits mentions another candidate, Alexander Konge, a little-known poet whose verse, obviously prefuturist, appeared in a joint collection, *Plennye golosa* ("Captive Voices"), published in St. Petersburg in 1912. Livshits describes Konge as being influenced by French poets and Khlebnikov, but he was never accepted by the rest of the group. Livshits also associated at this time with the avant-garde composer who called himself Arthur Vincent Lourié (Arthur in honor of Schopenhauer, Vincent in honor of Van Gogh) and who desired to open a new era in music. Prokofieff and Stravinsky were beginning to be considered passé by some of the young composers during that time, and the quarter-tone technique was much in vogue (in a way, a development of ideas proclaimed by Kulbin in 1910). Artur Sergeyevich Lourié (1892–1966) planned to divide musical tones into even smaller subdivisions, but unfortunately no instruments could play music for intervals of one-eighth tone and less. Livshits describes Lourié as a provincial snob, who cared little for the futurists, but associated with them, and never called himself a futurist "out of foppishness." He proudly considered himself a Russian Pratella. Livshits knew little about music, but thought Pratella a more articulate writer of manifestos than Lourié.

During the winter of 1913–14, the cubo-futurists unexpectedly received support from academic circles. Victor Borisovich Shklovsky

(1893———), who studied philology at the University of St. Petersburg and dabbled in sculpture, became closely associated with Kulbin, the Union of Youth, and finally the cubo-futurists. Though not a member of the group, he was a useful ally. It was Shklovsky who added to the prestige of futurism by delivering, in the Stray Dog cabaret, a lecture in which futurism was presented as doing the necessary work based on the general laws of the evolution of language. This lecture was later published as a pamphlet entitled *Voskreshenie slova* ("Resurrection of the Word," St. Petersburg, 1914). Basing his ideas partly on those of the great philologist, Alexander Potebnya, Shklovsky described the dying of the image in all words, resulting in their becoming algebraic signs, whose "inner form" is ultimately not felt by those using them. The old forms in art are dead, he asserted, because they have become habitual, and the habitual does not enter our consciousness. Only a creation of new, unfamiliar forms can bring back a vision of the world and raise the objects from the dead. One way to create these new and startling forms is to distort words, as people do in moments of excitement, and creating new forms through word distortion is exactly what futurists are doing, each in his own way. The new language they are creating is difficult and incomprehensible, but so was the language of poetry in older times. Perhaps someone else, and not the futurists, will create a new art, adds Shklovsky rather cautiously, but nevertheless they are on the right road. Shklovsky impressed not only his audience, but the futurists themselves, many of whom probably never dreamed that their work could be discussed with quotations from Aristotle and references to the troubadours and to the ancient Sumerian language. Later Shklovsky was to elaborate on some of these ideas in his famous theory of "making it strange" as the basis of art. The formalist school in criticism and philology, one of whose leaders Shklovsky was later to become, was to preserve this alliance with Russian futurism, and Shklovsky's lecture in the Stray Dog may be considered its beginning.

The end of 1913 was marked by futurism's most ambitious venture in the area of the theater. It had its beginnings in July when a group of futurists held a conference in Usikirko, Finland, which was called rather grandiloquently "vserossiiskii syezd bayachei budushchego" ("The All-National Congress of Futurist Writers"). Little is known about the proceedings of, and the participants in, this "congress," but soon a "declaration" [41] appeared in the Petersburg press bearing the signatures of Kruchenykh, Malevich, and Matyushin, and announcing the decision of the congress to organize a futurist theater under the name of "Budetlyanin." The production of plays by Khlebnikov, Mayakovsky, and Kruchenykh was planned. It is appropriate to note that during the same summer a theatrical journal *Maski* ("Masks") printed an article by a certain B. Shaposhnikov, "Futurizm i teatr," [42] which expressed dissatisfaction with the existing theater and acquainted the reader with Marinetti's ideas on the subject. Also during the same summer, Mayakovsky published in a Moscow cinema journal the first of three articles[43] on the problems of movies and the legitimate theater. In them he attacked the realistic theater in general, and the Moscow Art Theater in particular, as photography and slavish imitation of nature (and nature, according to Mayakovsky, does not contain beauty; beauty is created by an artist). He prophesied a victory of the cinema over the theater, a triumph symbolizing the progressive victory of the machine over realism. Mayakovsky was not to be actively involved with the cinema[44] until after the Revolution, but his only prerevolutionary dramatic work was produced in December in St. Petersburg.

The Union of Youth sponsored four performances of futurist works in the Luna Park in St. Petersburg. Two of them, on December 2 and 4, were performances of Mayakovsky's tragedy *Vladimir Mayakovsky,* and the other two, on December 3 and 5, were of Kruchenykh's opera *Pobeda nad solntsem* ("Victory over the Sun"). Proving to be the sensation of the season, both productions played to full houses despite exorbitant prices. Mayakovsky not only produced and directed his tragedy, but played in it the starring role of Vladimir Mayakovsky. Other roles were played by university students, coached by him personally: he did not want any professional actors.

Mayakovsky's tragedy is in two acts with a soliloquized prologue and epilogue. In the prologue, Mayakovsky appears before the audience as "perhaps the last poet" in an expressionistically distorted, tragic city. Calm, mocking, and fearless, he proclaims his hatred for the rays of day (which sounds almost like the favorite theme of the symbolist Fyodor Sologub) and promises to "reveal our new souls in words as simple as mooing," which will bring the people life-affirming happiness ("you will have grown lips for huge kisses"), and to provide a universal language. In this short monologue, Mayakovsky manages to touch on some of his own basic themes and aspects, as well as those of Russian futurism as a whole (urbanism, primitivism, and antiaestheticism; the themes of hysterical despair, of lack of understanding, and of the soul of a new man and the souls of things). In the rest of the play, the prophet-like figure of the poet, superior to, but sympathetic toward, the people, remains; but whatever action there is in the tragedy is carried by grotesque abstractions of people (a man without an ear, a man without a head, etc.) or by chorus-like groups. Some of the supporting characters have important soliloquies assigned to them. These characters, however, with the exception of the "ordinary young man," are nothing but fragments of the lyric self of the poet, Vladimir Mayakovsky, even when, on the surface, they seem separate from, or antagonistic to, him.

In the first act, "the holiday of the beggars" develops into something between rebellion and madness, though the rebelliousness never acquires distinct political overtones. The end of the act, when the objects "take off the rags of worn-out names," is preceded by a magnificent spectacle of urbanistic despair with gobbets of spit being transformed into human cripples, and the appearance of a piano player who is "unable to pull his hands out from between the white teeth of the enraged keyboard." The second act takes place in the same city, now liberated from the tragedy of its existence; but it is also, as always with Mayakovsky's portrayals of future centers of utopian harmony, tinged with dullness and boredom. Mayakovsky, crowned by the people, is embarrassed at being entrusted with all of human sadness: a long line of people bring him their tears of various sizes, and at the end he departs from the city with a valise full of these tears, "leaving his soul on the lances of the city, shred by shred." In the short epilogue, Mayakovsky once more appears before the audience and nonchalantly tries to dismiss the tragedy of the work and to scandalize the onlookers by his buffoon-like attitude. (This buffoon theme is reminiscent of certain of Vadim Shershenevich's poems.) "Sometimes the thing I like most is my surname, Mayakovsky," are his last words.

Taken as a whole, "Vladimir Mayakovsky" not only represents a deepening of Mayakovsky's preceding work, but also points toward his celebrated series of poems about tragic love, beginning with

) v shtanakh ("A Cloud Wearing Trousers," 1915) and ending he postrevolutionary masterpiece *Pro eto* ("About That," 1923). Maj kovsky's tragedy is a work of great lyric power and freshness, even though it lacks the structural clarity of his later major works. The seemingly unrestrained lyricism of its spoken lines is cleverly balanced with the almost classic manner of its presentation: events seldom happen on stage; instead, various characters describe them in soliloquies not unlike those spoken by the messengers in ancient tragedies. On the other hand, the Marinettian theme of the modern city is handled by Mayakovsky in an unmistakably Slavic manner, with heavy emotionalism, the no-one-understands-me attitude, and the good old search for a soul in everything.

After Mayakovsky's tragedy, Kruchenykh's opera *Victory over the Sun,* for which M. Matyushin wrote the music, reads like boring nonsense. The only interesting part is the prologue, written by Khlebnikov, with his amusing attempts to make Russian theatrical vocabulary sound really Russian by means of clever neologisms. The opera is in two acts, each divided into several scenes. Among the characters are futurist Strong Men who begin and conclude the opera by proclaiming the endlessness of futurist progress. The world will perish, but there will be no end for us, they sing at the end. The four unequal scenes of the first act are a haphazard sequence of arias, monologues, dialogues, and choruses depicting the struggle of the forces of the future and the past. A fight against the sun (also touched upon by Mayakovsky in his tragedy)[45] is at the center of the play. In the very first scene the Strong Men call the sun "a birth giver to passion" and express the desire to hide it behind a dusty curtain. Later on, the sun is first stabbed and then captured, and the chorus celebrates this victory over the sun by singing:

> In smoke and haze
> And fatty dust
> The blows strengthen
> We get stronger like pigs
> Our faces are dark
> Our light comes from inside
> We are warmed by the dead udder
> Of the red dawn
> BRN   BRN

The pig motif here is characteristic of Kruchenykh's antiaesthetic efforts. Hard-to-pronounce consonant clusters like the one at the end of the song are to be found not only in the rest of the opera, but also in much of his poetry. In other arias, one can find neologisms and transrational language, both in pure form and in combination with existing Russian words; the latter may appear in meaningful or meaningless combinations. The alogical effect is further intensified by alogical situations, sometimes reminiscent of nonsense rhymes. Occasionally Kruchenykh demonstrates his own linguistic theories, as, for instance, in the aria of the Traveler, where the amputation of endings from words of neuter and feminine gender (*ozer* from *ozero* ["lake"] and *bur'* from *burya* ["storm"]) signifies that "everything has become masculine" in the future. Nor does he hesitate to borrow ideas from his fellow futurists: the contrasting of *myach* ("ball") and *mech* ("sword") is taken from Khlebnikov. Among the characters of the play one finds a combination of Nero and Caligula, symbolizing the old world, a Traveler through the centuries who is just back from the thirty-fifth century, the Herostratic figure of the Ill-Intentioned One (probably a satire on contemporary critics), and the Quarrelsome One (Zabiyaka). The second act, which takes place in the "Tenth Lands" of the future, portrays the difficulties of mankind trying to adapt itself to the new way of life. People are afraid of being strong, some are unable to live with the new lightness of breath and commit suicide, and the Fat One (whose head is two steps behind the rest of his body) bitterly complains about architecture, climate, and the fact that now everybody has a bald head. Optimism prevails, however, in the transrational song of the Aviator, who crashed but survived, and in the final arias of the Strong Men.

There exist several memoirs that describe in detail the auditions and rehearsals of both works, and try to recapture the opening night atmosphere. Among them are those of the first performers of the roles of the woman with a tear and the man without an ear in the Mayakovsky play (the latter also played the Ill-Intentioned One in the opera).[46] The casts were recruited through an advertisement in a newspaper, which discouraged professional actors, and consequently most of those auditioning were university students. They read Mayakovsky's lines like prose, which was painful to the poet. Kruchenykh wanted from his performers a special kind of reciting "with a pause after every syllable." In *Vladimir Mayakovsky*, the "slightly slanted" sets were designed by Shkolnik, a member of the Union of Youth, and Pavel Filonov made costumes for everyone (except the poet himself) which consisted of two painted shields for each performer. The actor, sandwiched between these shields, was supposed to move only in a straight line. Livshits praised highly the sets for the opera, designed by Malevich in a pure abstract style, for creating a truly transrational effect, which, in Livshits' opinion, Kruchenykh failed to realize in his text. Matyushin's music seemed to one listener to be like "a distorted Verdi," and the singers tried deliberately to sing flat. Matyushin himself described the preparation and the performance of both works.[47] He wrote about the inept chorus of seven people, hired only two days before, of whom only three could sing, and about the out-of-tune piano, which replaced the orchestra and was delivered only hours before the opening night performance. There were only two rehearsals. Matyushin had a high opinion of Kruchenykh's opera with its "complete break between concepts and words," whereas Mayakovsky disappointed him by "not once tearing the word away from its meaning." Matyushin termed Mayakovsky an impressionist.

All four performances (two of the tragedy and two of the opera) were sold out, and the audiences expected a lively exchange. Many celebrities—among them Alexander Blok—came to see the Mayakovsky play. Mayakovsky later described the first night as a fiasco,[48] but it was actually a great personal success for him, for it established his reputation in literary circles. Hissing and applause alternated during the evening, and critics in their reviews predictably blamed the futurists in a blasé manner for not presenting anything really new and found Mayakovsky's manners bad. One critic wrote of Mayakovsky's "unbearable way of pronouncing sentences separately, as if hurling them out one after another, and ending them in a singsong manner."[49] One actor who was in the audience that night was so "excited and moved"[50] by the performance he later described in his memoirs that he obviously misunderstood the futurist character of the production and saw it through symbolist glasses. There is no reason to assume that he was an exception. He writes about the "semimystical lighting" of the stage and about the audience that tried but was unable to laugh at the living puppet characters. Kruchenykh's opera also received hisses, much to the author's delight; some in the audience jumped up, shook their fists, and shouted, "You're an ass yourself!" Someone even hurled an apple, but generally the performances passed in an atmosphere of good-natured laughter and mirth. After these early December productions, the newspapers continued to play up futurism even more; but there were no more attempts to produce futurist works on stage until after the Revolution of 1917. *Vladimir Mayakovsky* was soon published as a separate volume, as was *Victory over the Sun* with musical examples.

On April 26, 1914, Shershenevich published "A Declaration about the Futurist Theater" in the newspaper *Nov.*[51] There is scarcely a serious phrase in this boisterous document, which dismisses not only the usual scapegoat, the Moscow Art Theater, but the movies and the avant-garde attempts of young theatrical directors like Meyerhold. Shershenevich accuses the theater of eclecticism and of keeping its real force, the actor, subordinated to other people. The ideal theater should be based on movement, and Shershenevich's slogan is "down with the word," which is to be replaced by "intuitive improvisation."

The attempts of futurists to invade the motion picture field were less spectacular and less consistent. In addition to the articles mentioned above, Mayakovsky wrote one film script, but it was never accepted or even returned to the author. After the Revolution, however, he wrote scripts and starred in films. During this time, there was only one known futurist film, "A Drama in Futurist Cabaret No. 3," created by Goncharova and Larionov, who also acted in it. Among the other participants we find Mayakovsky, the Burliuk brothers, Shershenevich, and Lavrenev.

The climax of the interest of the Russian reading public in futurism was reached when Filippo Tommaso Marinetti himself came to Russia in 1914. This visit was made upon the invitation of Genrikh Edmundovich Tasteven (d. 1916), the Russian delegate to the Parisian *Société des grandes conferences,* who had been the managing editor of the famous symbolist magazine *Zolotoe Runo* ("The Golden Fleece") and who was soon to publish one of the first Russian books about futurism. Marinetti eagerly accepted the invitation, hoping to establish during his visit a contact with Russian futurists and thus to extend his futurist empire to the faraway East. Russian futurists were not known to him by name alone. When Mayakovsky, in his lecture in Moscow on November 11, 1913, attacked the Italians as "men of fist and fight," [52] refused to subscribe to Marinetti's onomatopoeic theories and practices, and proclaimed Russian futurism's independence from its Western counterpart, Marinetti was informed of the fact and quickly responded with a letter to the Russian newspaper *Russkie Vedomosti*[53] refuting Mayakovsky's statements. Before coming to Russia, Marinetti sent Russian futurists his manifestos for study. He was coming with five years of stormy futurist history behind him, the outlines of which were reported in the Russian press, but neither his poetry nor his prose were known in translation to the general reader. On the whole, however, Russians had been rather well informed about the new movement. As already indicated, it was as early as March 8, 1909, that the newspaper *Vecher* ("Evening") told its readers about Marinetti's first historic manifesto in *Le Figaro* (February 20).[54] Then, toward the middle of the same year, a certain R. Rabov published a two-column item in a literary magazine[55] wherein he quoted from the manifesto and stated that the new movement derived from modern Europe's "athletic upbringing" and saw futurism's essence in its glorification of the instinct. There followed articles by B. Shaposhnikov and I. Rosenfeld, discussing the theatrical aspects and the intuitivist roots of futurism, respectively, in *Masks*.[56] *Apollon* acquainted its readers with all aspects of the movement beginning with 1910, through both their Italian correspondents (several "letters from Italy" by Paolo Buzzi) and their Russian contributors (among them the famous poet Mikhail Kuzmin, who found futurism "vague, heterogeneous, accidental, and inconsistent," in issue no. 5, 1910). Competing with this, another influential journal, *Russkaya Mysl*, printed in December, 1913, an article describing Italian futurism written by the Italian writer and poet, Sibilla Aleramo (see p. 158). Vadim Shershenevich, as noted above, was both enthusiastic about, and critical of, Marinetti, to whom he devoted a chapter in his book *Futurism without a Mask*. Even earlier, in June, 1912, the second issue of *Union of Youth* printed, for the first time, Italian futurist manifestos in Russian translation.[57] One could add the less important but fascinating facts that a leading poet of Russia, Valery Bryusov, printed his poems in the Italian futurist magazine *Poesia* in 1910, and that Umberto Boccioni, a leading futurist artist, spent several months in Russia before the birth of futurism.

Of definite historical interest are two articles by Anatoly Lunacharsky, who was destined to be the first Soviet minister of culture. In 1913 he was a little-known journalist who contributed to Kievan and St. Petersburg dailies. In *Kievskaya Mysl*,[58] for example, he rather condescendingly informed his readers about Marinetti, whom he credited with some talent but still labeled a "literary super-Nozdrev" (a character from Gogol's *Dead Souls*) and an "ultracivilized super-Repetilov (a character from Griboyedov's *Wit Works Woe*). In another article,[59] Lunacharsky gave a vivid firsthand impression of Marinetti's appearance at a dispute during an exhibition of Boccioni's works.

Marinetti arrived in Moscow on January 26, 1914,[60] and was met at the station with great respect by the Russian literati (including Tasteven and A. N. Tolstoy); but of those present only Shershenevich could claim a connection with futurism.[61] In fact, if Marinetti's primary purpose in coming to Moscow was to meet local futurists, he selected the worst possible time and place, because Mayakovsky, David Burliuk, and Kamensky were still on their tour, and most of the other futurists lived in St. Petersburg at that time. On each day of Marinetti's stay in Russia, local newspapers carried articles about futurism, and eagerly reported his every word. One paper reported that he called the Kremlin an absurd thing and expressed the desire (after having been shown the old execution block on Red Square) to see the place "where heads are chopped off now." When asked his opinion of Russian art, he queried, "Does it exist?" He termed Tolstoy hypocritical and Dostoevsky hysterical, and, in short, tried to behave like a "terrible" futurist. But he was in Russia, where any foreign guest was welcome and where any "Frenchman from Bordeaux" [62] could expect red-carpet treatment. Moreover, his hosts did everything to make his appearances as uncontroversial as possible. Kulbin published a letter to the editor of a St. Petersburg paper[63] denying, allegedly on Marinetti's request, the press reports that Marinetti had expressed some "negative or funny remarks about Russian antiquity." Such a request hardly sounds like Marinetti, who tried to be at his futurist best in his lectures, repeating his well-known appeals to burn the museums and to despise women; but the audiences (including women) applauded the darling foreigner for his temperament. Reporters were enthusiastic about Marinetti's delivery and especially about the art with which he read his own sound-imitative poetry and were only mildly critical of his theories; but they never missed the chance to remind the domestic futurists that here at last was a genuine futurism that could be treated seriously.

The whole situation was hardly to Marinetti's taste, and he probably missed the *volupté d'être sifflé*. He delivered two lectures in Moscow, one on January 27 and the other on January 28, and the only discordant note was the interview with Mikhail Larionov, printed in a Moscow newspaper just before the visitor's arrival, in which Larionov invited his fellow Russians to hurl rotten eggs at Marinetti for his betrayal of futurist ideals. Larionov's failure to explain the nature of this betrayal gave rise to a lively exchange of opinions on the pages of Suvorin's newspaper *Nov*, which was particularly active in exploiting Marinetti's visit. Shershenevich, who in the same paper tried to get as much publicity for himself from this visit as possible (he published two articles about Marinetti just before his arrival), branded Larionov's behavior as *nekulturny*, and he was supported in this view by the abstractionist painter Malevich. Probably the accusation of *nekulturnost* (dreadful for any Russian) was too much even for the wild Larionov, because he hastened to explain that the rotten eggs were meant figuratively. Nevertheless, he declared that Marinetti was old hat and that his lionization by nonfuturists was proof enough of this fact. Shershenevich answered again and repeated his *nekulturnost* charges. One critic compared Marinetti to a bottle of champagne and praised his oratorical abilities, but found his lecture "devoid of content and proof." Another one termed the fact that Marinetti did not scandalize anyone, but rather entered Moscow as a triumphant conqueror, a scandal in itself for a futurist.[64] Two subsequent lectures were given on February 1 and 4 in St. Petersburg. During the latter Marinetti did admit that there were futurists in Russia and that the soil there was ready for the growth of futurism; but this confirmation had its ironic aspects in that a day or so before the Italian poet's first St. Petersburg lecture, Khlebnikov and Livshits resisted Kulbin's efforts to display unanimity in offering hospitality to the distinguished visitor (and Kulbin was supported by Nikolai Burliuk, Matyushin, and Lourié). Both poets saw humiliating overtones in Marinetti's visit. He seemed to them to affect the pose of a general who had come to inspect one of his remote garrisons. For this reason the usually shy

and aloof Khlebnikov printed a hostile leaflet, which he wrote with
Livshits, and tried to distribute it before the February 1 lecture. He
was stopped by Kulbin, who almost started a fight with Khlebnikov.
Here is the text of this leaflet in translation:[65]

Today some natives and the Italian colony on the Neva's banks, out of
private considerations, prostrate themselves before Marinetti, thus betraying
Russian art's first steps on the road to freedom and honor, and placing the
noble neck of Asia under the yoke of Europe.
Persons who do not want any collar on their necks will be calm observers
of such a black deed, as they were during the shameful days of Verhaeren
and Max Linder.
Persons of strong will are aloof. They know the laws of hospitality, but
their bow is tightened and their foreheads show anger.
Foreigner, remember, you are in another country!
The lace of servility on the sheep of hospitality.

V. Khlebnikov
B. Livshits

The events hinted at in the second paragraph are previous visits of
foreign celebrities—a famous Belgian poet and a French movie star,
respectively. The allusion in the last sentence refers to the little-known
passage in Gogol's *Dead Souls* where smugglers, with the customs
officials' connivance, hide Brabant lace under a false second fleece of
live sheep.
A split among Russian futurists was also indicated by the developments following the publication in the newspaper *Nov* (February 5)
of a letter to the editor,[66] over several signatures, in which any connections between the Italian and the Russian varieties of futurism, except
the name, were refuted. The attitude to be taken toward the distinguished visitor was, however, not prescribed in this letter, and its
readers were offered complete freedom to choose any form of greeting
from offering Marinetti flowers on the railroad platform to throwing
rotten eggs at him. The authors also mentioned that Russian independence from the Italians was formulated as early as in *Sadok sudei
II*, which simply was not true. Later some of the futurists, who then
lived in St. Petersburg and whose signatures were under the *Nov* letter (Nikolai Burliuk, Kruchenykh, and Matyushin), published a
letter in the newspaper *Den* (February 13) in which they categorically

denied their authorship of the February 5 letter. There followed still another letter. This one, written in Moscow and signed by Bolshakov, Mayakovsky, and Shershenevich, appeared in *Nov* on February 15. This latter group, while also stressing Russian independence, nevertheless emphasized a parallelism between the two schools: "Futurism is a social big-city-born movement which by itself abolishes all national differences. Poetry of the future will be cosmopolitan." [67] This letter identified the actual authors of the February 5 letter as only David Burliuk and Kamensky and questioned their honesty in using the signatures of the others. The most interesting aspect of the February 15 letter is the uniting of Mayakovsky with two former Mezzanine members in an alliance directed against his fellow Hylaeans.

On the personal level, the Hylaean disagreements were probably never serious. Only three days before the appearance of the February 15 letter, both David Burliuk and Mayakovsky participated in a public discussion in the Polytechnic Museum and showed no animosity. More important, both attended Marinetti's final lecture in Moscow (to which he returned on February 9) on February 13 and created an incident during the discussion when Mayakovsky, wearing a red tuxedo, expressed his displeasure at the debate's being conducted in French, which he called "a public muzzling of Russian futurists." [68] On February 17 (i.e., after the publication of the second *Nov* letter), Burliuk and Mayakovsky again took part in a public discussion and were apparently on good terms. The occasion was a lecture entitled "Fact and Fiction about Woman." Mayakovsky appeared on the stage wearing a multicolored blouse and carrying a whip in his hand. When police suggested that he go home and change his clothes, he obeyed and came back wearing an orange jacket. After this appearance, Burliuk, Kamensky, and Mayakovsky continued their big tour, described earlier; nevertheless, there was some significance in the combination of Bolshakov, Shershenevich, and Mayakovsky. The latter was probably fed up with Hylaean primitivism, for which he had little use, and the possibility of creating a "genuine," urbanist futurism obviously appealed to him. Besides, both Shershenevich and Bolshakov became close to the Burliuk group at this time (see chap. 5). They were not only printing their work in Hylaean publications, but Shershenevich was even entrusted with editorial duties. Boris Pasternak says in his memoirs that this "inner" alliance of the urbanists lasted at least until the summer of 1914.[69]

Livshits' memoirs present a detailed description of Marinetti's stay in St. Petersburg, with an account that goes considerably further than newspaper reports or other individual reminiscences.[70] His portrayal of Marinetti mixes satire with respect. On the one hand, he stresses the guest's "European superficiality" and mocks his tendency to lecture the Russian "provincials." The description of Marinetti's last St. Petersburg lecture acquires humorous overtones as Livshits, who visited Marinetti in his hotel before the lecture, describes how uncomfortable and restrained in his Italian gesticulation the lecturer was because of his trousers, which burst in "the most critical place" just before the appearance and had to be fixed with pins. At that time Livshits was of the opinion that Marinetti already belonged to the past and that Russian futurism was ahead of the Italian movement in many respects. He saw in Marinetti's manifestos either a past stage or half measures, and thought Marinetti's philosophy uninteresting. The lecture seemed to him merely a rehash of old statements and an imposition of Italian domestic affairs on Russia and the rest of Europe. "How little did our declarations resemble this purely political program," commented Livshits. He found in this program "a romantic idealization of the present" rather than a religion of the future. Contemptuously, Livshits adds, "In the West, all these destructions of syntax, abolitions of some parts of speech, and liberated words might have seemed extreme," but Russians already had all this behind them. On the other hand, Livshits had a high regard for Marinetti because he "lived his futurism" and "acted within it"—in short, he was not the hypocrite that one could expect a European to be. Even more important is Livshits' admission of "the indisputable fact" that "we coincide with the Italians in postulating certain formal and technical tasks and, to a degree, in our poetic practice."

The most interesting part of Livshits' reminiscences is his description of a supper in honor of Marinetti at Kulbin's. It took place immediately after Marinetti's first St. Petersburg lecture, and all those who were invited did attend the supper with the exception of Khlebnikov, who remained adamant in his anti-Westernism. The supper went well: Marinetti recited from his *Zang Tumb Tuum* to everybody's satisfaction, and the host called the guest's attention to the fact that the word FuTurisM contains all initials of Marinetti's name. Livshits had a long conversation with Marinetti which the Italian guest of honor began by suggesting that the Russians and the Italians, despite their racial differences, should join forces in their common cause, the fight against "passéism." Livshits replied that there were different kinds of passéism, and that in Russia the past never pressed so heavily on modern art as it did in Italy. "We have never had a Michelangelo," he explained, "and our native sculptors are either mediocre or non-Russian." Then Livshits tried to explain to the Italian the importance of Khlebnikov, but without success. Creation of neologisms seemed an insignificant accomplishment to Marinetti, who immediately reminded Livshits that the Italian futurists had, in addition to creating neologisms, destroyed syntax, used verbs in the infinitive only, and abolished adjectives and punctuation. To Livshits, however, all these achievements seemed superficial. "You wage a war against the individual parts of speech and never go beyond etymology," he said; and he added that a grammatical sentence is nothing but the outer form of logical statement, and that, despite all Italian innovations, the connection of the logical subject and predicate remained untouched. "One cannot destroy syntax in your way," he concluded. When later Kulbin, who also participated in the conversation, mentioned *zaum*, Marinetti became interested for a selfish reason: "But this is nothing but our *parole in libertà* ["liberated words"]," exclaimed he. Then Livshits decided to take the initiative in this seesaw argument and accused Marinetti of a contradiction between what he wrote and the manner in which he recited it publicly, stating that during recitation he smuggled back into it what he had destroyed in its writing. Here Marinetti had to retreat, but he claimed that declamatory aspects were only a temporary substitute in the process of the destruction of syntax. He asserted that after *immaginazione senza fili* has been introduced, the first series of analogies will be dropped, and, with only the second series remaining, the firm foundation for the new, intuitive vision of the world will be established. Ideal poetry, he continued, which does not yet exist, will be one uninterrupted chain of analogies of the secondary order, completely irrational, and it will be necessary for the poet to be "obsessed with matter" to create it. For Livshits this mention of "matter" was the signal to proclaim once more Russian superiority over a West notoriously insensitive to poetic matter (*material*). After all, he exclaimed, Russia already has Khlebnikov, before whose "abysses of the protoplastic [*pervozdannogo*] word even a Rimbaud is a child"; but he confessed the impossibility of translating Khlebnikov in the best manifestations of his genius. Marinetti tried to dismiss Khlebnikov's work as archaism that did not reflect the rhythms of modernity, but Livshits found in this lack of appreciation only another proof that Marinetti's "l'ossessione lirica della materia" (*Manifesto tecnico della letteratura futurista*) was nothing but an empty phrase. "You destroyed punctuation in the name of the new beauty of Speed," he continued to attack, "but we spit on any beauty." At this point, Marinetti became obviously irritated, and, unable to produce any more trumps, accused the Russians of being lazy and lacking mobility. Livshits countered with: "We are more consistent than you. We abolished punctuation five years ago [he had the first *Sadok sudei* in mind], but not in order to create another kind of punctuation to replace it; we wanted to emphasize that the verbal mass is uninterrupted, that its essence is cosmic." This assertion was too much for Marinetti, and he wearily accused Livshits of preaching metaphysics, a subject totally unrelated to futurism. But Livshits still went him one better by asking what futurism had to do with the occupation of Tripoli.

This excellent example of a confrontation between East and West was not the last contact between Marinetti and his Russian counterparts, and with Livshits in particular. The Italian Futurist spent several evenings in the Stray Dog cabaret, and before his second St. Petersburg lecture he again proposed to Livshits a united front. Livshits admits that he never betrayed to the visitor the fact that the origin of the name "futurism" was nothing but an accident in Russia. Marinetti would be terrified if he knew that, he adds. Even before Marinetti left St. Petersburg, Livshits and Lourié, disappointed by the second lecture (on futurism in arts and music), decided to organize a recital that would be a Russian answer to the arrogant, but provincial, West. It took place on February 11 and consisted of two lectures: "Shared Aspects of Italian and Russian Futurism" by Livshits and "Italian Futurist Music." Livshits stressed the fact that Italian futurism presented itself as a new canon in all fields of art, whereas the Russians shunned all formulas. The Italians had a program; the Russians, concrete achievements. In the rest of his one-and-a-half-hour lecture, Livshits described the West and the East as two completely different systems of aesthetic vision. Russia was presented as an organic part of the East, and the lecturer drew parallels between Russian icons and Persian miniatures, Russian and Chinese popular lithographs, Russian *chastushka*'s ("popular ditties") and Japanese tankas. But the most important distinguishing characteristic was, for Livshits, the Russian intimacy with the artistic media, something lacking in a West that, because of this lack, was approaching a crisis in aesthetics. The lecture ended with appeals to wake up and recognize Russian superiority over the West. Livshits was rewarded with the applause of the audience, which made him uneasy because he felt that his grandiose cultural metaphysics was, with mistaken approval, taken for political chauvinism.

It is appropriate to remember that the ideas Livshits expressed in this lecture go back to the leaflet manifesto published by him in Russian, French, and Italian at the very beginning of 1914, nearly a month before Marinetti's arrival. The signatories of the manifesto were, in addition to Livshits, Lourié and George Yakulov, an artist who had just returned from Paris, where simultaneism was the vogue at the time, both in poetry and in painting. Livshits was skeptical about Cendrars's and Apollinaire's recent experiments in this direction; and Yakulov considered himself robbed by Robert Delaunay, who, he claimed, stole his ideas, so they decided to write a manifesto under the title "We and the West." In this manifesto Europe was declared to be in a state of artistic crisis, one of whose manifestations was a current interest in oriental art. The West was represented as organically unable to understand the East, having lost the idea of the precise limits of art. European art was found to be not only archaic, but also incapable of developing in a new direction, yet desperately trying to create a priori aesthetics for a nonexistent art. Russia, on the other hand, was presented as building on "cosmic elements" and moving from subject to object. The manifesto ended with the positing of several abstruse aesthetic points, first those common to all arts, then, in three adjacent columns, specifically those for painting, poetry, and music. To give an illustration, Livshits demanded for poetry "a differentiation of the masses of various degrees of rarefaction: the lithoid, fluid, and phosphenoid ones." Among Yakulov's demands there was one for "a negation of conical construction as trigonometrical perspective." [71] The French version was sent to Apollinaire and appeared in *Mercure de France* (CVIII, April 16, 1914, pp. 882–883). "Quelques esthètes russes ont lancé un manifeste," wrote Apollinaire in his brief remarks; and he commented, with ironic puzzlement, "Il est vrais que *la negation de la construction d'après le conus* est tout un programme." Livshits, at any rate, wrote later in his memoirs that the ideas expressed in the leaflet manifesto were more convincing as part of the preliminary verbal arguments than in their final form on paper. He also admitted that his ideas were the result of meditating on Marinetti's theories. The fact that Russian and Italian futurists coincided in their technical aspects, but were different otherwise, made him think that the Russians were not free of nationalism, which had only been driven deep inside. It was ironic that Livshits, the most European of all the Russian futurists, came to the conclusion that "we should recognize ourselves as Asians and rid ourselves of our European yoke." [72]

Thus Marinetti's visit led to the beginning of a disintegration of Russian futurism in the movement's finest hour and when interest in it was at its height. It was as if the guest clearly showed the Russian futurists not only how different they were from Italian futurists, but how they differed among themselves as well. Livshits soon ceased to appear in futurist collections. Khlebnikov broke with Hylaea angrily after some of his friends showed tolerance toward Marinetti. In his letter of February 2 to Nikolai Burliuk in which he did not spare either the addressee ("untalented windbag"), or Kulbin ("madman," "scoundrel"), or Marinetti himself ("this Italian vegetable"), he once more stressed the Russian chronological priority ("We've been jumping into the future since 1905") and added, "From now on I have nothing in common with members of Hylaea." [73] Soon Khlebnikov left for his native Astrakhan in disgust and there became preoccupied with mathematics of history once more. He also began to dream about the Platonic organization of a Society of Globe Presidents. He probably did not know that Marinetti also dreamed of government by painters, poets, and musicians. In 1916, however, Khlebnikov became more tolerant and admitted Marinetti and H. G. Wells into his Martian parliament as guests and gave them the right of deliberative vote. He also made up with his Hylaean friends that year.

Marinetti was obviously disappointed by his Russian tour, and soon after his return home is known to have called the Russians "pseudo-futurists" who live in *plusquamperfectum* rather than in *futurum.*[74] But prewar Italian futurism was nearing its end, too; and Papini's article in *Lacerba,* which is usually considered the beginning of the split in the ranks, appeared on February 15, 1914. The split became final one year later. For Marinetti, his "post-Russian" periods were less spectacular, pathbreaking, or just plain interesting than his earlier years, so his Russian trip marks the point after which a slow decline begins. If one is to believe some sources, he came into direct contact with Russia once more, as an officer in the Italian division that was crushed, together with the German troops, at Stalingrad during World War II.[75]

Marinetti's visit, reported in newspapers, review articles, and books, naturally aroused interest in Italian futurism in Russia. Only a month or so before his arrival, a leading journal, *Russkaya Mysl* ("Russian Thought"), printed, in translation, the eight-column article "Futurism in Italy," [76] written by the Italian authoress Sibilla Aleramo. In it, Aleramo is mildly critical of the movement, but on the whole she welcomes its arrival, which, in her opinion, adds new and genuine talents to Italian literature. Incidentally, the author states that the real interest in futurist activities in Italy dates only from the spring of 1913, which roughly corresponds to the Russian situation. She gives a few details on the history of Italian futurism and describes in one paragraph the main tenets of futurist artists, among whom she truly appreciates only Boccioni. Aleramo mentions "the undeniable talent" of Marinetti and finds his similar to Verhaeren, Hugo, and Kipling. Then she summarizes the content of some of the works, mentioning not only those of Marinetti, but those of Palazzeschi, Folgore, and Buzzi as well.

Articles in the best Russian periodicals, which coincided with, or appeared in the wake of, Marinetti's visit and were written by Russians, normally combined an attempt at informative objectivity in description of the facts with poorly concealed irritation in evaluation of futurist works and activities. Such, for instance, was the long article "Italian Futurism," printed in *Vestnik Evropy* and sent from Rome by the well-known journalist, Mikhail Osorgin.[77] Osorgin quotes extensively from Marinetti's manifestos and gives perhaps the most detailed biographical account of the movement leader which ever appeared in Russian. He translates pieces from Marinetti's works written according to the method of "liberated words" (which even the futurist Shershenevich was unable to do when translating futurist manifestos). He does not deny Marinetti's talents, but says that his best work is nonfuturist. Osorgin does not neglect futurist music and painting, expounding their theories and surveying in detail the work of representative composers and artists. His judgment is, however, condescendingly negative, and he accuses the futurists of inconsistency, self-advertisement, and pornography, and prophesies that the end is near for the whole movement. A similar letter from Rome, written by a reporter, was printed in the March issue of another monthly, *Sovremennyi Mir,* under the title "Pseudofuturism." [78] The author, M. Pervukhin, wrote his verbose article from an aesthetically conservative, "honest" position, and mostly repeats the accusations, so familiar from the daily press, that the futurists consciously fooled the public and that the movement resembled Andersen's naked emperor. Occasionally he displays an ignorance of the facts and he must have felt ill at ease when he later discovered that Valentine de Saint-Point was a woman and the granddaughter of Lamartine, which certainly adds piquant overtones to her preaching of lust. Like Osorgin, Pervukhin sees the end of futurism in the near future, but he also predicts the arrival of a genuine, nondestructive futurism. He does not see any soil for futurism in Russia. Finally, *Vestnik Znaniya* (no. 5, 1914) published an article by the distinguished philologist Baudouin de Courtenay under the title "Galopom Vpered" ("At Full Speed Ahead"), which was a quotation ("A galoppo! . . ."), from Marinetti's "Contro la Spagna passatista." Baudouin de Courtenay showed an interest in Russian domestic futurism. On one occasion he entered into polemics with its theories (see chap. 5), and he even consented to serve as chairman at one of its public debates. In this essay, as Osorgin had done before him, Baudouin de Courtenay recognizes Marinetti's talent in his early works, but not in his onomatopoeic futurist writings. He even allies himself with Kruchenykh in his critique of some aspects of Italian futurism. For Baudouin de Courtenay futurism is an amorphous phenomenon, and he anticipates the development of many different trends within it. Russian futurism is, in his opinion, more avant-garde than its Italian counterpart, because it is not satisfied with destruction of syntax, but tries to destroy the very word. He also states that futurism as an idea originated in Russia before Italy, though he is not specific in this assertion. Many of Baudouin de Courtenay's judgments and statements were obviously taken from Kulbin, to whom he refers several times. Incidentally, he quotes from Marinetti's conversation with Kulbin the former's assertion that the Italian futurists are of this earth (*zemnye*), whereas the Russians are too abstract in their aspirations.

An example of a negative reaction to Marinetti can be found in the writings of the Russian symbolist George Chulkov, who saw in Italian futurism "little poetry, little literature, but much moralism upside down," and, behind its brisk appeals, nothing but the depression and boredom of an empty soul.[79]

Genrikh Tasteven, who was the main power behind Marinetti's invitation to Russia and the organization of his lectures, published in 1914 in Moscow a book entitled *Futurizm: Na puti k novomu simvolizmu* ("Futurism: On the Road to a New Symbolism"). In this rather confused treatise he does not separate Italian and Russian futurism. Futurism is for Tasteven *the* ideological movement of his time and the dominant artistic force that has replaced the decadent ideals of the recent past and helps mankind to see "the new beauty of the Earth." He writes at some length about Mallarmé's influence on futurism and even defines the latter as "Mallarméism upside down." The main traits of futurism for him are the creation of neologisms, "subordination of words to the rhythm of verse [whatever that means]," and destruction of syntax. Far from seeing in futurism nihilist features, he describes the movement as an attempt at a new synthesis, a new faith, an unconsciously religious movement, its essence being moral, rather than aesthetic. Tasteven's conclusion, as anticipated in the subtitle of his book, is that futurism is the new symbolism that will be able to realize the long-desired synthesis of arts.

There were few translations of Marinetti's nontheoretical works, and his poetry, to the best of my knowledge, has been translated into Russian only once.[80] Vadim Shershenevich, who obviously prided himself on being the only Marinettist among the Russian futurists, translated and published two of Marinetti's longer works (both in Moscow and both in 1916). His translation of *La Bataille de Tripoli* appeared in an edition designed for the general public (thus exploiting the anti-Turkish trend of the work).[81] The translation is preceded by Shershenevich's preface in which he praises Marinetti and characterizes him as a man "who uses his pen as excellently as his sword." But later Shershenevich shows his independence and stresses Marinetti's lack of consistency, which he does not regard as a vice. He also condescendingly remarks that certain aspects of Italian futurism, such as its nihilism, may seem novel to the West, but in Russia they have been known since the publication of Turgenev's *Fathers and Sons*. Marinetti's portrayal of war, however, satisfies Shershenevich more than those by Leo Tolstoy and Garshin, because in Marinetti's work the chaos of war grows directly out of the chaos of style. The book also contains Marinetti's 1911 manifesto on war and his statements to the press in connection with his war reports. The other work by Marinetti which Shershenevich translated is *Mafarka le futuriste*.[82] The quality of the translation is poor, so that the work is clumsy and occasionally tasteless, as in the passage where Mafarka calls his mother *mamochka* in Russian.

The first complete translation of an Italian futurist manifesto was the work of the publishers of *Union of Youth*. Tasteven's *Futurism* has an appendix containing translations of Marinetti's first manifesto, the manifesto on *immaginazione senza fili* and *parole in libertà*, the proclamations "Contro la Spagna passatista" and "Contro Venezia passatista," and Valentine de Saint-Point's *luxure* manifesto. The most comprehensive collection of European futurist manifestos in Russian is Shershenevich's book, *Manifesty italyanskogo futurizma* ("Manifestos of Italian Futurism), published in Moscow in 1914. In his preface, the translator says that he took all the texts from the publications of the Milanese Direction du Mouvement Futuriste, failed to get hold of two or three, and decided not to translate two. Actually, this collection lacks about ten futurist manifestos published by that time. Shershenevich allowed himself to change and omit passages in his texts at will and was at times maladroit in his translations (*sensibilité*, for example, is rendered by *chuvstvovanie*). In addition to all the manifestos published previously by Union of Youth and by Tasteven (minus the two proclamations), Shershenevich included Pratella's manifesto on music, Boccioni's manifesto on sculpture, Marinetti's "Technical Manifesto of Futurist Literature" of 1912 and the supplement to it, Russolo's "Art of Noises," Carrà's "Painting of Sounds, Noises, and Smells," and, finally, Marinetti's "Il Teatro di varietà." The same year, Marinetti's lectures, collected in *Le Futurisme* in a translation by M. Engelhardt,* were published in Moscow.

The question of direct Russian borrowings from Marinetti remains to be explored. His demand that literature become a voice of the twentieth century could not but appeal to some Russians. There are too many echoes of Marinetti's ideas in the preserved outlines of Mayakovsky's lectures (as well as in his early urbanist poetry) to be dismissed as mere coincidence. One reporter wrote,[83] for example, that Mayakovsky demanded whistles (which in Russian correspond to boos) during his public appearances and declared that he felt a "lust for whistles," a statement that obviously derives from Marinetti. Use of various typefaces in the poems and prose of Ignatyev and David Burliuk, and Ignatyev's attempt to introduce mathematical symbols and musical notations into poetry are likewise reminiscent of Marinetti. Marinetti's "daily spittings on the altar of Art" sound like Burliuk or Kruchenykh, and the very title of *A Slap in the Face of Public Taste* sounds like Italian futurism. Kruchenykh's enjoying himself in the mud next to a pig echoes Marinetti's pleasure after being thrown from his car into the gutter. And there are other evidences of Italian influence upon Russian futurism, such as Livshits' destruction of syntax in his prose and the glorification of intuition in the writings of ego-futurists, practices that are largely Marinettian. But to prove that all these similarities are the result of direct influence is not so easy. The only clear-cut examples of Marinetti's influence on the work of Russian futurists are Shershenevich's writings of 1914 to 1916, which are described later.

After the Revolution, interest in Marinetti did not stop. Additional Marinetti manifestos (on tactilism and on speed) were printed in two issues of *Sovremennyi Zapad* ("Modern West"), and articles about him appeared in magazines and encyclopedias. One critic (N. Gorlov) even tried to consider him and Mayakovsky as similar poetic phenomena.[84] Nikolai Aseyev, a prominent poet of the second futurist wave (see chap. 6), not only saw a production of a Marinetti play during his visit to Italy in 1927 (when Aseyev was already a well-known Soviet literary figure), but was introduced to the author. Both the play and its author aroused in Aseyev nothing but pity—or so he wrote.[85] After 1928, interest in Marinetti seems to have ceased in Russia.

THE YEARS OF FLOWERING

5

The beginning of 1914 saw no decrease in futurist publishing activities. One after another, four miscellanies appeared in print: *Moloko kobylits* ("The Milk of Mares"), *Rykayushchii Parnas* ("Roaring Parnassus"), *Pervyi Zhurnal Russkikh Futuristov* ("The First Journal of Russian Futurists"), and the second edition of *Dokhlaya luna* ("The Croaked Moon"). All of them except *Roaring Parnassus* were published by the Literary Company of Futurists, Hylaea, and were marked "Moscow," even if David Burliuk actually printed them in Kherson. Later, the name of this publishing enterprise was changed to the Publishing House of the First Journal of Russian Futurists. It also published such individual efforts as Mayakovsky's tragedy, the first volume of Khlebnikov's works, and Livshits' only futurist collection, *Volchye solntse* ("The Sun of the Wolves"). Simultaneously, there existed the small publishing enterprise of G. Kuzmin and S. Dolinsky, which had earlier made possible the publication of *A Slap in the Face of Public Taste* and then followed it with *The Missal of the Three*. In addition, they published seven of Kruchenykh's ventures: the two editions of *A Game in Hell*, *Old-Time Love*, *Worldbackwards*, *Hermits*, *Pomade*, and *Half Alive*. At approximately the same time, Kruchenykh published in St. Petersburg, where he had moved, his own and Khlebnikov's books under the imprint "Euy." Among these books was his opera, *Victory over the Sun*. He also announced a two-volume collection of Vasily Kamensky's works, which was to include his earlier flop, *The Mud Hut*, but never materialized. Finally, there was another St. Petersburg enterprise called Zhuravl ("the Crane"), whose moving force was M. Matyushin and which counted *Sadok sudei II* among its credits. Retrospectively, Zhuravl also considered the historic first *Sadok sudei* among its publications, despite the fact that in 1910 the name "Zhuravl" did not yet exist. A third *Sadok sudei* and some additional works by Kruchenykh were slated for publication but never appeared. Zhuravl published, however, *The Three*, *Roaring Parnassus*, and all three of Elena Guro's books.[1] Last to complete the picture, the editions of the Union of Youth must be mentioned. This group published three issues of their magazine (the fourth was in preparation but never appeared) and a few books on art by their members, as well as a book of translations from Chinese poetry—all before 1914. David Burliuk's booklet attacking a prominent art critic (see p. 181) was also published by the Union of Youth.

Although the miscellanies of 1914 were, in some respects, more or less deficient in their literary content, each of them was an event in the history of Russian futurism, and all of them were marked by the desire to form a united futurist movement in Russia. On the other hand, however, the influx into some of these collections of mediocre poetic products, especially some of the verse by the Burliuks, and the lack of progress in aesthetic theory can be considered as signs of deterioration at the very moment when Russian futurism seemed to have reached its climax.

It is difficult to say precisely when *The Milk of Mares* appeared, except that it was at the beginning of 1914. At any rate, it seems that the material for this book was gathered, with a few exceptions, after the first edition of *The Croaked Moon* had gone to press. At that time the publishers intended to entitle this collection with the neologism "Miristel," a title that only Khlebnikov could have created. It was changed to *The Milk of Mares* probably because the latter sounded more Hylaean while still retaining a Khlebnikovian quality.[2] The surprising thing about *The Milk of Mares* and the subsequent *Roaring Parnassus* is that Igor-Severyanin participated in both. In both instances, it was obviously a last-minute decision, based on his short-lived alliance with the Hylaeans, made while the latter were on the Crimean leg of their tour. Severyanin's name had not been mentioned in the announced lists of contributors which preceded publication, and in both books his poems were printed on the final pages. Otherwise, these two miscellanies had in common the fact that all participants were rather underrepresented, with the exception of the Burliuks. Forty-six of David Burliuk's poems were printed in the first miscellany, and fifty-seven appeared in the second. *The Milk of Mares* was illustrated by the two Burliuks and by Alexandra Exter. The editor, David Burliuk, tried to make this book look avant-garde typographically and often used different typefaces for different poems. He probably exhausted the possibilities of the provincial printing house in Kherson, yet he showed little imagination. In general, each poem is printed in one kind of type (there are only two instances where boldface is used for one or two words), and nowhere does Burliuk come near the elaborate typographical combinations employed by the Italians at the same time (which Burliuk was most likely trying to emulate in this book, but which he knew of only through hearsay). Handwritten mimeographed texts and drawings reminiscent of Kruchenykh's publications are inserted in two places.

There is no formal manifesto in *The Milk of Mares,* but an excerpt from Khlebnikov's private letter to Vyacheslav Ivanov, a leader of Russian symbolism, under the title "Instead of a Preface," was obviously meant as a manifesto and shows the growing nationalistic trend within futurism. This trend found its clearest expression in the writings of Khlebnikov and in the activities of Livshits just before he left Hylaea. In printing Khlebnikov's letter, Burliuk obviously intended to impress the public with a "summit" exchange of ideas between the leaders of two literary movements. The excerpt is highly interesting, not only as a guide to understanding Khlebnikov's "Otter's Children," a major work printed in *Roaring Parnassus,* but also as a theoretical statement. Khlebnikov affirms here the superiority of the Man of the Continent (in contradistinction to the Man of the Coast), thus indicating a shift in the relative importance of Europe and Asia favoring the East. He anticipates Russian participation in this process, but deplores his countrymen's present indifference to Russia's past deeds. Khlebnikov ends with a pessimistic remark that at present only translations and imitations can be printed in Russia. The poems by Khlebnikov, which follow this prefatory item, are almost all nationalistic or pan-Slavic in their content, form, and tone. There are some valuable pieces among them, but Burliuk edited them in a most atrocious way, publishing some without endings (which he must have omitted after not being able to read them from the manuscripts) and many with typographical errors. The dramatic idyll "Selskaya druzhba" ("Rustic Friendship") is the only sizable work among them.[3]

David Burliuk's own poems, which, this time, carried no opus numbers, belong mostly to his early work and demonstrate his close ties with nineteenth-century Russian poetry. Only here and there are they marked with futurism, perhaps as the result of a last-minute retouch; and very often it is difficult to distinguish this "futurism" from a simple lack of verbal awareness. Nikolai Burliuk's twelve poems, presented as a cycle under the title "Ushcherblennost" ("Decline"), are hardly better. They are inarticulate, monotonous, and imitative, and resemble the poems of his brother to such an extent that they might just as well have been signed by David.

The rest of the book is occupied by one poem by Mayakovsky (with his usual big-city theme), three by Kruchenykh (of which only "The Song of a Witch Doctor," consisting of a column of semimeaningful words, is mildly interesting), two by Livshits (rather mannered, but carefully constructed), and one by Severyanin, who in the Hylaean company tried hard to be scandalous and defiant and to express his contempt for high society. Special mention should be reserved for Vasily Kamensky, who appears here for the first time after his self-imposed silence and displays in his five poems both a degree of freshness and the influence of Khlebnikov. Some of his poems are based on sound echo; others follow the procedures of Khlebnikov's "Incantation by Laughter" (but with a songlike charm of their own); still others (e.g., "Slovoisko") are an attempt to blend words having syllables in common. The most original among them is "Chugunnoe zhitye" ("Pig-Iron Life"), which has force and atmosphere; it later became a part of Kamensky's novel about Razin (see chap. 7).

The next miscellany, *Futuristy: Rykayushchii Parnas* ("Futurists: Roaring Parnassus"), appeared in St. Petersburg in January, 1914. In addition to works by those who contributed to *The Milk of Mares*, one can find here two posthumous poems by Guro and the work of such Petersburg artists as Ivan Pougni (who designed the cover), Pavel Filonov, and Olga Rozanova. The book was published with money supplied by Pougni's wife. It now seems incomprehensible that the publication was promptly confiscated by the Committee of Press because of the alleged pornography in Filonov's illustrations. A close examination of these pictures, done by one of the most fascinating, though still little appreciated, Russian artists of the twentieth century,[4] does not reveal anything that even by a great stretch of imagination could be considered objectionable: they are austere representations of human figures, betraying the influence of Russian icons. Only ten copies of the book could be secretly carried out of the printing house, and thus *Roaring Parnassus* is probably the greatest bibliographical rarity among the major futurist publications.

Roaring Parnassus begins with a violent attack on the rest of contemporary literature, an attack that hardly deserves any discussion, since it consists mainly of insults: no theoretical issues are involved. This on-the-offensive stance probably resulted from a fear that futurism might lose its initial revolutionary fervor and become just another poets' movement in Russia. The very title "Idite k chortu" ("Go to Hell!") is defiant to an extreme: here the Hylaeans and Severyanin dissociate themselves not only from the symbolists, who still dominated the literary scene, and from the Acmeists, who made their first organized appearance in 1913, but also from the Ego-groups as well. The Acmeists are described as "a pack of Adams with partings in their hair" who "try to attach an Apollonian . . . label to their faded songs about samovars from Tula and toy lions." The symbolists are referred to as the "crawling little old men of Russian literature [*literaturochki*]," some of whom, for commercial reasons, welcomed futurism, hoping "hastily to make for themselves, out of the sparks of our defiant poetry, an electrical belt for intercourse with the Muses." Fyodor Sologub and Valery Bryusov are singled out for special attacks. The former is portrayed as covering his "balding little talent [*oblysevshii talantik*]" with Severyanin's hat. Of Bryusov the manifesto's authors wrote: "Vasily Bryusov habitually chewed the poetry of Mayakovsky and Livshits on the pages of *Russian Thought*. Stop, Vasya, this is no cork for you!" Such a statement combines a sarcastic reference to Bryusov's inherited cork business with the unfounded rumor that his Roman-sounding first name, Valery, was invented to replace the pedestrian Vasily. The manifesto ends with the following words: "Today we spit out the past which sticks to our teeth and makes us sick and tired, and we announce: (1) all futurists are united only in our group; (2) we have dropped the incidental labels of 'ego' and 'cubo' and have formed a united literary company of futurists." The latter statement placed the Petersburg Herald and the Moscow Mezzanine of Poetry outside Russian futurism; and these two groups were described as "a herd of young men, formerly without definite occupations, who now pounce upon literature and show their grimacing faces." Only a month later, however, the two leading Mezzanine poets, Shershenevich and Bol-shakov, were accepted into Hylaea.

Those attacked in the *Roaring Parnassus* manifesto were deeply offended. Most of them had taken the insults in *A Slap* rather good-naturedly; but this time they were hurt, and the indignation of the Petersburg literati was aroused. Sologub was especially insulted by the fact that Severyanin, whom he had presented to the world as his protégé, had participated in the manifesto's writing. (They later made up.) Gumilev, the leader of the Acmeists, felt hurt, too, and broke off personal relationships with all futurists except Nikolai Burliuk, who had refused to sign the manifesto.

Almost half of *Roaring Parnassus* was taken up by more than fifty poems by David Burliuk under the general title, "Doitel iznurennykh zhab" ("A Milker of Exhausted Toads"). Selected for its shock value, this title is probably the only really successful thing in the whole work. If, on the whole, these poems are of better quality than those printed in the earlier collection and do sound more futurist, still they lack distinction or novelty. In these fragmentary pieces, Burliuk tries oc-casionally "to kill the moonlight" (to quote from Marinetti), but he cannot conceal the fact that his verse is essentially symbolist, or even presymbolist. To make it look avant-garde, Burliuk uses antiaesthetic imagery, explanations of metaphoric periphrases in footnotes, large print for "key words," omissions of punctuation and prefixes, mathe-

nbols, and, less frequently, meter mixing, neologisms, and ʒal incongruities. But occasionally one finds a personal touch ık's gruesome themes, in his insistent, grimly primitivist и̗о̗.̗.̗.̗ / and even in his vague, but involved, metaphorical structures. There is also some individuality in his predilection for archaic diction.

A much more interesting contribution was made this time by Nikolai Burliuk in his "mystery" entitled "Kovcheg vesny" ("The Ark of Spring"). This cycle (two prefatory poems with titles and ten numbered poems forming the main body of the "mystery") consists primarily of Petersburg cityscapes, which are followed by country landscapes and a few "on-the-road" poems with images based on railroad travel. The cycle begins in the expected manner, combining convention with minor eccentricities. There is a quiet symmetry in this beginning, emphasized by the prevalent *abba* rhyming, and it is occasionally reminiscent of Rilke. Burliuk also reminds one at times of Khlebnikov, but a lyric Khlebnikov. The most original thing about Burliuk's cycle is its development from the absolute clarity and symmetry of the first poems to a pantheistic entanglement at the end. Lucid stanzas about autumn give way to verse that is fragmented at will, has vacillating and sometimes disappearing meter (so that parts of the cycle actually become prose), and shows a certain loosening of rhyme and syntax and a deliberate, involved imagery. This gradual transition from a harmonious, traditional artificiality to an introspective confusion, which is constantly reflected in the texture of the work, is a real achievement.

Mayakovsky's two poems immediately follow the manifesto, and he is especially in tune with it in the first of these, his violently defiant "Nate" ("Take This!"). The second work, about a man who starts a riot in a barbershop by asking the barber to comb his ears, is the poem now well known under its later title "They Don't Understand a Thing." Kamensky, in his six poems, displays all aspects of his poetry, both thematically and structurally: he tries sound echoes, neologisms, antiaesthetic diction, and oriental color in imagery and in language. One poem is an inverted pyramid of words created by dropping a letter or two from each word and forming below it from the letters that remain another meaningful word. In the poem about a naked youth, there is a primitivist theme; in another, the poet writes about his profession, aviation; and in the lullaby-like "Kolybaika," whose

170

verse is inspired by children (the type introduced by Guro), the *zaum* direction is evident.

Tribute is paid to Guro in *Roaring Parnassus* in a critical miniature, written in her manner by, of all people, Kruchenykh. On the other hand, Guro's own poetry, printed here, bears a resemblance to Mayakovsky's. Livshits writes, as expected, in his own tradition, perhaps best described as an aesthetic hermeticism, which combines clarity of form with obscurity of content. (Two of the three poems by Livshits selected for inclusion in *Roaring Parnassus* had been printed before in *The Milk of Mares*.) Severyanin's two poems are carefully chosen to harmonize with the manifesto. One of them attacks Leo Tolstoy, among others, for a few uncomplimentary opinions about Severyanin's poetry;[5] the other is a familiar Severyanin exercise in self-aggrandizement ("Venus gave herself to me," "I am the reincarnated Napoleon," etc.). The book ends rather unexpectedly with a one-page table of correspondences between musical tonalities and Russian vowels. The name of the author of this table, Elachich, does not appear in any other publication of this time.

The artistic backbone of the book is, as usual, a work by Khlebnikov, who, probably through Burliuk's inadvertence, is here called Vladimir. In addition to "Mudrost v silke" ("Wisdom in a Snare"), which is a charming and ingenious attempt to reproduce the singing of forest birds with letters of the alphabet, *Roaring Parnassus* contains one of his most ambitious attempts to merge poetry, prose, and his theories on the mathematical foundations of history. Though not a masterpiece, "Deti vydry" ("The Otter's Children") is an important work. Here Khlebnikov once more shows that while his colleagues were busy rebelling against the past and the present and were expending so much energy trying to create a new art, he walked his own path with absolute naturalness. This man was completely immune to most of the influence that shaped the poetry of his contemporaries, but he was deeply touched by traditions that were habitually neglected or ignored. Only Khlebnikov could conceive a work that begins in a clear, lucid prose (patterned after the stage descriptions that precede the acts in dramatic works and based on the cosmogonic myths of the Orochi, an obscure Siberian tribe) which gradually develops into poetry, becomes prose again, and ends in the self-centered image of the island of Khlebnikov, which serves as a meeting place for the shades of the great men of history. "The Otter's Children," belonging to the genre called by the poet "transtale," presents a sequence of six unequal parts, designated by him as "sails"; and it moves from the prehistoric times of the Orochi (this portion is surprisingly reminiscent of German romantic comedy) to the portrayal of Russian conquests before the formation of the Russian state. This movement is interrupted by a story, written in brilliant, Gogol-like prose, about the death of the Cossack leader Palivoda, who is ambushed by Crimean Tartars. A crucial meditation about time and history, with an admixture of chess imagery, has as its backdrop the sinking *Titanic*. The ending, which consists principally of a dialogue between Hannibal and Scipio, contains a magnificent invective directed against the two apostles of determinism (so hateful to Khlebnikov), Karl and Charles (i.e., Karl Marx and Charles Darwin). The verse sections are written in the mixture of meters characteristic of Khlebnikov's other longer poetic works and are handled here in a virtuoso way.

The *First Journal of Russian Futurists*, whose issue number 1–2 [6] appeared in Moscow in March, 1914, was the first and last large-scale attempt to unite all Russian futurists under the same cover. It was planned as a bimonthly and was the result of a *rapprochement* between Hylaea and the former Mezzanine of Poetry, whose members had been dismissed by the Hylaeans only a short time before as practitioners of a phony futurism. In a way, it *was* a unification of *all* futurists, because at the time this issue was prepared, in February, 1914, ego-futurism did not exist, and Centrifuge had not yet appeared. The Soviet novelist Boris Lavrenev, once a member of the Mezzanine of Poetry, mentions in his memoirs [7] that the meetings of the Moscow ego- and cubo-futurists took place in 1913 at his, Lavrenev's, apartment, and that the two Burliuks, Shershenevich, Kruchenykh, Bolshakov, Tretyakov, and Khrisanf were present. Lavrenev also says that the meeting was called on Shershenevich's initiative. This attempt to unite obviously never went smoothly, but, for lack of documentation, one can only deduce and sometimes simply guess the details. Shershenevich was probably alarmed by Ignatyev's death (after which the Petersburg ego-futurist group disintegrated), and he decided to enter into an alliance with the cubists despite all differences and despite past exchanges of insults. He evidently hoped to assume leadership someday, which he thought he deserved because of his education and his "correct" understanding of futurism. The only Hylaean Shershenevich respected as a poet was Mayakovsky, so he, with the help of Bolshakov, openly tried to separate Mayakovsky from the Burliuks and the others. In so doing, he hoped to form a distinctly urbanist futurist group in Russia, which could then draw closer to the western European modernist movements. He never succeeded, but he made a good try, as we can judge from his letter (written with Mayakovsky) to a newspaper, directed against Burliuk and Kamensky (see chap. 4), from his active role during Marinetti's visit, and from his editorial activities in the *First Journal* and in the second edition of *The Croaked Moon*.[8] Shershenevich's wooing of Mayakovsky seems to have led to a split in the Mezzanine group, because the name of Khrisanf does not figure among the actual or prospective contributors to the *First Journal* (Lavrenev's and Tretyakov's do). On the other hand, all the Hylaeans are listed, although Kruchenykh gave nothing for publication in this issue, and Livshits' single poem is evidence of only token participation. As Khlebnikov was breaking with the Hylaeans by the time the magazine was prepared for publication, he is represented in it, probably without his permission, by a haphazard selection: an atrociously edited "birds fragment" previously published in *Roaring Parnassus*, some short prose, a list of neologisms, and a few fragments printed in a chaotic manner. Only one poem by Severyanin is included. Even Nikolai Burliuk has here just seven of his poems, which are only mildly interesting and demonstrate none of the devices he himself praises in his important theoretical essay printed in this issue.

The list of prospective contributors to the *First Journal* contains the names of Ivan Aksenov, who later became a member of the Centrifuge group, Rurik Ivnev, N. Kulbin, and, in its later versions, that of Marinetti himself. Among the artists who took part or agreed to take part, one finds the familiar names of the Russian avant-garde of the period, such as the two Burliuks, Malevich, Matyushin, Yakulov, and Exter, and also Fernand Léger. The rest of the list is composed of unknown names, some of them female and most of them nothing but Shershenevich's pseudonyms. On the editoral board, Mayakovsky was supposed to be in charge of poetry; Kamensky, of prose; D. Burliuk, of the arts and literature (*sic*); and Shershenevich and Bolshakov, of criticism. David Burliuk is mentioned as the publisher, and Kamensky, as the chief editor of the magazine; but so far as this first (and last) issue is concerned, the man in complete charge was Shershene-vich, because Burliuk, Kamensky, and Mayakovsky were still on tour and could visit Moscow only briefly.

Far from considering himself a newcomer who ought to be cautious and modest in his first steps, Shershenevich gave his own poetry star billing, printing it near the front of the issue, immediately after Mayakovsky's (which might be another proof of his intent to "steal" Mayakovsky). He also filled the critical section with reviews praising himself to the skies, and he squared his accounts with a Moscow group of young poets to which Pasternak belonged. Burliuk later regretted delegating responsibilities to Shershenevich and apologized in his letter to Livshits, who had a dim view of this alliance with the Mez-zanine and who had not been consulted by Burliuk in advance.[9]

Shershenevich's eleven poems in the *First Journal* do not represent anything new after one has read his poetry in the Mezzanine editions. He is here the poet of the big city and of the "modern" soul, whose nervousness and hysteria usually find expression in the images of a heart trampled upon. He tries to achieve the same kind of dissonant dynamism that can be observed in the paintings of the Italian futurists; and he displays a veritable parade of artistic devices, from filling his verse with urbanist similes, metaphors, and hyperboles to attempting to write accentual verse (which he considered "free verse") with a wide variety of unusual rhymes. In both thematic and metrical aspects, Shershenevich shows a resemblance to Mayakovsky, but one should not hasten to draw conclusions about the latter's influence; future investigations may even prove the reverse. At any rate, the mutual influence of these poets may safely be suggested, which only confirms the suspicion that an alliance of Mayakovsky-Shershenevich-Bol-shakov was in the making and that it had a very good foundation. Despite some similarities to Shershenevich, Bolshakov, as before, shows more subdued qualities. He is softer and more complex than his friend, although they actually write about the same subjects and both look for ways to expand the area of Russian imagery and rhyme.

David Burliuk, as usual, is not underrepresented in the *First Journal*, and this time he makes an even more consistent attempt to instill avant-garde features in his poetry. He uses all the typographical devices that he did before, but in larger number, and adds a few more, such as printing the predominant sounds (usually consonants) in large letters for emphasis, or printing only part of a word and filling the rest of it with dots. In his "railroad poems" (Burliuk's specialty), he indicates the movement of the train with a snakelike curve in the block of the printed text, thus anticipating some devices of e. e. cummings. Anti-aesthetic themes and imagery are consistently emphasized. The very first poem is full of manifesto-like declarations that "poetry is a worn-out whore" and "beauty is sacrilegious[?] trash." In the others, Burliuk tries to shock his readers by likening his soul to a saloon, by describing a woman giving birth as "opening her belly," and by printing words like "excrement" and "rat" in large type. There is also "a stiletto piercing the guts of a child," and in other poems one can enjoy "smelling the sweaty armpit of a cloud," or an eye that comes out; and the poet likens himself to a human embryo preserved in alcohol after an abortion. Burliuk was unaware that, when he described the train as raising its skirt and making water, he was simply repeating the great eighteenth-century poet Derzhavin (whose Autumn does practically the same thing). The alogical is also stressed in Burliuk's poetry, which is often based on a cataloging of images without semantic or even grammatical connection.

Mayakovsky, as usual, is represented by only a few poems, and they are, predictably, very good; but their placement in this publication deserves attention. Two of his poems open the issue, followed by the work of Shershenevich and Bolshakov. These two poems show some Mezzanine qualities: the no-one-in-this-world-understands-me theme and what can be termed a futurist dandyism.[10] The other two poems by Mayakovsky included in the *First Journal* are placed at the very end of the poetry section, and these are more in tune with the ideals of *A Slap* ("The street is caved in like the nose of a syphilitic," and the poem attacking Tolstoy).

The most original poetic contribution to the *First Journal* belongs, however, to Kamensky. His six poems predictably are based on oriental motifs and on the theme of aviation (in addition to some gypsy motifs) and contain some efforts to *épater les bourgeois* with coarse language. In them he uses typographical devices with more variety and imagination than did Burliuk. Especially interesting is his one "ferro concrete" poem (this genre is described and analyzed later), in which the visual element predominates over all others to such a degree that the poem can hardly be read aloud.

Experiments of this kind find a theoretical foundation in the essay "Poeticheskie nachala" ("Poetic Principles"), written by Nikolai Burliuk with David's collaboration. It is not, strictly speaking, a theoretical work, because whenever Nikolai touches on theoretical issues, he blurs outlines, makes jumps, and seems to be just jotting down personal notes. This essay, however, does emphasize the idea that the qualities of a word vary as a function of the way it is written or printed. Burliuk gives interesting examples. He draws attention to the fact that certain words are more closely tied to being written by hand than others (e.g., a man's name, which so often appears as a signature). He mentions medieval handwritten books and discusses the role that color and other visual aspects play in them. He also speaks about the ancient Alexandrian poets (Apollonius Rhodius, Callimachus) who gave original visual shape to poetic texts. Burliuk deplores the fact that modern poets are unaware of the aesthetic value of mathematical and other signs and quotes Rimbaud's famous sonnet on vowels. He even suggests a poetic meaning of smell as in perfumed love letters and gives an example of his own discovery that cemetery inscriptions on stone "sound" different from those on brass. The rest of the essay is disposed of rather quickly and unsystematically, but Burliuk does try to connect word with myth (and thus is the only futurist to think along these rather symbolistic lines, or to posit mythmaking as a necessary requirement for the creation of new words). He only touches on the problem of accident in poetry, regretting that *lapsus linguae* is in neglect whereas another "child of accident," the rhyme, still reigns supreme. The essay ends with appeals (this time by David Burliuk alone) to create a new alphabet and to cultivate the art of the grammatical mistake.

No less interesting, but less concerned with the problems of the futurist movement as a whole, is Khlebnikov's short dialogue "Razgovor Olega i Kazimira" ("A Conversation between Oleg and Kazimir"), in which the law of the quintuple repetition of a sound is proclaimed for poetry, and the special nature of the first sound in a word is emphasized. Somehow the functioning of these "first sounds" reveals for Khlebnikov the way in which destiny works within language and points the way to the future. It is no accident, Khlebnikov says, that the names of almost all continents begin with the letter *A*, making one think that in the protolanguage *A* denotes dry land. He insists that the ancient Greeks and Romans continue to live on in the present Germans and Russians, as shown by the first consonants in their names. Khlebnikov refuses, however, to take foreign languages into consideration, which leads him to assume that the names of Goethe and Heine begin with the same letter (they do in Russian).

The rest of the critical portion of the *First Journal* consists of polemical writings by Shershenevich—under his own name and pseudonyms—in which he talks back to critics, sometimes for purely personal reasons, and is concerned mainly with going them one better. Of special interest are Nikolai Burliuk's (and Shershenevich's) polemics with Marxists and liberals, whom they accuse of not understanding poetry and of violating the very ideals of freedom that they preach by persecuting futurists, whose only aim is freedom in the sphere of art. Forgetting for a moment that he is still a part of Hylaea, N. Burliuk labels his enemies "Asians," using the term derogatively. He also calls them the worthy descendants of "the spiritual enslavers" of the Russian past such as Belinsky, Pisarev, and Chernyshevsky (i.e., the leading radical literary critics of the nineteenth century whose work is still a cornerstone of Soviet aesthetics).

The central part of the critical section of the magazine is, however, "Pozornyi stolb russkoi kritiki" ("A Pillory of Russian Criticism"), an anthology of negative statements about Russian futurists in the Russian periodicals of 1913. It was compiled with commentary by Livshits and David Burliuk and was intended to appear much earlier as a pamphlet; when it was printed in the *First Journal* it already looked dated, says Livshits in his memoirs. The main value of this collection is precisely in the fact that so much contemporary reaction (otherwise not easily available, since it is scattered in newspapers) is gathered here. The sources are not identified; only the names and pen names of the authors are given. Some of the items were written by well-known journalists of the time (Homunculus, A. Izmailov), but most are the work of obscure reporters who were very often illiterates and ignoramuses and who expressed their indignation at the futurist "outrage," or made fun of futurist poetry, occasionally ineptly parodying it. They accuse futurists of being charlatans, madmen, untalented hacks, literary hooligans, and/or swindlers; sometimes they deny futurists their claim of novelty and point out that similar things were done before them by the Russian decadents. A curious inclusion in this anthology is

Sergei Bobrov, who had earlier criticized the Hylaeans in a Petersburg Ego publication and who was soon to start his own brand of futurism in Moscow. On the whole, the compilers display here little of the thriving on controversy so typical of the Italian futurists; and, in a rather undignified manner, they pathetically complain about the negative attitude exhibited toward them by critics who "persecute everything that is fresh, young, kind, and pure." The last two adjectives are hardly in tune with the trend created by the futurists themselves, especially as shown in Burliuk's own poetry printed in the very same issue of the *First Journal*.

The review portion was written by Shershenevich under a half-dozen pen names and by his friends. The reviews extol Shershenevich himself for his *Extravagant Scent Bottles* (this particular review was written by Yuri Egert, and it contains the best description of Shershenevich's poetry), reasonably praise Bolshakov's *Heart Wearing a Glove*, and devastatingly criticize the Lirika group and all its recent publications[11] (this group was to form Centrifuge in a short while). Even in those reviews where Shershenevich's authorship cannot be identified with certainty, one easily notices the qualities so characteristic of his criticism: excessive caviling and a flaunting of his considerable knowledge of Russian and western European literature. The magazine ends with a report on a public lecture about futurism and with Matyushin's valuable article about the details of the preparation and the stage performance of two futurist works in St. Petersburg in December, 1913.

A second edition of *Dokhlaya luna* ("The Croaked Moon") appeared in the spring of 1914, and deserves special mention here because it was not an exact reprinting of the edition of the year before. Shershenevich was entrusted with editing and publishing it in the absence of Burliuk, and he behaved as ruthlessly as he had with the *First Journal*. Livshits' theoretical essay opens the book as before, but the new editor did not care even to correct the misprints in it. He also relegated Livshits' poems to the middle of the book (in the first edition, they directly followed the essay), and pushed the works of Kruchenykh and Nikolai Burliuk even further back, placing seven of his own poems immediately after the essay. In these poems, as before, Shershenevich juxtaposed the city of skyscrapers (and thus hardly Russian) with the human psyche (there is one poem where the naked human soul is tied

Nikolai Kulbin. Self-portrait. 1914.

Photograph of David Burliuk.
Ca. 1915.

Vasily Kamensky. Drawing by
V. Mayakovsky. 1917.

Velimir Khlebnikov. Portrait by
V. Mayakovsky. 1915.

Photograph of Elena Guro. 1912(?).

Photograph of Elena Guro. 1912(?).

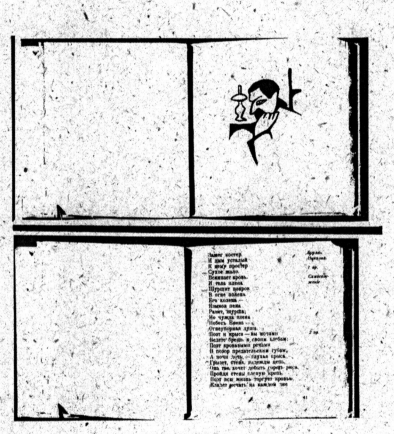

Four pages from *Sadok sudei* (1910), with drawing of Nikolai Burliuk
by Vladimir Burliuk.

Benedict Livshits. Painting by Vladimir Burliuk. 1912.

Members of Hylaea. From left to right: Kruchenykh,
David Burliuk, Mayakovsky, Nikolai Burliuk, Livshits. 1913.

Alexei Kruchenykh.
Drawing by N. Kulbin. 1913.

A page from Kruchenykh's
Pomade (1913).

Photograph of Igor-Severyanin. 1912.

Photograph of the ego-futurist Areopagus. Standing (from left to right): Kryuchkov, Gnedov, Shirokov. Seated: Ignatyev. Early 1913.

РАЗВОРОЧЕНЫЕ ЧЕРЕПА
ЭГО ФУТУРИСТЫ
IX

Душа, причудовъ
полная,
Перевороты
дѣлаетъ:
На бѣломъ ищетъ
черное,
А въ черномъ
видитъ бѣлое.

Constantine Olimpov. Drawing by Ilya Repin on cover of *Shattered Skulls* (1913).

ЗАСАХАРЕ КРЫ

ЭГО-ФУТУРИСТЫ

V

Cover of *Zasakhare kry* (1913). Drawing by Lev Zak.

ВАСИЛИСКЪ ГНѢДОВЪ.

Огнянна свита.

Гриба будик цари чіпіг—
Здвіна на хам ляки,
Коли за гичь будан цікавче
Тарасъ Шерченко будяче скавче—
Гуля ласкавъ стогма регота двірка
Свитила заіла сонкэ.
Байдры шлига шкапік рука
На дьготі сила хмара—
А з зірок поів опару

Перша эго—футурня пісня
на украіньской мові.
Усім набридли Тарас Шевченко.
Та гопашникъ Кропівницькій.
Ніхто ни збреше, що Я свидачій,
Забувъ украйців.

Громовая линія простора
На лосиных спинах башмаки
Расписался молнией по небе.
Сизотѣлый воевода Василиск.

Шекспиръ и Байрон владѣли совмѣстно
80 тысячами словъ—
Геніальнѣйшій Поэтъ Будущаго
Василискъ Гнѣдовъ ежеминутно
владѣетъ 80000000001 квадратныхъ словъ

Тско-литографія   Т-ва „СВѢТЪ".
СПБ . Невскій   проса. д. 136

1913.

Vasilisk Gnedov and a page from *Sky Diggers* (1913).

—но выслушай!..

Н. В. ИГНАТЬЕВЪ.

Слѣдомъ за...

...сердце простужено Подождите вы меня узнаете скорѣй-бы счетъ Падаетъ Какъ въ лифтъ ѣхать или не. Хочу. Отдаться. Доминику; Пишешь пишешь, а денегъ не платятъ Скажите, какая птица и нашимъ и вашимъ Зажгите электричество—„Всецѣло Вашъ" не думаетъ, мнѣ извѣстно онъ открещи порода даетъ себя „Витязь"!!! Витязь WI барышня будьте пожалуйста четыреста Шопенгауэръ въ шагренѣ сорокъ четыре двадцать девять Двадцать десять двадцать одиннадцать двадц.. Witjaz Шit достаточно? Сдачи не надо...

Ivan Ignatyev and a page from *Strike!* (1913).

Месонин Поэзіи

Крематорій Здравомыслія

Cover of *Crematorium of Common Sense* (1913).

Two pages from *The Croaked Moon* (1913), with drawing by David Burliuk.

А. Крученыхъ и В. Хлѣбниковъ

СЛОВО
КАКЪ ТАКОВОЕ

Cover of Khlebnikov and Kruchenykh's *The Word as Such* (1913), with drawing by K. Malevich.

Vladimir Mayakovsky. Portrait by David Burliuk. 1925.

Sample of Matyushin's music in Kruchenykh's opera *Victory over the Sun* (1913).

Marinetti. Drawing by
N. Kulbin. 1914.

Photograph of (from left to right). Mikhail Larionov, Natalya
Goncharova, Ilya Zdanevich. 1913.

Benedict Livshits. Drawing by David Burliuk. 1911.

Kamensky's ferroconcrete poem "Constantinople" (1914).

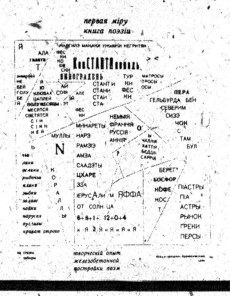

Cover of Kamensky's *Tango with Cows* (1914).

Page from Kruchenykh's *Explodity* (1913).

Sergei Bobrov. Silhouette by E. Kruglikova. 1922(?).

Р

УКОногъ

Nikolai Aseyev. Portrait by David Burliuk. 1920.

Grigory Petnikov. Drawing
by N. Tyrsa. Late 1920's.

Photograph of Bozhidar. 1914.

Photograph of Constantine
Bolshakov. Mid-1920's.

Boris Pasternak. Silhouette
by E. Kruglikova. 1922(?).

Cover of Aksenov's *Picasso and Environs* (1917).
Drawing by A. Ekster.

The dead Velimir Khlebnikov. Drawing by P. Miturich. 1922.

Photograph of Pasternak
and Mayakovsky. 1924.

Photograph of David Burliuk. 1928.

ТЕРЕНТЬЕВ
друг трех глютов

(вариант m 1919)

Page from Kruchenykh's *Universal
War* (1916). Collage entitled
"Battle between Mars and
Scorpio" by Olga Rozanova.

The group "41°"
Drawing by I. Terentyev.

Page from Kruchenykh's
Melancholy in a Robe (1919).

Page from
Zdanevich's *Dünkě*
for Rent (1919).

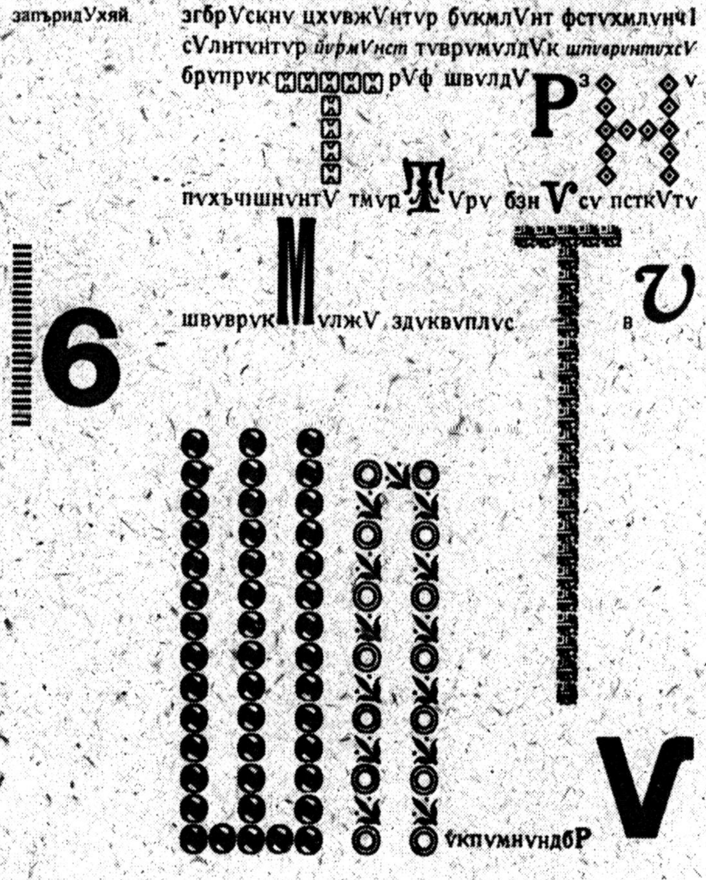

запърид Ухяй.   згбр Vскнv цхvвжVнтvр бvкмлVнт фстvхмлvнч1

сVлнтvнтvр *йvрмVнст* тvврvмvлдV.к *шпvврvнтvхсV*

брvпрvк ◨◨◨◨◨ рVф швvлдV ⬦⬦⬦ v

пvхъчiшнvнтV тмvр ⬛Vрv бзн V сv псткVтv

швvврvк ⬛ vлжV здvквvплvс ⬛ в

6

vкпvмнvндбР

V

Two pages from Zdanevich's

1   иЕ.   иО   пърипупОфка
2   сухЕряя.   грОпса   сипОфка
3   хЕрик.   хвОпс   каралЁк
4   михИрсы.   навОжат   жапиндрОи
5   хихИре.   сквОжа   пърижапиндр°и

                                           трупЁрды
                                           сабОрам

1   иЕ.   иЭ.   иО
2   вЕсика.   шЭсика.   гОпса
3   вЕрик.   шЭрик.   гдОпс.
4   вУрпи.   зашЭриш.   гдАрфа
5   вУрпь.   пшЫрая.   дАст

1   иА
2   нАстика
3   стыкАм. и. и
4   кастыйчЯ
5   стынчЯм

1   Ы.   Ы
2   рЫкаси. вЫкаси
3   рЫкам. бЫкам. и. и
4   рцхОня. бабАги
5   шхОру. вавАк

Ledentu as a Beacon (1923).

Igor Terentyev. Self-portrait. *Ca.* 1928.

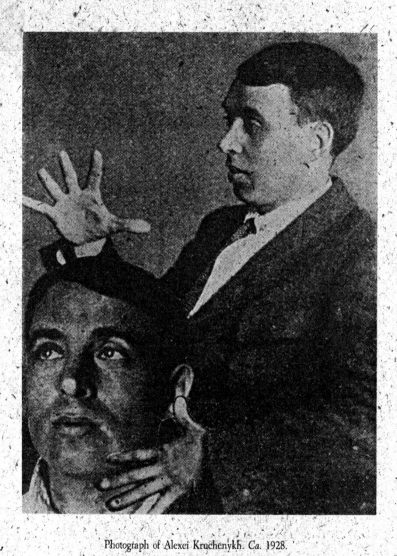

Photograph of Alexei Kruchenykh. Ca. 1928.

Photograph of Vadim Shershenevich. Ca. 1924.

to the tails of cars and dragged about in the early Middle Ages manner of tying people to the tails of horses). Despite all the nasty things said about these poems later by Shershenevich's reluctant allies like Livshits, they are among his best and serve to underscore once again the fact that Russian twentieth-century poetic metaphor and rhyme cannot be studied without taking into consideration not only Shershenevich, but Bolshakov as well (at whose expense Shershenevich showed some modesty, placing his four poems at the very end of the book). Shershenevich not only reshuffled; he also dropped a few works from the first edition to make room for himself. Livshits was especially indignant because Khlebnikov's three works (among them, a whole play) were dropped, and by whom? By the one who only recently was referred to in the manifesto of *Roaring Parnassus* as "a young man without definite occupation." Burliuk was indignant, too, about Khlebnikov; but the real reason for his pique was probably the fact that Shershenevich did not spare him either. He reduced the number of David's contributions by nine, and also dropped one of Nikolai's stories. There was no mention of Hylaea on the cover, nor did the phrase "the only futurists in the world" appear on the title page of the second edition. Unlike the first edition, the second contained two poems by Vasily Kamensky, one being a typical folk-song-like paean to life with many neologisms and sound echoes; and the other, unexpectedly for this onetime antiurbanist, containing electricity, ferroconcrete, X rays, advertisements, sparks from a streetcar, oxygen, the radio, the telegraph, and—this time predictably—aviators.

The purpose of the second *Croaked Moon* was not only to demonstrate a strengthened, "unified" futurist movement in Russia, but also to point with pride to previous achievements: the lists of published books at the end of the collection contain titles of nearly thirty publications issued by five different publishers. There is also an announcement here that David Burliuk, described as "a member of the Paris Academy of Arts" (a most unlikely alliance), is opening a studio in Moscow and accepting students. It was in May of 1914, immediately before the beginning of World War I, that he moved his family from the Hylaean south to the vicinity of Moscow, where he acquired a small estate. It was obviously the time of great expectations; but, as later developments show, the second *Croaked Moon* actually marked the end of the period of flowering of prerevolutionary Russian futurism.

One more product of the flourishing remains to be described: the publication, on a long sheet of paper (it was meant to be a scroll), of seven futurist manifestos under the title *Gramoty i deklaratsii russkikh futuristov* ("Charters and Declarations of Russian Futurists"). This scroll appeared sometime during the first half of 1914 in St. Petersburg and contained four reprints: the manifestos from *A Slap in the Face of Public Taste* and *Sadok sudei II*, Kruchenykh's *Declaration of the Word as Such*, and *We and the West*, written by Livshits and his friends. The remaining pieces were by Kulbin (two manifestos) and Gnedov, the latter at this time making attempts to enter the cubo-futurist group after the disintegration of his ego movement. Judging from the neologistic name of the publishing enterprise, "Svirelga," which also happens to be the title of one of Gnedov's poems, he probably was one of those directly responsible for publishing this scroll.

In his first manifesto,[12] written in short, notelike sentences, Kulbin first stresses the constructive meaning of the activities of the Russian avant-garde and their love for the artistic medium. At the very beginning of poetry he places "the pure word," without an admixture of music, plastic elements, or philosophy, but he foresees a synthesis at the end. Like many futurists of this time, he emphasizes the role of the graphic element and writes about the importance of "the letter," with an admonition not to translate poetry into another language, but rather to transliterate it. His second manifesto, entitled "What Is the Word" and subtitled "The Second Declaration of the Word as Such," again stresses the importance of "the letter," calling it "the flesh of the word," and assigns colors to consonants (the red *R*, the yellow *ZH*, the blue *S*, the green *Z*, the gray *KH*, the yellow-black *G*, and the black *K*). In it Kulbin also says that every vowel has its musical pitch, but all these aspects are secondary when compared with the exclusively "verbal" ones.

Interesting is Vasilisk Gnedov's own manifesto under the title "Glas o soglase i zloglase" ("Manifesto about Consonance and Dissonance"), in which he opens "a new road for thousands of years" in the area of rhyme, which "for thousands of years [*sic*]" had been purely musical in nature. Gnedov proclaims "the rhyme of ideas" which could be a consonance (horseradish–mustard) or a dissonance. A second scroll, devoted to "Free Music," announced at the end of this publication, never materialized.

An account of the activities of Russian futurists during this time would be incomplete without brief mention of their writings on the problems of the arts. David Burliuk, for example, published in 1913 a twenty-page pamphlet, *Galdyashchie "benua" i Novoe Russkoe Natsionalnoe Iskusstvo* ("The Noisy Benois and the New Russian National Art"). This rambling work is written in the form of a dialogue between Burliuk himself and one of the leading artists, art critics, and art historians of that time, Alexander Benois (whose name was spelled by Burliuk with a lowercase *b* to show contempt). Actually, it is no dialogue at all, but rather Burliuk's comments about Benois's criticism of the Russian avant-garde over a period of several years. Quotations (or semiquotations) from Benois are given in smaller print, and in his comments, Burliuk tries to demonstrate that Benois has evolved from an ignorant open foe of the new art to a wolf in sheep's clothing who now hypocritically recognizes it, while actually continuing to hate it. There are, however, a few interesting statements in this booklet. For instance, Burliuk exclaims: "We discovered this new art for them [the conservative art critics] in Western painting. We howled and yelled, expressing our enthusiasm for Cézanne, Gauguin, and Van Gogh, who opened our eyes—not so that we should imitate them, but to the possibility of freedom." Then Burliuk summarizes the lessons Russians have learned from the West in the following way: There is no one definite concept of artistic form and beauty; therefore, things like "good taste" and "good drawing" are lies and despotisms, and the application of content and ideology to art is a crime. Thus, one must negate the old and search for the new. The only recognized authorities are Nature and Self.

As to Mayakovsky, from May to December of 1914, he published, mostly in the Moscow newspaper *Nov*, eleven articles on both poetry and the arts. His ideas may be summarized as follows: Realism has nothing to do with genuine art, and an artist has no right to moralize or reproduce reality in his works. Art is based on free play. With the advent of World War I, Mayakovsky becomes increasingly nationalistic to the point of chauvinism in his articles. He demands that the artists discover the artistic soul of Russia, so that "the bold will of the

East" can be "dictated to the senile West"; he also wants them to create an art of the present, which can be of help to those fighting the war. In his articles on literature, Mayakovsky continues to preach the gospel of the word, proclaiming it the only aim of a poet, who must find the freedom "to create words from other words." This process is also described as "creation of a language for the people of the future." One source of this creation is folk poetry; and, in Mayakovsky's opinion, his fellow futurists, like Khlebnikov and Kruchenykh, do take inspiration from "the native primeval word, from the anonymous Russian song." Partly in contradiction, Mayakovsky continues to extol urbanism ("The nervous life of the cities requires quick, economical, abrupt words"), or suddenly declares: "It's for life that we need words; we don't recognize useless art." This latter statement sounds like an anticipation of the postrevolutionary Mayakovsky in his Lef period, when he sponsored utilitarian art; and, against the background of the rest of his statements on aesthetics, this condemnation of "art for art's sake" looks like an exception. Otherwise, Mayakovsky can be described as an aesthete, though a rugged one. In the most memorable article of the series, "Dva Chekhova" ("The Two Chekhovs"), he clearly raises his voice against "the great ideals of the good" preached in the nineteenth century by the liberal and radical Russian critics and declares content "a matter of indifference" as far as art is concerned. He praises Chekhov for understanding that "it does not matter what one pours into a vase, wine or slop." "An idea does not give birth to words, but the word, to the idea," he continues, and Chekhov's works are nothing but "solutions to verbal problems." On the whole, however, even if Mayakovsky writes his essays in clear, strong, and sometimes almost oratorical prose, he fails as a theoretician of the movement, obviously unable to present a consistent or original system of aesthetics.

To round out the picture, we should report on an attempt of one artists' group to claim leadership in avant-garde poetry, an attempt that again emphasizes the close interrelations between painting and literature. This effort came from Mikhail Larionov, who was first a pioneer of impressionist painting in Russia, then started the neo-primitivist trend, and finally wound up with "rayonism," which was entirely his own creation. Larionov was a fascinating, but difficult, person; and the reader of this book has already observed him as he illustrated Hylaean books, broke with Burliuk, and threatened to pelt the visiting Marinetti with rotten eggs. Like the Hylaeans, Larionov and N. Goncharova began to turn away from the West and to proclaim Russia's artistic independence, based mainly on the icons and on primitive art. Unlike the Hylaeans, however, Larionov preached a militant eclecticism (i.e., recognition of all past and present art styles and their free mixture). In this connection, Larionov was probably the first in Russia to declare that Italian futurism was old hat.

The man who helped Larionov and Goncharova formulate their theories was Ilya Mikhailovich Zdanevich (1894———), the son of a French teacher from Tiflis (Tbilisi), the only poet in the Larionov group, and, in his later development, one of the most dazzling figures of Russian futurism, who has not yet received the attention he deserves. Zdanevich never recognized the Hylaeans, who were for him hopelessly old-fashioned and imitative, and made an exception only for Khlebnikov—with some reservations, however.[13] In 1913, Zdanevich published in Moscow a book, *Nataliya Goncharova [and] Mikhail Larionov,* which is still the best and the most detailed account of the first dozen years of their painting, containing many reproductions and lists of their works. In his preface to the book, Zdanevich (who chose the pseudonym of Eli Eganbyuri, which is partly the result of reading his name as spelled in Russian longhand from a French point of view) gives an interesting survey of Russian art with a touch of neo-Slavophilism. He praises the Tartar yoke in Russia for its beneficent influence on native art, and accuses Peter the Great of practically destroying national tradition and of splitting Russian culture between the city and the country through his reforms. Zdanevich does not condemn Western influences as such, however, and notices that the Western influence on Russia in the field of poetry was, on the whole, good (for him, the climax of nineteenth-century poetry was Tyutchev). In painting, however, the results were disastrous; and the Russian countryside, superior in its culture to the city, could never be properly approached by Russian painters because they lacked the taste and craftsmanship. Awakened by the French artists of the turn of the century, Larionov and Goncharova finally reversed the situation and discovered the true Russian art. At the end of the book there is an announcement of a forthcoming edition of a collection of rayonist poetry, which never appeared.

In July, 1913, the Larionov group published the book *Oslinyi khvost i mishen* ("The Donkey's Tail and the Bull's Eye"), which includes a rayonist manifesto and two essays on art. The book ends with an article signed by S. Khudakov, which represents the group's opinion on literary matters and dismisses "the majority of the litterati who call themselves futurists" as nothing but "renovated decadents." One after another, the author disqualifies Khlebnikov, Kulbin, Mayakovsky, and Kruchenykh (though he does term the latter two "spontaneous and gifted"), and Kruchenykh is accused of borrowing his ideas from Larionov. The ego-futurists and the Mezzanine of Poetry are treated no better. The only poet who is highly praised by S. Khudakov is Anton Lotov, whose book *Rekord* ("Record"), illustrated by Goncharova, is described as having appeared in only forty copies and as being already sold out. It seems impossible to identify S. Khudakov (probably a pseudonym), but one Soviet scholar insists that Lotov was Zdanevich himself.[14] The matter is not helped by the fact that no library in Russia seems to have *Record* on its shelves. At any rate, Lotov is presented as a poet who was once under the strong influence of Marinetti, but has now completely overcome it. The three poems by Lotov given *in toto* in the article resemble Kruchenykh's attempts to write in disjointed letters, syllables, and invented words, or Kamensky's poems that reproduce the sound of oriental languages. One poem is written in consonants alone. Khudakov also says a few complimentary things about the poetry of Constantine Bolshakov, especially his "Esmerami, verdomi . . . ." Then mention is made of the existence of a whole group of young rayonist poets, and three completely unknown names are given with examples of their poetry. In these poems words go like rays in different directions from the basic, horizontally printed sentence;[15] letters of one bigger word form various smaller words; Cyrillic and Latin alphabets are mixed; type of various sizes is used; and words (or syllables) are placed inside squares, triangles, and tilted rectangles. Periods, commas, exclamation points, question marks, arrows, and complex broken lines build their own patterns. Kruchenykh, in his article in *The Three*, accused these poets of plagiarism; and he had a point, though his devices and those of the rayonists do not precisely coincide. The work of the rayonists is essentially more rationalist, abstract, even geometrical, than that of

Kruchenykh. The rayonist poets themselves seem to be the invention of Khudakov (whoever he was).

Zdanevich also assisted Larionov in creating the new aesthetics of *vsechestvo* ("everythingism"), based on the ideas mentioned above; in November, 1913, he delivered a lecture on the subject in Moscow. The very word was his invention. It is hard to say whether this idea (like rayonism) had anything to do with poetry. Some memoirists describe Zdanevich as the only "everythingist" in existence.[16] Otherwise, Zdanevich is credited with the discovery of the now famous Georgian painter of signboards, Niko Pirosmanishvili, and with writing the now unavailable declaration in which an American shoe was proclaimed superior to the *Venus de Milo*. He also published, together with Larionov, a manifesto in the Christmas issue of the popular magazine *Argus* in 1913 under the title "Pochemu my raskrashivaemsya" ("Why We Paint Our Faces"). Painting faces, which was introduced by Larionov before the Hylaeans did it, is presented here as a merging of life and art and of art's invasion of life, based on the synthesis of illustration and pure decoration. Examples of painting on a right and on a left cheek are given (with letters, numbers, and hieroglyphs). Larionov and Goncharova left Russia for France in 1915 and remained there until their deaths in 1964 and 1962, respectively. After 1914 Zdanevich emerged again only in 1918, when he and Kruchenykh organized a *zaum* group in Tiflis, in the Caucasus (see chap. 7).

During what may be called the years of Russian futurism's flowering, several individual books of verse by futurist poets were published, among them *The Sun of the Wolves* by Livshits. The appearance of his only futurist collection was an anachronism, because at the time of its publication this Hamlet of Russian futurism was already leaving the movement. Livshits was a key figure of Russian futurism, and, at the same time, a lonely figure and a brief guest within the group. When Livshits published his first book, *The Flute of Marsyas* (Kiev, 1911), Bryusov ironically wrote in his review[17] that this collection had come ten years too late to attract any attention. Bryusov knew best, of course, because the book is written mostly in Bryusov's own early decadent manner. In the prefatory poem, Apollo's reign is declared to be doomed, with descendants of Marsyas, once defeated by the sun-god, taking over in the cold world of the night that is approaching.

One is further reminded of Bryusov by Livshits' cold eroticism and the witches, lamias, incubi, and the like that populate his poems (a few poems, such as "The Nymphomaniac Rondeau," or "The Somnambular Rondeau" with its "phallus-like chimneys," had to be dropped from the publication, obviously because of the censorship). But Livshits has his own theme, too, which clearly comes to the fore in the central cycle of the book entitled "Pan and Eros," describing a new, transformed world after the death of Pan. Heterosexual love, with its tortures and distortions, is abolished, and the planet is inhabited by hermaphroditic mankind which worships the moon. Livshits glorifies this phase as "the triumph of Eros," where sterility and beauty go hand in hand. Livshits was also a pupil of Rimbaud, and some of his poetry here even sounds as that of Rimbaud might have sounded had he written it in Russian (one critic was later to speak about Russian futurism's "close ties" with Rimbaud).[18] The book ends with translations from Rimbaud, Corbière, and Maurice Rollinat.

For the beginning poet, Livshits displays excellent technique, especially evident in his handling of the rondeau and in his original use of hyperdactylic rhymes; even Bryusov had to admit in his review that the poems were "skillfully made." Another influential critic, Nikolai Gumilev, found Livshits' verse "flexible, dry, and sure" and saw in this book "not only promise, but achievement as well," though he chided the author for such "inartistic themes" as sterility.[19] Livshits was already thinking about a second book to be entitled "Komya" ("Lumps"); but, as we have already seen, he met Burliuk and became a Hylaean. Three years after the publication of The Flute of Marsyas, Volchye solntse ("The Sun of the Wolves") was published in Moscow in 1914, probably the last futurist book with the name of Hylaea on its cover.

The Sun of the Wolves, whose title derives from Corbière's phrase soleil des loups, used in "Paysage mauvais," is Livshits' only book without thematic unity. The very idea of a theme was practically a taboo for Livshits at that time, possessed as he was by the desire to reveal the inner flesh of the word. Still, one discovers the familiar motif of the moon, as well as that of Hylaea (four times). Some poems are love poems; others present reality transfigured as it might be to one under the influence of hashish, for example, the landscape with "the porcelain cherubs, who sway lightly in their sleep, and whose elbows rest on the clouds." It would be wrong to look for obvious or hidden significance in this poetry: meaning comes and goes in these brightly colored, smoothly written combinations of words and images, which seem far away from each other, but still somehow connected.[20] These poems probably belong to the most conscious efforts by a futurist to write nonobjective poetry, carefully constructed according to the methods of avant-garde painting. Livshits was obsessed with "objective criteria," and the subjective method of Rimbaud was no longer acceptable to him. His ambition was to "shift" or dislocate the usual, but without doing violence to the relationships between the compositional elements. He wanted the creation of "a second semantic system that would be a correlative of the first one" (it begins to sound like T. S. Eliot) so that the result would not look like a rebus to be solved (unfortunately, very often it did). Luckily, we have in Livshits' memoirs a detailed description of how he wrote one of his short poems, which, without this explanation, would remain rather obscure. Here is a prose translation of this poem, entitled "Warmth":

> Open the nut belly,
> You, slow-moving executioner of a Bushman:
> Until your death it will not dissolve,
> The foam of your old-woman worries.
>
> From the eternally yellow side
> More embraces are due;
> Give blessings to the foot of a child,
> Which falls into dreams like a sail.
>
> And peacefully prostrating yourself,
> Try not to know that, sinking behind the leaves,
> In the night of the mounds, a peacock tail
> Drills the openings of the eye sockets.

Livshits later wrote:[21]

Approaching such poems [as "Warmth"], I already knew what I was able to transfer into them from the area of the neighboring art [i.e., from painting]: *relationships and mutual functional interdependence of composing elements.* It was rather too general, but still it offered some guidance. Armed with the canon of a shifted construction, I began to work on an *interieur.*

In the upper left corner of the painting, there is a brown chest with one drawer pulled out and a bent female figure rummaging in it. To the right of this, there is the yellow rectangle of a wide-open door leading into a room lit by a lamp. In the lower left corner, there is a nocturnal window with a blizzard raging outside. Such were the elements of *The Warmth,* as anyone could visualize while standing on the threshold of the bedroom [of Burliuk's mother]. One had to shift all this by metaphor, hyperbole, or epithet, without, however, destroying the basic relationship between the elements. The Armenian in a well-known joke, who paints a herring green "so that no one would recognize it" was for me at that time a stern warning. How could I "shift" the picture and not degrade it to the level of a jigsaw puzzle? It was not difficult to imagine the chest of drawers as a Bushman in whose open belly a slow-moving executioner (i.e., a housekeeper looking for something in a drawer) was rummaging. It was "the aberration of the first degree," according to my terminology of that time. It was not difficult to stop the whirling disc of the snowstorm behind the window and to decompose it into the seven colors of the spectrum, making a peacock tail out of it; and this was "the aberration of the second degree." It was much more difficult to push the poles in two opposite directions in order to increase the distance between the elements of warmth and cold (i.e., the yellow rectangle of the door and the dark-blue window, respectively) and not to break the chain, not to destroy the contact.

It was necessary to restrain the play of centrifugal forces by using centripetal ones—by introducing, say, in the window, the image of a nocturnal burial mound with a skull and by counterbalancing it, in the rectangle of the door, with the image of a cradle and the leg of a baby sticking out of it. Thus the whole was kept in the framework of the original composition. So I maneuvered between the Scylla of the Armenian joke and the Charybdis of the symbolic system of Mallarmé.

Livshits complains that such procedures led him finally too far away from sound and in the direction of the silent word. Many poems of the book, however, are heavily, though exquisitely, orchestrated, playing, in the manner of a pun, on identical sound of different roots or word combinations, reminiscent of Khlebnikov or of the later Kuzmin. Words echo each other, epithets are selected for their strangeness, phrases are often nothing but strings of images barely connected in meaning. The way they are put in a line and the way they are "foreshortened" seem to be more important than what they denote, and the consonantal richness of the lines often forms a pleasant contrast to the clearly dissonant rhyme of the type *trúpik–trópik.* But

Livshits never tries to be forceful or antiaesthetic, as did his fellow futurists, and for this reason some critics accuse him of simply parading as a futurist, while actually being an Acmeist.[22] Nothing could be more wrong, because very few futurists went further in loosening traditional poetic semantics than Livshits; but his poems had a pleasant sound, and for many this trait was not to be associated with futurism. Livshits himself praised Khlebnikov for "a discovery of language in its liquid state." He explained:

In this state the words do not yet have a precise, final meaning. Only recently having been phosphenes (the music of the retina!), and now already being fluids (its plastic art!), they change their light shapes while both continually approaching the objects of the "real" world and continually moving away from it. The secret irrational ties between the objects are not the pain of muteness for us anymore, but the joy of the first name giving. On the border of the fourth dimension—the dimension of our times—one can speak only in the language of Khlebnikov.[23]

Though Livshits himself admitted that the way of the "liquid state" was only for Khlebnikov, he was, nevertheless, very skillful in creating "phosphene" poems, as may be seen in many pieces in *The Sun of the Wolves*; thus he was far from being an Acmeist. Livshits himself wrote that Acmeism was unacceptable to him because of its impressionism, its tendency to narrative, and its underestimation of composition in a cubist sense.[24] In 1919, Livshits saw in *The Sun of the Wolves* "samples of a new syntax," but considered it "a book of general tasks rather than of individual achievements." [25]

While refusing to be labeled an Acmeist, Livshits also disliked being called a futurist and resented David Burliuk's accepting this term so easily and without consulting anyone. Although, to keep the party discipline, he wore his black jabot at futurist public appearances and tried to speak as defiantly as anyone, he was too serious to enjoy all this "harmless iconoclasm," as he called it. Proud and intolerant, he was filled with the desire to find and formulate "the merciless truth of the new art," and the naïve joy of his friends that this happened to be their day was "egocentric empirism" for him. He refused to write the text of the manifesto in *A Slap* because the principles of the movement were unclear to him (as they really were to all futurists), and he did not want the theory to be ahead of practice, no matter how much Burliuk wanted to make "a Marinetti" of him. Also, Livshits knew the past too well to want to "throw it overboard," and he considered it hypocritical to debunk Pushkin while keeping his books under the pillows. Among his fellow futurists, he respected only Khlebnikov. There was a "state of mutual Platonic hatred" between him and Guro, who was too unearthly for him. Kruchenykh got on his nerves, though publicly Livshits called him "a poet not without interest." And the first poems of Mayakovsky, in which Burliuk recognized a genius, left Livshits cold. The term futurism "choked him like a collar," and he painfully recognized after the conversation with Marinetti that the top hat he was showing the guest "did not contain the rabbit." Writing the anti-Western manifesto with Yakulov and Lourié was for him the beginning of a withdrawal from the movement; the war accomplished the rest.

In 1914 Livshits was drafted, and was later wounded and sent to his native Kiev to convalesce. While there, he published, in 1922, a slim volume of only nine poems, *Iz topi blat* ("Out of the Swamp"). The title is, of course, a quotation from Pushkin's celebrated poem *The Bronze Horseman*, and this poetry of Livshits' has more than one thing in common with the work of Pushkin. The resemblance lies in Livshits' admiration for the city of St. Petersburg, especially for its architecture, and in the dark mood coming from the awareness of unresolved conflicts inherent in the city. Here Livshits becomes a part of the Russian literary tradition that had given birth to works by Gogol, Dostoevsky, and Biely about St. Petersburg; but he molds tradition to suit his own die. Most poems in the book have specific buildings, squares, or canals as their subjects, and one even examines the grille of the Kazan cathedral; but the all-pervading theme is that of "the Medusa of the swamps" being held in control, but not definitely conquered, by the surrounding stone. Thus *Out of the Swamp* is another of the books by Livshits built around a single theme. The image of the Medusa had been discovered by him in the summer of 1914 during his increasing alienation from futurism. It was then that he saw in St. Petersburg "the untamed element" protesting Emperor Peter's grand mistake, and he recognized in it only "a European mask on the face of the Medusa of swamps." The poems are all written in traditional four-foot iambics (but with a special predilection for only two stresses in a line), sound slightly rhetorical, and resemble the

Russian classical ode. They betray the poet's recent avant-garde experiments only obliquely, but Livshits himself saw in the poems of this book "a deformation of the semantic and emotional aspects of the word—the task that until now has not attracted the attention of Russian poets." [26] It is not, however, conventional poetry. What can be called the Alexandrian element was always typical of Livshits. If in the earlier collections it was mostly noticeable in Livshits' attraction to rare or intricate poetic forms (such as acrostics), here it can be seen in a wealth of historical and artistic allusions.

Livshits' best collection of verse was published in Moscow in 1926 under the title *Patmos*. Practically every poem in this book is a masterpiece. Rooted in the Russian nineteenth-century tradition of philosophical vision (Tyutchev and Baratynsky), these poems are unhurried, dark-colored meditations on the nature of poetry. Livshits, not unlike some Russian symbolists, tries to penetrate into the regions where poetry just begins, or is about to begin, and "where the very root of sound is corroded by eternal darkness"; but he also refuses to go inside the word and accepts "the sweet offense of the three dimensions." This last statement sounds like one more rejection by Livshits of his futurist youth, but in the texture of the poems one can find some traces of futurism, for example, an occasional neologism or a rarely used "nonbeautiful" image. Frequent motifs are those of sleep and dream, of silence and sound; and there is a central feminine image in the *Patmos* verse which takes the shape of the Muse, of Psyche, or of a dancing girl (an alme or Salome). There is a distinct occult atmosphere in this poetry, and also a predilection for alchemic images. For Livshits *Patmos* was the peak, both artistically and spiritually, not just a manifestation of his final poetic maturity, but also an individual realization of a synthesis of the main Russian twentieth-century poetic trends. One suspects inner ties between this poetry and the later and best poetry of Mikhail Kuzmin and Osip Mandelstamm, who were both close friends of Livshits'. All three of them, in addition to specific similarities of poetic texture, themes, and the like, created a poetry that, more than any other, deserves to be called neoclassical[27] because of its combination of simplicity of outline, great complexity of thematic treatment, and allusions often based on Greek mythology and history.

Two years later, Livshits put together all four of his books and, adding many previously unpublished poems to each part, published them under the title of *Krotonskii polden* ("Crotonian Noon," Moscow, 1928). This book, although combining different phases of the poet's development, has a unity of its own in showing the poet's ascent from sculpture (*The Flute of Marsyas*) through painting (*The Sun of the Wolves*) and architecture (*The Medusa of the Swamps*, as he now named his third book) to poetry (*Patmos*). It is an impressive achievement which entitles Livshits to a place of honor in Russian twentieth-century poetry near such poets as Vyacheslav Ivanov, Kuzmin, Mandelstamm, and Khodasevich. There is irony in the fact that neither Livshits' contemporaries nor our own generation has noticed this important poet. *Patmos* was met with silence and so was *Crotonian Noon*. Livshits remains for everybody a secondary futurist, whose poetry is deservedly forgotten, though his memoirs (*The One-and-a-half-eyed Archer*, Moscow, 1933) may be an important historical source. In this book Livshits bitterly calls himself "a literary failure who doesn't know how fame begins."

In the 1920's Livshits evidently made his living by translating, and editing translations of, contemporary French prose (Giraudoux, Duhamel, Pierre Hampe, etc.). His translations of French poetry, which are among the best in Russian literature, were collected in 1934 in the book *Ot romantikov do syurrealistov* ("From the Romanticists to the Surrealists"). An enlarged second edition followed in 1937 under the new title *Frantsuzskie liriki XIX i XX vekov*. Some time later, Livshits became a victim of Stalin's purges and his very name disappeared. In 1940, a scholar[28] who wrote about the history of Russian futurism not only refrained from speaking about Livshits while describing the events in which the latter was directly and actively involved (for instance, his participation with Khlebnikov in writing and distributing the anti-Marinetti leaflet), but also dropped his name from a quotation, where Mayakovsky mentioned him. Now he is rehabilitated, like many similar nonpersons of modern Russian literature, but the circumstances of his death are still unknown. The rediscovery of Livshits' best poetry is unlikely in the foreseeable future: it is completely devoid of what the Soviet critics like to call "progressive features."

If Livshits deserted futurism for good, Khlebnikov deserted it temporarily. As we have seen, he left Hylaea because some of its

THE YEARS OF FLOWERING

members showed tolerance toward Marinetti during the latter's visit.[29] His leaving was something that futurists could hardly admit publicly because Russian futurism without Khlebnikov was like Bolshevism without Lenin, so they continued to publish and praise him. As many as four of Khlebnikov's books were published in 1914, three of them being collections of verse (his first ones). Two were published by Euy (i.e., by Kruchenykh in St. Petersburg): *Ryav!* and *Izbornik stikhov.*

Ryav! ("Roar!") had the subtitle "The Gauntlets, 1908–1914," but despite these defiant words on the cover, the content of the book was rather peaceful, with the poem "Vila i leshii" ("A Vila [a Slavic nymph] and a Wood Goblin") being the central work. This whimsical and highly disorganized description of a flirtatious teenage dryad and an old Slavic satyr is one of Khlebnikov's most representative examples of a primitivistic Slavic idyll. Another, and different, primitivist work is "Mirskontsa" ("Worldbackwards"), whose title is identical with Kruchenykh's earlier edition, but which, otherwise, has nothing in common with that book. This short drama by Khlebnikov begins with a dead man having fled from his own funeral and continues as his life and that of his wife flow by from end to beginning, concluding with a scene showing both in baby carriages with balloons. There is also a dramatic fragment, "Asparukh," about a Bulgarian troop leader of the seventh century and his wars with Greece. The rest of the book is occupied by reprints, in entirety or in fragments, of works previously published in futurist miscellanies. The collection begins and ends with nonliterary material: it opens with a reprint of Khlebnikov's 1908 chauvinistic appeal to the Slavs ("Russian horses know how to trample the streets of Berlin with their hoofs"), and the concluding piece is a short utopian essay about railroads.

Izbornik stikhov ("Selected Poems") is twice as big as *Roar!* and is divided into two parts. The first, which was prepared for printing by Khlebnikov himself, contains poems that had been printed before; the second consists of works (both old and recently written) being published for the first time. Among the poetry of the second part, one finds neologistic pieces, poems reproducing the spirit of ancient Slavic times, verse experimenting with compound rhyme, and poetry about witches. The book concludes with meditations on philological, historical, and even ornithological topics. The theme underlying these meditations is mathematical relations in history as revealed through dates, and Khlebnikov borrowed material to support his theory and enhance this theme from such diverse sources as Manchurian Tatar beliefs and northern Russian dialects.

The most ambitious attempt to present Khlebnikov's poetry was made by David Burliuk in *Tvoreniya 1906–1908* ("Creations, 1906–1908"), on whose cover are the names of both the First Journal of Russian Futurists (as the publishing enterprise) and Hylaea (above the title). Probably never during his lifetime (and even after his death) was Khlebnikov so unrestrainedly extolled as in Burliuk's preface to *Creations*. In it he is called "the father of futurism," "a genius," and "the one who pointed out new ways in poetry," and leading Russian poets are blamed for not having discovered him in time. More lyrical, but no less superlative, is another preface, written by Vasily Kamensky and sandwiched between the beginning and the end of Burliuk's preface. Kamensky points out the national character and importance of Khlebnikov's work and his modern handling of the word. He also hints at the elements of sainthood in Khlebnikov's personality. Khlebnikov is praised for having liberated "the word as such," and toward the end is compared to the verbal ocean on whose coast other futurists stand and only make some use of the waves the tide brings. The dates on the cover are, of course, a part of Burliuk's effort to prove that Russian futurism antedated its Italian counterpart. Actually, many works in the book are definitely of much later origin. On the other hand, while saying that Khlebnikov began to write poetry in 1905, Burliuk did not know that it had happened even earlier (about 1903). Different faces and sizes of type, reminiscent of *The Milk of Mares*, were used to emphasize the heterogeneity and chaotic character of Khlebnikov's work ("He is chaotic because he is a genius," Burliuk says in his preface); and to prove further that Khlebnikov was no "typewriter poet" who carefully preserves his own manuscripts, Burliuk prepared the whole edition with an utmost lack of care. Texts run together, poetic jottings are mixed with finished poems and mere fragments, and, in one instance, we are given the end of a poem whose beginning was printed four years earlier under a different title ("The Crane"). In most of these pieces, Khlebnikov shows his familiar preoccupation with neologisms and primitivist themes. There is also one work written in stylized prose, in which scenes from modern times and from seventeenth-century Russia are interwoven ("Uchilitsa" ["The Co-ed"]).

"Chortik" ("Little Devil") is the longest work in this one-hundred-page-long collection. Burliuk's dating it "1906" is particularly ridiculous because Khlebnikov at that time had not yet moved to St. Petersburg, the setting for this drama. Though it is presented as being satirical of the *Apollon* circle, there is nothing about *Apollon* in this rather overlong play (which may be just the first act of a projected longer drama), and its satire is directed against the modern city that has lost the taste and feeling for fantasy and fable. Satire is aimed even more directly at contemporary education (approximately in the same manner as in Khlebnikov's poem "Malusha's Granddaughter"). Toward the end this theme develops into patriotic meditations on the decline of the true Russian spirit. Though "Little Devil" is hardly one of Khlebnikov's best major works, it is interesting in its mixing of modern city life and pagan mythology. Its characters include the Devil, who is the protagonist of the play, the ancient Russian god Perun, and Hercules and Hera. There is no action but rather a succession of short and long soliloquies, in prose and in poetry. There is even an admixture of choruses. Sometimes it seems to be almost a parody of the second part of Goethe's *Faust*.

Khlebnikov was furious when he saw the way in which his works were presented in *Creations* (as well as in the *First Journal* and in *The Stopper*) and wrote a letter to the editor, which, however, was never mailed. He accused the Burliuk brothers of distorting his texts and of printing things not meant for, and not worthy of, publication without asking his permission. He demanded that publication of *Creations* be stopped and threatened the Burliuks with court action.

Khlebnikov's fourth book was published in St. Petersburg by Matyushin at the end of 1914 (though marked "1915" on the cover) after World War I had already begun. It bore the title *Bitvy 1915–1917 gg.: Novoe uchenie o voine* ("Battles of 1915–1917: A New Teaching about War"). The outbreak of war had obviously inspired Khlebnikov to share some of his historical mathematics with the reader. He presented ample material—whole pages that consist of nothing but columns of dates of historical events from ancient Egypt to modern times. Khlebnikov's conclusion is that the numbers 317 and 365 underline human history, whereas 28 has a connection with personal destinies, separating generations of contrasting philosophies and ways of life. On this basis he tries a few predictions. The booklet starts with a preface written by Kruchenykh who tried to present Khlebnikov's calculations as the essence of futurism: "Only we, now futurists, now Asians, venture to take into our hands the handle of historical numbers and to turn it as if they [the numbers] were a coffee grinder."

By this time and in contradistinction to the actions and attitudes of Livshits and Khlebnikov, Kamensky's desertion was a thing of the past. Now he was back and ready to continue actively and faithfully. The tour across Russia gave him confidence and made him forget past disappointments. He rejoined the group at a time when it definitely had switched from the impressionism of the old days to new, avant-garde techniques; and Kamensky not only welcomed the change, but wanted to proceed even further in this direction. He probably went further than any other Russian futurist in using the graphic aspects of words. Burliuk used different prints and signs in his verse, but his poems were still meant to be read. In Kamensky's ferroconcrete poems, the visual aspects virtually eliminate all others, and it is nearly impossible to read these poems aloud. Although Kamensky himself printed various poems under the heading "ferroconcrete poems," one should draw a line between those that are regular poetic texts, made unusual only by varied and fanciful use of typographical print, and those that are almost purely visual. Kamensky exhibited some of these almost exclusively visual "poems" with Larionov's group in 1914 at the exhibition named "No. 4." [30] Examples of such poems are "Constantinople," his poems about a nightclub, a museum of modern art, a circus, a skating rink, and a bathhouse, and perhaps, in a sense, those about the telephone and the flight of airplanes. For Kamensky, a poem is, in this instance, a square occupying a page and is divided into segments (stanzas) of different shape and size. The title of a poem can, as a rule, be found in the upper central segment, where it is printed larger than other words, but still is not separated from the rest of the poem. The segments are filled with groups of letters (or, less often, with individual letters, numbers, dots, and circles), which are printed in different typefaces; sometimes these letter groupings are words and sometimes they are only parts of actual words. Often these groupings are arranged in columns only one word in width. These columns are sometimes simple lists of words or word fragments, one under the other, and sometimes the result of dropping one letter from the preceding word to form another meaningful word below, a device used by Kamensky more than once.

Though we lack the kind of detailed, firsthand explanation of any of these ferroconcrete poems which Livshits gave us of his "Warmth," there is an article by Andrei Shemshurin in *Strelets* ("Archer," no. 1 [1915]) which presents a partial exegesis of one of them, based on a conversation with Kamensky himself. Shemshurin saw the particular poem with which he is concerned, "Constantinople," in the one-leaf edition, printed on yellow sateen, the main body of the poem forming a square. Above this square was printed "the first book of poetry for the world" and below it were the words, "To be pasted on walls and fences," and Kamensky's favorite slogan, "Poetry is the nuptials of words." The poem is based on Kamensky's impressions of his visit to Constantinople. The part *stanti* in the title is singled out in larger print (he heard that this was a colloquial form of the city's name) and is the basis of a "word column" in which one letter is omitted in each succeeding word. The other words in the segment list what the poet saw in the port, with some of these words starting word columns of their own. Occasionally, words are both divided into syllables and, simultaneously, blended together (e.g., *ko-fe-ski* ["coffee and fezzes"]). The symbols > and < denote ebbs and floods of crowds on the waterfront. In the triangle to the left of the main segment, the mysterious "short *i*" that appears both at the top and at the bottom of the segment is "a strange sound" the poet heard in the port and at first mistook for the cries of sea gulls, but which turned out to be the shouts of begging boys. The words here are mostly Turkish (or so Kamensky said), one of them being a street name. Some signboards consisted of a T-shaped symbol, so one finds the solitary letter *T* in this segment, too. Also there is a column that makes a teasing, rhyme-like sentence: *Enverbei/ ne/bei/golu-be/i* ("Soldier, don't strike the pigeons"). In another segment, impressions from mosques suggest the beaks of herons to Kamensky, and we find both "beaks" and "herons" among the words here, though some of them are used in oblique grammatical cases (usually, Kamensky prefers nominatives) and some of them rhyme. The three strange words at the bottom, the poet claims, are Turkish and denote "various densities of light." Next to this segment is a tiny triangle in which the incomplete words "Hagia Sophia" can be read.

These represent the poet's fleeting thought of the famous church while looking at the mosques. The long rectangle in the lower part of the poem-square consists of a column of italicized words, many of them similar in sound or morphology; this column is an imagined "translation" of a song heard by the poet. He did not understand a word of it, but decided it must have been about donkeys, fishermen, boats, the bay, sea gulls, sails, and so on. Shemshurin does not explain why this column is headed by the Russian soft sign: presumably the song was soft or made the poet feel soft. The next segment has only three elements: the word "mullahs" printed horizontally, the word "corals" placed vertically, but with a slight diagonal slant (a series of dots extends to the right of it), and a large capital N from the Latin alphabet. Shemshurin explains that Kamensky saw on the streets many mullahs, who seemed to him one and the same person met over and over again, so he became superstitious and began to fear for his sea voyage home. His fear of the unknown is represented by N; the corals are a talisman for luck. Another tiny triangle holds only a question mark, symbolizing the poet's perplexity at alien life and foreign words, some of which are printed in a column of the adjacent segment. Several of these words are said to be the names of Russia and other European countries (although actually only Germany and England are there), and they form another column. At the very bottom of the square is a series of added numbers and the chain of words, *I ya i ya* etc. ("and me and me, etc."), both extending from one segment into another, the former representing winning numbers in a game of dice; the latter, the poet wishing himself luck. The O-like symbol means that the temperature in the city fell to zero during the night. Shemshurin leaves unexplained a part of the poem filled with both Russian and Turkish words, some of which are geographical names from beyond the borders of Turkey (Jerusalem, Jaffa), probably indicating the poet's wish to continue his travels.

Kamensky's other ferroconcrete poems do not differ in their structure from "Constantinople." Actually, in spite of their bizarre appearance, they are essentially impressionistic. This typically impressionistic quality is particularly noticeable in the poem having as its subject a gallery of modern paintings.

The poems that are not divided into segments show more variety and imagination than those that are. For instance, the telephone poem

is probably the most diversified futurist poem of the period from a typographical point of view. It consists of onomatopoeia (imitating the
ringing of a telephone), many numbers (the telephone number, the
time of the meeting, dates, numbers of houses and of automobiles),
and a series of street impressions. A funeral procession complete with
mourners, horses, and the hearse—the latter being represented by an
elongated o lying on its side—is very graphically depicted by the different letters in the word "procession." There is also some originality in
Kamensky's poem describing his airplane flight over Warsaw, with
the direction to read it from the bottom to the top. The lines become
shorter and shorter, forming a pyramid and ending in a single letter,
thus representing the pilot's gradual ascent and disappearance from
sight. The lines consist of meaningful sentences, but their beginnings
and endings are sometimes cut off. Diversity of print is also descriptive
—of the crowd at the airport, of the plane shaking before takeoff, and
so on.

In addition to printing his ferroconcrete poems in the *First Journal
of Russian Futurists*, Kamensky included them in two of his books,
both "pentagonal" (i.e., with the upper right corner cut off), printed on
wallpaper with flowers, and illustrated with drawings. Both appeared
in Moscow in 1914. The first one, published in March and illustrated
by David and Vladimir Burliuk, had *Tango s korovami* ("Tango with
Cows") for its title.[31] The letters of the title and the subtitle ("ferroconcrete Poems") are placed on the cover in such an involvel way that
they are scarcely legible. In addition to the poems described or mentioned above, the book contains the title poem "Tango with Cows,"
which is printed in various typefaces, is written in free verse, and combines the familiar futurist practice of using insulting statements to
shock the audience with a heavy pessimism, so uncharacteristic of
Kamensky; in this instance, it is simply an imitation of David Burliuk.
There is also a poem in the book which was allegedly written by
Kamensky when he was only eleven years old.

The other book, *Nagoi sredi odetykh* ("The Naked One among the
Clad"), has a coauthor, Andrei Kravtsov, a doctor whom Kamensky
met during the famous futurist tour through the Russian provinces.
Kravtsov never published anything after this book; nor, it seems, did
he join any futurist groups. His five rhymed contributions slightly resemble Burliuk's verse in that they are essentially conventional, cliché-

ridden poems (in this instance, mostly with erotic themes) in which
Kravtsov tries very hard to appear avant-garde through the use of occasional "daring" imagery ("I dip my nerves into the blood of my
heart") and typographical means. All Kamensky's ferroconcrete poems
in this collection are reprints. Kamensky illustrated *The Naked One*
with circus scenes and portraits of Kravtsov and himself.

After the Revolution, Kamensky published two more ferroconcrete
poems in the miscellany *1918* (Tiflis, 1917).* The Soviet scholar N.
Khardzhiev sees in Kamensky's experiments of this kind "a true parallel to the experiments of Apollinaire [i.e., his "simultaneous" poems]
and of the Italian futurists." [32]

In the complex history of Russian futurism, where the number of
desertions, breaks, and alliances might have exceeded the number of
members in individual groups, there was one person who could be
called a paragon of loyalty and consistency: Kruchenykh. Both the
hesitant Livshits and the hit-or-miss David Burliuk tended toward
extremes, the former being too demanding, and the latter, capable of
cheapening and confusing the movement's aims. And Khlebnikov,
despite his stature, was too much a lone searcher. In any of the futurist
preoccupations, be it the rejection of the past, a fight against literary
rivals, or an investigation of the possibilities of "the word as such" in
its graphic appearance, phonetic flesh, and morphological skeleton,
Alexei Kruchenykh was never behind any of his confreres. And although he had less education, sophistication, and talent than some
of them, he actually became the futurist theoretician by default; it is
perhaps to him that futurism owes its sustained identity and the fact
that it managed to stick to essentials.

During 1913 and 1914, Kruchenykh published under the imprint
"Euy" several books in which he both continued and developed what
he had started in his earlier, mimeographed primitivist editions. In
Kruchenykh's irrepressible fighting spirit, as well as in his successful
evolving of nonobjective techniques out of primitivism, one can see the
"classical" features of Russian futurism.

Vozropshchem ("Let's Grumble," 1913), illustrated by K. Malevich
and O. Rozanova, was, for a change, typographically normal, but practically no punctuation was used and some lines were printed only in
capital letters. The book consists mainly of three longer-than-a-page
pieces, which are poetry, drama, and prose, respectively. The whole

book may be described as an exercise in alogism, bordering (especially in the third piece) on automatic writing. The dramatic fragment is an especially good example and may be called a predecessor of modern dramas of the absurd, in many respects more avant-garde and consistent than its descendants. It begins with a brief parenthetical preface attacking the Moscow Art Theater, "that respectable refuge of triviality." The alogical quality increases throughout the play. At first the words spoken by the characters have some semblance of meaning, but this is constantly violated by the irrelevant intrusion of grammatical incongruities, strange words, or fragments of words. During the soliloquy of the Woman, who seems to be the protagonist, the bed rises into the air, and, later, objects begin to fly around. Toward the end of her monologue, the Reader begins to recite a *zaum* poem, which, according to the directions, must be read fast, in high pitch, and with the voice often dropping and gliding. At this point, the Woman's monologue becomes an unintelligible sequence of words unfinished or not begun, of auxiliary words, alogical neologisms, and actual Russian words (often misspelled or ungrammatically connected) in combination with meaningless syllables, letters, and numbers. The play ends with the actors leaving the stage, and Someone at Ease begins to read Kruchenykh's old *zaum* verse.

Typically for Kruchenykh, *Let's Grumble* contains some criticism and polemics. In a short essay, Kruchenykh comes close to proclaiming Turgenev one of the predecessors of futurism; and in the final, manifesto-like statements, he dismisses the Italian futurists, praises "the Moscow futurists" [i.e., the Hylaeans] for being the first to write in a "free, transrational, and universal language," and contemptuously refuses Severyanin the right to call himself a futurist (Kruchenykh's condemnation came only a few months before an alliance with Severyanin was made).

Let's Grumble, called by one critic an example of "cretinism," [33] met with resistance in other futurist quarters. Shershenevich, in one of his Mezzanine editions, was not so much impatient with Kruchenykh's "soporific verse" and "foul language only slightly softened by literature," as with his calling himself and his friends "futurists," and accused him of acting under false pretenses.[34] In October, 1913, Shershenevich did not know that in February, 1914, he would be an ally of these "pretenders."

Vzorval' ("Explodity"), illustrated by Malevich and Kulbin (who drew Kruchenykh's portrait for this edition), was issued sometime in June, 1913, in St. Petersburg, and in its appearance continued the tradition of Kruchenykh's earlier mimeographed editions. All texts were printed by hand (pencil or rubber stamp) in a haphazard manner on sheets of different size and color. The emphasis here is on "free language," so the first page displays the nonexisting word *belyamato-kiyai* written across the page, and some of the ensuing poems are merely sequences of words, without meaning, but often carefully organized in sound. Some of them sound like Russian children's counting rhymes or folk riddles. Theoretically, *Explodity* is important because it is here that Kruchenykh refers for the first time to the glossolalic manifestations among Russian religious sectarians as predecessors of his own *zaum* (*The Three,* with Kruchenykh's article, appeared about two months later). He quotes a sequence of meaningless words by V. Shishkov, a member of the flagellating Khlysty sect and sees in them "a genuine expression of a tormented soul." For Kruchenykh, such "speaking with tongues" is proof that man resorts to a free, "transrational" language "in important moments." Kruchenykh places his own poems written in *zaum*—one of them consisting of vowels only—after his argument for the existence and use of a transrational language.

The source of Kruchenykh's theories, in this instance, is an article he never mentions: "Religious Ecstasy in Russian Mystical Sectarianism." Written by D. G. Konovalov, it was serialized in *Bogoslovskii Vestnik* ("Theological Herald," 1907–08) and gives many examples of *zaum avant la lettre* produced by sect members in moments of ecstasy. One of them says: "I speak I don't know what and even in languages I don't know." [35] Among examples of such speech are sequences that result from the speaker's dropping one letter from a word to form the next word in the sequence (e.g., *Mikhailo, ikhailo,* etc.), one of the favorite practices of Vasily Kamensky. Konovalov also writes about a German pastor who felt the desire "to possess the gift of tongues." After his articulation apparatus began to work without his will, he recorded what he thought to be Chinese. The examples cited look like what Khlebnikov called "the language of the gods" in his *Zangezi* (1922). Kruchenykh was obviously inspired by this passage from Konovalov's article—whether he had firsthand knowledge of it or not—when he wrote at the end of his essay in *Explodity:* "On April 27, at 3 P.M., I mastered all languages in a momentary flash. Such is a poet of modern times." This statement is followed by poetry written by Kruchenykh allegedly in Japanese, Spanish, and Hebrew. The "Japanese" lines (written, of course, with Russian letters) do sound remotely Japanese to a Russian who does not know the language; the Spanish lines bear no resemblance to Spanish; and Kruchenykh's Hebrew is simply an exercise in pulling the reader's leg: he writes the Russian word *shish* ("fico") in large letters stylized in such a manner that they look Hebrew. It is in this essay, too, that Kruchenykh, probably obliquely influenced by Marinetti, announces: "Out of implacable contempt for women and children, our language will contain only the masculine gender." His application of this principle can be observed in the libretto to the opera *Victory over the Sun.* Kruchenykh did not bother, however, to be consistent in this respect: even the title of this book looks feminine (like the Russian words *pechal', dal',* etc.). Thus, in *Explodity* Kruchenykh continued his theoretical investigation of *zaum* and tried to establish its historical genealogy after he had written, in December, 1912, his first poem in *zaum* ("Dyr bul shchyl"), and had tried, in April, 1913, to give it its first definition in his *Declaration of the Word as Such* (see pp. 130–131).

As was true of *Explodity,* Kruchenykh's other book, *Porosyata* ("Piglets"),[36] was published in two editions. The first appeared in 1913 and was illustrated by K. Malevich. The book had as its coauthor an eleven-year-old girl, Zina V. Thus infantilistic primitivism in its authentic variety is stressed here (cf. Khlebnikov's efforts to print the poetry of a thirteen-year-old girl in *Sadok sudei II* and Kamensky's printing of poems he had written when he was eleven). Zina's contribution consists of three items: an anecdote about a philosopher in the WC, a superbrief story about four pigs in a pocket, and a longer, surrealistic dream in which a bear and a catfish are planted in a garden like trees or bushes. The themes or motifs (WC, garbage, pigs) make one slightly suspicious of Zina's authenticity, since they are so typical of Kruchenykh's own work. The second portion of the book is occupied by Kruchenykh's own poems of various content and structure. Some of them are primitivistic; some, almost impressionistic; others, surrealistic in their alogical, dreamlike quality; one poem is purely abstract and is composed of meaningless, outlandish words, syllables, and consonantal clusters. Another poem, entitled "Russia," is a paean to the piggishness of Kruchenykh's native country; it sounds almost like a parody of Tyutchev's famous poems about the spiritual, holy Russia. In the second edition, Kruchenykh added to these poems a revised version of his notorious pig poem originally published in *Union of Youth* (no. 3). The book ends with a "Miscellany," where the most interesting item is one in which Kruchenykh attacks Pushkin. He calls Pushkin's "Folktale about a She-Bear" (misquoting it, to be sure) the bard's best work because Pushkin really had nothing to do with its composition, but simply imitated Russian folkloric traditions.

Also published in 1913, Kruchenykh's *Chort i rechetvortsy* ("The Devil and Poets") was a sixteen-page pamphlet, a critical essay. It is written in a rather annoying tone, reminiscent of earlier decadents and impressionists. In its contents, however, it is an important example of the futurists' direct literary polemics with the symbolist school and with the Russian literary tradition in general. Russian literature before the futurists is declared to have been devil-obsessed and unduly eschatological. "Like children in a fairy tale, writers lost their way in the three hairs on the devil's head and so never entered the lands of the word as such." Kruchenykh makes a jeering survey of Russian literature from Gogol and Dostoevsky to the symbolists, who took the devil theme and the end of the world (especially as manifested in the theme of St. Petersburg) too seriously, whereas the devil was nothing more than a mere flea. Lermontov is accused of a hyperbolization and a glamorization of this "flea" in his *Demon*, and Leo Tolstoy receives most mocking treatment in the ironic description of his efforts to catch the flea first and then to make peace with it. The arrival of the futurists is portrayed as the end of the devil era in Russian literature. Kruchenykh's own *Half Alive* and *A Game in Hell* are given as examples of a correct approach to the theme, because in them the author does not succumb to the devil. Kruchenykh later reported that he had discussed this essay with Khlebnikov before its publication and that Khlebnikov had made some corrections in the text. There was a second edition of *The Devil and Poets*.

The book entitled *Utinoe gnezdyshko durnykh slov* ("Duck's Nest of Bad Words") was most likely published in 1913.[37] Here Kruchenykh put emphasis on other futurist specialties: an antiaestheticism and a coarseness in content and form. This book was printed in long-hand, mimeographed on sheets of gray cardboard, and illustrated by Olga Rozanova in a style reminiscent of later abstract expressionism. Its preface is a four-line poem:

My impostor-like shouts
Are a wash of profanity.
No preface is needed:
I'm all good, even in my cussing.

Images of nonsense, ugliness, violence, and coarseness pervade the book: stench, an executioner, a plague, cannibalism, hanging nipples, a dead worm, spit, vomit, an idiot, and belching are among them. The vulgar imagery and vocabulary are in harmony with Kruchenykh's cultivation of irregularities in the formal aspects of language: wrong case endings, deliberately incorrect word stresses (*mysléi, nevestý*), heterotonic or heterosyllabic rhymes, and carelessnes in spelling. The central work of the booklet is a long poem under the title "The F Ray," which has only vague outlines of a story and reminds one of Khlebnikov's grim fantasy "The Crane," also about a machine that destroys people.

Kruchenykh's first book of 1914 (January) differs from the others in that both the handwritten texts of the poems and the profuse illustrations by O. Rozanova and N. Kulbin are mimeographed in four colors. The book, entitled in a *zaum* manner *Te li le,* is filled with previously published works, or fragments of them, by Kruchenykh and Khlebnikov (mostly from *Pomade* and *A Slap*). Poems are written on the pages in all possible ways, and individual words or their parts may be printed in different colors. The infantilism of *Piglets* was continued in 1914 by the publication of *Sobstvennye rasskazy i risunki detei** ("Children's Own Stories and Drawings").[38]

Kruchenykh's last book of this period is *Stikhi V. Mayakovskogo* ("Poetry of Mayakovsky"). It is written in a long-winded and confused way, and its lyric commentary on Kruchenykh's fellow futurist poet is not very interesting. Quotations make up half of the book, and Mayakovsky is presented as a boxer (i.e., a poet with heavy fists) and an apache, who combines rudeness with sentimentality and gives expression to the "yearnings of the modern savage." Contemporaneity is proclaimed to be only a stage in the futurist development, and the theme of madness in Mayakovsky's work is explained away as mere frightening tactics: "We know the rays of madness better than Dostoevsky and Nietzsche, but it will never touch us." Mayakovsky is constantly compared with the symbolists, to their disadvantage, and even with Pushkin. In contrast with Bryusov, Mayakovsky is described as the genuine poet of the big city with a deep understanding of the nature of inanimate objects and one who enters the inner life of that city and lives through it, instead of merely contemplating it. With all its shortcomings, Kruchenykh's book is the first book about Mayakovsky and is thus entitled to a place of honor in the now enormous literature on this poet. Unfortunately, present-day Russian students of Mayakovsky too readily ignore this pioneering book, which is also a typical example of futurist criticism, always so partial to fellow futurists, in contrast with symbolist criticism and its efforts to be impartial.

The impact of futurism on Russian literature became noticeable during 1913 and 1914. The resulting literature "around futurism" may be roughly divided into the works by futurist satellites, who established personal contact with individual futurists or with groups but never became regular or active members; the poetry and prose of imitators of futurism; and futurist forgeries and hoaxes, suspected or actually exposed. Some of these hardly deserve to be called literature (much less poetry) and were created by semiliterates, cranks, jokers, or hopeless mediocrities, but a brief account of them is of definite historical interest.

The "greatest" name among the satellites is that of Vadim Bayan (V..Sidorov; d. 1966), who was a host to the Hylaeans and Igor-Severyanin when they toured Crimea and who participated as a poet in their evenings. In 1914 Bayan published an impressive-looking volume in one of the best publishing houses in St. Petersburg under the title *Liricheskii potok: Lirionetty i barkarolly* ("Lyric Torrent: Lirionettas and Barcarollas"). Playing it safe, Bayan not only provided the book with two prefaces, by Severyanin himself and by a then well-known novelist, I. Yasinsky (the latter being simply a well-meaning but essentially patronizing personal letter to the author), but also printed some poems by Fyodor Sologub and Sologub's wife which they had written in Bayan's personal album. At the end of the book there is some music written to two of Bayan's texts. His is a poetry of sweet sounds and glib verse, full of exotic and erotic daydreaming ("a necklace of women"). The greatest influence is, predictably, Severyanin, from whom Bayan takes self-glorification, frequent use of foreign words (sometimes without understanding their meaning), and rare neologisms. Some untoward criticism in the papers gave rise to a leaflet by Bayan in which he called himself "an aristocrat of the spirit" and defiantly dismissed his critics as a "malicious literary mob." [39] After the Revolution, he changed his manner to one of loud and coarse shouts studded with hyperboles, not unlike Mayakovsky's. One essay in a miscellany published by Bayan in the Crimea in 1920 (*Obvaly serdtsa* ["Avalanches of the Heart"]) glorified Severyanin, Mayakovsky, and Bayan as the three all-time giants of futurism; the essay was signed by a completely unknown feminine name, probably Bayan's own pseudonym. [40] Later he switched to writing *chastushka's* for Soviet villages. [41]

Pavel Kokorin was a peasant encouraged by Severyanin in his poetic ventures. From 1909 to 1913 he published in St. Petersburg four books of very mediocre poetry, full of clumsy and illiterate lines, folksy in form and content, but occasionally betraying Severyanin's influence. One of his books was noticed by Bryusov, who even managed to see a "freshness" in it. [42] One of Kokorin's poems appeared in the ego-futurist collection of 1912, *Eagles over the Abyss*. Kokorin's first real attempt to appear "modern" did not come until his fourth book, [43] *Muzyka rifm: Poezopyesy* ("Music of Rhymes: Poesopieces," 1913), whose subtitle is definitely ego-futurist. Despite its poor quality, the book is rather unique in concentrating heavily on two- and one-foot-line poems and on poems filled with internal rhymes. His previously announced plan to publish eight more books of verse never materialized, and nothing was heard of him after 1913.

Like Kokorin, Pavel Korotov was a contributor to one of the ego-futurist miscellanies (*Vsegdai*). He lived in Kharkov, where he published in 1914 a slim book of varied contents, *Predzaly futury: Intuity* ("Anterooms of the Future: Intuittas"). Korotov was an ambitious man of little talent. In his poems he imitates at least four of the leading ego-futurist poets, mixing clumsy neologisms à la Gnedov with Severyanin-like mannerisms. He also tries prose in which impressionism is combined with a grotesque alogism reminiscent of both Ignatyev and Shershenevich. At the end, in an essay answering his critics, he defiantly defends his idea of ego-theater, proposed in *Vsegdai*, and attacks Stanislavsky. Otherwise, his poetry is printed in different type-faces and reveals his attempts to be "arythmic."

Pavel Filonov, on the other hand, followed cubo-futurism in his *Propeven' o prorosli mirovoi* ("A Sermon-Chant about Universal Sprouting"), which he illustrated himself. The book was published in March, 1915, by M. Matyushin in St. Petersburg (then already called Petrograd). The work is a kind of a Slavic cantata or oratorio with the first singer (*zapevala*) and the supporting voice (*podgolosok*) being among the protagonists. The work is in two parts, both based partly on the folk song about Ivan the Steward (Vanka Klyuchnik), and partly on the events of the current war. There is no discernible action in this drama, and the characters deliver one monologue (or aria) after another. The main theme of this obscure work seems to be that life and love will finally sprout through the chaotic debris left after the ravages of war and death. Ivan and the Princess are among the main forces of good, whereas evil is represented by the Germans, the decayed Commendatore (from *Don Giovanni*), and such minor characters as the Police Agent. The play is written in rhythmic prose, or free verse, reminiscent of Russian liturgical chants and works of medieval Russian literature. The language is neologistic, with Khleb-nikov's influence showing, but Filonov remains nonetheless original, mixing his neologisms freely not only with existing Russian words but also with foreign ones. Like Kruchenykh, he uses word fragments. Unlike Khlebnikov, whose neologistic prose or poetry usually has a clear and, more often than not, logical structure, Filonov's sentences often seem not to be sentences at all but rather to be chains of words, distributed as a painter would distribute colors on his canvas. The whole results in utter obscurity, but leaves a strong and haunting impression on the reader, similar to that of Filonov's own paintings. Khlebnikov considered *Sermon-Chant* the best work about the war.

The following half-dozen poets do not seem to have been in any direct personal contact with other futurists and thus present a good example of the impact of futurist ideas, in whatever form these ideas influenced these poets, on the periphery, both qualitative and geo-graphic, of Russian poetry. Practically all the books they wrote, or had their works published in, appeared in 1914, when the futurist movement in Moscow and St. Petersburg had reached its climax; and

these authors, in most instances, vanished from literature after publishing one or two books of verse (some of them might have been
drafted and killed in the war). In most instances, too, it was poetry
of little promise, to put it mildly, and some of the poets may safely
be termed provincial cranks who saw their chance in futurism. Futurism at that time became the talk of the town to such a degree that
a distinguished bibliographer, who listed all these opera under the
heading "Futurist Verse," [44] also included under the same heading
the title *Linyi–Katr Bra 1815 g.*, which seemed to him to be perfect
zaum, but was actually a solid and painstaking scholarly work by a
historian about Napoleon's campaigns in Belgium (*Ligny and Quatre-
Bras in 1815*).

Among futurist imitators in Moscow, there is one Vladimir Vishnyakov, the author of the allegedly posthumous book, *Golybye ugli*
("Blue Coals"), in which decadent themes and motifs (expectation
of, and welcome to, death; heavy eroticism) are sprinkled with ego-
futuristic devices. The subtitle of the book is *Lirizy*. There are a few
neologisms (even Khlebnikovian ones) and foreign words. The poems
are rather weak and almost semiliterate, but Vishnyakov does strike
his own note in a peculiar combination of romantic clichés and prosaic details, especially in the area of sex, which must have sounded
"shameless" in 1914. Afterward at least seven booklets* of Vishnyakov's
patriotic or monarchistic verse appeared, the latest of them dated 1916.

Another futurist follower in Moscow was Vladimir Gorsky, who
made his debut in 1913 with *Chernye lenty* ("Black Ribbons"), which
demonstrated a satisfactory technique for a beginner and the use of
such decadent themes as delirium, suicide, a lunatic asylum, Christ in
a brothel, and city prostitutes. In his second, and last, book of verse,
Tango: Poezy (1914), Gorsky not only walks the ego-futurist road,
but, more specifically, imitates Shershenevich's and Bolshakov's poetry
in imagery and in a preoccupation with original rhyme. His poems
display the typical ego-futurist predilection for foreign words and the
ego-futurist kind of urbanism (elevators, cars, streetcars, skating rinks),
but they also contain "powdered phrases." In one poem, Gorsky expresses the desire to promenade on Kuznetsky completely naked, and
this is, perhaps, the peak of his futurism. He was an ambitious man,
however; and, judging by the announcement at the end of the book,
he thought of starting his own movement of "presentism," both with

a book of poems and with a theoretical treatise, but this ambition was never fulfilled. Critics called Gorsky "Shershenevich's ape," and Shershenevich, they said, was, in turn, Severyanin's ape; and this provoked Shershenevich to some polemics.[45] A book called *Pisanka futurista Sergeya Podgayevskogo* ("Jottings of the Futurist Sergei Podgayevsky")* also appeared in Moscow (and also in 1914). In it Podgayevsky announced that "there are no more fleas and untalented poets," and some critics detected Kruchenykh's influence.[46]

In St. Petersburg, Nikolai Cherkasov published in 1914 the book *V ryady: Poema i poezy* ("Join the Ranks: A Long Poem and Poesas"), printed without the use of some letters (yat, hard signs). One can find here a few futurist traits, such as deliberate prosaisms, sound echoes, onomatopoeia, and neologisms, as well as the theme of the city and an antiaesthetic vocabulary in combination with archaisms; but it is difficult to reduce Cherkasov to any particular brand of futurism or to futurism in general, because in his poetic salad one can find anything. Cherkasov exhibits his lack of formal education in his obviously unconsciously incorrect use of words and stresses and in his calling *terza rima* a triolet, but his poems do possess a degree of wild originality which cultivation would probably have killed. Some poems ("A Praise to the Dash," "Snails," and a few others) are simply unlike anything else in Russian poetry. His next book, *Vyshe! Liremy* ("Excelsior! Lyremas." 1916), published after the author had spent some time in a military hospital because of a war wound, shows much less originality, although in it Cherkasov makes a stronger effort to look like a futurist, entitling a whole portion "Ego." Though one can detect Olimpovian and Severyanin-like traits in some of Cherkasov's verse, he jealously guarded his independence and not only parodied Severyanin's "Pineapples in Champagne," but also made an uncomplimentary allusion to him in his preface. The same year saw the publication of another, and probably the last, book of Cherkasov's "lyremas," *Iskaniya dukha: Liremy i dissony* ("Spiritual Searchings: Lyremas and Dissonas").*

There were at least three examples of futurist imitation in provincial cities. Anatoly Fioletov published in Odessa in 1914 the book *Zelenye agaty: Poezy* ("Green Agates: Poesas"). This "sweet" poetry combines such predecadent and decadent poets as Fofanov and Balmont with Severyanin, and is full of "fairy tales," "dreams," "castles of daydreams," "beauty," and typographical indentations. At times, however, Fioletov remembers what "real" futurism ought to be and writes about electricity, automobiles, concrete, and streetcars in a modern city, and even becomes, very briefly, antiaesthetic, mentioning "the croaked sunset." Ego-futurist self-glorification appeals to Fioletov particularly, and he consistently spells "I" with a capital letter and in the last poem of the book follows Severyanin exactly ("I am Fioletov, I am a prophet").

In Rostov-on-Don, a certain Leonid Sklyarov, after publishing in December, 1913, a book of atrocious, illiterate, and cliché-ridden poetry (and plagiarisms) under the title *Prizraki: Esteticheskie stikhi* ("Phantoms: Aesthetic Poems"), decided a month later to switch to futurism and printed the pamphlet *Otkroveniya yuzhnogo futurista Leonida Sklyarova* ("Revelations of the Southern Futurist Leonid Sklyarov"), which, for the most part, expresses contempt for the crowd and announces the inevitable coming of the reign of futurism. Futurists are, for Sklyarov, the sons of the Sun and Venus, mad geniuses who achieve in this life "a chaotically aesthetic self-indulgence" (one of the few positive statements in this manifesto); and they will build, on the fragments of this existence, a new life "of madness and spirit" and of idleness. The manifesto also contains a demand to open the lunatic asylums and it defends painting on human faces. This half-baked attempt to formulate a theory of futurist anarchism was never put into poetic practice.

Finally, in remote Kerch, also in 1914, the most respectable effort to follow futurism was made by George Shengeli in his first book of verse, *Rozy s kladbishcha* ("Roses from a Cemetery"), subtitled *Poezy*. Like Fioletov, Shengeli follows Balmont as well as Severyanin, and his futurism of rare neologisms and self-glorification is difficult to distinguish from decadence: death, alcohol, opium, witchcraft, necrophilia, and an obsession with precious stones. Shengeli, unlike most of the other poets who are discussed in this chapter, shows good technique and education; and his knowledge of Verlaine, Baudelaire, and Edgar Allan Poe seems to be firsthand. In Kerch, he must have been the center of cultural activities on its most avant-garde front (and certainly no one in Kerch before him—or even after him—dared to proclaim the phallus a vessel of truth).

On the whole, all this poetry, no matter what its merit (and most of it falls under what Russians call "graphomaniac poetry"), demonstrates one interesting fact: despite all the efforts of the Hylaeans, in 1914, futurism for many people meant ego-futurism, which had, ironically, already ceased to exist. Russian ego-futurism can be found in the writings of Ukrainian futurists, too. Although it is not my aim to give here an account of the development of futurism in Ukrainian poetry, it may be pointed out that in the book *Kvero-futurizm*, published in Kiev in 1914 by perhaps the best-known Ukrainian futurist, Mikhail Semenko, there are ego-futuristic features, but he also wrote in the Kruchenykh vein, using fragments of words instead of whole words.

No survey of the impact of futurism on Russian society is complete without taking into consideration futurist forgeries and hoaxes. In some instances, it is difficult to say what is a hoax and what is an honest attempt to write in the futurist manner. It is worth noting, too, that the object of forgery is exclusively cubo- rather than ego-futurism, obviously because the public found the Hylaeans more extreme and harder to swallow. The best known of these literary frauds was *Neofuturizm*, published in 1913 in Kazan. It is a big book of about a hundred pages, and nearly a quarter of it is occupied by a manifesto, "Nemnogim, kotorye poimut nas" ("To the Few Who Will Understand Us"), signed by A. Gribatnikov (the pen name that also appears under some of the poems and drawings in the book). In the manifesto, the "neofuturists" divorce themselves from the rest of the avant-garde ("they are seeking; we have found"), but they do not reject it: Burliuk is accepted; Khlebnikov is called a genius. Many concrete ideas are taken from the Hylaeans (Burliuk's appeal to establish a museum of signboards, for instance), and there are examples of almost verbatim borrowings from Mayakovsky's lectures. The object of the hidden parody both in the manifesto and in the works displayed in the book is not only the Hylaeans, but also the Union of Youth and the Larionov group. The drawings are very crude imitations of primitivism and sometimes of rayonism and cubism. Like the Hylaeans, the neofuturists reject the past—from Leonardo da Vinci to Pushkin, Tschaikovsky (to whom—no doubt deliberately—the *Kreutzer Sonata* is ascribed), and Bryusov. They attack realism and entitle some of their drawings in a highly technical way, just as had Burliuk (example: "A *Leit*-Line Conceived in a Thracian Way"). In the poems,

there is a well-concealed parody of Khlebnikov (neologism, primitivism with hunting themes), and a more obvious one of Kruchenykh
(poems printed in longhand, reproduction of foreign languages, non-
standard forms, je-m'en-fiche–ism). Places of writing are given under
some poems, as well as under some references in the manifesto, to
create the impression that the neofuturists are widely traveled and
well known in Europe through Marinetti-like scandals. There is a
note of anti-Semitism in the fact that some of the names given for
the authors are Jewish, and Jewish features are caricatured in the
portrait drawings of these poets. Some of the futurists were taken in
by neofuturists. Though no one accepted or welcomed them, they
were seriously discussed in the seventh miscellany of Ignatyev, but
Shershenevich dismissed them contemptuously as illiterate and inconsistent pseudo–fellow travelers (he suggested that the third letter
in neofuturists is not needed, which makes them, in Russian, "nonfuturists" [nefuturisty]).[47] The Hylaeans were less gullible: Kruchenykh called neofuturist art "scribbling on a fence by a drunken
shoemaker" and made fun of the serious discussion of them by A.
Chebotarevskaya.[48] Nikolai Burliuk, who was warned of the hoax
in advance, added two pages to his brother's anti-Benois pamphlet
to expose this "provocation."

Also noticed by the "real" futurists was the publication Chempionat
poetov ("Championship of Poets")* by the group of the same name
in St. Petersburg in 1913. Six completely unknown poets participated
in it with poems, some of which make one suspect a parody of the
Hylaeans (one poem is ostensibly written by a gorilla; in another,
"ganglike, freakish [oravourodnye] Hyperboreans" are mentioned).
The book was crowned by a kind of manifesto entitled "A Breach in
the Reader's Head," which is obviously a descendant of the title A
Slap in the Face of Public Taste. In one of his reviews, Shershenevich
called the Championship poets "a few clever mediocrities" who "have
nothing in common with futurism."[49] A little later, probably still in
1913, the same group published another booklet, Vsedur': Rukavitsa
sovremenyu ("Unistupidity: A Gauntlet to the Present"), which contains only two short poems, signed by two names familiar from the
previous edition and characterized by neologisms and word fragments.
They are followed by a rather inarticulate essay in which modernity
is declared at a freezing point and contemptuously called "unistupid-

ity." Even futurism is dismissed as ephemeral. The Championship is described as using the methods of boxing in poetry; but, since the group dismisses even the word, all that remains is matter, whose expression is not necessary.

No doubts exist as to the fact that *Ya: Futur-almanakh vselenskoi samosti* ("Me: Futuro-Miscellany of Universal Selfhood"), published in Saratov in 1914, was a hoax. This book poses as a type of ego-futurism (one poem is even dedicated "with contempt and hate" to Mayakovsky), but it parodies both ego- and cubo-futurism. The manifesto proclaims "psychofuturism," and is written with the hyperbolic self-praise typical of Severyanin and Olimpov. Parody can easily be discerned in the numerous neologisms (both in the manifesto and in the poems) which do not bring about the usual "toned-down semantics" or a partial destruction of meaning, but are simplistic and unnecessary translations from normal Russian into a language of grotesque coined words. Satire is noticeable in the funny names of the participants. The metric structure of the poems is very traditional: the parodists did not think of reproducing the typically futurist breaking-up or complication of conventional meters. In the poems and prose of the book, futurist poetry is reflected in typographical tricks, neologisms, excessive onomatopoeia, omissions of commas, *zaum* words, inconvenient combinations of sounds, and archaic admixtures. One finds word columns (as in Kamensky), monostichs (as in Gnedov), the reverse narrative (as in Khlebnikov and Kruchenykh), and poems shaped like pyramids and diamonds. Quite recently, a Soviet magazine printed brief reminiscences on this matter by the practically unknown E. Efremov[50] as part of the officially sponsored campaign to discredit avant-garde literature in the eyes of the literary youth, who, it is alleged, are inordinately attracted by it. Efremov begins with a conversation between two young men overheard in a streetcar. One of the men has just discovered *Me* and concludes that Saratov used to have "a strong futurist group." Then Efremov tells the real story, claiming to be a firsthand witness. He relates that *Me* was quickly sold out and that a second edition followed. A hundred people came when the public appearance of the group was announced in the papers, and then L. Gumilevsky, one of the Saratov literati, declared that the whole thing was a hoax and that its aim had been to unmask the charlatanry of futurism. Efremov also says that "the Moscow futurists" recognized their Saratov colleagues—a fact not confirmed by any reliable source and extremely unlikely, as could be seen from the previous hoax cases. It was only too obvious that this publication was a forgery. The moral of the Soviet journalist is predictable: Contemporary movements, like abstract art, are based on deception.

A booklet by two unknowns, Lev Markov and Alexander Durov, Jr., *Kabluk futurista: Stihi*[51] ("High Heel of a Futurist: Poems"), with the subtitle written in Latin letters, also has the appearance of a hoax. It was published in Moscow in 1914, and Shershenevich's review[52] said that the book revealed the idea of futurism as a sixth-grade schoolboy might have imagined it. Although writing poetry about pinching heels may be an effort to imitate Kruchenykh and the fact that some words are printed in boldface may remind one of Burliuk, and although the image "the sidewalk of my tormented soul" brings to mind the Mezzanine of Poetry, the book on the whole bears no resemblance to futurism, but is rather the kind of humorous nonsense found in popular weekly magazines of that time.

L. Burov wrote a booklet, *Futuristicheskie stikhi* ("Futurist Poems"), which appeared, of all places, in Yampol (there are at least four towns with this name in the Ukraine) in 1913. The introduction to the book, written in free verse, is a manifesto that attacks the past, complains about the present, and announces the future based on "holy Intuition." The ten poems in the book are all miniatures with huge spaces between the lines. The imagery is absurd, but the content is almost invariably impressionist. Captain Lebyadkin from Dostoevsky's *The Possessed* could have written such poetry, had he been alive between 1910 and 1920. It may be the work of an honest poetic crank, and not a hoax. Here is an example of one of these "futurist poems," which is a worried meditation on the problem of alcoholism:

> Zlaki, zlaki!
> Zreyut draki!
> Paki, paki?
> Layut sobaki.
>
> (Grain, Grain!
> Brawls are ripening!
> Again, again?
> The dogs are barking.)

An obvious hoax is *iglY koMFortA sverkh-futuristA AntonA puP* ("Needles of Comfort by the Superfuturist Anton Bellybutton"), which was published in 1914 in St. Petersburg, by the same publishing house that printed many of Kruchenykh's books of the same period. It might even be the work of the printer who set Kruchenykh's books and who decided to make fun of such poetry. All he could see in Kruchenykh was the latter's frequent antiaestheticism, so the parodist filled his poems with pus, vomit, dung, lice, belching, bedbugs, hiccups, saliva, smelly feet, blackheads, constipation, rectums, and dried cockroaches (which the poet says he likes to chew), but employed clear, conventional meters. In all this poetry, final rather than initial letters of the lines are capitalized, and these letters usually form regular patterns; this capitalization scheme may be ingenious, but one cannot find it in any poetry by a known futurist. The detractors of Kruchenykh, who often refuse him the right to belong to literature, ought to read his books after this parody to realize his achievement.

Another work that must be discussed among the imitations, parodies, and hoaxes is *Vsyas': Pervaya i edinstvennaya futurnaya mirodrama Artamona Popova* ("Allhood: The First and Only Futurous World Drama by Artamon Popov," St. Petersburg, 1914). Unlike Anton Bellybutton, the author of this is a crank with some education, and his work is probably no hoax and can hardly be called "futurist" because this solemn and pretentiously pseudoprofound drama aims rather at mystical symbolism and conscientiously continues the tradition of the second part of Goethe's *Faust*. Popov himself explains in a preface that his work is not futurist, but "futurous" (*futuryi*), which means "opening a road for future mankind." Nevertheless, he follows futurists in his self-glorification, and his language is full of clumsy neologisms, which, however, decrease in number after the first act.

Futurism became one of the favorite topics for humorists, especially in the first months of 1914. For example, S. I. Zak published in Odessa, in 1914, a book of humorous stories. One of these stories, "Futurist ponevole" ("A Futurist in Spite of Himself"), is about a young man who is called a futurist by his friends when he joins them in a restaurant after a date and they notice he has forgotten to remove lipstick from his face. More satirical and direct in its intent is the story "Poslednii futurist" ("The Last Futurist") in a 1914 collection[53] by the popular humorist, O. L. d'Or (I. L. Orsher). The story describes a "utopia" i.e., the rather unglorious and shabby near-future of the futurists, when the public finally tires of them. The protagonist of the story is Kruchenykh, now an insignificant high school teacher, who still remembers the good old days of scandals and publicity when he was "a leader of ego-futurists" [sic] and rejected the Pushkin Prize offered him. Kruchenykh tells about the destinies of his friends: Khlebnikov is writing captions to illustrations for a popular magazine, Mayakovsky has become a respectable citizen and has an office job, and so on. One can find the futurist theme in the verse of Sasha Chernyi, the most popular humorist-poet of the period. Finally, there were some spoofs in drama form. The well-known humorist Arkadii Averchenko wrote a play, "Gore ot futurizma" ("Woe from Futurism," the title alluding to "Woe from Wit," the famous nineteenth-century comedy by Griboyedov). Also in 1914 there came out a parodistic play by I. Zhdarsky, *Kabare futuristov* ("Futurists' Cabaret"), with the subtitle, "A Performance for the Mentally Ill." This caricature aims at both Mayakovsky's tragedy and Kruchenykh's opera, and was obviously written in the wake of the performances. It also parodies Khlebnikov's neologistic prose in the prologue to the opera. Often Zhdarsky simply quotes from both works. In the middle, there is an attempt to "translate" the famous description of the river Dnepr by Gogol into the language of futurist literature.

Critical reaction to Russian futurism was abundant and varied. By May, 1915, a reviewer had written that "there exists an immense literature on futurism." [54] The bulk of these writings was, of course, to be found in the papers, and these are probably the least interesting. "The Pillory of Russian Criticism" in the *First Journal* gave a correct image of it: it was, more often than not, a mixture, or an alternation, of virulent animosity and derision with strong overtones of bad faith. A different picture was presented by the so-called thick journals, which at that time were so indicative of the thinking and the moods of the Russian intelligentsia. These monthlies did try to approach the problem with objectivity and an honest desire to understand, though with varying degrees of success.

Literary criticism in *Russkaya Mysl* ("Russian Thought") was then almost entirely in the hands of the former number one Russian symbolist poet, Valery Bryusov, and he was among the first to pay serious attention to futurism. As seen above, Bryusov first noticed futurism in its ego variety in 1912 and saw in it a "desire to give expression to the soul of modern man, who is a big-city dweller." [55] He also pointed out the difference between the ego-futurist image of the city with its automobiles and boudoirs and the image drawn by Émile Verhaeren, then the most influential urbanist in poetry. Bryusov even delved into futurist imagery and vocabulary. At that time, ego-futurism included only the signatories of "The Tables," and even Ignatyev had not yet become a part of it. When Bryusov wrote about futurism again, in March, 1913 (*Russkaya Mysl*, no. 3), both of its groups were in full bloom. Bryusov was the first to divide Russian futurists into Moscow and Petersburg groups, and made an objective, though cautious, approach toward both their theories and their poetic practices. He found the Muscovites (i.e., the Hylaeans) more specific in their aspirations than the Ego-group, but added that the claims for novelty made by both groups were dubious. In theory, both repeated Marinetti; in practice (and here Bryusov displayed his own erudition), futurists were unaware that their "discoveries could be found not only in Mallarmé, Rimbaud, Poe, and Balmont, but also in Russian eighteenth-century poetry and even in the work of some Latin poets of the third and fourth centuries A.D. The main criticism of Bryusov pursues the following line: Nothing is obligatory in poetry, be it logical content, ties with surrounding reality, or even beauty (on the pages of *Russian Thought*, this statement sounded almost like heresy), except what he calls "expressivity" (i.e., emotional or intellectual impact on the reader), and it is this quality that Bryusov, in general, misses in futuristic works. Bryusov sees, however, originality in the futurists' "verbal expression" (*slovesnoe vyrazhenie*) and finds their "form" more interesting than their content. On the whole, Bryusov's taste proved to be conservative, and he was unable to accept even the best of the Hylaean poetry, though he nodded approvingly at the second-rate Shirokov. While giving futurists much unnecessary advice (e.g., build on tradition; get rid of extremes), Bryusov ends on an optimistic note and sees "some kind of truth" in futurism despite all its shortcomings, thus anticipating by almost three years the well-known appreciation by Gorky. The article concludes with the first bibliography of Russian futurism, which consists of fourteen entries. Five months later, while continuing his survey of contemporary trends in poetry, Bryusov even went so far as to suggest to the young imitators of symbolism (whom he called "eclectics") that they undergo "the healthy influence of futurism"—that they (1) depict contemporary life, and (2) handle the poetic medium in a new manner; but he adds that, to have this "healthy influence," futurism must free itself from "the hands of Khlebnikov, Kruchenykh, and Gnedov, who distort the Russian language." [56]

The article by V. Kranikhfeld in the April issue of the socialist *Sovremennyi Mir*[57] was a direct answer to Bryusov, and shows that the latter's attitude was felt by the intelligentsia to be too friendly and almost pampering. Kranikhfeld explains Bryusov's attitude by establishing family relationships between Bryusov, the father of decadence in Russia, and the futurists, its latest manifestation. In Kranikhfeld's opinion, futurists do not forge a new tongue for poetry, but rather stick out their tongues at society and find a ready audience in the new generation of socially deaf egocentrics.

In July, another critic, A. Redko, devoted to futurism the last part of his survey of contemporary Russian poetic trends, which was printed in the populist *Russkoe Bogatstvo* ("Russian Wealth").[58] In it he connects futurism genealogically with Russian symbolist decadence, but sees its originality in its rejection of beauty. For Redko, futurism shares its important traits (the absurd as a manifestation of freedom, a preoccupation with the "beastlike" subconscious, a striving toward other worlds) with many other modern European trends in art (and Redko considers cubism the expression of a "beastlike" soul), but he praises the futurists for their consistency and their lack of hypocrisy. He is neither hopeful nor panicky, and considers the whole movement to be a passing fancy. This article received qualified praise in Kruchenykh's *Piglets*, despite the fact that Redko had made no distinction between the cubo- and Ego-groups and had called them both ego-futurist (he continued to do so as late as 1915 when neither the cubo nor the ego variety was still in existence).

The article by the Marxist critic V. Lvov-Rogachevsky in *Sovremennik* ("Contemporary")[59] hardly deserves mention, because he merely repeats the clichés of the daily press about futurism and makes many factual errors of his own. It is ironic that this article, perhaps the first mention in the socialist press of Mayakovsky, who was later pro-

claimed in Soviet Russia as the greatest of socialist poets and one of
the all-time greats in world poetry, dismisses him as "a most untalented
poetaster" (*bezdarneishii virsheplët*).

Much more important was the long essay, printed in issue number
22 of *Shipovnik* (1914) and written by Kornei Chukovsky,[60] then a
popular critic. This brilliant piece is based on Chukovsky's lecture,
dating from the end of 1913 (or earlier), which was frequently and
successfully delivered by him in different cities. (He gave it so
often that finally the futurists reproached him, saying that without
them he could not have made his living.) Chukovsky might not have
created, but he securely categorized, the now familiar division of the
Russian futurists into ego and cubo. He displays in this essay his
usual popularizing splendor, his art of good quotation, his heavy
irony, and his relative inability to penetrate deeply into his subject.
He begins with a fine portrayal of Severyanin, but concludes that the
Ego-group only pretends to be futurist, being simply a type of modern
poetic eclecticism, an ephemeral phenomenon, and is miles apart from
the cubo-futurists (Chukovsky's differentiation between these two
branches of futurism later became a cliché of writers for encyclopedias). Still both groups wear the same kind of uniform, adds
Chukovsky, the name of the tailor being Marinetti. The critic was
probably the first nonfuturist who paid any serious attention to *zaum*;
but, as with neologism, he denies futurists the right of priority, since
neologism is typical of little children's language, whereas *zaum* is protolanguage, rather than a language of the future. Thus, once more
futurists are futurists in name only, which is further emphasized by
their predilection for archaic subjects and orientalism. Chukovsky
sees in Russian futurism three aspects: urbanism, primitivism, and
anarchistic rebellion, the latter being the most typically Russian trait.
His final conclusion is that the whole movement should be called
"antifuturism," and he contrasts its poets with his favorite, Walt
Whitman, who, in his opinion, is the real futurist of world literature.
Chukovsky's essay is further strengthened by his attempt to give a
short history of futurism in Russia (which he begins with the publication of Khlebnikov's laughter poem) and by his providing, at the end,
an anthology of futurist poetry with his comments. Later Chukovsky
reprinted this essay in his collection *Litsa i maski* ("Faces and Masks,"

St. Petersburg, 1914) and still later enlarged it into a small book, *Futuristy* ("Futurists," Petrograd, 1922).

In 1914, discussion of futurism in the press continued without slackening. As before, the most important things were said by Bryusov on the pages of *Russkaya Mysl*. In his "Zdravogo smysla tartarary" (roughly, "Common Sense Consigned to Hell"),[61] Bryusov presents a dialogue of five literati in a restaurant after a futurist lecture, one of the participants being "a moderate futurist" of the Shershenevich variety. The dialogue is well written and gives an unusually vivid reflection of the literary arguments of that period. Bryusov not only makes his characters alive dramatically, but also very cleverly scatters his own opinions among them, thus making each one of them express a part of the truth; but he identifies himself most closely with a literary historian, whose summing up is as follows: (1) any poetry is primarily a combination of words, but futurists have cheapened this esoteric truth, which should be kept hidden from laymen; (2) all literary history is an alternation of content-oriented and form-oriented schools, but each time they are repeated with more sophistication, so futurism is a historically legitimate phenomenon, coming after content-oriented symbolism; (3) in its rejection of content, futurism is wrong, because a combination of words cannot exist without being supported by content, which has to be expressed symbolically.

It is interesting that the editor of *Russkaya Mysl* found it necessary to counterbalance the "biased" Bryusov with an article by E. Lundberg, "O Futurizme" ("About Futurism"), in the same March issue. The author of this article calls the futurists "a small group of extravagant innovators" and finds in their poetry aesthetic untidiness, bad taste, clichés, a poverty of imagination, and mercenary motives, especially in the works of the cubo-futurists. In their aesthetic theory, Lundberg sees pretentiousness and ignorance, and he compares futurism to an inept chess player who, nevertheless, might win the first game with an experienced one. He refuses to see any achievements in their practice and prophesies a quick end for them.

Also in March, 1914, A. Redko published in *Russkoe Bogatstvo* his second article on futurism,[62] which, incidentally, begins with his defending himself against the reproaches that he had treated that subject too seriously in his earlier article. He insists that, despite scandalmongering and self-advertising, futurism is a part of modern man's search. Arguing with Bryusov, however, Redko sees in the very appearance of futurism an indication that the previous, symbolist generation failed in its mystical quest. This assertion of symbolism's failure becomes a part of Redko's main argument about the false claims of modernism, revealed in the futurist extremes more clearly than ever before. For this reason, he must present futurists as new mystics seeking supernatural mysteries in the absurd and deluding themselves in this search. And he feels that realism will probably be the winner as a result of this crisis of modernism.

In May, Bryusov published still another article on futurism, "God russkoi poezii" ("A Year of Russian Poetry").[63] At the beginning he describes the past year (from April, 1913, to April, 1914), as the "futurist" year in Russian literature, but his verdict is, on the whole, more severe than before. Perhaps one reason for his being more critical was that Bryusov was hurt by the manifesto printed in Roaring Parnassus. This time he divides futurism into the moderate and the extreme elements. The moderate futurists, represented by the Mezzanine of Poetry, give form to the content they consider new and they follow Marinetti's cult of today in their poetry, though they may disagree with him in their theory. There are important differences in their poetry, too; the Russians refuse to reject the theme of love, stressing "soul" (as befits good Russians), and are far from the technical daring of the Italians. The extreme futurists, on the other hand, among whom Bryusov places not only many Hylaeans, but Gnedov as well, reject Marinetti, "discover" things discovered long ago, or achieve a novelty that has nothing to do with poetry. Pointing out their bad manners, Bryusov denies them the right of opening new roads in art. Referring to his own recent article, Bryusov continues: "Even if there is some kind of truth in the doctrine of 'the word as such,' still the preachers of that doctrine do not see this truth and are unable to reveal it in their poetry." He makes exceptions only for Mayakovsky (for his originality, imagination, and poetic skill) and for Guro. After this, Bryusov bids farewell to the subject of futurism, little knowing that after the Revolution, shortly before his death, he would write one more article on the topic,[64] in which he would acclaim Khlebnikov as a poetic revolutionary and appreciate futurism for its realization of the part played by language in poetry. To conclude, one should also mention three jocular epigrams by Bryusov, dating from 1913 and written as classical elegiac distichs. One of them patronizingly reminds futurists that the idea of "the word as such" was taken by them from him, Bryusov; another one, about a futurist who writes beautiful but unintelligible verse, is probably directed at Livshits; and Bryusov obviously had Kruchenykh in mind in the third when he said to a futurist poet that his nauseating words were unnecessary because one could buy purgatives in any pharmacy.

Of special interest are the two newspaper articles by Baudoin de Courtenay which appeared soon after the publication of Kruchenykh's *Declaration of the Word as Such.*[65] In "Slovo i 'slovo'" ("Word and 'Word'"), Baudoin de Courtenay gives examples of neologisms and *zaum* from Kruchenykh's and Khlebnikov's works and calls them the result of a linguistic and an aesthetic chaos in their creators' heads. He emphasizes the necessity of referents for words; otherwise they are not words. He claims that he himself is able to produce "for hours on end" *zaum* words with various colorings, but it is not speech, nevertheless, only phonetic excrement. In the second article, "K teorii 'slova kak takovogo' i 'bukvy kak takovoi'" ("Toward a Theory of the 'Word as Such' and the 'Letter as Such'"), Baudoin de Courtenay calls Kruchenykh's *Declaration* "a conglomeration of words" and accuses him of an ignorance of elementary linguistic truths when he confuses alphabetical letters with speech sounds. The scholar declares that the theory of the musical pitch of vowels is not new and that the theory of the relationship between colors and consonants is an old fantasy. As to the futurist preoccupation with letters, he says that "letters do not have, and cannot have, any direct relationship to poetry" and refers Kruchenykh to the fact of the existence of oral folk poetry.

Mention should be made of the article by N. Abramovich, "O futurizme v literature" ("On Futurism in Literature"), printed in the magazine *Novaya Zhizn* (no. 5 [1914]). For Abramovich, there is no revolution or even struggle in literature, except on the surface; and after this superficial struggling, the new schools come back to the old truths, which are eternal. He respects Marinetti and his futurism, which is a legitimate offspring of history in Italy; but he considers it not an artistic movement, but rather an ideological trend in modern thought. Russian futurism is for Abramovich a bunch of little boys ("a rumpus room of Russian literature") whose activities are overpublicized by the press. He makes exceptions only for Ivnev, Guro, and Livshits, who are for him real dreamers and searchers. A year later Abramovich made his article a chapter in his very mediocre *Istoriya russkoi poezii* ("History of Russian Poetry," vol. 2, Moscow, 1914)— which is, incidentally, still the only book of its kind in Russia—and substituted the name Kryuchkov for that of Livshits.

One may also note the attempt of the well-known Pushkin scholar N. Lerner to find a predecessor of futurism in Vasily Egoryevsky, a poetic crank of the nineteenth century.[66] Vladislav Khodasevich, who was to become one of the major poets of the twentieth century, also wrote about Russian futurism in 1914 in a survey of Russian poetry of the period.[67] He had words of praise for Severyanin, but refused to see any important talents among the Moscovites. He found only lines "that are not bad" in Mayakovsky, Khlebnikov, and Burliuk.

In 1914 there appeared six books devoted more or less directly to the subject of Russian futurism. Tasteven's *Futurizm* is mentioned above in connection with Marinetti. In it, Tasteven discusses Russian futurists in a haphazard way, calls *zaum* a vulgarization of Mallarmé's ideas, and connects Kruchenykh and Gnedov not only with Mallarmé, but with Plato as well. He mentions the cubo-futurists and the "neofuturists" (treating the latter quite seriously) and calls them "the Bolsheviks of futurism" (in three years Mayakovsky and some of his friends would be glad to hear that, but in 1914 they might have felt ill at ease). Though Tasteven considers the cubo-futurists more radical than Marinetti in their poetic practice, they are for him out of touch both with modernity and with the future.

Much more detailed in its analysis of Russian futurism is the book of a Kievan critic, Alexander Zakrzhevsky, *Rytsari bezumiya (futuristy)* ("The Knights of Madness [Futurists]," Kiev, 1914), which grew out of his lecture in Moscow in December, 1913. After this lecture, Zakrzhevsky was reputed to be a "futurist-lover" and, therefore, appealed to the futurists. As a treatise on the nature of futurism, Zakrzhevsky's book is as unsatisfactory as Tasteven's. Being aware of a stagnation in Russian literature after the crisis of symbolism, but absolutely lacking critical sobriety, the author is ready to welcome futurism as a destructive force, "a golden ray of the future in the swamp of the present," without penetrating very deeply into its theories or practices. It is another version of the "they've got something" accept-

ance of futurism. Wishful thinking alternates with nonsense and inconsistency in Zakrzhevsky's theoretical chapters; nevertheless, the book
is the first historical account of the movement by an outsider, though
it concentrates primarily on Severyanin and ego-futurism, in which
Zakrzhevsky sees "rebellion for rebellion's sake." He discusses at some
length Gnedov, Ignatyev, and Olimpov, as well as the Mezzanine
poets. Among the Hylaeans, however, only Guro and Kruchenykh
attract the critic's attention. Kruchenykh as poet, theoretician, and
critic receives a one-chapter treatment. His *The Devil and Poets* is
praised as "more than a satire" and as "a mine laid under the whole of
Russian literature." Zakrzhevsky even discusses "Championship of
Poets" in a long footnote and is ready to proclaim Ivnev as the greatest
poet of futurism.

The book by N. P. Rozanov, *Ego-futurizm*, published in Vladikavkaz (of all places!) in 1914, is an attempt to inform the public about
the movement on the basis, mainly, of other people's writings in Russian monthlies and to dismiss the futurists, except Severyanin, as
hopeless mediocrities. Unfortunately, Rozanov's book itself is not
only worse than mediocre, but it also teems with factual errors and
sheer illiteracy. Despite his rather specific title, the author treats Russian futurism in its entirety, including Hylaea and the Mezzanine (he
was probably misled by Redko's articles).

There is also the eight-page booklet by K. Morozova (*O Futurizme*
["About Futurism"], 1914), published by a group of students in
Kaunas, Lithuania. It is a rather naïve attempt to tell "in their own
words" about the essence of futurism as "objectively" as possible. The
first part might have been written from notes taken during a lecture
by a futurist or a futurist sympathizer (there is no record, however, of
futurists paying visits to Kaunas at this time). It is followed by a
synopsis of Baudoin de Courtenay's views on futurism, which are
negative, and of those of the distinguished literary historian Semyon
Vengerov, who also tries to be "objective."

The general confusion about futurism was further increased by the
appearance of Dr. E. P. Radin's book *Futurizm i bezumie* ("Futurism and Madness," St. Petersburg, 1914), in which he draws parallels between certain aspects of futurist theory and practice on the one
hand and medical observations of the thought processes and behavior
patterns of the mentally ill on the other. The doctor finds an analogy

in "starting points," in the methods of handling the word (paraphasia, etymologization, etc.), and in artistic forms (Dr. Radin compares pictures produced by madmen, children, and avant-garde painters). Dr. Radin's excursions into literary analysis are inept, and his ability to critically interpret paintings and drawings is limited, to say the least. At the end he is overcome by scientific objectivity and states that there is not enough data to declare the futurists mentally ill, but he warns that theirs is a dangerous road.

Finally, there is the curious book written by a Moscow art patron, Andrei Shemshurin, under the title *Futurizm v stikhakh V. Bryusova* ("Futurism in V. Bryusov's Poetry," 1913). Shemshurin tries to prove the nonsensical point stated in the title with an energy deserving better application; but he makes a few penetrating concomitant observations on futurism, and his understanding of *sdvig* ("shift, dislocation") anticipates what Kruchenykh was to write about it several years later. Shemshurin states that futurist poetry is characterized by alogism and a multiplicity of meaning. This latter quality would be called "ambiguity" today; and, not knowing that it is an ingredient in any poetry, Shemshurin easily "proves" that Bryusov was a futurist by its presence in his works.

Reaction to futurism was not, of course, exhaustively expressed in the articles and books written by more or less professional critics. It would be interesting to know what statements were made about futurism by the leading poets and writers of the time, but there is little material available. Valery Bryusov, as is indicated above, expressed himself more fully than anyone else in this respect. We know Blok's attitude only from his diaries, published posthumously. He reports, for instance, on March 25, 1913, that he read aloud to his family Severyanin's poetry, and adds "I underrated him before. . . . His is a genuine, fresh, childlike talent." "These days," he continues, "futurist disputes, with scandals. I didn't go. The Burliuks, whom I haven't seen yet, scare me away. I am afraid there are more bad manners [khamstvo] here than anything else [in D. Burliuk]. In general, however, futurism may be a more important thing than Acmeism. . . . I suspect that Khlebnikov is significant. E. Guro deserves attention. Burliuk has fists." Later Blok said: "What if we were taught how to *love* Pushkin *in an new way*, not by Bryusov, Shshchegolev, Morozov, and so on, at all [Blok enumerates here the contemporary

Pushkin scholars], but . . . by futurists. They scold him in a new way and he becomes dearer in a new way." [68] Blok also mentioned Khlebnikov and Mayakovsky by name in the first version of his "Zhizn moego priyatelya" ("Life of My Friend"), his cycle poems.

It has been said before that another major symbolist poet, Fyodor Sologub, wrote a welcoming preface to Severyanin's *Goblet Seething with Thunders*. In his poetry of 1913, which was later published in volume 17 of his *Collected Works* under the title "Ocharovaniya zemli" ("Spells of the Earth"), there are several triolets on futurist themes (mostly about futurists who paint their faces). Severyanin's "betrayal" in *Roaring Parnassus* cooled Sologub's enthusiasm for a brief time. In April, 1915,[69] he called all futurists, except Severyanin, "people of small talent," walking "a false road," and he found their works "unreadable and extremely boring."

Leonid Andreyev, one of the most popular authors of the period, at first expressed to an interviewer (probably in 1913) a favorable opinion about futurism and called it "the birth of a great future." [70] In May, 1915, however,[71] he not only expressed his disappointment in another newspaper interview and said that the futurists failed to produce anything of value, but also described himself as disgusted with their antics when so serious a situation as the war existed.

Finally, futurism was condemned in July, 1914, in the newspaper article "Eshche odin shag gryadushchego khama" ("Another Step of the Coming Boor"),[72] written, to be sure, by the famous author Dmitri Merezhkovsky. Merezhkovsky, while not mentioning Russian futurism specifically and mainly arguing with Marinetti, treats the "liberal" defenders of futurism, like Bryusov, with sarcasm for their meek acceptance of the destruction of all values in a most vulgar form. For Merezhkovsky, futurism is insignificant as an aesthetic fact, but ominously important as a life phenomenon, being a first test of the eschatological end of mankind.

At the end of 1913, in Moscow, another futurist group came into existence. Its name was *Tsentrifuga* ("Centrifuge"). This group was a curious and complex phenomenon. It appeared only a few weeks before the first signs of the disintegration of Russian futurism became visible. The death of Ignatyev in St. Petersburg dealt a mortal blow to ego-futurism; Marinetti's visit to Russia brought to the fore serious differences inside the cubo-futurist group; and "the Mezzanine of Poetry was disbanded after a brief existence. One fails to find in Centrifuge the step-by-step development toward a simple and clear goal which can be observed in Hylaea; it does not show the aesthetic unity or clarity of the Mezzanine of Poetry; and there was no ideology behind its writings comparable to that underlying the work of the ego-futurists. Nor did Centrifuge have any of ego-futurism's appeal: no one outside the group was under its influence. On the other hand, there are some points of similarity between Centrifuge and some futurist groups: its strong ties with contemporary avant-garde painting are reminiscent of Hylaea, and it exhibits a European orientation as did the Mezzanine before it. As to ego-futurism, there was hardly a member of that Petersburg circle who did not print his poems in Centrifuge publications. More than that, one finds in these publications the works of quite a few former Mezzanine poets and even of a few Hylaeans, and it is difficult to separate the actual members of the Centrifuge from those who simply were guest contributors to its publications. One gets an impression that practically anybody could enter Centrifuge except its bête noire, Vadim Shershenevich.

Centrifuge had an involved history (and, by futurist standards, a rather long one: the group lasted for about four years), and must be considered if one wants to understand what Russian futurism really was. Boris Pasternak and Nikolai Aseyev were members, and this fact alone makes Centrifuge significant. In the literature about Russian futurism, one often comes across the statement that Centrifuge had strong ties with Russian symbolism. More precisely, it was, in its initial stages, a frankly symbolist group; and it is amusing that even at its beginning it showed some futurist features, whereas later, having entered the futurist mainstream, it retained some remnants of symbolist aesthetics.

There is a scarcity of memoirs dealing with Centrifuge, and most of the information about its prehistory comes from Pasternak's autobiographical writings. It all began about 1907 with a circle that formed around Yulian Pavlovich Anisimov (1889–1940). A general's son and the grandson of the famous folklorist Gilferding, Anisimov both painted and wrote poetry. He even worked with Henri Matisse. He had an excellent education, an appealing personality, and many direct contacts with European cultural life because his ill health forced him to spend his winters abroad. He was probably the first one in Russia to notice Rilke and to begin to translate him. Other contemporary German poets (e.g., Richard Dehmel) were read and translated in Anisimov's circle, which at first received the nonsensical name of *Serdarda*. It was not, however, a literary group, but rather a kind of salon where poets, writers, musicians, and artists met. Pasternak, incidentally, entered the circle as a musician. Sitting at a piano, he improvised musical portraits of those who arrived; poetry was only a "weakness" for him at that time.

Anisimov took part in the well-known symbolist-oriented publishing enterprise Musagetes and was close to another modernist-minded publishing business in Moscow called Halcyon. At Musagetes, a group of young poets formed a circle around the famous symbolist poet Andrei Biely mainly for the purpose of studying verse rhythms. In 1913 Anisimov became the head of a group that split from Musagetes, without breaking with it, and started a short-lived publishing enterprise financed by their pooled resources. Both the group and the enterprise were given the name "Lirika." Anisimov was by that time the author of *Obitel'* ("Monastery"), a book of quiet poetic watercolors elaborating the theme of Russian piety. Blok, Tyutchev, and especially Rilke (who was represented by six translations) can be felt, in various ways, in this poetry, which is simple, melodious, and monotonous. An atmosphere of sad, sighing fatigue permeates the book, which is full of religious symbolism and vocabulary. Also in 1913, Anisimov published his translation of Rilke's *Das Stunden-Buch.*[1]

The group's first and only miscellany, *Lirika,* appeared in the first half of 1913. Eight young poets each printed five poems in the book. The symbolist orientation of the group was clearly suggested at the beginning with a quotation taken from Vyacheslav Ivanov. There are few bright stars among the poets, and their poems in this publication differ little in quality, mood, or theme from those of Anisimov. These poets were Vera Stanevich (Anisimov's wife), Semyon Rubanovich (who tranlsated Verlaine), and Sergei Rayevsky (who wrote under his real name, Durylin, among other things, a book about Richard Wagner in Russia). There was also Alexei Sidorov, a slightly more varied, though hardly less eclectic or more exciting, poet.[2] There are, however, three poets in the book who attract attention even in this small selection. Sergei Bobrov, for example, shows a syntactic and rhythmic variety bordering on virtuosity in his epigraph-studded, tight, and lightly moving "metapoetry," which betrays a careful study of the poets of Pushkin's time. One of the poems, "Zavet" ("Legacy"), is clearly a poetic manifesto of this neosymbolist group ("Blessed symbolism has revealed coasts and woods for us"). Even more arresting is Pasternak's contribution, which shows both the traits of his poetry which are by now familiar and those that are unfamiliar to the average Pasternak reader of our days. Similes built on everyday details are unmistakably Pasternakian and so are his élan and catachreses. In metrics, however, he betrays Bobrov's influence. Rilke is also present in Pasternak's verse; unlike his friends, Pasternak does not imitate, but rather approaches Rilke in some of his imagery, especially when he pictures inanimate objects as being alive. The third poet is Nikolai Aseyev, who was later to make so prominent a name for himself in Soviet poetry. His interesting, but clumsy, poetry in *Lirika* hardly hints at his subsequent development. It is amusing to see this poet, who was later so strongly Slavic-oriented, being here so much under German influence. He seems to live in the world of E. T. A. Hoffmann, and even his ballads remind one of Uhland, rather than of A. K. Tolstoy, the Russian balladeer.

Bobrov, Pasternak, and Aseyev were the only Lirika poets who individually published books of verse during 1913 and 1914. The most mature among these books is Bobrov's *Vertogradari nad lozami* ("Gardeners over the Vines") which appeared in May, 1913. Sergei Pavlovich Bobrov (1899———) entered Lirika with the reputation of "a Russian Rimbaud"[3] and thus, in a way, represented a French current in this largely German-oriented group. In a few months he was to publish what was perhaps the first Russian article about Rimbaud,[4] which showed a thorough knowledge of Paterne Berrichon's books on the subject, as well as of Rimbaud's own letters. He also showed that he had attempted to translate the French poet: some epigraphs are in poetic Russian, and Bobrov later planned publication of Rimbaud's poems, *Les Illuminations,* and *Une Saison en enfer,* but this idea never materialized. The article also shows Bobrov's acquaintance with other poets of French symbolism. He writes about the "pungent and incorrect language of Mallarmé," mentions characteristics of Corbière, Laforgue, and Charles Cros, and finds examples of Rimbaud's influence in Russia (Bryusov, Annensky).

Gardeners over the Vines is an impressive achievement for a beginning poet. Though there is little spontaneity in Bobrov's verse, it grows on one with repeated readings. Here is a poet who enters literature with complete technical equipment and a knowledge of the Russian poetic heritage, both old and immediate. The very first poem, a programmatic ghazel about symbolic gardeners, not only imitates, but also rivals, such a past master of this form as Vyacheslav Ivanov. Bobrov stuns the reader with his amazing literary erudition, which he generously displays in numerous epigraphs (nearly always in the original) to his poems. One can find here Lerberghe, Aloysius Bertrand, Corbière, Baudelaire, Rimbaud, Villon, Nerval, Novalis, Hoffmann, Fet, Baratynsky, Pushkin, Yazykov, V. Ivanov, and Konevskoi, to give only an incomplete list. This book can be called symbolist in more than one respect. First, it is full of imitations, often clever ones, of the senior Russian symbolists. "Postsymbolist," however, would be a better word. Bobrov is a pupil of Bryusov, Ivanov, and Biely who does not rebel against his teachers, who learned from them everything he could technically, but who cannot conceal his indifference toward their metaphysics. For this reason, Bobrov feels more attracted to Ivan Konevskoi (1877–1901), the "unkempt" symbolist pioneer who died early, and to Mikhail Kuzmin, the symbolist maverick whose lightness and transparency are occasionally duplicated by Bobrov in his verse.

Bobrov's preoccupation with metrics is definitely of symbolist origin. After having been trained in the Musagetes circle by Biely himself, he developed into a theoretician whose name now cannot be ignored by any student of Russian metrics. In his poetry, Bobrov delights in practicing the unusual or the nonallowed metric effects (especially, $\smile\smile\smile\smile'$ in iambic tetrameter when the first word has more than one syllable). He also practices metrical substitution, fills his lines with as many "pyrrhics" as possible, likes to place words in such a way that theses are stressed, and makes close neighbors of lines and stanzas of different metric structure. Poetics even invades imagery in Bobrov's poetry, and one finds poems in which "catachresis," "alliteration," "oxymoron," and "anacoluthon" are the real heroes.

If a part (and particularly the first portion) of *Gardeners* is written in the manner of Russian symbolism, if not of early decadence, in the rest of the book Bobrov appears as a pupil of the poets of Pushkin's time and a sincere admirer of that period. He strives to approach its classical simplicity and borrows lexically from such poets as Baratynsky. Some of his metrical mannerisms are simply a development of Tyutchev's (metrical) "slips." Bobrov's greatest object of veneration among these poets is, however, Nikolai Yazykov, probably the most neglected first-rate poet of Pushkin's time. It is interesting that futurists (let us remember Shershenevich in addition to Bobrov) tried to establish a cult of Yazykov. Bobrov is attracted by even less well-known figures of Pushkin's period ("The deceptive destiny of [Vasily or Fyodor?] Tumansky and [Mikhail] de la Rue fills me with joy"), and his habit of dedicating so many of his poems to his friends and contemporaries also reminds us of the early nineteenth century.

Bobrov cannot help being a theoretician. There is a section of notes in *Gardeners* in which one finds a whole treatise written by Bobrov in an attempt to justify his erratic metrical procedures by a comparison with other, mostly unconvincing, examples from Russian poetry. He is apt to draw the reader's attention to the fact that he used a "tribrachoidal" pause in one line or that some of his poems consist of one sentence only, or that the sonnet on page so-and-so is not a sonnet at all. He explains in which of his poems he applied the method of Aloysius Bertrand or imitated Dante Gabriel Rossetti.

Finally, in *Gardeners* there is an essay on book illustration. Printing was a hobby with Bobrov, and he always tried to make his books typographically arresting and appealing. Often he illustrated his books himself and he designed the covers for all Centrifuge publications. In this instance, the illustrations are by Natalya Goncharova. The quality of her two-color, semicubist designs gives Bobrov's essentially conservative book an avant-garde appearance. The essay, written partly in an unpleasantly conversational manner reminiscent of Dostoevsky's "underground man," praises Goncharova's drawings as a new, and the only valid, type of book illustration, which interprets the poetry in its own, nonliterary way. Probably without knowing that he would apply this term to himself in a matter of a few months, Bobrov uses the word "futurism" while discussing Goncharova's work. The book was considered partly futuristic by at least one provincial reviewer.[5]

Bobrov's aesthetic theories are not so easy to deduce from his early —or, for that matter, even his late—writings. Most of these writings present an eclectic conglomeration gleaned from his tremendous reading. The heterogeneity and fuzziness of his ideas are only partly covered by a smoke screen of aggressiveness and arrogance which he displays before the intimidated reader. On the other hand, he was doubtless a man of intellectual ability who had few rivals within the framework of Russian futurism.

As early as the beginning of 1913, Bobrov printed in *Trudy i dni* ("Works and Days") an ambitious essay, "O liricheskoi teme" ("Concerning the Lyric Theme").[6] This abstruse treatise was an attempt to create a new poetics and bordered on being a manifesto. Clearly Bobrov's goal was a "revaluation of all values," but he was reappraising within the context of Russian symbolism—and his reappraisal was printed in a first-class symbolist journal. Here, practically all traditional tenets of Western or domestic symbolism undergo Bobrov's reconsideration, deepening, correction, or direct assault: music as substance of poetry, word magic, *correspondances,* relation of symbol and allegory, and V. Ivanov's theories of ascending and descending symbolism. Bobrov analyzes the concept of *lirika,* which for him is not a kind of poetry, in addition to epic and drama, but a "special element of poetry," its "principal means and source of creation," its third indispensable hypostasis in addition to content and form. There is a "break" in the middle of the creative process, caused by a "lyric activity of the soul," which gives birth to poetry, or else poetry degenerates into mere "gestures" of either content or form. Even talented poets may build their poetry on such "gestures," but Bobrov resolutely rejects it if it lacks the "lyric quality," which he tries to define and approach (or, rather, demonstrate) in eighteen different ways. Refusing to follow the example of the famous symbolist leaders, refusing either to fall victim to an old-fashioned aestheticism (Bryusov), or to equate poetry with religion (V. Ivanov), or to become mired in the swamps of preliminary metaphysical consideration (Biely), Bobrov is on his way to what we now call "structural analysis" in his attempt to define poetry. He never achieves his aim, mainly because he becomes bogged down in swamps of his own. In addition to poetics, he draws from mathematics, chemistry, and even from psychophysics. He takes illustrative material from a dozen sources, extending from the Veda to the medieval Belgian mystic, Jan van Ruysbroeck; but he often fails to say what he illustrates as he becomes intoxicated with names: the familiar Bertrand, Rimbaud, Nerval, Novalis, Lerberghe, Yazykov, Tyutchev, Baratynsky, Konevskoi, and Hoffmann. These emerge as his standards of excellence. Finally, the reader is annoyed, realizing that the author has failed to define the quality he extols so much and that he has used indiscriminately dozens of terms without making them clear. For instance, he takes it more or less for granted that everybody understands what he means by "symbol" (large and small), "symbolics," "symbolization," and "symbolism." Actually, what Bobrov tries to say here amounts to the simple "a poem should not mean, but be"; but he says it in many unnecessary words and in at least four different languages. Still, "Concerning the Lyric Theme" cannot be dismissed easily. It remained Bobrov's credo even after he switched to futurism, and many details of this essay are the best clues to what he wanted to achieve in his poetry. Indirectly, some of Bobrov's ideas affected the early work of Aseyev and Pasternak, who began in some respects as his pupils. As an example, the title of one of Pasternak's poems, "Liricheskii prostor" ("Lyrical Expanse"), is a quotation from Bobrov's essay.

When several months later Bobrov wrote a preface to Aseyev's *Nochnaya fleita* ("Nocturnal Flute"), he had moved further away from symbolism. While repeating the well-known commonplace of symbolist criticism that any real art is symbolist, he credits Russian symbolism only with establishing the idea of unity between form and content. "Universal symbolism cannot dry up, but the symbolism of yesterday is drying up before our eyes in the latest books of its leaders." Ironically repeating the symbolist slogans, Bobrov continues: " 'Art is not only art!'—and look—well, now reap what you have sown—nobody knows now what art is, nobody believes in it." For himself and his friends, Bobrov sees the following way out: "To understand the meaning of the internal study of structures [*skhemy*] of lyrical movements in a poem and then to give oneself to the pure lyrical element [*lirika*] while tirelessly developing the essential maximal metaphorism." [7] Historically speaking, adds Bobrov, this solution means "back to Yazykov." Here he is only half a step from naming his art something else, and the name was to be "futurism."

The first published volume of poetry by Nikolai Nikolayevich Aseyev (1889–1963), then a student of the School of Commerce in Moscow who had already published a few conventional poems,[8] was *Nocturnal Flute*, a slim volume of only eighteen poems which makes a curious impression. It is his least Aseyev-like book, because it is too Western and too literary, and, paradoxically, the most futuristic book of the Lirika group. As in his poems printed in *Lirika* (none of which was included in this book), there is much of Hoffmann and a Hoffmannesque mood in *Nocturnal Flute*, which must be partly the result of Bobrov's influence. Even more of Bobrov can be seen in the epigraph (in French!) from Bertrand, in the numerous dedications to his Lirika colleagues, and in his attempts at a display of erudition, something that he hardly possessed at that time. Certain motifs point in the direction of Pasternak, from whom the young Aseyev seems to have borrowed his sunrises and sunsets. *Nocturnal Flute*, in short, is an imitative and immature book, whose author sometimes desperately tries to hide banality under the cloak of obscurity. Nevertheless, even at that time Aseyev had a considerable technique. His metrics are varied and his neologisms more daring than those of Bobrov. Occasionally, one can even discern qualities or trademarks of the later and familiar Aseyev, such as his predilection for song and for archaic words.

The poetry in *Nocturnal Flute* can be called futuristic in the sense that it employs the theme of the big city, which, for the most part, takes on a fantastic shape so that the Hoffmannesque element verges on expressionist urbanism. In one poem, a man comes out of a shop window; in another, a night ride in a car is presented hyperbolically. The last poem in the book includes the image of a "midnight flute" that begins "a crazy song," thus explaining the book's title. Motifs of madness and of the sky seem to be Aseyev's favorites. Two features appear with some consistency and give Aseyev's poetry an air of originality: the use of families of images throughout a poem, and a predilection for pairs of alliterated words. The book concludes with a postscript written in lyric prose and preceded by two lengthy epigraphs from Hoffmann, and in it the theme of the big city is stressed once more. The ideas of Bobrov, who wrote a preface to the book, are echoed by Aseyev in the postscript when he mentions "The Lady of the Big Metaphor."

As could have been expected, the most striking and genuinely novel first book by a member of Lirika was that of Boris Leonidovich Pasternak (1890–1960). It is strange that this book did not attract attention when it appeared and even more so that it has been habitually dismissed or ignored by all subsequent critics of Pasternak. He himself later regretted that he had published it.[9] It is true, of course, that the twenty-three-year-old poet shows here a certain lack of precision resulting from his inexperience, but otherwise there is nothing to be ashamed of. Talent and originality of the first rank are visible in practically every poem. The book, entitled *Bliznets v tuchakh* ("Twin in the Clouds") and containing a preface by Aseyev,[10] appeared at the very beginning of 1914. It consisted of poems written during the summer vacation in 1913 after Pasternak graduated from the university. He was at that time the young Pasternak who was "poisoned by modern literature" and "crazy about Biely." [11] He had delivered in the Musagetes circle a paper ("Symbolism and Immortality") in which he asserted the symbolic nature of any art. The title of his first book, as he says, reflects "the symbolist vogue for cosmological obscurities" (the twin motif undergoes a series of astronomical, astrological, and other transformations in the poems of the book). But even at that early time, Pasternak aimed at some kind of antiromantic symbolism and already adhered to his favorite idea of subjectivity in any art.

Probably the most noticeable feature of *Twin in the Clouds* is a hypertrophy of imagery, which might reflect an eager following of Bobrov's ideas ("the big metaphor"), but it is also a spectacle familiar from Pasternak's later poetry with tropes crowding and jostling one another in a seemingly haphazard way. Then there is the thrice familiar Pasternakian merger of nature and self, colored by his unmistakable exuberance and his proclivity for making inanimate objects come to life ("the profile of midnight"). Abrupt transitions of meaning, resulting in ellipsis, can also be found in the poetry of *Twin in the Clouds,* as can many technical devices that Pasternak was to use in his poems for many years. For instance, he does not go far away in his search for similes and takes them from his immediate surroundings ("my eye is like a cornered weathercock"). He is apt to select words for their sound rather than for their meaning (despite the statements of his late years that he was always content oriented).[12] He likes the unusual, though not necessarily tricky, rhyme (*verv'– verf'*). Even metrically, he displays little details that were to remain with him to the end of his days—though Bobrov's influence is here clearly noticeable in lines based on a metrical philosophy of the fewer accents the better and in the use of choriambs.

Pasternak relishes words rarely, if ever, used in poetry before him, and he places them ostentatiously in rhyming positions; but, on the whole, lexical and metric features are less distinctive than metaphorical wealth in the early Pasternak. Often his poetry is an absolute reign of metaphor, and only gradually, from context, does it become clear that "the chorus" in the poem of the same title is not a chorus, but morning.

Development is everything, and this is probably the imprint of Pasternak the musician. Many of Pasternak's poems are built according to the same pattern. A theme (often in metaphorical garb) is given; then it is developed in a double way: (1) syntactically, that is, sentences (or, often, it is one complex, poem-long sentence, in Bobrov's fashion) extend and ramify so that the reader begins to see nothing but moving and branching-out clauses whose lexical filling seems to be secondary, if not irrelevant, and (2) these syntactical frames are filled, almost at whim, with little details, also often presented as metaphors. Thus syntax and tropes form the flesh and blood of this difficult poetry. Themes and motifs are combined in a complex way. In "My Sadness," for example, the motifs of "I" and "you" are first intertwined and later resolved in a finale of loneliness.

Perhaps because of this essentially musical method, Pasternak greatly favors the juxtaposition of contrasting images (e.g., day and night) or things that grow and develop. Many of the poems are about the gradual arrival of day or night, in the country or in the city; about transitions from light to darkness and vice versa, and in one poem it is the transition from childhood to adulthood. So much emphasis on contrast and transition often results in images of a fragmented reality in flux, dislocated by imagery, and thus this poetry is an anticipation of Pasternak's own later definition of art as a record of a dislocation of reality by emotion.

If a label can be given to Pasternak's art, it is expressionism; and, properly speaking, Pasternak and Mayakovsky are, in different ways, the truest Russian representatives of this aesthetic kind,[13] which was born (but never actually identified) on the frontier of symbolism and futurism. The sources of Pasternak's early poetry are complex and not entirely clear. Further investigations are needed, and these may disclose Annensky, Tyutchev, and Blok in Pasternak's poetic genealogy. *Twin in the Clouds* may delight an admirer of Pasternak's with several "firsts." Here is his first train poem ("Vokzal" ["The Station"], which is probably the best poem in the book), the first winter in Pasternak's verse, his first rain, and his first metapoetry.

The publications of Lirika had little resonance. Bryusov called them "eclectic" and saw little of their professed symbolism in the poetry ("rather, a primitive romanticism"), but, nevertheless, connected them with Biely's verse school.[14] The *Enchanted Wanderer* welcomed the new group in vaguely encouraging terms;[15] but Shershenevich subjected all the publications of Lirika to murderous criticism. First, in *Vernissage*, he called them "symbolist trash";[16] alter, in the *First Journal of Russian Futurists*, in reviews that were edited, if not necessarily written, by him, he contemptuously and rudely dismissed Pasternak and Bobrov as boring imitators and accused Pasternak of stealing from nine poets (including Shershenevich). No traces of Yazykov were found in Aseyev's poetry (as was claimed by Bobrov), and Anisimov's (and others') translations from German were branded as *nekulturnye*.[17] Shershenevich also reviewed Pasternak's *Twin in the Clouds* in a nonfuturist magazine under his own name in order, perhaps, to prove that the nasty reviews in the *First Journal* were not penned by him. Still, despite crediting Pasternak with an "indubitable search for new ways" and a "broadening of poetic vocabulary and themes," he insisted that the defects outweighed the good qualities, listing among the former the very things Pasternak proudly displayed: mixing of diction and "Bobrovian" metrics.[18]

In addition to the books already mentioned, Lirika published only A. Sidorov's translation of Goethe's *Geheimnisse* (the work that Pasternak later tried to translate, too). Nothing else appeared, though plans were ambitious. Nearly every member planned publication of one or more books of verse, prose, or translations. Pasternak intended to publish a book of essays, "Symbolism and Immortality." Especially elaborate were the translation projects: Bertrand's *Gaspard de la nuit*, medieval Catholic hymns, Plutarch of Chaeronea, Jakob Böhme Novalis, and several books by Rilke. These translations never appeared; nor did the second Lirika miscellany, which was to be devoted entirely to contemporary German poetry.

Some time in the spring of 1914, a book under the strange name *Rukonog* ("Brachiopod"[?]) went on sale in Moscow; the group that published it included Bobrov, Aseyev, and Pasternak, and called itself "Centrifuge." Among the literary news items printed at the end of the book was an inconspicuous announcement about the dissolution of the Lirika group as of March 1. The notice said that within the group two trends had become apparent and had divided it. One of the resulting parts formed the publishing enterprise Centrifuge; the other intended to continue under the name of *Strelets* ("Archer").[19] The members of Centrifuge did not call themselves futurists, but there are enough indirect indications in the book that they considered themselves as such. At any rate, the press immediately labeled them futurist and they never protested.

Rukonog was not, however, the first publication of Centrifuge; neither was it the first manifestation of the group's (or its members') futurist inclinations. As shown in chapter 3, Sergei Bobrov printed his poetry and an essay dated fall, 1913, in the St. Petersburg ego-futurist miscellany *Shattered Skulls* while still a member of Lirika and received "star" treatment: his poetry and criticism took up half the edition and were placed at the beginning.[20] The essay made a scathing attack on the Hylaeans, after expressing some neosymbolist ideas on the essence of poetry, which differed little from what was said by Bobrov in his "Concerning the Lyric Theme."

Bobrov's essay was soon republished as a booklet under the name *Liricheskaya tema* ("The Lyric Theme") with Bobrov's own drawing and Centrifuge's imprint on the cover. The bulk of this thirty-page pamphlet was a simple reprint of the familiar essay, containing no essential changes; but it was now accompanied and buttressed by a preface and a few scholarly notes at the end. The preface sounded like a manifesto, especially in its repeated "we" and its contemptuous references to "professors of academies," but it contained no new ideas. Among the notes, Bobrov reprinted his essay from *Shattered Skulls*, omitting the entire polemical part. The pamphlet's publication embodied a paradox: while constituting a complete break with symbolism, it did not show a single change in Bobrov's neosymbolist aesthetics of two years before. The imprint of Centrifuge was there with all its futurist connotations, but the word "futurism" did not appear anywhere. It seems that Bobrov, like Shershenevich, simply realized that to be "modern" one had to be—or, rather, to be called—futurist. On the other hand, the very fact of presenting an old symbolist essay as a futurist manifesto is full of implications, raising again the problem of relationships between Russian symbolists and futurists: were they "fathers and sons," or simply two stages of the same process? One fact is clear: by 1914 any postsymbolist group with avant-garde aspirations or claims had to join the ranks of domestic futurism.

The birth of Centrifuge, as Pasternak recalls, "was marked by endless bickering throughout the winter." [21] Nevertheless, Bobrov made it a constant habit to soft-pedal any unpleasant happenings within his group. Centrifuge, for example, continued to advertise the old Lirika publications to the very end.

Because memoirs about Centrifuge are practically nonexistent, one must concentrate almost entirely on the study of its publications, and *Rukonog* was its first unambiguous appearance as a group. The cover looked rather futuristic. The letters of the title were of four different sizes. On the top there was a rhymed cuplet printed in the following way:

> In   the center of a reef there's a fugue
> Be happy   CENTRIFUGE.

Down below there stood: "Moscow the first turboyear—4191," which suggested that 1914 (printed in reverse) was the beginning of a new era. Finally, the title shared space with the name Centrifuge printed in such a way that C (Russian Ц) contained, in a manner of a vessel, all the rest of the letters in three rows with a comma at the very bottom.

So far as content is concerned, Centrifuge does what one would expect: claims that it follows a "true" futurism, attacks its enemies (i.e., nonfuturists and pseudofuturists), and tries to impress its readers with the number and the quality of its members. *Rukonog's* most noticeable characteristic is a strong ego-futurist orientation: it begins with a one-page announcement of the death of Ignatyev, who elsewhere is called "the first Russian futurist" and, in a short preface to four of his poems, is presented as almost a martyr of futurism. There is also Bobrov's poem in memory of Ignatyev. In addition to the late leader of the Petersburg futurists, all other Areopagites and signatories of the "charter" (i.e., Gnedov, Shirokov, and Kryuchkov; see p. 75) are gathered in *Rukonog*. Moreover, one comes across Rurik Ivnev, who had found it possible to participate in both Ignatyev's and Shershenevich's publications and who this time offered some of his most futuristic verse.

Probably considering his previously published *The Lyric Theme* enough of a theoretical foundation, Bobrov now concentrates heavily on polemics rather than on theory. Only one shot is fired in the direction of symbolism, and the victim is the insignificant, though active,

CENTRIFUGE

symbolist poet, Ellis. The most devastating fire is aimed at Hylaea. In fact, the polemical manifesto (styled in an ego-futurist fashion as a "charter" [*gramota*]) does not spare the cubo-futurists, calling them "an insolent, high-handed gang that misappropriated the name of Russian futurists," "traitors and renegades," "pretenders" with "forged passports," "a corporation of Russian mediocrities," "slanderers" and "cowards," and finally "passéists." In one passage, the charter clearly suggests, without naming them, that the Hylaeans are criminals and that their place is in Siberia. The reason for so violent an attack, unprecedented even in futurist circles, can be found in the book review section, where Bobrov, under a pseudonym, leaves no stone unturned while answering criticism of Lirika publications printed in the *First Journal of Russian Futurists,* and even appeals to the Moscow city administration to take care of the sewer-like stench coming from the pages of that Hylaean publication. Of course, the one who is spared least is Shershenevich, whose alliance with Hylaea is mentioned with contempt and scorn and whose poetic abilities are dismissed entirely. Bobrov, paying Shershenevich in kind, calls him a literary thief, states that he was once refused entrance into Lirika, and reports that his first book was mercifully edited by an unidentified Lirika member.

To return once more to the charter, Centrifuge does not condemn all Hylaeans and even exempts Khlebnikov and Mayakovsky from the "corporation of Russian mediocrities" in an obvious attempt to split the group. Its members certainly knew that Khlebnikov had broken with his friends by that time, and their desire to attract Mayakovsky and Bolshakov to their circle becomes clear from several critical statements printed in *Rukonog* and elsewhere. They finally succeeded with Bolshakov and almost succeeded with Mayakovsky, whose participation in Centrifuge publications was announced more than once. Pasternak describes in his memoirs an attempt to establish peace when Bobrov and Pasternak, on the one hand, and Shershenevich, Bolshakov, and Mayakovsky, on the other, met in a Moscow café.[22] The charter was signed by, in addition to the core of Centrifuge (i.e., Bobrov, Pasternak, and Aseyev), Ilya Zdanevich, who otherwise never printed a line in this or any other of the Centrifuge publications.[23] The signing by Aseyev is an ironic fact, since at the time he was already an enthusiastic admirer of Khlebnikov's and Mayakovsky's and later became a friend of many of the Hylaeans. It is also worth noting

242

that Marinetti is called in the charter "the commander in chief of the futurist troops" and Severyanin acquires the title of "senior Russian futurist." It is not explained how this differs from the title, the "first Russian Futurist," awarded Ignatyev.

Pasternak's essay "Vassermanova reaktsiya" ("Wassermann Test"), which directly follows the charter, is deceptive. It begins as an ambitious theoretical treatise, but all initial meditations on the loss of the aristocratic in art lead only to a contemptuous exposé of that bête noire of the Centrifugists, Vadim Shershenevich, who is presented as a victim of the unfortunate democratization of poetry with the result that now anybody, even Shershenevich, can call himself a poet. Pasternak touches only on the subject of "true futurism" to which he admits Khlebnikov, Mayakovsky (with reservations), Bolshakov (in part), and the Petersburg ego-futurists. He never defines this "true futurism," neither does he include himself or Bobrov among the futurists (which seems a deliberate tactic on Bobrov's part, since nowhere in the book is the group called "futurist"). The most interesting passage in Pasternak's essay concerns a doctrine of imagery which develops out of his dismissal of Shershenevich and is a good key to Pasternak's own poetry: "The origin of Shershenevich's metaphors lies in the fact of similarity, or, less often, in the associative ties based on similarity—never on contiguity. It is only in the phenomena of contiguity,[24] however, that one finds the inherent features of coercion and mental dramatism, which could be justified metaphorically."

Since both the charter and Pasternak's essay are polemical acts of revenge, the poem "Turbopean" ("Turbopaean") is the only manifesto of a positive nature. This anonymously printed poem is sandwiched somewhere in the middle of the book between signed poems of the participants, but it is emphasized with italics. Actually, it is nothing but a joyful go-ahead to the new group, describing the noise of the centrifuge and its threat to the unidentified "bullheaded ones" (*mednolobye*), written in a gay meter and in an odd, partly agrammatical mixture of neologisms and archaic words. One passage reads: "And high above the world, Aseyev, Bobrov, and Pasternak sit."

Among the new names in the book are those of Elizaveta Kuzmina-Karavayeva, who was later to become in exile the legendary Mother Maria, the poetess-nun who sought and found martyrdom in a German concentration camp. Her poetry is not at all futurist. Also there is Bozhidar who makes his debut here with a single poem. It attracts attention because of its strange appearance: it is printed in large letters, some of which are Cyrillic and some Latin. Despite pronunciation instructions at the beginning, it is difficult to understand why, for example, all *v*'s and all *n*'s had to be printed in a non-Russian alphabet. Nearly every word occupies a separate line. Otherwise, it is a rather conventional poem reminiscent of the symbolists.

While the poems of the Petersburg ego-futurists hardly add to their reputation, the contributions of the founders of the group arouse interest even when they are not at their best artistically. Aseyev clearly embarks here on his period of songlike Old Slavic stylizations, while Pasternak briefly makes use—not without Aseyev's influence—of a different idiom, especially in those poems where he tries to suggest medieval Moscow through word choice. Bobrov, particularly in his "oratorio," "Lira lir" ("Lyre of Lyres"), tries a little too hard to be avant-garde. This cycle of poems, which proclaims the desire to open "the gate of endless meanings," is a hymn to the arrival of New Poetry and it is filled with technological and geometrical imagery mixed with metaphysical overtones so that it almost succeeds in sounding like the work of a futurist Tyutchev. At the end of the book, and separate from the rest of the poetry, there is another cycle of poems written by Bobrov, but signed with the pseudonym Mar Iolen, which was probably meant as a mystification. Partly, however, Bobrov used this pseudonym in order to move even further into the realm of avant-garde poetry. Neologisms and colloquialisms are used more freely here, meter is handled in a more radical manner, and the rhyming words are even more remote in sound than in "Lyre of Lyres" (which also experimented in rhymoids). But Bobrov's agrammaticism and his desire to create "endless meanings" result in an inarticulateness that sounds like a cross between Gnedov and Ignatyev.

The press met *Rukonog* with its usual derision. Everybody, including Bryusov, called the new group futurist. Bryusov found in Centrifuge a special trait, "the desire to connect their activities with the artistic work of preceding generations." [25]

Two years went by before the formation of another little group and small publishing enterprise, *Liren* ("Lyroon"),[26] by Aseyev and a young provincial, Grigory Petnikov. Though Aseyev was grateful to Bobrov and tried to be loyal to him almost to the end, he probably never felt comfortable among his supereducated, West-oriented fellow Centrifugists in Moscow and became more and more attracted to the Slavic orientation and verbal laboratory of Khlebnikov and by the personal magnetism of Mayakovsky. With his own provincial background and his poetic temperament and keen interest in historical and neologistic aspects of the poetic word, Aseyev was a born Hylaean, and later he must have considered the *Rukonog* charter the greatest mistake of his youth.

The birth of Lyroon seems to have taken place during the summer of 1914 in Krasnaya Polyana, a little place near Kharkov where the family of Sinyakov lived. The three Sinyakov sisters became closely connected with the futurist movement: Pasternak, Aseyev, and Khlebnikov were in love with them at different times. Aseyev married one of them, Oksana; Khlebnikov wrote about them in his poems. One of them, Maria, an artist, illustrated several futurist publications.

Petnikov lived in Kharkov and so did Bozhidar. The activities of Lyroon began with the publication in 1914 of two slim volumes of verse, Aseyev's *Zor* and Bozhidar's *Buben* ("Tambourine"), in their appearance reminiscent of Kruchenykh's handwritten mimeographed pamphlets. The books were printed in Kharkov but marked as published in Moscow, and were followed by a book of Novalis' *Fragmente* in a translation by Petnikov.*

It was not until August, 1915, that Lyroon's manifesto appeared in the form of a preface to a joint edition of poetry by Aseyev and Petnikov, *Letorei* (which means approximately "the one who soars, or hovers, in the summer"). Entitled "A Few Words about *Letorei*" and signed, not with the authors' names, but with the name of the group, Lyroon, it begins with the following words: "A vision of the word has haunted mankind since prehistoric times. In the word, man becomes aware of himself." Mildly colored by neologisms and archaic words, the essay further continues to describe the world of language as superior to and larger than the world of visible things. This language is "flexible and strong," but everything depends on its "equipment" (*osnastka*), and it can be equipped with intellect, beauty, or life. Intellect fills the word with poison, and such a word stings and then dies; beauty makes the word fly over the world to be repeated by many lips; but both of them [the intellectual word and the beautiful word] are inferior to the "live" word, whose life is "only in the combination

245

of sounds, which remain with people for centuries and reveal themselves suddenly in the harmonies of roots in the tongues of various races." Such a word may live, without being repeated, for a long time "like fire in wood." In the meantime, people are satisfied with the "cold and worn" common currency of words, produced by the "miserable classics." Innovation is proclaimed as the only responsibility of an artist; and, for the true artist, its goal will not be to produce another ism, but to assert his own individual will. Only verse can give birth to the real word, and this verse does not have to be metrical or rhymed: "It is without the bones of meter! It is without the dessert of rhyme!" The manifesto ends with an assertion of the "wild word."

Thus Lyroon developed as a curious Hylaean offshoot of Centrifuge. While Centrifuge combined ego-futurist and symbolist features, Lyroon embraced primitivism and a preoccupation with words, while at the same time ignoring (in fact, almost rejecting) metrical considerations, so dear to Bobrov. In practice, this program amounted primarily to the creation of neologisms and the use of rare words, both invariably of Slavic color or origin.

Bobrov was, naturally, cool to the whole idea, but never allowed the existence of Lyroon to develop into, or look like, a split in the ranks of Centrifuge. Condescendingly reviewing *Letorei,* he called the manifesto a repetition of "the doctrines of the late Hylaea of which everybody is so sick and tired." [27] Bobrov, however, chose to overlook Aseyev's activities in this group and even advertised Lyroon books in Centrifuge publications. Later he printed Petnikov in the second Centrifuge miscellany, though he always held a dim view of his poetic abilities. On the other hand, Lyroon planned to publish Bobrov's poetry. Not until 1917 did some of the latent animosities come to the fore when Lyroon bitterly accused Bobrov of tampering with Bozhidar's works. [28]

In April, 1915, Lyroon decided to publish "Slovoved" ("Wordician"), a journal of prose, poetry, and criticism. According to Aseyev, it was to deal with "live language," excluding everything that was "technical" or "artistic"; "It will be a midwife of language." [29] Organization of the publishing venture dragged on until the fall of 1916, and the journal never appeared. Among the prospective contributors, in addition to Aseyev and Petnikov, were Khlebnikov, Mayakovsky, Kruchenykh, D. Burliuk, Ivnev, and Matyushin. Thus Aseyev managed to get in touch with those Hylaeans whom Bobrov could never accept. The contact with Matyushin led to the advertising of Zhuravl books on the pages of Lyroon publications. Both Petnikov and Aseyev became admirers and disciples of Khlebnikov.

From 1916 on Lyroon became more and more Khlebnikov-oriented, first publishing the manifesto *Truba Marsian* ("Trumpet of the Martians") inspired by him, then publishing a separate edition of his play *Oshibka smerti* ("Death's Mistake"), and regularly printing his work in its miscellanies, such as *Vremennik* (the venture joined toward the end by Gnedov) and *Lyroon*. The latter appeared in 1920, and by that time the group also seems to have attracted Pasternak, who not only printed a few poems with them, but also planned to publish, under their imprint, a book of verse, "Kvintessentsii" ("Quintessences"), which never materialized.

The three early books of Aseyev's published by Lyroon show clearly his development as a futurist poet. In them, Aseyev quickly grew into a major force within the Russian avant-garde, and his poetry of this period had an appeal that his later and more mature works could never capture. In spite of being drafted into the army in 1915, he remained active in literature from 1914 to 1917, publishing four books of verse and printing his poems in several late futurist miscellanies. While in the army, he continued to write and even read his obscure poems to his fellow soldiers, who, he says, listened readily.[30]

Perhaps it was good for Aseyev to tear himself loose from the excessive intellectualism of Centrifuge and thus to find his own place in poetry. Having grown up in the family of a provincial insurance agent in the small, but ancient, town of Lgov (Kursk area), he hardly had much use for Rimbaud and Bertrand. In fact, his enthusiasm for poetry was nurtured in his adolescence on popular anthologies, often filled with melodramatic trash. But he also had favorites on a much higher level, and, like Khlebnikov, was early struck by the "light, dancelike rhythms of A. K. Tolstoy's poems"[31] and by the fantastic quality of Gogol's Ukrainian stories. Even then, however, he was miles away from the sneering Bobrov and from Pasternak, who was lost in the intricacies of his own soul and in the neo-Kantian philosophy. Aseyev's was probably the greatest, if not the only, gift of song among the Russian futurists, and Bobrov saw in his poems "radiant musicality and the gift of magic."[32] Pasternak once said that of all his colleagues of those years only Aseyev possessed a mature style.[33] A confirmation of this maturity could be the fact that Aseyev's four books of verse published between 1914 and 1916 can be analyzed as a unit. Already in *Zor* he is no disciple; even when he borrows here or later (and he does it often), he assimilates. *Zor* (a word probably built on the Old Russian root meaning "see"), published in 1914 in a "handwritten" edition containing only seven poems, is one of Aseyev's most striking books. It was followed by *Letorei*, a joint publication with Petnikov, in 1915. Later, in 1916, Lyroon published Aseyev's *Oi konin dan okein* (Gypsy for "I Love Your Eyes").[34] The same year, Bobrov, probably in order to compensate for Aseyev's absence in the second Centrifuge miscellany, published his *Oksana* (the name of Aseyev's wife) where only thirteen poems were new; the other forty-six were selected by Aseyev from those previously printed in books or periodicals. Among these books, Aseyev's work appears most uneven and forced in *Letorei* and most consistent in poetic quality in *Oi konin dan okein,* and exhibits the greatest originality in *Zor.*

Many of Aseyev's poems are not only songlike, but are poetic recreations of songs, usually exuberant and full of abandon. He says in his autobiography that his early reading of Alexei K. Tolstoy gave him the desire to write something equally "gay, tempestuous, and teasing." [35] He may try metric irregularities or even go too deep into the area of abrupt and uneven rhythms (as in *Letorei*), but he is at his best when his rhythm is clear and his tempo fast. When he slows down or complicates, he is apt to sound crude; therefore, one would guess that the principles of Lyroon which suggested the ignoring of meter were not Aseyev's invention.

Aseyev's predilection for "antiquity and the motherland" (*starina i rodina*)[36] is apparent in a liberal sprinkling of Slavic exoticism and Old Russian stylization (songs of the Cossacks, prayers to old pagan gods, etc.) throughout his works. Vocabulary is, however, the main means he employs to achieve this atmosphere: Old Russian, Russian dialect words, and Ukrainian and Polish linguistic color (Aseyev planned to write a book called "Southwestern Speech"). He made an interesting confession that he used to "swallow" page after page of the Old Russian chronicles and took many of his words from them.[37] A careful check might reveal, however, that the majority of these words are neologisms that only pretend to be Old Russian, Ukrainian, and Polish words, and Aseyev is here more a pupil of Khlebnikov than a poet-scholar. Add to this Old Russian atmosphere the use of old grammatical forms (frequent vocatives, dual number, and others) and a sizable number of Slavic place-names and personal nouns, and Aseyev stands perhaps as the greatest futurist de-Europeanizer after Khlebnikov, a fact that may surprise a reader of his *Nocturnal Flute*. And it was not a "conversion": some poems, unusually rich in Slavic lexical color, are dated 1912 and 1913 (i.e., the time of his *Lirika* membership and even before). In *Zor*, however, he attempts to pass this trait off as genuine futurism, and in the "stage directions" between his poems, presents a satirical portrait of Valery Bryusov, who, like a beggar, gathers into his sack some of the Slavisms spilled by the generous, youthful Aseyev.

Earlier poems showed Aseyev's tendency to alliterate neighboring words. Now this predilection becomes phonetic excess, where all words are directed toward an identical sound quality (*kto preet, predkam predan, vpered prikhodit prezhde*), or lines may rhyme all the way through, rather than only at the end. This practice caused one critic to remark that Aseyev showed "the highest achievements in phonetics." [38] In one poem, this looking for phonetic similarity becomes a theme with a touch of blasphemy: the poet "hears" within the notice *Prodazha ovsa i sena* ("Sale of oats and hay") on the market signboard the words from a prayer *ottsa i syna* ("Father and Son"). Add to his alliterative tendency his clever onomatopoeia (e.g., the cries of sea gulls in his "Hungarian Song") and unusual rhyme (including compound and broken), and his poems become feasts of verbal color and sound.

Khlebnikov's influence has been mentioned: Slavic themes and neologisms are evidence enough and Aseyev would be the last to deny it. But other little details and devices can be found which demonstrate the same influence. When, for instance, Aseyev applies Khlebnikov's theories of internal declension, he does it with real lyric charm and with no hint of laboratory work. Mayakovsky also begins to be heard in Aseyev's verse, especially in the crudities, in the passages in which the author defies God, and in compound rhymes and exclamations. Occasionally, the hyperbolic treatment of the love theme reminds one of Mayakovsky.[39] Such evidence of "outside" influences does not make Aseyev a complete renegade. There is still much of

Centrifuge in his poems: emphatic metaphoric quality, nonfusion of syntax and content, deliberate obscurity, and the echo of Pasternak.

Two themes stand out in Aseyev's poetry. One is war, at first stylized in the familiar Slavic way, then shaped in the mold of World War I with all its violence and devastations hyperbolized. Sometimes war imagery is applied to a poem that is not about war at all. The other theme is that of "theomachia," open or veiled, and for this reason *Letorei* was temporarily banned.

Aseyev's next book was published in the Far East in 1921. He had been sent to Siberia in 1917 on military orders. The Revolution took place while he was on his way, and *Bomba* ("The Bomb," 1921) was his categorical futurist "yes" to the Communist Revolution. It also marked his participation in the Vladivostok futurist group *Tvorchestvo* ("Creation"), which included David Burliuk and Tretyakov. Aseyev had a long and prolific career in Soviet poetry which stretches roughly from the Lef group and the blind following of Mayakovsky to the end of his days as the "grand old man" of Soviet poetry.

For all his loyalty to the Soviet regime, Aseyev never renounced futurism in his heart even when it was declared completely unacceptable. It is true that in 1923 he dismissed everything he had written before that date as mere exercises,[40] but shortly before his death in 1963 he included practically all his prerevolutionary books in a five-volume collection, and he printed the earliest versions of all his futurist-period poems. To be sure, it was possible to do this in post-Stalinist Russia; but even under Stalin, Aseyev wrote (in 1940) a long poem about Mayakovsky (and received a Stalin Prize for it) in which he spoke with nostalgia about the good old futurist days, discussed Burliuk and Kruchenykh with warmth, and wrote about Khlebnikov with adoration.

The publisher of Lyroon books, Grigory Nikolayevich Petnikov (1894——), first came in touch with futurism in 1913 when the touring futurist trio visited Kharkov where he, the son of a railroad employee,[41] studied music. In 1914 Petnikov began to pursue Slavic studies at the University of Moscow and later received a degree in law at Kharkov. He planned to enter Lirika, and that group had announced publication of a book of his, a translation (in collaboration with Bobrov) of *Heinrich von Ofterdingen* by Novalis, his favorite author. He made his real literary debut[42] in *Letorei*, where his fifteen poems appear alongside fourteen by Aseyev. These poems are written in a language that is an unpalatable mixture of archaic and newly coined words, only occasionally brightened by a standard Russion word (and in only one instance by a whole stanza written in Russian). This excess of neologisms results in utter obscurity, an obscurity that is further intensified by ellipsis and alogism. In the printed texts, Petnikov places capital letters where they are not expected (a practice reminiscent of Burliuk's experiments). Still the general content of this poetry is clear, even if many details are not: nature is its constant subject.

One can see in Petnikov's poetry more connection with the ideas expressed in the *Letorei* manifesto than in Aseyev's, which makes one suspect that Petnikov was its actual author. For instance, it is Petnikov, rather than Aseyev, who consistently practices freedom from meter and rhyme. (See also the image of trees hiding fire in one of the poems of his subsequent book, which repeats one of the images in the manifesto.) On the whole, all these poems are immature, artificial, and sterile. The book's planned freedom, which is not sustained by the poet's inner freedom, makes a painful impression. Petnikov himself must have realized its inadequacies as evidenced by the fact that he omitted it from his record and designated his fifth book of verse in 1928 as his fourth one.

This unpromising debut was not an accurate reflection of Petnikov's talent, as we can judge from his later books, which, though published after the Revolution, consist mostly of his poems written between 1913 and 1917. Strangely enough, the themes and the formal features of these poems remain almost the same as in *Letorei,* but most of them are the work of a poet of talent and originality. Two books, *Byt pobegov* ("The Daily Life of Sprouts") and *Porosl solntsa* ("Shoots of the Sun"), were published in Moscow in 1918 under the Lyroon imprint. This intellectually concentrated, masculine, and strongly optimistic poetry has nature as practically its only subject. Seasons (especially the spring), thunderstorms, fields, and night and day are constant themes and sources of imagery, which makes Petnikov look like a twentieth-century Tyutchev. Roots, moisture, fruits, birds, trees, stars, sap, bark, foliage, sky, and grass appear in one poem after another, sometimes as objects of description, sometimes as parts of the numerous metaphors. Only seldom are words like death, love, and fate glimpsed behind all that scenery. Part of this nature, however, wears the garb of neologism, which, though less abundant than in *Letorei*, still remains Petnikov's main poetic device. As in Khlebnikov, neologism helps to create a picture of rustic paganism and to suggest an Old Russian (or, rather, an Old Slavic) atmosphere. If for Aseyev neologisms are mostly bright lexical colors, Petnikov's new words are often abstract ideas, and he obviously strives for semantic precision; but, since he seldom deciphers these words, they appear, as in Khlebnikov's works, with "toned-down semantics." As an exception, Petnikov calls *vechernyaya pechal'* ("evening sadness") what he only a line before presented as *vechal'*; but it is difficult to see "the fast current of individual human consciousness" [43] in *mnestr*, which is formed from an oblique case of "I" and the name of a rapid Russian river, the Dnestr.[44] Most of these neologisms seem to be nouns (*upevy, vema, divesa, olyb', krasotina*), and they are often modified by standard Russian adjectives. Khlebnikov described Petnikov's poetry as "a severe blade of reason that governs the world," and Livshits wrote that Petnikov "had a feeling for . . . remote roots [of Russian words] that rest in the entrails of our protolanguage." [45] It is necessary to add that Petnikov also uses a considerable number of Ukrainian words. Some poems are built more conventionally on Russian folklore and on religious symbolism, and in them Petnikov sounds very similar to such so-called peasant poets as Kluyev and Esenin.

Khlebnikov is Petnikov's model not only in neologisms, in some compound rhymes, in tautologies, and in certain images, but also in his constant mixing of meters. Such mixing was one way for Petnikov to achieve the proclaimed free form, so that in one poem several metrical transitions from the classical iamb to free verse may be observed. Petnikov is similarly free in his rhyme (an aspect worthy of special study) and employs many unorthodox kinds, including heterosyllabic and heterotonic, and he often shocks by avoiding rhyme where it is expected. He also has a special predilection for assonance, of which he may be the most important practitioner in Russian poetry.

To these features one should add Petnikov's frequent lack of syntactic connection between words and an agrammatical quality. Parts of his poems are indissoluble clusters of metaphors expressed in opaque neologisms that defy analysis.

Despite the Slavic appearance of Petnikov's poetry, many of its roots are to be found in the western European poetic tradition. Probably the key to his *Naturphilosophie* is the German romantic poet and philosopher Novalis, a partial translation of whose *Fragmente* Petnikov published by Lyroon as early as 1914. In 1913 he also translated Novalis' *Die Lehrlinge zu Sais* (which he eventually published in 1920), and the echoes of this work can be found both in Petnikov's poems and in the *Letorei* manifesto (especially in the ideas of nature made animate and of ties between poetry and nature). He translated other works by Novalis (e.g., *Blütenstaub*), as well as the prose of Friedrich Schlegel and Rilke. Thus Petnikov is a Slav brought up on German romantic philosophy, and as such is not such a rarity if one recalls the intellectual history of nineteenth-century Russia. We have already seen the role played by Hoffmann in Centrifuge; still it is amazing to find so much German influence in a disciple of Khlebnikov's. The whole picture is further complicated by the fact that Petnikov had read Mallarmé and planned an edition of his poems in Russian translation. Future studies may establish connections here, too. Bobrov wrote of Petnikov, "Who needs homespun Mallarmés like this?" [46] Petnikov also translated Rimbaud, but his interest in, and knowledge of, German poetry seems to have a much greater scope, comprising as it does Walter von de Vogelweide and Franz Werfel.

Unfortunately, Petnikov never managed to publish collections of his essays (one such book was to be about the epithet), though he often announced them; they would have clarified his aesthetics still further. As a poet, however, he is undeservedly little known: his complex and serious work is an indisputable achievement. There is a similarity between his work and that of Livshits, another futurist intellectual and introvert with a European background. The difference, of course, lies in the fact that Livshits was of French orientation and an aesthete, rather than a metaphysician, with his work built around culture, not nature. Petnikov's Westernism, intellectualism, and education would have made him a perfect Centrifuge member, which, astonishingly, he never became (although he printed one poem in that group's *Second Miscellany*).

Petnikov's last book of verse to be published by Lyroon was *Mariya zazhgi snega* ("Mary Set the Snows Afire," Petrograd, 1920), in which he continued in his old vein. In 1922 Lyroon ceased to exist. Petnikov, who took an active part first in the Civil War (on the Red side) and then in Soviet cultural life,[47] gradually moved from nature poetry to verse about the Revolution, Red guerrillas, and industrialization, and took to quoting Lenin, not Rimbaud, in his epigraphs. His poetry, however, continued to be complex and partly obscure, and he has been praised for not descending from the level of poetic algebra to that of arithmetic.[48] He yielded to Pasternak's influence (especially in *Nochnye molnii* ["Nocturnal Lightnings," Leningrad, 1928]). He was very active in translating German writers and folklore. The peak of his success under the Soviets was the publication of a collection of his poetry (including some new verse) under the title *Molodost mira* ("Young Age of the World") and of a volume of translations of his poems into Ukrainian, both in 1934. Another collection, *Izbrannye stikhi* ("Selected Poetry") was published in Moscow in 1936. Some of his early poetry appeared in interesting new versions in these collections. After 1936 Petnikov faded away, only occasionally publishing such uncongenial books as anthologies of popular humor, translations of Ukrainian and Belorussian fairy tales, and retellings of Greek myths for children. His first book after a long interval, *Zavetnaya kniga* ("A Book Dear to My Heart," Simferopol, 1961), contains some new poetry, which is an accommodation to Soviet poetic standards and is almost painful in its obvious mediocrity. Petnikov was not represented in the anthology of the best in Soviet poetry (in two big volumes) published in 1958, which makes one suspect that he was in disfavor, if not in exile, at that time.

The third member of the Lyroon group, Bozhidar (né Bogdan Petrovich Gordeyev, 1894–1913), a teacher's son who planned to study philosophy at a university, died immediately after the group was organized. He became a diligently cultivated legend for his colleagues, especially for Aseyev, who saw in Bozhidar's poetry "the first knocking of mankind at the doors of the unavoidable" and in the poet, the first romantic victim of futurism, almost a martyr, "the youth who fell from a galloping horse at the very beginning of the great war against death" [49] (destruction of death by the men of the future is one of the favorite themes of Russian futurists, especially Khlebnikov, Aseyev, and Mayakovsky). As to Bozhidar's first and only book of poems, *Buben* ("Tambourine"), it is more a curio than an achievement. Its first edition,* published by Lyroon as a "handwritten" book in 1914, consisted of only nine poems, written primarily in Russian letters but with some Latin ones included. Its subject matter is varied and includes war pictures, pagan dances, psychological sketches, and one grotesque inspired by Hoffmann. Bozhidar displays a keen interest in neologism, unusual rhyme (he is one of the few Russian poets who rhymed the end of one line with the beginning of another), strange consonantal effects, unusual stanzas, and a play with word stress. In contrast with Aseyev and Petnikov, Bozhidar seems to mix his poetic ingredients at random so that the final result sounds absurd. He produces lexical and metrical "cocktails" with boyish abandon, and is perhaps the one futurist of his time to produce effects similar to those later introduced by the Dada poets; and therein lies his strongest claim to originality.

Bozhidar's greatest interest was in the area of metrics. Even more than Bobrov, he was fond of metrical substitution (e.g., use of an anapest foot in an otherwise iambic line) and other unusual metrical effects. The texts of his poems include signs for pauses, "triplets," and the like, and he discusses these devices at length in his treatise on versification, *Raspevochnoe edinstvo* ("Rhythmic Unity"), published by Centrifuge posthumously in 1916. There are some correct observations in this book, but on the whole it is now dated and looks amateurish. It is interesting primarily because of the quaint prose Bozhidar uses: he invents new, "more Russian" words for every metrical term (e.g., he calls a pause *vymolchanie*), so that the final result reminds one of the most outlandish experiments of Admiral Alexander Shishkov (1754–1841) at the beginning of the nineteenth century to purge Russian language of foreign words. Bobrov provided the book with a preface and commentaries, and his occasionally critical attitude aroused the wrath of Aseyev and Petnikov, in whose eyes Bozhidar could do no wrong. Bobrov reviewed *Tambourine* in the *Second Centrifuge Miscellany,* and while lamenting his untimely death, he also mentioned Bozhidar's methods of studying internal rhyme with the help of trigonometry. These studies were never published.

Lyroon considered another of Bozhidar's books of poetry but never published it. It did issue, however, a second edition of *Tambourine* in 1916, this time in usual print, still with pauses, but without marks for "triplets." Two poems were added to this second edition, and it included a metrical commentary and an enthusiastic epilogue by Aseyev. After this, Bozhidar ceased to interest anyone. If Aseyev and Petnikov achieved a certain fusion of elements, resulting in the first instance in a poetic flow and splash, and in the second, in a static drawing, Bozhidar's poetry is heterogeneous and seemingly incongruous. All three of them, however, wanted to create a new poetic language and thus approached the most ambitious aspiration of the Hylaeans.

While Lyroon was so active, Centrifuge was in the doldrums and published practically nothing in 1915. Finally Bobrov found money to continue, but before he was able to do so, there was an interlude in the history of his group during which he was connected with Peta (a neologism built from the verb *pet'*, "to sing"), a publishing enterprise of Fyodor Platov, an owner of a movie theater. Judging by what he wrote, Platov was a man of superhuman ambition and no talent, one of those whom the poet Khodasevich labeled "geniuses below zero." He would deserve no more than a mere mention in this study were he not so typical of his time and of the cranks who were often attracted by futurism (as they are by any avant-garde movement in any country). Platov published at the beginning of 1915 (under the Centrifuge imprint) *Blazhenny nishchie dukhom* ("Blessed Are the Meek") in which he called himself a futurist and tried to reconcile Christ and Nietzsche. A better idea of the caliber of this author can be gleaned from his *Tretya kniga ot Fedora Platova* ("The Third Book According to Fyodor Platov"), published in 1916 by Centrifuge and soon after that seized by the police. In this opus, with the help of mathematical formulas, quotations from the Bible, and statements such as "lack of faith is faith" and "pessimism is optimism," Platon fights socialism, the petty bourgeois, the music of Scriabin, and whatnot, and preaches a mixture of anarchism, neo-Nietzscheanism, hermaphroditism, obsession with death, and what the author calls "mystical masturbation." The whole message amounts to proclaiming Fyodor Platov the Messiah of the Third Coming, and the book is full of such statements as "By Fyodor Platov through Fyodor Platov toward Fyodor Platov" or "Woman is a field in the wheat of dysentery." There is something reminiscent of ego-futurist manifestos in the abrupt, elliptic verses of his "gospel." With Platov's money, Bobrov could continue Centrifuge, but before doing so he participated briefly in Platov's own enterprise, Peta.

Peta's first and only collection, *Peta,* appeared in Moscow at the very beginning of 1916. Its editor in chief was Alexander Lopukhin, a second-rate artist (some of his drawings, in the manner of the early Russian decadents, appear in the book) with literary ambitions. He printed both poetry and prose in the book, the first being conventional trash parading as avant-garde, the latter, an imitation of Platov. Platov, obviously the moving force behind the enterprise, shows himself in all his universality. He bestows on mankind a lengthy, prophetic semidrama, three poems (in which he vulgarizes the futurist concept of transrational poetry, i.e., *zaum*), sixteen "commandments" in gibberish on the mathematical foundation of sentence construction, and one undistinguished drawing. There are three more unknown names, probably Platov's cronies who also wanted to make their contribution to the treasury of Russian poetry, of whom only Evgeny Shilling deserves mention with his overly long exercise in the primitivist absurd, based mainly on *bout-rimé* technique. This company is joined by Aseyev and Bobrov, the latter laboriously mixing urbanism, violence, and alogism in his poems. There is also Bolshakov, who by that time had decided to forsake his friend Shershenevich. Bobrov disapproved of Lopukhin and company, and he certainly kept his opinion about Platov to himself; but for some strange reason, this excessively exacting critic saw some merit in Shilling and later printed his poetry in the *Second Miscellany*.[50]

Peta would have been nothing but a pathetic and rather inglorious episode in the history of Centrifuge were it not for the fact that among the names of the nine participants on the cover is that of Khlebnikov, printed larger than the rest. His only poem, later a part of his "Voina v myshelovke" ("War in a Mousetrap"), is a magnificent example of Khlebnikov's new, antiwar trend. His "star billing" obviously betrays the efforts of Centrifuge to woo the most valuable members of the disintegrating cubo-futurist movement. This impression is further strengthened by the fact that Aseyev's only book review in *Peta* is a paean to Mayakovsky for his *Cloud Wearing Trousers*, which had just appeared. Nowhere did the *Peta* poets call themselves futurists (continuing the tradition of Centrifuge), but, in a rather opportunistic way, they printed on the cover, right over the title, Maxim Gorky's recent phrase about futurists, "They've got something!" (The circumstances surrounding this event are discussed in chap. 7.) It obviously did not discourage them that Gorky explicitly meant Mayakovsky, Kamensky, and David Burliuk.

The critical portion of *Peta* was entrusted to Bobrov, and he did his job in his usual unappealing manner (only more so), sneering, gesticulating, and showing off. He is cruel to poor poetry, though *Peta* is full of it, and is patronizing in his praise. He terms "hopeless" the poetry of the youthful Boris Kushner, whose work he was planning to print in the next Centrifuge miscellany, and practically wipes out Samuil Vermel ("I haven't read such trash in a long time"), with whom he was later to form an alliance and whose book of verse he planned to publish. On the other hand, Bobrov reviews his own book under a pseudonym and finds it "new and essential." Worth mentioning are Bobrov's other attacks on Russian symbolism ("a swampy forest, which only recently looked like a park of Louis XVI") and his defense of Picasso.

After this miscellany, Peta published only a book of Bolshakov's poetry, but some of its unfulfilled plans were interesting: a book by Mayakovsky, four pamphlets by Khlebnikov, and "phonobooks" with recorded readings by Mayakovsky, Khlebnikov, Aseyev, and, of course, Platov.

In *Vtoroi sbornik Tsentrifugi* ("Second Centrifuge Miscellany," May, 1916), Bobrov finally managed to present Centrifuge as a group once more. Although of the twenty-five names proudly displayed on the title page at least nine belong to Bobrov himself, the book contains nearly seventy poems by fourteen poets. Actually, only two of them (Bobrov and Pasternak) are Centrifugists, with Aseyev absent this time. The Petersburg ego-futurists are not so numerous now (Shirokov, Olimpov), but the Muscovites of ego-futurist orientation, such as Ivnev and Bolshakov, are so generously represented that the overall impression is almost that of the resurrection of the Mezzanine of Poetry, which is the last thing Bobrov would have wished. Nevertheless, the atmosphere of the intimate, "interior" urbanism prevails in the book, and even such poets as Petnikov do not contradict it. Khlebnikov's two (and again, marvelous) poems look foreign in such an ambiance. Platov's radical mixing of folklore, alogism, and *zaum* can be easily dismissed as boring nonsense. There are also the late Bozhidar, Shilling, M. Struve, and Maia Cuvillies (actually, Maria Kudasheva, the future wife of Romain Rolland) with five poems in French. Bobrov supplies almost a third of the poetic output with his twenty-four poems (counting translations from Rimbaud and other

French poets), which he again prints under two names. As Bobrov, he offers slightly expressionistic poems, mostly about war, in which he strives to be utterly free in his rhythm and rhyme and refuses to adhere to any poetic device consistently, which only makes his poems faceless. Even more avant-garde are the poems published under the name of Mar Iolen, in which Bobrov indulges in free verse, exclamations, agrammaticism, and alogism. A touch of hoax is added to these poems in the indication of place where they presumably were written ("Atlantic Ocean," "Klondike").

On the whole, the *Second Miscellany* does not live up to its name or reputation. Associations with twentieth-century technology scarcely go beyond the title page with its "fifth turboedition" and "third turboyear," and any further mentions of modern technology are drowned in the hysterical self-pity of an Ivnev or the powdered dandyism of a Bolshakov. Bobrov's talkative preface, "K chitatelyu" ("To the Reader"), is so elusive and allusive that it says nothing in two pages, and the only clear statement in it is the last sentence: "There are no guides to CENTRIFUGE." On the other hand, another implication of the name "Centrifuge," that of separating the cream of poetry from less valuable writings, is canceled by the fact that members of the Russian futurist elite are not adequately represented here.

Bobrov does not make things simpler in his criticism, which fills two-thirds of the book. His only programmatic essay, "Philosophical Stone of a Fantast," after many gestures and innuendos, makes only one idea relatively clear: Bobrov's ideal is a "fantast" who starts from simple and clear things and arrives at an "essential confusion." He does not define this confusion, but (again allusively) illustrates it with examples from Hoffmann (who else?); and, after generous quotations from his own poetry, arrives at nothing. In another essay, Bobrov enters into a polemic with Rossiyansky without naming him and completely rejects the latter's definitions of presymbolism, symbolism, and futurism (see chap. 3), insisting that futurism *is* content-oriented. From time to time, one senses that Bobrov has at least some laudable intentions, refusing, as he does, to commit himself to any definite futurist program, and stressing the idea of genuine poetry, rather than of a contemporary and an avant-garde one at any price. At other times, however, one cannot get rid of the impression that Bobrov's arguments are sheer intellectual snobbery and that he has nothing essential to say, and, therefore, puts up a smoke screen of supererudition and critical abuse in an effort to impress everybody, while hiding under a legion of pen names (Bik, Ts. f. G., Aigustov, Sargin, Chagin, Serzhant, Yurlov, S. P. B., S. B., and probably a few more). It is interesting to note that practically all of Bobrov's theorizing comes in the form of review or reply, as if he were unable to develop a positive idea independently.

Surprisingly, Bobrov makes no obvious attacks on futurists outside Centrifuge (as he had done in *Rukonog*), but restricts his critical remarks to those publishing in his editions. Perhaps he considered Hylaea already dead, as he had said in a review in *Peta* a while before. He does not spare the symbolists, however. On various occasions, leading symbolist poets are treated scathingly, ironically, or at least ambiguously; but it is the lesser figures of the symbolist milieu on whom he turns his utmost scorn. Still he cannot conceal that his own ambition is to become what the symbolist pioneers were ten years earlier, and perhaps his hidden desire is to be what they have now become, namely, recognized and respected classics. For this reason he lets it slip out that "in ten years historians of literature will shine our shoes" and for this reason the review section of the *Second Miscellany* is a conscious imitation of that of the leading symbolist periodical of the recent past, *Vesy* ("The Balance"). He even invited one of the former critics of *The Balance*, Boris Sadovskoi, to contribute an essay, and Sadovskoi, though contemptuous of other brands of Russian futurism, complied in his best manner: he once more delivers a few punches to the icons of the sacrosanct tradition of nineteenth-century democratic and liberal criticism (Belinsky and his school).[51] And Bobrov adds a few punches of his own. Though he calls the criticism section of the book "the Centrifuge's thresher" and compares it to a dreadnought that in one salvo fires "50,000 kilograms of contempt, mockery, and insult," it is nothing but an imitation; and Bobrov ever remains a neosymbolist. Even the kind of books Bobrov reviews (mystical writings of Jakob Böhme, academic editions of the poets of Pushkin's time) remind one of *The Balance*, though here Bobrov may have the additional intent to display his universality and show the university professors that he, a futurist, is more scholarly than they.

Pasternak also appears in the capacity of a critic, and in the essay "Chernyi bokal" ("Black Goblet") he copes with the problem of futurism more directly than Bobrov, but still follows the latter too much in his ideas and even in his mannerisms to produce anything clear-cut. Like Bobrov, Pasternak is allusive and metaphorical to an extreme, and every sentence of his leaves a reader puzzled as to whom he actually has in mind and what he actually means. Contemporaries seemed to be of a similar opinion, and Shershenevich, a futurist himself and Centrifuge's whipping boy, called Pasternak an "abstruse [*zamyslovatyi*] critic." Pasternak does not deny, however, that he speaks in the name of futurism, though he credits the symbolists, whom he calls "impressionists," with labeling them so, as well as with claiming them (i.e., the futurists) as their children. Attacking the "popular" theories of futurism (he means Shershenevich and his book *Zelenaya ulitsa* ["Green Street"]), he rejects the Marinettian concepts of speed and contemporaneity as cornerstones of futurism, but finds in the futurist "abbreviations" a "transformation of the temporal into the eternal." He sees in futurism "impetuosity, insistence, and lightning-likeness," but ascribes it not to any efforts to be "contemporary," but rather to the "lyrical assault on reality." The futurist absolute is *lirika* (i.e., the primary essence of poetry), which had been explored earlier by Bobrov. Separating himself from "the symbolist impressionists," as well as from futurist "vulgarizers," Pasternak also draws a line between futurist poets and heroes of history (hinting here at the soldiers fighting the war at the moment) in their task of giving shape to the future.

There is also an essay by the late Bozhidar, analyzing the early poetry of Bobrov and showing such penetration into, and empathy with, this poetry that one is unable to fight the suspicion that Bobrov wrote the essay himself. Bolshakov helps Bobrov with reviews, and not only applies the latter's ideas, speaking about *lirika* and "lyric expanse," but strikes a rather Judas-like attitude toward the poor Shershenevich while reviewing his book and gently accuses his former friend of popularizing Mayakovsky's and his (Bolshakov's) poetic discoveries.

Sergei Bobrov was an active leader, but a spiteful and unpleasant person who antagonized most people and finally, toward the end of 1915, could write with satisfaction that "fortunately, with every new year, there are fewer and fewer people around." [52] One memoirist recalls Bobrov (without naming him) as "an unsuccessful poet" who liked to destroy the young poets with his bile and to discourage them, and "would ban poetry if he could." [53] On the other hand, Nikolai Aseyev, who admits that in time he became cool toward Bobrov, still calls him "exacting and zealous in matters of literature." [54] Pasternak portrays him as a leader eager to maintain group discipline in his ranks, who guarded his (Pasternak's) purity and got him into trouble with the senior symbolists as soon as they started to show their benevolence to the young poet.[55] Part of Bobrov's personality clearly comes through in his critical writings, which are aggressive, mordant, arrogant, often in poor taste, and occasionally, not quite honest. While reading them, one becomes particularly tired of Bobrov's consistent snobbery: for him, almost everybody is a provincial or an ignoramus. At his best, he is a subtle, but not profound, critic with a strongly developed analytical mind, but one unable to synthesize his ideas.

Bobrov's theories must be assembled piece by piece. By his nature, he was primarily a writer of negative reviews and needed somebody's book as a starting point to express his own ideas apropos. Actually, he never added anything essential to what he had said in his *Lyric Theme,* but imposed those ideas on his co-Centrifugists (Pasternak, Bolshakov). His ego-futurist orientation decreased markedly after *Rukunog,* and in the *Second Miscellany* one no longer finds the Ignatyev cult, Severyanin (the "senior Russian futurist") gets quite a dressing down from Bobrov for his latest book, *Pineapples in Champagne,* and is declared to be the end of the preceding era.[56] Some hints of Bobrov's theories can be found in his *Zapiski stikhotvortsa* ("Notes of a Poet," Moscow, 1916),[57] published by Musagetes (thus, even the futurist Bobrov did not break contact with his symbolist cradle). These theories are mostly technical. Bobrov envisions the disappearance of rhyme, for instance, and its replacement by "assonance" (a rather broad term for him, because it covers all deviations from regular rhyme). He even prescribes the use of such "assonance" in two-fifths of a poem, while the remaining three-fifths should not use rhyme whatsoever (and he followed this practice in his own poems). Metrically, Russian verse evolves, as Bobrov sees it, from the classical iamb distorted by "triplets" and other kinds of metrical substitutions to "lines of rhymed prose." The old iamb, which Bobrov composed to perfection, is not dismissed or abused, but is declared to be excellent for hiding defects, while the new, ametrical poetry is said to allow no cheating. Still, Bobrov's gods belong to the time of the greatest flourishing of the classical iamb (i.e., the first half of the nineteenth century). His book contains a paean to Yazykov,[58] and later, in a fashion quite different from that of Hylaea, he exclaims: "Pushkin . . . what a weighty and honey-like sweetness fill this beautiful name." Baratynsky and Tyutchev were two other models for Bobrov, and he could rival any scholar of his time in knowledge and understanding of their work. Neither does Bobrov reject symbolism, though he walks his own paths through this area and establishes a cult of Ivan Konevskoi, an act not inconsistent since this symbolist pioneer might be called the closest to futurism. In Konevskoi's poetry, Bobrov sees "an ascetic, almost holy, self-deepening" and exclaims: "O, if Russian poetry could only flow in this glorious and pure riverbed!" Bobrov's most futurist book of verse, *Lyre of Lyres*, begins with the poem glorifying Konevskoi.

In his approach to versification, Bobrov was a scientist who believed in a mathematical exploration of the medium and thus was an immediate predecessor of the Russian formalists. He even tried (without much success) to investigate statistically the consonants in Russian verse and said: "We can hope that a hypothesis that can be applied to poetry, analogous [to those of physics], will appear in the future and will explain to us the origin of metaphorical energy through accumulations and collisions of a certain amount of labial or guttural consonants." [59] Bobrov's special and constant preoccupation, however, was metrics, in which he remained the disciple of Andrei Biely, one who assimilated also all the shortcomings of his teacher's theories. Most essays in the *Notes of a Poet* deal with meter and rhythm. Following Biely, Bobrov once described in detail a Pushkin poem for a periodical devoted to Pushkin scholarship and published a pamphlet on some difficult aspects of Pushkin's verse.[60] At the end of the 1960's it is easy to point out that all this analysis is terribly dated and often questionable in its major features,[61] but the interest itself is so characteristic that some critics in the 1920's saw preoccupation with rhythmic problems as the only shared characteristic of the entire Centrifuge circle.[62] Among his unfulfilled projects was the publication of a book to be called "Osnovy stikhovedeniya" ("Foundations of Verse Science") and of a dictionary of Pushkin's rhymes.[63]

As a poet, Bobrov was, of course, not "unsuccessful," but rather unjustly neglected. (Pasternak considered him "a genuine poet.") In this respect, he had much bad luck even at the height of his activities and power. His two books following *Gardeners over the Vines,* though announced in 1914, were not published until 1917. Both finally appeared with the Centrifuge imprint, and one of them, at least, was an anachronism in 1917, containing as it did Bobrov's prefuturist verse written in 1913. Its title was *Almaznye lesa* ("Diamond Forests"), and its sources, predictably, are to be found in Russian poetry of Pushkin's time and in French symbolist poetry (Rimbaud, Bertrand). Bobrov felt this book represented a totally new stage in his development, but the works in it actually show an intensification of traits evident in his earlier work. Despite his search for true *lirika,* Bobrov practically always ignored erotic poetry and concentrated on philosophical meditation, especially in this dry, abstract, but original and excellently written, book about the Soul and the Heart in Life; but Bobrov is almost exclusively interested in the upper regions of this life with its landscape of the heights and its rarefied air. "Nonexistence" begins in those regions, but they still are not the "beyond" of most Russian symbolists. It is true that Bobrov was interested in mystical writings; but his was an intellectual curiosity, and he searched for artistic devices and not for mystical ideas. *Diamond Forests* contains poetry of an outward simplicity, with a geometrical economy and an uncluttered perspective, as well as newly synthesized clichés of the poetry of Pushkin's time; but it is inherently complex and built on ellipsis and grammatical dislocations. On the whole, however, it is still a symbolist book.

It is difficult to describe Bobrov's subsequent, and last, book of verse, *Lyre of Lyres,* his only book that can be considered futurist. It contains poetry written between 1913 and 1916. He is elusive here, and deliberately employs a different style in practically every poem to avoid being stereotyped and to show that futurism is more than a fixed set of literary devices. In fact, Bobrov sounds much more "conventionally" futurist in the prose of his preface and his epilogue to the book, where he, in a barker's tones, invites the audience, which is not going to understand anyway, to run on "the torn brains" of his poetry, and he foresees their criticism that it does "not sing" and is "meaningless, mad, close to a mockery." In one of the poems he warns: "My speeches will be unintelligible." The latter may be partly true, but one would look in vain for traces of real madness in Bobrov's poetry.

It is calculated and even rhetorical, and it is only *the theme* of confusion which appears frequently within it, not confusion itself. Lack of repetition is carried to an extreme. One can find here the familiar soul in the heights, which would arouse nothing but scorn in Marinetti, a very Marinettian speed ("I don't have time to describe everything"), the expressionistically presented war, and some idyllic landscapes. Sometimes Bobrov selects "contemporary" themes, such as motion pictures; sometimes he appears metaphysical and abstract. Classical meters alternate with what he calls "elusive meter." Phonetic asceticism gives way to a play on identical roots or to Khlebnikovian neologism. Onomatopoeia is used in the poem about a train, where the movement of the train is also reproduced rhythmically. In this concrete instance, Bobrov acted quite knowledgeably: elsewhere[64] he lectured the "naïve" Bryusov who thought a train moved trochaically; according to Bobrov, a train leaves the station in choriamb, then moves in paeonospondeics, anapest, and the first bacchius, switching to iambic dimeter with "the third foot truncated" (as if such a thing were possible) just before the stop. Two more books of verse by Bobrov were announced but never appeared: "Delta" and "Dyshu" ("I Breathe").[65]

After the Revolution, Bobrov practically stopped publishing poetry and, for a time, specialized in his familiar bilious, devastating criticism (e.g., he delivered a most scathing attack on Alexander Blok),[66] published in some leading Soviet periodicals, as usual, under many pseudonyms. He spared his old friends, though, and praised Aseyev to the skies.

The last book published by Centrifuge was, unexpectedly, Bobrov's first novel, *Vosstanie mizantropov* ("Uprising of the Misanthropes," Moscow, 1922), written in avant-garde prose deriving from Biely and Laurence Sterne, and continually filled with epigraphs (including even a quotation from Tolstoy in French) and allusions (including attacks on Shershenevich). The book begins as an obscure and complex mélange, metaphorical, full of quotations, nervous and meandering, mixing narrative planes and vocabulary, and finally developing into science fiction. This genre with an admixture of mystery was continued in *Spetsifikatsiya iditola* ("Specification of the Iditol," Berlin, 1923) and *Nashedshii sokrovishche* ("The One Who Found a Treasure," Moscow, 1931), adventure stories about the intrigues of wicked capitalists and murderous Catholic priests in the West. Later he published translations, books on popular mathematics, and an adaptation for children of the *Chanson de Roland*. In 1964 *Literaturnaya Gazeta* congratulated him on the seventy-fifth anniversary of his birth. In 1966 Bobrov published an autobiographical story of a childhood, *Malchik* ("A Little Boy").

In 1916 Centrifuge honored some if its new members with publications of their verse. Constantine Bolshakov, an ex-Mezzanine member and an ex-Hylaean, who, since 1915, had been serving in the army, saw the publication of his first collection of selected poems, *Solntse na izlete* ("Sun at the End of Its Flight"), containing poetry from his earlier *Heart Wearing a Glove* and cycles of poems printed previously in the futurist publications of several groups, and ending with poetry inspired by the war. The book shows his development from an effeminate, French-oriented follower of Severyanin to the louder, Mayakovsky-like poet of the streets cultivating hyperbole, "realized" metaphor, and compound rhyme. The influence of Mayakovsky (or was it a trend shared by Bolshakov and Mayakovsky?) began even earlier in Bolshakov's long poem, *Poema sobytii* ("The Poem of Events"), published in February, 1916, by Peta. Not only the imagery and the rhyme, but the rhythmical features and the phraseology remind readers of Mayakovsky's longer poems. This poem, written between November, 1914, and January, 1915, is a requiem for Bolshakov's friend killed in the war, whose own poem, in a collage manner, is included in Bolshakov's work.

After Bolshakov returned from the war to Moscow, he wrote prose exclusively[67] and for a time belonged to Mayakovsky's group, Lef. In 1927, he published three books of short stories,[68] largely conventional, but well written and occasionally strong and vivid, in the manner typical of the Soviet prose of the 1920's. Even more interesting are his two novels, *Sgonoch* ("Those Who Were Wiped Off"),[69] about the defeat of the White Army (in which the author evidently served), written in mildly experimental prose, and a novel about Lermontov.[70]

The work of another former Mezzanine poet, Rurik Ivnev, was published by Centrifuge in 1916. His book of poetry *Zoloto smerti* "Gold of Death") is permeated with motifs of despair, hopelessness, rot, and dirt and adds little to the poet's familiar image, except that these themes pile up here without relief. This book probably belongs among the most decadent in Russian poetry, with urban surroundings serving as a background for details of death and morbidity (hospital, suicide, worms in a grave, etc.), finally culminating in "the sweet-sounding phrase: I'll die." It is absolutely nonfuturist verse.

Ivnev's last prerevolutionary book was the already mentioned *Samosozhzhenie* ("Self-Immolation," Petrograd, 1917), based largely on his three previous booklets with the same title. For nearly a hundred pages he alternates masochistic and hysterical poems about one's own sinfulness with no less hysterical prayers to God. It was an ironic summing-up, on the very threshold of the Revolution, for a poet who not only was soon to become secretary to Lunacharsky (the Soviet minister of culture), but also was to accept the Revolution, at least on the surface. He was to play a rather important part in imagism,[71] which was led by Shershenevich, after which he turned to writing potboilers.[72] Except for translations of Georgian poets, he emerged again as a poet only in the 1940's and then after World War II with three collections of verse.[73]

Though Boris Anisimovich Kushner (1888–1937), a young man from Minsk, contributed only one poem to the last Centrifuge collection, he should be mentioned here briefly. In his literary debut, *Semafory* ("Semaphores," Moscow, 1914), a slim volume of naïve and inept poetry, he tried hard belatedly to join the neosymbolist forces (especially in his ambitious long preface), but he found little encouragement from Bobrov. Then Kushner switched to cubo-futurism and published *Tavro vzdokhov* ("A [Cattle] Brand of Sighs," Moscow, 1915), a long poem that is interesting in its imitation of perhaps all the aspects and devices of Russian futurism one after another in encyclopedic fashion. Having formed his own publishing enterprise, Kushner published a historicophilosophical treatise on Jewry[74] and planned to published a book by Pasternak (*Sovremenniki srednevekovya* ["Contemporaries of the Middle Ages"]), probably about the war. He also played a part in shaping formalist criticism.

After the Revolution, Kushner became an active figure in Soviet leftist groups (Art of the Communes, IMO, Lef) and a prominent cultural commissar. His disappearance from the literary scene in the 1930's was probably connected with the political purges of the time. Kushner's small, but tangible, contribution to futurism is to be found in his attempts to write futurist prose[75] in *Samyi stoikii s ulitsy* ("The Staunchest One from the Street") and in *Miting dvortsov* ("Rally of the Palaces"), both published in Petrograd, in 1917 and 1918, respectively.

The first and only book Pasternak published under Centrifuge auspices was *Poverkh baryerov* ("Above the Barriers").[76] It was also one of the last books published by the group. It appeared in 1917, carried an epigraph from Swinburne, and contained nearly fifty poems. *Above the Barriers* is the beginning of the Pasternak we know; and in his next four (and much more famous) books of verse, he added little that was new. All basic elements of his style and poetic vision are present here in developed and unmistakable form. It is mainly a book of poetic landscape, usually of the city and its suburbs in all four seasons (but there are also quite a few Ural landscapes); and if there is any other theme, it is, more often than not, presented through nature (thus, the motifs of war and revolution are drowned in details of landscape, as they are in his *My Sister Life*).

Nature, for Pasternak, is, first of all, detailed and alive. Minute details, as observed before, are mostly "unromantic" (and Pasternak was conscious of this fact),[77] and they usually depict whatever is portrayed in his poetry as being in a state of change or transition. It is "instantaneous painting, depicting motion." [78] Even in Pushkin, Pasternak sees "impulsive depiction" (*poryvistaya izobrazitelnost*).[79] In *Twin in the Clouds*, the instant of change was often presented in an abstract, ready-made syntactical frame. In *Above the Barriers*, Pasternak introduces motivation: abrupt syntactic changes are now justified as the excited talk of a man who is out of breath. Pasternak is an emotional impressionist, so he usually abandons the classical impressionism of a Monet, which belies his professed "unromanticism" and "objective thematism" (e.g., "but the streets are made of dreams").[80] "Soul" is a constant image in Pasternak's poetry, but it is not an inhabitant of those premetaphysical heights, as with Bobrov; Pasternak's soul rushes along the streets and displaces everything. Thus, with Pasternak all things are concrete, everyday, and precisely observed; and all of them, at the same time, are slightly dislocated, slanted, and distorted. Both the dynamism described above and the very presence of that soul contribute to the general impression that everything is alive, but the main means for creating this impression is the time-honored device of personification. Thus, "the Urals give birth to [*rozhaet*] the morning"; the snowflakes "identify" a passerby;

under the snow, "the Adam's apple of the earth" is visible; the woods perspire; a garden has bad breath or even feels sick at its stomach "because of miles of stillness"; nights play chess on a parquet floor; and the piano keyboard is transformed into a flock of birds the poet feeds. On the other hand, sometimes there is an objectivization of abstract things ("a lump of morning lies [*valyaetsya*] behind the wardrobe"). The effect of such devices is intensified by the generally surprising imagery (the courtyard in winter is "like a condemnation to exile"), often coming in clusters of metaphors with similes ("February burns like cotton, gulping spirits and choking") and mixing everyday details with history and literature (the massacre of St. Bartholomew, the Tatar yoke, and a reference to Dante). Conversational diction, occasional selection of words because of their sound, and a predilection for rare words and rare rhymes are also familiar features of the later (or the earlier) Pasternak. As in much of his later poetry, Pasternak's verse is full of that disorganized motion within an enclosure which can be so fittingly described by the nearly untranslatable Russian words *mechetsya* and *tychetsya*.

Some less familiar aspects of Pasternak's style also appear in *Above the Barriers*, and one of them is a more frequent use of enjambment than is usually associated with him. It would be interesting to analyze in detail the poems in this book, which Pasternak never reprinted. Of course, he could have considered them inferior, but they also present a new quality, a road the poet could have taken, but did not. For instance, these poems are seldom about nature, they are longer than the usual Pasternak poems, and they mix lines of unequal length and of different meters.

On the whole, *Above the Barriers* can hardly be dismissed as an immature product of Pasternak's early days. It contains, for instance, such a masterpiece of rhythm as "Metel" ("Snowstorm") with its stuttering repetitions and the intensifying atmosphere of foreboding it creates.

The question is raised sometimes as to whether or not Pasternak ever was a futurist, but it comes principally from critics who lack an understanding of, or sympathy with, avant-garde art and who are full of the best intentions to rehabilitate his honest name.[81] Russian futurism, however, was flexible, varied, and contradictory, and any effort to reduce it to the aspirations or achievements of only one group or of a single person are bound to end in the worst possible simplifications and distortions. It is true that Pasternak said he was indifferent to futurist efforts to create a new poetic language, and for him the "music of words" was not purely "acoustical," but was based on the relation between sound and meaning.[82] One should, however, approach cautiously such statements by the Pasternak of the 1930's or even the 1950's, who was in the habit of forgetting that he himself wrote poetry that was hardly less avant-garde than Kruchenykh's. Besides, Pasternak had a tendency to underestimate the Hylaeans in both his early, militantly fratricidal critiques and his latter-day pronouncements.[83] He did say that all his life he was "oriented toward content," [84] but so were the members of Centrifuge—and which futurist group, to a large measure, was not? What really was uncomfortable for him in futurism was not its aesthetics, but rather the behavior of his futurist colleagues; and he did suffer (like Livshits in Hylaea) from their belief that it was a necessity to flaunt and strut and to keep the chip on one's shoulder for fear of being called a sissy. The complexity of Russian futurism makes it possible even to deny that Mayakovsky and Khlebnikov were futurists, and such attempts have been made always with less than convincing results.[85] As to Pasternak, in *Above the Barriers* the abundance of violence and antiaestheticism in his imagery would suffice to put him next to Kruchenykh and David Burliuk. His moon is "twangy" (*gundosyi*) and "hoarse-voiced" (*siplyi*); his thaw "retches, hacks" (*kharkaet*), and "hiccups"; his bay [of water] "clings to the meadow like a tick." He smells "the stench . . . of sky" and sees "a fetid heap of red clouds." His blood corpuscles bite like rats. And this is only one feature Pasternak shares with other futurists. In addition, he develops a futurism of his own, which is not surprising for the man who wrote about the true and false varieties of futurism in his "Wassermann Test."

In 1915 Centrifuge acquired a new member, Ivan Alexandrovich Aksenov (1884–1935), who, unlike Ivnev and Bolshakov, soon became a central figure in the group, similar in importance to Bobrov, Pasternak, and Aseyev. Unfortunately, the group was nearing its demise, and Aksenov could not develop fully his considerable abilities as a poet and a theoretician (and possibly a leader). In 1916, his book of poetry *Neuvazhitelnye osnovaniya* ("Invalid Foundations") was published by Centrifuge. Before that, he had written another one under the title "Kenotaf" ("Cenotaph"), but had destroyed it. Judging by one poem from "Cenotaph" quoted in full at the beginning of *Invalid Foundations*, this earlier manuscript showed strongly the influence of Andrei Biely's *Urna* ("Urn"). *Invalid Foundations* is a brilliant and difficult book, and it is one of the few genuinely avant-garde works published by Centrifuge. It is poetry that is partly based on personal association, but is primarily shaped in the manner of a painting. Words are placed in it like color, in contrast with or in addition to the previously used shade. Applying such a procedure, Aksenov does not neglect word meaning, but he uses semantics also as a color, a line, an element of texture.

Here is one of Aksenov's poems in translation:

> Impervious evening is glorified again
> Absolute amulet
> Onto the disillusioned and satiny
> Trace inductive to the sky.
> And, by improvident prospects,
> Those imagining guilt, without realizing it.
> Water feels dusty,
> And so does the fire in the garden running
> Through the ashtray.
> Birds going to explosions.
> On the frozen,
> There is the dated sign of last revelations—
> The head is ready to hide under the snow, the wing;
> It is visible because of the spray, too.
> Changing round.
> About the withered noise and the voltage of lamps,
> About the incurable ground
> Which died before living:
> It made a circuit, shortly, and got fame through books,
> Plaited together,
> Atoned world.
> The reason is unknown.

Within this poem, one sees a landscape, or rather a cityscape, a view from a window, but its elements are shifted, rearranged, certain things omitted—and, above all, the entire picture is painted with words that are apparently unrelated to it. The outward appearance of his words is of primary importance for Aksenov, so he chooses long and slightly quaint words (e.g., *neukosnitelnyi*, or *nepredusmotritelnyi* in this poem) and is especially fond of a foreign vocabulary, which he often Russifies (e.g., *vernissirovat, semishopot, klerdelunshchik*). He also likes to attach rare adjectives of foreign origin to Russian nouns ("Erymanthian fear," "apotropical arms"). It is a consciously West-oriented poetry, and Aksenov never strives for Slavic color as did Khlebnikov, Aseyev, and Petnikov. Often his diction takes on a sci-entific or technical shading when he adds words like "coordinates" and "entropy," and even complete mathematical formulas. The allusive quality is further strengthened by quotations (from Tolstoy, from Go-gol) emerging from a poem and by carefully selected epigraphs, which suggest a wider and a more esoteric erudition than that of Bobrov. In this book they are from Shakespeare, Bobrov, Max Jacob, Guido Cavalcanti, and John Webster. All this is presented in rhymed free verse (with unorthodox rhyme) in combination with some varieties of accentual verse (though one part of the book employs regular meters and rhymes).

One important source of Aksenov's poetry is French cubism. The quotation from Max Jacob in *Invalid Foundations* is certainly not accidental, but Aksenov borrowed directly from painters, too. Even his use of unorthodox printing methods may have been inspired by cubist paintings (in one instance, the print is such that from behind one sentence, another, of biblical origin, emerges). Intercrossing planes is Aksenov's favorite device; he enjoys intertwining high diction with newspaper style, not as a mixture of words, but as a counterpoint of sentences. In one poem he obviously tries to achieve an effect similar to that of a multiple-exposure photograph. The two poems that end the book ("La Tour Eifel" I and II) seem to be poetic variations on Delaunay's well-known painting (Aksenov did plan a book on Delaunay). Finally, Aksenov was the author of the first (and, until recently, the only)[86] Russian book about Picasso, *Pikasso i okrestnosti* ("Picasso and Environs," Moscow, 1917), also published, and provided with twelve reproductions, by Centrifuge. *Picasso and Environs* is an original, penetrating, and fascinating book, which begins with four fragmentary chapters revolving around Picasso and barely touching him. Actually it is a book on aesthetics, also containing a polemical treatise, which consists of anecdotes, aphorisms, quotations, remarks, and insights. As a conscious paradox, Aksenov turns to the actual analysis of Picasso's art and artistic evolution only in the essay that forms an appendix to the book; but it is so subtle and thoroughly professional that it deserves translation into other languages even now, fifty years after publication.[87] Alexandra Exter, the artist who played a part in the poetic formation of Benedict Livshits, designed a cubistic cover for the book. She also illustrated Aksenov's book of poetry with two cubistic etchings. Publication of an album of her drawings was planned by Centrifuge.

All things said, Aksenov emerges as an important figure of late prerevolutionary Russian futurism. He represents a curious fulfillment of ego-futurism, which no ego-futurist proper could have accomplished. Aksenov's mild urbanism, alternating city interiors with cityscapes, is truly Western and genuinely refined, especially as offered in his dry, moderately humorous, conversational idiom. Severyanin and his followers could only dream of such an achievement, lacking, as they did, education and a firsthand knowledge of the West, and presenting, therefore, only a vulgarization, a caricature, or a homespun imitation. Like most futurists of the ego variety, Aksenov does not take words apart and does not even stress the "internal form" of the word to excess; but he does play on the semantic color of words in a cubistic way, and he prefers figurative verbal cross sections or intercrossings, rather than factual ones. In this sense, he still deserves to be called a cubo-futurist more than any of the Hylaeans, who seldom, if ever, really achieved cubistic effects in poetry.

As a Centrifugist, Aksenov was a rhythm worshiper. In fact, rhythm was for him the very spine of any art: "Art is the construction of stable likenesses of what one has experienced emotionally by means of the rhythmic arrangement of the medium one selects"; "The foundation of art is not beauty (which does not even exist in nature), but rhythm." These two statements are typical of Aksenov.[88] In the distant future, however, Aksenov envisioned a complete disappearance of art, because the people would be so highly organized rhythmically that a mere contemplation of mathematical formulas would give them aesthetic satisfaction.[89] He wrote, but could never publish, articles on "experimental metrics," and he studied the contemporary theoreticians of verse diligently (Paul Verrier, Pierre Rousselot, Eugene Landry, Edward Wheeler Scripture, among others). Like Bobrov, Aksenov admired Pushkin and felt that any good Russian verse had to be written according to the laws of Pushkin's verse.[90]

Aksenov's other book published by Centrifuge was *Elisavetintsy* ("Elizabethans," Moscow, 1916). He was a pioneer in the translation (into Russian) and the study of Elizabethan drama other than that of Shakespeare and Marlowe. This first volume contained John Ford's " 'Tis Pity She's a Whore," John Webster's "The White Devil," and Cyril Tourneur's "The Atheist's Tragedy." Two more volumes were in preparation. Toward the end of his life, when his poetry was completely ignored, Aksenov was widely respected in Russia for his contribution in this area, as well as for his studies of Shakespeare.[91] In contradistinction to Bobrov, who considered theater an inferior art,[92] Aksenov was attracted to both drama and theater. In 1918 Centrifuge published his imitation of an ancient tragedy, *Korinfyane* ("The Corinthians"). It is Aksenov's version of the Medea story, written for "an imaginary theater" and preceded by an interesting preface that dismisses traditional Russian (and German) versification as "artificial and perverse," whereas English, French, and Polish verse are considered as based upon the "organic rhythmization of speech." In the tragedy itself, the most fascinating thing, besides "the quotation method" and consistent anachronisms, is the choruses, which are excellent examples of Aksenov's own futurist poetry. Later he developed a close relationship with the famous director, Vsevolod Meyerhold, and not only translated European plays for a production in the Meyerhold theater, but also worked on theoretical problems of the theater.

Otherwise, Aksenov's biography after the Revolution included a brief membership in the Communist party, chairmanship of the All-Russian Union of Poets (an apolitical organization known as "Sopo"), and teaching at the university level. He also belonged first to the short-lived poetic group, *Moskovskii Parnas* ("Moscow Parnassus"), which included Bobrov and Shilling, and later joined the famous constructivists. His poetry, which became in the meantime more conservative, appeared until the beginning of the 1930's in various miscellanies, both before and after the publication of his last book of verse, *Serenada* ("Serenade," Moscow, 1920).* Now Aksenov is forgotten in Russia, and the recent literary encyclopedia did not include him.

Though books bearing the Centrifuge imprint continued to appear until 1920, the group itself seems to have ceased to exist around the end of 1917. A third miscellany,[93] with the prominent participation of Aksenov and a promised contribution by Mayakovsky, but otherwise without any changes, was announced, but never appeared. Neither did "Tsentrifuga—Pushkinu" ("The Centrifuge—To Pushkin"), under the editorship of Valery Bryusov appear; but this projected volume demonstrated once more not only the presence of a Pushkin cult within the group, but the continuing ties of Centrifugists with symbolism as well. Centrifuge members also thought of publishing a bimonthly, "Vestnik Tsentrifugi."

7 DECLINE

In the preceding chapters I have attempted to show that it is incorrect to regard (as many still do) the evolution of Hylaea as the only history of Russian futurism. After the Revolution of 1917, the former Hylaeans regrouped, absorbed some non-Hylaeans (Aseyev, Pasternak, Tretyakov), made a strong bid for literary power in the young Soviet state, and generally created the impression that they alone represented (and had represented) the futurist movement in Russia. Subsequent memoirs have contributed further to this: Kamensky alone wrote no less than four books of memoirs, covering again and again the good old cubo-futurist days.[1] There is no doubt, of course, that the Hylaeans were the *central* futurist group: they started the history of the movement; on the whole, they produced the greater poets and the most flamboyant personalities; and they dominated the literary stage more consistently. In a sense, they also illustrate better than any other group the gradual disintegration of the movement before the Revolution. This final phase, which coincided with World War I, was ambiguous, combining, as it did, both a decay in vigor and a growth in prestige.

Despite the continuing negative attitude of the daily press, the recognition of futurism on the part of the literary elite became obvious during these last years. The futurists showed up in literary salons and paid visits to literary luminaries (Blok, Sologub, Gumilev, and Akhmatova). They ceased to appear in print as a militant group, but published their work individually as they saw fit. It was said of them in 1915: "Critics write about them, readers buy their books, and everybody talks about them." [2] Still this seemingly ideal situation did not satisfy the heroes of the day, and Kamensky, for instance, showed a touchiness about being attacked so unlike the classical futurist "joy in being booed." [3] Poets who had once been proud of being outcasts now yearned to become part of the literary establishment. It is especially noticeable in scattered reports of brief summer sojourns of the leading cubo-futurists at the *dacha*'s of their avant-garde allies or sympathizers in Kuokkala, Finland. It was there that some of these futurist "monsters" were introduced to the most celebrated realist painter of Russia, Ilya Repin, and they behaved so well that he found them "polite and peaceful." [4]

Living, however, became difficult for futurists. The war distracted their audiences. Sensing this loss, David Burliuk tried to correct the situation by organizing, on October 14, a lecture, "War and Art ," accompanied by a poetry recitation by Mayakovsky and Kamensky; but despite the fact that the place (the Polytechnic Museum in Moscow) was the scene of one of their past triumphs, the public did not come. Both Burliuk and Mayakovsky, commuting between Moscow and St. Petersburg, tried to earn money by painting portraits of wealthy customers. They also participated in the avant-garde exhibition entitled "1915" (end of March) and managed to sell a few paintings. They wrote articles for newspapers (mainly *Nov*). Kamensky was commissioned to write a biography of Evreinov. Mayakovsky gambled and played billiards.

One sign of the recognition of futurists was their admission to the famous Stray Dog night club,[5] where the literary and artistic elite of

St. Petersburg gathered at that time. Wealthy outsiders (contemptuously called "apothecaries" by those who "belonged") were admitted to the club and were charged exorbitant prices for a night of looking at celebrities and perhaps hearing them sing or recite. By 1915 the futurists had become the main attraction at the Stray Dog. In the best futurist tradition, Mayakovsky, on February 11, 1915, scandalized the "apothecaries" and all those "who have a bathroom and a warm WC" by reciting his poem "Vam!" ("You There!"), in which he contrasted the horrors of the war with their comfortable life in the capital. The poem ended with the stanza,

> Should I be sacrificing my life
> For you, who love nothing but dames and grub?
> I'd rather be serving pineapple soda
> To the whores in a bar,

after which ladies fainted and their escorts threatened the poet. Other appearances were, however, much tamer, and all of them were dutifully reported in the press. A few days later, for instance, there was another Mayakovsky reading, during which the poet not only recited his poetry, but also delivered a lecture on futurism (the sort of occurrence that is hard to imagine in a European or American nightclub). Also in February, and again at the Stray Dog (which was closed by police in March, 1915), there was a celebration of the appearance of the first issue of *Strelets* ("Archer").

Archer was a perfect example of the new trends. Published by an enterprising man with some literary ambitions, Alexander Emmanuilovich Belenson,[6] this miscellany brought together, for the first time, almost the complete Hylaea membership (David and Vladimir Burliuk, Kamensky, Mayakovsky, Kruchenykh, Livshits, and Khlebnikov) under the same cover not only with some of their fellow avant-gardists in other fields (Arthur Lourié, O. Rozanova, Kulbin, M. Sinyakova) and with benevolent outsiders (N. Evreinov, A. Shemshurin), but also with such influential and established figures of twentieth-century Russian modernism as Alexander Blok, Fyodor Sologub, Mikhail Kuzmin, and Alexei Remizov. The celebrities received much more space in the book than the futurists; but, nevertheless, the general impression was not that of famous men giving a chance to youth, but rather that of youth elbowing aside its elders. This displacement was especially noticeable in the amusing juxtaposition of Blok's life-weary excerpt from his "Life of My Friend" and Burliuk's cheerfully barbaric "Plodonosyashchie" ("The Fruit-Bearing Ones") with its paean to the "pregnant man" at the Pushkin monument.

> I like the pregnant man.
> How good-looking he is here near the Pushkin monument,
> Wearing a gray coat,
> Poking stucco with his finger,
> And not knowing whether a boy or a girl
> Will come out of his malicious seed.[7]

Also amusing was the fact that the "elders" tried in *Archer* to appear more avant-garde than they had in their earlier work, whereas the futurists made no compromises. Sologub presented some not very successful translations from Rimbaud's *Illuminations;* Blok mentioned, with tired irony, the names of Khlebnikov and Mayakovsky in his free verse poem (he later dropped these lines), and even his translation of Rutebeuf's *Le Miracle de Téophile* contained a glossolalic incantation passage that, in such a context, easily looked like *zaum.*[8]

The most widely represented futurist in the book is Kamensky, whose impressionistic prose piece "Poemiya o Khatsu" ("Poemia about Hatsu") is an exercise in exotic primitivism, bringing together some of the poet's favorite themes (the circus and aviation) and using onomatopoeia and neologism generously. He calls himself a "songsmith of shapely words whose figures resemble naked girls," and he even "carries his soul, clad in a bearskin," to a "radioactive female"; but he is unable to control his often manifested tendency to become trivial and cheap. Much more successful are Kamensky's excursions in the area of children's language and his Russian "river pirate" songs with their coarse abandon, later included in his novel about the famous Cossack rebel Razin. Burliuk's other poem repeats in verse what the *Sadok sudei II* manifesto had said about vowels and consonants. Kruchenykh, in his only poem, elaborates on death and madness expectedly along the lines of the antiaesthetic grotesque; but Livshits, on the contrary, strikes a non-Hylaean pose with his one neoclassical poem about the environs of St. Petersburg. Mayakovsky displays a rather hysterical obsession with sex in an excerpt from his famous *Cloud Wearing Trousers,* then still in progress (with God-defying passages omitted by the censors); and Khlebnikov is represented by the first half of the charming idyll "Selskaya ocharovannost" ("Rural Enchantment"). Other items of interest are Shemshurin's detailed analysis of Kamensky's ferro concrete poems (see chap. 5) with the conclusion that futurism amounts to a portrayal of impressions, Evreinov's attack on the Moscow Art Theater, Lourié's proposal for the notation of quarter-tone music and Kulbin's extensive essay on cubism which details its prehistory and periodization, describes its essence, and criticizes its theoretical and practical aspects. An interesting detail of Kulbin's essay is his mention of the visit to Russia in 1910 of Arnold Schönberg, who is characterized as "a Burliuk in music."

Special mention ought to be made of the article "Angliiskie futuristy" ("English Futurists"), by Zinaida Vengerova (1867–1941), the sister of the famous scholar and a critic in her own right, who regularly informed the Russian reader about new trends in European literature. It is actually an interview with Ezra Pound, who angrily disclaims being a futurist, and calls himself both a vorticist and an imagist. The ideas expressed by Pound in his conversation with Vengerova are well known: a definition of "vortex," a rejection of both past and future, and art living in the present, but "only the present that is not subordinate to nature and does not just stick to life and limit itself to a perception of whatever exists, but creates a new, living abstraction out of itself." Vengerova portrays Pound as "tall, slender, and blond, with his long hair tossed back, having angular features, a large nose, and light eyes that never smile" as he "snatches a pencil and a piece of paper, [and] . . . sketches a funnel depicting a vortex and makes mathematical calculations that show the movements of the vortex in space." She also anlyzes the manifestos in *Blast*, and condemns them as theories not supported by poetic practice. She sees in *Blast* nothing but an imitation of "French futurism" (i.e., Apollinaire). She also gives examples, in Russian translation, of short poems by Pound himself and by H. D.

The appearance of *Archer* caused a minor sensation, and the press interpreted it in various ways. Some considered this "a Pyrrhic victory for futurism," since the futurists behaved well amid "proper" symbolist society, dealing no slaps and even allowing an explication of their poetry. Others found this "alliance between futurism and symbolism" not an accident and saw in it a sign of "a decided shift of literature in the direction of the limitless sovereignty of the word." Still others shouted shame on the symbolists for socializing with literary hooligans.[9] Sologub even decided to publicly explain[10] that he had never dreamed of such an alliance and that it was the futurists who had come knocking at his door; besides, he considered all futurists, except Severyanin, to be people of little talent. Sologub's statement contradicts Kulbin's letter, which says that Blok, Sologub, and Kuzmin did show sympathy toward the futurists and welcomed them.[11]

A year and a half later, in August, 1916, the second issue of *Archer* made its appearance and showed the "alliance" to be far from flourishing. Two-thirds of the book was occupied by Kuzmin's novel about Cagliostro; Sologub contributed only another small piece from *Illuminations*; and Blok was absent. Also missing were practically all the futurists. If one discounts Khlebnikov (who, after all, was represented only by the end of the poem whose beginning had been printed in the preceding issue), futurism was represented by Mayakovsky alone. His contribution was his poem "Anafema" ("Anathema"), later renamed "Ko vsemu" ("To Everything"), an outburst of unrequited love, full of hyperbolic animalism and religious imagery. A new contributor was the controversial Vasily Rozanov with two short essays attacking radicalism and the Jewish domination of Russian criticism. The liberal press was incensed, and one critic[12] saw some "logic" in the apparent union between the "left and right radicals," with the result that Rozanov's anti-Semitism and Mayakovsky's "paean to rape" appeared under the same cover. Mayakovsky had to defend himself and broke with *Archer* by writing a letter to the editor of a daily paper. After the Revolution, Belenson published the third and last issue of *Archer* in 1923, in which there appeared practically no futurist pieces.

Another recognition of the futurists by "respectable literature" was also connected with *Archer,* but in an oblique way. The central figure was the famous Maxim Gorky, whom the Hylaeans had dismissed in the *Slap* manifesto as one of those who wanted nothing but a *dacha* on a river—a tailor's dream. In the winter of 1914–15, David Burliuk and Kamensky, who were desperately looking for more earnings and connections, met Gorky. Gorky obviously liked them personally and even gave Burliuk one of his books with the inscription: "They sing their song, and we shall continue ours" (*Oni svoe, a my svoe*). The two futurists evidently complained to Gorky of being persecuted by the Russian press, and he was not against pretending, for a few minutes, that the three of them belonged to the same camp. Considering the futurists' plebeian background and attitudes, the whole thing was not entirely insincere on his part. Burliuk and Kamensky soon introduced Mayakovsky to Gorky. Gorky was present when Mayakovsky read from his *Cloud Wearing Trousers* in the Stray Dog. Finally, on February 25, 1915, when the appearance of *Archer* was being celebrated in the same nightclub, Gorky suddenly rose, went to the stage, and, pointing at the futurists, proclaimed, "They've got something! [*V nikh chto-to est!*]." He also added a few words about their youth, energy, search for new ways, and acceptance of life. For the futurists, this was a gift from on high. Even Peta (as was seen in chap. 6) put Gorky's words on the cover of its book, although Gorky had had Peta in mind least of all and perhaps never even knew of its existence. Gorky's public appearances after his return to Russia from Capri a year earlier had been few, so the press not only reported the events that took place at the Stray Dog that night, but began to discuss them, mostly reproaching Gorky. Since everybody kept repeating his vague phrase "they've got something," Gorky found it necessary to explain. In April, his short article "O futurizme" ("About Futurism"), with some deletions by the censor, appeared in *Zhurnal Zhurnalov* ("Journal of Journals").[13] It began as follows:

> There is no Russian futurism. There are simply Igor-Severyanin, Mayakovsky, Burliuk, V. Kamensky. There are talented people among them, and in the future they will "cast aside the tares" and grow into a definite entity. They know little; they have seen little; but they will, no doubt, become wiser, will start working and learning. They are subjected to much abuse, and this is doubtless a great mistake. What they need is not abuse, but simply a humane approach, because even in their shouts and invectives there is something good.

Gorky especially singled out Mayakovsky and toward the end of the article expressed a hope that Russian youth would perhaps refresh the stagnant atmosphere of contemporary Russian life.

Such words could hardly satisfy those who wished to discredit futurism (or, for that matter, the futurists themselves, but they wisely kept silent), and Gorky's former friend, the tremendously popular writer Leonid Andreyev, took him to task in an interview in a daily paper.[14] Admitting that he himself had been optimistic about futurism in the past, Andreyev resolutely said that he did not see any hopes for the movement now. The war had proved to be a real test for its members, and they had not withstood it. Instead, they had revealed their philistine souls to the world and had showed that they were nothing but entertainers for the bourgeoisie. Andreyev appealed to all those who loved literature to draw a line between themselves and the so-called futurists.

There were also attempts to "find pearls in the dunghill" of futurism, and one critic[15] paid posthumous honor to Guro. He declared her the only genuine futurist in existence, one who was able to understand the soul of the city, who got into the very essence of things, who knew the real spirit of the language, and who possessed the gift of simplicity. The critic not only separated Guro from her "poseur friends," but compared her with Bunin (not in the latter's favor).

Probably the most notable discussion of futurism in 1915 took place on the pages of the magazine *Golos Zhizni* ("Voice of Life," Petrograd) when it published Victor Shklovsky's learned article "Predposylki futurizma" ("Premises of Futurism").[16] In the article Shklovsky developed some of his old ideas (see chap. 4), but his defense of futurism was now much more confident. Using examples from Russian and English folk poetry, he showed how the ability of words to evoke a poetic image could fade and die, and related this process to that of the automatization of the reader's reception of poetic words and phrases from the past (this time, Pushkins works served as examples). Additional examples from architecture, sculpture, and the applied arts proved, for Shklovsky, that old art forms die. On the other hand, attempts by futurists to break old words and to create new ones make poetic language live again. Wrote Shklovsky, "This is an incomprehensible and a difficult language; one cannot read it as one reads a newspaper, but our demand that poetic language be understandable is too much a habit." And he went on to give examples of deliberately or essentially obscure poetry in the songs of primitive men, in religious chants, in *dolce stil nuovo,* and so on. Shklovsky's conclusion was that futurist poetry did not differ in its procedures from the general laws of language. In his article, Shklovsky even went so far as to make respectable that bogey of the press, *zaum*. He defined it as "the language that is, so to speak, personal, with words having no definite meaning, but affecting the emotions directly." To those who thought that the futurists were simply pulling the audience's leg with their gibberish, Shklovsky quoted from French scholars and Russian poets (including Pushkin) who believed that the sounds of the language express emotions. He also gave examples of natural *zaum* in the practice of religious sects, in children's language, and in folk and popular songs. Shklovsky's final conclusion was that *zaum*, though outside language, was not outside art.[17]

Shklovsky's "pro" opinion was counterbalanced, however, in the same issue by a "con" article, which, though it was an answer to Shklovsky's essay, preceded it. Written by Dmitri Filosofov, a well-known critic from the Merezhkovsky circle, it was entitled "Razlo-zhenie futurizma" ("The Disintegration of Futurism"). Filosofov reproached Shklovsky for missing the point and for failing to prove that the futurists were good poets; rather he was "hanging a lot of ancestral portraits on the naked walls of the futurist palace," which, in Filosofov's opinion, was a dubious service to those who claim the future as their own. In reality, he continued, futurism is at an end, with its heroic era behind it. The initial scare has proved to be unfounded: the futurist "flood" filled only a puddle, where now frogs are croaking. "Futurists have not conquered; they have become a part of the crowd." The very fact that Shklovsky mounted an academic defense was, for Filosofov, proof of futurism's failure.

The discussion did not end there; a few issues later, Victor Khovin, the editor of the neo-ego-futurist *Enchanted Wanderer*, attacked Filosofov, but his more-Catholic-than-the-pope attitude could hardly appeal to Mayakovsky and his friends. In fact, Khovin's article[18] was an even sharper reproach to the futurists than was Filosofov's. With fanatic extremism, Khovin declared that real futurism, far from being dead, had not yet made its appearance. He asserted that futurism was not a literary school, but the entire rejection of the dominant literary forces. The fact of rebellion was more important than any theories or even poetic practice, and Khovin missed precisely this rebellion. He saw much more consistency, grandeur, and heroism in Marinetti than in the Russian futurists, and he appealed to them to become real futurists (i.e., to cease to entertain the crowd and to go underground).

To be sure, Khovin's admonition was rather ephemeral, but the whole situation did contain the seeds of the decline of Russian futurism as a movement. The danger signs were there: recognition by representatives of the literary establishment, a general loss of vehemence and intensity within the movement itself, and some opposition from the left to this hitherto furthest-left literary group in Russia. A survey of futurist joint publications in the years remaining before the Revolution only confirms this picture and shows that, once Russian futurism had achieved a degree of success, it failed to maintain its initial freshness of outlook and was gradually watered down through compromises, opportunist alliances, and failure to produce new aesthetic theories.

Two of these futurist joint editions were published by, or with the help of, Samuil Matveevich Vermel (1890———), who had some, but evidently not enough, money for such ventures. Vermel was a Moscow aesthete and theatrical figure who organized an academy based on ideas similar to those of Evreinov, where many disciplines, including juggling and the "grotesque," were, or were supposed to be, taught and where pupils danced or mimed to Kamensky's recitation of his own poetry. Near the beginning of 1915, Vermel published a book of poetry, *Tanki* ("Tankas"), perhaps the first attempt to introduce this Japanese form into Russian—an achievement slightly diminished by the fact that the poems had little merit. Some of these tankas also found their way into *Vesennee kontragentstvo muz* ("The Vernal Forwarding Agency of the Muses"), the miscellany Vermel published with David Burliuk in May, 1915. Despite some indifferent contributions from little-known and unknown poets making futurist gestures (Belenson, Varavvin), or from frankly nonfuturist poets (Kanev), the book was the last full-scale demonstration of futurist strength. Most poets of Hylaea were represented in it (except Livshits and Kruchenykh), and it was enriched by the cream of Centrifuge (Aseyev, Pasternak, Bolshakov). The large pages of this book of more than one hundred pages are filled with impressive poems, and there are drawings by David and Vladimir Burliuk, and by Aristarkh Lentulov (among them one sketch for a set for Mayakovsky's tragedy). In addition to art, there are prose, drama, and criticism pieces. Even music is represented with two pages of "Composition pour violon et piano" by Nikolai Roslavets (1880–1944).[19]

The poetry is generally of good quality. Kamensky, expectedly, is intoxicated with aviation in his four flight poems, which he fills with various types of verbal echoes, neologisms, and even the sounds of birds. Mayakovsky seems to have found in the war an even better vehicle than the city for his self-hyperbolization and hysterical emotionality. The most interesting among his three contributions is "Ya i Napoleon" ("Me and Napoleon") with its "heliomachia"; and the most artistically successful is "Voina obyavlena" ("War Is Declared"), a masterpeice of "phonetic" stridor. Nikolai Burliuk contributed only one poem, but his two prose miniatures are quite remarkable in that their impressionism is transformed into surrealism. The well-developed and varied technique exhibited by Burliuk in these two pieces makes one regret that this underestimated writer was soon to disappear from literature, after having displayed a talent of unusual promise. Pasternak published three poems (two of which were later included in his *Above the Barriers*) and so appeared for the first time under the same cover with Mayakovsky. Aseyev was represented by only one poem, written with war as its theme. Bolshakov presented a six-poem cycle, "Gorod v lete" ("City in Summer"), dedicated to Mayakovsky "in memory of May, 1914," [20] and later to be included in the collection *Sun at the End of Its Flight*. These six urbanist "nocturnes" present the city as a mixture of lust and decay, "electricity and dust"; and they strike an original note on what could be termed "futurist sentimentalism," combining the most divergent influences and traditions both inside and outside futurism. Finally comes David Burliuk with a generous selection of his verse, prose, and criticism under the general title "Zdravstvuite, Mlle Poeziya" ("Hello, Mlle Poetry"). On the whole, it is a poetic salad, combining all possible styles (including those very far from futurism) and demonstrating Burliuk's omnivorousness once again. As usual the poems are often "modernized" by the omission of prepositions and by an occasional lack of punctuation. Sometimes there are naïve exercises in simple alliteration offered with the air of unveiling this time-honored device to the amazed world. This interest in texture, which Burliuk simply transfers to poetry from the area of his real achievements, painting, is exemplified in the frequently quoted poem:

The *a*-sounds are wide and spacious;
The *i*-sounds are high and adroit;
The *u*-sounds are like empty pipes;
The *o*-sounds are like the curve of a hunchback;
The *e*-sounds are flat, like sandbanks;
Thus I have surveyed the family of vowels, laughingly.

Burliuk is at his best in earthy primitivism when he, in the midst of all this boring eclecticism, throws in a line about "the wide, fertile, female pelvis," or gives a poem a title like "A Singing Nostril" ("Poyushchaya nozdrya"). The only prose piece attributed to him seems to be the work of his brother and sounds almost too "sissy" to have been written by David himself.

Despite its occasionally provocative, even cocksure, tone, Burliuk's article (which closes the book) "Otnyne ya otkazyvayus govorit durno dazhe o tvorchestve durakov" ("From Now on I Refuse To Say Nasty Things Even about the Work of Fools") is actually an admonition to be reasonable. In the fact that the futurists' creations are now hanging side by side with conservatvie paintings Burliuk sees that "the public, even if it has not understood it, has, at least, accepted cubism, futurism, and the *creative freedom*." [21] He sees a similar phenomenon in *Archer*, "where futurists stick like cockroaches in between the solid, moist logs of symbolism." Emphasizing that he is not representing any literary party, but expressing his own opinion, Burliuk appeals to critics and the public to become tolerant and "good-natured" and to recognize the right of any kind of art to exist. Alluding to the war, Burliuk even waxes patriotic and begins to preach that great Russia needs a lot of art: "The amount is the main thing; quality will come along by itself." This idea is expressed even more clearly in the subtitle, "An Aesthetically United Russia."

Amid all the urbanism, Hylaeanism, and reactions to war, Khlebnikov's early (1908) play comes as an anachronism. His "Snezhimochka" ("Snowchild-Baby") is a "Christmas fairy tale" about the daily life of wood spirits and goblins who live in harmony and friendship with the surrounding flora and fauna. Predictably, there is much folklore and archaic color in this short play, and its mythology seems to grow out of neologisms, generously created by the poet. But this idyllic world is, from time to time, invaded by stupid humans; even worse, the Snowchild-Baby, everybody's darling, leaves for the city.

There she is arrested by the police and finally dies, but not before she has rekindled the pagan Slavic spirit among the people. Khlebnikov's literary derivation here is clearly A. Ostrovsky's play *The Snow Maiden*, and symbolist drama. Burliuk printed in *The Vernal Forwarding Agency of the Muses* only a part of the play under an incorrect title and with many distortions. He also predated it 1906.

The alliance of Burliuk and Vermel was short-lived. The next issue, whose title was to be "The Autumnal Forwarding Agency of the Muses," never appeared. There is nothing to indicate that their other project, a joint art-theater academy, was fully realized either. In Vermel's next publishing venture, Burliuk was only a contributor, not a copublisher. This miscellany, *Moskovskie mastera* ("Moscow Masters"), came out in April, 1916, and was, in its appearance, perhaps the worst "betrayal" of early futurist ideals. It reminds one of the best "aesthete" publications of the period, with its good paper and type, "beautiful" drawings by Lentulov which precede and follow the works, and mounted color reproductions. Futurism went not only conservative, but deluxe as well. Actually, it is difficult to speak about futurism in connection with *Moscow Masters*. The very brief, manifesto-like preface is extremely general and vague:

> The Moscow Masters do not know of any art except the one they are creating themselves now. While inventing form, the poets do not neglect lyricism; painters, the picturesque; musicians, musicality. Moscow, which has created Russian art, admires the mastery of its painters, poets, and musicians. . . .

Poetry opens *Moscow Masters,* and no poet (except the publisher himself with his rather clumsy attempt to revive the eroticism of Ovid in the Moscow of 1916) is represented by more than three poems. And the result is futurism according to Vermel: nothing is offensive, almost everything is smooth, or tries to be so. Livshits is inspired by St. Petersburg's classical architecture; Ivnev continues his watercolor moaning; Bolshakov displays his urbanist dandyism; Nikolai Burliuk, in his last appearance in print, reminds one of the baroque; Kamensky works in his usual folk song–like manner; Aseyev offers a conversation between two warships in drama form (thus anticipating at least two well-known poems of the later Mayakovsky) and a haunting poem built on Khlebnikov's "inner declension"; Varavvin is at least varied in his futurist apprenticeship. Even David Burliuk sounds almost like a member of the Mezzanine of Poetry in his poetic meditation about lingerie. The champion is easily Khlebnikov with his two short masterpieces, "Eta osen takaya zayachya" and "Ni khrupkie teni Yaponii," showing him at his softest, tenderest, and most lyric.

The new name accepted into futurist ranks in *Moscow Masters* is Tikhon Vasilyevich Churilin (1892–1944). Churilin made his debut in literature as early as 1908, but was noticed only in 1915, when his *Vesna posle smerti* ("Springtime after Death"), with illustrations by N. Goncharova, appeared in Moscow and created a minor sensation in some literary circles. It is a bizarre book, containing, on the whole, rather poor poetry, but highly interesting in the way it combines primitivism and decadence. There is real (not just poetic) madness in Churilin's poems; and this quality, together with the dream reality of some of his poetry written in 1913, probably qualifies him as being one of the genuine Russian surrealists *avant la lettre*. The themes of the book never leave the area of the macabre: one's own funeral, death, violence, blood, suicide, and insanity follow one another unrelieved. Technically, Churilin achieves special effects by a simple repetition of words and phrases and by his use of conversation fragments and of exclamations, which sometimes produce an impression similar to stream of consciousness. Judging by the epigraphs, his masters are mostly symbolists, especially Andrei Biely, but their influence does not deprive Churilin of originality. Probably the best-known poem of his whole poetic career was "Konets Kikapu" ("Kickapoo's End"), a grotesque study of death and loneliness.

In *Moscow Masters*, Churilin printed an introduction to his long poem "Yarkii yagnenok" ("The Gaudy Lamb"), which combines bright colors and luxuriance of sound with echoes of Russian folklore and Old Russian literature, and also two strange short poems, whose quality can be described only as obscure simplicity.[22] After the Revolution, Churilin joined Lyroon and published there at least one book, the slim *Vtoraya kniga stikhov*[23] ("The Second Book of Verse," 1918), which, though dedicated to Petnikov, is filled with the gaudiest and loudest poetry in Russia, nearly bursting with paronomasias. Later, Churilin was active in the Communist underground in the Crimea during the Civil War and all but abandoned poetry. He was also connected with the Proletcult movement in Soviet literature, but his name disappeared as early as the 1920's. His poetry was printed for the last time in 1922; his criticism, in 1925. Then, unexpectedly, his verse was published in 1940.

Moscow Masters stands out among futurist collections because of its generous representation of futurist prose, to which more than thirty pages of the book are devoted. Rurik Ivnev's "Belaya pyl" ("White Dust") is a story about a genteel lady who gives herself to the postman on the spur of the moment. The story is constructed around a careful confusion of memories, impressions, motives, and characters (and even their "variants"), with occasional intrusions by the author himself. On the verbal level, however, the story is conventional. Vasily Kamensky's excessively lyric "Zima i mai" ("Winter and May"), on the other hand, is full of neologisms. This *Lolita*-like story of love between a sixty-five-year-old fisherman and the fourteen-year-old daughter of a factory manager is sophomoric in its mixture of pretentious verbosity, pseudoprofundities, and bad taste, and, in a way, is a version of his earlier novel, *The Mud Hut*. The *pièce de résistance* of the prose section (and, in fact, of the whole book) is Khlebnikov's short novel "Ka" (the Egyptian word for soul), which is perhaps his crowning achievement in prose. Written in 1915, this tale about Ka, or rather, about the narrator's ka (defined as "the shadow of a soul, its double, an envoy to the people who come to the snoring master in his dreams"), consists of nine little chapters and is a masterpiece of Khlebnikov's "irrealism." Ka's main quality is that he has "no obstacles in time," and so moves from one dream to another. The theme of time, with which Khlebnikov was so preoccupied, is ever present in the work, where both the ka and its master, the author, move freely from the Egypt of the XVIII dynasty to the Moslem paradise, and this movement allows Khlebnikov to introduce a host of characters ranging from Mohammed to African monkeys. Adventures alternate with clear, but fantastic, visions; simplicity goes hand in hand with the incredible; the story of a murder stands in no conflict with the author's strange, but not heavy, humor. Calculation and nonchalance are combined in this fragile and crisp story of the migration of souls; childishness is inseparable from scholarship. One can find here Egyptian, Arabic, Chinese, Japanese, Mexican, Indian, and many other elements. Besides the narrator and his ka, the famous pharaoh, Ikhnaton, is a principal character. He is murdered twice—once by his priests and again, in one of his reincarnations as a monkey, by a Russian merchant in Africa. The woman of the story is Laili, the heroine of the famous twelfth-century Persian poem, and she speaks in classical hexameters and writes Japanese tankas on a beach pebble that is another reincarnation of Ka.

Khlebnikov's prose places him predominantly, but not exclusively, in the Pushkin tradition. It is lucid and economical, but occasionally Khlebnikov indulges in rhythmic prose or in an imitation of scientific prose, or mixes his narrative prose with drama and verse. He even attempts a bit of monkey language. In "Ka" there are numerous unforgettable details, for example, a bathing girl crossing the transparent figure of Ka, or a whole picture reflected in a toenail of Laili, or a parrot quoting Pushkin in darkest Africa, or the passages about sleeping while walking and about a card game played against the Universal Will. Khlebnikov obviously planned to continue the "Ka" project, and wrote, in 1916, more prose along the same lines, but only fragments have been preserved. He himself considered "Ka" one of his central works.

Otherwise, in addition to more of Roslavets' music and to Vermel's fragmentary and not very original ideas on theater, there is some criticism in *Moscow Masters*. Vermel himself, under the pseudonym Chelionati, tries the role of the chief theoretician; and, though he avoids speaking about futurism, he labels the past decade "a renaissance in Russian poetry" whose characteristic trait is attention to the word and to its study. "The word's shape, the combination of letters in it, their appearance, and their sound are more important than any possible meaning. . . . Since the word is tonal or graphic material, one can increase it, fragment it, or simply invent it (transrational language)." Inspiration comes now not from classical antiquity or from the West, but from the Russian language itself. After his discussion of futurism and the word, Vermel makes a sympathetic survey of those whose work appears in *Moscow Masters,* placing Khlebnikov at the head as a poet who not only has a complete mastery of the language, but foresees its future and acts as its liberator. Vermel mentions only two noncontributors, Mayakovsky and Pasternak, and the latter's style is summarized as "perception checked by the attentive, cutting intellect." In his own tankas, Vermel sees "a road to a broad succession of words of Russo-oriental forms" (i.e., he tries to secure

place in the East-oriented, late Hylaea). A second article
work of the artists who participated in *Moscow Masters,*
d, by D. Varavvin, analyzes Khlebnikov's versification. The
ostly by Vermel, discuss recent works by Mayakovsky,
Kamensky, Bobrov, and Churilin, as well as futurist miscellanies or
periodicals such as *Letorei* and the *Enchanted Wanderer. Moscow
Masters* closes with a "chronicle" of the future plans and past activities of its participants. For instance, in November, 1915, in the Tower
(Vermel's theater studio, so called in imitation of the famous Petersburg symbolist salon), the tenth anniversary of D. Burliuk's artistic
career was celebrated (with Kamensky reading a paper); and a lecture
by Khlebnikov, "Past, Present, and Future of the Language," wherein
he expressed the idea that numbers may replace words, was heard.

Moscow Masters was intended to be a periodical, but its first issue
was also its last. In fact, Vermel was able to pay the printing house
for only two hundred copies, so the remaining eight hundred never
went on sale.

In the meantime, there was some futurist activity in St. Petersburg
(now renamed Petrograd), where, in December, 1915, a slim, sixteen-
page miscellany, *Vzyal: Baraban Futuristov* ("Took: A Futurists'
Drum"), made its appearance. It was probably the only almanac published with the participation of the former Hylaeans which really
sounded and looked futurist. Its cover was made of wrapping paper,
with grains of stone and pieces of wood in it, and the content was
properly militant and loud. The money for the publication was do-
nated by Osip Maksimovich Brik (1888–1945), a graduate of the law
school, who at that time had no literary ambitions, doubted poetry's
right to exist, and planned to publish detective stories about Nat Pin-
kerton, then widely popular in Russia. Brik's sister-in-law, later known
as Elsa Triolet (Louis Aragon's wife), introduced Mayakovsky to him
in July, 1915; and in no time the Briks' apartment became the headquarters of futurism in Petrograd (or rather, a futurist salon with Brik's
wife Lilya as a would-be Russian Mme Récamier). Their later *ménage
à trois* with Mayakovsky is still a subject of gossip in Russia, though
little of the gossip appeared in print. Eventually Lilya did achieve immortality through Mayakovsky; perhaps only Petrarch devoted so much
of his poetry to one woman. Osip Brik found his place in literature,
too, ultimately becoming one of the prominent formalist critics. In

addition to Mayakovsky and Khlebnikov, Brik and his wife had among their regular guests Victor Shklovsky, the ubiquitous Ivnev, and Victor Khovin. One time Brik invited mathematicians for Khlebnikov's lecture on the mathematical foundations of history, and they were interested, though puzzled. Brik published two of Mayakovsky's longer poems, *Cloud Wearing Trousers* and *The Backbone Flute*.

Took was planned as a showcase for Mayakovsky who appeared there as a polemist, the star poet (Khlebnikov, Kamensky, Pasternak, Aseyev, and Shklovsky being represented by one short poem each), and the main object of discussion. The book begins with the piece of invective that had caused such turmoil at the Stray Dog, where Mayakovsky had recited it almost a year before; the heavily censored Part 1 of his *The Backbone Flute* is to be found here, too, though it is printed without a title, but with a dedication to Lilya Brik. The recently published *Cloud Wearing Trousers* is praised and discussed in the articles by Shklovsky and Osip Brik. Shklovsky sees a major event in the appearance of a "young and live poet" amid a literature that has become divorced from life. He regrets that censorship has prevented Mayakovsky from printing passages that give "the political creed of Russian futurism," but adds that "love, wrath, the glorification of the streets, and a new mastery of form" can still be found in Mayakovsky's writings. For Shklovsky, *Cloud Wearing Trousers* marks the arrival of a new beauty and the new man, who knows how to shout, a virtue utterly neglected among the Russian intelligentsia brought up on Chekhov. Brik's review juxtaposes quotations from the symbolists, aimed at demonstrating their dreamy, mannered effeminacy, with excerpts from Mayakovsky which are full of virility and earthiness, and compares the former to pastry and the latter to daily bread. Brik misses no opportunity to promote the poem, and exclaims: "Go, line up and buy Mayakovsky's book."

The central place in *Took* is occupied by "Kaplya degtya" ("A Drop of Tar"), subtitled "A Speech To Be Delivered at the First Chance," and this manifesto is the only one Mayakovsky wrote by himself. Despite its aggressive tone, "A Drop of Tar" is ambiguous. The author tries both to be rude and to stick to the rules of good behavior; he cannot conceal the disintegration of futurism, but he still wants to proclaim its victory. The manifesto was obviously a response to widespread discussions about the "death of futurism" (similar to that in *Golos Zhizni*). At first, paradoxically, Mayakovsky admits this death. He cannot but see that the boisterous quarrels of the good old days when there was so much "gay smashing of decanters on empty heads" have given way to the boring debates of old men. Nostalgically, Mayakovsky recalls *A Slap in the Face of Public Taste* and its manifesto which, he says, urged futurists to "(1) crush the regulations that act as an ice cream freezer, making ice of inspiration, (2) break the old language that is unable to keep pace with the gallop of life, and (3) throw overboard the old greats from the ship of modernity." For Mayakovsky, the war that was going on was a confirmation of the prophecy contained in that anarchistic program. It had become clear that a poet or an artist could not portray war by antiquated, genteel means. Life itself follows futurism, he continued, and begins to create new words ("Petrograd," which replaced "St. Petersburg," is an example). "Today everybody is a futurist. . . . Futurism TOOK Russia in a mortal grip." [24] Having thus built up his crescendo, Mayakovsky explains that futurism's death was actually its victory, because it was now "spread like a flood in all of you." He concludes the manifesto thus: "But if futurism has died as the idea of the chosen ones, we do not need it anymore. We consider the first part of our program, the destruction, finished. So do not be surprised if, instead of a jester's rattle, you see the blueprint of an architect in our hand. . . ."

As if to illustrate the last point, *Took* contained two highly interesting contributions by Khlebnikov, both standing outside his strictly poetic activities. One of them, "Bugi na nebe" ("Buoys [?] in the Sky"), continues the poet's familiar exploration of the mathematical foundations of the universe. He laments that while the laws of space have been established, no one has bothered to study time. Khlebnikov tries to establish similar laws governing time, and half of his essay consists of algebraic formulas (he calls one of these laws "a boomerang hurled at Newton"). He again applies these laws to the histories of various nations and also concentrates on the lives of individual persons (Pushkin and Mlle Marie Bashkirtseff). "Predlozheniya" ("Proposals"), on the other hand, is a fine example of Khlebnikov's utopianism and pacifism. Among the twenty-six proposals there is the ironic suggestion that we should number thoughts ("there are so few of them") as we do houses. Then, instead of delivering an imitative speech at court, a lawyer would have only to show a card with a number relating to thoughts already expressed in the speeches of Cicero, Othello, and the like. "Then languages will be reserved for the arts alone and will be freed from the offensive load. The ears are tired." There are also proposals to single out Iceland as a place for eternal war (thus leaving the rest of the world in peace), to use sleep bullets in battles, to divide mankind into "inventors" and others, to give any- one the right to have a room in any city (which would have been wonderful for Khlebnikov, who was constantly on the move), to introduce a numbering system based on 5 and expressed in letters of the alphabet, and so on.[25] Brik planned, but never published, another miscellany, "Eshche Vzyal" ("Took Once More").

In the meantime, the tireless David Burliuk found another "angel" in George Zolotukhin, a wealthy landowner from the Tambov region who dabbled in poetry. Burliuk said later with a sigh that had he found Zolotukhin earlier, the entire history of Russian futurism "would prob- ably have been brighter, richer, and wider." [26] Zolotukhin, however, had gambled away much of his wealth and was close to bankruptcy at the time Burliuk met him. In 1915 Zolotukhin published a huge book of his own poetry entitled *Opaly* ("Opals"), which imitated the excesses of Russian decadence or the Romantic poetry of the nine- teenth century. It is silly, illiterate, clumsy, and in bad taste, but never boring, and can be enjoyed in the same way one enjoys boners or "camp." Ironically, the book included one antifuturist poem. With Zolotukhin's money, Burliuk published the last Hylaean miscellany, *Chetyre ptitsy* ("Four Birds"). The birds in question were Khlebni- kov, David Burliuk, Kamensky, and Zolotukhin himself, in that order. One critical futurist edition sarcastically called these birds "a singing one, a fighting one, a domestic one, and a stuffed one." [27] The book appeared in Moscow sometime before November, 1916, and contained only poetry.

Zolotukhin was generously represented in the collection; and, with the eagerness of a neophyte, he plunged into futurism without reserva- tions. He imitates Burliuk, Mayakovsky, and Kamensky; attacks the critics "who will never understand"; and embraces antiaestheticism, primitivism, the futurists' Slavic orientation, and even their calls to arms. The very first poem in the collection is entitled "The Verse of the Future." For Zolotukhin, futurism can be equated with maximum sound saturation. Rich and unusual rhyme predominates in his work

*(laty–Pilaty, goreli–gore li, grokhnut–grog minut, privez dochku–
zvezdochku, malykh–poymala ikh, metamorfozami–morfiya rozami,
etc.)*, and "root" alliteration is applied frequently *(Kolesa Kolinoi
kolesnitsy)*; but when Zolotukhin wants more striking effects, he
rhymes whole lines:

> Vypivayut bez ostatka
> . . . .
> Vypi voyut besa sladko

or

> Bystruyu zavorozhu Dianu gonboyu,
> Vystroyu zabor zhuti. A nu kon boyu!

Zolotukhin called this device "echoism-euphonism" and must rank first
in all of Russian poetry in its use.

Burliuk probably did not suspect that his own twelve-poem cycle
in *Four Birds* was to be his last poetic appearance before the readers
of Russia's capitals.[28] The poems are united under one title, "Kata-
falkotants" ("Catafalquedance"), and are called, in Zolotukhin's verse,
"free and distinct anthems sung in a cemetery" (which may be a free
rendition of Burliuk's own words). Actually, there is little new in
Burliuk's exercises in the macabre, the sepulchral, and the funereal—
exercises built on the contrast between a romantic phraseology and
the antiaesthetic content. Not only coffin makers and graves, but
muddy autumnal landscapes and even cannibalism are present. In
terms of technique, however, Burliuk once again goes no further than
his "compactwords" and the omission of prepositions. A curious touch
is that Burliuk here is obviously West-oriented, quoting Cervantes,
Huysmans, and Rollinat (in French) and introducing motifs of a
declining Rome into his poetry. So much education does not become
him, and he ends up looking like a poor copy of Igor-Severyanin.

Kamensky appears hardly more impressive than Burliuk with his
annoying excesses of pseudo-Russian style. He claims, in one poem, to
"forge sound from words," and he certainly is not satisfied with mere
words, sometimes resorting to a whistle; but in all this mixture of
sun-praising, shoulder-slapping, loud and brightly colored paeans to
youth, beauty, and freedom, the poet merely strives to be futuristic by

means of neologism and onomatopoeia. Actually, despite all his ferro-concrete experiments, Kamensky throughout his life never left the initial, impressionistic stage of Russian futurism. In 1915, when Maya-kovsky contemptuously dismissed (in his *Cloud Wearing Trousers*) most of contemporary poetry as "some kind of brew made of loves and nightingales," he unwittingly included his friend Kamensky. Kamen-sky occasionally attempts a non-Russian exoticism (and, like Burliuk, cannot help looking like a parody of Severyanin):

> There, in the shadow-southern cool of bananas,
> The cockatoo, the sonorician, is musicking.
> I will dance with a Negro girl until scarlet mists,
> And I will fall with her into a basket of maize.

Khlebnikov, on the other hand, is represented by one of his most successful and strongest poem cycles, despite Burliuk's editorial dis-tortions and misprints and the ridiculous titles and subtitles he at-tached, such as "Rayonism," "Soundism," "Sans-Jumpism," which do not have anything to do with either the content or the form of these poems. Most of these poems are full of violence, but one poem begins with a description of forest flora and ends in a pagan love ritual. As usual, Khlebnikov makes excursions into the Russian past (and in one of these poems there is a parade of ancient Russian nautical terms); but one poem, "Bog 20 veka" ("God of the Twentieth Cen-tury"), is a restrained paean to modern technology. Africa and Rus-sia, war and idyll, primitivism and the age of factories and electricity —all can be found in these twelve poems. Khlebnikov also tries new techniques, like reverse rhyme (*bese–sebe*), or imperatives formed from names like Genghis Khan, Zarathustra, Mozart, and Goya (the resulting tour de force has become a favorite of the anthologists).

If one were to consider the group that published *Sadok sudei* back in 1910 the nucleus of Russian futurism (and, in many respects, it was), then its demise came with *Four Birds*—a rather inconclusive ending, three dots rather than a full stop. Centrifuge still existed, of course, but more on paper than in reality. There were some activities in Kharkov with Petnikov as the moving force and Khlebnikov as a banner (see below), but these had more in common with the post-revolutionary than with the prerevolutionary development of Russian futurism. The individual poets who created the futurist movement continued to develop, however, and it was at this time that some of them proved that they did not need a movement to lean upon. From now on, we shall concentrate on their personal destinies and their artistic evolution, if any, with brief epilogue-like descriptions of their postrevolutionary activities.

War never became a cornerstone of Russian futurist ideology as it did for the Italians. Some of the Russians took a patriotic stance as individuals, but even that lacked permanence. For others, the war was an inevitable poetic theme or source of imagery. One thing is clear: futurism suffered from the war more than any other poetic school, not only in terms of the ebb of public interest, but simply because it thinned futurist ranks. Almost all the poets were of draft age. Even though not all of them got to the front line (and only one, Vladimir Burliuk, was killed), many could not avoid mobilization: Aseyev, Aksenov, Bolshakov, Nikolai and Vladimir Burliuk, Gnedov, Khlebnikov, Mayakovsky, and probably a few more. Some of them did manage to participate in futurist publications while in uniform.

The most pathetic of these war victims was the man whom, ideologically, the war suited best, the Germanophobe, Khlebnikov, who eagerly awaited the moment when "the Russian steeds" would "trample the streets of Berlin." [29] Despite all this militancy and notwithstanding the constant warrior imagery of his poetry, Khlebnikov was a soft-spoken, withdrawn, and eccentric man. Impractical and childish to the point of absurdity, he moved through life like a sleepwalker, jotting down poetry and mathematical formulas on pieces of paper and losing them along his way. Shortly before the war, he was seized by what his friends called a "hunger for space" and began to wander, crossing Russia from north to south more than once. He went home to Astrakhan in March, 1914, quarreled with his relatives, and returned to St. Petersburg; but at the end of the year he was in his native city again only to leave in the spring of 1915. David Burliuk gave him shelter in his recently acquired home near Moscow for two summer months, but at the end of 1915 Khlebnikov could be found in St. Petersburg (Petrograd) again, attending the "Latest Futurist Exhibit of Paintings, 0.10," visiting the Finnish *dacha*'s of literary and artistic notables, and being proclaimed the "king of Russian poets" at a party at Brik's. In March, 1916, he was seen at another futurist exhibit in Moscow. Amid all this hectic activity, he obviously went through a crisis and expressed his loneliness best in a letter: "Now I'm quite positive that there is no one around who can understand me. . . . I must break with my past and start looking for new things." [30] It was during one of his routine visits to Astrakhan that he was drafted (on April 8, 1916). Finding himself an enlisted man in the 2d company of the 93d reserve infantry regiment was the shock of his life, because perhaps no other Russian poet was less suited for army life than Khlebnikov. He began to mail desperate pleas for help to his friends, among them to Kulbin, who had connections in the army. He wrote Kulbin that he could not remain a soldier because he had already sworn an oath to Poetry, and he complained that "the monotonous and heavy profanity [in the barracks]" was killing his feeling for language. "I am a dervish, a yogi, a Martian—anything but a private in a reserve regiment." [31] But even Kulbin could do little, and only the ensuing Revolution finally gave Khlebnikov a chance to step back into civilian life.

In this context, Khlebnikov's most important poem of the period was "Voina v myshelovke" ("War in a Mousetrap"), a sequence of nearly thirty shorter poems, written, for the most part, between 1915 and 1917 (and many of them printed in futurist miscellanies, as well as in newspapers), but put together under one title only in 1919 and published posthumously in 1930 in his first collected edition. This work could become the bible of modern war protesters, and Khlebnikov their prophet, if only they knew about it: it combines his avantgarde technique, the antiwar theme, and an orientation toward youth. Khlebnikov laments the fact that the young people sent to the war "have become cheaper than land, than a barrel of water, than a cart filled with coal," and shouts shame to mankind, suggesting it forget hypocrisy and take lessons in cannibalism. But war is something that can be eliminated, and Khlebnikov announces a military campaign against death, which would put a muzzle on the universe to prevent it from biting "us, the youth." What he has in mind is finding the mathematical laws to regulate history. For this purpose, he wants to establish first "a state of twenty-two-year-olds," who are "free from the stupidity of their elders." There is an unusual richness of poetic intonation in this poem, from the declamatory cosmic and self-glorifying passages to the lilting love passages with their sound repetition.

Much of Khlebnikov's poetry of 1914–1916 has been irretrievably lost, but what is left shows a distinct change. On the whole, he abandons neologisms to concentrate on rhyme and paronomasias. Paronomasia is far from being a poetic embellishment for him; he seems to observe intently what grows out of language if he, say, changes a vowel while leaving the consonants intact, or puts together different words of the same meaning. He always seems to explore rather than to try to achieve perfection, and his manuscripts are the despair of scholars. A poem is for him a process, not a thing. Even without neologisms, however, Khlebnikov's vocabulary is easily the richest in Russian literature: not only does he use rare dialect words, but his lines teem with names of people and places. His phenomenal and unorthodox erudition is seen everywhere, and it extends from ancient Chinese history to the mathematical treatises of Gauss. If in the preceding periods elusive meanings were born out of newly coined words, now Khlebnikov's lines are based on firm "content"; but thoughts are so compressed and are presented through such unusual imagery that one is constantly dazed and exhausted by the poet's elliptical jumps, though one is forced to admit "the amazing simplicity of the so-called obscurity of Khlebnikov." [32] Perfect examples of this "simple obscurity" are Khlebnikov's intimate poems, written mostly for the women he knew, which are full of personal, hardly decipherable allusions.

Folklore, Slavic antiquity, and the idyll continued to attract Khlebnikov; but the themes of war, death, history, and the nature of time came more and more to dominate his poetry. Khlebnikov was the only futurist who not only thought and talked about the future, but tried to do something about it as well. His practice-oriented imagination and the inextricable merger of his poetry with his projects and research gave reason for some to consider him a madman;[33] but he was simply more of a poet than all his friends, whose pictures of the future were invariably "acted out" with more or less conviction and with more or less irresponsibility.

Another of Khlebnikov's themes, defiance of death, found expression in one of his dramas, *Death's Mistake*, which was published by Petnikov under the Lyroon imprint, with the addition of a few short poems, at the end of 1916 (though marked "1917" on the cover).

It is written in a primitivistic manner and has an ending that reminds one of comedies by the German romantics (Ludwig Tieck, for example) who aimed at a destruction of stage illusion. During a feast in a tavern, with Miss Death presiding over a dozen guests, the thirteenth guest knocks at the door and is reluctantly admitted. Since there are no extra wine glasses, Death has to lend him her head, becomes blind, mixes beverages, and dies herself. As is frequently true of Khlebnikov's works, this play has points in common with the Russian symbolist tradition, but the theme itself is well known from the work of other futurists (i.e., Aseyev, Petnikov, Mayakovsky).

Khlebnikov, who is still for many a creator of inarticulate nonsense and gibberish, actually created new meanings all his life and tried to make both history and language clearer and more manageable. We have already seen with what persistence he continued to write and publish essays on both subjects in futurist joint collections and in individual publications. One of the latter, *Vremya mera mira* ("Time Is a Measure of the World"), an extended version of his article printed in *Took,* appeared in Petrograd at the beginning of 1916. In this book, by the way, the author foresees the victory of numbers over words and counts among those who shared the same view Leibnitz, Novalis, Pythagoras, and Ikhnaton. He admits, however, that "the word, though it is no tool for thinking anymore, will remain [as a medium] for art." Mathematics always fought with language for Khlebnikov's affection, and it was certainly his greater ambition to "discover the laws of time" than to leave his name in the history of poetry.

Throughout the war years and even before, Khlebnikov collected an enormous amount of numerical data and asked his friends to help him. "I need books with numbers in them," [34] he wrote to one of them. He was interested not only in the dates of historical battles, but also in the number of steps a German infantryman takes in a minute. In May, 1914, he wrote Kamensky: "Jot down the days and hours of your emotions . . . and namely their angles, turns, climax points. I will build an equation." [35] He studied the chronicle of Pushkin's life, and his own diary of 1915 contains many birth dates and exact records of when he fell down, when he felt exhilarated, and what dreams he had. Matyushin and Petnikov watched Khlebnikov's work with intense interest, and the former helped him publish the results. In December,

1914, Khlebnikov expected large naval battles (on the basis of Islamic victories in the eleventh and twelfth centuries) which never came; and, like a true scientist, instead of being despondent, he immediately began to look for mistakes in his calculations. The search for "the central number that would connect all phenomena" brought him to 365 ± 48, which, in most instances, took the form of 317. No matter how one regards Khlebnikov's efforts in this field, behind them is the truly futurist dream of a free man, a man who will know the laws of existence and will be able to regulate his life. Determinism was always hateful to him (see his "Malusha's Granddaughter"). "The great sacred forest of numbers," whose rustling Khlebnikov professed to hear, showed him that "a breath from the same mouth of time covers both the windowpanes of stars and those of human destinies; the same laws work in both." [36] Khlebnikov continued his calculations until his death, and it was two years before his death, while wandering through southern Russia during the Civil War, that he changed his whole system, built with such patience throughout the years, and came to the conclusion that everything could be reduced to only two numbers, 2 and 3, in various powers. The results were published posthumously in three consecutive booklets of *Otryvok iz dosok sudby* ("A Fragment from the Boards of Destiny").

To specialists, Khlebnikov's linguistic theories may look no less fantastic than his historical calculations, but they are another cornerstone of his poetry and, therefore, demand attention. Besides, they are truly fascinating and not so devoid of genuine insight into the matter as one would, at first, suspect. Their foundation is a firm belief that the sound of a word is deeply related to its meaning. Similar "magical" theories can be found elsewhere, even in other twentieth-century writings; but Khlebnikov, true to himself, tried to do something about it. Starting with the axiom that the first consonant of a word root expresses a definite idea, he gradually formulated those ideas (mainly in a series of articles written in 1915 and 1916) for all consonantal letters of the Russian alphabet. Finding, for instance, that about forty words in Russian dialects and related languages which denote dwellings begin with the letter x (kh), he concluded that the idea behind x must be an outer surface that protects the something within from outside movements. Similarly, the idea of the Russian ch (written in Russian as one letter) was for him that of a vessel (*cháshka*, "cup"; *chulók*, "stocking," etc.). To demonstrate the idea behind *l*, Khlebnikov even wrote a poem full of words beginning with an *l* and invariably expressing a vertical movement that finally spreads across a surface. The idea that consonants themselves express ideas and thus form a kind of proto-protolanguage was full of implications for Khlebnikov. The most important of these was that language thus proved to be a bearer of inherent wisdom that had only to be uncovered. Originally, Khlebnikov believed, language did express everything directly and clearly, and "one savage understood another";[37] but later all the clarity and directness were lost in everyday usage. The task was to distill the language by scientific means to obtain those original meanings and then to build on this foundation a universal language that would, by itself, lead to a cessation of wars because people would understand one another, and wars would not be necessary. Khlebnikov finally called this language *zaum*, borrowing the term from Kruchenykh, but giving it a new meaning. For Kruchenykh it was a free, but often emotionally expressive, combination of sound, devoid of full meaning; for Khlebnikov, it was the basic meaning expressed in the purest and most direct way. Khlebnikov once translated a passage from *De bello Gallico* into *zaum*, but never really attempted to use it extensively.[38] His most ambitious efforts to demonstrate *zaum* are contained in his two postrevolutionary works, *Zangezi* and "Tsarapina po nebu" ("A Scratch across the Sky"). One should add, too, that, despite their "magical" aspects, Khlebnikov's linguistics have much in common with the ideas of a "philosophical language," relatively widespread in Europe during the seventeenth and eighteenth centuries.

Khlebnikov's utopianism found expression in another of his undertakings of this period. As early as the spring of 1914, he dreamed of a Platonic society consisting of the best men living on this earth, and he called it "the government of the presidents of the globe." The idea was that this would be "the government of time," rather than the mere "governments of space," and that it would finally dictate its will to the latter. Petnikov was probably the first who became enthusiastic about the idea, and he still had similar ideas as late as the 1930's. Together with Petnikov, Khlebnikov formed, in February, 1916, in Moscow, the Society of 317 and wanted to enroll H. G. Wells in it. When in August and September, 1916, he got a month's furlough, he went directly to Kharkov, where Aseyev (as well as Petnikov) happened to be, and they decided to start a periodical. It was at this time that they also published, in the form of a scroll, another manifesto (written entirely by Khlebnikov) under the title *Trumpet of the Martians*. In addition to the author, Petnikov, and Aseyev, the manifesto was signed by Aseyev's sister-in-law, Maria Sinyakova, and by Bozhidar, who had been dead for two years, but was deemed a suitable cosignatory. It was the first nonliterary Russian futurist manifesto, since it addressed the people in general and had to do with time as the fourth dimension and with organizing youth into one universal union or state. This manifesto may be considered the father of numerous undertakings and poetic works that, during both revolutions and during at least the first years afterward, resorted to self-glorification and to pronouncements on a planetary scale. One of the key sentences in *Trumpet of the Martians* was, however, camouflaged from the censorship: instead of *my bogi* ("we are gods") there stood *my bosy* ("we are barefooted") with a not very clear parenthetical clue that there was a misprint in a consonant. The most memorable passage in the manifesto is the sentence wherein Khlebnikov divides all people, rather fittingly, into *izobretáteli* ("inventors") and *priobretáteli* ("acquirers"). The former are described as a special breed, united in the state of time; the latter follow the laws of family and commerce and have "one speech: I eat." The future is described as the time when "a transman [*zachelovek*] wearing a carpenter's apron saws time into boards and handles his tomorrow in the manner of a lathe operator."

The same group (minus Sinyakova) published in Kharkov, at the end of 1916 (but it was marked "Moscow, 1917"), the first issue of *Vremennik* ("Chronicler"). A slim publication of merely six pages of small print, it contained some poetry and two articles on linguistics by Khlebnikov, as well as poetry by Petnikov, Aseyev, and Bozhidar. Most of the material is properly "Martian" (i.e., it speaks of time and is full of expectations for the future). Aseyev apes Khlebnikov in his quasi-philological essay about prefixes and their meaning, and grammarians would raise their eyebrows if they knew what Aseyev considers prefixes. An interesting piece is Khlebnikov's letter to two Japanese students. The Japanese boys had printed a letter in the Russian daily press expressing the desire to get in contact with Russian pen pals of the same age. Khlebnikov saw in their letter not only an answer to his desires to organize youth into a state of time, but also an opportunity for a congress of Asians. He adds: "I could understand more easily a young man from Japan who speaks Old Japanese than I could some of my compatriots who speak modern Russian." Following the letter, there are thirteen problems to be discussed at the congress, most of them echoing *Trumpet of the Martians*. Among them are the construction of a railroad around the Himalayas and the breeding of predatory beasts "to prevent the transformation of humans into rabbits." *Chronicler* ends with a survey, which combines reporting literary news and book reviews. Three more issues* of *Chronicler*, with similar content, were published during 1917 and 1918, and the publisher of the last one was Vasilisk Gnedov, who emerged briefly at this time before his final disappearance from literature.

The issues of *Chronicler*, as well as *Trumpet of the Martians*, were only formally an activity of the Lyroon group. Actually, at this time, one can speak about the final split of Hylaea into the old Burliuk faction, primarily primitivist and painting-oriented, and still characterized by its shock-the-bourgeois tendencies, and the Khlebnikov group, utopian and language-oriented, where the mentor was surrounded by young poets who had never belonged to the original Hylaea group.

One more disciple of Khlebnikov's ought to be mentioned here, though he never printed his work in prerevolutionary futurist publications. His name is Dmitri Vasilyevich Petrovsky (1892–1955). He met Khlebnikov in 1916, lived with him in the same room in Moscow, then met him again in Astrakhan, Tsaritsyn, Petrograd, Kharkov, and Moscow. He wrote interesting memoirs about these meetings and captured the spirit of Khlebnikov in his own early poetry better than any other Russian poet.[39] Younger poets, like Petrovsky, Petnikov, and Aseyev, were much closer to Khlebnikov and worshiped him quite unrestrainedly, whereas there was always a touch of insincerity whenever Burliuk, Kamensky, or Mayakovsky began to praise "their own genius."

Khlebnikov's theories of time, which could so easily qualify him as a crank in the eyes of many, were received seriously by this second futurist generation; for Petrovsky, for example, they "opened the bliss of feeling and perceiving oneself as a meaningful, complex part of the endlessly complicated cosmic formula." [40] Probably what appealed to the Russian intelligentsia in these ideas of Khlebnikov's was their combining positivism with the cosmic mood of approaching revolution. This combination attracted both the unemotional, West-oriented Petnikov, and Petrovsky, a well-balanced Ukrainian. Petrovsky later became a noticeable figure in Soviet poetry, and at the First Congress of Soviet Writers he appealed to his colleagues to accept Khlebnikov into the Soviet pantheon.

The five years Khlebnikov lived under the new Soviet regime were his most prolific and mark his period of greatest creative maturity. Language and time, Utopia, the Orient, rustic life, and Slavic mythology still attracted him; but it was in his poems on civil war and revolution that he achieved a new dimension and showed the rare ability that was his, a direct poetic vision of events and things. [41] After Khlebnikov died of malnutrition somewhere at the edge of a country dirt road, his legend began to grow; his poetic reputation, to flourish; his books, to be published; and his works, to be studied. It is significant that Mayakovsky's group claimed him less wholeheartedly than did some others, and the attitude they manifested toward him was one of respect rather than either of love or of understanding. It has even been suggested that Khlebnikov's *budetlyanstvo* was basically different from what was known as Russian futurism. [42] After the problems of *Nachlass* were more or less settled, Khlebnikov's work went through the stages of textual controversy and of posthumous persecution, and was banned in part for political reasons. At the time of this writing, Khlebnikov is reluctantly accepted as a fact of life by literary officials, but his avant-garde features are diligently de-emphasized. He is adored, however, by many young poets, and interest in him outside Russia is growing.

An assessment of Khlebnikov is still difficult. A few people protect themselves by calling him an idiot. The majority of educated Russians have begun to realize that he was one of the major figures of the Russian prerevolutionary poetic renaissance. Nevertheless, such broad evaluations seem insufficient; Khlebnikov refuses to remain in a pigeonhole, forces one to approach him again and again, and continues to grow in stature with each revaluation. It is quite possible that Russian poetry will be divided someday into the Lomonosov, Lermontov, and Khlebnikov periods. But Khlebnikov is more than a historical figure and an influence. He is at his most fascinating as an artist, and he is easily the most original poet Russia ever produced, whose very unevenness is a system and whose "mistakes" are legitimate elements of his high artistry. Khlebnikov's poetic imagination is unbelievable, almost inhuman; the reader is often unable to keep pace with it and gives up, exhausted. His poetic range, be it ideas, themes, or devices, is enormous, and he easily dwarfs all his colleagues: even Mayakovsky looks conventional, narrow, and monotonous next to him. Still, Khlebnikov's genuineness and inherent importance are elements for the future to reveal completely, and in this sense he remains a true futurist. In one of his poems (incidentally, not included in any collection of his works) he said, perhaps prophetically:

> All will be forgotten by mankind,
> After it arrives in the land of futurism;
> But, I, for my courage,
> Will be honored with a bizarre monument.[43]

For Vladimir Mayakovsky, the war years were a period of amazing poetic growth and achievement. It was at this time that he entered Russian literature as an independent poetic force and was recognized by such powerful figures as Maxim Gorky and Alexander Blok. He also became a professional man of letters, accepting jobs from newspapers and magazines. In October, 1916, an edition of 2,000 copies of Mayakovsky's first full-scale collection of verse (and his fifth book), *Prostoe kak mychanie* ("Simple as Mooing"), was published by a "real," nonfuturist publishing house (his previous editions were from 300 to 600 copies). In short, Mayakovsky ceased to play the role of an outcast in Russian literature. Some of this success may be attributed to Gorky; but, on the whole, his part in Mayakovsky's career has been unduly exaggerated by Soviet scholars. As was his habit, Gorky briefly showed enthusiasm for the young man's work;[44] but otherwise they were different in practically every respect, and later became complete strangers.

At first, the war caught Mayakovsky's imagination. He volunteered, but was rejected because of his police record. Then he wrote superpatriotic verse for popular war propaganda posters and postcards (e.g., "Germania grandiosa = mania grandiosa"). In 1915, he moved from Moscow to Petrograd, where in October he was conscripted into the army and became a draftsman in the military automotive school that became a refuge for several futurists, among them Shklovsky and Brik. Mayakovsky's poetic evolution is often described as a gradual realization that war was a massacre, which is sometimes ascribed (without much foundation) to Gorky's beneficent influence. The real picture was more complex. Mayakovsky welcomed the war as excellent subject matter for a futurist, and from the very beginning he treated it in a variety of ways. In some poems it was "the hygiene of the world" (which had more than mere coincidence in common with Marinetti's idea); in others, it appeared in its negative aspect as a destroyer of the lives of average people. There was no evolution from this first view of war to the second; they coexisted peacefully in Mayakovsky's work. In both instances, war was an excellent pretext for displaying a huge voice and violent, hyperbolic imagery. In poems of the second kind, Mayakovsky reveled in emotional outpourings, mixing sentimentality with hysterical raving. But one should not look for ideological significance in any of these works. As late as June, 1916, Mayakovsky complained to Blok in a telephone conversation that he (Mayakovsky) had written too much about the horrors of war without seeing them firsthand and wondered how they really looked.[45] At any rate, Mayakovsky, as a poet and a futurist, saw in the war an artistic challenge and an untapped poetic treasury more varied, more effective, and more modern than the big city he had used previously.

While still in Moscow, Mayakovsky had a brief job with the newspaper *Nov*, and wrote for it in November, 1914, more than a dozen articles on poetry and art. He made several clear statements in those articles (despite occasional inconsistencies). For Mayakovsky, the traditional (i.e., realist and symbolist) art and literature failed to meet the challenge of war artistically because they were conventional, effeminate, and non-Russian. On the other hand, war was proof that the Russian avant-garde had been right all along. "Try to paint the war, this rosy-cheeked beauty who wears a bright, blood-colored dress—try to do it with your gray, gravelike palette which is suitable only for making portraits of wood lice and snails," [46] he challenged the traditionalists. He was not worried about the destructive side of the war, because after it a new life would blossom on the ruins, which would need a new art. Mayakovsky not only repeated in these articles the old slogans from *A Slap*, but occasionally echoed Marinetti despite the fact that he hoped someday to "dictate to the senile West the bold will of the East." [47]

Another opportunity came Mayakovsky's way in Petrograd, when one of the leading humorous weeklies, *Novyi Satirikon* ("The New Satyricon"), began to print his poetry regularly. The publisher of the magazine was the popular humorist Arkady Averchenko, whom the *A Slap* manifesto had contemptuously dismissed, and so Mayakovsky's working for him now was a kind of Canossa. But for Mayakovsky the magazine proved also to be an excellent school of satire, of which he was to make extensive use from then on; and he handled satire as an exercise in the grotesque, which he later enlarged and emotionalized into the picture of the lonely poet surrounded by the big city's insensitivity, usually taking the form of gluttony. In some of these poems, Mayakovsky brings to one's mind Gogol's famous "pig muzzles." The best among them is perhaps the poem about the bandleader in a restaurant, who, before committing suicide, literally uses his music to beat up the disgusting diners. Among the lyric gems of this period, the best is unquestionably Mayakovsky's other essay in loneliness, "Skripka i nemnozhko nervno" ("The Violin and a Little Nervously"), in which the poet sees much in common between himself and the violin in a café ("I, too, yell, but I cannot prove a thing") and asks her to marry him.

Next to war, the love theme helped Mayakovsky to find himself as a poet, and it also belongs to the period under consideration. Love is hardly a theme for a futurist, Marinetti would have remarked, and it was never sounded very loudly in Russian futurist poetry, though some futurists did not avoid it (Aseyev, Kamensky, Pasternak). But even within this context Mayakovsky cuts an exceptional figure, invariably emphasizing the tragic aspects of love (aspects infrequent or lacking in his own life). The love theme reigns supreme in three of the four major works written by Mayakovsky during the war. To this day, the most famous among them is *Oblako v shtanakh* ("Cloud Wearing Trousers"), with the title ironically suggesting a combination of tenderness and earthiness in the poet. This poem brought its author real recognition, though it was published (by Osip Brik in September, 1915, as an individual edition) in a ridiculously mutilated form. At the end, for example, censorship left nothing but six pages of dots. The poem is in four cantos, and three years after publication

1915

Mayakovsky himself explained it as a quadruple rebellion: down with your love, down with your art, down with your social structure, and down with your religion. Whether or not the author had so explicit a plan in mind when he was writing the poem, it certainly inaugurated his second futurist phase, deepening, as it did, the pure aestheticism of his first phase in both an emotional and an intellectual direction. In many respects, however, there are connections between this poem and the earlier tragedy, *Vladimir Mayakovsky*. The section dealing with love is a triumph of Mayakovsky's art. From the gong-like beginning to the concluding heart-on-fire scene, there is not one word too many, and the tension of the hero's waiting for the girl in a hotel room is almost unbearable in its intensity: he melts the windowpane with his forehead while watching the rainy night in the city outside and waiting for his tardy date; and when she arrives, the hotel doors clatter like teeth. The tragic situation is basically similar in all three of Mayakovsky's long poems about love: the girl marries (or stays with, or goes to) another man because he is a better provider. But in Mayakovsky, the surface reasons, which may be downright adolescent, do not count; what is important are the intensity and the dynamism of his emotion and his art. The love theme is continued in the fourth part, in which the hero asks for another girl's[48] body "as Christians ask: Give us this day our daily bread." Rejected again, he turns, as an outlet, to defying God; but his defiance amounts to a few disrespectful words and a threat to knife Him, and then he quickly cools off. Though, based on the poem thus far, one might accuse Mayakovsky of being a schoolboy ready to sob at his mother's knees because a classmate refused to give him a date, everything is saved by a magnificent image of the deaf universe at the end of the poem.

If the first and last cantos of *Cloud Wearing Trousers* are clear and simple, the ideological parts sandwiched between them are fragmentary, contradictory, and not quite articulate. It was obviously easier for Mayakovsky "to turn himself inside out so that nothing is left but lips" than to preach. The stance is that of a nihilistic prophet, of a "shout-on-his-lips Zarathustra," or of "the thirteenth apostle" (which, incidentally, was the original title for the poem, banned by the censors). The most explicit passage, and one that is, therefore, often quoted, is the one where the street is described as "tongueless" and abandoned by cowardly poets. The people of the street, "students, prostitutes, and contractors," as well as other "prisoners of the leprosarium, the city," deserve a new kind of poetry, which should combine "the noise of factory and laboratory" with things of immediate and direct individual concern ("I know that a nail in my shoe is more nightmarish than Goethe's fantasy"). The poets have failed in this task because they traditionally sing only "a girl, a love, and a flower under dew." Such poets are exemplified by the "chirping" Igor-Severyanin, of whose popular success Mayakovsky was becoming increasingly jealous. Mayakovsky, on the other hand, knows that the time has come "to crush the world's skull with brass knuckles." Though mocked by the present (and here, in his hunger for tragedy, Mayakovsky goes a little too far and even calls his own public appearances on the tour of 1913–14, thoroughly enjoyed by him, "the Golgothas of audiences"), he sees the arrival of "1916 wearing the thorny crown of revolutions" and he wants to light the way with his own bleeding soul trampled into a banner. Much fuss has been made about this prediction by people who always forget that Khlebnikov made a more precise prophecy to this effect back in 1912. Moreover, the visualized revolutions bear no socialist traits, and are described as being lustily anarchistic ("you, strollers, take your hands out of your pockets, take a rock, a knife, a bomb"). The political theme, however, is less presented through seditious appeals than suggested through quasi-political imagery: the clouds are likened to striking workingmen; the sky frowns like Bismarck; the sunset is red like the "Marseillaise"; the night is black like Azef, the notorious double agent. And it is imagery in general which stuns one most of all and sticks in one's memory even after the context is forgotten: the final stroke of midnight falls like the head of one who has been decapitated; a word jumps out of the poet's mouth like a prostitute from the window of a burning brothel; jumpy nerves really jump from the bed and start a tap dance; the poet uses the sun as a monocle and walks Napoleon on a leash like a Boston terrier.

There is no preaching in *Fleita-pozvonochnik* ("The Backbone Flute"), which was published in February, 1916. It is a poem of tragic love par excellence. The title is explained in the lines: "Today I am going to play a flute, which is my own spine." One may note here that Mayakovsky's poetry, which so often sounds like a trombone

A Cloud: love

solo with percussion accompaniment, frequently contains images of the "tender" flute and the violin. The title originally selected was "Stikhi ei" ("Verses for Her"), "her" being the now famous Lilya Brik, Osip's wife, who almost to the poet's death was to play the role of his Muse and who, in real life, became, in a sense, Mayakovsky's wife. She survived the poet by four decades and devoted her life to the study and promotion of his work. At the time of *The Backbone Flute*, she was described as "brown-eyed, bigheaded, beautiful, red-haired, and light-footed";[49] and she obviously, even at that remote time, relished the idea of becoming the Laura or Beatrice of the Russian twentieth century. She quickly had *The Backbone Flute*, this shout of Mayakovsky's soul, bound in lilac Elizabethan brocade[50]—and it was published again by that broad-minded man, her husband.

The Backbone Flute is half as long as *Cloud Wearing Trousers* and perhaps twice as forceful. It is certainly a supreme achievement to sustain a loud, anguished groan of love through three hundred lines without becoming monotonous. Love in this poem is hell and torture; symbols of madness, despair, and death run through it. The poet's thoughts are lumps of coagulated blood; he wants to crush his head on the pavement, and he drinks wine from his skull.[51] Suicide as a motive appears here distinctly for the first time in Mayakovsky's work. He blames God here again, but he oscillates between a satire of, and a prayer to, the one whom he calls the "All-High Inquisitor." Hyperbolism can be found here not only in individual tropes or in phrases calling this love the last love on earth, but also in the magnificent tale of the chase of Lilya (who is named in the poem) around the globe, which is reminiscent of both Andrew Marvell and the Keystone Kops. The poem is also the first real display of the compound rhyme that was to become one of Mayakovsky's trademarks. Aseyev wrote in his review that Mayakovsky's rhymes shine like the muzzles of revolvers.[52] Large-scale contrasts (between the crown and St. Helena, the king of universe and chains) make the poem resemble an eighteenth-century Russian ode, but the I-cannot-afford-you finale is an anticlimax. Present-day Soviet critics interpret this ending as an exposé of capitalism's inhuman nature since it bases human relationships only on money and property, but the poem is clearly a hyperbolization of a personal predicament. Mayakovsky's

[handwritten annotation: War as the hygiene of the world]

denunciation of capitalism did not really start until after the Revolution.

A radically new departure was the mammoth, five-canto *Voina i mir* ("War and Universe"), which Mayakovsky spent the whole of 1916 writing but was able to publish in a separate edition only after the Revolution. Though different, *War and Universe* does resemble his other major works of the period: it is loud and hyperbolic—and Mayakovsky succeeds in sustaining these qualities until the end without boring the reader. Like other works of his, it has a prologue and a dedication. In the prologue, the poet appears as the herald of the future. The dedication, to be sure, is to Lilya, and in it Mayakovsky rather pathetically begs for her compassion because he has been drafted and might be killed in the war. But these familiar features do not cancel the essential difference: except in those introductory sections, the poet seldom intrudes in person and never with personal problems. Instead, he becomes "objective," concentrating on events rather than on his own emotions. But this does not preclude emotionality as the way to present ideas and events. On the contrary, the poem is a parade of oratory with exclamations, strong words, an accumulation of sound, and larger spaces between the rhymed endings than ever. Still the emotion is rhetorical, rather than individually human. Trying to achieve a wider variety of color, Mayakovsky resorts to typographical tricks, so dear to many of the futurists. He uses large print, prolongs vowels in his words, fragments his lines more than ever before, and introduces passages of music (church chants, a tango ["El Choclo"], the roll of a drum).

The compositional plan of *War and Universe* is as clear as it can possibly be, with each of the five sections fulfilling a distinct function. The beginning is a grotesque picture of prewar mankind, engrossed in eating, drinking, and lust, with its soul "gnawed by the ruble." Many motifs of Mayakovsky's *New Satyricon* poetry are gathered and intensified here, culminating in the spectacle of a day giving way to a night, which is presented also through the symbols of filth and lechery. Thus war is inevitable as "hygiene of the world." "If people are not gathered into platoons, if their veins are not opened, the contaminated earth will die." The most arresting episode in *War and Universe* is related at the beginning of the third canto, where the

313

poet invites Nero to watch World War I, which is presented as a gladiators' fight, and the tension before the beginning of military action is likened to a coitus. It is also in this third canto, however, that the mood changes from a spectator's breathless expectancy to the despair that must result from seeing blood endlessly spilled. As is his habit, Mayakovsky satirically depicts "another world," where the soul of a slain soldier fails to find any gods: they fled, frightened by the war. The fourth canto offers the familiar sight of Mayakovsky's compassionate breast-beating with almost Dostoevskian overtones. The poet takes upon himself the guilt and admits his responsibility for all the cruelties perpetrated by man, but he also expresses the hope that there will be born a new breed of men who will surpass God in goodness and charity. From here on, there comes a transition to the picture of a happy future on this earth after a general resurrection. Bones rise from the mounds and are covered with flesh; severed limbs search for their owners. In this time of peace and plenty, cannons graze like cattle, czars walk under the supervision of nannies, and Cain plays checkers with Jesus Christ. The poem ends in an apotheosis ("Slava! Slava!") of the kind one finds at the end of many Russian operas. In *War and Universe*, Mayakovsky's attitude definitely changed from his initial futurist acceptance of war to pacificism, though the Marinettian attitude was not entirely absent and definitely not condemned. It is even said that in the final Utopia, "in every youth, there is the gunpowder of Marinetti."

One could argue whether or not Mayakovsky's next major poem, *Chelovek* ("Man"), belongs to his prerevolutionary work. It was begun as early as 1916, but in its final form it bears the imprint of the Soviet era, especially in its portrayal of "the other man" as the posterlike figure of the Sovereign of Everything, the epitome of capitalism. *Man* is one more recounting of Mayakovsky's "inextinguishable fire of unimaginable love," and it contains such familiar things as a Whitmanesque self-glorification, the theme of suicide, a satirical portrayal of life in paradise as *zalizannaya skuka* (sleeked-down boredom) where angels sing "La donna è mobile." A plethora of religious imagery is applied, as usual, to the poet rather than to God (in fact, the story of *Man* is a parody of the life of Jesus). This poem achieved quite a reputation. Mayakovsky recited it before some of the literary elite in 1918, and it made a strong impression. For Pasternak it was "a thing of extraordinary depth and elevated inspiration,"[53] but his is an exaggerated assessment. It is true that the poem sums up the earlier period and forms a bridge to Soviet times, but the author claims here more than he actually accomplishes. *Man* lacks the freshness of *Cloud Wearing Trousers*, the intensity of *The Backbone Flute,* and the splendor and inner scale of *War and Universe;* and it seems verbose when compared with any of the three. As to the intellectual content, this aspect was never Mayakovsky's forte.

There is a queer combination of simplicity and complexity in Mayakovsky. His "primitive" emotions are complicated by self-parody, by the conflict of the lyric with the antilyric (Jakobson), and by his gambling spirit. He belongs among the most original Russian poets of all time, one whose presence can be sensed immediately, not only from his rhyme and rhythm and from his stepwise divided lines, but from the very tone of his voice. Of his many qualities, two may be singled out as his most essential characteristics. Psychologically, there is the ever-present desire to achieve the extreme in any area, which results in his hyperbole, his planetary scale, his visions of the future, his frequent visits to heaven and hell (in familiarity with the topography and population of those regions, his only rival is probably Swedenborg), his communism, and his cultivating of the "unpoetic." Formally, the key to Mayakovsky is asymmetry, which explains the shape of his lines, his rhyme system, and his lexical dissonances. Some may be annoyed by the relative poverty of his vision of the world and his psychological and spiritual immaturity; others may be repelled by the soapbox quality of some of his poetry, or by his gaudy colors. But Mayakovsky was a born poet. He created his own poetic universe and his own system of poetics. More than that, he was a supreme *poetic* intellect, which resulted in his giving his unique poetic shape to any topic essayed, whether love for Lilya or for Lenin, praise of baby pacifiers in a rhymed ad, or invention of an obscene impromptu. From this viewpoint, there is no truth in the statement that Mayakovsky destroyed the poet in himself by writing editorials in verse.

Mayakovsky's postrevolutionary development is too rich in material to be adequately surveyed here even briefly, but practically all its sources (even those of his propaganda writings) are to be found before the Revolution, when his poetic system took shape. When a certain simplicity of syntax and diction came later, during the Soviet time, it

all themes before REV

315

ally a change, but an inevitable ripening of what had already fruition. Still, there is much to appreciate and to enjoy ..g the works of Mayakovsky's Soviet period, with the poem *Pro eto* ("About That") and the plays probably deserving particular attention.

When the democratic revolution came in February, Mayakovsky greeted it by talks about an art free from politics; but when the Bolsheviks seized power, he quickly accepted their line that art should be subordinated to politics. Hysteria soon disappeared from his writings, and a certain good-naturedness and peace of mind settled in. He was not an outcast, no rebel anymore, but the servant of a just cause. The lost child in Mayakovsky always needed a nanny to lead him by the hand, be it Burliuk, Lilya, or the Communist Party. Not that his problems completely vanished after the Revolution. For instance, his kind of futurist communism was frowned upon by Lenin, who was a man of rather philistine tastes and simply could not stand Mayakovsky's poetry (fortunately, in those good old days, a poet did not have to worry about such things). Mayakovsky was often attacked by numerous more-Communist-than-thou critics. He wrote propaganda posters during the Civil War, later headed the futurist group Lef, wrote many poems, and traveled abroad. The most unexpected and ironic episode of his entire life came when, during his travels, he fell in love with a White *émigré* girl in Paris. She refused to follow him back to Soviet Russia; he was refused a visa to go to see her again. This was probably the immediate, though hardly the only, cause of his suicide in 1930, which stunned all Russia.

In 1935, ten words of praise by Stalin did more for Mayakovsky's reputation than all thirteen volumes of his works. One result was that there are now more statues of Mayakovsky in Russia than of Garibaldi in Italy. Politically, this recognition by Stalin (who privately did not enjoy Mayakovsky's poetry) was a stroke of genius. While Stalin decreed that Soviet literature was to be based on the impossible and backward foundations of the so-called socialist realism, the looming figure of Mayakovsky almost redeemed Soviet poetry in the 1930's and later. His poetic stature nearly made readers forget that he was surrounded in Soviet poetry by so many dwarfs. But unwittingly Stalin thus also helped the cause of the Russian avant-garde, because no righteous interpretation could destroy or even tame the explosive force within Mayakovsky's poetry. By now, this force has been largely spent, and Mayakovsky has become a bookshelf classic and a figure of the past. Yet even now he is held in esteem by many young poets (though not by the wide masses of people, who could never "understand" his poetry). Stalin's remark, naturally, increased the scholarly attention given Mayakovsky, but only quantitatively. An almost immeasurable amount of worthless, and occasionally illiterate, trash has been written about poor Mayakovsky in the past thirty-five years. The law of the vacuum explains why the best research on the poet's work has been carried out by mathematicians (a cybernetic investigation of his metrics), or why the best criticism of it has been written outside Russia (Jakobson, Stahlberger).

Mayakovsky's futurism remains for Soviet scholars an uneasy fact, and they try to dispose of the problem either by declaring it a mistake of his youth, or by insisting that even while belonging to this wicked movement, he was actually alien to it. For any unprejudiced person, however, it is clear that Mayakovsky is a classic example of a futurist before or after the Revolution. He considered himself a futurist all his life[54] and was perhaps more loyal to the main tenets of A Slap than any of his friends: the self-oriented word, "standing on the block of the word we," a hatred of the past, the urbanism, neologisms, the antiaesthetic and antimetaphysical attitudes, and an enthusiasm for technology remained with him throughout his poetic career, changing shape but not essence; and there is no other label for such a combination than "futurism," even if it is true that Mayakovsky's futurism was of a conservative variety (for instance, he never entered the area of zaum).

In exercising leadership over the futurist movement, Mayakovsky differed greatly from Khlebnikov. Khlebnikov merely pointed ways to solutions; Mayakovsky solved the problems, but in his own individual way, because, ironically, he was an artist in the traditional sense: he felt compelled to put a finish on what he did. This trait, incidentally, reduced Mayakovsky's influence and made him less of a maître, even during his posthumous deification: it is easy to imitate Mayakovsky, but it is practically impossible to follow him. There was another difference between the two poets: Mayakovsky was a vassal; Khlebnikov was a king.

three Burliuk brothers were sooner or later lost to Russian futurism. The athletic Vladimir, after graduating from an art school in 1915, received his commission, was inducted into the active army, and was killed by a bomb near Saloniki in 1917. The scholarly Nikolai served in the army, then married a woman who was a wealthy landowner, and seems to have been liquidated by the Reds in 1920.[55] David, being the eldest brother, was spared military service. Contrary to the futurist Bohemian tradition, he was a family man and an excellent provider. When he met with shortages during the war, he abandoned his recently acquired estate near Moscow and, in 1915, went with his family to the Urals, where he combined art and business, painting prolifically and supplying the Russian army with hay. After the Communist Revolution he returned to Moscow and, for a time, was active in such enterprises as the futurist nightclub Pittoresque (fall, 1917, to spring, 1918). He also toyed, unsuccessfully, with the idea of bringing his art closer to "the masses": he nailed one of his pictures to a house wall.

The starvation and anarchy in the Moscow of that time did not long suit Burliuk, so, in April, 1918, he joined his family again; but at that time, even the remotest areas of Russia had begun to feel the Civil War, so Burliuk's family started moving across Siberia with the head of the family painting, lecturing, and trying to eke out a living until they reached Vladivostok.[56] On his way he even published his first collection of verse, *Lyseyushchii khvost* ("A Balding Tail," Kurgan, 1918),* now one of the rarest of futurist editions. Vladivostok proved to be an oasis for futurists. As the presence of foreign troops there made the situation more stable than in other places, Burliuk began to flourish again, reciting verse in the cabaret Bi-ba-bo and organizing exhibits while strolling around in trousers having legs of different colors. In these activities he was joined by the veteran futurists Tretyakov and Aseyev, as well as by a few newcomers (N. Chuzhak, Sergei Alymov). When Vladivostok became Soviet, they organized a futurist group, *Tvorchestvo* ("Creation"), around the magazine of the same name.

When the Japanese drove the Bolsheviks farther west and when Tretyakov and a few friends settled in Chita, continuing some publishing activities, Burliuk was not among them. He was already in Japan, painting and organizing exhibits of his work. After two years in Japan (1920–1922), Burliuk finally moved to the United States in September, 1922. America promised to be a good place for Burliuk, who knew how to find patrons of art and how to attract attention. He went to parties wearing a top hat and a strangely colored vest, with an earring in his left ear, a wooden spoon in his buttonhole, and a bird on a tree painted on his cheek. He preached something he called "radiofuturism," which, ideologically, amounted to preaching "soul" to materialistic Americans, while producing paintings reminiscent of the Italian futurists. America was not overly impressed. Depression put an end to most of Burliuk's activities, though he stubbornly continued to paint throughout the most difficult years, while also working for a pro-Soviet Russian newspaper in New York, *Russkii Golos*. Mayakovsky visited him during his famous American trip in 1925. In 1930 Burliuk became a citizen of the United States. It was not until after the end of World War II that he achieved financial success, and was able to buy a home in Hampton Bays, Long Island, and to spend his winters in Florida. He began to travel around the globe, busily exhibiting his paintings, and once noted with pride that he had sold all of his more than 16,000 canvases. In 1956, he accepted an invitation to visit Russia with all expenses paid; and before his death he visited his native country again.

In America, Burliuk never abandoned literature. In 1923 he gave money to a fellow writer so that he could publish Burliuk's poetry collection "Beremennyi muzhchina" ("The Pregnant Man") in Berlin, but the prospective publisher spent the money for his return trip to Russia. In New York, Burliuk entered the literary cooperative Hammer and Sickle, a group of nearly forty poets, writers, and artists united by their Soviet sympathies. They published, in 1924, the miscellany *Svirel sobveya* ("Reed Pipe of the Subway"), filled with unbelievably poor poetry, mostly expressing the authors' disgust with, and terror of, the city of New York. The more avant-garde members of Hammer and Sickle organized in the same year a short-lived group which they called the American Lef, and they published from August to October, 1924, three issues of *Kitovras,* named after Kamensky's publishing enterprise (see p. 330). *Kitovras* boasted about twenty contributors and was published by a certain V. Vorontsovsky, who demonstrated his abilities as both a poet and a theoretician. Burliuk wrote poems and theoretical articles for the periodical, in which the old futurist slogans of antiaestheticism, urbanism, and "pure form" were given with a Communist slant.[57]

Perhaps disappointed with group enterprises, Burliuk began to publish individually in 1924 and did so until his death, first under his own name and then under that of his wife. Some of these publications were books and pamphlets on the arts: *Russkie khudozhniki v Amerike* ("Russian Artists in America," 1928); *American Art of Tomorrow,** 1929; and a small monograph on the famous Russian artist Nikolai Roerich (*Rerikh,* 1929). Burliuk also published prose, usually based on his Siberian and Japanese experience. Verbose, sloppy, and uninteresting, showing little, if any, talent, the prose is contained in the following editions: *Voskhozhdenie na Fudzi-san* ("Climbing the Fuji-san," 1926); *Morskaya povest* ("A Sea Tale," 1927); *Po Tikhomu okeanu* ("Across the Pacific," 1927);* *Oshima,* 1927; and *Novelly* ("Stories," 1929). The last of these, seemingly not written by Burliuk himself, is probably the work of his wife.

Burliuk's American collections of verse usually combined poetry written in his adopted country with that written and even published before his emigration from the Soviet Union, and were often illustrated with his own drawings. He also published in 1932 an anthology, *Krasnaya strela* ("Red Arrow"), which contained reminiscences about Mayakovsky and a large selection of Russian poets. His first American collection was *Burlyuk pozhimaet ruku Vulvort Bildingu* ("Burliuk Shakes Hands with the Woolworth Building," 1924). It marked the author's twenty-fifth anniversary of artistic activities (from then on, anniversaries became Burliuk's favorite pastime) and contained his very first poem. It was followed by *Marusya-san* (1925), whose title combined the first name of Burliuk's wife with a Japanese affix. Here one finds his Siberian, Japanese (including one haiku), and New York verse, and some of it sounds, oddly enough, ego-futurist. *Desyatyi Oktyabr* ("The Tenth October," 1928) consisted of a long poem extolling the anniversary of the Bolshevik Revolution and recalling some of its events. Burliuk at first wrote in the form of a cantata libretto, with choruses, solos, and even speeches; then he changed to what he considered film technique. The poem is followed by an essay about poets who anticipated the Revolution in their works. Another publication in which Burliuk tried very hard to assure Soviet Russia of his loyalty was the booklet containing two long poems, *Tolstoy [and] Gorky*

(1929). The first one, commemorating the one-hundredth birthday anniversary of Leo Tolstoy (whom Burliuk had thrown overboard sixteen years before), called that author "a meek Bolshevik"; the second, on the occasion of Maxim Gorky's sixtieth birthday, praised Gorky's achievement. Incidentally, in *The Tenth October* Burliuk even went so far as to say that he, Burliuk, became a futurist only after reading Gorky's works.

The most ambitious of Burliuk's books was *Entelekhizm* ("Entelechism"), published in 1930 to commemorate futurism's twentieth anniversary. In its theoretical section, the man who never failed to mention that he was "the father of Russian futurism" made a belated attempt to contribute something essential to the movement's ideology. The book was also a bid for leadership in Soviet literature, where, in Burliuk's naïve opinion, futurism was still the wave of the future. Obviously wanting to update and to deepen the futurist doctrine of 1912, Burliuk quoted and discussed not only philosophers but scientists (Pavlov) as well. The result is, however, self-contradictory and confused, and even borders on being semiliterate. "Entelechism" is not even given a passable definition. The one thing that does emerge is Burliuk's desire to write some words backward (though in this practice he is borrowing from Khlebnikov) and to oversaturate lines with sound, a device not new, even for Burliuk. Burliuk sent hundreds of copies of *Entelechism* to Russia at a time when his family often had little to eat, but the book impressed no one. One of his correspondents, Igor Postupalsky, a student of futurism and the author of a book about Burliuk, frankly confessed that he could not comprehend the treatise.[58] More interesting, though not necessarily good, are the numerous poems by Burliuk which fill the rest of *Entelechism*. In them, Burliuk finally, and again belatedly, appears as an urbanist with his sketches of New York life, usually emphasizing its social contrasts. There are also poems that are pure technical exercises (mostly of the "mirror type," i.e., palindromes); present too is his familiar antiaestheticism ("the teats of the sky," "the snotty city," spitting on the sky, etc.) and a nostalgia for Russia.

In 1932, Burliuk published another commemorative collection, this time for his own fiftieth anniversary, under the title *1/2 veka* ("Half a Century"). This book is interesting primarily because it presents the largest selection of Burliuk's poetry written in Japan;[59] it prints some poems from the "The Pregnant Man" (which had never materialized), and reprints all poems from the first *Sadok sudei* in reworked versions intended as improvements. A curious trait noticeable here is the aging futurist's accent on culture and education. Burliuk uses classical motifs, translates Moréas and Mallarmé, and quotes in four foreign languages from a variety of poets and philosophers from Plato to Baudelaire, ridiculously distorting the originals.

It was at this time that Burliuk began to publish writings about himself by Soviet authors, for whom it was then difficult to discuss futurism in their own country. Thus he published two books by the art critic Erikh Gollerbakh, *Iskusstvo Davida Burlyuka* ("The Painting of David Burliuk," 1930),* and *Poeziya Davida Burlyuka* ("The Poetry of David Burliuk," 1931); one book by Igor Postupalsky, *Literaturnyi trud Davida D. Burlyuka* ("The Literary Work of David D. Burliuk," 1931); and Benedict Livshits' *Gileya* ("Hylaea," 1931), which two years later became the first chapter of his book of memoirs, *The One-and-a-half-eyed Archer,* published in Russia.

Finally Burliuk stopped publishing books and pamphlets and launched a periodical, *Color and Rhyme,* which eventually reached its sixtieth issue. *Color and Rhyme* is an encyclopedia of Burliuk. Printed sometimes in Russian, but mostly in English (i.e., in Burliuk's kind of English), and varying in size from four to one hundred pages, it offers reproductions of Burliuk's paintings (as well as those of his friends), reviews of his exhibits, letters written to him (among the correspondents: Rockwell Kent, Henry Miller), his recollections, biographical data about him and his family (he considers himself a descendant of Genghis Khan), and reports about his travels. There are also extensive selections from his wife's diaries about their everyday life, from which one learns, for instance, that at 10:30 A.M. on August 5, 1930, one of Burliuk's front teeth was extracted. From time to time, one comes across Burliuk's own poetry, and in number 55 (1964) there is the largest selection of it since *1/2 veka.* One can say little of this verse except that Mayakovsky probably would turn in his grave if he were able to read his friend's nonpoetry about nightingales, dreams of the lake, Chopin nocturnes, ecstasies, zephyrs, and Diana and Hecate. In almost everything Burliuk printed in *Color and Rhyme,* his warm and pleasant, but chaotic, personality is reflected; and although a student can find a rich amount of information, this information is often unreliable. Burliuk is apt to misquote even himself, and as to his bibliographical data, they are sometimes more than 50 percent wrong or misleading.

Burliuk's poetry has been described more than once in earlier chapters of this book. Critics found in it a continuation of the French *poètes maudits*, "aestheticism upside down," "vulgar diction," "absurdization of archaic clichés," and "magnificent cynicism." [60] One critic (Gollerbakh) made the correct observation that Burliuk's poetry produces the impression of having been written by many different poets. [61] Eclecticism is probably his most salient feature. He accepts everything and assimilates nothing, so that his verse occasionally resembles a garbage pail where melon peels, bread crusts, paper fragments, and whatnot are floating. He is really original and even good only in a very few lustily optimistic poems that combine a good-natured menacing quality with something like a rumbling in the intestines, and this feature practically disappears in his postrevolutionary poetry. When one reads Burliuk's poetry book after book (and such an exercise is no fun at all), wading through torrents of dull and clumsy verse which seldom betrays a feeling for language and in most instances is utterly non-avant-garde, one is at a loss to explain how he could have written a few relatively successful poems. Perhaps Burliuk the poet resembles an archer who shoots without aiming and sometimes hits the bull's-eye through sheer chance.

The story of the postrevolutionary Burliuk is pathetic in its ambiguities and ironies. He started it with loud fanfares of self-advertisement and, after that, never failed to remind the reader that he was "the great Burliuk," "the future[!] pioneer of world modern art," "a legend of Soviet art," "well known everywhere on all five continents of our globe." [62] But recognition was slow in coming, even in the field of painting where Burliuk did have a real claim to distinction. In all books on modern art Burliuk remains just a name in enumerations of the participants in the first "Der blaue Reiter" exhibit. In a recent book on Russian avant-garde art, [63] Burliuk occupies, perhaps unjustly, a secondary place. When he wrote in a poem,

> Books are written about you,
> You are mentioned in encyclopedias—
> You're on the roof, my child, [64]

323

he could hardly forget that he himself commissioned and published those books and that a mention in an encyclopedia does not necessarily constitute "worldwide recognition." [65] He became an ardent collector of mentions of himself, and a friend of his (whom he calls "my Boswell") dutifully reported to Burliuk that in one book he is mentioned twice whereas the names of Rubens, Gauguin, and Modigliani appear only once, and Chagall is not mentioned at all.[66]

Another disappointment was connected with Burliuk's stake in the future of Soviet Russia. In his daydreams, which were strengthened by the reality of the depression, he was evidently convinced that a proletarian revolution in the United States was inevitable and that thereafter he would triumphantly return to Soviet Russia as the recognized leader of revolutionary futurism. "I am a genuine Bolshevik in literature," he wrote, and more than once one is reminded that he always "defended the interests of the Union of Soviet Socialist Republics under the difficult conditions of capitalist encirclement" in the "country of predatory capital." [67] Again no one was impressed in Russia, and no one bothered to publish the memoirs he sent there. From afar, Burliuk could not see that his campaign against "understandable art" was a lost cause. Besides, it was not easy to anticipate in New York the zigs and zags of Stalin's policy in Moscow. For instance, just when Burliuk changed his usual "father of Russian futurism" on the covers of his books to the better-sounding "father of Russian proletarian futurism" (and when he, no doubt, was glad to read in Postupalsky's book that "Burliuk may become a part of proletarian literature"),[68] the Politburo suddenly turned against proletarian tendencies and abuses in literature. In one of the subsequent editions, Burliuk had to adorn himself with the vaguer title of "father of Soviet Russian futurism." But he refused to give up: later he went so far as to renounce futurism and to glorify Pushkin and said that he saw light in socialist realism.[69] Again, no one over there was impressed.

Contradictions were bound to begin flourishing in Burliuk's writings. The man who in 1913 made it his specialty to debunk Raphael now called him "forever a symbol of genius";[70] the atheistic lecturer of the 1930's who considered Christianity "a mass psychosis" [71] of history proudly announced after World War II that he "belonged to the church";[72] a futurist demanded that a museum of futurism be founded in Russia and monuments erected to the pioneers of the movement.[73]

Emphasis on his own greatness finally got mixed with bitter complaints not only about not being recognized, but about being robbed as well. Burliuk began to accuse some Soviet writers of using his idea of "compactwords" and other, mostly imaginary, inventions[74] while failing to give him credit and forgetting that he had begun to employ these devices as early as 1907 (which was not true).

When the Mayakovsky cult was started by Stalin, Burliuk saw in it the greatest chance of his life. The man who claimed to be well known everywhere on the globe was ready to settle for being a footnote to Mayakovsky. After all, Mayakovsky had admitted in his autobiography that it was Burliuk who discovered him and "made him a poet." [75] This admission soon became hyperbolized in Burliuk's imagination to the statement that now "every Soviet child knows Burliuk." [76] Another of Mayakovsky's remarks, that about Burliuk having been his "real teacher," underwent an even more bizarre exaggeration. Burliuk, a primitivist and a former "overthrower" of the past, forgot the bird he painted on his cheeks and began to parade as a scholar, a polyglot, and "a connoisseur of French poetry" who educated Mayakovsky, the wild genius, by incessantly reading to him poetry in Greek, Latin, French, German, English, and Japanese.[77] How Burliuk could have known Japanese (or English) in 1911 remains a secret, but his own level of education and "scholarship" comes through at least in part in his spelling of names in Color and Rhyme, where one finds "George Rouo," "Gauptman," "Maria Van Rielke," and even that "great Portugeuse poet, . . . Camdens Luciades."

The sad truth is that the man who launched Russian futurism, and whose very name sounded futurist to a Russian ear, has never been an avant-garde artist. Even in painting, he went no further than cubism, and there is strong reason to believe that cubism was for him just a means of scandalizing his Russian audiences in 1912 and 1913. Later he gradually became more and more conservative and finally settled on a mixture of Van Gogh and some Russian version of Henri Rousseau. He declared himself "the founder of abstract expressionism," [78] but elsewhere admitted that this movement was alien to him[79] and generally showed complete indifference to American art when it came into its own after World War II. His professed rejection of the artistic past was firmly founded on his thorough lack of knowledge of that past; one can almost say that his lack of education was a primary factor in his becoming and remaining a futurist. His poetry has always been a chaotic conglomeration of the clichés of various periods of Russian literature, a fact that was especially obvious in his postrevolutionary work when the early futurist trappings and gestures were no longer consistently applied. The eclectic-conglomerate character of his work was evident even earlier, but naïve tricks like the occasional omission of prepositions and the use of large print and "compactwords" deceived some critics (and the poet himself) into believing that Burliuk was an innovator.

Throughout 1914 Vasily Kamensky worked on his second novel, *Stenka Razin,* based on the life of the famous Cossack rebel of the seventeenth century. Razin had always been a favorite subject of Russian folk poetry, and he attracted the attention of poets (among them Pushkin); but there does not seem to have been a novel about him before Kamensky's, the main reason being, of course, the fact that Razin was still in the state of excommunication imposed by the Russian church. Among the futurists, Khlebnikov valued Razin most. Kamensky's novel was published with Zolotukhin's money in November, 1915 (the year on the cover was 1916), and quickly sold out. Kamensky later claimed that the second edition did not materialize because of pressure from the political right.

Stenka Razin (Stenka is a diminutive for Stepan) is clearly Kamensky's central work, and it demonstrates both the strongest and the weakest sides of the author's talent. The author's aim was "to present the essence of the Russian soul . . . in the single figure of Stepan Razin," which was possible because "Razin lives in every soul." [80] Like *The Mud Hut, Stenka Razin* is a lyric novel wherein poems and songs constantly alternate with various kinds of prose, including epically narrative, purely lyrical, and factually historical. One of Kamensky's favorite ideas of that period was "creating life out of song," which was, of course, one of the main tenets of the symbolist movement. His Razin arises not from history (the historical passages are invariably dull and almost irrelevant), but from those numerous Russian songs that extol and glamorize this chief of Russian river pirates. Even here Kamensky goes his own way, occasionally giving his own version of a well-known episode. For example, in the famous drowning of the Persian princess, Razin is completely cleared of wanton cruelty: she does it herself.

One of the principal themes of *Stenka Razin* is Razin and song. Not only do songs abound in the novel, but most of them are supposed to be Razin's own creations. In fact, Kamensky makes Razin a man with two souls, that of the leader and that of the poet, who regrets that future generations will remember him as a pirate rather than as a creator of songs and a "transformer of life." Thus Razin = Volga = Russian land = Russian song = Russian soul is developed into a predictable self-glamorization of Russians as the people of extremes and innate artistry, wild abandon and youthful sweep, childlike purity and animalistic strength. Such a paean to Russia had an enhanced patriotic significance during the war years. "I know of no deeper awareness than being a Russian," exclaims Kamensky.

Attraction for the non-Russian East is, however, also a part of Kamensky's "futurist romanticism." Persian scenes and songs (written in an imaginary Persian language) create the atmosphere of a fairy tale, with Kamensky thus entering the time-honored Russian tradition that extends from the folk epics to Rimsky-Korsakov's music. The novel's lyric, rhythmic prose (which obviously derives from such perennial favorites as A. K. Tolstoy's novel *Prince Serebryanyi*) soon wears thin. It is so full of kitsch *à la russe* (the variety known in Russian as *susalnost'*) that no amount of neologism can save the situation. The book has too much lilt and garish folkloric color. The overall operatic atmosphere is perhaps another quality that makes the novel so hard to swallow. Razin, for instance, sings songs and plays his dulcimer nearly everywhere: during the battle, in bed with the princess, and in the cage on his way to his execution. What makes the novel a partial success (and a genuinely futurist work) are its crowd scenes. Kamensky draws them by means of columns of words or short phrases, which produce onomatopoeic effects or consist of all kinds of shouts, Russian and non-Russian, creating the image of a robbing and cursing, loud, multicolored, and coarse mob very effectively. Some of the songs project the same quality.

After the Revolution, Kamensky rewrote the novel. He added more historical chapters, cut many lyric passages, and changed the title of the work to the more respectable-sounding *Stepan Razin*. This second edition appeared in 1919, and in 1928 there was a third one with additional changes.

The war years were a time of considerable personal success for

Kamensky. After his participation in the futurist tour of 1913–14 revealed to him his talent for public appearances, he continued this kind of activity. His poetry began to be written with an eye for effective public recitation, and the showman more often than not substituted himself for the poet. Trying to dodge the draft, Kamensky moved to the resort areas of the Caucasus and the Crimea and began a long and pleasant lecture and recital tour. In his lectures he appealed to the rich, the idle, and those not directly involved in the war to be like children, to hear the music of the waves of Eternity; to rejoice, laugh, and love; to sing songs and read his, Kamensky's, poetry; and to lead a beautiful and free life. In the Caucasus, he once recited his poetry from horseback in a circus, dressed like Stepan Razin. He also made friends with the Georgian and Armenian futurists.

Kamensky's constant companion at this time was Vladimir Robertovich Goltsshmidt, a colorful peripheral figure in Russian futurism who also lectured and wrote poetry in which he showed the strong influence of Kamensky and a complete lack of talent; but he did not have too much literary ambition and called himself "a futurist of life." In his lectures he appeared as a self-styled prophet of a new life full of health, sun, and joy. His message was largely antiurbanist, and he demonstrated it by refusing to wear hats and collars. During his appearances, Goltsshmidt wore a pink silk tunic and a golden hoop over his forehead, but what made him famous was his breaking heavy wooden boards against his own head, which was his way of demonstrating "the sunny joys of the body." The method worked, and some ladies rushed to the stage afterward and shouted: "Vladimir, we are sick people of the city! Show us the way to a sunny life." During the Civil War, Goltsshmidt, like David Burliuk, found himself in the Far East, where he even published in 1919 (in Petropavlovsk, Kamchatka) his book *Poslaniya Vladimira zhizni s puti k istine* ("Epistles of Vladimir to Life from His Road to the Truth"), which consisted of his lectures and a few poems. His main activity in the Far East seems to have been jumping from departing ships while fully dressed, to the amazement of the passengers, and then swimming to shore. He was last seen in Japan.

While touring in the Caucasus, Vasily Kamensky published in 1916 in Tiflis his first large (140 pages) collection of verse under the title *Devushki bosikom* ("Barefooted Girls"). Twenty of these poems had been previously printed in the various futurist miscellanies described above. The rest is familiar Kamensky, with his folklore, his interest in the language of little children, his Asian exoticism, his neologisms, and his onomatopoeia. There is also some verbal experiment, such as, for instance, poems built on one root, in the Khlebnikovian vein, or one-line poems with no space between words. There are also many poems connected with his tour: landscapes, drinking toasts, and mementos of his casual, resort-type affairs with women. Sometimes, Kamensky adopts the manner of Igor-Severyanin.

Another book published by Kamensky before the Revolution was *Kniga o Evreinove* ("Book about Evreinov," Petrograd, 1917), which, he claims, he was commissioned to write. It is an account of Evreinov's life and his ideas on the theater in such overly enthusiastic terms that it probably made uncomfortable reading for Evreinov himself.[81] As to Kamensky, nowhere else does he demonstrate his essentially impressionistic nature and his alienation from Hylaea more clearly than in this book, which is filled with "prayers to Art," lyric outpourings on the transformation of life by beauty, and all kinds of exuberant banality. He even praises Evreinov for creating a theater of old drama, thus completely disregarding the manifesto in *A Slap*. Some of Kamensky's ideas here fit ego-futurism rather than Hylaea. Evreinov later returned the compliment by publishing in 1922 in Moscow the slim, fifteen-page book, *Teatralizatsiya zhizni* ("Theatralization of Life"), which is still the only book about Kamensky and is written in the best tradition of mutual admiration. Evreinov praised Kamensky as a poet who had achieved a complete merger of his life and his art (other examples: Diogenes, St. Francis of Assisi, and Leo Tolstoy). Incidentally, he reported that *Stenka Razin* was written on tree bark, in a forest, on handkerchiefs, newspaper margins, and so on, and that type was actually set from this unorthodox manuscript. He also says that Kamensky made quite a work of art out of his own blanket, a multicolored bed covering containing pieces of many different kinds of fabric and adorned with inscriptions, little bells, clipped pictures, shells, and whatnot.

During the interval between the two Russian revolutions of 1917, Kamensky blossomed out more than any of his colleagues. He left the Caucasus for Moscow, where he embraced anarchistic doctrines and found himself a mistress in Mrs. Filippov, wife of the Moscow mil-

lionaire baker. Her money made it possible for him to support Khlebnikov, Mayakovsky, and even Burliuk during the lean revolutionary
months, and to organize the publishing enterprise Kitovras (named
after the wise monster of the medieval Russian apocryphal legend, who
was unable to make detours and always went straight ahead disregarding obstacles). Two books by Kamensky carry the Kitovras imprint,
and both appeared in Moscow in 1918. One of them was a book of
memoirs and theory, *Ego-Moya Biografiya velikogo futurista* ("His-My
Biography of the Great Futurist"), with a dedication to Mrs. Filippov,
seven prefaces, three portraits of himself, and one of his father and
mother. Although Kamensky here, as in all his other memoirs, is guilty
of distorting facts,[82] this book is his most interesting autobiographical
work because it is the most sincere one. Otherwise, it is a familiar
presentation of himself as a poet-child-genius-prophet, to which the
label of superanarchist is now added.

In *His-My Biography of the Great Futurist,* Kamensky preaches
his affirmation of the individual, predicts the eventual abolishment of
books, and rejects political freedom in the name of spiritual freedom.
Basically, however, his concept of the poet is a hundred years old,
borrowed, probably unwittingly, almost entirely from Pushkin. It is
based on the division of the poet's self into social and creative parts
(thus explaining the "his" and "my" of the title) and on the juxtaposition of the poet to the crowd. The book is full of enthusiasm for
the Revolution, which "gave her blessings to all futurists," who are
described as "revolutionaries who suffered much from czarism." Despite instances of ridiculous self-aggrandizement, the book is a valuable introduction to Kamensky's work and explains some of the symbols found in his poetry. In theory, Kamensky imitates (rather clumsily) Khlebnikov in his doctrine of the "letter" as a monad of poetic
creation, in his ideas of onomatopoeic *zaum* and of word creation, and
in his utopian projects. Kamensky tries to create as much surface
"futurism" as possible, and he uses typefaces of different sizes and
many capital letters, mixes prose and verse, and even attempts avant-
garde prose built on neologism and grammatical incongruity.

Perhaps simultaneously with this work, there appeared another collection of Kamensky's verse, *Zvuchal' vesneyanki,* which may be
roughly translated as "Sound-Song of the Pipe of Spring." There are
very few items in this book which cannot be found in his previous

collection of verse, from which Kamensky reprinted more than twenty poems. He alternates the theme of welcoming the Revolution with religious motifs, and drowns superficial experimentation (some use of mathematical symbols, demonstration of the meaning of individual letters) in the flood of conventional poetry glorifying himself or his girls and cronies. The influence of Igor-Severyanin is apparent here to a considerable degree. The book includes Kamensky's poetic "decree" about writing poems on fences, painting the walls of houses, playing music from balconies, and otherwise celebrating revolution; but, more significantly, it also prints for the first time *in toto* his long poem about Razin, here called "Serdtse narodnoe Stenka Razin" ("Stenka Razin, the Heart of the People"). Although this poem marks the beginning of Kamensky's indiscriminate exploitation of the Razin theme, it is also one of his artistic successes, despite the fact that most of the sixty fragments that make up the poem are nothing but songs and poems from the already published novel. The mere act of subtraction makes all the difference here, however, showing clearly the questionable value of the novel's prose and demonstrating that the real skeleton of the novel was contained in these barbaric and forceful miniatures in verse. In the same year Kamensky published this poem again in a separate edition. Later, as with the novel, he renamed it "Stepan Razin" and rewrote (and occasionally shortened) it for many editions, separate and collected, in the years 1927, 1932, 1939, 1948, and 1961. The first version remained the best, the subsequent ones being marred by the omission of the original anarchistic flavor and a reduction of the colorful *zaum,* as well as by the more "correct," official historical interpretation of Razin.

Filippov's money also helped Kamensky and Goltsshmidt to organize the futurist Café of Poets in Moscow, where they and Mayakovsky recited their poetry with Burliuk before black marketeers, anarchists, and secret police; but soon after the October Revolution Filippov's property was expropriated by the Bolsheviks, despite his leftist sympathies. Kamensky quickly realized that anarchism was a dangerous creed to espouse and became an all-out supporter of Soviet communism. He was even imprisoned by the Whites in Yalta in 1919, a fact that he always proudly reiterated afterward. He lived in Moscow and on his farm in the Urals and traveled extensively throughout Russia, lecturing and reciting his poetry. Lenin liked his poetry. Kamensky belonged to the Lef group headed by Mayakovsky from 1923 to 1925 and indulged in some *zaum,* but was criticized for it[83] and finally switched to "understandable" poetry. Before his death Kamensky published more than twenty-five books, but he was ready to publish many more and complained in 1932 in a letter to Burliuk in the United States that he still had enough manuscript material to fill twenty volumes.[84] In 1927 he dreamed of being the first reporter on the moon. During the last fifteen years of his life, from 1945 until his death in 1960, he was paralyzed.

Kamensky's writings during Soviet times were many and extremely uneven. He exploited his *Stenka Razin* also in the theatrical field, publishing the play several times[85] in different versions (one was even produced by Tairov) and also eventually changing it from "Stenka" to "Stepan." The version of 1923, for example, ended with the singing of the "International" and the expectation of world revolution. In the 1920's several of Kamensky's plays were produced in Russian theaters, both in the capitals and in the provincial cities; later he stopped writing dramas, perhaps having realized that he totally lacked talent in this area. He also wrote and published a few crude propaganda plays for village and factory amateurs.[86]

As a pendant to his Razin poem, Kamensky also wrote two long historical poems about two more rebels of the past who became heroes in the Soviet pantheon. The poem about Pugachev ("Emelyan Pugachev") first appeared in 1931, though Kamensky had treated the same theme six years before in a play. Eight years later the poem became the basis for a libretto, first of an oratorio and then of an opera. There are pages in the poem which are as strong and impressive as any in Kamensky's work. It is poetry of violence and rebellion, based on folklore and loud sound, and influenced by Mayakovsky and Khlebnikov, but, on the whole, overly long. It was followed in 1934 by the poem about Ivan Bolotnikov ("Ivan Bolotnikov"), which betrays a marked decline.

Kamensky was also an indefatigable memoirist who reminisced about his early days and the time of futurism in *Put entuziasta* ("The Road of an Enthusiast," Moscow, 1931), and covered the same material with special emphasis on Mayakovsky in *Zhizn s Mayakovskim* ("Life with Mayakovsky," Moscow, 1940), which was one of the many books published on the tenth anniversary of Mayakovsky's death.[87] He also wrote potboilers: for instance, a "European" adventure novel (with an admixture of philosophy), *27 priklyuchenii Khorta Dzhois* ("Twenty-Seven Adventures of Hort Joyce," 1924), and the biographical *Pushkin i Dantes* ("Pushkin and D'Anthès," 1928). The latter (which was a play before it became a novel) stands out as being unbelievably bad in all respects, even among the extremely uneven works of Kamensky.[88]

Finally, Kamensky tried to be a good Soviet poet and diligently followed all twists and turns of official policy: he wrote poetry about industrialization, construction of power dams, and collectivization of agriculture, for the five-year plans and against the Church and religion. To show his zeal, he resorted in many of these works to the most primitive manifestations of enthusiasm with the result that some of them are among the most exclamatory poems in Soviet literature. The worst examples of his servility before Stalin are to be found in his collection *Rodina schastya* ("Country of Happiness," 1938) and in his verbose "novel in verse," *Mogushchestvo* ("Might," 1939), written at the height of the purges and glorifying the happiness and eternal youth of the Soviet people. In the former, he exclaims: "I am twenty; you are twenty; everybody is twenty" (he was fifty-three at that time). In 1934, Kamensky was rewarded with a selected edition of his poems (*Izbrannye stikhi*) and with one containing only his longer poems (*Poemy*).[89] Shortly before his death in 1961, he was honored with another edition of longer poems (*Poemy*)[90] in Moscow and with publication of *Leto na Kamenke* ("Summer at Kamenka"), which borrowed its title from an earlier book of his of different content and represented the first publishing of a selection of his prose (including even a shortened version of his *Mud Hut*); it was published in his native Perm. Scholarly prefaces to both editions (which appeared after his death) praised Kamensky's literary output during the Soviet time. Finally, in 1966, a selection of Kamensky's poetry (surprisingly containing even a few genuinely futurist poems) appeared in the well-known series "The Poet's Library."

It is hard to find, however, anything of real value or novelty in Kamensky's prolific poetry after *Zvuchal' vesneyanki* except a few pages in historical poems or a very few shorter poems, such as his phonetic masterpiece "Katorzhnaya taezhnaya" ("Convicts' Song in the Taiga"), which he published first in the fourth issue of *Lef* and then added to later editions of his Razin novel and poem, or his "Okhotnichii marsh" ("A Hunter's March") with its rhythmic force-fulness. Hunting and fishing, for example, were used over and over by Kamensky *ad nauseam* in too many works, as repetition became his main characteristic. The final verdict on Kamensky's achievement seems to be that he watered down the few elements of real originality which he possessed in the flood of writing he indiscriminately pub-lished. Perhaps he was a poet only by temperament, and his poetry lived only by reflecting some of his vivid personality, or the lively and unspoiled background (the Urals) of this colorful extrovert.

After the war began, Kruchenykh added four more titles to his already impressive list of publications. Most of them continued to elaborate on the theme of "a futurist book." Perhaps the wildest of them was *Zaumnaya gniga* ("Transrational Book," 1915). Its title contains a deliberate misprint of the Russian *kniga* ("book"), which produces unpleasant connotations by its association with such words as *gniloi* ("rotten") and *gnida* ("nit"). The book's cover has a big ace of hearts pasted on it, and on the ace there is a big, white, real button. Almost half of the book consists of O. Rozanova's multicolored engrav-ings of card figures: jacks, queens, kings (in which color combinations are never used more than once). These pages almost regularly alternate with pages on which are printed *zaum* poems or simple inscriptions. Planned total disorder and deliberate silliness prevail in the book. Pages are of different size, color, and texture; texts or pictures are placed in the usual way or upside down. Words are written by hand or stamped; they fill a page or leave most of it blank. The last page of the book is devoted to the *zaum* poetry of a new poet who is identified only by his last name, Alyagrov. His poetry is a conglomera-tion of known words, word fragments, distorted and invented words, and individual vowels. Stresses are denoted by italicized vowel letters. There is a certain tendency toward internal rhyme, and some deliberate use of unusual letter combinations. On the whole, Alyagrov's *zaum* is original and interesting, but his debut was, unfortunately, his last appearance as a *zaum* practitioner.[91] Under his real name, Roman Jakobson, he is, of course, now known to quite a few people.

Also in 1915 and also in Moscow there appeared Kruchenykh's second full-scale venture into literary polemics, *Tainye poroki aka-*

demikov ("Secret Vices of Academicians"), printed in the usual typographical way.[92] The bulk of the book is another of Kruchenykh's attacks on Russian symbolism and its nineteenth-century predecessors (Lermontov, V. Solovyev). This time Symbolism is accused of practicing escapism and of being obsessed with death, and its romantic themes of proud solitude, despair, and transformation of life by dream are ridiculed and deglamorized. Kruchenykh mocks at "the mystical lily of all the loners of flesh and spirit and proud freaks, ecstatic sigh-producers and whisperers, lazybones and cowards with dried-up little legs, decadents and symbolists who made 'this world' incorporeal in the name of their own defective flesh." He also touches on the modernist theater of Oscar Wilde, Maeterlinck, and Alexander Blok; briefly investigates such philosophical predecessors of Russian symbolism as Kant, Schopenhauer, and Nietzsche; praises Elena Guro while insisting on the *zaum* foundation of her work; and compares the romantic and neoromantic moon with the futurist "croaked moon," concluding that the moon is dead and ought to be discarded as worn-out toothbrushes are. The most interesting part of Kruchenykh's treatise deals with style and phonetics. He declares that the sound of Russian poetry from Pushkin up to (and including) the symbolists does not go beyond the hissive *"s-s-s-s"* and monotonously sissy *eni,* which he demonstrates with examples. For Kruchenykh, such sound is nothing but "creeping slime," and he likens it to the "whistle in sleep," "monotonous, thin, and sucking in." Futurist verse, on the other hand, is "a bold fight with sabers." Kruchenykh is not satisfied with modernist "patches on the old" fabric either, and says that "it is more honest to switch to *zaum,* to a completely new language," which precludes any "deals with artistic conscience." The part of the book which acquired notoriety and made Kruchenykh even more of a favorite target of the critics[93] was his comparison of Pushkin's poetry with a random laundry bill, which, he declared, was superior to Pushkin in its sound organization.

There were two more collaborations of Kruchenykh with Olga Rozanova, both having war as their main theme, *Voina* ("War," 1915),* described as containing "colored cuttings," and *Vselenskaya voina* ("Universal War," 1916). The latter had a huge hard sign on its cover, and twelve of its fourteen pages had geometrically shaped cutouts in various colors pasted on paper. The remaining two pages belonged to Kruchenykh. In a short preface, he described the book as the "poetic *zaum* shaking the hand of the pictorial *zaum*" and preached "violent nonobjectiveness" (while criticizing the inadequacy of the term "suprematism"). Kruchenykh also gave the figures titles, all printed separately under the general, Orwellian title "Universal War Will Take Place in 1985." The individual titles, such as "The Battle of the Futurists with the Ocean," "Germany in the Dust," "The Battle of India and Europe," "Destruction of Gardens," and the like, were, in many instances, followed by Kruchenykh's own *zaum* poems printed mostly as columns of words and displaying the author's tendency to use strong and crude words. Here, as an example, is the poem that follows the title "Battle of India and Europe":

> driving
> ruffian
> fluff
> so
> baby
> reason
> rat
> unshoed the armchair

Like Kamensky, Kruchenykh dodged the draft by "modestly retiring to the Caucasus" [94] sometime during 1916. There he found work at a railway construction site but had enough time for literature. The Caucasian period in Kruchenykh's life coincided with one of the most fascinating, though little-known, episodes in the history of Russian futurism. One might say that the inexorable development of what is known as Russian futurism from impressionism through primitivism to abstractionism found here the final point beyond which it never went. In strictly chronological terms, it was postrevolutionary Russia, but there are enough reasons to include it in this book: it was the clearest crystallization of futurism's avant-garde elements and its evolutionary, if not necessarily aesthetic, climax. Moreover, the Bolsheviks came to the Caucasus relatively late, in 1920–21, so the 1917 date is not really applicable here.

The Transcaucasia, and especially Tiflis (now Tbilisi), the capital of Georgia, had become a literary and artistic oasis of Russia by the time Kruchenykh arrived there (or *dokatilsya* ["rolled in"], as he described it in colloquial Russian).[95] Power passed from the representatives of the Provisional Government to the nationalists and then to the Mensheviks. Foreign occupation forces (German, British) also played their role. But governmental and military affairs affected the life of the ordinary people very little, and for those living in Transcaucasia at that time, the Civil War was a conflict that raged elsewhere. Fleeing this war, many artists found temporary refuge in Tiflis. All poetic persuasions were represented: the famous symbolist Balmont was there, and the then still popular Acmeist Sergei Gorodetsky even organized a Tiflis branch of the Guild of Poets (S. Rafalovich, V. Elsner, and others),[96] which published almanacs and counted poetry-writing generals among its members. Many other poets from Osip Mandelstamm to Agnivtsev and the future constructivist, Agapov, also turned up in Tiflis from time to time. Publishing enterprises existed in abundance; clubs and salons flourished. But the Bolsheviks put an end to all these activities when they established control in that area. Many poets went into exile; the ones who remained switched to the winning side.

Futurism found especially fertile soil in Tiflis. First of all, some of the most significant Georgian poets of the time (Paolo Yashvili, Titian Tabidze) then considered themselves futurists and formed their own group, the Blue Horn. Armenians had their own futurists (Kara-Darvish). The Kamensky-Goltsshmidt tour had created an interest in Russian futurism. Then Kruchenykh arrived. Kamensky and Kruchenykh, two fellow former Hylaeans, published one joint collection, *1918.** Kamensky, however, soon left for Russia. Another futurist figure from Russia was Rurik Ivnev, but he remained aloof and did not participate in any futurist activities in Tiflis. These activities centered in the nightclub "Fantasticheskii kabachok" ("The Fantastic Tavern"), where noisy gatherings took place. Kruchenykh, Ilya Zdanevich (the former "everythingist" and Larionov's companion), his brother, Kirill Zdanevich (an artist), and Igor Terentyev lectured and recited their verse there and formed a group called "41°." This group, however, was not the only local representative of futurism. There was, for instance, the short-lived magazine *Feniks* ("Phoenix"),* published by a futurist who did not belong to 41°, Yuri Degen, who allegedly was later executed by the Reds for belonging to a "counterrevolutionary" organization.[97]

Kruchenykh was in Tiflis off and on for three years. Upon his arrival there, he immediately assumed a leading position and began publishing prodigiously. In Tiflis alone, if we are to believe his auto-bibliography,[98] he published, between 1917 and 1919, about forty booklets, most of them mimeographed pamphlets with titles varying from something like *Blue Eggs* or *Nosebreakers* to the frankly trans-rational *Ra-va-kha*, *Tsotsa*, and *F'nagt*. As one of Kruchenykh's friends wrote: "There is no end, and will be no end, to these publications."[99] Practically all of them are now unavailable even in the best libraries in Russia; in fact, they had become bibliographical rarities by 1923.

The name "41°" has never been properly explained.[100] Perhaps it had something to do with the latitude and longitude of Tiflis. Also, it is one degree stronger than vodka and is the body temperature (centigrade) that may be fatal. Terentyev also suggested that it is 40 (the biblical 40 days and 40 nights; 40 thousand brothers from *Hamlet*, etc.) plus 1 for no reason at all. The group, though in existence from the end of 1917 to 1920, did not formally announce its formation until 1919. The majority of its publications likewise appeared in 1919, when the group published the first and only issue of the newspaper *41°*,* in which it printed the following manifesto:

> The company 41° unites the left-bank [avant-garde] futurism and affirms *zaum* as the obligatory form of manifestation of art. The aim of 41° is to make use of all great discoveries by its contributors and to put the world on a new axis. The newspaper will be a haven of the events in the life of the company, as well as a cause of constant troubles. We are rolling up our sleeves.[101]

This manifesto was signed by Ilya Zdanevich, Kruchenykh, Igor Terentyev, and a certain Nikolai Chernyavsky.

On November 12, 1917, even before "the company" acquired a name, it began its activities with lectures on *zaum* by both Kruchenykh and Zdanevich. There followed a series of appearances by Kruchenykh and Zdanevich consisting of recitations of their own poetry and/or lectures. Kruchenykh himself said later[102] that futurist verse was aimed at a listening audience; and, according to an eyewitness (Tretyakov), he was "a brilliant reader of his own work."[103] Kruchenykh's "co-zaumnik," Igor Terentyev, was more specific in his description: "He [Kruchenykh] shouted out words full of juicy dullness and brought the listeners to the verge of fainting with his monotonous construction of sentences." [104] Such appearances were a weekly affair, and most of them took place, beginning in January, 1918, in the Fantastic Tavern. The lectures were, predictably, on futurism and particularly *zaum*, the poets' own and their colleagues' work, and attacks on *proshlyaki* (i.e., "pastniks"), a category that might have included anyone from the nineteenth-century poet Tyutchev to a contemporary Bryusov. Kruchenykh later published many of his Tiflis lectures in Baku and in Moscow; some of these lectures were nothing but his old writings (*The Word as Such, Secret Vices of Academicians*). Zdanevich was most interesting and varied in his choice of themes, which included *zaum*, Italian futurism, futurism in painting, the *zaum* theater, the relationship between spelling and pronunciation, and so on. In May, 1918, they were joined by Terentyev who delivered a lecture on Kruchenykh, Mayakovsky, and other subjects. It is appropriate to note here that the "zaumniks" of 41° not only considered themselves more advanced than other futurists, both in theory and in poetic practice, but openly criticized their colleagues and predecessors. For Terentyev, for example, Kruchenykh was really new, whereas both Khlebnikov and Mayakovsky were merely "renovators" and passé. Kruchenykh, on the other hand, not only dismissed Blok and Severyanin, but found suspicious romanticism in Mayakovsky, who, according to Kruchenykh, indulged in "anal shifts" (see p. 342) and was willing to write to order, all of which practically amounted to a futurism under false pretenses. Kruchenykh even dared attack Khlebnikov, that icon of futurism (an act he later tried hard to justify). In addition to their own publications, the members of 41° printed their work in *Phoenix*, in *Chimes* (*Kuranty*, another short-lived magazine and also the name of a publishing enterprise), and in the *Tiflis Sheet* (*Tiflisskii Listok*), a newspaper.

Amid all this hustle and bustle, Kruchenykh was the central figure and the epitome of futurism. For the first time in many years he had the leading role, and this gave him wings. The effect was more than superficial: it was in the Caucasus that Kruchenykh matured theoretically, and his later Moscow publications, which look so impressive, are the direct result of his Tiflis years. Afterward, he only repeated and ruminated on what he had created there. The method of careful examination of each futurist book would not work with the Kruchenykh of this period both because there were so many of them and because they are largely unavailable. For this reason, these books are treated as an entity in the paragraphs that follow.

As to the type of publication, Kruchenykh continued to develop what, in many instances, he had tried before: a disorderly, offbeat, individualist book. It could be a book where avant-garde illustrations predominated. Thus in *Uchites khudogi* ("Learn Art," 1917), there are more drawings (imitating David Burliuk and Larionov) by Kirill Zdanevich than poems by Kruchenykh. These poems, which are either *zaum* or antiaesthetic, are sometimes adorned by the poet's own little drawings. In fact, some of the poem's words occasionally disintegrate into syllables or disjointed letters, often unpronounceable, and thus become more a part of the pictorial, rather than the poetic, aspect of the book. Other books could be variations of Kruchenykh's "handwritten" publications. Such is his *Malokholiya v kapote* ("Melancholy[105] in a Robe," 1919), whose pages are mostly covered with material printed by hand (in the usual manner, i.e., from left to right and from top to bottom), or typed on an old typewriter. Only the cover (in black) and the first page (in green) are typographically printed, and these employ type of various sizes. Finally, there are books printed typographically in their entirety. Similar books had been published by Kruchenykh before, but he had never displayed so much imagination or variety in his use of print. Both were missing, however, when he later reprinted some of his Caucasian poetry in Moscow. Obviously, the printing houses in Tiflis were both more cooperative and more patient. The idea itself surely came from Ilya Zdanevich who was a past master in matters of typographical art.[106] This kind of book was represented by *Lakirovannoe triko* ("Lacquered Tights") and *Milliork* (probably a merger of "million" and "New York"), both published in 1919.

All these books could be classified variously in terms of the material included. Whereas some of them consist of poetry or criticism (or mix both) by Kruchenykh, others may be joint publications, often without any indication to this effect on the cover. In the past, Kruchenykh had worked in this way with Khlebnikov and with modernist painters, who might have acted not only as illustrators, but also as essayists (see *Secret Vices of Academicians*). In Tiflis, Kruchenykh's collaborator was often Terentyev, who, for example, provided marginal notes and

comments, printed where subheadings usually appear, to all Kruchenykh's poetry in *Lacquered Tights* (all these notes were removed
when Kruchenykh later reprinted most of the poems in Moscow).
For example, *Ozhirenie roz* ("Obesity of Roses," 1918?) belongs to
Terentyev as much as it does to Kruchenykh, though the former's name
does not appear on the cover. It begins with Kruchenykh's lively analysis of Terentyev's poetry, which is followed by a kind of platonic
dialogue between the two poets. There follow several specimens of
Terentyev's poetry, while Kruchenykh himself is represented by only
one poem and an excerpt from a play written in *zaum*.

From this time on, a book by Kruchenykh was likely to consist of
almost anything, and a typical publication might contain a preface (his
own or someone else's), a current manifesto, a reprint of an old essay
(sometimes with minor changes), one or several new essays with a
thorough discussion of his own or his colleagues' poetry (favorable)
or of poetry written by symbolists or Pushkin (unfavorable). Such
essays were likely to contain polemics, an answer to a recent review,
theoretical definitions or classifications, historical information on futurism, letters from friends, and other people's essays (printed as excerpts
or in their entirety). The same book was likely to feature at least some
poetry by Kruchenykh (new or old, unchanged or revised), or by his
friends, and so on—and all this in any order. In these writings,
Kruchenykh often generously explicates his own poetry, which otherwise would probably never be properly understood by posterity; the
three cornerstones of his aesthetics are *sdvig* ("shift"), *faktura* ("texture"), and *zaum* ("transrational language").

Faktura was probably first explored by Kruchenykh in 1919 in
the pamphlet *Zamaul'* (an untranslatable *zaum* word), and on the
whole it is an attempt to apply to literature what David Burliuk had
found in painting in *A Slap*: a rich and varied typology of painting
surfaces. The same subject was commented upon in *Milliork,* and
finally resulted in a manifesto published in 1923 in Moscow in a
pamphlet entitled *Faktura slova* ("Verbal Texture"). Kruchenykh
went into particular detail in trying to establish different kinds of
sound texture in words: tender, heavy, coarse, harsh, muted, dry, or
moist. Of course, his sympathies lay with unpleasant textural effects,
and he argued that after a prolonged domination by euphony
(*sladkoglasie*), "picrophony" (*gorkoglasie*) and even cacophony

341

(*zloglasie*) should be encouraged and practiced, giving as an example of the latter his own "Dyr bul shchyl." In addition to phonetic texture, Kruchenykh identified syllabic, rhythmic, semantic, syntactic, graphic, colorific, and lectorial textures. Kruchenykh's favorite consonantal sound was z, which he considered harsh and piercing, and he delighted in filling his poems with it, often substituting it for other, "legitimate" consonants in a word. Such, for example, is his book *Zudesnik* ("Itch-ician," Moscow, 1922). Finally Kruchenykh developed his sense of texture to such a degree that it bordered on the imaginary, rather than on the imaginative (see, for example, his analysis of a Mayakovsky line, in which he sees a progression "from the muted *bu* through the dampened *bryu* to the resounding *bey-ey*").[107]

One particular minor observation in the area of verbal texture became Kruchenykh's hobby, and he developed it into a branch of poetics. He called it *sdvigologiya* or "shiftology." As shown before, the Russian word *sdvig*, which means "shift" or "dislocation," was a term used by avant-garde artists, and through them it came to be used by the futurists in poetry. In a wider sense it includes all conscious violations and distortions of traditional aesthetics, whether it be in the plot or in the metrics. Kruchenykh, however, had something else in mind when he used the term. When two Russian words, which are often likely to be polysyllabic, meet, the back part of one of them and the front part of the other may form a new, usually unwanted but nonetheless meaningful, word. For instance, the underlined syllables in the phrase "gro*my lo*mayut" ("thunders break") form *mylo*, which means "soap" in Russian. Russian schoolboys knew this before Kruchenykh and enjoyed composing ditties in which completely innocent words produced, after a collision, vocables with a clearly obscene meaning. As a matter of fact, Kruchenykh arrived at his great discovery in a similar way.[108] His *Melancholy in a Robe* (first a lecture, then a pamphlet) was planned to be a shocker: in it he tried to demonstrate with quotations from all Russian literature that poets and writers, whether they wanted to or not, produced *sdvigi* of sexual and scatological meaning (the latter was not difficult to do, *kak* being the Russian conjunction for "as" or "like"). Even the name of Gogol's famous character, Akaky Akakievich, was, for Kruchenykh, an excellent proof of this point. Igor Terentyev echoed Kruchenykh, insisting that "the anal nature of Russian protoroots was indubitable." [109] Enlarging his idea of *sdvig*, Kruchenykh came to find in it both a proof of the inadequacy of the classics and an important poetic tool. Unconscious poetic shifts in Pushkin's poems were condemned as faulty technique (*zapletayushchiisya yazyk*, i.e., "mumbling speech"), or gleefully examined as a revelation of the subconscious mind. Kruchenykh himself, however, began to use such shifts consciously in his own verse in many forms, often emphasizing them typographically. He also postulated them theoretically as a basis for any poetry. His critical writings began to abound in mental acrobatics, as he made semantic redistributions in any lines he came across. For example, the line from the work of the non-futurist poet Sergei Rafalovich, *Spletya khulu s osannoyu*, which means "having interlaced abuse with a hosanna," became in Kruchenykh's hands *Spletyakhu lu sosannoyu*. In this form, the first word retains its meaning ("interlacing" or "weaving"), but gets an unexpected Old Russian verbal ending; the second word is interpreted as a fragment of the name Lulu; and the last word either reminds one of another name, Susanna, or contains the root "to suck." Later at the Linguistic Circle in Moscow, Kruchenykh read a paper on the kinds of shifts which result in "anal eroticism." "The paper stirred a lively discussion among the young scholars," reported Kruchenykh in a deadpan manner.[110]

Kruchenykh may easily be accused of everything from having a dirty mind to being ignorant of linguistics. His learned critics (Vysheslavtseva, Shor),[111] however, never quite managed to refute him convincingly. The very existence of a minor folklore based on shifts proves that it is a legitimate poetic device, though the Victorian-minded Soviet folklorists would be the last to admit it.[112] Kruchenykh's weakness lies elsewhere. He made his *sdvig* hunting a parlor game rather than a poetic tool and often based it on an artificial, and an utterly nonfuturist, understanding of Russian verse prosody. Nevertheless, he was amusing in the highest degree, and the respected Bryusov could never quite explain his own lapse that resulted in the line, exposed by Kruchenykh, *I shag tvoi zemlyu tyagotil* ("And your step was a burden to the earth"), which, in pronunciation, acquired also the meaning of "Your donkey was a burden to the earth." [113] Also, Kruchenykh's *sdvig* puts under question the concept of the word boundary (*slovorazdel*), which is still accepted by many scholars.

Kruchenykh's most noticeable, though by no means his only, contribution to Russian poetry and poetic theory was his creation, exposition, and promotion of a "transrational language" (i.e., *zaum*). As noted above, he wrote (December, 1912) and printed (January, 1913) the first poem in pure *zaum*, and he was the first to mention it in a manifesto (April, 1913). In the Caucasus *zaum* was his main interest and the cornerstone of the activities of the 41° group.

A book could be written about the essence and the various kinds of *zaum*. The subject is complicated, and Kruchenykh himself contributed much to the confusion regarding the word with his inconsistencies and imprecisions. Still, there is no excuse for the abusive and incorrect current usage of the word, when even dictionaries define it as "gibberish" or "nonsense," and scholars resort to the adjective *zaumnyi* as soon as they do not quite understand a poem.[114]

Early futurists sought to completely overhaul the poetic language by creating neologisms and, theoretically, by stressing the concept of the "self-oriented word" or "the word as such." From overhauling, it was only one step to an entirely new language, in which the existing phonemes would form new words of a nonreferential nature, but, nevertheless, be expressive or enjoyable "by themselves"—as line and color might be in purely nonobjective painting. Delight in strange and incomprehensible words existed long before futurism (for example in children's counting rhymes); the belief that speech sounds in certain combinations or accumulations may affect our senses emotionally or aesthetically was not limited to the futurists alone. What Kruchenykh and his colleagues did was to declare that such nonreferential words were the very basis, as well as the flesh and blood, of poetry and the guarantee of its "liberation." Many aspects of such an idea were dear to futurist hearts. For instance, *zaum* looked like the outer limit of poetry, its extreme and pure manifestation, where sound creates meaning (or meanings) and is not subordinated to it. It also put a definite emphasis on the word as an artistic medium rather than as a means of communication. Tretyakov later wrote that "Kruchenykh was the first to chop the compact firewood of words into bars and chips, and with indescribable delight he was inhaling the fresh smell of speech wood." [115] Besides, all this did have the appearance of ultimate freedom, and Igor Terentyev said: "In *zaum* one can howl, squeak, ask for the unaskable, and touch the unapproachable subjects . . . one can create for oneself, because the mystery of the transrational word's birth is as deep for the author's consciousness as it is for any out-sider." [116]

In 1921 Kruchenykh formulated his ideas in his second manifesto, published first in Baku and later often reprinted by him in many of his publications in full, or in abbreviated form. A complete translation of it follows with my comments in brackets (the parentheses are Kruchenykh's):

DECLARATION OF TRANSRATIONAL LANGUAGE

1. Thought and speech cannot catch up with the emotional experience of someone inspired; therefore, the artist is free to express himself not only in a common language (concepts), but also in a private one (a creator is individual), as well as in a language that does not have a definite meaning (is not frozen), that is *transrational*. A common language is bind-ing; a free one allows more complete expression. (Example: *go osneg kaid*, etc.) [This is a verbatim transplant of the first paragraph from the 1913 *Declaration of the Word as Such*; the example is from Kruchenykh's own poem printed first in the *Union of Youth*, number 3, and later reprinted in *Explodity*.]

2. *Zaum* is the primary (both historically and individually) form of poetry. At first comes a rhythmic, musical agitation, a protosound (a poet ought to write it down, because it may be forgotten in the course of fur-ther work).

3. Transrational speech gives birth to a transrational protoimage[117] (and vice versa), which cannot be defined precisely. For example: the amorphous bogey, gorgon, mormo; the nebulous beauty Ylajali; Avoska and Neboska [the What-About and the How-About], and so on. [This beautiful woman is from Hamsun's novel *Hunger*; the pair of names is from Russian folk-lore.]

4. Transrational language is resorted to

a) When the artist produces images that have not yet taken definite shape (in him or outside).

b) When it is not desired to name an object, but only to suggest it: "He's kind of like this," "He has a four-cornered soul"—here a common word is used in its transrational sense. Also belonging here are invented names of characters, nations, localities, cities, and the like. For example: Oile, Bleyana, Vudras and Baryba, Svidrigaylov, Karamazov, Chichikov, and others (not, however, the allegorical ones like Pravdin, Glupyshkin, where the meaning is clear and definite). [The examples, respectively, refer to the names of imaginary lands in a poem by the symbolist poet

F. Sologub, and in a story by Myasoyedov in *Sadok sudei*, and to the names of characters in Gorodetsky,[118] Dostoyevsky, and Gogol. Then, in parentheses, are given the names of a character from Fonvizin's comedy, *The Minor*, and of the funny character in early Russian movies[119]—something like Mr. Truth and Mr. Stupid.]

c) When one loses one's mind (hatred, jealousy, rage).

d) When one does not need it—religious ecstasy, love (a gloss of an exclamation, interjections, purring, refrains, a child's babbling, affectionate names, nicknames—such *zaum* can be found in abundance in the works of writers of every school).

5. *Zaum* awakens and liberates creative imagination, without offending it by anything concrete. Meaning makes the word contract, writhe, turn to stone; *zaum*, on the other hand, is wild, fiery, explosive (wild paradise, flaming tongues, glowing coal).

6. Thus one should distinguish between three forms of word creation:
  I. The transrational *a)* sung and incanted magic.
        b) "revelation (naming and depicting) of invisible things" [120]—[i.e.] mysticism.
        c) musical-phonetic word creation—[i.e.] orchestration, texture.
  II. The rational (its opposite is the mad, the clinical, which has its own laws, establishable by science; what is, however, beyond scientific cognition belongs to the area of aesthetics, of the aleatory [*naobumnoe*].
  III. The aleatory (alogical, fortuitous, a creative breakthrough, mechanical combination of words: slips of tongue, misprints, lapses; partly belonging here are shifts of sound and meaning, national accent, stuttering, baby talk, etc.).

7. *Zaum* is the most compact art in the length of the way from perception to reproduction, as well as in its form. For example: *Kuboa* (Hamsun), *Kho-bo-ro*, etc. [*Kuboa* is a word invented by the hero of Hamsun's *Hunger*. The last sequence of words is the beginning of Kruchenykh's own *zaum* poem printed in *Learn Art*].

8. *Zaum* is a universal art, though its origin and initial character may be national. For example: hurrah, euhoe, and so on.

Transrational works may result in a worldwide poetic language which is born organically, and not artificially like Esperanto.

Kruchenykh also divided *zaum* into three kinds, depending on the artistic intent: verbal fun (*veselaya zabava*), preoccupation with verse texture, and insight into the mysteries of poetry and the universe. The last part shows that the zaumniks were on their way to some kind of aesthetic "totalitarianism," and Igor Terentyev did write once that "any poet is a zaumnik," [121] whether he knows (or likes) it or not. In a similar way, Russian symbolists some ten years earlier had insisted that any great art cannot avoid being symbolist.

There are many more aspects of the *zaum* Kruchenykh spoke of (stress on the unexpected and the unusual in sound, desirability of mixing *zaum* with the usual language, etc.), but they could be discussed only in a special study. One thing, however, remains to be mentioned. For Kruchenykh and most of his colleagues, the emotional essence of *zaum* was obviously in the center. "A strong emotion shatters all words. The not yet frozen element speaks a melted language, that is, a transrational one," he wrote. Tretyakov also saw in *zaum* "the creation of a language of pure emotions." "When a strong emotion is present," continues Kruchenykh, "the meaning of the words becomes unimportant; it may even be forgotten. A man in passion confuses words, forgets them, distorts them, uses wrong words, but the emotional aspect still remains the same, and this constitutes the transrational side of the matter." In the same book (*Fonetika teatra* ["Phonetics of Theater," Moscow, 1923]), however, Kruchenykh, rather anticlimactically and almost prosaically, states that in a " *zaum* word there are always fragments of various [non-*zaum*] words (concepts, images), and they result in a new, transrational image, which is not clearly definable." [122]

Khlebnikov's concept of *zaum* was essentially different from Kruchenykh's, though they may occasionally touch each other. After years of meditation about the nature of language "molecules" (i.e., speech sounds, especially consonants), and knowing the power of the word as manifested in charms and incantations, Khlebnikov dreamed of taming this power and of turning transrational language into a rational one, but with a difference. Unlike the languages we use, this one would be the universal language[123] of pure concepts clearly expressed by speech sounds. One is almost tempted to speak in terms of the Apollonian versus the Dionysian, or the classical versus the Romantic, when comparing Khlebnikov's theory of *zaum* with that of Kruchenykh.

In 1921 Kruchenykh could speak about the existence of the *zaum* school in Russian poetry, which boasted, in addition to the four members of 41° and such established figures as Khlebnikov, Guro, and Kamensky, several younger people, most of them painters: Malevich, Filonov, Alyagrov, Rozanova, Varst, Khabias, and Vechorka.[124] To these Kruchenykh adds Petnikov and Aseyev. One might also mention the solitary figure from Petrograd, Alexander Vasilyevich Tufanov (1877–?).[125] But Kruchenykh's triumph was short-lived: his school had only a few more years to go. He failed to take into consideration Karl Marx's statement that the "name of a thing does not have anything to do with its nature. I know absolutely nothing about the man, if all I know is that his name is Jacob." [126] An amusing temporary epilogue to the whole business was a recent article by a young Soviet critic, who discussed *zaum* from the cybernetic point of view. He had come to the conclusion that it contained the richest possible amount of information because its redundancy is close to zero; then he became frightened and concluded by saying, "Well, this is an obvious *contradiction in adjecto, ergo* . . ." [127]

Surprisingly, there is little *zaum* in Kruchenykh's largest collection of verse (nearly fifty poems), *Lacquered Tights,* to which the author obviously attached importance, reprinting almost the whole book later in *Shiftology of Russian Verse,* where he also explained certain poems. The book as a whole is disappointing: Kruchenykh is a poet to relish in little doses or in extreme manifestations such as *zaum.* Here he is boring. Nevertheless, the book is a good, though one-sided, illustration of both Kruchenykh's Caucasian period and the 41° atmosphere. Kruchenykh listed in a later book the following trademarks of futurism: richness of sonic orchestration, gaudy metaphorism, variety of rhythmic patterns, and structure based on shift.[128] In this book he tried to apply all of these, but without much success: dullness reigns on its pages despite his efforts to shock the reader with ugly words, stun him with print of all sizes, and play innumerable verbal tricks on him. The fact remains that Kruchenykh was much more capable as a critic than as a poet. Paradoxically, his intentions are clearer in his content than in his form.

The familiar stress on coarseness is present in *Lacquered Tights.* We come across "fisticuffs of chords," "a shudder of a rotten egg," "the mattress that champs twenty times under kisses," and frequent allusions to Russian swearwords. Rendering the classical heritage unaesthetic is part and parcel of this tendency to crudeness, and in one poem Kruchenykh not only calls the goddess of love *Afroditka* (i.e., attaches a contemptuous colloquial suffix to her name), but also adds to the name the epithet *mokronosaya* ("runny-nosed"). Also, the foam from which the goddess was born (*pena*), becomes *penka* (the "skin" on milk), and it appears in close proximity to *slyuna* ("saliva"). Kruchenykh was convinced that "all absurdities and nightmares come true in our days," [129] and it is no surprise, therefore, to find in his verse "brocade sabers," "seltzer legs," or sentences like "Destiny and all grocery shops are betrothed to me." If in the classical fable a mountain brought forth a mouse, in one of Kruchenykh's poems exactly the reverse happens. His friend Terentyev wrote about him: "No one before him printed such grandiose nonsense," [130] and this nonsense occasionally acquires a surrealistic quality. Not all of it, however, comes from consciously applied illogicality; some imagery of this kind originates in exercises in sound. For instance, in the line "Every piece of myself is emeraldly obscene," the next to the last word (in Russian, *izumrudno*) was chosen only for its harshness of sounds.

Many poems in *Lacquered Tights* will remain incomprehensible forever, because of the private jokes and allusions contained in them. Terentyev and Kruchenykh himself are not necessarily helpful with their comments or notes, which are likely to be absurd. Had one reproached Kruchenykh for the boredom his book produces, he would not have been dismayed, because even that was planned, and mediocrity was as much an ingredient of his rejection of the past as were ugliness, disorder, and the inconsistencies of his poetry and criticism. Terentyev praised some of Kruchenykh's lines, saying, "They contain absolutely nothing, they are a great nothing, an absolute zero." The same Terentyev wrote, "Kruchenykh allowed himself every impermissible deed." [131] These comments have Dostoyevskian overtones. Svidrigaylov in *Crime and Punishment* experiences the consequence of the maxim "Everything is permitted," and ends in absolute boredom and suicide. Kruchenykh was saved from tragedy because from the very beginning he accepted mediocrity.

In *Explodity* (1913) Kruchenykh printed on one page two lines: "I forgot to hang myself; I'm flying off to America." He was not humble, however; Kruchenykh loved the limelight and advertised himself with an uncanny anticipation of modern Madison Avenue methods. In Tiflis, an "Institute for the Study of Kruchenykh" (probably a hoax) was founded, and in Baku the book *Stikhi vokrug Kruchenykh* ("Poems around Kruchenykh")* was published in 1921. Terentyev published a book about him, *Kruchenykh grandiozar* ("Kruchenykh the Grandiozaire," Tiflis, 1919). Finally, after moving to Moscow, Kruchenykh published a collection of essays about himself, most of which had originated as papers read at Tiflis literary gatherings, entitled *Buka russkoi literatury* ("The Bogeyman of Russian Literature," Moscow, 1923). The authors of the essays were Sergei Tretyakov, David Burliuk, Tatyana Vechorka, and Sergei Rafalovich. In 1925 the second edition of this book appeared with the title *Zhiv Kruchenykh!* ("Kruchenykh Is Still Alive!"), with Boris Pasternak as an additional contributor.

The most unmistakable artistic achievement among the members of 41° may be credited to Ilya Mikhailovich Zdanevich (1894——), who in one of his publications predicted the year of his own death, 1973. Tiflis was his home; he was born there, the son of a teacher of French. Later he studied law in St. Petersburg, and lived also in Moscow and Paris. He has already been mentioned as an "everythingist" (*vsek*), as the author of a book on Goncharova and Larionov, and as a participant in Marinetti's reception; but his major contribution to futurism came later, at the time discussed in this chapter, in the form of a dramatic pentalogy *aslaablichya* ("ăs'pĕktsŭvŭdun'kē"). The donkey image does connect these five plays, the animal appearing in them either as one of the dramatis personae, or as a brief reference (or implication) in the text. Zdanevich called the whole thing a *vertep,* thus emphasizing its primitivistic nature. *Vertep* was a form of puppet folk theater of Ukrainian origin, which mixed episodes from the Bible with comic scenes of everyday life. In Zdanevich's work, a comical absurdity prevails and the religious theme remains in the background, occasionally manifesting itself in parodistic and blasphemous passages. Also in the tradition of folk theater is the figure of the Master (*khozyain*), who begins each play with a short talk with the audience, providing hints as to the possible meaning of the play. These talks are always clever imitations of spoken Russian, but a clear meaning emerges from them only occasionally, for sentences overlap or are broken and what results is nonsense that sounds like Russian. The Master sometimes sums up the action in the middle of a play in brief sentences, and it is he who announces the appearance of the characters and the end of each *dra* (as Zdanevich called his dramatic works). The spoken element is further enhanced by the fact that every word, including stage directions and the title, is given in a phonetic transcription with word accents suggested by capital letters or italics. The text itself is not Russian, but *zaum,* and it is perhaps the most consistent and large-scale use of *zaum* in Russian futurist literature. Its verse texture is occasionally emphasized by clear meter, phrase repetition, and even rhyme. The *zaum* changes from play to play and from character to character, and Russian is not completely excluded from it. Russian words may appear unexpectedly for shock purposes and for comic effects. Also, in the best tradition of 41°, there is some amount of "anal eroticism," parts of the invented words consisting of, or suggesting, Russian roots of scatological, uretic, and sexual meaning. Kruchenykh spoke of Zdanevich's *dra* as being a good example of *zaum* used for "verbal fun" and an exhilarating pastime,[132] and humor is the main element in practically all these plays. They are permeated with mockery and absurdities, and many things are said with tongue in cheek. Hoaxes and private jokes also find a place in them. Another common trait of these *dra*'s is their resemblance to opera, the plays abounding in choruses, duets, trios, and other ensembles.

The first *dra* in the cycle was written in 1916 in Petrograd and published in May, 1918, in Tiflis, by the publishing enterprise Syndicate even before 41 ° acquired its name.[133] It was "Yanko krul' albanskai" ("Yanko, thə kĭng ūv ălbānĭə"), and it was ostensibly written in Albanian, with the revealing admission that this Albanian "derives from his own," that is, Zdanevich's (*idet at yvonnava*). The action is simple: a gang of Albanian bandits forces Yanko, a sexless creature, to become a king. Because he is frightened, they glue him to the throne. He tries to unglue himself with the help of a German doctor (a typical figure of folk theater), but the bandits surprise them and kill Yanko.

Gay absurdities prevail in the *dra*. One of the Albanians has a Russian name (breshkabreshkófskai); among the characters are a flea (which does not speak a word) and something called *svabódnyi shkipidáry* ("free turpentines"); and the doctor speaks a parody of German. But the funniest part of the play is its *zaum*. The Albanians, for example, speak or sing, for the most part, nothing but the Russian alphabet (i.e., words consisting of Russian letters in alphabetical order, organized into smaller or larger, pronounceable or unpronounceable, units, delivered with different intonations). For variety's sake, they are occasionally interrupted by groans that suggest defecation. There is much more variety in the speech of the main characters, where one can find sequences of invented words which produce the illusion of morphology with their *zaum* "endings," utterly fantastic long verbal formations (like *vykikhakabukú*), distorted Russian phrases, and some real words or names ("donkey," "guitar," Casablanca). Outlandish and familiar, mono- and polysyllabic, easy or hard (or impossible) to pronounce—all these characteristics combine in a rich mélange. The best parts are Yanko's soliloquies, especially the first one, when he reacts to his capture with words resembling a child's language, or the one where he tries to unglue himself and whines with words bursting with vowels.

The next play is "Asel naprakat" ("Dŭn′kē for rent"), written in 1918 and printed in 1919 [134] in the miscellany dedicated to an actress, Miss Melnikova (see below). Terentyev explained in his book about the life and work of Ilya Zdanevich, *Rekord nezhnosti* ("Record of Tenderness," Tiflis, 1919), that the Yanko play symbolized dryness (hence the cover "of the color of gall turned to stone" and requests for water by the doctor and Yanko himself). The second play, on the contrary, is full of "tenderness and softness," with the "saliva of love" [135] in it. It is the most compact of all Zdanevich's plays, having only four characters: the heroine, Zokhna; her two suitors, named simply A and B; and the ass, whose only sounds are several hee-haw shouts in a trio with the suitors. The plot involves one of the suitors who is transformed into an ass, and this makes him even more attractive for Zokhna, who then falls in love with him. Together the suitors plot to substitute a real ass for the transformed suitor Zokhna loves, and she enters wearing a bridal gown and makes love to the ass. Then A explains the situation to her, and Zokhna makes love to A. For some reason, both A and B stab themselves to death after a duet, and the *dra* ends with Zokhna's lament.

Avoiding interpretation, despite the Master's suggestion that in this play there is something behind all this (*nesprosta*), we still can easily notice a few qualities about "Dŭn′kē for rent" which set it apart from *Yanko krul' albanskai*. The *zaum* has a definite oriental flavor. While remaining bizarre, it is more pronounceable than in the first play, even in such monstrosities as *zhavyukhalipipókhakha*. There is also an attempt to create the language of lovemaking for some scenes, and its billing and cooing are suggested by suffixes of endearment, "iotation," and a plethora of palatalization in consonants. In duets and trios Zdanevich emloyed a method of great significance for his subsequent publications. He used bigger letters for the sounds, spoken or sung, which the characters had in common, while the rest was printed in two or three stories, thus making whimsical typographical figures. Often the visual seems to be dominant over the aural. The two illustrations, made by the author himself and representing the main characters of the play, are almost entirely made of letters and are reminiscent of Dada compositions.[136]

The first of Zdanevich's plays to be published (in 1919) under the imprint of 41° was *Ostraf paskhi* ("Easter eyeland"); Terentyev described it as an escape from the "Ibsen-like unresolvedness" of the preceding *dra*.[137] Zdanevich must have had in mind the actual Easter Island in the Pacific with its unintelligible inscriptions and primitive stone statues, and some of his *zaum* here might be an imaginary Polynesian dialect. The two male characters, however, are clearly Russian: the sculptor (*vayach*) and especially the merchant, with his language consisting of invented roots attached often to normal Russian verbal and case endings, or to suffixes of endearment. He is described as "a considerable ass," while the sculptor is "even worse than that." The action takes place in "a shop of stone coffins," and two and a half stone statues carry on a conversation in *zaum* which is very ingenious and highly individualized. Since, as one of the characters explains, "Easter is the negative indicator of death," the play has a happy ending—rather unexpectedly because up to this time some of the characters have devoted themselves to killing the others. But they all are resurrected, mostly with sprinkled blood of various origin. Terentyev found "gaiety" in this play, and Kruchenykh also admired the "uninterrupted death and resurrection."[138]

The next play is the only one to which no commentary is available by either the author or his friends, but that does not mean we cannot understand it. The play is *zgA YAkaby* ("ăz thō zgah") and it was Zdanevich's last play to be published in Russia (still in Tiflis, in September, 1920). It is an important new departure in his work because

it marks the abandoning of primitivistic principles. It is a play of classical symmetry on the theme of reality and illusion with little action
and many shades, in which the author unexpectedly reveals himself
as an introvert. One is almost tempted to say that this play occupies the
place in Zdanevich's works which *Berenice* does in Racine's. *Zga* is a
very rare Russian word whose meaning ranges from "darkness" to
something like "a little bit," but here it is the name of a person who
has characteristics of both sexes. The action develops between Zga's
awakening and falling asleep again. Zga looks into a mirror that, at
first, seems to be the only other character in the play. The protagonist
speaks here a kind of *zaum* which sounds closer to Russian than in
any of Zdanevich's other works, and the Mirror's speech has a spicy,
oriental flavor. After the Mirror comes to life and performs a dance
with the hero(ine), there appears a new character, Zga in the Mirror,
who eventually gets transformed into As Though Zga. From here on,
it is only natural to expect the formation of a fifth personage, As
Though Zga in the Mirror. The Mirror, which is the source of all
these troubles, is finally broken, Zga in the Mirror dies, and the
original Zga happily returns to sleep. One of the more interesting
passages is the scene of fortune-telling with its gypsy color and the
use of names from Russian playing cards.

The edition of the Zga play showed an increasing concern with the
appearance of a book. Zdanevich colored his pages and inserted
between them thin sheets of lilac paper. The verbal notation also
became more sophisticated, with more signs used for the reproduction
of phonetic subtleties. Both aspects were further developed in the
final part of the series, *lidantYU fAram* ("Ledentu as a Beacon"),
perhaps written in Russia, but published in 1923 in Paris. The play
in this edition is preceded by a table of symbols with a description as
to how the sounds they stand for should be pronounced (one of them
is a click of the tongue). The table even lists features of pronunciation
for which no symbols are given, such as vowel length, staccato, pitch,
and so on. In respect to typography, the book is probably the most
luxurious one in the world, with hundreds of different sorts of letters
used so that the pages become visual works of art in which letters and
page numbers jostle one another, fly, jump, and somersault. The
book was published under the pen name of Iliazd (contraction of Ilya
Zdanevich), which was ever after to stay with him. The play is

dedicated to the memeory of Mikhail Ledentu, an obscure Russian avant-garde artist (d. 1917) who is made the hero of this *dra*.

Ledentu as a Beacon is a synthesis of all Zdanevich's previous trends and motifs. It is mocking and satirical, but, like the Zga play, it investigates the nature of reality, this time in its relation to art. The *dra* begins with the Spirit (bearing the neologistic name of Zaperedukhyái) muttering a soliloquy over the body of a dead woman. The Spirit's words do not contain vowels, and this omission is supposed to suggest firmness. The villain of the piece is a realist painter (*peredvizhnik*), defined as a "grass plucker," and presented as a lisping phony. He paints the portrait of the dead woman, "the living image of her," thus parodying this favorite phrase of approval used by the defenders of realism (*dokhluyu kak zhivuyu*). Then comes Ledentu, who represents genuine, liberated art, and he paints an "unlike" portrait of the same lady. Significantly, when this unlike portrait touches the woman (both portraits come to life in the course of the play) she is resurrected; and another of Zdanevich's lovemaking duets follows. As the "unlike" portrait kills the "lifelike" one, a chain of murders begins in which even the Spirit dies, but at the end the forces of life are resurrected. The play ends with a magnificent ensemble for eleven voices, or rather two separate ensembles superimposed one upon the other in the manner of Verdi's *Falstaff*: the harmonious trio of the living is echoed by the dissonant octet of the dead. These forces of death are so numerous because they include the Greek chorus of this "optimistic tragedy," which is composed of five ugly realism-loving women, usually singing in quintet. They are neologistically defined as *truperdy*, a word that successfully combines necrosis with scatology, and their individual names are mostly rare Russian folk words with sexual anatomical meanings. Their quintets are models of linguistic and poetic virtuosity, showing clarity, richness, and strong individualization of each part. One of them speaks and sings in vowels only; another, in a hissive lisping; still another, in abrupt and primitive tones, adding clicks of the tongue to her words; and the last two are enormous viragoes who speak in coarse and unpleasant idiom. The *zaum* in this play is unbelievably inventive, expressive, and funny, with some words borrowed from Khlebnikov (*manch, shakadam*) and Aseyev (*zor*). The play, which combines slapstick with the solution of aesthetic problems, may be considered the oddest literary work of Russia, but it is unquestionably a masterpiece of the Russian poetic avant-garde.

Zdanevich found himself an expatriate after he was sent to Paris to organize an exhibit of modern Russian art. A change of directives from Russia killed the project, and Zdanevich, probably disappointed but also defiant, remained in France.[139] He became a member of the Dada movement. He wrote a *zaum* ballet whose production was planned but never materialized (the sets were to be designed by Matisse).[140] But Zdanevich's main occupation became preparing small editions for collectors in which originality and taste rivaled the offbeat quality of the content. Most of them were illustrated by such artists as Picasso, Braque, Giacometti, Chagall, Matisse, and Arp, among others. Such are *Le frère mendiant, Afat* (1940), *Prigovor bezmolviya* ("Sentence to Silence," 1963).* The last two contain Zdanevich's later poetry, all in sonnet form. Both these sonnets and the sequence of four-foot iambic quatrains, *Pismo* ("A Letter," 1948, written 1946), show Zdanevich's growing conservatism. They are written not in *zaum,* but in standard Russian; they are elegiac and mostly lament unrequited love. But they are printed without punctuation and their sentences and meanings are blurred in outline and slightly obscure and ungrammatical; their diction is heterogeneous and occasionally the romantic clichés are interrupted by colloquialisms and archaic words producing a certain strangeness. A similar strangeness is experienced by the reader of Zdanevich's Russian novel *Voskhishchenie* ("Rapture," 1930) which, on the surface, is a novel of adventure with its action developing in an imaginary country. But in the background outlines of a novel of ideas with semi-Rousseauistic overtones can be discerned, and more than once one comes upon the theme of *zaum.* In 1949 Zdanevich published an unusual work under the title *Poésie de mots inconnus,* an anthology of *zaum* presenting both European Dadaists and Russian futurists under the same cover (Russian words transliterated with Latin letters). Among the Russians one finds not only the 41° poets and Khlebnikov, but also Boris Poplavsky, a Russian *émigré* poet.[141]

Unlike Kruchenykh and Terentyev, Zdanevich never published his theoretical writings. In 1947, however, Georges Ribemont-Dessaignes, the well-known Dadaist, wrote an eight-page pamphlet which was published as a commentary in French to Zdanevich's *Ledentu as a*

Beacon. Aside from a description of the action, the booklet contains passages about *zaum*, which are obviously by Zdanevich himself, and a version of the history of Russian futurism beginning in 1912 and marked in 1914 by the movement's split into futurism proper and the *zaum* school of 41°. *Zaum* is defined as a "language of Russian appearance whose words and onomatopoeias are of such a nature that they allow for the support within themselves of several meanings of concomitant sonorities." It is a Russian invention, but can be imagined in any other language (with poorer results, however, since Russian is ideal for *zaum*). In *zaum*, the article continues, every word consists of more or less supported, numerous senses of various orders and levels, the concrete and the abstract, the particular and the general. A reader of *zaum* opens a door within himself and gives birth to images based on his memory and power of evocation, but his creative role is as limited as that of the author of *zaum*, because no one is the master of a *zaum* word after it has come into existence. A new world emerges, "new creatures live like stars, and they sing like the gesturing, impassioned hands of the deaf-mute." These new words are also described as being both destroying and self-destructive, copulating with and devouring one another, bringing within themselves particles of eroticism and pride, bestiality, intelligence, or stupidity.

No matter how interesting Zdanevich's Dadaist ties may be,[142] exploring them in detail is beyond the scope of this book. His greatest poetic achievement can be summed up without reference to those ties, because it is clearly contained in his five *zaum* dramas. These *dra*'s are based on a solid tradition that includes not only folk theater and opera, but also, perhaps unwittingly, some plays by Ivan Krylov and Kozma Prutkov as well. Some of Zdanevich's *zaum* in the plays bears coincidental resemblance to Gnedov's poetry in *Sky Diggers;* but primarily Zdanevich is to be praised for the purity and excellence of his *zaum*, which was never used before or after him in a major work of such proportions and on so large a scale. Kruchenykh's short exercises in *zaum* may have a forcefulness and an individuality of their own, but on the whole, they are a spotty affair, containing only a few hits and oh so many misses, based, as they were, on pure accident. Zdanevich evidently never subscribed to the aleatory theories of his colleagues; he was a "classicist" of *zaum*, which he constructed and balanced in an elaborate manner. It is genuinely persuasive. Zdanevich displays in it unbelievable verbal imagination, and he never repeats himself. In a sense, it is a creation of genius; however, only Zdanevich can tell where in his *zaum* the bizarre sonority ends and the onomatopoeia, or another more complex meaning, begins. Not that such conventional considerations matter.

The poetic output of the remaining member of the 41° trio, Igor Gerasimovich Terentyev, is unimpressive, but he deserves attention as an active theoretician and a militant polemicist. Some of Kruchenykh's later theorizing in Moscow may have drawn heavily on Terentyev's work (and we know that Terentyev welcomed plagiarism).[143] Valuable critical insights can be gathered from both of Terentyev's books about his colleagues (*Kruchenykh the Grandiozaire* and *Record of Tenderness*), and they also reveal his own aesthetics. Terentyev was primarily an apostle of the absurd and an apologist for aggressive mediocrity. He valued Kruchenykh, whom he also extolled in verse, for "the naked nonsense" found in his lines. He also praised "the father of *zaum*" for his being "outside style, outside everything that guarantees good quality (*zavedomo khoroshei marki*), even if this quality be futurist." In the same book Terentyev calls the absurd (*nelepost*) "the only lever of beauty and a poker of creativeness," and *zaum* was for him "an even greater nonsense" than the simple absurdity expressed by the means of common language. Some of Terentyev's ideas may be gleaned from his marginal "transnotes" in Kruchenykh's books, where one comes across such admonitions as "read faster, don't think," or "even if you don't like what you read, keep on reading and suffer." [144] In more or less developed form, Terentyev's ideas are to be found in two booklets and one essay.

Terentyev's first published "treatise" was *17 erundovykh orudii* ("17 Nonsensical Implements," Tiflis, 1919), with the categorical statement on the cover: "There are no misprints in this book." It begins with an apologia for mistakes. Only when the dictatorship of reason is absent does art—which is the absurd, the nonsense, the naked miracle—begin. The main principle is to think with one's ear and not with one's head. What follows is a more extreme defense of the well-known tenet of Russian formalist critics that the laws of poetic language are different from those of the language used as a tool for communication. Terentyev formulates it in one sentence as "similar sound means similar meaning" and demonstrates this idea with fascinating examples from Pushkin's *Eugene Onegin* and from folk riddles, where sound is shown living its own life and revealing the true meaning of the work better than the "content." This statement leads to the assertion that any poet is transrational whether he knows or wants it or not. Poetry of the 41°, Terentyev says, can be used in seven different ways: as an exercise for the voice, as material for linguistics, as a potential source for new words, as "relaxation for fatigued sages," as a means of disavowing men of the past, as a modern theory of verse in a nutshell, and for fertilization of language (in *zaum*, sound rots and thought sprouts). After presenting interesting neo-Marinettian theories of modern rhythm, Terentyev concludes with his pet idea of 41° being or having to be a more progressive stage of avant-garde poetry than the futurism of Mayakovsky, Khlebnikov, and Kamensky. Elsewhere (in *Kruchenykh the Grandiozaire*) he compared Kruchenykh's *Victory over the Sun* with Khlebnikov's *Death's Mistake* in favor of the former and contemptuously designated encyclopedias as the proper place for the history of Russian futurism. The book ends with eighteen absurd or semiabsurd points of advice (including the "seventeen[145] implements") whimsically printed and accompanied by quotations from futurists. They range from "making heartbeat and unmotivated laughter" from another's stolen coat to drinking wine alone after 11 P.M. or "reading poor literature."

Terentyev's "Marshrut sharizny" ("Route of Globeness"), whose title is based on a quotation from Kruchenykh, was published by Kruchenykh in his own *Shiftology of Russian Verse* (1923), but it was written during the Tiflis period. Here the author defends chance in art. The straight line is the invention of reason, whereas poetry has always deviated from it toward "casual strangeness" (*nebrezhnaya strannost*). Poetry has always used the time-honored device of contrast, which prevents it from unpoetically shooting straight at the target. With tongue in cheek, Terentyev even includes David Burliuk's "The Fruit-Bearing Ones" in this tradition. He declares that contrast, with its obvious juxtaposition or substitution of the ugly for the beautiful, is dead, and that it has been replaced by the law of chance or the "route of globeness," which he explains as follows:

Around the globe, facing in the direction of a creative idea, there blows "the wind of lethargy." Thus, hitting the target becomes possible only when one shoots in the opposite direction (i.e., at random). In this instance, the idea will circle the globe, twice deviating from a straight path because of the wind, and will describe a figure eight while crossing exotic and strange countries.

Terentyev's most ambitious theoretical pamphlet was the typographically elaborate (rivaling in this respect Zdanevich's *Ledentu as a Beacon*) *Traktat o sploshnom neprilichii* ("Treatise on Total Indecency"), published probably in 1920. Entire words or their parts are printed here in special, sometimes bizarre, print; some letters are lying on their sides, Latin letters are mixed with Cyrillic ones, and the letters *kh, y,* and *yu* are systematically singled out as typical for the true Russian idiom. Often, typographically emphasized parts reveal similarity to, or identity with, taboo words. The "treatise" is written in a conversational manner with a constant emphasis on the *zaum* possibilities of each word, so that sentences become strings of similarly sounding words. Thought seems to grow out of sound. *Tvorchestvo* ("creation") contains *vor* ("thief"), so beauty is thievery; and Iscariot was certainly the most sincere (*iskrenny*) man, and so on. There is the familiar attack on reason, followed by a debunking of nineteenth-century metaphysical philosophy. History is presented as the reign of reason giving way to madness (decadents, futurists) and finally arriving in the era of *bzypyzy,* a *zaum* word borrowed from Zdanevich's *Easter eyeland* and symbolizing here funny and ugly nonsense. Terentyev defends this grotesque word on three grounds: (1) it is stupid, (2) it is disgusting, but (3) it may mean things like "our daily bread." There are many phrases like "hemorrhoidal heights of the theory of knowledge" and "the vomit of thought," or sentences like "Every word of a poet sticks in the middle of a street like a disgrace—like a dogs' wedding near a café." Contemporaries, from Blok to Mayakovsky, are dismissed as an effeminate lot, whereas "we pour carbolic acid on every word." It does not occur to Terentyev that he is belatedly repeating ideas that, even in Russia, were about ten years old when he wrote about them. He develops them, however, into the theory of the "naked fact" which replaces the antiquated "thing-in-itself," the "eternal feminine," and "solving the accursed problems," and which is "devoid of meaning, useless, evil, featureless [*nikakoi*], uncomfortable, and plain." Finally, a theology *sui generis* is developed by Terentyev: God, whose fourth person is "complete indecency," is declared a predecessor of 41°, because it follows from the Bible that the world was created at random (*naobum*). Curiously echoing the doctrine of the Russian Acmeists, Terentyev then glorifies the world around him and even says that if another divinity comes here to judge our God, Kruchenykh, Zdanevich, and he are willing to share with Him the defendant's box as accessories to everything He created. The booklet ends with the author's prophesying the arrival of the time when (after priests, generals, capitalists, and proletarians, in that order) artists such as atheists, idiots, *agents provocateurs*, beggars, and idlers will rule the world.

Terentyev's poetry adds little to what can be found in Kruchenykh's, but it does stress the absurd even more. There is pure *zaum* among the former's poems (e.g., "K zanyatiyu Palestiny anglichanami" ("To the English Occupation of Palestine"), but usually Terentyev mixes *zaum* with Russian, as he does in "Serenkii kozlik"—perhaps his best poem—whose lines come as a result of "muttering out." Some of Terentyev's poetry is scattered through Kruchenykh's books, but the larger and more representative part is found in his only book of verse, *Kheruvimy svistyat* ("The Cherubim Whistle") and in the miscellany dedicated to Melnikova. *The Cherubim Whistle* (Tiflis, 1919), published by the Kuranty ("Chimes") enterprise, contains less than ten poems, and the opening one, "Moi pokhorony" ("My Funeral"), may perhaps serve as the best example. It has *zaum*, the absurd, much antiaesthetic imagery (the sun having a migraine, the pavement's callouses, horses eaten up by moths), and onomatopoeia depicting the tramping of horses, the howling of the wind, and the whistling of cherubim. At the end of the book, the poet gives this advice: Never miss the chance to say a stupid thing.

The poems in the Melnikova miscellany have the general title "Gotovo" ("Ready"), and most of them are more arresting in their typography than in their content. They are full of verbal associations (*sinitsy, gusenitsy, devstvennitsy, listvennitsy*), word distortions (*pliavaki*), words flowing into one another, taboo and ugly words ("my poetry, flourish, you daughter-of-a-bitch"), and pure *zaum* (*Yuya yayakaya*). Random epithets ("the maternity meridian") appear frequently, and the dominant principle remains the absurd stringing of images:

> Pull the reel of verse along the main street
> Across the provincial malady
> When a frog gives birth to an oyster
> In the liver of Leonardo da Vinci.

Following Kruchenykh, Terentyev moved later to Moscow and became a member of Mayakovsky's group, Lef. He published no more books, however. His planned "Grammar of Transrational Language," announced in one of the 41° publications, was never printed. In an article contributed in 1928 to one of Kruchenykh's publications (*15 let russkogo futurizma* ["Fifteen Years of Russian Futurism"]), Terentyev defended *zaum* from the attacks of the "proletarian" critics and made references to Lenin, while claiming that *zaum* was both materialistic and dialectical. At that time Terentyev was active in Leningrad as the director of the theater of the House of Press, which, he wrote, was based on *zaum*. It was obviously also partly based on the good old "anal" theories of his friend Kruchenykh, because those fortunate enough to see his production of Gogol's *Inspector General* report that the comedy began with all officials sitting on toilets and the mayor punctuating his soliloquy with pauses for groans of defecation. It is not known what happened to Terentyev after 1928.

Although 41° meant Kruchenykh, Zdanevich, and Terentyev, there was another name under their manifesto, that of Nikolai Chernyavsky. Kruchenykh described him in *Obesity of Roses* as a collector of folktales and a zaumnik whose poetry defies typographical reproduction. Some of Chernyavsky's verse was printed in the Melnikova miscellany. Visually it reminds one of Zdanevich's ensembles in some of his dramas: it is printed as three-line structures in which the largest letters are three lines high so that a part of the letter appears in each of the three lines. Shorter letters are shared by only two lines, or appear in only one. Each line must be read separately, and each one has its own meaning.

Even after 41° ceased to exist, its former participants published books with its imprint. Kruchenykh proudly tried to demonstrate the group's "global" impact by listing the names of its members on the back cover of his book like this: Kruchenykh (Russia), Terentyev (Georgia), Zdanevich (Germany and France). Zdanevich sent Kruchenykh some excerpts from his forthcoming play, "Ledentu as a Beacon," and Kruchenykh printed them as short poems in *Phonetics of Theater* (1923). Zdanevich still publishes his books in Paris with "41°" on their title pages.

Even if 41° was the most avant-garde group of Russian futurism, a better idea of the futurist movement in Transcaucasia at that time can be gained from the miscellany devoted to Miss Melnikova, an actress and obviously the center of the local avant-garde society. It was published under the title *Sofii Georgievne Melnikovoi* ("To Sofia Georgievna Melnikova") by Fantastic Tavern in 1919 in a deluxe edition. It is profusely illustrated, and much detailed information about the activities of local futurists is given at the end. In addition to Zdanevich, Terentyev, Kruchenykh (whose contribution roughly coincides with what he included in *Lacquered Tights* and *Milliork*), and Chernyavsky, the miscellany contains the poetry (in the original) of the Armenian futurist, Kara-Darvish, and of the Georgians Robakidze, Tabidze, and Yashvili. As for the rest, three minor figures should be mentioned.

"Ubiistvo na romanticheskoi pochve" ("Murder on Romantic Grounds") by Vasily Abgarovich Katanyan (1902——) is a cycle of ten short poems which the author also published in the same year in a separate edition. It is a lyric love story in which this provincial beginner poet cannot quite make up his mind whether to follow cubo-futurist antiaestheticism or to settle for ego-futurist preciosity, with the result that his verse generally sounds like that of a second-rate Bolshakov when it does not sound like that of a second-rate Mayakovsky. On the one hand, there are gallant kisses on a girl's glove, her l'Origan perfume, "the smarting smell of English cigarettes," pink liqueur, Baudelaire, and even snowflakes on an autumn day; on the other hand, Katanyan boasts a "saliva-dripping sky," a "pockmarked dawn," a "rotten-through love," and a "revolutionary riot." All this mixture of images is presented in traditional verse, sometimes even in Alexandrines, with almost no deviation from grammatical correctness. Katanyan is now well known in Soviet literary circles as the compiler of the chronicle of Mayakovsky's life (and the husband of Lilya Brik).

The style of another local poet, Alexander Mikhailovich Chachikov (1894———), is characterized by a similar discrepancy. In his "Nastuplenie na Mossul" ("Attack on Mossul"), he makes Mayakovsky-like gestures in the introduction, while the rest of the poem (about the heroic deeds of his compatriots in World War I) is in the tradition of Pushkin's *Poltava*. Also in 1919, Chachikov published a slim book of verse, *Krepkii grom* ("Solid Thunder"), some of which is in the familiar precious quasi–western European vein and is reminiscent of so many poets from Gumilev to Severyanin. The rest, however, is more successful and original in its exploitation of oriental color. The most interesting part of the book is Kruchenykh's preface. In it Kruchenykh translates some of Chachikov's poems into *zaum* and says amusing things about both the transrational and the anal aspects of Tyutchev's poetry. In Chachikov, Kruchenykh hears "the resonant metallic sound of the Caucasian soil and the juiciness of thick wine." In 1922 Chachikov headed the Academy of Verse in Batumi. Later he published poems, primarily on Caucasian themes, but his main work was in the film industry.

A cycle of poems by Tatyana Vladimirovna Vechorka (d. 1965), entitled "Soblazn afish" ("The Temptation of Posters"), opens the Melnikova miscellany. These poems are filled with backstage and dressing-room images. Like Katanyan and Chachikov, Vechorka demonstrates her education and her knowledge of European poetry. Like them, too, she writes in the ego-futurist tradition of drawing-room atmosphere and foreign words. Vechorka was no newcomer to poetry, having published in Tiflis in 1918 her first collection, *Magnolii* ("Magnolias"), in which Akhmatova-like poetry of the feminine soul is combined with Russian dandyism ("Beardsley and Goya are close to my soul"; "I like to sip at Kuzmin's verse"; "At dawn I dream of being a mistress of Guy de Maupassant"; "I again leaf through Mallarmé's *Divagations*"). One "esquise," however, was even then dedicated to Kruchenykh, whom she called *bessrebrennik s ulybkoi iezuita* ("an altruist with a Jesuit's smile"). In 1919 Vechorka published *The Temptation of Posters* in book form, adding several short poems and one long one on the theme of homosexual love to the original cycle; most added poems display a cautious futurism, and different print is used for each poem. Like Kruchenykh, Vechorka moved to Baku and later to Moscow. In Baku she stood closer to futurism than ever before or after. Together with Khlebnikov and Kruchenykh, she published the miscellany, *Mir i ostalnoe* ("The World and the Rest," 1920),* and prepared for print a book of *zaum* poems, which, unfortunately, never appeared. For Kruchenykh's edition of Khlebnikov's notebook (1925), she contributed her valuable memoirs about Khlebnikov in Baku. At this time she added her real name, Tolstoy, to her pen name, Vechorka, and began to call herself Vechorka-Tolstoy. She became a member of the Moscow Guild of Poets, under whose imprint she published in 1927 *Tret dushi* ("Third of a Soul"), which, despite some avant-garde rhyme, two or three images (like "the moon is like an enormous cutoff fingernail") and such "modern" subjects as a flight in an airplane, a newspaper office, and childbirth, marked Vechorka's turn from futurism to more conventional poetry.[146]

After the Bolshevik takeover, Kruchenykh continued to work for a time at railroad construction in Baku, then found a job with the agency, Rosta, and wrote for the newspapers. There was still enough literary atmosphere during this short period: Gorodetsky moved to Baku from Tiflis; Vyacheslav Ivanov was teaching at the local university; and Khlebnikov too was there. But it was nothing like the heroic time of 41° in Tiflis. All Kruchenykh published in Baku were the declaration on *zaum*, about twelve little pamphlets, and probably a few newspaper articles.

In August, 1921, Kruchenykh arrived in Moscow and at once plunged into a whirlpool of activities. Moscow was hungry, but it throbbed with cultural excitement in all areas. Literary groups mushroomed; there were more than a hundred publishing enterprises; poets seemed to be more numerous than readers of poetry; and the avant-garde saw a chance of becoming a ruling party in the arts. Kruchenykh's friends—Mayakovsky, Aseyev, Tretyakov, Kushner, and Osip Brik—were influential, and some of them were already Communist Party members. Kruchenykh immediately initiated a series of publications, recitations of his verse, and literary disputes. The ideas he defended and advertised were, however, not new; now and then he merely added a Soviet tinge to what he had written and preached in the Caucasus. Naturally, his first ventures were of a *zaum* nature, and the abstractionist Alexander Rodchenko illustrated some of his editions: *Tsotsa,* *Zzudo,* and *Zaum*. The latter (which appeared in September, 1921), for example, except for the typographically reproduced Baku declaration, consists of pages covered with large words or just plain letters and syllables written by hand in every possible way and position. One page has no letters at all, but rather five straight strokes of the pen made in a haphazard way.

Subsequent publications, however, were all printed typographically, but even at that, they never approached the variety and imagination of the Tiflis-published books. The book *Zaumniki* ("Zaumniks") appeared in 1922 and offered a few poems by Khlebnikov and Petnikov, but most of it was occupied by Kruchenykh's *zaum* and not so *zaum* poems, theoretical essays, reprints of declarations, and factual reports about futurism in the Caucasus and in Moscow. Many of Kruchenykh's poems are about the seasons, are written in free verse, and are filled with onomatopoeia and heterogeneous imagery, aiming at dynamism and a destruction of sweetness (rot, poison). Kruchenykh colors his verse with sound effects of an alliterative or assonant kind, suggests special intonation for reciting (indicates prolongation of vowels, breaks words into hyphenated syllables for a staccato effect), and applies, though sparingly, *zaum* devices (extra letters, letter substitutes). Unusual printing effects are also used.

Zaumniks was followed in 1922 by two books of poetry, *Golodnyak* (a neologism built on the root "hunger") and *Zudesnik* ("Itch-ician"). The former contains some of Kruchenykh's poetry inspired by the famine of 1921–22; as for the remainder of the poetry, both books are filled with exercises in texture (especially, Kruchenykh's favorite z-orchestration), as well as with *zaum*. There is also some surrealist prose. These two editions were followed in 1926 by another, and Kruchenykh's last typographical, book of poems, *Kalendar* ("Calendar"), which reprinted, though often in a new arrangement, most of his previously published "seasonal" poetry. The book deserves special attention, however, because of Pasternak's preface, which is both an admission of Kruchenykh's significance and a rejection of his method. It is also the only serious criticism Kruchenykh received during his lifetime. Describing his impression of the author's own reading of these poems to his friends (and Kruchenykh was an excellent reader of his work and even received applause for his *zaum* verse in an audience of soldiers), Pasternak writes: "Illusion of literature was vanishing. Memory of meaning was dying out like the recollection of a ridiculous pretension quickly withdrawn. There was a faint whiff of theater, but in its circus aspect. All categories had slipped away. What remained was only the pungency of general excellence (naturalistic, two minutes long) as shown by talented impersonators. Fluent, fragmented observantness made us laugh during passages devoid of direct comedy, and, through this laughter, broad, typical pictures of nature floated into our consciousness, one after another, evoked by an abrupt, almost sleight-of-hand gesture, akin to the art's basic element, which is hoodwinking." Kruchenykh's role in the sphere of art is to Pasternak curious and edifying: "You are on its very edge. One step, and you are outside it (i.e., in raw philistinism, which has more fancies and whims than it is credited with). You are a living bit of art's imaginable frontier. Even its crudest formula, the formula of effect, . . . is broader than the area you have delimited for yourself."

On the title page of *Zudesnik* there was the number 119, and from then on Kruchenykh began to count his books, a practice in conflict with his own previously professed wastefulness.[147] He probably began to feel himself a classic of sorts, or simply realized that he had published so much and felt an understandable, childlike joy at his accomplishment.

The year 1923 saw the organization by Mayakovsky of Lef, the group whose ideology comes closest to "Communist futurism." This group included such veteran futurists as Aseyev and Tretyakov, plus peripheral figures from the past who had suddenly achieved prominence, like O. Brik and Kushner. There were also newcomers, like B. Arvatov. Kamensky and Kruchenykh did belong to the inner circle, but they never played an important or productive part in the group's publication, *Lef* (1923–1925). Kruchenykh's place in a group like Lef is easily explained, for it accepted so-called technical processing of words;[148] still Mayakovsky seems to have soft-pedaled the excesses of the good old times so as not to arouse distrust in the authorities; thus Kruchenykh's poems appeared only a few times on the pages of *Lef* and only twice in its later continuation, *Novyi Lef*.

Parallel to Lef and preceding it by more than a year was an organization called MAF (Moscow Association of Futurists); it was also a publishing enterprise, and included roughly the same people as Lef. This group was less concerned about adjusting itself to Communist ideology, and, as it tried to organize publishing ventures outside Soviet Russia (in Latvia and Germany), the "M" in its name suggested the eventual *mezhdunarodnaya* ("International"). Its chief theoretician was obviously Kruchenykh, who published three books in its "series on theory." As usual, these treatises were apt to contain anything—from poetry to self-advertising quotations—in addition to the main, theoretical part. The first treatise was *Faktura slova* ("Verbal Texture," 1923), which included Kruchenykh's declaration on the subject, a specific demonstration of textural devices, and a reprint of twelve pages from *Golodnyak*. Number 2 was *Sdvigologiya russkogo stikha* ("Shiftology of Russian Verse," 1923), a real giant among Kruchenykh's books with its fifty pages and its presentation in detail of his ideas on "shift," as well as numerous examples of its undesirable or its beneficiary aspects.[149] The third and last book in the series was *Apokalipsis v russkoi literature* ("Apocalypse in Russian Literature," an allusion to the title of an essay by the famous symbolist Andrei Biely), which was nothing but a reprint (with some changes and additions) of Kruchenykh's old polemical essays, *The Devil and Poets* and *Secret Vices of Academicians*, as well as of his first three declarations. With only a few changes Kruchenykh reprinted the entire book once more in 1925 under the title *Protiv popov i otshelnikov* ("Against Priests and Hermits"), thus joining the official antireligious campaign on the slimmest of pretexts that the symbolists he attacked in the essays were "priests of literature" (*popy ot literatury*).

The official line of Lef was better reflected in Kruchenykh's *Lefagitki Mayakovskogo, Aseeva i Tretyakova* ("Lef Propaganda by Mayakovsky, Aseyev, and Tretyakov," 1925), with examples printed *in toto* and accompanied by a discussion of their effectiveness, and in *Yazyk Lenina* ("Lenin's Language," 1925), which classified Lenin's style and tried to establish its sources. The book went through three editions, the last one being called *Priemy leninskoi rechi* ("Devices of Lenin's Style," 1928). Kruchenykh—like Kamensky—also wrote a few propaganda plays for amateur village dramatic groups.[150]

Kruchenykh continued to preach futurism and *zaum*, though he found few new things to say about it. His *Fonetika teatra* ("Phonetics of the Theater," 1923), including Kushner's preface, his own historical sketch of the *zaum* movement, and an actor's interpretation of a Kruchenykh poem, was illustrated mainly by examples of his and his Tiflis colleagues' writings. The book even bore the imprint of 41° and had at its end a list of that group's publications. Its main point, though, was Kruchenykh's claim that *zaum* was to become the language of the modern theater and film and was thus to be the first step toward a universal language. There were in it also several examples of his own *zaum* poems, usually built on the sound of non-Russian, oriental tongues. A second edition of this book was published in 1925. Later, in 1928, Kruchenykh also published the curious book *Govoryashchee kino* ("Talking Movie"), subtitled "The First Book of Verse about the Movies." The title is misleading, because the book was actually about silent motion pictures (in 1928!); Kruchenykh wanted to marry the art of making silent films to a "talker," poetry, by giving his free-verse impressions of several Russian and foreign films. The book also contained a short history of Russian futurism in the form of a movie script.

Sobstvennye rasskazy detei ("Stories by Children," 1923) was an anthology of children's writings in verse and prose collected by Kruchenykh in 1921 and 1922 with some material added from his similar prerevolutionary publication. *500 novykh ostrot i kalamburov Pushkina* ("Five Hundred New Witticisms and Puns by Pushkin," 1924) was an ambitious debunking of Pushkin on the basis of Kruchenykh's theory of shift; it also contained another declaration, his fourth, this time on the subject of shift.[151] In another 1925 publication, *Zaumnyi yazyk u Seifullinoi, Vs. Ivanova, Leonova, Babelya, I. Selvinskogo, A. Veselogo i dr.* ("Transrational Language in the Work of Seifullina . . . et al."), the prose of some popular writers of the 1920's was analyzed, and it was claimed that their work owed its success to their use (often unconscious or rudimentary) of *zaum*. Here Kruchenykh widened the idea of *zaum* beyond recognition. Dialect words, onomatopoeia, the use of familiar words with new and surprising meanings, an illiterate distortion of the word's form or meaning, neologisms, and foreign words—all become *zaum,* where Kruchenykh sees "the word's independent life" and where the word affects one more through its sound than through its content. The Freudian "declaration number 5" closes the book, proclaiming the triumph of *zaum* in contemporary literature and life. At the end of this manifesto, Kruchenykh wrote: "As long ago as 1913, we, the futurists, sketched the theory of verbal relativity—a concentration on sound, a toning down of semantics, a stress on the subconscious—thus rejuvenating the world. A rainbow of shift images; a coalfield under the layers of everyday." In 1927, he reprinted the book under a new title, *Novoe v pisatelskoi tekhnike* ("New Things in Writing Technique"), adding only a new preface.

At the very end of 1925, all Russian readers were stunned when the famous poet Sergei Esenin slashed his wrists and then hanged himself in a hotel room. Kruchenykh immediately responded to the suicide (thus adding to a flood of literature on Esenin after his death) with a booklet, *Drama Esenina* ("Esenin's Drama"),* published, as were many of Kruchenykh's books of that time, by the All-Russian Union of Poets. The book evidently found an eager audience, because Kruchenykh followed it in 1926 with no less than nine more books on the subject,[152] all of them privately printed. The books explored all possible aspects and angles of Esenin's work and personality, the causes of his death, and his social and literary influence. Kruchenykh could not refrain from literary polemics, demonstrating how much healthier and less suicide-prone futurists were than Esenin and his group. Some of these books went through two or three editions. They scandalized some readers, and they did contain repetition and passages that were in bad taste, but Kruchenykh also showed himself a critic of considerable penetration (e.g., in showing how death-ridden Esenin's poetry was).[153] In one of the books (*Gibel Esenina*), a jocular *zaum* poem was printed which, surprisingly, did not find its way into any of the collections of Esenin's verse:

> Tar-ra-el'
> Si-liu-ka
> Eskh
> Kry
> chu
> chok
>   sesenin.

In some of these books the theme of Esenin was intertwined with the then eagerly discussed theme of "hooliganism." Kruchenykh was attracted to this theme even before Esenin's death, when he first printed in Lef number 3 (and then published, in 1925, as a book), his long, fantastic poem, *Razboinik Vanka Kain i Sonka Manikyurshchitsa* ("The Robber Ivan the Cain and Sonka the Manicure Girl"). The book also contained Kruchenykh's last published declaration, this time on Lef ideals versus the rest of contemporary literature. Then later he published *Na borbu s khuliganstvom v literature* ("Let's Fight Hooliganism in Literature," 1926), a series of polemical essays, and *Chetyre foneticheskikh romana* ("Four Phonetic Novels," 1927), where a new version of the Cain poem was followed by three others and a glossary of slang terms. One of the new poems was "Dunka rubikha" ("Dunka the Chopper"), based on an actual octuple murder.

Ironically, when Kruchenykh decided to celebrate the victory of futurism in Russia in his *15 let russkogo futurizma 1912–1927* ("Fifteen Years of Russian Futurism, 1912–1927," 1928), the death knell for futurism was already tolling; the book was to remain his last typographically published one (with "no. 151" on the title page). There was in it valuable autobiographical material by the veterans Tretyakov and Kruchenykh, as well as by futurist fledglings (e.g., S. Kirsanov), exuberant anniversary poetry, historical documentary material, praise of Khlebnikov, attacks on Maxim Gorky, and so on.

Once the Communist Party had made it clear that it did not want any futurism in Soviet literature, Kruchenykh's fall was abrupt, although he survived personally. Friends succeeded in making him a member of the Union of Soviet Writers, which meant having an apartment and eventually getting a pension. Kruchenykh could not stop publishing, however, though he continued it only as a hobby, resorting, as in the old days, to mimeographed handwritten editions. But there was a difference: these later works did not aim at shocking the reader and they never went on sale, being distributed among a hundred or so friends and colleagues. The former "bogey man of Russian literature" found himself in the position of a dusty archivist, who published, from time to time, some materials from the seemingly inexhaustible treasury of his personal collection and his memory.

Actually, Kruchenykh had begun his anthologist and memoirist activities much earlier by publishing, in 1925, *Zapisnaya knizhka Khlebnikova* ("Khlebnikov's Notebook"). Now, with the help of a handful of Khlebnikov's admirers, he published thirty isues of *Neizdannyi Khlebnikov* ("Unpublished Khlebnikov," 1928–1933). There were also reminiscences about Mayakovsky (*Zhivoi Mayakovsky* [Mayakovsky in Life"], 1930), an anthology of his friends' impromptus and literary parlor games (*Turnir poetov* ["A Tournament of Poets"], 1929), and even bibliographies (e.g., *Knigi N. Aseeva za 20 let* ["Twenty Years of Books by N. Aseyev"], 1934). Kruchenykh also continued to publish his own verse. For example, in 1930, there were *Ironiada* and *Rubiniada*, in which he mixed jazz and love, vigorous avant-garde gestures, and poorly concealed old-fashioned melancholy, and he used no *zaum*. After 1934, judging by all available information, no more publications came from Kruchenykh,[154] and he is said to have been teaching art to high school students. Now retired, he is mostly preoccupied with the transfer of his rich collection of rare editions to state archives. His eightieth anniversary was recently celebrated with a soirée in his honor, but the press was silent about it.[155]

All other prominent futurists had their normal share of success, recognition, or oblivion; but Kruchenykh, almost from the start, was relegated by "serious" critics to nonliterature, and he seemed to enjoy his position. Thus his name is not to be found in the reference book on literary miscellanies published from 1917 to 1928,[156] which was his most active period in terms of individual books, because the editors and publishers of such joint collections probably refused to include him. The recent formidable bibliographical work by K. Muratova[157] omits him entirely—though it has an entry on David Burliuk —and most literary encyclopedias ignore him, despite the fact that "Kruchenykh" was, and still is, a famous name. In the 1920's he was at least mentioned. In 1922 Sergei Bobrov called his work "a hysterical expectoration into the reader's eyes of all the disgusting trash that comes to the author's mind." [158] Later he was merely mentioned in surveys of his friends' work and then only as "a pathetic caricature of Khlebnikov who brought to absurdity the latter's theory and practice," or as one of the "poetasters, . . . with his *zaum* exercises which have nothing to do with poetry." [159] Even Kruchenykh's former friends in later days either dismissed him as "coprolalic" (Livshits), or coolly mentioned him as "an extreme anarchist" (Kamensky).[160] Only Aseyev had courage to call Kruchenykh "a genuine virtuoso of the word," [161] and, in his Mayakovsky poem, he went so far as to say:

> Now
> It would be appropriate to begin a chapter on Kruchenykh
> But I'm scared:
> The aristocracy of the press will start howling.
> The next result:

A loss of readers . . .
It's a pity.
One ought to know who Kruchenykh was.

From the perspective of fifty years, the role of Kruchenykh becomes
clear, and it is much more significant than that of many whose names
fill the pages of encyclopedias and textbooks. Of course, Kruchenykh
had his limitations. He was not always literate, imagined more than
he actually saw, displayed false subtlety, cursed without inner strength
to support his curses; but he also deserves respect—and not only for
a deeper loyalty to futurism than any of his fellow futurists ever
showed. It is almost a miracle that this man, who possessed neither
great poetic talent nor a superior intellect and was led only by his
instinct, came so close (and closer than his friends) to what futurism
was really all about. He created the "classical" type of a futurist book.
He was the only true futurist polemicist, stimulating and fun to read.
He was really consistent in his rejection of the past, not only denying
conventional beauty, comprehensibility ("I myself don't understand
myself"),[162] order, and respect for his reader, but also the poetic quality as well.

Kruchenykh's greatest contribution, however, remains his dream,
and perhaps even some of his practice, of *zaum*, which is both a fascinating and challenging idea and which brought futurism to its climax and logical end. The idea of a "true" poetic language, which
would speak directly through its form, had wide appeal. Even Mayakovsky, who never practiced *zaum* per se, confessed once to a friend
that in one of his perfectly "understandable" poems from his Soviet
period the real solution of the poetic problem was accomplished on
a transrational plane.[163] Nevertheless, Kruchenykh is said to have once
admitted privately that *zaum* was like pepper and salt: One cannot
eat food without them, but they alone are not food. In the history of
this disappointment with *zaum*, the name of Khlebnikov, expectedly,
looms much higher than that of Kruchenykh. In 1919, in "Svoyasi"
("Pro Domo Sua"), Khlebnikov wrote: "While I was writing them,
the *zaum* words of the dying Ikhnaton, "manch, manch," almost
hurt me; I couldn't read them without seeing lightning between them
and myself. Now they are nothing to me. I don't know why." And

in his notebook Khlebnikov jotted down: "A work written entirely with the New Word does not affect the consciousness. Ergo, its [the New Word's] efforts are in vain." [164]

Only one leading figure of prerevolutionary Russian futurism remains unaccounted for: Vadim Shershenevich. He was last seen in a brief alliance with Hylaea and as an object of virulent criticism on the part of Centrifuge. In the years remaining before the Revolution, Shershenevich found himself alone, an ostracized man whose only loyal futurist friend seems to have been Sergei Tretyakov. Shershenevich was, however, not inactive. If one includes the two translations of Marinetti mentioned above, he published six books during this late phase of Russian futurism while printing his work in various publications.

Among these works the least futurist was a selection from the major books of Jules Laforgue, in a not very successful Russian translation done in collaboration with Valery Bryusov and N. Lvova. The title, *Feericheskii sobor,* was taken from one of Laforgue's books (*Le concile féérique*) ("Altsiona," Moscow, 1914). Shershenevich provided the book not only with commentaries and a bibliography, but with an introductory essay, which characterized Laforgue as a poet of the city and of its speed and ennui (*toska*), as well as a genuine dandy—in short, all that Shershenevich himself wanted to be in his poetry. In 1918, he published another book by Laforgue under the title *Pyerro** (probably a translation of *Pierrot fumiste*).

If in his earlier *Futurism without a Mask* Shershenevich offered information and criticism, in *Zelenaya ulitsa* (literally "Green Street," but meaning something like "Running the Gauntlet") he does his best to appear as a theoretician. The book appeared in 1916 in Moscow but, for the most part, seems to have been written in 1914. It begins, in the Mezzanine tradition, with an "ouverture" (i.e., a preface), written in the form of a conversation between the author's poetic and critical selves and his friend who is also a poet (the latter is probably Tretyakov, to whom the book is dedicated). In this *ouverture* Shershenevich asserts that he does not mind being called a futurist, but he stresses his independence. The futurist theory satisfies him, so he accepts the label. His futurism, however, is still a select one, including the works of Tretyakov, Bolshakov, Ivnev, Guro, and

Marinetti, and some of Mayakovsky's. The rest of Hylaea is dismissed either as an artistic failure or as nonfuturist. Severyanin is now refused the designation "futurist" and is defined as "a mixture of cheap Parnassianism and Massenet." For those who know that Shershenevich became, after the Revolution, one of the leaders of imagism (*imazhinizm*), it may be interesting that the roots are to be found in this book, where he declares, in the preface, that "images are before all else" and even calls himself an *imazhionist*. Later in the book he takes up the theme again and defines a poetic work as an "uninterrupted series of images."

There are in *Green Street* several passages taken verbatim from *Futurism without a Mask*, but it is essentially a new book, though the subject matter discussed here remains practically the same: realism, symbolism, scientific poetry (Acmeism is now ignored), the relationship between form and content, aspects of poetics. It is ostensibly a quiet discussion of poetry by a well-read eclectic who presents an apologia for the modern in literature. He borrows from a variety of sources beginning with Pushkin and going all the way to Potebnya, Marinetti, and even Khlebnikov, and sees the task of a contemporary poet in "the expressive reproduction of the dynamics of the modern city." For this, one must find the rhythm of modern times, and Shershenevich's own method is "polythematism" and "insubordination of images to the leading image." "Each line carries a new image in its womb, which is sometimes a direct opposite of the preceding one. All these images follow a maximum of disorder." If in *Futurism without a Mask* futurism was declared, for all practical purposes, not yet existent in Russia, in *Green Street* there is, nonetheless, a clear line drawn between its Italian and Russian varieties, the former being *ars vivendi*, a social movement, whereas the latter represents a revolution in art and therefore is ahead of its Italian counterpart. Futurism is described as poetry of the city ("the chaos of the streets, the city traffic, the roars of the stations and ports"), "the entire fullness and speed [*poln' i bystr'*] of modern life," and as being earth-oriented. In terms of aims, however, futurism is a "from," and not a "toward," movement and is an appeal to abandon habit and stagnation.

The book has a second part that presents a contrast to the first. Claiming that "critical rods [*shpitsruteny*] left bloody marks on my soul," Shershenevich is here, for the most part, talking back to his critics, who range from obscure newspaper reviewers of his prefuturist verse to Pasternak and Bryusov, and he often tries to prove his point with Pushkin or with Dahl's dictionary. The book ends with a manifesto-like "Two Last Words," which is one of the clearest examples of Marinetti's influence on Shershenevich; it preaches urbanism, extols speed, rejects the past, and glorifies the machine. But Shershenevich also rejects primitivism and nationalism and declares that there is no meaning or content in poetry and there should be none.

At approximately the same time, Shershenevich collected most of his futurist poetry published after *Carmina* into one book and called it *Avtomobilya postup'* ("Automobile Gait"). It appeared in 1916, but had been completed, including the preface, as early as the summer of 1914. Later he added only a section of poems about the war, not all of them futurist. As a whole, despite the inclusion of some ego-futuristic poetry, the book is an impressive collection (of almost one hundred poems), strongly Marinettian both in the poems and in the preface, sorted into five sections entitled "Exclamatory Skeletons," "Lunar Cigarette Butts," "Freckles of Joy," "In the Folds of the City," and "The Sacred Trash of War." The preface, which is probably Shershenevich's most complete identification with Marinetti, likens itself to an automobile horn which both attracts the attention of the passersby and gives a sportsman a chance to gain speed. In his *Romantic Face Powder*, Shershenevich had coyly written that no one would need his book, whereas here he states the direct opposite in a newly acquired tone of brashness and arrogance. Being contemporary through and through is the chief merit of his poetry, he says. Poetry has left Parnassus. Since the advent of urbanism with its dynamics, its speed-beauty, and its "inner Americanism," there is no longer room for "moonlight trifles," "people forward stuff," ivory towers, and rhymed rhetoric. "We have lost the ability to understand the life of motionless statues, but the movement of the bacilli of cholera is comprehensible and exciting to us." Some poems in the book, which are here printed for the first time, further intensify the picture of the modern city, called by Shershenevich in one poem "a hysterical mazurka of the clouds." The general impression is that of a baroque urbanism, where shrillness and disorder are the main aims and where metaphors and prosopopeias never tire of stressing violence, madness, lust, and ugliness. All this is rather obvious; Shershenevich is a poet without mysteries or *je-ne-sais-quoi*'s and thus may easily be translated into foreign languages, and he may even look in translation more important poetically than he really is. It is interesting that some of his early drawing-room poetry is now retouched, with, for example, the epithet "exotic" replaced by "obscene" and *pishu* ("I write") giving place to the more modern *stuchu* ("I type"). One can also find in this occasionally childish, and always too loud, conglomeration one of the themes of the more mature Shershenevich, the emptiness of the human soul ("My soul is an ashtray full of cigarette butts"); but at this stage another theme seems to preoccupy the author: "I am an important telegram that the world must deliver to the future."

Also in 1916 there appeared *Bystr'* ("Swifthood"), a "monological drama," which, Shershenevich says in the preface, was written in 1913 and 1914. Predictably set in the city with its stone buildings, crowds, shouts, and noises, it presents a series of soliloquies by a futurist poet (*lirik*), who is interrupted by numerous arguing or admiring people, machines, and objects. The poet both attracts and puzzles people in his appeals to them to understand the city and to abandon the past. The soliloquies bear most of the traits of Shershenevich's poetry. In them, streetcars are "electrical sharks," motorcycles are likened to "fleas in the hair of mongrel dogs," women "flow out of doorways like saliva," and rhymes "crawl like lice." There are also occasional parodies of contemporary nonfuturist poetry. Essentially, however, *Swifthood* is a poor imitation of Mayakovsky's tragedy *Vladimir Mayakovsky,* from which Shershenevich borrows motifs, background details, occasional phrases, and the method of the hyperbolic grotesque, especially in the stage directions (a woman jumps from a roof before beginning to speak, and the poet himself grows to enormous size). Another source from which Shershenevich borrows is Marinetti. The poet, for example, harangues against old men ("You are nothing but food leavings, each of you is about fifty") or against culture ("Mankind is about to die of diarrhea of books"). There are also many examples of rather uninteresting sound imitations, obviously patterned on Marinetti.

These three books were written during the heroic period of futurism, and all three of them were significant contributions to the movement, but they were published too late, during a time when people were interested in other things. Afterward Shershenevich issued only a popular edition of Yazykov's poetry with a rather academic preface.[165]

Shershenevich's postrevolutionary imagist period, which made him a celebrity, is too rich to be handled adequately here. After the imagist movement disintegrated around 1927, Shershenevich found some literary work in the Soviet film industry, and after 1928 he stopped publishing. Shershenevich's prerevolutionary futurism is all but forgotten, but it deserves attention and is worth scholarly scrutiny for many reasons. The chief among them is that he forms a bridge between ego-futurism and Hylaea, and it was he who made the most consistent attempt in Russia to build on Marinetti's legacy. And he had many other foreign connections. Together with Livshits and Bobrov, he was in the vanguard of the Russian futurist assimilation of European modernism.

To be complete, this history must mention, at the very end and rather anticlimactically, a group of young poets in Odessa. The group, which had no name, published five collections of poetry between 1914 and 1917. The first, *Shelkovye fonari* ("Silk Lanterns," 1914), included the work of six poets, written in a mélange of styles, imitating modernist trends of the twentieth century beginning with symbolism. Among these poets, George Tsagareli, a Georgian, stands closest to Severyanin; in a poem, "To Igor Severyanin," he compares the latter's appearance in poetry to the coming of the Messiah. Tsagareli remained with the group to the end, featuring oriental color and exoticism in his later poems. Another permanent member was Isidor Bobovich, an imitative poet of Acmeist orientation. The group stabilized in 1915, when these remaining two poets were joined by Peter Storitsyn, who seems to have assumed the publishing duties. This group's second publication was *Serebryanye truby* ("Silver Trumpets"), wherein all the contributors seem to have gone Acmeist and most of them imitate Gumilev to the last comma. Among these imitators was Eduard Bagritsky (1885–1934), the poet destined to become a classic in Soviet poetry. The only clear ego-futurist present was Anatoly Fioletov (see chap. 5).

Also in 1915 the group published its third book, *Avto v oblakakh* ("Auto in Clouds"), in which it made its strongest futurist bid. The cover boasted crudely drawn city buildings through which newspaper columns could be seen. For most participants, futurism was obviously *le dernier cri,* with which they did not quite know what to do and which, in some instances, they did not even take seriously. Bobovich's poems suddenly were filled with cavemen and Mongolian conquerors crushing lice, and even mentioned the smell of urine in a zoo. Storitsyn sang a paean to the automobile, "the benzine Pegasus," and Bagritsky invented a futurist alter ego and published his most "avant-garde" poetry, reminiscent of Mayakovsky and Shershenevich, under the female name of Nina Voskresenskaya. It almost seems a hoax, but Bagritsky's "Hymn to Mayakovsky" was published in the same book under his real name. The genuine futurist orientation is seen, however, on the pages occupied by the non-Odessa-ites, Sergei Tretyakov and Shershenevich. "Auto in Clouds" was noticed even in the capitals, and a reviewer in Petrograd called the group "the Oscar Wildes of the Deribasovskaya Street," adding that if "futurism is fashionable, you can be sure that the provincial youth will start singing in a futurist manner; in Archangelsk and in Erevan, the gloomy Dobrolyubov and the shaggy Marx will disappear from the walls, replaced by the glorified Igor-Severyanin and Marinetti." [166]

The Odessa group, however, had second thoughts, and its next publication, *Sedmoe pokryvalo* ("Seventh Veil"), was a step back to the more conservative idioms of Acmeism and others, but the two main varieties of futurism also remained between its hospitable covers. The members of the group were preparing another publication, "Ametistovye zori" ("Amethyst Dawns"), in which Rurik Ivnev was supposed to be added to the familiar participants, but instead they published in the spring of 1917 their fifth and last collection, *Chudo v pustyne* ("Miracle in the Desert"), which was nothing but a compilation of poems published earlier. The exceptions were certain poems written by Tretyakov, those by Shershenevich, and the book's *pièce de résistance*, the first printed version of the fourth chapter of Mayakovsky's *War and the Universe*.[167]

CONCLUSION●

The history of Russian futurism does not end with this book. Its evolution after 1917 was, however, sufficiently peculiar to deserve another book, or perhaps a series of essays. The ego-futurist and neosymbolist varieties of futurism disappeared completely, but the cubo-futurists never gave up. David Burliuk, Kamensky, and Mayakovsky, the trio that made the famous tour of 1913–14, tried to adapt themselves to the period of "oral literature," since publishing was well-nigh impossible during the Revolution, and organized a futurist nightclub in Moscow; but famine and anarchy soon put an end to that enterprise. For a few years afterward, the avant-garde in the Russian capitals manifested itself mostly in the sphere of the pictorial arts, rather than in poetry, Mayakovsky being the only poet of importance who was there—and even he devoted most of his time to producing propaganda cartoons. Futurist literature was mainly created on the periphery of Russia. Petnikov became an active publisher in Kharkov; Kruchenykh and Company flourished in Tiflis; Khlebnikov was wandering across the Russian south scribbling in a huge ledger he carried with him (fortunately it has been preserved, and it includes some of his best poetry).

In the meantime, an important group formed in the far east, where David Burliuk, Aseyev, and Tretyakov published the magazine *Tvorchestvo* ("Creation") in Vladivostok. Most members of Creation subsequently moved to Chita, and from there finally to Moscow, where they, together with N. Chuzhak, joined Mayakovsky. By that time (around 1922), Kamensky and Kruchenykh were also in Moscow. Together with Pasternak, Shklovsky, Brik, and several less important personalities, they first organized MAF, and then the well-known group Lef (a contraction for "The Left Front of the Arts") which published a magazine of the same name.

The history of Lef is a fascinating story of attempts to create an avant-garde art and literature based on, and helpful to, communism. It is also the story of fierce literary battles and defense against the attacks of the orthodox proletarians and other groups. Lef disbanded in 1925, then was revived in 1927 under the name Novyi Lef ("The New Lef"). Finally, shortly before his death, Mayakovsky was pressured into abandoning the group he had created and going to Canossa by joining the "proletarians."

Within the framework of the Russian poetic avant-garde, two more organizations claim most of the attention. They both disclaimed futurism, but both would be unthinkable without it. One of them was the Imagists (1919–1927), a group of Bohemian anarchists headed by Shershenevich and Esenin; the other was the Constructivists (1923–1930), which combined characteristics of Lef with those of the prerevolutionary Centrifuge (Aksenov, incidentally, was one of the members). Almost to the end of the 1920's anarchist individualism (imagism, biocosmists), on the one hand, and constructive attempts to create a close-to-life, technological literature (Lef, constructivism), on the other, were the prevalent forms of futurism, if we use this term in a broad sense.

Immediately after the Revolution, numerous short-lived avant-garde groups emerged, which, though lacking in artistic significance, are highly interesting historically, but have never been studied. Among them *nichevoki* ("nothingists"), fuists, and expressionists deserve special attention. Usually each of these grouplets and "trendillos" took one or two features of the "classical" futurism and tried to build on it, while producing deafening, though mercifully brief, noise. The end of Russian futurism is probably to be found in *obereuty* (a contraction of sorts for Association of Real Creativity), which included Kharms, Zabolotsky, Oleinikov, and Vvedensky, who published little of their Dada-like, primitivist, absurd poetry; but their influence still continues in the verse of some Soviet poets.

It would be wrong to think that the official Communist ban and personal persecution were solely responsible for the end of futurist poetry in Russia. There was resistance to it from several poetic groups, usually of a neoclassical orientation, which attacked futurism in an "honest" way, that is, not from the position of power. One example is the miscellany *Chet i nechet* ("Even and Odd"), published in 1925 in Moscow. Its contributors, Filipp Vermel, S. Spassky, A. V. Chicherin, and G. Vinokur, among others, fought the destructive and "anticultural" tendencies of futurism and described themselves as "those who escaped the stifling futurist captivity." [1]

Can any conclusions be drawn from the history described in this book? Not the conclusions one makes after a thorough analysis, but those that come by themselves. I must confess that while writing I naturally and easily came to some such conclusions and even made some discoveries. I was surprised, for example, to find that so-called cubo-futurism had gone through three consecutive and clear, though occasionally overlapping, stages of development: impressionist, primitivist, and word-oriented. Moreover, this evolution can be found, though less clearly, in other groups. I was not prepared to find Centrifuge so complex, ego-futurism so significant, or 41° so fascinating. I distinctly saw that Marinetti's futurism was much more of an influence in Russia than is customarily thought, and more than the Russian futurists wanted to acknowledge. There were also minor surprises: Mayakovsky's alliance with the dandyists and the rich prehistory of the postrevolutionary imagist, Shershenevich, not to mention discoveries of important bodies of poetic work (Livshits, Bobrov, Petnikov, Aksenov, and others), which are so habitually ignored by the critics and literary historians. In some instances, futurism was richer than I knew. For example, contrary to the statement of Maya-kovsky that futurist prose was undeveloped and secondary,[2] I came across interesting and varied futurist prose that awaits an anthologist. Problems of comparative literary history also emerged spontaneously and cried for a close scrutiny. Mallarmé and Rimbaud clearly seem to be tied more to Russian futurism than to Russian symbolism. Laforgue and even Novalis made their appearances in this context, and the history of Russian Hoffmannism is definitely incomplete without Centrifuge.

During the discussion of futurism in Russia, first from 1913 through 1916 and then from 1918 through 1928 many statements were made, some of them self-contradictory. Futurists were called "rapists who mock at the word, castrate it, and exterminate its soul" (Polonsky), and "the turtledoves from the Ark of the future" (D. Burliuk).[3] The meaning of futurism has been stated in even more varied terms. Contemporaries defined it as "negation of the present in the name of the future" (Tasteven), "rebellion against everything without excep-tion" (Chukovsky), "an heir and a continuer of Nietzsche" (Zakrzhev-sky), and "a pretentious mixture of the *recherché* and the semiliterate" (Z. Hippius).[4] Even formalist scholars could not agree, calling futurism "poetry of the canonized bared medium" (Jakobson), "an abandoning of the middle verse culture of the nineteenth century" (Tynyanov), and "a *sui generis* illness of art" (Zhirmunsky).[5] Com-munist critics also differed and saw in futurism "populism with a revolutionary trend in the atmosphere of reaction" (Shapirshtein-Lers), "a rebellion of emotion against the old way of life" (Gorlov), "a child of the rotten bourgeois regime" (Serafimovich), and "a protest by a part of the Bohemian literati against traditional aesthetics" (Malakhov).[6] I find especially apt the admission of a former Polish futurist that what fascinated him most in futurism was the awareness that "one can do with the word anything one likes."[7]

Can anything be said about the essence of Russian futurism once one is acquainted with its history? Twelve years ago, acting according to Robert Frost's motto of "courage before experience," I tried to describe futurism as stress on the word, as making the word the real protagonist of poetry, and more important, as poetry growing out of the word.[8] Of course, any poetry is word-oriented, but futurism is consciously and, I would add, aggressively so. A knowledge of history complicates the picture. We have seen in this book how futurism now trod the path of individualism and intuitivism, now embraced the way of "verbal construction." Guro, Severyanin, and Zdanevich coexisted in this movement, as did urbanism and rustic Slavophilism. This complex conglomeration, in which there was not only poetry and prose, but ideology, aesthetics, literary theory, and polemics, contained elements of impressionism, expressionism, neoprimitivism, constructivism, abstractionism, dandyism, theosophy, and so forth. It all began with talks about the liberation of art, or about the new art (an even vaguer idea which, as is often true in such instances, was anything but new), and here few people (notably, the rigorous Livshits) avoided slipping into an impressionist neodecadence. The appearance of the word "futurism" brought even more confusion, because it could be interpreted in a variety of ways, from a preoccupation with the future of mankind to an imitation of Marinetti.

Another complicating factor was the role of symbolism. For Bobrov, futurism was largely neosymbolism; but in Mayakovsky's eyes, any symbolism was old hat. The fact that even futurists themselves could not agree on an interpretation of, or an attitude toward, symbolism belies the Soviet theories about futurism being a Procrustean bed for young poets; actually it was the most flexible of all poetic doctrines in Russia. One should stop looking for clear outlines or purity of any kind in this movement, which simply united virtually all those who considered themselves "modern" at that time. The shortest, though not necessarily the most helpful, historical definition of futurism might be "a postsymbolist movement in Russian poetry of 1910–1930 which, roughly, put under the same roof all avant-garde forces." It does not matter how different those forces were. Even in the most compact and united of all futurist groups, Hylaea, there were clearly two factions, the Burliuk faction and that of Matyushin, not to mention less important centrifugal tendencies. In short, the description habitually offered by Soviet critics of the innocent but misguided Mayakovsky on the one side and a villainous, monolithic futurism trying its best to seduce this future "socialist-realist" on the other is only a figment of their imaginations.

But in all this seeming disorder there was a direction, of which many participants were hardly aware. "Impressionism" was gradually overcome, and poetry slowly moved toward "the pure word." This groping movement toward the "ideal" can be found in all futurist groups, but only Khlebnikov and Kruchenykh with his 41° friends occasionally came close to realizing it. The fact that even they did not always remain pure-word poets proves nothing. Pure meter seldom occurs in versification (at least in Russian), but it is real—and so is pure futurism. The relationship between meter and rhythm is a good, though not perfect, analogy to the relationship between the ideal futurism and the historical futurism. And I hope to be forgiven for occasionally revealing my impatience, when, in my opinion, history moved too slowly or too imperfectly in pursuing the ideal.

It is easy to repeat the banality that movements do not mean much, that they come and go, but good poetry remains. Of course, the poetic achievements of Khlebnikov, Mayakovsky, and Pasternak are monumental, futurism or no futurism. But let us not forget the existence of another kind of life—those formations, both elusive and cumbersome, which we denote with words ending in "ism." These group/trend/school movements are the despair of the scholar and a nuisance to an honest reader; but they do exist, they have a heart (not always easy to locate), they are born and die, and after death they often leave strong and formative memories. I am hardly a Hegelian, but the history of Russian futurism seems to me an imperfect and disorganized manifestation of a clear aesthetic idea, that of poetry growing directly from language: "Ideas are not thoughts, they are a special kind of reality" (Lossky).

ABBREVIATIONS

Katanjan	V. Katanjan. *Majakovskij: Literaturnaja xronika.*
LN	*Literaturnoe Nasledstvo.*
NP	Velimir Xlebnikov. *Neizdannye proizvedenija.* Moscow, 1940.
Pasternak, *Proza*	Boris Pasternak. *Proza 1915–1958: Povesti, rasskazy, avtobiografičeskie proizvedenija.* Ann Arbor: University of Michigan Press, 1961.
POV	*Poščečina obščestvennomu vkusu.*
PS	Benedikt Livšic. *Polutoraglazyi strelec.* Leningrad, 1933.
PSS	V. V. Majakovskij. *Polnoe sobranie sočinenij v 13 tomax.* Moscow, 1955–1961. 13 vols.
PŽRF	*Futuristy: Pervyj žurnal russkix futuristov.* Moscow, 1914.
RM	*Russkaja Mysl'.*
Sdvigologija.	A. Kručenyx. *Sdvigologija russkogo stixa.* Moscow, 1923.
SP	*Sobranie proizvedenij Velimira Xlebnikova.* Leningrad, 1928–1933. 5 vols.
Xardžiev.	N. Xardžiev. Either of the two articles in *Majakovskij: Materialy i issledovanija.* Moscow, 1940.

NOTES

1. Impressionism

[1] The name "futurism" was, and still is, a misnomer, a label applied from the outside and only later accepted by the participants. A similar thing happened with other terms in Russia ("decadence," "formalism"), and in Europe ("fauves"). Some futurists were frankly unhappy about the name applied to their movement. See, e.g., in *PS*, p. 282: "The word *futurism* was, for us, the result of illegitimate birth: the movement was a stream of diversely directed wills characterized, above all, by the unity of their negative aim." Also note the caution displayed by some scholars: "die . . . literarische Gärung, die häufig unter der Spitzmarke 'Futurismus' vereinigt wird" (R. Jakobson, "Randbemerkungen zur Prosa des Dichters Pasternak," *Slavische Rundschau,* no. 6 [1935], p. 357).

[2] Efforts have been made to consider both symbolism and futurism as parts of a whole, with no clear border line between them. See, for instance, Professor Dmitrij Tschiževskij's preface to his anthology *Anfänge des russischen Futurismus* (Wiesbaden, 1963), p. 9.

[3] For instance, Xlebnikov was welcomed by Vjačeslav Ivanov and Kuzmin; Brjusov and Sologub gave their go-ahead to Igor' Severjanin and printed their own poetry in ego-futurist publications; Guro was invited by V. Ivanov and Blok to participate in symbolist publications; Livšic was welcomed into Russian poetry by Brjusov (and by Gumilev). Some contemporaries were aware of these connections, and on at least two occasions Valerij Brjusov was declared "the futurists' elder brother" (B. Sadovskoj, *Ozim'* [Petrograd, 1915], p. 24), or even a "futurist" A. Šemšurin, *Futurizm v stixax V. Brjusova* [Moscow, 1913]). Also see (as quoted in K. Močul'skij, *Valerij Brjusov* [Paris: YMCA Press, 1962], p. 48) how similar Brjusov's concept of decadence in 1897 was to later futurist programs.

[4] There is no history of Russian symbolism in any language, and it seems there will be none for some time, unless someone outside Russia undertakes the project.

[5] The best introduction to these interrelationships is N. Xardžiev's "Majakovskij i živopis' " in *Majakovskij: Materialy i issledovannija* (Moscow, 1940). Also very valuable is B. Livšic's *Polutoraglazyj strelec* (Leningrad, 1932), especially the first chapter.

[6] *Studija impressionistov*, p. 11.

[7] David Burljuk once considered organizing an exhibition of paintings by writers.

[8] One critic has suggested the reverse: Xlebnikov's influence on contem-

porary painting (Vel., "V. Xlebnikov: Osnovatel' budetljan," *Kniga i Revoljucija*, no. 9–10 [1922], p. 23).

[9] *PS*, p. 17.

[10] This aspect is not ignored in this book. See especially the sections on Seršenevič, Bobrov, and Petnikov. There has been some research on Majakovskij by Soviet scholars in this regard. The best study is by V. Trenin and N. Xardžiev, "Poètika rannego Majakovskogo," *Literaturnyj Kritik*, no. 4 (1935), which also includes a discussion of David Burljuk. Burljuk reprinted this article in his *Color and Rhyme*, no. 35. See also *PS*, p. 46.

[11] For example, Xlebnikov's and Aseev's poetry had among its sources the poetic works of Aleksei K. Tolstoj; Majakovskij's verse could be connected with Russian liturgical chants (see Pasternak, *Proza*, pp. 40–41); ego-futurism claimed Fofanov and Loxvickaja as ancestors; N. Jazykov attracted both Sergej Bobrov and Šeršenevič; I have been told that some futurists were interested in the work of Semen Bobrov (1767–1810). In some futurist poetry there are similarities to eighteenth-century Russian poetry (that of Trediakovskij, Lomonosov, Deržavin). It is curious to note in this connection that Italian futurism was also found to echo baroque poetry, especially that of Marino (see Rosa Trillo Clough, *Futurism* [New York: Philosophical Library, 1961], pp. 45–46).

[12] For instance, Kručenyx and David Burljuk. The latter returned to impressionism in his late paintings done in the United States. Even Vasilij Kamenskij, a nonprofessional, exhibited in March, 1909, at the "Impressionisty" exhibition, a pointillist painting, "Birches," which he even managed to sell.

[13] Professor D. Tschižewskij has attempted to bring some clarity to the problem of impressionism in Čexov's work (see his "Über die Stellung Čechovs innerhalb der russischen Literaturentwicklung," in *Anton Čechov, 1860–1960: Some Essays*, ed. T. Eekman [Leiden, 1960]). The entry on impressionism in Volume III of the recently published *Kratkaja Literaturnaja Ènciklopedija* (Moscow, 1966) by the Soviet critic P. Pavlievskij distinguishes between the realist and the decadent varieties of impressionism and sees its basic quality in "the absence of any a priori accepted form and in the desire to portray an object through fragmentary strokes, fixing momentarily each sensation. Those strokes are laid on in apparent disorder, and they do not seem to follow one another; the whole reveals, however, their concealed unity and interconnections" (p. 111).

[14] "Karl V," *Zolotoe Runo*, no. 4 (1906), p. 62.

[15] N. Gumilev did, however, once link Zaicev and Guro (see *Giperborej*, V, 29).

[16] R. Jakobson, *Novejšaja russkaja poèzija*, p. 38.

[17] See *PŽRF*, p. 157. Also note that Livšic (*PS*, p. 281) lists "the futurists' impressionist approach to reality" as one cause of his disagreement and eventual break with the movement.

[18] V. Pjast, *Vstreči* (Leningrad, 1929), p. 249.

[19] *Studija impressionistov*, p. 12.

[20] Kamenskij, *Put' èntuziasta*, p. 100.

[21] Sklovskij, *Tret'ja fabrika*, p. 48.

[22] N. Evreinov, *Original o portretistak*, p. 67.

[23] *Kul'bin*, Izdanie obščestva Intimnogo Teatra (St. Petersburg, 1912).

[24] *PS*, p. 77.

[25] See "Smes'," *Apollon*, no. 1 (1913).

[26] G. Ivanov, *Peterburgskie zimy* (Paris, 1928), pp. 23–31. For Kul'bin, see *Color and Rhyme*, no. 55, pp. 25–28.

[27] "Ègo-futuristy i kubo-futuristy," *Šipovnik*, XXII (St. Petersburg, 1914), 127.

[28] Šklovskij, *O Majakovskom*, p. 24.

[29] Kamenskij, *Put' èntuziasta*, p. 109.

[30] He himself chose to spell his last name this way in English.

[31] Different sources give at least four different birthplaces for D. Burljuk. In this respect he is closer to Homer than any other Russian poet.

[32] *Burljuk požimaet ruku Vul'vort Bildingu* (New York, 1924), p. 5.

[33] Much material on this subject can be found in *Color and Rhyme*, published by Burljuk in the United States, especially in nos. 31, 43, 50, 51–52, and 57.

[34] *PS*, p. 33.

[35] *Vesna*, first a miscellany, then a weekly, was in existence only three months before the police closed it on the grounds that Šebuev's own poetry was pornographic.

[36] Kamenskij, *Zizn' s Majakovskim*, p. 5.

[37] *SP*, VI, 282.

[38] *NP*, p. 289.

[39] See Sergei Makovskij, *Na Parnase Serebrjanogo veka* (Munich, 1962), pp. 145–175.

[40] *NP*, p. 354.

[41] *PS*, pp. 47, 115, 129.

[42] See N. Abramovič, "O futurizme v literature," *Novaja Zizn'*, no. 5 (1914), p. 113.

[43] See *Literaturnoe Nasledstvo*, LXV, 405–406.

[44] *Slovo kak takovoe*, p. 5.

[45] *Literaturnaja Ènciklopedija*, II (Moscow and Leningrad, 1925), 268.

[46] *Slovo kak takovoe*, p. 3.

[47] *Sojuz molodeži*, no. 3, p. [83].

[48] N. Xardžiev and T. Gric, "E. Guro (K 25-letiju so dnja smerti)," *Knižnye Novosti*, no. 7 (1938), p. 41.

[49] *PS*, p. 133.

[50] V. Xovin, "E. Guro," *Očarovannyj strannik*, [Vol. V] (St. Petersburg, 1914), pp. 6–8.

[51] For Pilnjak, see L'vov-Rogačevskij *Novejšaja russkaja literatura* (6th ed.; Moscow, 1927), p. 392; also *Molodaja Gvardija*, no. 6–7 (1922), p. 309; for Poletaev, see Aseev, *Začem i komu nužna poèzija*, p. 192.

52 Xardžiev and Gric, *op. cit.*, p. 40; *Literaturnoe Nasledstvo*, LXV, 405–406.

53 Quoted by Xardžiev and Gric, *op. cit.*, p. 41.

54 *Color and Rhyme*, no. 31, p. 22.

55 The second edition of *Doxlaja luna*, p. [131], however, described *Sadok sudej* as "sold out," though the "remaining copies" were said to be on sale at the address given.

56 *Apollon*, no. 12 (1910), pp. 57–58.

57 See *NP*, p. 398.

58 *PS*, p. 18.

59 ½ *veka* (New York, 1932), pp. 5–7.

60 *NP*, pp. 361–362.

61 See V. Pjast, *Vstreči*, pp. 73–75, where Gej, rather unexpectedly, is declared "chronologically the first futurist artist."

62 Dmitrij Jazykov, who lived at the beginning of the nineteenth century, also omitted jat' and hard signs from his work (see P. A. Vjazemskij, *Stixotvorenija* [Leningrad: Sovetskij Pisatel', 1958], p. 429).

63 *RM*, no. 2 (1911), pp. 228, 230.

64 See *Apollon*, no. 5 (1911), pp. 111–112.

65 *PSS*, XII, 40.

66 *Put' èntuziasta*, p. 109; *Èntelexizm*, p. 3.

67 Kamenskij, *Junost' Majakovskogo* (Tiflis, 1931), p. 4.

68 *Put' èntuziasta*, p. 113.

69 *SP*, V, 291; *Put' èntuziasta*, p. 121; *SP*, V, 302.

70 Vel., "Xlebnikov-osnovatel' budetljan . . . ," *Kniga i Revoljucija*, no. 9–10 (1922), p. 25.

2. Hylaea

1 The year 1911 is printed on the cover of the book. "Predates" were widespread at the time, so that a book very often actually appeared during the last months of the year preceding the one indicated on its cover. Publishers followed this practice to make a book look new longer.

2 *Put' èntuziasta*, p. 124.

3 Such mixing of prose and poetry was not very original, however, because even in Russian literature one can find precedents such as Karolina Pavlova's *Dvojnaja žizn'* (1848) and other examples. In western European literature it was, of course, a time-honored tradition with well-known examples extending from *Aucassin et Nicolette* and *La Vita Nuova* to *Heinrich von Ofterdingen*.

4 This study, coming as it did after Burljuk's participation in so many modern art exhibits, was a necessary bow to academic art in order to obtain a diploma, without which making money through painting would have been difficult, if not impossible.

5 Aleksandra Aleksandrovna Èkster, Léger's pupil, frequently lived abroad, and her art evolved from impressionism to cubism. She took an active part in

Russian avant-garde painting. After the Revolution, she was connected with the Kamernyj Theater in Moscow.

[6] The suggestion of V. Pjast (*Vstreči,* p. 246) that *Gileja* derives from *gil'* ("nonsense") belongs itself to the category of *gil'*.

[7] *PS,* pp. 29, 43, 26.

[8] *Ibid.,* p. 40.

[9] Livšic, *Gileja* (New York, 1931), p. 8.

[10] *PS,* p. 57.

[11] *Studija impressionistov,* p. 9.

[12] Camilla Gray, *The Great Experiment: Russian Art, 1863-1922* (London: Thames and Hudson, 1962), p. 94.

[13] A detailed analysis (and the Russian titles of the enumerated works) may be found in my *The Longer Poems of Velimir Khlebnikov* (Berkeley and Los Angeles: University of California Press, 1962).

[14] At the end of 1910 and the beginning of 1911, Izdebskij organized his second "Salon," which this time exhibited only the Russian avant-garde in Odessa and Nikolaev. Like the first "Salon," this exhibit brought financial losses to the organizer.

[15] *15 let russkogo futurizma,* p. 57.

[16] *Ibid.,* p. 24.

[17] S. Tret'jakov sees, however, in *Starinnaja ljubov'* "a pulling-up of the genteel album poetry's skirt" (*Buka russkoj literatury,* p. 5).

[18] This edition, which boasted a new cover by Larionov, abandoned the "handwriting" method of the preceding versions and used typographical print of various shapes and sizes.

[19] Lunev seems to have been Kručenyx's pseudonym for some of his collaborations with Xlebnikov, but he also used it later for work written by himself alone. In some instances this name is also found under the poems written by Xlebnikov alone. At any rate, the situation is complex. N. Xardžiev considers all three Lunev poems to be Xlebnikov's (*NP,* p. 405), but Kručenyx reprinted one of them under his own name in the later *Tè-li-lè.*

[20] Later, in *Sdvigologija,* p. 35, Kručenyx saw a "menace" in the final line of the poem. In *Zaumnyi jazyk u Seifullinoj . . .* (p. 28), he described the poem as a "hollow and heavy series of sounds, having a Tartar tinge." Burljuk later (in *Kitovras,* no. 2, p. 4) distorted the first line into *dyrbulščol* and deciphered this line as *dyroj budet lico sčastlivyx oluxov.*

[21] *PS,* p. 133.

[22] See *PŽRF,* p. 106.

[23] Kručenyx describes (in *Zverinec* [Moscow, 1930], pp. 13-14) some circumstances of the creation of the manifesto: "We wrote it for a long time, argued over every phrase, every word, and every letter." Kručenyx claims to be the author of the famous "throwing Puškin etc." phrase, but says that Majakovskij changed the original *brosit'* to *sbrosit'.* Otherwise, Majakovskij said, it could mean that the classics were on the ship by themselves, whereas *sbrosit'* would imply taking them to the ship by force and throwing them from it.

Kručenyx contradicts some sources (Livšic) and claims that Xlebnikov was the author of some sentences (e.g., the one about the block of the word *we* and, strangely enough, the one containing the skyscrapers). Xlebnikov did not want to sign the manifesto if the offensive mention of his admired mentor, Kuzmin, was not removed. A promise to him to do so was not fulfilled.

[24] Kručenyx at first used Aleksandr as a part of his pen name (under the manifesto in *Poščečina*, and also in *Troe*), then dropped it and used his real first name, Aleksej, or the initial A. Occasionally he put Aleksandr in parentheses, after Aleksej (as in his *Deklaracija slova kak takovogo*).

[25] *PS*, p. 50.

[26] *Ibid.*, p. 128. I have been told that Kandinskij, in a letter to a newspaper, later protested against his inclusion in the book and called the whole thing "hooliganism."

[27] *SP*, II, 7.

[28] The reaction of the daily press to *Poščečina* was predictably either derisive or indignant. Reputable journals, however, decided not to react to the "hooliganism." Thus there was no review in *Apollon*, and *RM* waited until March, 1913 (i.e., fifteen months), before it decided to discuss the manifesto and the book. It is interesting that France spoke about *Poščečina* not much later, when *Mercure de France* ([Nov.–Dec., 1913], p. 202) was puzzled by the desire of some Russian poets to "biffer Pouchkine, sour le prétexte, assez inintelligent du rest, qu'on le trouve hiéroglyphique et incompréhensible."

[29] It may be appropriate here to mention that as early as 1910 Kul'bin exhibited samples of the handwriting of famous Russian writers and singers (for example, Chaliapin), and this part of the exhibit attracted larger crowds than the paintings.

[30] *PS*, p. 139.

[31] In *Kitovras*, no. 2, p. 7, Burljuk calls such a method *mozaika nesoglasovannostej*.

[32] Sergej Tret'jakov (*Buka russkoj literatury*, p. 5) was later to describe enthusiastically the initial words of the sequence (*sarča kroča*) as containing *parča* ("brocade"), *saryn'* ("gang"), *ryčat'* ("to roar"), and *krov'* ("blood"), "thrown together like a bold pattern in one carpet-like stroke."

[33] About this alliance (as well as about the production of Majakovskij's tragedy, described in chap. 4), see the memoirs of L. Ževeržeev in *Majakovskomu: Sbornik vospominanij i statej* (Leningrad, 1940). Ževeržeev gives April as the month for the appearance of the third issue of the magazine.

[34] It was printed earlier in the leaflet *Poščečina obščestvennomu vkusu*.

3. Ego-Futurism and the Mezzanine of Poetry

[1] I made this mistake in my *The Longer Poems of Velimir Khlebnikov* (Berkeley and Los Angeles: University of California Press, 1962), pp. 8–9, in which the entire first chapter seems deficient to me now because it is not based on firsthand knowledge.

[2] Severjanin seldom missed an opportunity to use this odd hyphen in his pen name, and in this practice he was imitated by his followers (Graal'-Arel'skij).

[3] In *Mirrèlija*, p. 111.

[4] See Joshua C. Taylor, *Futurism* (New York: Museum of Modern Art, 1961), p. 9.

[5] *Utro Rossii*, Feb. 5, 1911; *Russkaja Mysl'*, no. 7 (1911); *Apollon*, no. 5 (1911). Brjusov paid attention to the "strange title" and saw in the book "a tendency to renovate language" by using "the slang of boulevardiers," "bold metaphorism," and "courageous neologism." "Sometimes ridiculous, but there is no denying some kind of cheerfulness and bravery," he added (p. 24).

[6] Actually, Olimpov is credited with having invented the word *poèza* and with having used it for the first time on the funeral wreath for his father, Fofanov, on May 19, 1911 (see Ignat'ev, *Ègo-futurizm*, p. 5).

[7] The first ego-futurist, according to Severjanin (*Padučaja stremnina* [Berlin, 1922], p. 22), was Ibsen.

[8] Professor Tschiževskij characterizes these formulas in his *Anfänge des russischen Futurismus* (Wiesbaden, 1963), p. 54, as "die Umkehrung der traditionellen 'Bescheidenheit-Topos.' "

[9] Such announcements in those days were usually made in leaflets mailed to the newspapers.

[10] *RM*, no. 3 (1913), p. 125. Ignat'ev later repeated this assertion (*Ègo-futurizm*, p. 3).

[11] *Orly nad propast'ju*, p. 2.

[12] *Mirrèlija*, p. 140.

[13] *RM*, no. 7 (1912); *Pis'ma o russkoj poèzii*, p. 146.

[14] Blok, in *Sobranie sočinenij*, VII (1963), 93–94; VIII (1963), 380.

[15] *Pis'ma o russkoj poèzii*, p. 128.

[16] For instance, in *Stožary*, no. 1 (1923), one can find his play in verse,* and in no. 3, a long poem.*

[17] It might be appropriate to say here that neologism, although handled more skillfully and understood more profoundly by some Hylaeans, was more widely used by the ego-futurists. These latter (especially Ignat'ev) used it not only in poetry, but in essays and criticism as well.

[18] *Orly nad propast'ju*, p. 2.

[19] Bibliographies list it as a book, but no library has it.

[20] Not to be confused with the Saratov hoax (see chap. 5).

[21] The number of visitors was actually very small.

[22] I was unable to find this place; it is possible that it does not exist.

[23] From the kind of paper called *papier vergé*.

[24] On futurists and Whitman, see K. Čukovskij, *Uot Uitmèn: Poèzija grjaduščej demokratii* (Moscow and Petrograd, 1923), pp. 161–162.

[25] Sologub's interest in ego-futurism seems to be deeper than a personal enthusiasm for Severjanin's poetry; an essay entitled "Ja: Kniga soveršennogo samoutverždenija" has been preserved among his MSS.

²⁶ Širokov made his literary debut in *Nižegorodec* in September, 1911. His verse subsequently appeared in many issues of this newspaper.

²⁷ See, e.g., Pjast, *Vstreči*, p. 264, where Olimpov is described as "terror-inspiring, with disheveled blond hair."

²⁸ In addition to those mentioned in the text, the following titles of 1913–1922 are listed by Olimpov on the cover of one of his books (it is difficult to say whether all of them were published): *Otdyx, Èpoxa Olimpova, Glagol Roditelja Mirozdanija, Proèmij Roditelja Mirozdanija, Isxod Roditelja Mirozdanija, Parrèzija Roditelja Mirozdanija,* and *Anafema Roditelja Mirozdanija.*

²⁹ See *Novaja Russkaja Kniga* (Berlin), no. 1 (1922), p. 42.

³⁰ Ignat'ev calls this piece (in *Ègo-futurizm*, p. 14) "an automatic creation [*mexaničeskoe tvorčestvo*]," and he may be its author.

³¹ See S. Makovskij, *Portrety sovremennikov* (New York, 1955), pp. 333–358.

³² The imprint (a naked man about to take wing with something like roses underneath) on all editions of the *Peterburgskij Glašataj* from then on was also by Zak.

³³ See *PS*, p. 200.

³⁴ Pjast, *op. cit.*, p. 263; *Smert' iskusstvu*, p. 2; B. Tomaševskij (*Stilistika i stixosloženie* [Leningrad, 1959], p. 182) is wrong in his account of Gnedov's recitation. What he describes is not "Poèma konca," but another, untitled, one-letter poem from the same book by Gnedov.

³⁵ Gnedov's *Kozij slašč: Futurnalii* (St. Petersburg, 1913) was listed in a Brjusov review (*RM*, no. 3 [1913], p. 125) as having been printed, and "Vernissaž" announced his *Vertikal'nye guby* as being on sale; but neither these two titles nor *Gory v čepce*, mentioned in Ignat'ev's *Èšafot egofutury*, can be found in any library. They were probably never published.

³⁶ Volume XIII of Majakovskij's *PSS* even lists him as "Peter" instead of "Pavel" and gives no dates, although his autobiography (written for Professor S. Vengerov) is on file at the Institute of Russian Literature. After the Revolution, Širokov was a journalist, worked for Rosta, and never left Leningrad.

³⁷ Šklovskij mentions Gnedov in his *Tret'ja fabrika*, p. 50. In 1917 Gnedov appeared at the futurist nightclub in Moscow with Majakovskij, Kamenskij, Burljuk, and Gol'cšmidt and took part in *Gazeta futuristov*. In 1918 he published at least one issue of *Vremennik* (Xlebnikov, Aseev, Petnikov, Petrovskij). Petnikov printed his poetry in 1919 in *Puti tvorčestva*.

³⁸ The Hylaean *Pervyj Žurnal Russkix Futuristov*, p. 139, described him as "a modest symbolist who works at the *Petersburg Herald*—no one knows why."

³⁹ The author of popular novels.

⁴⁰ *SP*, II, 294. The Centrifugist *Rukonog* cites approaching bankruptcy as at least one cause of his suicide (p. 4).

⁴¹ *RM*, no. 7 (1912), p. 20.

⁴² Čukovskij, "Ègo-futuristy . . . ," *Šipovnik*, XXII, 120; Šeršenevič, *Futurizm bez maski*, p. 87n; Tasteven, *Futurizm*, p. 24.

⁴³ *PS*, pp. 86, 89.

44 Čukovskij, *op. cit.*, p. 107; A. V. Bagrij, *Russkaja literatura XIX-pervoj četverti XX vv.* (Baku, 1926), p. 307.

45 *Color and Rhyme*, no. 55, p. 6; in his poem "Na farme" on page 18 the influence of Severjanin is obvious—and this is not the only example.

46 *Al'manaxi izdatel'stva Al'ciona*, I (2d ed.; Moscow, 1914), 217; *Šipovnik*, XXII (St. Petersburg, 1914), 100; Z. Gippius, *Živye lica* (2 vols., Prague, 1925), I, 108–113.

47 Čukovskij, *op. cit.*, pp. 99–100.

48 A. Amfiteatrov (see *Kritika o tvorčestve Severjanina*, p. 99).

49 *Ibid.*, p. 35.

50 *Poèty Estonii* (1928) and five more books of translations from individual poets.

51 *Crème de Violettes* (Jur'ev, 1919); *Tragedija titana* (Berlin, 1925). In Russia, such collections were *Poèzokoncert* (Moscow, 1918) and *Za strunnoj izgorod'ju liry* (Moscow, 1918).

52 In addition to those named in the text, we might add *Pühajõgi* (Jur'ev, 1919), *Vervèna* (Jur'ev, 1920), *Menestrel'* (Berlin, 1921), *Mirrèlija* (Berlin, 1922), *Feja Eiole* (Berlin, 1922), *Solovej* (Berlin, 1923), and *Adriatika* (Narva, 1925); the first and the fifth books in this enumeration contain Estonian themes. Autobiographical poetry forms a special group: *Padučaja stremnina* (Berlin, 1922), *Kolokola sobora čuvstv* (Jur'ev, 1925), and *Rosa oranževogo časa* (Jur'ev, 1925). Among the posthumous publications of Severjanin, those in *Ogonek*, no. 29 (1962), and in *Novyj Žurnal*, no. 83 (New York, 1966), deserve mention.

53 Aleksis Rannit, who knew Severjanin well, insisted on this date of his death in his letter to me of February 6, 1967.

54 There is no room here to refute this inclusion of Gippius in the decadent movement; this classification is one of the most persistent clichés of Russian criticism, both inside the Soviet Union and abroad. Actually, it is enough to look at a few pages of her *Literaturnyj dnevnik* to be convinced of her totally negative and utterly contemptuous judgment of this movement (in which she included Aleksandr Blok). Gippius' token participation in *Očarovannyj strannik* (no. 3) is therefore to be considered a tongue-in-cheek affair: in her only poem ("Banal'nostjam") printed in this publication, she defends old-fashioned, trite rhymes and thus fights against the decadent overrefinement of poetic form.

55 Incidentally, she was Livšic's wife (as well as Andrej Belyj's niece).

56 Ada Vladimirova published the following books of verse: *Dali večernie* (1913); *Nevypitoe serdce* (1918); *Kuvšin sinevy* (1922); *Stixotvorenija* (1927); *Liven'* (1929).

57 In *Knižnyj Ugol* (no. 5), Xovin repeated his accusations, not only reproaching Maksim Gor'kij for being silent under the Communists, whereas under the Czar he had told the truth, but also attacking Majakovskij and his friends for reprinting old works in a futurist anthology (*Ržanoe slovo*, 1918) with a preface by A. Lunačarskij, then the minister of culture. Xovin called the very fact of such a preface "a slap that hit the futurists themselves." I

have been told that Xovin somehow became an *émigré,* but I was unable to confirm this report or find any details on his life after the seventh issue of *Knižnyj Ugol.* Even the dates of his birth and death are unavailable.

58 Lavrenev never published his "Ekzotičeskij korablik," announced by the Mezzanine of Poetry.

59 Šeršenevič's critical contributions to *Vernissaž* were two reviews, one exposing the illiteracy of the "neofuturists" (see chap. 5), and the other (under the pen name of L'abbé Fanferluche) dismissing the publications of the Lirika group (see chap. 6).

60 See Gumilev, *Pis'ma o russkoj poèzii,* p. 140.

61 *Ibid.,* p. 170.

62 The transition from symbolism to ego-futurism is noticeable in Šeršenevič's poetry printed in the almanac *Krugovaja čaša,* published in the spring of 1913 by seven young poets living in Moscow (among them were the previously mentioned Čajkin and Sidorov). Šeršenevič here not only dedicates one poem to Širokov, but also mentions electricity and the telephone—probably a very modern thing to do in 1913. Later, Šeršenevič included only one of these poems in his futurist collection *Avtomobil'ja postup'* (see chap. 7), the one with the image of a "bald-headed moon [*mesjac plešivyj*]." There is also one rhyme (*Èzele–grezili*) in these poems which has obviously been taken from Xlebnikov.

63 *Zelenaja ulica,* p. 84.

64 I. Aksenov, "K likvidacii futurizma," *Pečat' i Revolucija,* no. 3 (1921), p. 90.

65 E.g., the reviewer in *Žatva,* V, 301–302, who found *Carmina* merely inept, could not find words to express his disgust not only with *Èkstravagantnye flakony* ("most ordinary, pretentious, and tasteless nonsense written in a poor semiprose"), but with all Mezzanine publications ("Why is this all called 'futurism,' and not simply 'poor poetry'?").

66 See Spasskij, *Majakovskij i ego sputniki,* p. 47, where Šeršenevič is portrayed as having the ambition to become "a futurist Brjusov."

67 In the verse epigraph to the book (perhaps of his own composition), Šeršenevič speaks about "the futurist express" coming to replace the "symbolist trojka."

68 Šeršenevič, *Zelenaja ulica,* p. 92.

69 Only Trenin and Xardžiev briefly mention him in this context ("Poètika rannego Majakovskogo," pp. 188–189) in a very limited manner: "Xrisanf builds all his poetry on punning rhymes." In 1920, Zak left Russia and, after a short stay in Florence, settled in Paris. His painting is described in Pierre Courthion's *Léon Zack* (Paris: Le Musée de Poche, 1961). He continued writing poetry, which he never published. It is still available only in typescript —M. Rossijanskij, *Utro vnutri: Stixi (1916–1962)*—and really deserves more than a mention in a note. In his late poetry Zak has grown into an important poet who, ironically, is still completely unknown even to the literati of the Russian emigration. His is a perfect example of introspective philosophical and

religious poetry which *as a whole* grows out of the words and is based entirely on paronomasia. In a way, this book is the goal toward which all futurist poetry was moving but, paradoxically, could never achieve to such an extent on Russian soil. Human wisdom and depth in relation to the world and God are combined in this poetry with lightness of touch which, nevertheless, does not come into conflict with the richness of verbal texture.

[70] Aksenov, *op. cit.*, p. 90.

[71] *Mozaika* was called an "immature, decadent book" by S. Gorodeckij (*Rec'*, no. 146 [1911], p. 3); Gumilev, who tried to be courteous in his review, still had to admit that Bol'šakov's prose was "worse than weak" (see *Pis'ma o russkoj poèzii*, pp. 115–116).

[72] In this characteristic Tret'jakov strikes an original note, not only anticipating much of the early Soviet poetry, both futurist and nonfuturist, but also refuting the idea expressed by N. Ul'janov ("Ob odnoj neudavšejsja poèzii," *Vozdušnye Puti*, III [New York, 1963]) that futurism "never sang the machine." Ul'janov further asserts that Russian poetry never portrayed a moving train, car, or ship, which is completely unfounded. One need only remember N. Kucol'nik (to whose text Glinka wrote his marvelous "Poputnaja pesnja") and P. Vjazemskij, not to mention such twentieth-century poets as Bagrickij, Šeršenevič, and Severjanin.

[73] Tret'jakov's most important verse collections of the Soviet period are *Jasnyš* (Čita, 1922), *Itogo* (Moscow, 1924), *Oktjabreviči* (Leningrad, 1924), and *Ryči, Kitaj* (Moscow, 1926), the last not to be confused with his famous play with the same title, produced by V. Mejerxol'd. Tret'jakov was one of the Communist experts on China and wrote many essays about that country. His autobiography is included in Kručenyx's *15 let russkogo futurizma*.

4. Cubo-Futurism

[1] See V. Katanjan, *Majakovskij, Literaturnaja xronika* (2d ed.; Leningrad, 1948), p. 44.

[2] *Ibid.*, p. 45.

[3] "I nam mjasa," *Nov'*, Nov. 16, 1914.

[4] See Livšic, *PS*, p. 155.

[5] V. Brjusov, "Novye tečenija v russkoj poèzii," *RM*, no. 3 (1913), p. 124.

[6] This terminology took root, but things soon got mixed up when the Muscovite groups, Mezzanine of Poetry and Centrifuge, took the ego-futurists' side and when Xlebnikov and Kručenyx settled in St. Petersburg. Still later, there was more of this type of confusion.

[7] Livšic, *op. cit.*, p. 155.

[8] *Ibid.*, p. 282.

[9] A. Dymšic, "Vladimir Majakovskij," *Zvezda*, no. 5–6 (1940), p. 156, is an example of the former opinion. The latter view is represented by V. Trenin and N. Xardžiev, *LN*, II, 157.

[10] V. Šeršenevič, *Futurizm bez maski* (Moscow, 1914), pp. 73–74.

[11] K. Čukovskij, "Ėgo-futuristy i kubo-futuristy," Šipovnik, XXII (St. Petersburg, 1914), 95–154. It was then reprinted in his book of critical essays, Lica i maski (St. Petersburg, 1914), pp. 93–136, and finally became the book Futuristy (Petrograd, 1922).

[12] PSS, I, 366.

[13] See, e.g., Pir vo vremja čumy, p. [18].

[14] In "Novye tečenija v russkoj poèzii," RM, no. 3 (1913).

[15] N. Xardžiev, "Zametki o Majakovskov," LN, LXV (Moscow, 1958), 419–420.

[16] See SP, II, 10.

[17] This poem was, however, printed earlier in Sojuz molodezi, no. 3 (March, 1913).

[18] The first of these lines is taken, almost verbatim, from Vjačeslav Ivanov (cf. his "Ropot" in Ėros [St. Petersburg, 1907], p. 35).

[19] See SP, V, 257.

[20] Both quotations from NP, p. 361.

[21] This passage refers to Petr Uspenskij's Tertium Organum, a work to which Kručenyx was most likely introduced by Matjušin.

[22] Kručenyx's knowledge of the glossolalia of religious sects derives from D. G. Konovalov's article, "Religioznyj èkstaz v russkom mističeskom sektantstve," printed in Bogoslovskij Vestnik, especially from the portion printed in the April issue of 1908.

[23] It is doubtful that Kručenyx read even so much as a line by Kant (or Plato). The image of Kant sitting behind a screen is perhaps taken from a poem by Aleksandr Blok, "Sižu za širmoj" (published in 1909).

[24] A much shorter piece under the same title, also signed by Kručenyx and Xlebnikov, was not published at that time (see it in SP, V, 247). It stresses the idea that a poetic work is primarily based on the word and rejects tendentiousness. Italian futurism (which is described as imitative of Russian) is accused precisely of this tendentiousness and of the inability to match theory with artistic practice. Another document, "Bukva kak takovaja," written by the same authors, also remained unpublished until much later (SP, V, 248–249); it proclaimed the importance of handwriting in poetic works.

[25] As in the poem "Pamjatnik" which concludes the book. R. Jakobson told me its last stanza is definitely by Xlebnikov.

[26] As I was unable to obtain the original leaflet, I translated from the text printed by Kručenyx several months later in the scroll Gramoty i deklaracii russkix futuristov (see chap. 5). The declaration, as Kručenyx himself claims, was written in April, 1913, but the material published later in Troe and Slovo kak takovoe had obviously been written before it. He wrote the latter, together with Xlebnikov, sometime early in 1913; and Xlebnikov reacted from Astrakan' to Deklaracija slova kak takovogo, sent to him by Kručenyx, in August, 1913.

[27] NP, p. 367. Let us add, too, that for Kručenyx the very appearance of y (the Russian letter for u) suggested a lily.

[28] It appears that the word *rečetvorcy* was seriously considered as a possible name for the Hylaean group.

[29] Descriptions of this futurist tour can be found in a variety of sources, such as Katanjan's chronicle; *PSS*, I, 366–367; memoirs by Livšic and Kamenskij; and finally in the excellent summing-up in an article by N. Xardžiev, "Turne kubo-futuristov 1913–1914 gg.," in *Majakovskij: Materialy i issledovanija* (Moscow, 1940), pp. 401–427.

[30] *PSS*, I, 368.

[31] See Al. Karcev, "Majakovskij i drugie," *Novoe Russkoe Slovo* (New York), May 3, 1964.

[32] In 1908 and 1909, while in his teens, Majakovskij was jailed twice: for working in a Communist underground printing house and for planning the escape of female political prisoners.

[33] In Samara, the local official who received them refused to believe that the first parts of their names were David Davidovič, Vasilij Vasil'evič, and Vladimir Vladimirovič, respectively, and thought these were a futurist trick.

[34] Katanjan, p. 61.

[35] V. Kamenskij, *Ego-moja biografija velikogo futurista* (Moscow, 1918), p. 131.

[36] A. Kručenyx, *15 let russkogo futurizma, 1912–1927 gg.* (Moscow, 1928), p. 60.

[37] In "God russkoj poèzii," *RM*, no. 5 (1913); quoted here from V. Brjusov, *Izbrannye sočinenija v dvux tomax*, II, (Moscow, 1955), 258.

[38] See Aleksandr Zakrževskij, *Rycari bezumija*, p. 10.

[39] *Apollon*, no. 1 (1913), p. 42.

[40] "Smes'," *Apollon*, no. 1 (1913).

[41] See some quotations from this declaration in *NP*, pp. 396–397.

[42] *Maski*, no. 7–8 (1912–13), pp. 29–33.

[43] See *PSS*, I, 275–285.

[44] See Angelo Maria Ripellino, *Majakovskij e il teatro russo d'avanguardia* (Torino, 1959), pp. 248–249.

[45] The image of heliomachia is also found in other early poems by Majakovskij and in Xlebnikov's writings (*solncelovy*). Matjušin thus interprets this symbol in the opera: "The Strong Men, who are men of the future, are victorious over the sun of cheap appearances and have lit their own inner light" ("Futurizm v Petersburge," *PŽRF*, pp. 153–157).

[46] O. Matjušina, "Negasimye iskry," *Zvezda*, no. 10 (1959), pp. 165–167; and K. Tomaševskij, " 'Vladimir Majakovskij,' " *Teatr*, no. 4 (1938), pp. 137–150.

[47] *PŽRF*, pp. 153–157.

[48] *PSS*, I, 22 (*prosvistali ee do dyrok*).

[49] P. Jarcev, "Teatral'nye očerki: Teatr futuristov," *Reč'*, Dec. 7, 1913.

[50] A. Mgebrov, *Žizn' v teatre*, II (1932), 274.

[51] The text of the declaration was later reprinted by the author in his *Zelenaja ulica* (Moscow, 1916), pp. 54–61.

⁵² *PSS*, I, 367.

⁵³ Xardžiev, p. 417.

⁵⁴ Panda, "Futuristy," *Večer*, no. 269.

⁵⁵ R. Rabov, "Futurizm: Novaja literaturnaja škola," *Vestnik literatury tovariščestva Vol'f* (Moscow), no. 5 (1909), pp. 120–121.

⁵⁶ B. Šapošnikov, "Futurizm i teatr," *Maski*, no. 7–8 (1912–13), pp. 29–33; I. Rozenfel'd, "Intuitivizm i futurizm," *Maski*, no. 6 (1913–14), pp. 17–26.

⁵⁷ Entitled simply "Manifest futuristov," it is actually the famous manifesto of the futurist artists of April 11, 1910, and it is followed by the text of the address to the audience at their first Parisian exhibit.

⁵⁸ "Futuristy," *Kievskaja Mysl'*, May 17, 1913; later reprinted in Lunačarskij's *Sobranie sočinenij*, V (Moscow, 1965), 270–275.

⁵⁹ "Sverxskul'ptor i sverxpoèt," *Den'*, July 29, 1913.

⁶⁰ Some non-Russian sources mention an earlier visit of Marinetti's to Russia (see, e.g., Graziella Lehrmann, *De Marinetti à Maiakovski* [Fribourg, 1942]). There must be some misunderstanding behind this.

⁶¹ On page 112 of the miscellany *Petrogradskie večera*, III (1914), there is a description of Marinetti's arrival, as part of a serialized novel by Tat'jana Krasnopol'skaja (Šenfel'd), which, contrary to historical fact, includes, but does not name, Majakovskij among the welcoming committee: "A local six-foot poet in a short, bright, striped blouse, with crazy eyes in the face of a degenerate."

⁶² "Francuzik iz Bordo" is the famous phrase from Griboedov's classic comedy *Gore ot uma* (III, 22), often quoted to satirize the willingness of Russian educated society to lionize any foreign visitor.

⁶³ *Reč'*, no. 30 (Jan. 31, 1914).

⁶⁴ Čužoj, "Moskovskie otkliki: Šampanskogo butylka," *Reč'*, no. 29 (1914); Ja. Tugendxol'd, "Zapozdalyj futurizm (k priezdu Marinetti)," *Reč'*, no. 31 (1914).

⁶⁵ See *SP*, V, 250.

⁶⁶ Reprinted in Kamenskij, *Žizn' s Majakovskim*, pp. 112–113.

⁶⁷ *PSS*, I, 369.

⁶⁸ Katanjan, p. 59.

⁶⁹ Pasternak, *Proza*, pp. 39, 269.

⁷⁰ *PS*, chap. 7.

⁷¹ *Ibid.*, p. 203.

⁷² *Ibid.*, p. 255.

⁷³ *NP*, pp. 368–369.

⁷⁴ *NP*, p. 476; *LN*, II, 157. Otherwise, Italians remained discreetly silent about their Russian counterparts in the wake of Marinetti's visit. *Lacerba* for 1914, e.g., does not mention them, except for a three-paragraph report on page 109 of the issue of April 1, "Marinetti in Russia," which notes his eight "triumphal lectures" (there were only five), in the country in which, for several years, "s'agitano e prosperano numerosi gruppi di futuristi russi"; describes

the Russian translation of *Le Futurisme* as a best seller; and claims that Marinetti, "not having been lulled by the great multitude of female Russian hearts," is organizing an exhibit of Italian futurist paintings scheduled to open in November.

[75] See *Kratkij slovar' literaturovedčeskix terminov* (Moscow: Učpedgiz, 1952), p. 139. A letter to D. Burljuk, published in *Color and Rhyme*, no. 55 (1964), even states that Marinetti was a Russian prisoner of war.

[76] "Futurizm v Italii," *RM*, no. 12 (1913), pp. 16–19.

[77] "Ital'janskij futurizm," *Vestnik Evropy*, no. 2 (1914), pp. 339–357.

[78] "Psevdofuturizm," *Sovremennyj Mir* (March, 1914), pp. 122–174.

[79] G. Čulkov's "Marinetti," printed first in January, 1914, in *Otkliki* (the literary supplement to the daily paper *Den'*), was later reprinted in Čulkov's collections of essays, *Včera i segodnja* (Moscow, 1916) and *Naši sputniki* (Moscow, 1922). Both books also include a criticism of domestic futurism in "Opravdanie simvolizma": Čulkov sees in Hylaea a sign of the disintegration, decline, and moral fatigue of contemporary culture. He divides futurism into the following groups: (1) Marinettism (mechanization of life, antihumanism); (2) pseudofuturism, i.e., neodecadence (where he places Šeršenevič without naming him); (3) Hylaea. Čulkov condescends, however, to polemics with Kručenyx's essay in *Troe*.

[80] By Il'ja Èrenburg in his *Poèty Francii* (Paris, 1914), pp. 106–107. This is "Mon cœur de sucre rouge" from Marinetti's *La ville charnelle* with two portions in the middle and the entire final portion omitted. Šeršenevič's intention to publish *La Conquête des étoiles* and some other works by Marinetti in Russian translation was never realized.

[81] *Bitva u Tripoli (26 oktjabrja 1911 g.), perežitaja i vospetaja F. T. Marinetti,* "Universal'naja biblioteka" (Moscow, 1916).

[82] *Futurist Mafarka: Afrikanskij roman* (Moscow: Severnye dni, 1916).

[83] Homunculus [pseud. of David Zaslavskij], whose review is quoted on page 121 of *PŽRF*.

[84] *Sovremennyj Zapad*, no. 1 (St. Petersburg, 1922), pp. 132–138; no. 3, pp. 192–196; B. Percov, "Marinetti—fašist i futurist," *Krasnaja Nov'*, no. 8 (1927), pp. 214–225; *Literaturnaja Ènciklopedija*, VI, 800–804; *Bol'šaja Sovetskaja Ènciklopedija*, 1st ed., XXXIX, 354–356; N. Gorlov, *Futurizm i revoljucija: Poèzija futuristov* (Moscow, 1924). To this, one can add that the famous theatrical director Aleksandr Tairov criticized Marinetti's "music hall" theories and called them revolutionary only on the surface in his *Zapiski režissera* (Moscow, 1921), pp. 180–181. Also, the self-styled leader of Russian expressionism, Ippolit Sokolov, considered Majakovskij, Šeršenevič, Bol'šakov, and Tret'jakov "purebred Marinettiists" (see his *Èkspressionizm* [Moscow, 1920], p. 5, and his *Bunt èkspressionista* [Moscow, 1919], p. 4). Viktor Xovin spoke about "Russian Marinettiism" as early as the winter of 1914 ("Futurizm i vojna," *Očarovannyj strannik*, no. 6, p. 7). Most recently there was an article about Marinetti by Z. M. Potapova in *Kratkaja Literaturnaja Ènciklopedija*, IV (1967), 616–617.

⁸⁵ See *Razgrimirovannaja krasavica* (Moscow, 1928), pp. 176–180; also in Aseev's latest collected works, V, 344–347.

5. The Years of Flowering

¹ *Šarmanka* does not, however, have the name "Žuravl'" on its cover.

² Xlebnikov used the phrase "moloko kobylic" in his utopian essay "My i doma" (see *SP*, IV, 275).

³ For more details about the longer poems of Xlebnikov see my *The Longer Poems of Velimir Khlebnikov* (Berkeley and Los Angeles: University of California Press, 1962).

⁴ About Pavel Nikolaevič Filonov (1883–1942) and his art (with reproductions of his paintings), see "The Art of Russia That Nobody Sees," *Life* (March 28, 1960), pp. 68–70; Troels Andersen, "Pavel Nikolajevič Filonov" in the Danish magazine *Signum*, no. 4 (1963), pp. 20–31; Camilla Gray, *The Great Experiment: Russian Art, 1863–1922* (London, 1962), p. 183. Also see D. Burljuk's novel (in English), "Filonov," which occupies the entire issue of his *Color and Rhyme*, no. 28 (1954), pp. 1–28. In Russian, Filonov briefly appears as Rogov in Olga Matjušina's novel *Pesn' o žizni* (Leningrad: Molodaja Gvardija, 1946), pp. 106–111, 125–126. For an interpretation of Filonov's work, see I. I. Ioffe, *Sintetičeskaja istorija iskusstv* (Leningrad, 1933), pp. 482–484.

⁵ See I. F. Naživin, *Moja ispoved'* (Moscow, 1912), p. 446.

⁶ As the next issue, which was being prepared in March, 1914, never appeared, *PŽRF* may be considered a miscellany, and not a periodical.

⁷ See *Novyj Mir*, no. 7 (1963), p. 230.

⁸ In "I nam mjasa" (see *PSS*, I, 313–315), Majakovskij clearly rejects both Severjanin and Kručenyx, but he shows a point of contact with Šeršenevič, whose poetry he included in his recitations while on tour.

⁹ *PS*, p. 199.

¹⁰ This dandyism, which derived mainly from Mixail Kuzmin (who wrote a preface to a Russian edition of Jules Barbey d'Aurevilly) and from the Petersburg ego-futurism, was another important basis for Majakovskij's alliance with the Šeršenevič-Bol'šakov duo. It is possible that the long poem "Don Juan," written by Majakovskij in the middle of 1916 and then destroyed, was dandyist. Even David Burljuk was not against this method of attracting attention, and both he and Majakovskij may be seen in photographs wearing top hats and gloves, with Burljuk also sporting a lorgnette. After the Revolution, both eventually switched to a "proletarian" appearance.

¹¹ Šeršenevič later insisted (in his *Zelenaja ulica*, p. 89) that he was not the author of the reviews that so offensively criticized the first books by Bobrov and Pasternak. He did not, however, reveal the name of the real author.

¹² My copy of the scroll is defective and seems to lack several lines at the beginning of Kul'bin's first manifesto.

[13] About Zdanevič in this period see S. Spasskij, *Majakovskij i ego sputniki* (Leningrad, 1940), pp. 15–21.

[14] N. Xardžiev (see his article on futurism and the arts in *Majakovskij: Materialy i issledovanija* [Moscow, 1940], p. 375) declares that Anton Lotov was a pseudonym of Il'ja Zdanevič. Zdanevič himself, however, denies this claim —and even denies knowing any Lotov—in his letter to me. *Rekord* is unavailable not only in Russian state libraries, but in private collections as well. As I have heard, even Xardžiev's personal collection does not contain it, and this collection is supposed to be the most complete one on futurism. Was Lotov not a pseudonym for Larionov? Did *Rekord* exist at all?

[15] Similar rayonist poems could later be found among Apollinaire's "calligrammes"; but much earlier Russia had similar phenomena in the work of the seventeenth-century poet Simeon of Polock.

[16] V. Pjast, *Vstreči*, p. 263, also names the "group" of universalists (*vselenniči*, i.e., the word created by Xlebnikov) represented by the completely unknown Grinič.

[17] *RM*, no. 7 (1911), p. 23.

[18] Igor' Postupal'skij, *Literaturnyj trud D. Burljuka* (New York, 1931), p. 8.

[19] See *Pis'ma o russkoj poèzii* (Petrograd, 1923), p. 113.

[20] Čelionati, in *Moskovskie mastera* (Moscow, 1916), p. 81, called Livšic *stroitel' slov dalekix*.

[21] *PS*, pp. 49–50. All other nonverse quotations, unless otherwise specified, are from the same book.

[22] Šeršenevič, *Futurizm bez maski*, p. 82, and especially A. P. Selivanovskij, *Očerki po istorii sovetskoj poèzii*, p. 74.

[23] *PŽRF*, p. 103.

[24] *PS*, p. 281.

[25] "V citadeli revoljucionnogo slova," *Puti Tvorčestva*, no. 5 (Xar'kov, 1919), p. 46.

[26] *Ibid.*

[27] Despite these neoclassical leanings, Livšic continued to consider himself a Hylaean, even after the Revolution. In "V citadeli revoljucionnogo slova," he repeated his ideas previously expressed in "Liberation of the Word." Writing about his own poetry, Livšic declared: "I imagine the whole totality of verbal units as an uninterrupted mass, one organic whole, in which I distinguish parts of unequal, so to speak, 'specific weights' of states, of various degrees of rarefaction. Those differences depend on the sound aspect of the word being more or less tied to its conceptual or emotional content, and they are located on a scale whose base coincides with our practical conversational word circulation, whereas the top touches the area of pure sound. For this reason the highest type of structure is for me the one where words are matched according to the laws of inner affinities, freely crystallizing on their own axes, and do not look for an agreement with the phenomena of the external world or of the lyric self." From here, Livšic proclaims the task of the destruction of syntax.

[28] See *Majakovskij: Materialy i issledovanija*, pp. 402, 419, 425.

²⁹ It was probably shortly before this break that Xlebnikov wrote the essay *!budetljanskij* (published posthumously in *SP*, V, 193), in which he sharply rejected Russian symbolism on nationalistic grounds. The piece looks like a draft of a manifesto for some of the Hylaean collections. It contains *Slap*-like attacks on Puškin (*iznežennoe perekatipole, nosimoe vetrom naslaždenija tudy i sjudy*) and L. Tolstoj (Xlebnikov calls the ox that marches toward the slaughterhouse and does not resist the butcher Tolstoy's first teacher). The title shows that the author does not subscribe to the foreign label of "futurism."

³⁰ In *Žizn' s Majakovskim* (Moscow, 1940), p. 140, Kamenskij describes his work displayed at that exhibit. It was called "A Fall from an Airplane" and consisted of a 4-pound metal weight, with a face painted on it, hanging on a wire from a hook about an inch away from a sheet iron background. Below, fragments of the airplane were suggested in a puddle of blood (minium). One was supposed to pull the corner of the "painting," then the "head" hit the iron and produced "thunder." Majakovskij explained to the spectators that it was "not a painting, but a gay game" portraying Kamenskij's thunder of joy at having survived the crash.

³¹ The tango was a rage of the day (see Šeršenevič, *PŽRF*, p. 92). Cf. the title (*Tango*) of a book by V. Gorskij. Pasternak (*Proza*, p. 40) calls the period a "reign of tango and skating rinks."

³² *Majakovskij: Materialy i issledovania*, p. 386.

³³ *Sovremennik*, no. 7 (1913).

³⁴ *Pir vo vremja čumy*, p. [17].

³⁵ See n. 22, chap. 4.

³⁶ The second edition of *Explodity* appeared the same year; that of *Piglets*, in 1914.

³⁷ At the end of *Vozropščem*, it is listed as appearing in June, 1913, but in 1925 Kručenyx listed it among the publications of 1914 (in *Zaumnyj jazyk u Sejfullinoj* . . .).

³⁸ In 1923 Kručenyx published a different book with a similar title, *Sobstvennye rasskazy, stixi i pesni detej*.

³⁹ *Literaturnyi cirkuljar* (1914).

⁴⁰ See also his miscellany *Scrublennyj poceluj* (1922), to which K. Bol'šakov contributed some poems.

⁴¹ *Kumačevye guljanki* (Moscow and Leningrad: Molodaja Gvardija, 1927).

⁴² "Segodnjašnij den' v russkoj poèzii," *RM*, no. 7 (1912), p. 22.

⁴³ His first three works were *Pesni i dumy* (1909), *Fantastičeskaja jav'* (1910), and *Pesni devušek* (1912).

⁴⁴ I. V. Vladislavlev [Gul'binskij], ed., *Bibliografičeskij Ežegodnik*, Vol. IV, *Sistematičeskij ukazatel' za 1914* (Moscow, 1915), p. 171.

⁴⁵ *Zelenaja ulica*, pp. 82–83.

⁴⁶ S. Bobrov in *Rukonog*, p. 43.

⁴⁷ "V zaščitu futurizma," *Vernissaž* (Moscow: Mezonin Poèzii, Sept., 1913), pp. [26–28].

⁴⁸ *Porosjata* (2d ed.), p. 15.

⁴⁹ *PŽRF*, p. 139.

⁵⁰ "Saratovskie psixofuturisty" *Neva*, no. 7 (1963), pp. 182–183.

⁵¹ This word is printed with Latin letters precisely in this way.

⁵² *PŽRF*, p. 139.

⁵³ *Deševaja jumoristiceskaja biblioteka Novogo Satirikona*, no. 16 (Petersburg, 1914).

⁵⁴ *Sovremennik*, no. 5 (1915), p. 290.

⁵⁵ *RM*, no. 7 (1912), p. 20.

⁵⁶ *RM*, no. 8 (1913), p. 79.

⁵⁷ Vl. Kranixfel'd, "Literaturnye otkliki. 80 tysjač verst vokrug sebja," *Sovremennyj Mir*, no. 4 (1913), pp. 96–112.

⁵⁸ A. Red'ko, "U podnožija afrikanskogo idola," *Russkoe Bogatstvo*, no. 7 (1913), pp. 179–199.

⁵⁹ V. L. L'vov-Rogačevskij, "Simvolisty i nasledniki ix," *Sovremennik*, no. 6 (1913), pp. 271–279.

⁶⁰ See n. 11, chap. 4.

⁶¹ *RM*, no. 3 (1914), pp. 83–95.

⁶² "Sredi ustremlenij k neponjatnomu i nepostižnomu," *Russkoe Bogatstvo*, no. 3 (1914), pp. 217–250.

⁶³ *RM*, no. 5 (1914), pp. 25–31.

⁶⁴ "Včera, segodnja i zavtra russkoj poèzii," *Pečat' i Revoljucija*, no. 7 (1922), pp. 38–68.

⁶⁵ *Otkliki*, nos. 7–8 (1914).

⁶⁶ N. Lerner, "Praščur russkogo futurizma," *Golos Žizni*, no. 15 (April 8, 1915), pp. 19–20; later repr. in his *Rasskazy o Puškine* (Leningrad, 1929).

⁶⁷ "Russkaja poèzija: Obzor," *Al'manax izdatel'stva Al'ciona*, I (2d ed.; Moscow, 1914), 213–217.

⁶⁸ A. Blok, *Sočinenija v dvux tomax*, II (1955), 452–459.

⁶⁹ "F. K. Sologub o futurizme," *Birževye Vedomosti*, April 23, 1915 (evening edition).

⁷⁰ N. Rozanov refers to this interview on page 31 of his *Ègo-futurizm*.

⁷¹ "L. Andreev o futurizme," *Birževye Vodomosti*, May 4, 1915 (evening edition).

⁷² *Russkoe Slovo*, June 29 (July 12), 1914, p. 3. Later Merežkovskij printed it in his book of essays, *Nevoennyj dnevnik 1914–1916* (Petrograd, 1917), pp. 79–90.

6. Centrifuge

¹ Anisimov's second book of verse, *Večer* (1916), never went on sale. After the Revolution he worked in museums. His third book, *Zemljanoe* (Moscow, 1926), shows a change in manner, content, and influence (Morgenstern, Xlebnikov), and is primitivistic. Anisimov occasionally printed translations that varied in subject from American Negro poetry to James Joyce.

² Sidorov was the only one who printed his work with other groups (*Vernissaž*) or publishing undertakings (*Krugovaja čaša*).

3 Pasternak, *Proza*, p. 24.

4 Žizn' i tvorčestvo Artjura Rimbo," *RM*, no. 10 (1913), pp. 127–154. "Bateau ivre" excites Bobrov more than anything else: "It is a ribbon of a phantastic telegraph transmitter which clicks out, one after another, fragmentary statements. Nothing can compare with the wild magnificence of this prophetic delirium."

5 Quoted on page 207 of *Vtoroj Sbornik Centrifugi* from the newspaper *Priazovskij Kraj* as having said, ". . . a mixture of Puškin, Tjutčev, and French poets sprinkled with the cologne of futurism and strewn with the pepper of the 'Donkey's-tail-ism.' "

6 *Trudy i dni*, no. 1–2 (1913), pp. 116–137.

7 *Nočnaja flejta* (Moscow, 1914), pp. 3, 4, 5.

8 Aseev previously printed poetry in the miscellany *Pervocvet* (Moscow, 1912).

9 Pasternak, *Proza*, p. 33.

10 Aseev's preface, adorned with an epigraph borrowed from Jazykov, presents Pasternak as a worthy heir to the symbolists, especially to the "one and only, the unforgettable Konevskoj." There is also a muffled attack against the "young men with French accents who lead a dissolute life in Russian poetry," which is clearly aimed at the Mezzanine of Poetry.

11 Pasternak, *Proza*, p. 18.

12 *Ibid.*, p. 32.

13 Pasternak was analyzed from this viewpoint by I. I. Ioffe, *Sintetičeskaja istorija iskusstv* (Leningrad, 1933), pp. 468–476.

14 "Novye tečenija v russkoj poèzii," *RM*, no. 8 (1913), p. 75.

15 No. 3, pp. 17–18.

16 P. 28.

17 Pp. 140–147.

18 *Svobodnyj Žurnal* (Nov., 1914), pp. 134–135.

19 Not to be confused with the Petersburg semifuturist miscellany published under the same title by A. Belenson (see chap. 7). Also compare the title of Livšic's memoirs, *Polutoraglazyj strelec*, derived from a painting by D. Burljuk.

20 Later Bobrov insisted (*Rukonog*, p. 43) that he never was an ego-futurist, but his statement in *Razvoročennye čerepa*, which he later claimed was misinterpreted by Hylaeans, does sound ambiguous. Also, Ignat'ev sent two poems to Bobrov in November, 1913, to be printed in *Rukonog*. These facts suggest that the split in Lirika took place well before March 1, 1914.

21 Pasternak, *Proza*, p. 269.

22 *Ibid.*, pp. 39, 269–272.

23 In a letter dated November 27, 1964, Zdanevič claims that he signed the manifesto simply "out of friendship."

24 Later it was Roman Jakobson who brilliantly demonstrated this metonymic nature of both Pasternak's poetry and prose ("Randbemerkungen zur Prosa des

Dichters Pasternak," *Slavische Rundschau*, no. 6 [1935], pp. 357–374).

[25] Quoted from the preface to Pasternak, *Stixotvorenija i poèmy* (Moscow and Leningrad, 1965), p. 26n.

[26] Originally, Aseev planned to give the title "Liren' " to his next book of verse (to be published by Centrifuge).

[27] *Peta*, p. 38.

[28] *Vremennik*, p. [6].

[29] See *NP*, p. 480.

[30] Aseev, *Sobranie sočinenij v 5 tomax*, I (Moscow, 1963), 11.

[31] *Ibid.*, p. 8.

[32] *Pečat' i Revoljucija*, no. 2 (1921), p. 203.

[33] Pasternak, *Proza*, p. 17.

[34] Despite Aseev's (*op. cit.*, p. 64) claims that these words are Gypsy, I could not find them in a Gypsy-Russian dictionary; however, in 1917 (*Vremennik*, p. [6]) Aseev suggested the title was in Tadzhik.

[35] Aseev, *op. cit.*, p. 8.

[36] *Ibid.*, p. 9.

[37] *Ibid.*

[38] Igor' Postupalskij, *Literaturnyj trud Davida D. Burljuka* (New York, 1931), p. 8.

[39] Bobrov later made the rather farfetched assertion (*Pečat' i Revoljucija*, no. 2 [1921], p. 203) that Aseev combines the heavy, tortuous speech of Xlebnikov, the seductive, sweet coquetry of Severjanin, and the point-blank, morbid garishness of Majakovskij with symbolism.

[40] See the preface to Aseev's *Izbran'* (1923).

[41] See Petnikov's biography in *Zavetnaja kniga* (Simferopol', 1961). The emphasis on *trudovaja sem'ja* on page 147 sounds suspicious, and Ju. Tera-piano is perhaps closer to the truth when he writes (in "Grigorij Petnikov," *Russkaja Mysl'* [Paris], June 10, 1961) that Petnikov's father was a colonel.

[42] The source in note 41 also gives 1914 as Petnikov's literary debut, but I was unable to obtain more specific information.

[43] *SP*, V, 232.

[44] *Porosl' solnca*, p. 4.

[45] *SP*, V, 223; *Puti Tvorčestva*, no. 5 (1919), p. 44. Petnikov's use of familiar Russian words (often geographical names) with a new meaning based on their root is interesting. His *litva* derives from *lit'*; *rus'*, from *rusyj*; *golub'*, from *glub'*; etc.

[46] *Pečat' i Revoljucija*, no. 2 (1921), p. 207.

[47] Starting with the fourth issue, Petnikov was a member of the editorial board and later the editor of *Puti Tvorčestva*, the magazine published in Xar'kov in 1919–20, where he printed the works of Xlebnikov, Guro, Pasternak, Božidar, Livšic, and Gnedov.

[48] In the anonymous preface to his *Izbrannye stixi* (Moscow, 1936), p. 8.

[49] "Posleslovie" in *Buben* (2d ed; Moscow, 1916), pp. 27, 28–29.

[50] In 1922 Šilling printed his poetry in the collective edition of the members

of the Union of Poets (*Sojuz poètov: 2 sbornik stixov*), and described himself as a "centrifugist."

⁵¹ Sadovskoj, like Bobrov, was an enthusiast of Jazykov (see, e.g., his article in *Petrogradskie večera*, no. 3 [1914]).

⁵² *Lira lir*, p. 63.

⁵³ Sergej Spasskij, *Majakovskij i ego sputniki* (Leningrad, 1940), p. 48.

⁵⁴ Aseev, *Začem i komu nužna poèzija* (Moscow, 1961), p. 277.

⁵⁵ Pasternak, *Proza*, p. 36.

⁵⁶ See *Vtoroj sbornik Centrifugi*, p. 99; *Lira lir*, p. 63.

⁵⁷ Some bibliographies list the second volume of *Zapiski stixotvorca*, but it was never published. The MS was lost in the 1920's in a publishing house.

⁵⁸ Bobrov also published the pamphlet *N. M. Jazykov o mirovoj literature* (Moscow, 1916), a collection of Jazykov's literary opinions and judgments. In the preface Bobrov characterizes Jazykov's work as "a reaction to the insufficient revolutionary quality of Puškin's form" (p. 4).

⁵⁹ In the essay, "Soglasnye v stixe," in *Zapiski stixotvorca* (p. 84).

⁶⁰ "Opisanie stixotvorenija 'Vinograd,' " *Puškin i ego sovremenniki*, XXIX–XXX (1918), 188–209; *Novoe o stixosloženii A. S. Puškina* (Moscow: Musaget, 1915).

⁶¹ Like Božidar, Bobrov "solves" the problems of accentual verse mainly by seeing in it "triplets" and pauses. Also, he applies Greek terms too generously, and sometimes misleadingly. He often does not take into consideration non-standard stress in Russian words and therefore discovers "deviations" from classical verse where there are none. Despite all his erudition, he is ignorant of much of Russian eighteenth-century poetry (a shortcoming that he, of course, shares with his period), where he could find unexpected support or correction for some of his statements.

⁶² E.g., S. Malaxov, "Russkij futurizm posle revoljucii," *Molodaja Gvardija*, no. 10 (1926), p. 172.

⁶³ In 1964–65 Bobrov published, after a long period of silence, three long articles on metrics and poetics (see *Russkaja Literatura*, nos. 3–4 [1965]).

⁶⁴ In his *Novoe o stixosloženii* . . ., pp. 28–29.

⁶⁵ Some of the poetry in these two books did appear in miscellanies (*Moskovskij Parnas II, Sopo I, Vesennij salon poètov*).

⁶⁶ *Pečat' i Revoljucija*, no. 1 (1921), pp. 146–147.

⁶⁷ One can, however, find a few poems scattered through periodicals (e.g., *Xudožestvennoe Slovo*, no. 2 [1920]). Bibliographies also mention Bol'šakov's book *Koroleva Mod* ("Queen Maud [?]") (Moscow, 1917), but I was unable to obtain it.

⁶⁸ *Sud'ba slučajnostej, Golyj fakt*, and *Put' prokažennyx*.

⁶⁹ Moscow, 1927. Also published in Riga in 1931 as *Konec dobrovol'českoj armii*.

⁷⁰ *Begstvo plennyx ili istorija stradanij i gibeli poručika tenginskogo pexotnogo polka Mixaila Lermontova* (Xar'kov, 1929). The other version of the novel was *Car' i poručik* (Riga, 1930).

[71] As an imagist, Ivnev published *Solnce vo grobe* (poetry) and *4 vystrela* (criticism), both in Moscow in 1921.

[72] This judgment does not include his first novel, *Nesčastnyj angel* (1917), which is connected with his poetry. *Ljubov' bez ljubvi* (1925) and *Otkrytyj dom* (1927) portray the life of the literati in the Caucasus. *Geroj romana* (1928) depicts the Russian emigration as a stinking swamp.

[73] *Moja strana* (1943), *Stixi* (1948) and *Izbrannye stixi* (1965). About Ivnev and his "drawer" poetry, see the interesting memoirs of V. Pastuxov in *Opyty*, V (New York, 1955); also G. Ivanov, *Peterburgskie zimy* (Paris, 1928), pp. 153-159.

[74] *Rodina i narody* (Moscow, 1915).

[75] *Miting dvorcov* was reprinted in the futurist anthology *Ržanoe slovo* (Moscow, 1918), and Kušner's active part in Lef caused Majakovskij (*PSS*, XIII, 57) to include his name among the very few (according to Majakovskij) who tried futurist prose: Xlebnikov and Kamenskij. Actually Kušner's heavily alliterated rhythmic, and occasionally rhymed, prose derives from Andrej Belyj as much as from Majakovskij (in imagery).

[76] It should not be confused with Pasternak's later book (1929) which, though published under the same title, was basically different from this first version. The 1929 edition does contain many poems from the 1917 edition, but they are, in most instances, rewritten almost beyond recognition. Eighteen poems are omitted, and many are included which were written either earlier (*Lirika*) or later than 1917.

[77] Pasternak, *Proza*, p. 281.

[78] See Pasternak, *Stixotvorenija i poèmy* (Moscow and Leningrad, 1965), p. 625.

[79] Pasternak, *Stixi 1936-1959* . . . (Ann Arbor, 1961), p. 159.

[80] Pasternak, *Stixotvorenija i poèmy*, p. 625.

[81] For example, V. Vejdle (see Pasternak, *Stixi i poèmy 1912-1932*, pp. xxvii-xliv) lauds the poet for getting out of the blind alley of "modernism" and considers the futurism of Pasternak's early days to be only skin-deep and something like measles. The venerable critic finds this futurism, however, only in the two poems printed in *Rukonog* ("Cygane" and "Mel'xior"), and he obviously has not read *Bliznec v tučax* attentively. Much more naïve and hardly qualified to discuss the problem is Irina Bušman (*Sbornik statej posvjaščennyx tvorcestvu . . . Pasternaka* [Munich, 1962], p. 209), who categorically denies the presence of any avant-garde qualities in Pasternak's poetry. Both Bušman and Vejdle use the term *zaumnyj* incorrectly. On the other hand, the futurists valued in Pasternak "his unusual vocabulary, his stunning [*ogorašivajuščie*] semantic dissonances, and his dynamic rhythms" (Kamenskij, *Žizn' s Majakovskim*, p. 112). They also saw in his poetry "semantic breaks [which] were superimposed by the momentum of rhythm," whereby "dissimilar things converged and words changed their meaning in a musical way" (Šklovskij, *Žili-byli*, p. 274).

[82] Pasternak, *Proza*, p. 13.

⁸³ In "Oxrannaja gramota" (*Proza*, p. 278), he calls Majakovskij's friends "a hastily collected and always nearly indecently mediocre clique." If he means Hylaea, the description is not fair: they were connected by personal friendships not found elsewhere in Russian futurism, and none of them (with one possible exception) were mediocre.

⁸⁴ Pasternak, *Proza*, p. 32.

⁸⁵ Ju. Tynjanov spoke about Xlebnikov in these terms ("O V. Xlebnikove"); much of Soviet criticism interprets Majakovskij in this way.

⁸⁶ The second one seems to be I. Golomštok and A. Sinjavskij, *Pikasso* (Moscow, 1960).

⁸⁷ Especially interesting is his discovery of the baroque element in Picasso, and his is perhaps the first Russian apologia of the baroque in the twentieth century. The recent arguments of Soviet scholars echo his findings on the subject.

⁸⁸ Both are from *Pikasso i okrestnosti*, p. 5.

⁸⁹ *Ibid.*, p. 6.

⁹⁰ *Ibid.*, p. 22.

⁹¹ See, for example, his *Gamlet i drugie opyty* . . . (Moscow, 1930) and the posthumous *Elizavetincy, Stat'i i perevody* (Moscow, 1938). The title of this posthumous publication lacks the stylization of the prerevolutionary *Elisavetincy*.

⁹² *Peta*, p. 39.

⁹³ This volume was to be illustrated not only by Russians (Gončarova, Ėkster, Arxipenko), but also by Soffici. Judging by the title of Bobrov's essay in their projected miscellany, "Peterburgskie teoretiki," he planned a continuation of his fight against other avant-gardists. Despite his earlier alliance with the ego-futurists, Bobrov was a Muscovite patriot ("Russia has been and will be in Moscow," *Zapiski stixotvorca*, p. 22).

7. Decline

¹ Also see Majakovskij's letter of September 1, 1922, to an unnamed addressee (Trockij?) (*PSS*, XIII, 56), in which he makes cubo-futurists of several poets who at the time in question clearly belonged to other groups.

² A. Tinjakov in *Veršiny*, no. 16 (1915), p. 18.

³ See his letter to the editor entitled "O gonenii na molodost'" in *Žurnal Žurnalov*, no. 2 (1916), p. 17.

⁴ K. Čukovskij, *Iz vospominanij* (Moscow, 1959), p. 361.

⁵ There is much about the Stray Dog in Xlebnikov's unfinished *poèma* "Žut' lesnaja" (see *NP*, pp. 231–243).

⁶ In 1914 Belenson published in St. Petersburg his mediocre *Zabavnye stiški* with Kul'bin's illustrations, a book that clearly belonged to the tradition of Russian dandyism. His second book was *Vrata Tesnye* (Petrograd, 1922).* Belenson's poetry printed in *Strelec* appeared later in his third book, *Bezumija* (Moscow, 1924), which does contain some poems touched by originality. Bel-

enson also collected his postrevolutionary newspaper columns on the theater, art, and literature in *Iskusstvennaja žizn'* (Petrograd, 1921).

[7] This obviously inspired the postrevolutionary fuist, Boris Nesmelov, to write his *poema Rodit' mužčinam*, which appeared as a book in April, 1923, in Moscow.

[8] A. Remizov had his own touches of futurism in what he printed in *Strelec*: the author's drawings in the text, infantilism, special stress on speech intonation, and a collage-like technique.

[9] *Sovremennik*, no. 5 (1915), p. 286; D. Krjučkov in *Veršiny*, no. 20 (1915), pp. 15–16; Tinjakov, *op. cit.*, in this order.

[10] In *Birževye Vedomosti*, April 23, 1915 (evening edition).

[11] Cited in Kamenskij, *Put' èntuziasta*, p. 212.

[12] Nebukva, in *Žurnal Žurnalov*, no. 35 (1916).

[13] No. 1 (1915), pp. 3–4.

[14] See chap. 5.

[15] K. Kova, "Sled obreten," *Pesni Žatvy*, I (Moscow, 1915), 447–454.

[16] No. 18, pp. 6–8.

[17] In 1916 Šklovskij published another article on *zaum'*, "Zaumnyj jazyk' i poèzija" (*Sborniki po teorii poèticeskogo jazyka*, I), which he republished in *Poètika* (1919).

[18] "Golos iz podpol'ja," *Golos Žizni*, no. 22, pp. 6–8.

[19] Roslavec wrote music to texts by Severjanin, Bol'šakov, D. Burljuk (who, in his turn, illustrated some of Roslavec's sheet music), and even Gnedov.

[20] Possibly the month when they became friends.

[21] These italics appear in the original.

[22] Also in 1916 Čurilin printed in *Al'manax muz* the poem "Krotkij katarsis," which combines a love theme with religious imagery and is built on paronomasia.

[23] Sometimes incorrectly presented in bibliographies as *L'vu bars* (which is actually the title of the first poem in the book). Bibliographies also credit Čurilin with the book *Konec Kikapu*, allegedly published by Liren' in the same year. I was unable to verify the connection with the previously printed poem of the same title, and to ascertain whether this book was published at all. In 1940 another book by Čurilin appeared (see bibliography), but I have been unable to obtain a copy of it.

[24] This key sentence is printed in boldface with the word "took" in large capital letters, thus explaining the title of the miscellany.

[25] Xlebnikov's later projects included a fascinating essay on city planning and the architecture of the future ("My i doma"), suggestions to paint the sky with multicolored cannon smoke, and a proposal to treat people medically by making them stare into the eyes of animals (snakes, toads, or dogs, depending on the illness).

[26] *Color and Rhyme*, no. 31, p. 31.

[27] *Vremennik*, p. [6].

[28] Burljuk's later participation in *Vesennij salon poètov* (Moscow, 1918)

consisted of only two poems, and his poetry published in Siberia, which in-cluded two [?] editions of *Lysejuščij xvost,* never really reached the European part of Russia.

²⁹ See *Rjav,* p. 3.

³⁰ *NP,* p. 371.

³¹ *SP,* V, 310.

³² Jurij Oleša in V. Xlebnikov, *Zverinec* . . . (Moscow, 1930), p. 4.

³³ It is hardly necessary to refute such considerations, which are often noth-ing but the defense mechanisms of narrow and/or closed minds. With a very few exceptions dating from the revolutionary time, Xlebnikov's poetry is re-markably balanced and healthy. As to his personal sanity, he *was* examined by a psychiatrist in 1919, who found him sane, though he did not deny a certain deviation from the psychiatric norm. Xlebnikov's associations, though slow, were judged to be of high quality (V. Ja. Anfimov, "Klebnikov v 1919 g.," in *Trudy Tret'ej Kzasnodarskoj Kliničeskoj Gorodskoj Bol'nicy,* vypusk I (1935), pp. 66–74.

³⁴ Sergej Spasskij, *Majakovskij i ego sputniki,* p. 72.

³⁵ *NP,* p. 369.

³⁶ *Otryvok iz Dosok sud'by,* List 2-j, p. 25; List 3-j, p. 37.

³⁷ Spasskij, *op. cit.,* p. 71.

³⁸ Xlebnikov was not consistent in his terminology, calling his *zaum'* "a language of the stars." On one occasion, however, he suggested that he was making a distinction between these two terms.

³⁹ Petrovskij's memoirs were first printed in *Lef,* no. 1 (1923), then ap-peared as a book *Povest' o Xlebnikove* (Moscow, 1926). His poetic debut took place in 1920 with *Pustynnaja osen',* a huge book of immature, but extremely promising, poems. Petrovskij's poetry originates not only in the "quiet" fu-turism of Xlebnikov and Guro, but in Rilke as well (plus several other foreign roots). He writes about autumnal nature and God according to the method of drafts and excerpts in his modest, absorbed, mystical, slightly inarticulate verse, characterized by soft obscurity. Petrovskij resolutely accepted the Revolution and, being a seminary student and the son of a Černigov priest, had to do something about his "social origin." He worked as a lathe operator in 1917 and was a Red guerrilla in the Ukraine. He later participated in Lef and Pereval. His later poetry became more firm and glib, but lost much of the earlier originality. The theme of the word continued to connect him with Xlebnikov, but in imagery he drew closer to Pasternak. In his numerous Cos-sack songs and poems about the Civil War he differs little from the run-of-the-mill Soviet poets of the 1920's. Among his additional books of verse, *Poedinok* (Moscow, 1926) and *Gal'ka* (Moscow, 1927) deserve attention. He also wrote prose.

⁴⁰ Petrovskij, *Povest' o Xlebnikove* (Moscow: Ogonek, 1926), p. 6.

⁴¹ For biographical information and an extensive description and analysis of Xlebnikov's *poèmas* of this time, see chaps. vii–ix of my *The Longer Poems of Velimir Klebnikov.*

[42] Vel., "V. Xlebnikov: Osnovatel' budetljan," *Kniga i Revoljucija*, no. 9–10 (1922), p. 25.

[43] It concludes *Slovo kak takovoe.*

[44] About Gorkij's customary "sobbing on any poetic vest," see Majakovskij's autobiography (*PSS*, I, 23).

[45] See Aleksandr Blok, *Zapisnye knižki 1901–1920* (Moscow, 1965), p. 306.

[46] *PSS*, I, 309.

[47] *PSS*, I, 336.

[48] Despite the same name (Marija), she is another girl. See R. Jakobson, "Novye stroki Majakovskogo" in *Russkij Literaturnyj Arxiv* (New York, 1956), p. 200.

[49] V. Sklovskij, *Žili-byli* (Moscow, 1964), p. 267.

[50] *Ibid.*, p. 272.

[51] Compare Xlebnikov's drama *Ošibka smerti* and his poem "Napisannoe do vojny," as well as D. Burljuk's painting *Svjatoslav XX veka* (Tret'jakov Gallery).

[52] *Peta*, p. 46.

[53] Pasternak, *Proza*, p. 284.

[54] As late as October, 1929, he clearly stated: "We do not denounce all our past work as futurists" (*PSS*, XII, 510).

[55] My guess is that he was on the White side in the Civil War. Soviet sources give 1920 as the year of his death; in Western sources there is complete confusion in this respect. Katherine Dreier (*Burliuk* [New York, 1944]), who wrote her book on David's firsthand information, says that both Vladimir and Nicolaj were killed in World War I in 1917, the latter on the Rumanian front. Camilla Gray (*The Great Experiment*), who is probably the worst source so far as dates are concerned, describes Nikolaj as having been killed in 1915. The genealogical tree on the cover of *Color and Rhyme*, no. 59, drawn by David, gives 1929. When I asked David Burljuk at a personal meeting about the circumstances of Nikolaj's death, he was evasive, but later wrote me on February 25, 1964, that his brother "byl likvidirovan v zapas, v dosku."

[56] He sent his description of the artistic and literary life of Siberia during this time to Berlin, where it was printed ("Literatura i xudožestvo v Sibiri i na Dal'nem Vostoke [1919–22 gg.]," *Novaja Russkaja Kniga*, no. 2 [1922], pp. 44–48).

[57] Kitovras published a small anthology of contemporary futurist-oriented Russian poetry, *Segodnja russkoj poèzii* (New York, 1924).

[58] *Color and Rhyme*, no. 53, p. 2.

[59] In his poems about Japan, Burljuk uses many Japanese words, spelled with Russian letters, as he uses English words in the poems in *Èntelexizm.*

[60] See N. Xardžiev, "Zametki o Majakovskom," in *Literaturnoe Nasledstvo*, LXV, 403; V. Trenin and N. Xardžiev, "Poètika rannego Majakovskogo," *Literaturnyj Kritik*, no. 4 (1935), pp. 171–189; E. Gollerbax, *Poèzija Davida Burljuka* (New York, 1931), p. 15; Čelionati in *Moskovskie Mastera*, p. 81.

[61] Gollerbax, *op. cit.*, p. 15.

[62] *Color and Rhyme*, no. 39, p. 6; no. 40, p. 8; no. 57, p. 1; no. 37, p. 8; no. 40, p. 18.

[63] Camilla Gray, *The Great Experiment*.

[64] *Color and Rhyme*, no. 55, p. 46.

[65] *Ibid.*, no. 58, p. 1.

[66] *Ibid.*, no. 40, p. [20].

[67] *Èntelexizm*, p. 11; *Krasnaja Strela*, p. 3; *Èntelexizm*, p. 5.

[68] Postupal'skij, *op. cit.*, p. 13.

[69] *Color and Rhyme*, no. 37, p. 9; no. 49, p. 8.

[70] *Ibid.*, no. 30, p. [11].

[71] Burljuk, "Pravila igry," *Kitovras*, no. 2, p. 3.

[72] *Color and Rhyme*, no. 33, p. [3].

[73] *Èntelexizm*, p. 3.

[74] *Desjatyj Oktjabr'*, p. 24n; see also *Èntelexizm*, p. 9.

[75] *PSS*, I, 20.

[76] *Color and Rhyme*, no. 37, p. 8.

[77] *Ibid.*

[78] *Ibid.*, no. 47, p. 6.

[79] *Ibid.*, no. 33, p. [9].

[80] *Ego-Moja biografija velikogo futurista*, pp. 153, 28.

[81] Vsevolod Mejerxol'd, who correctly considered Evreinov a theatrical amateur, reviewed the book in *Birževye Vedomosti*, Feb. 10, 1917 (morning edition), writing that Kamensky not only exaggerated Evreinov's importance, but also thus compromised Evreinov's ideas.

[82] In *Žizn' s Majakovskim*, e.g., he gives 1907 as the date of publication for the first *Sadok sudej*.

[83] See, e.g., the article by Sosnovskij, "O jakoby revoljucionnom slovotvorčestve," *Na postu*, no. 2–3 (1923), pp. 247–250.

[84] *Èntelexizm*, p. 3.

[85] In 1919, 1923, and 1925. The Razin and the Pugachov plays were printed together in *P'esy* (Moscow, 1925). The play, "Zdes' slavjat razum," was printed in no. 2 (1923) of the miscellany *Vozroždenie*. Many plays, such as "Parovoznaja obednja" (1920), credited with being the first Soviet factory propaganda play, were never published.

[86] The "village" plays, *Kozij zagon* (1926), *Sel'kor* (1927), and *Na postu* (1927), appeared in individual editions.

[87] Autobiographical material can also be found in the preface to the collection of verse *I èto est'* (Tiflis, 1927). The novel in verse, *Stavka na bessmertie*, printed in issues 1 (1922) and 2 (1923) of *Vozroždenie*, is slightly autobiographical. *Junost' Majakovskogo* (Tiflis, 1931) should also be added.

[88] The leading poet and critic of Russian exile, Vladislav Xodasevič (who also was an outstanding Puškin scholar), wrote a sardonically contemptuous review of the book ("Sovetskaja kljukva") in the newspaper *Vozroždenie* (Paris), July 12, 1928. Xodasevič probably read this book in the Berlin edition printed in Latvia.

[89] Smaller collections had appeared before: *I èto est'* (Tiflis, 1927); *Saryn' na kičku* (Moscow, 1932); *Stixi o Zakavkaz'e* (Tiflis, 1932).

[90] In between there were *Tri poèmy* (Leningrad, 1933), *Ural'skie poèmy* (Sverdlovsk, 1935), *Rodina scast'ja* (Moscow, 1938), *Stixi i poèmy* (Tiflis, 1945), *Izbrannoe* (Leningrad, 1948), *Izbrannoe* (Moscow, 1958), and probably a few more.

[91] With the exception of several lines of his *zaum'* prose, quoted by Kručenyx in the miscellany *Zaumniki* (Moscow, 1922). This prose is based on the syntax of newspaper ads.

[92] The book was illustrated by I. Kljun. In addition, essays by Kljun and Malevič conclude the book.

[93] See, for instance, the review by A. Tinjakov in *Reč'*, Oct. 5, 1915.

[94] Kručenyx, *15 let russkogo futurizma* . . . , p. 60.

[95] *Ibid.*

[96] See G. Èristov, "Tiflisskij Cex Poètov," *Sovremennik* (Toronto), no. 5 (April, 1962), pp. 30–33. Also see S. Gorodeckij, "Iskusstvo i literatura v Zakavkaz'e v 1917–1920 g.g.," *Kniga i Revoljucija*, no. 2 (1920), pp. 12–13.

[97] Degen published at least four books during this short time (*Ètix glaz* [1919], *Smert' i buržuj* [1919], *Ottepel'* [1920], *Volšebnyj ulov* [1922]), most of them in Tiflis under the Feniks imprint. He also contributed to the miscellanies *Neva* (1919) and *Putešestvie Sergeja Gorodeckogo v Batum* (1919).

[98] As this autobibliography was printed at the end of his *Zaumnyj jazyk u Sejfullinoj* . . . , it does not go beyond 1924. The titles were not numbered, but were arranged chronologically. There are chronological and other errors (e.g., *Lakirovannoe Triko* is listed as a mimeograph edition). Some published books did not get into the bibliography, and some of those that are listed, one assumes, probably were never published. Knowing Kručenyx's publishing habits, one also assumes that much of the material from those rare Tiflis publications got into later ones, published in Moscow and now, for the most part, readily available.

[99] Terent'ev, *Kručenyx grandiozar'*, p. 7.

[100] See *Traktat o splošnom nepriličii*, p. 4.

[101] The newspaper was not available to me, but the manifesto was reprinted later in *Zaumniki* (Moscow, 1922).

[102] *Zaumniki*, p. 12.

[103] *Buka russkoj literatury*, p. 16.

[104] *Kručenyx grandiozar'*, p. 2.

[105] The word *maloxol'nyj* means something like "nuts" in modern Russian slang; in this title, however, *maloxolija* has additional sexual connotations and perhaps should be translated as "postcoital tristesse."

[106] Burljuk would certainly claim priority in this matter, but actually the first attempt to combine print of different sizes in one poem could be traced to V. Trediakovskij (1703–1769) (see *Russkaja èpigramma* [Leningrad: Sovetskij pisatel', 1958], p. 33).

[107] *Sdvigologija*, p. 7.

415

[108] A predecessor of Kručenyx's in discussing such *sdvig* was A. Šemšurin in his *Futurizm v stixax Brjusova* (Moscow, 1913). Brjusov pointed this out himself in *Pečat' i Revoljucija*, no. 1 (1923), p. 77.

[109] *Kručenyx grandiozar'*, p. 13.

[110] *Zaumniki*, p. 24.

[111] *Poètika*, III (Leningrad, 1927), 59n; *Pečat' i Revoljucija*, no. 6 (1924), pp. 220–222.

[112] A good example of such "Victorianism" can be found in the preface by V. Anikin to the recent new edition of the famous collection of Russian folk riddles by D. Sadovnikov (*Zagadki russkogo naroda* [Moscow University, 1959], p. 3): "Some texts are marked by that 'naughtiness' of thought which does not fear ambiguities. Because of this, many texts that would look extremely embarrassing in print had to be deleted from the collection."

[113] See *Pečat' i Revoljucija*, no. 1 (1923), pp. 76–77.

[114] Even if we agree that *zaum'* means one thing (which it does not), it may result in only one kind of poetic obscurity. Ellipsis, alogism, and the absence of a key are among the others. We really need a good typology of poetical obscurities.

[115] *Buka russkoj literatury*, p. 4.

[116] Terent'ev, *Kručenyx grandiozar'*, p. 13.

[117] It is curious that Vjačeslav Ivanov, in his "K probleme zvukoobraza u Puškina" *Moskovskij Puškinist*, II [Moscow, 1930], 96), assumes *zaumnaja reč'* in the primary stages of Puškin's creative process.

[118] Kručenyx slightly distorted the name of one of Gorodeckij's Slavic gods of fertility. In the latter's *Jar'*, the first name reads "Udras."

[119] Those were actually French movies about Cretinetti, Russianized by the man who released them, Xanžonkov (see V. Mixalkovič, "Glupyškin, kto on?" *Sovetskij Ekran*, no. 12 [1966], p. 17).

[120] A quotation from the definition of faith in the prerevolutionary official textbook on religion, deriving from St. Paul.

[121] *17 erundovyx orudij*, p. 7

[122] *Fonetika teatra*, pp. 7, 40; *Buka russkoj literatury*, p. 5.

[123] Kručenyx was not against joining this universal language march, especially after the Revolution (see *Fonetika teatra*, p. 12), but his vision of *zaum'* as fragments of existing words of a given language floating in a pool certainly contradicts such claims. As to the kind of *zaum'* created by Kamenskij, and also practiced by Kručenyx, which is an imitation of foreign tongues, it is nothing but foreign language from a Russian viewpoint. Compare Julian Tuwim's similar effort, "O mowie rosyjskiej," which sounds perfectly Polish to me.

[124] Varst was a pen name of Varvara Stepanova (1894–1958), an artist from the Jack of Diamonds group, who later participated in Lef and was Rodčenko's wife. Xabias' real name was Nina Komarova; she published a booklet of "non-objective" (*bespredmetnaja*) poetry in 1922 (*Stixetty*), which rather deserved to be called "nongrammatical" and was saturated with sex. Večorka is discussed later in chapter 7.

[125] Tufanov made his appearance with a book of verse and prose, *Ëolova arfa* (Petrograd, 1917), which was a belated revival of Russian decadence by an erudite crackpot and had more than a trace of ego-futurism. Later, he re-emerged with the treatise *K zaumi* (Petersburg, 1924) in which *zaum'* was declared to be the seventh art. Tufanov tried to base his theory of *zaum'* on the "immanent teleology of phonemes" and claimed to broaden what Guro, Kručenyx, and Xlebnikov had started (for example, orientation to languages other than Russian). The theories were demonstrated in poor, cerebral verse which utilized Cyrillic and Latin alphabets, meters of classical antiquity and of Russian *častuški*, and vowel length and musical stress. His last book was *Uškujniki* (Leningrad, 1927), in which he tried to add Bergson, Einstein, and Novgorod history to the formulations of *zaum'*, but showed some merit in the heavily stylized poems based on Old Russian material (*The Igor Tale*, etc.) and folklore.

[126] As quoted by E. M. Galkina-Fedoruk, "K voprosu ob omonimax v russkom jazyke," *Russkij Jazyk v Škole*, no. 3 (1954).

[127] V. Zareckij, "Obraz kak informacija," *Voprosy Literatury*, no. 2 (1963). More recently, a "sdvig" toward more mature discussion of *zaum'* can be observed in M. V. Panov, "O vosprijatii zvukov," in the collection of articles, *Razvitie fonetiki sovremennogo russkogo jazyka* (Moscow, 1966), pp. 155–162.

[128] *Zaumniki*, p. 12.

[129] *Ožirenie roz*, p. 7.

[130] *Kručenyx grandiozar'*, p. 1.

[131] *Ibid.*, pp. 1, 14.

[132] *Zaumniki*, p. 14.

[133] The play was performed privately, even before it was published (the publication in Petrograd having been barred by the censor, Rimskij-Korsakov, a son of the composer). The performance took place on December 16 (3), 1916, in the studio of B. N. Ėssen, an artist, and the author played Janko and Xozjain. Music for the performance was written by the famous poet, Mixail Kuzmin.

[134] It was performed later by a puppet theater in Paris as part of a performance devoted to the *émigré* poet, B. Božnev, in April, 1923. Zdanevič read the text. He also choreographed the second *baba*'s dance from his own *Ostraf pasxi*, also performed at the evening.

[135] *Rekord nežnosti*, pp. 10–12.

[136] Zdanevič says in his letter to me of June 10, 1966, that he learned about Dada only in the summer of 1920 in Batumi from a letter sent by a friend, an artist from Paris.

[137] *Rekord nežnosti*, p. 18.

[138] *Milliork*, p. 15.

[139] See Michel Seuphor, "Russia and the Avant-Garde," in *Selective Eye* (New York, 1956–57).

[140] As a result of the intrigue led by Louis Aragon and Elsa Triolet, Matisse

demanded that his sketches be returned. The name of the ballet was *Vodostrel* (*La chasse sousmarine*).

[141] This book was an attempt to prove the derivative nature of French "lettrism," which appeared at that time. Zdanevič's latest publication known to me is *L'art de voir de Guillaume Tempel* (1964), on the life of a German astronomer, based on his own extensive research. As to the seven unfamiliar titles enumerated by Zdanevič in *Ledentu as a Beacon*, they either remained unpublished or, perhaps, were never written.

[142] He is only briefly mentioned in major works on Dada (even less attention is paid to the other Russian Dadaist, Sergei Šaršun). Among well-known Dadaists, only Hugo Ball approaches *zaum'* in some of his poetry.

[143] *17 erundovyx orudij,* p. 12.

[144] *Lakirovannoe triko,* p. 4; *Milliork,* p. 5.

[145] Actually there were only twelve.

[146] Later, having dropped Večorka from her name, she wrote biographical novels (*A. A. Bestužev-Marlinskij* [Moscow, 1932; 2d ed., 1933]; *Povest' o Lermontove* [Moscow, 1957; 2d ed., 1959]) and edited Lermontov's poems.

[147] "Pročitav razorvi," *Slovo kak takovoe,* p. 12.

[148] *PSS,* XII, 280.

[149] Among the book's motley content, there is a letter to Kručenyx from a beginning futurist poet in defense of phonetic associations. The name of the poet has since become prominent in Soviet prose: Valentin Kataev.

[150] For example, *Kuma-zatejnica. Devič'ja xitrost'* (Moscow and Leningrad, 1927) and *Xuligany v derevne* (Moscow and Leningrad, 1927); plus a few others either written in collaboration (*T'ma*) or printed in collections for village theaters ("Roditel'skoe prokljatie," etc.).

[151] Ironically, the library at the University of California, Berkeley, lists the book as a work by Puškin, obviously misled by the modest "compiled by Kručenyx" on the title page.

[152] Among them, *Gibel' Esenina, Esenin i Moskva kabackaja, Čornaja tajna Esenina, Esenin xuligan,** *Vse o Esenine.**

[153] I observed this quality in my article "Legenda o Esenine" (*Grani,* no. 25 [1955], p. 158) with the air of discovery and was later put to shame by Kručenyx when I looked through his Esenin books. Kručenyx also correctly dismisses the Soviet poetry of Esenin as the weakest in his works—precisely the part of his output which has been so much praised by Soviet critics since his rediscovery and rehabilitation.

[154] *Knigi Aseeva* . . . has no. 236 on its cover. There is no reason to believe that this was Kručenyx's last publication, but despite all my efforts, *Ironiada* and *Rubiniada* (unnumbered and no. 178, respectively) are all I have from those published before it and after *15 let.* . . . Thus this is another large blank in Kručenyx's bibliography, in addition to the one created by the absence of his mimeographed materials of the Caucasus period. I have personally been able to obtain in book form, as a Xerox (or other kind of) copy, or on microfilm, sixty-seven of his "productions" (the figure increases if one also counts publi-

cations in almanacs, magazines, etc.), and I had an opportunity to read another seven, leaving two hundred that I have yet to see.

[155] Volume III of *Kratkaja Literaturnaja Ènciklopedija*, in a brief, but objective and well-informed item, suggests that a "discovery" of Kručenyx may not be far away. He is also beginning to appear in memoirs (see L. Libedinskaja, *Zelenaja lampa* [Moscow, 1966]).

[156] N. P. Rogožin, *Literaturno-xudožestvennye al 'manaxi i sborniki: 1918–1927 gody* (Moscow, 1960).

[157] *Istorija russkoj literatury konca XIX-načala XX veka: Bibliografičeskij ukazatel'* (Moscow and Leningrad, 1963).

[158] *Krasnaja Nov'*, no. 2 (1922), p. 354.

[159] A. Dymšic, "Vladimir Majakovskij," *Zvezda*, no. 5–6 (1940), p. 158; N. Stepanov, preface to the 1960 edition of Xlebnikov, p. 66.

[160] *Polutoraglazyj strelec*, p. 263; *Put' èntuziasta*, p. 197.

[161] "Na čorta nam stixi," *Oktiabr'*, no. 1 (1927), p. 146.

[162] *Milliork*, p. 1.

[163] *Smert' Majakovskogo* (Berlin, 1931), p. 18.

[164] SP, II, 9; V, 270.

[165] N. M. Jazykov, *Liričeskie stixotvorenija* (Moscow: Universal'naja Biblioteka, 1916).

[166] *Reč'*, Oct. 5, 1915.

[167] Perhaps a subsection is needed here on Russian formalism, the movement in Russian literary criticism and scholarship which was so intimately tied up with futurism in some of its ideas and through some of its representatives (Šklovskij, Jakobson), but a much more detailed discussion of its initial phases than I could possibly undertake has already been given in the excellent study by Victor Erlich, *Russian Formalism: History-Doctrine* (The Hague: Mouton, 1955).

8. Conclusion

[1] *Čet i nečet* (Moscow, 1925), p. 5.

[2] PSS, XIII, 57.

[3] V. Polonskij, "Literatura i žizn'," *Novaja Žizn'*, no. 1 (1914), p. 176; quoted in V. Kamenskij, *Junost' Majakovskogo* (Tiflis, 1931), p. 7.

[4] Tasteven, *Futurizm* (Moscow, 1914), p. 78; Čukovskij, "Ėgo-futuristy . . . ," *Šipovnik*, XXII, 130; Zakrževskij, *Rycari bezumija*, p. 37.

[5] Jakobson, *Novejšaja russkaja poèzija*, p. 9; Tynjanov, *Arxaisty i novatory*, p. 553; Žirmunskij, review in *Načala*, no. 1 (1921), p. 215.

[6] Šapirštejn-Lers, *Obščestvennyj smysl . . . futurizma*, p. 78; N. Gorlov, *Futurizm i revoljucija* (Moscow, 1924), p. 3; A. Serafimovič, *Sbornik neopublikovannyx proizvedenij i materialov* (Moscow, 1950), p. 454; S. Malaxov, "Čto takoe futurizm?" *Oktjabr'*, no. 2 (1927).

[7] A letter to me from Aleksander Wat dated May 21, 1964.

[8] "Mysli o russkom futurizme," *Novyj Žurnal*, no. 38 (1954), p. 174.

BIBLOGRAPHY

This bibliography, although reasonably exhaustive for the prerevolutionary period of Russian literature, is selective (in various ways) for the postrevolutionary futurist movement. Despite my efforts to avoid duplications in different sections, some of them were inevitable. An important essay included in one of the already listed futurist joint publications is not listed separately.

The bibliography is simplified in that it does not reproduce the title page of a work in its entirety, as is customary, but rather gives, when possible, four essentials: author's name, main title (with subtitle usually omitted), and place and year of publication. The year of actual appearance and the place where the book was actually printed, whenever discoverable, have been substituted for those appearing on the cover or title page. The abbreviations M for Moscow, L for Leningrad, N.Y. for New York, and P for either St. Petersburg or Petrograd are used. Works by futurists are listed in chronological order; writings discussing futurism and futurists are arranged alphabetically. Book reviews are included only if they can be considered full-length articles.

FUTURIST PUBLICATIONS

HYLAEA

MISCELLANIES PUBLISHED BY THE GROUP
OR WITH ITS PARTICIPATION

Studija impressionistov. P, 1910.
Sadok sudej. P, 1910.
Poščečina obščestvennomu vkusu. M, 1912.
Sadok sudej II. P, 1913.
Sojuz molodeži. No. 3. P, 1913.
Trebnik troix. M, 1913.
Doxlaja luna. M, 1913.
Troe. P, 1913.
Zatyčka. Xerson, 1913.

BIBLIOGRAPHY

Futuristy "Gileja" sbornik Moloko kobylic. Xerson, 1914.
Futuristy: Rykajuščij Parnas. P, 1914.
Futuristy: Pervyj žurnal russkix futuristov. No. 1–2. M, 1914.
Doxlaja luna. 2d ed. M, 1914.
Vesennee kontragentstvo muz. M, 1915.
Strelec. Vols. 1–2. P, 1915–1916.
Vzjal: Baraban futuristov. P, 1915.
Moskovskie mastera. M, 1916.
Četyre pticy. M, 1916.
Vremennik. Vols. 1–4. M, 1917–1918.

MISCELLANEOUS

Poščečina obščestvennomu vkusu. M, 1913. Leaflet.
Gramoty i deklaracii russkix futuristov. P, 1914.
Truba marsian. Xar'kov, 1916.

LITERATURE ABOUT HYLAEA

Brjusov, V. "Novye sborniki stixov," *Russkaja Mysl'*, no. 2 (1911).
Color and Rhyme. Nos. 31, 57.
Jarcev, P. "Teatral'nye očerki: Teatr Futuristov," *Reč'*, Dec. 7, 1913.
Kamenskij, V. *Put' èntuziasta.* M, 1931.
Livšic, B. *Gileja.* N.Y., 1931.
————. *Polutoraglazyj strelec.* L, 1933.
Spasskij, S. *Majakovskij i ego sputniki.* L, 1940.
Šklovskij, V. *Tret'ja fabrika.* M, 1926.
————. *O Majakovskom.* M, 1940.
————. *Žili-byli.* M, 1964.
Tomaševskij, K. " 'Vladimir Majakovskij,' " *Teatr*, no. 4 (1938).
Trenin, V., and N. Xardžiev. "Poètika rannego Majakovskogo," *Literatur-nyj Kritik*, no. 4 (1935).
Xardžiev, N. "Turne kubo-futuristov 1913–1914 gg." In *Majakovskij: Materialy i issledovanija* (M, 1940).

Velimir Xlebnikov (Viktor Vladimirovič Xlebnikov)
1885–1922

Učitel' i učenik. Xerson, 1912.
Rjav! Perčatki 1908–1914 gg. P, 1913.
Izbornik stixov 1907–1914 gg. P, 1914.
Tvorenija (1906–1908). M, 1914.
Bitvy 1915–1917 gg: Novoe učenie o vojne. P, 1915.
Vremja mera mira. P, 1916.

Ošibka smerti. Xar'kov, 1916.
Zangezi. M, 1922.
Otryvok iz dosok sud'by. Vols. 1–3. M, 1922–1923.
Stixi. M, 1923.
Neizdannyj Xlebnikov. Vols. 1–30. M, 1928–1933.
Sobranie proizvedenij. Vols. 1–5. L, 1928–1933.
Zverinec. M, 1930.
Izbrannye stixotvorenija. M, 1936.
Neizdannye proizvedenija. M, 1940.
Stixotvorenija i poèmy. L, 1960.

Al'vek. "Naxlebniki Xlebnikova." *In* Xlebnikov, *Vsem: Nočnoj bal* (M, 1927).
Anfimov, V. Ja. "Xlebnikov v 1919 g.," *Trudy Tret'ej Krasnodarskoj Kliničeskoj Gorodskoj Bol'nicy,* no. 1 (1935).
Aseev, N. "Velemir," *Literaturnyj Kritik,* no. 1 (1936).
Gofman, V. "Jazykovoe novatorstvo Xlebnikova," *Zvezda,* no. 6 (1935).
Jakobson, R. *Novejšaja russkaja poèzija.* Prague, 1921.
Jakovlev, B. "Poèt dlja èstetov," *Novyj Mir,* no. 5 (1948).
Kručenyx, A. "Azef-Iuda-Xlebnikov." In his *Milliork* (Tiflis, 1919).
Majakovskij, V. "V. V. Xlebnikov," *Krasnaja Nov',* no. 4 (1922).
Markov, V. "O Xlebnikove," *Grani,* no. 22 (1954).
———. *The Longer Poems of Velimir Khlebnikov.* Berkeley and Los Angeles, 1962.
Mirskij, D. "Velemir Xlebnikov," *Literaturnaja Gazeta,* Nov. 15, 1935.
Petrovskij, D. *Povest' o Xlebnikove.* M, 1926.
Tynjanov, Ju. "O Xlebnikove." In his *Problema stixotvornogo jazyka* (M, 1965).
Večorka, T. "Vospominanija o Xlebnikove." In *Zapisnaja knižka Xlebnikova* (M, 1925).
Vel. "V. Xlebnikov- osnovatel' budetljan," *Kniga i Revoljucija,* no. 9–10 (1922).
Vinokur, G. "Xlebnikov," *Russkij Sovremennik,* no. 4 (1924).
Zelinskij, K. "Derviš russkoj poèzii," *Znamja,* no. 12 (1957).
See also prefaces to some of the editions of Xlebnikov's works listed above.

Vladimir Vladimirovič Majakovskij
1893–1930

Ja. M, 1913.
Vladimir Majakovskij. M, 1914.
Oblako v štanax. P, 1915.

BIBLIOGRAPHY

Flejta pozvonočnik. P, 1916.
Prostoe kak myčanie. P, 1916.
Vse sočinennoe Vladimirom Majakovskim. P, 1919.
"Davno prošedšee," *Literaturnoe Nasledstvo,* vol. 2 (1932).
Polnoe sobranie sočinenij. M, 1934–1938. 13 vols.
Polnoe sobranie sočinenij. M, 1939–1949. 12 vols.
Polnoe sobranie sočinenij. M, 1955–1961. 13 vols.

Arvatov, V. "Sintaksis Majakovskogo," *Pečat' i Revoljucija,* no. 1 (1923).
Aseev, N. *Majakovskij načinaetsja.* M, 1940.
——. *Začem i komu nužna poèzija.* M, 1961.
Blake, Patricia. "The Two Deaths of Vladimir Mayakovsky." *In* Mayakovsky, *The Bedbug and Selected Poetry* (N.Y., 1960).
Brik, L. "Majakovskij i čužie stixi," *Znamja,* no. 3 (1940).
Burljuk, D. "Tri glavy iz knigi 'Majakovskij i ego sovremenniki.'" In *Krasnaja Strela* (N.Y., 1932).
Color and Rhyme. Nos. 31, 41, 49.
Čeremin, G. *Rannij Majakovskij.* M-L, 1962.
Erlich, Victor. "The Dead Hand of the Future." In his *The Double Image* (Baltimore, 1964).
Gofman, V. "O jazyke Majakovskogo," *Zvezda,* no. 5 (1936).
Gric, T. "Rifma Majakovskogo," *Literaturnyj Kritik,* no. 3 (1939).
Humesky, Asya. *Majakovskij and His Neologisms.* N.Y., 1964.
Iskusstvo, no. 3 (1940).
Ivanov-Razumnik, R. *Vladimir Majakovskij.* Berlin, 1922.
Jakobson, R. "Novye stroki Majakovskogo." In *Russkij Literaturnyj Arxiv* (N.Y., 1956).
——. *O cešskom stixe.* . . . Prague, 1923.
Kamenskij, V. *Junost' Majakovskogo.* Tiflis, 1931.
——. *Žizn' s Majakovskim.* M, 1940.
Katanjan, V. *Majakovskij: Literaturnaja xronika.* M. Several editions.
Kolmogorov, A. "K izučeniju ritmiki Majakovskogo," *Voprosy Jazykoznanija,* no. 4 (1963).
Kondratov, A: "Èvoljucia ritmiki V. V. Majakovskogo, *Voprosy Jazykoznanija,* no. 5 (1962).
Kondratov, A., and A. Kolmogorov. "Ritmika poèm Majakovskogo," *Voprosy Jazykoznanija,* no. 3 (1962).
Kručenyx, A. *Stixi Majakovskogo.* P, 1913.
——. *Živoj Majakovskij.* Vols. 1–3. M, 1930.
Literaturnoe Nasledstvo, vol. 65 (1958).
Majakovskaja, L. *Perežitoe.* Tbilisi, 1957.

Majakovskij: Materialy i issledovanija. M, 1940.

Majakovskij, 1930–1940: Stat'i i materialy. L, 1940.

Majakovskomu: Sbornik vospominanij i statej. L, 1940.

Metčenko, A. "Protiv sub'ektivistskix izmyšlenij o tvorčestve Majakovskogo," *Kommunist,* no. 18 (1957).

Naumov, E. V. V. *Majakovskij: Seminarij.* L. Several editions.

Pravda, Dec. 5, 1935.

Pravduxin, V. "Pis'ma o sovremennoj literature," *Sibirskie Ogni,* no. 2 (1922).

Ripellino, Angelo Maria. *Majakovskij e il teatro russo d'avanguardia.* Torino, 1959.

Rostockij, B. *Majakovskij i teatr.* M, 1952.

Smert' Vladimira Majakovskogo. Berlin, 1931.

Stahlberger, Lawrence. *The Symbolic System of Majakovskij.* The Hague, 1964.

Šengeli, G. *Majakovskij vo ves' rost.* M, 1927.

Šklovskij, V. *O Majakovskom.* M, 1940.

Ščerbina, V. "Otvet fal' sifikatoram," *Kommunist,* no. 11 (1958).

———. "Za pravdivoe osveščenie tvorčestva Majakovskogo," *Pravda,* March 25, 1951.

Trenin, V. *V 'masterskoj stixa' Majakovskogo.* M, 1937.

Trockij, L. *Literatura i revoljucija.* M. Several editions.

Vinokur, V. *Majakovskij novator jazyka.* M, 1943.

Vladimir Majakovskij: Sbornik I. M-L, 1940.

V. Majakovskij v vospominanijax sovremennikov. M, 1963.

Xodasevič, V. "O Majakovskom." In his *Literaturnye stat'i i vospominanija* (N.Y., 1954).

David Davidovič Burljuk
1882–1967

"Die 'Wilden' Russlands." In *Der blaue Reiter* (Munich, 1912).

Galdjaščie 'benua' i novoe russkoe nacional'noe iskusstvo. P, 1913.

Lysejuščij xvost. Kurgan, 1918.

"Ot laboratorii k ulice (Èvoljucija futurizma)," *Tvorcestvo* (Vladivostok), no. 2 (1920).

"Literatura i xudožestvo v Sibiri i na Dal'nem Vostoke (1919–1922 gg.)," *Novaja Russkaja Kniga,* no. 2 (1922).

"Pravila igry," *Kitovras* (N.Y.), no. 2 (1924).

"Otkrovenija v prostote, kraske i linii," *Kitovras,* no. 3 (1924).

Burljuk požimaet ruku Vul'vort Bil'dingu/K 25-letiju xudožestvenno-literaturnoj dejatel'nosti. N.Y., 1924.

BIBLIOGRAPHY

Marusja-san. N.Y., 1925.
Vosxoždenie na Fudzi-san. N.Y., 1926.
Morskaja povest'. N.Y., 1927.
Po Tixomu okeanu. N.Y., 1927.
Ošima. N.Y., 1927.
Desjatyj Oktjabr'. N.Y., 1928.
Tolstoj. Gor'kij. N.Y., 1929.
Entelexizm. N.Y., 1930.
1/2 veka. N.Y., 1932.
Color and Rhyme (N.Y.), nos. 1–60 (1930–1966).

David Burliuk: 55 Years of Painting. N.Y., 1962.
Dreier, Katherine. *Burliuk.* N.Y., 1944.
Evreinov, N. *Original o portretistax.* M, 1922.
Galič, Jurij. "Burljuk i drugie," *Dni* (Paris), Oct. 25, 1925.
Gold, Michael. *David Burliuk: Artist-Scholar, Father of Russian Futurism.*
    N.Y., 1944.
Gollerbax, È. *Iskusstvo Davida Burljuka.* N.Y., 1930.
———. *Poèzija Davida Burljuka.* N.Y., 1931.
Gray, Camilla. *The Great Experiment: Russian Art, 1863–1922.* London,
    1962.
Postupal'skij, I. *Literaturnyj trud D. Burljuka.* N.Y., 1931.
Salpeter, Harry. "Burliuk: Wild Man of Art," *Esquire* (July, 1939).
Svirel' sobveja. N.Y., 1924.
"Umer David Burljuk," *Novoe Russkoe Slovo* (N.Y.), Jan. 17, 1967.
Zavališin, V., "David Burljuk kak xudožnik i poèt," *Novoe Russkoe
    Slovo,* Jan. 28, 1967.

Nikolaj Davidovič Burljuk
1890–1920

Poetry, prose, and essays in *Sadok sudej; Poščečina obščestvennomu vkusu;
Sadok sudej II; Sojuz molodezi,* no. 3; *Trebnik troix; Zatyčka; Doxlaja
luna; Rykajuščij Parnas; Moloko kobylic; Moskovskie mastera;* and
Vesennee kontragentstvo muz.

Vasilij Vasil'evič Kamenskij
1864–1961

Zemljanka. P, 1910.
Tango s korovami: Železobetonnye poèmy. M, 1914.
Nagoj sredi odetyx (with A. Kravcov). M, 1914.

Sten'ka Razin (novel). M, 1915. Two other editions in 1919 and 1928 under the title *Stepan Razin*.
"O gonenii na molodost'," *Žurnal Žurnalov*, no. 2 (1916).
Devuški bosikom. Tiflis, 1916.
Kniga o Evreinove. P, 1916.
Ego-Moja Biografija velikogo futurista. M, 1918.
Zvučal' vesnejanki. M, 1918.
Serdce narodnoe—Sten'ka Razin (poem). M, 1918.
Sten'ka Razin (play). M-P, 1919.
Cuvamma. Tiflis, 1920.
Biblioteka poètov, p/r V. Kamenskogo (M), nos. 1 (1922), 2 (1923).
I èto est'. Tiflis, 1927.
Put' èntuziasta. M, 1931.
Izbrannye stixi. M, 1934.
Poèmy. L, 1934.
Tri poèmy. L, 1935.
Izbrannoe. M, 1958.
Poèmy. M, 1961.
Leto na Kamenke. Perm', 1961.
Stixotvorenija i poèmy. M-L, 1966.

Efremov, A. "V. Kamenskij," *Oktjabr'*, no. 11 (1933).
Evreinov, N. *Teatralizacija žizni.* M, 1922.
Gusman, B. "Vasilij Kamenskij," *Očarovannyj strannik* (P), no. 8 (1915).
Lunačarskij, A. "V. V. Kamenskij," *Izvestija*, March 26, 1933.
Rozanov, I. "Kamenskij i Kirsanov." In *Russkie liriki* (M, 1929).
See also prefaces to some of the editions listed above.

Elena Genrixovna Guro
1877–1913

Šarmanka. P, 1909.
Osennij son. P, 1912.
Nebesnye verbljužata. P, 1914.
See also Hylaean miscellanies; *Sbornik molodyx pisatelej* (P, 1905); *Puti Tvorčestva* (Xar'kov), no. 5 (1919), and *Liren'* (Xar'kov, 1920).

Kova, K. "Sled obreten," *Pesni Žatvy* (M), no. 1 (1915).
Matjušina, O. "Negasimye zvezdy," *Zvezda*, no. 9 (1959).
Xardžiev, N., and T. Gric. "Elena Guro (K 25-letiju so dnja smerti)," *Knižnye Novosti*, no. 7 (1938).
Xovin, V. "Elena Guro," *Očarovannyj strannik* (P), no. 5 (1914).

BIBLIOGRAPHY

———. "'Vetrogony, sumasbrody, letateli,'" *Očarovannyj strannik* (P), no. 10 (1916).

Benedikt Konstantinovič Livšic
1886–1939

Flejta Marsija. Kiev, 1911.
Volč'e solnce. M, 1914.
"V citadeli revoljucionnogo slova," *Puti Tvorčestva* (Xar'kov), no. 5 (1919).
Iz topi blat. Kiev, 1922.
Patmos. M, 1926.
Krotonskij polden'. M, 1928.
Gileja. N.Y., 1931.
Polutoraglazyj strelec. L, 1933.
Ot romantikov do sjurrealistov. L, 1934.
Francuzskie liriki XIX i XX vekov. L, 1937.

Aleksej (Aleksandr) Eliseevič Kručenyx
1886———

(Because of an enormous number of publications, the postrevolutionary list is substantially cut.)
Igra v adu (with Xlebnikov). M, 1912, 1913.
Starinnaja ljubov'. M, 1912.
Mirskonca (with Xlebnikov). M, 1912.
Poluživoj. M, 1913.
Pustynniki. M, 1913.
Pomada. M, 1913.
Slovo kak takovoe (with Xlebnikov). M, 1913.
Bux lesinnyj (with Xlebnikov). P, 1913.
Deklaracija slova kak takovogo. P, 1913.
Vozropščem. P, 1913.
Vzorval'. P, 1913, 1914.
Porosjata (with Zina V.). P, 1913, 1914.
Stixi Majakovskogo. P, 1913.
Čort i rečetvorcy. P, 1913, 1914.
Pobeda nad solncem. P, 1913. Prologue by Xlebnikov.
Starinnaja ljubov'. Bux lesinnyj (with Xlebnikov). P, 1914.
Utinoe gnezdyško durnyx slov. P, 1914. Two editions.
Tè-li-lè (with Xlebnikov). P, 1914.
Sobstvennye rasskazy i risunki detej. P, 1914.
Tajnye poroki akademikov (with K. Malevič and I. Kljun). M, 1915.

428

Republished in revised form as *Apokalipsis v russkoj literature* (M, 1923), and as *Protiv popov i otšel'nikov* (M, 1925).
Zaumnaja gniga (with Aljagrov). M, 1915.
Vselenskaja vojna. P, 1916.
Učites' xudogi. Tiflis, 1917.
Lakirovannoe triko. Tiflis, 1919.
Maloxolija v kapote. Tiflis, 1919.
Milliork. Tiflis, 1919.
Preface to A. Čačikov, *Krepkij grom*. M, 1919.
Zamaul'. Baku, 1921. Four issues.
Mjatež. Baku, 1921. Nine issues.
Deklaracija zaumnogo jazyka. Baku, 1921.
Zaum'. M, 1921.
Zaumniki (with Xlebnikov and Petnikov). M, 1922.
Golodnjak. M, 1922.
Zudesnik. M, 1922.
Faktura slova. M, 1923.
Sdvigologija russkogo stixa. M, 1923.
Fonetika teatra. M, 1923, 1925.
500 novyx ostrot i kalamburov Puškina. M, 1924.
Zaumnyj jazyk u Sejfullinoj. . . . M, 1925.
Jazyk Lenina. M, 1925.
Kalendar'. M, 1926. Preface by B. Pasternak.
Gibel' Esenina. M, 1926.
Čornaja tajna Esenina. M, 1926.
Četyre fonetičeskix romana. M, 1927.
15 let russkogo futurizma. M, 1928.
Govorjaščee kino. M, 1928.
Rubiniada. M, 1930.
Turnir poètov. Vols. 1–3. M, 1930–1934.

Buka russkoj literatury. M, 1923. 2d ed. under the title *Živ Kručenyx* (M, 1925).
Stixi vokrug Kručenyx. Baku, 1921.
Terent'ev, I. *Kručenyx—grandiozar'*. Tiflis, 1919.

EGO-FUTURISM

Igor'-Severjanin (Igor' Vasil'evič Lotarev)
1887–1941

(Of the thirty-odd early "brochure" publications, only samples are given.)
Gibel' "Rjurika." P, 1904.

BIBLIOGRAPHY

Iz 'Pesen serdca.' P, 1905.
Mimoza. P, 1906.
A sad vesnoj blagouxaet. P, 1909.
Intuitivnye kraski. P, 1909.
Kol'e princessy. P, 1910.
Električeskie stixi. P, 1911.
Ruč'i v lilijax. P, 1911.
Prolog ègo-futurizm. P, 1911.
Kačalka grezèrki. P, 1912.
Èpilog ègo-futurizm. P, 1912.
Gromokipjaščij kubok. M, 1913. Followed by eleven more editions.
Zlatolira. M, 1914. Followed by six more editions.
Pamajatka o nemeckix zverstvax. M, 1914.
Ananasy v šampanskom. M, 1915. Followed by four more editions.
Victoria regia. M, 1915. Followed by three more editions.
Poèzoantrakt. M, 1915. Followed by two more editions.
Vintik (with Vinogradov, Massainov, and Tolmačev). P, 1915.
Tost bezotvetnyj. M, 1916. Followed by one more edition.
Mimozy l'na (with Massainov). P, 1916.
Ostrova očarovanij (with Massainov). P, 1917.
Za strunnoj izgorod'ju liry. M, 1918.
Poèzo-koncert. M, 1918.
Crème de violettes. Tartu, 1919.
Pühajõgi. Tartu, 1919.
Vervèna. Tartu, 1920.
Menestrel'. Berlin, 1921.
Mirrèlija. Berlin, 1922.
Feja Eiole. Berlin, 1922.
Padučaja stremnina. Berlin, 1922.
Via sacra (with Adams, Beljaev, and Pravdin). Tartu, 1922.
Solovej. Berlin, 1923.
Tragedija titana. Berlin, 1923.
Kolokola sobora čuvstv. Tartu, 1925.
Rosa oranževogo časa. Tartu, 1925.
Klassičeskie rozy. Belgrade, 1931.
Adriatika. Narva, 1932.
Medal'ony. Belgrade, 1934.

Translations by Severjanin

H. Visnapuu. *Amores.* M, 1922.
Poèty Estonii. Tartu, 1928.

M. Under. *Predcveten'e.* Tallin, 1937.
H. Visnapuu. *Polevaja fialka.* Narva, 1939.
A. Rannit. *V okonnom pereplete.* Tallin, 1938.
———. *Via dolorosa.* Stockholm, 1940.

Adams, V. "Igor' Severjanin v Èstonii." In *Russko-evropejskie literaturnye svjazi* (M-L, 1966). An extended version in Estonian appears in *Keel ja kirjandus,* no. 8 (1966).
Kritika o tvorčestve Igorja Severjanina. M, 1916.
Krjučkov, D. "Demimondènka i lesofeja," *Očarovannyj strannik,* no. 1 (1913).
Oršanin, A. "Poèzija šampsanskogo poloneza," *Russkaja Mysl',* no. 5 (1915).
Petrov, G. "Meridiany družby," *Moskva,* no. 1 (1967).
Red'ko, A. "Fazy Igorja Severjanina," *Russkie Zapiski,* no. 3 (1915).
Smirenskij, B. "Poslednie stixi Igorja Severjanina," *Ogonek,* no. 29 (1962).
Šumakov, Ju. "Revnitel' prirody," *Prostory,* no. 23 (1966).
Tal'nikov, D. "Nedorazumenie v stixax," *Sovremennyj Mir,* no. 6 (1914).
Xodasevič, V. "I. Severjanin." In *Al'ciona,* Vol. I (M, 1914).

EGO-FUTURIST GROUPS IN ST. PETERSBURG

Peterburgskij Glašataj (newspaper). Nos. 1–4. P, 1912.
Oranževaja urna. P, 1912.
Stekljannye cepi. P, 1912.
Orly nad propast'ju. P, 1912.
Dary Adonisu. P, 1913.
Zasaxare kry. P, 1913.
Bej! no vyslušaj. P, 1913.
Vsegdaj. P, 1913.
Nebokopy. P, 1913.
Razvoročennye čerepa, P, 1913.
Očarovannyj strannik (P), nos. 1–10 (1913–1916).

Graal'-Arel'skij (Stepan Stepanovič Petrov)
1889——

Goluboj ažur. P, 1911.
Letejskij breg. P, 1913.
Povesti o Marse. L, 1925.

Georgij Vladimirovič Ivanov
1894–1958

Otplytie na o. Citeru. P, 1912.
Gornica. P, 1914.
Pamajatnik slavy. P, 1915.
Veresk. M, 1916. 2d ed. Berlin, 1922.
Peterburgskie zimy. Paris, 1928. 2d ed. N.Y., 1952.
Rozy. Paris, 1930.
Otplytie na ostrov Citeru. Berlin, 1937.
1943–1958 Stixi. N.Y., 1958.

Konstantin Konstantinovič Olimpov (Fofanov)
1890–1940

Aèroplannye poèzy. P, 1912.
Žonglery-nervy. P, 1913.
Akademija ègo-poèzii Vselenskogo futurizma. Riga, 1914.
Fenomenal'naja genial'naja poèma Teoman. . . . P, 1915.
Tret'e Roždestvo velikogo mirovogo poèta. . . . P, 1922.

Ivan Vasil'evič Ignat'ev (Kazanskij)
1882–1914

Okolo teatra. P, 1912.
Ègo-futurizm. P, 1913.
Èšafot ègo-futury. P, 1914.

Pavel Dmitrievič Sirokov
1893–1963

Rozy v vine. P, 1912.
V i vne. P, 1913.
Kniga velikix (with Gnedov). P, 1914.

Vasilisk (Vasilij Ivanovič) Gnedov
1890——

Gostinec sentimentam. P, 1913.
Smert' iskusstvu. P, 1913.

Dmitrij Aleksandrovič Krjučkov
1887–?

Padun nemolčnyj. P, 1913.

Cvety ledjanye. P, 1914.

Viktor Romanovič Xovin

Segodnjašnemu dnju. P, 1918.

LITERATURE ABOUT EGO-FUTURISM

Brjusov, Valerij. "Segodnjašnij den' russkoj poèzii," *Russkaja Mysl'*, no. 7 (1912).

Čukovskij, K. "Ėgo-futuristy i kubo-futuristy," *Šipovnik*, no. 22 (1914).

Ivanov, Georgij. *Peterburgskie zimy.* Paris, 1928.

Markov, V. "K istorii russkogo égo-futurizma." In *Orbis scriptus: Festschrift für Dmitrij Tschižewskij* (Munich, 1966).

Šeršenevic, V. *Futurizm bez maski.* M, 1913.

Tasteven, G. *Futurizm.* M, 1914.

Zakrževskij, A. *Rycari bezumija.* Kiev, 1914.

THE MEZZANINE OF POETRY

Miscellanies

Vernissaž. M, 1913.

Pir vo vremja čumy. M, 1913.

Krematorij zdravomyslija. M, 1913.

Vadim Gabrièlevič Šeršenevic
1893–1942

Vesennie protalinki. M, 1911.

Carmina. M, 1913.

Romantičeskaja pudra. P, 1913.

Èkstravagantnye flakony. M, 1913.

Futurizm bez maski. M, 1913.

Poems in *Krugovaja čaša.* M, 1913.

Avtomobil'ja postup'. M, 1915.

Bystr'. M, 1916.

Zelenaja ulica. M, 1916.

Krematorij. M, 1918.

Lošad' kak lošad'. M, 1920.

2 × 2 = 5. M, 1920.

Večnyj žid. M, 1919.

Kooperativy vesel'ja. M, 1921.

Translations by Šeršenevic

Manifesty ital'janskogo futurizma. M, 1914.

Žjul' Laforg. *Feeričeskij sobor.* M, 1914. Translation with Brjusov and L'vova.

BIBLIOGRAPHY

Marinetti. *Bitva u Tripoli*. M, 1915.
———. *Futurist Mafarka*. M, 1916.
Vil'drak i Djuamel'. *Teorija svobodnogo stixa*. M, 1920.

Xrisanf (Lev Vasil'evič Zak)
1892——
"Utro vnutri: Stixi 1916–1962 gg." Unpublished MS.

Courthion, Pierre. *Léon Zack*. Paris, 1961.

Konstantin Aristarxovič Bol'šakov
1895–1940

Mozaika. M, 1911.
Le futur. M, 1913.
Serdce v perčatke. M, 1913.
Koroleva Mod. M, 1916.
Poèma sobytij. M, 1916.
Solnce na izlete. M, 1916.
Sgonoč'. M, 1927.
Put' prokažennyx. M, 1927.
Begstvo plennyx. Xar'kov, 1929.

Rjurik Ivnev (Mixail Aleksandrovič Kovalev)
1893——

Samosožženie. Vols. I–III. M-P, 1913–1916.
Plamja pyšet. M, 1913.
Zoloto smerti. M, 1916.
Samosožženie. P, 1917.
Nesčastnyj angel. P, 1917.
Solnce vo grobe. M, 1921.
4 vystrela. M, 1921.
Ljubov' bez ljubvi. M, 1925.
Moja strana. Tbilisi, 1943.
Izbrannye stixotvorenija. Tbilisi, 1945.
Stixi. Tbilisi, 1948.
Izbrannye stixi. M, 1965.

Ivanov, G. *Peterburgskie zimy*. Paris, 1928.
Pastuxov, V. "Strana vospominanij," *Opyty* (N.Y.), no. 5 (1955).
Zelinskij, K. Preface to *Izbrannye stixi* (1965).

Sergej Mixajlovič Tret'jakov
1892–1939

Železnaja pauza. Vladivostok, 1919.
Jasnyš. Čita, 1922.
Oktjabrevichi. L, 1924.
Stixi: Itogo. M, 1924.
Ryči, Kitaj. M, 1926.
"Avtobiografija moego stixa." *In* Kručenyx, *15 let russkogo futurizma* (M, 1928).

Aseev, A. "Bespokojnyj talant," *Literaturnaja Gazeta,* June 21, 1962.

CENTRIFUGE, LIREN', AND OTHERS

MISCELLANIES

Lirika. M, 1913.
Rukonog. M, 1914.
Vtoroj sbornik Centrifugi. M, 1916.
Peta. M, 1916.
Liren'. M, 1921.

LITERATURE ABOUT CENTRIFUGE

Malaxov, Sergej. "Russkij futurizm posle revoljucii," *Molodaja Gvardija,* no. 10 (1926).

Sergej Pavlovič Bobrov
1899——

Vertogradari nad lozami. M, 1913.
"O liričeskoj teme," *Trudy i dni,* no. 1–2 (1913).
"Zizn' i tvorčestvo Artjura Rimbo," *Russkaja Mysl',* no. 10 (1913).
"Čužoj golos." In *Razvoročennye čerepa* (P, 1913).
Liričeskaja tema. M, 1914.
"Bumažnyj gorodok," *Sovremennik,* Dec., 1914.
Novoe o stixosloženii A. S. Puškina. M, 1915.
"Russkaja poèzija v 1914 g," *Sovremennik,* no. 1 (1915).
"Severjanin i russkaja kritika." In *Kritika o tvorčestve I. Severjanina* (M, 1916).
Zapiski stixotvorca. M, 1916.
N. M. Jazykov o mirovoj literature. M, 1916.
Almaznye lesa. M, 1917.

BIBLIOGRAPHY

Lira lir. M, 1917.
"Opisanie stixotvorenija Puškina 'Vinograd,'" *Puškin i ego sovremenniki,* no. 29–30 (1918).
Vosstanie mizantropov. M, 1922.
Specifikacija iditola. Berlin, 1923.
Našedšij sokrovišče. M, 1931.
Pesn' o Rolande (translation). M-L, 1943.
Arximedovo leto. Vols. I–II. M, 1959–1962.
"K voprosu o podlinnom stixe puškinskix 'Pesen zapadnyx slavjan,'" *Russkaja Literatura,* no. 3 (1964).
"Tesnota stixovogo rjada," *Russkaja Literatura,* no. 3 (1965).
"Sintagmy, slovorazdely i litavridy," *Russkaja Literatura,* no. 4 (1965).
Mal'čik. M, 1966.
"Russkij toničeskij stix . . . ," *Russkaja Literatura,* no. 1 (1967).
See also Bobrov's poetry in *Razvoročennye čerepa; Moskovskij Parnas; Vesennij salon poètov;* and *Sopo;* and his reviews in *Krasnaja Nov'; Pečat i Revoljucija;* and *Russkaja Literatura.*

Boris Leonidovič Pasternak
1890–1960

Bliznec v tučax. M, 1914.
Poverx bar'erov. M, 1917.
Sestra moja žizn'. Berlin, 1922.
Sočinenija. Ann Arbor, 1961. 3 vols.
Stixotvorenija i poèmy. M-L, 1965.

Anstej, O. "Mysli o Pasternake," *Literaturnyj Sovremennik* (Munich), no. 2 (1951).
Aseev, N. "Pis'ma o poèzii," *Krasnaja Nov',* no. 3 (1922).
Cohen, J. M. "The Poetry of Boris Pasternak," *Horizon,* no. 51 (July, 1944).
Cvetaeva, M. "Svetovoj liven'," *Èpopeja,* no. 3 (1923). Also in *Proza* (N.Y., 1953).
Èl'sberg, Zh. "Mirovosprijatie B. Pasternaka," *Na Literaturnom Postu,* no. 7 (1930).
Jakobson, R. "Randbemerkungen zur Prosa des Dichters Pasternak," *Slavische Rundschau,* no. 6 (1935).
Krasil'nikov, B. "Boris Pasternak," *Pečat' i Revoljucija,* no. 5 (1927).
Kručenyx, A. *Knigi Pasternaka za 20 let.* M, 1933.
Ležnev, A. "Boris Pasternak," *Krasnaja Nov',* no. 8 (1926). Also in *Sovremenniki* (M, 1927).

Mandel'štam, O. "Boris Pasternak," *Rossija*, no. 6 (1923).
Oblomievskij, D. "Boris Pasternak," *Literaturnyj Sovremennik*, no. 4 (1934).
Ocup, N. "Boris Pasternak," *Zveno* (Paris), no. 5 (1928).
Plank, Dale L. *Pasternak's Lyric: A Study of Sound and Imagery*. The Hague, 1966.
Postupal'skij, I. "Boris Pasternak," *Novyj Mir*, no. 2 (1928).
Proyart, Jacqueline de. *Pasternak*. Paris, 1964.
Rozanov, I. *Russkie Liriki*. M, 1929.
Ruge, Gerd. *Pasternak*. Munich, 1959.
Sbornik statej posvjaščennyx tvorčestvu Borisa Leonidoviča Pasternaka. Munich, 1962.
Selivanovskij, A. "Boris Pasternak," *Krasnaja Nov'*, no. 1 (1933). Also in *Poèzija i poèty* (M, 1933).
Vejdle, V. "Stixi i proza Pasternaka," *Sovremennye Zapiski*, no. 36 (1928).
Wren, C. L. "Boris Pasternak." In *Oxford Slavonic Papers*, Vol. II (1951).
See *also* prefaces to the collections listed above.

Fedor Platov

Blaženny niščie duxom. M, 1915.
Nazad čtoby moja istina ne razdavila vas. M, 1915.
Tret'ja kniga ot Fedora Platova. M, 1916.

Nikolaj Nikolaevič Aseev
1898–1963

Nočnaja flejta. M, 1914.
Zor. Xar'kov, 1914.
Letorej (with Petnikov). Xar'kov, 1915.
Četvertaja kniga stixov: Oj konin dan okejn. M, 1916.
Oksana. M, 1916.
Bomba. Vladivostok, 1921.
Stal'noj solovej. M, 1922.
Izbran'. M-P, 1923.
Izmoroz'. M-L, 1927.
Sobranie stixotvorenij. Vols. I–IV. M-L, 1928–1930.
Rabota nad stixom. L, 1929.
Dnevnik poèta. L, 1929.
Proza poèta. M, 1930.
Majakovskij načinaetsja. M, 1940.
Razdum'ja. M, 1955.

BIBLIOGRAPHY

Lad. M, 1961.
Sobranie socinenij. Vols. I–V. M, 1963–1964.

Kručenyx, A. *Knigi N. Aseeva za 20 let.* M, 1934.
Levin, F. "N. Aseev," *Literaturnyj Kritik,* no. 3 (1939).
Margolina, A. "O stixotvornoj sud'be Nikolaja Aseeva," *Oktjabr',* no. 11 (1940).
Mustangova, E. "Nikolaj Aseev," *Literaturnyj Kritik,* no. 12 (1935).
Plisko, N. "Tvorčestvo Nikolaja Aseeva," *Novyj Mir,* no. 4 (1941).
Sarnov, B. "N. N. Aseev." In *Istorija russkoj sovetskoj literatury v trex tomax,* Vol. II (M, 1960).
See *also* prefaces to some of the collections listed above.

Ivan Aleksandrovič Aksenov
1884–1935

Neuvažitel'nye osnovanija. M, 1916.
Elisavetincy. M, 1916.
Pikasso i okrestnosti. M, 1917.
Korinfjane. M, 1918.
Serenada. M, 1920.
"K likvidacii futurizma," *Pečat' i Revoljucija,* no. 3 (1921).
"K besporjadku dnja." In *Moskovskij Parnas,* Vol. II (M, 1922).
Gamlet i drugie opyty. . . . M, 1931.
Elizavetincy. M, 1938.
See *also,* for Aksenov's poems, *Moskovskij Parnas; Sopo; Literaturnyj Osobnjak; Xudožestvennoe Slovo;* and *Novye stixi.*

Grigorij Nikolaevič Petnikov
1894——

Letorej (with Aseev). M, 1915.
Byt pobegov. M, 1918.
Porosli solnca. M, 1918. 2d ed., 1920.
Kniga Marii-Zažgi Snega. P, 1920.
Nočnye molnii. L, 1928.
Molodost' mira. Xar'kov, 1934.
Vibrani poezii. Xar'kov, 1934.
Izbrannye stixi. M, 1936.
Zavetnaja kniga. Simferopol', 1961.
See *also,* for poems, *Puti Tvorčestva* (Xar'kov).

Translation by Petnikov

Novalis. *Fragmenty*. M, 1914.

Terapiano, Ju. "Grigorij Petnikov," *Russkaja Mysl'* (Paris), June 10, 1961.
See *also* prefaces to some of the collections listed above.

Božidar (Bogdan Petrovič Gordeev)
1894–1914

Buben. M, 1914. 2d ed., 1916.
Raspevočnoe edinstvo. M, 1916.
See also *Puti Tvorčestva*, no. 5.

Tixon Vasil'evič Čurilin
1892–1944

Vesna posle smerti. M, 1915.
Vtoraja kniga stixov. M, 1918.
Stixi Tixona Čurilina. M, 1940.
See *also* his poems in *Moskovskie mastera; Al'manax muz;* and *Gjulistan*.

Julian Pavlovič Anisimov
1889–1940

Obitel'. M, 1913.
Zemljanoe. M, 1926.

41°

Sofii Georgievne Mel'nikovoj. Tiflis, 1919.
41° (newspaper). Tiflis, 1919. One issue.
Mir i ostal'noe. Baku, 1920.

Èristov, G. "Tiflisskij Cex Poètov," *Sovremennik* (Toronto), no. 5 (1962).
Kručenyx, A. *Zaumniki*. M, 1922.
Malaxov, S. "Zaumniki," *Na Literaturnom Postu*, no. 7–8 (1926).

Kručenyx

See list of publications under Hylaea. See *also*, for a more extensive list,
Zaumnyj jazyk u Sejfullinoj . . . (M, 1925).

BIBLIOGRAPHY

Il'ja Mixajlovič Zdanevič (Il'jazd)
1894——
Natalija Gončarova. Mixail Larionov. M, 1913.
Janko kruľ albanskaj. Tiflis, 1819.
Ostraf pasxi. Tiflis, 1919.
zgA JAkaby. Tiflis, 1920.
LidantJU fAram. Paris, 1923.
Vosxiščenie. Paris, 1930.
Afat. Paris, 1940.
Pis'mo. Paris, 1948.
Poésie de mots inconnus. Paris, 1949.
Le frère mendiant. Paris, n.d.
Prigovor bezmolvija. Paris, 1963.
L'art de voir de Guillaume Tempel. Paris, 1964.

Ribemont-Dessaignes, G. Préface added to *LidantJU fAram* (Paris, 1947).
Seuphor, Michel. "Russia and the Avant-Garde." In *The Selective Eye* (N.Y., 1956–57).
Terent'ev, I. *Rekord nežnosti.* Tiflis, 1919.

Igor' Gerasimovič Terent'ev
Xeruvimy svistjat. Tiflis, 1919.
Fakt. Tiflis, 1919.
17 erundovyx orudij. Tiflis, 1919.
Traktat o splošnom nepriličii. Tiflis, 1920(?).
"Maršrut šarizny." In Kručenyx, *Sdvigologija russkogo stixa* (M. 1923).
See also Kručenyx's books: *Ožirenie roz* (Tiflis, 1918); *Zudesnik, Fonetika teatra;* and *15 let russkogo futurizma.*

Tat'jana Vladimirovna Večorka (Tolstaja)
D. 1965
Magnolii. Tiflis, 1918.
Soblazn afiš. Baku, 1920.
Tret' duši. M, 1927.

Vasilij Abgarovič Katanjan
1902——
Ubijstvo na romantičeskoj počve. Tiflis, 1918.

FRIENDS, ALLIES, AND IMITATORS OF FUTURISTS

Nikolaj Ivanovič Kul'bin
1868–1917

"Svobodnoe iskusstvo kak osnova žizni." In *Studija impressionistov* (P, 1910).
"Kubizm," *Strelec*, no. 1 (1915).

Evreinov, N. *Original o portretistax*. M, 1922.
Kul'bin. P, 1912.
Livšic, B. *Polutoraglazyj strelec*. L, 1933.
Pjast, V. *Vstreči*. L, 1929.

Viktor Borisovič Šklovskij
1893——

Voskrešenie slova. P, 1914.
Svincovyj žrebij. P, 1914.
"Predposylki futurizma," *Golos Žizni*, no. 18 (1915).
"Zaumnyj jazyk v poèzii." In *Sborniki po teorii poèticeskogo jazyka* (P, 1916).
"O poèzii i zaumnom jazyke," *Poètika* (P, 1919).
Tret'ja fabrika. M, 1926.
Žili-byli. M, 1964.

Boris Anisimovič Kušner
1888–1937

Semafory. M, 1914.
Tavro vzdoxov. M, 1915.
Rodina i narody. M, 1915.
Demokratizacija iskusstvu. P, 1917.
Samyj stojkij s ulicy. P, 1917.
Miting dvorcov. P, 1918. Also in *Ržanoe slovo* (P, 1918).
103 dnja na Zapade. M-L, 1928.

Georgij Zolotuxin

Opaly. M, 1915.
Èxizm. M, 1917.
See also *Četyre pticy*.

Samuil Matveevič Vermel'
1892——

Tanki. M, 1915.
Alximija teatra. Berlin, 1923.
See also *Vesennee kontragentstvo muz* and *Moskovskie mastera*.

Aleksandr Ėmmanuilovič Belenson

Zabavnye stiški. P, 1914.
Iskusstvennaja žizn'. P, 1921.
Vrata tesnye. P, 1922.
Bezumija. M, 1924.
See also *Strelec*, Vols. I–III (P, 1915–1923).

Ada Vladimirova (Olimpiada Vladimirovna Kozyreva)
1892——

Dali večernie. P, 1913.
Nevypitoe serdce. P, 1918.
Kuvšin sinevy. M, 1922.
Stixotvorenija. M, 1927.
Liven'. M, 1929.

Vladimir Robertovič Gol'cšmidt

Poslanija Vladimira žizni s puti k istine. Petropavlovsk, 1919.

Pavel Nikolaevič Filonov
1883–1942

Propeven' o prorosli mirovoj. P, 1915.

Dmitrij Vasil'evič Petrovskij
1922–1955

Pustynnaja osen'. N.p., 1920.
Poedinok. M, 1926.
Povest' o Xlebnikove. M, 1926.
Gal'ka. M, 1927.
Izbrannoe. M, 1956.

ODESSA GROUP

Šelkovye fonari. 1914.
Serebrjanye truby. 1915.
Avto v oblakax. 1915.
Sed'moe pokryvalo. 1916.

Čudo v pustyne. 1917.
Fioletov Anatolij. *Zelenye agaty.* 1914.

MISCELLANEOUS

Alymov, Sergej. *Kiosk nežnosti.* Xarbin, 1920.
Bajan, Vadim (V. Sidorov). *Liričeskij potok.* P, 1914. See also Bajan's
Sevastopol' miscellanies *Obvaly serdca* (1920) and *Srublennyj poceluj c
gub vselennoj* (1922).
Čerkasov, Nikolaj. *V rjady.* P, 1914.
———. *Vyše!* P, 1916.
———. *Iskanija duxa.* P, 1916.
Gorskij, Vladimir. *Černye lenty.* M, 1913.
———. *Tango.* M, 1914.
Kokorin, Pavel. *Muzyka rifm.* P, 1913.
Korotov, Pavel. *Predzaly futury intuity.* Xar'kov, 1914.
Podgaevskij, Sergej. *Pisanka futurista Sergeja Podgaevskogo.* M, 1913.
Skljarov, Leonid. *Prizraki.* Rostov-on-Don, 1913.
———. *Otkrovenie južnogo futurista Leonida Skljarova.* Rostov-on-Don,
1914.
Šengeli, Georgij. *Rozy s kladbišča.* Kerč', 1914.
Višnjakov, Vladimir. *Golubye ugli.* M, 1914.

FUTURIST HOAXES

Burov, L. *Futurističeskie stixi.* Jampol', 1913.
Cèmpionat poètov. P, 1913.
iglY komFortA sverx-futuristA AntonA puP. P, 1914.
Ja: Futur-al'manax vselenskoj samosti. Saratov, 1914. Two editions.
Markov, Lev, and Aleksandr Durov. *Kabluk futurista.* M, 1914.
Neofuturizm: Vyzov obščestvennym vkusam. Kazan', 1913.
V sedur': Rukavica sovremen'ju. P, 1913.

Burljuk, Nikolaj. "O parodii i o podražanii." *In* D. Burljuk, *Galdjaščie
'benua'.* . . .
Efremov, E. "Saratovskie psixofuturisty," *Neva,* no. 7 (1963).

DISCUSSIONS, DESCRIPTIONS, POLEMICS, AND
JUDGMENTS CONCERNING FUTURISM
AND ITS POETS

CONTEMPORARY

Abramovič, N. [N. Kadmin]. *Ulica sovremennoj literatury.* P, 1916.

BIBLIOGRAPHY

———. "O futurizme v literature," *Novaja Žizn'*, no. 5 (1914). Later a chapter in his *Istorija russkoj poèzii*, Vol. II (M, 1915).

Baudoin de Courtenay, I. A. "K teorii 'slova kak takovogo' i 'bukvy kak takovoj,'" *Otkliki*, no. 8 (1914). Repr. in his *Izbrannye raboty po jazykoznaniju*, Vol. II (M, 1963).

———. "Slovo i 'slovo,'" *Otkliki*, no. 7 (1914). Repr. in *Izbrannye raboty po jazykoznaniju*, Vol. II (M, 1963).

Brjusov, Valerij. "God russkoj poèzii," *Russkaja Mysl'*, no. 5 (1914). Repr. in *Izbrannye sočinenija*, Vol. II (M, 1955).

———. "Novye tečenija v russkoj poèzii," *Russkaja Mysl'*, no. 3 (1913).

———. "Zdravogo smysla tartarary," *Russkaja Mysl'*, no. 3 (1914).

Cournos, John. "Smert' futurizma," *Apollon*, no. 8–9 (1917).

Čudovskij, Valerian. "Futurizm i prošloe," *Apollon*, no. 6 (1913).

Čukovskij, Kornej. "Ègo-futuristy i kubo-futuristy," *Šipovnik*, no. 22 (1914). Repr. in his *Lica i maski* (P, 1914); later extended and revised, and published separately as *Futuristy* (P, 1922).

Čulkov, Georgij. "Opravdanie simvolizma." In *Včera i segodnja* (M, 1916). Later included in his *Naši sputniki* (M, 1922).

Filosofov, Dmitrij. "Razloženie futurizma," *Golos Žizni*, no. 18 (1915).

Gor'kij, Maksim. "O futurizme," *Žurnal Žurnalov*, no. 1 (1915).

Gumilev, Nikolaj. *Pis'ma o russkoj poèzii*. P, 1923.

Kranixfel'd, V. "Literaturnye otkliki," *Sovremennyj Mir*, no. 4 (1913).

Lundberg, Evgenij. "O futurizme," *Russkaja Mysl'*, no. 3 (1914).

L'vov-Rogačevskij, V. "Simvolisty i nasledniki ix," *Sovremennik*, no. 6 (1913).

Morozova, K. *O futurizme*. Kovno, 1914.

Polonskij, Vjačeslav. "Literatura i žizn," *Novaja Žizn'*, no. 1 (1914).

Radin, E. P. *Futurizm i bezumie*. P, 1914.

Red'ko, A. "Sredi ustremlenij k neponjatnomu i nepostižnomu," *Russkoe Bogatstvo*, no. 3 (1914).

———. "U podnožija afrikanskogo idola," *Russkoe Bogatstvo*, no. 7 (1913).

Rozanov, N. P. *Ègo-futurizm* [sic]. Vladikavkaz, 1914.

Sadovskoj, Boris. "Futurizm i Rus'." In his *Ozim'* (P, 1915).

Šemšurin, A. *Futurizm v stixax V. Brjusova*. M, 1913.

Šeršenevič, V. See Ego-Futurism

Šklovskij, Viktor. "Predposylki futurizma," *Golos Žizni*, no. 18 (1915).

———. *Voskrešenie slova*. P, 1914.

———. "Zaumnyj jazyk v poèzii." In *Sborniki po teorii poèticeskogo jazyka*, Vol. I (P, 1916). Later published in *Poetika* (P, 1919).

Tasteven, Genrix. *Futurizm*. M, 1914.

Xodasevič, Vladislav. "Igor' Severjanin i futurizm," *Russkie Vedomosti*, April 29 (May 1), 1914.

———. "Russkaja poèzija: Obzor." In *Al'manaxi izdatel'stva Al'ciona*, Vol. I (M, 1914).

Xudakov, S. "Literatura. Xudožestvennaja kritika. Disputy i doklady." In *Oslinyj xvost i Mišen'* (M, 1913).

Zakrževskij, Aleksandr. *Rycari bezumija*. Kiev, 1914.

POSTREVOLUTIONARY

Aksenov, I. A. "K likvidacii futurizma," *Pečat' i Revoljucija*, no. 3 (1921).

Bagrij, A. V. *Russkaja literatura XIX-pervoj poloviny XX veka*. Baku, 1926.

Bogdanovič, Nana. *Futurizam Marinetija i Majakovskog*. Belgrade, 1963.

Bowra, C. M. *The Creative Experiment*. London, 1949.

Brjusov, Valerij. "Včera, segodnja i zavtra russkoj poèzii," *Pecat' i Revoljucija*, no. 7 (1922).

Erlich, Victor. "Russian Poets in Search for Poetics," *Comparative Literature*, IV (1952).

Gorbačev, G. *Sovremennaja russkaja literatura*. L, 1928.

Gorlov, N. *Futurizm i revoljucija*. M, 1924.

Gusman, Boris. *Sto poètov*. M, 1923.

Ivanov-Razumnik, R. "Duša futurizma," *Kniga i Revoljucija*, no. 7 (1921).

———. "'Misterija' ili 'buff'?" In his *Tvorčestvo i kritika* (P, 1922).

Kogan, P. S. *Literatura velikogo desjatiletija*. M, 1927.

Lehrmann, Graziella. *De Marinetti à Maiakovski*. Fribourg, 1942.

L'vov-Rogačevskij, V. "Futurizm," *Literaturnaja ènciklopedija: Slovar' literaturnyx terminov v dvux tomax*, II (M-L, 1925).

———. *Novejšaja russkaja literatura*. Several editions.

Malaxov, Sergej. "Čto takoe futurizm," *Oktjabr'*, no. 2 (1927).

———. "Futuristy," *Na Literaturnom Postu*, no. 3 (1927).

———. "Zaumniki," *ibid.*, no. 7–8 (1926).

Markov, Vladimir, "Der russische Futurismus," *Lexikon der Weltliteratur im 20. Jahrhundert*. Vol. 1. Freiburg, 1960.

———. "Mysli o russkom futurizme," *Novyj Žurnal*, no. 38 (1954).

Mixajlovskij, B. *Russkaja literatura XX v. s 90-x gg. do 1917*. M, 1939.

Pjast, V. *Vstreči*. L, 1929.

Plisko, N. "Futurizm russkij," *Bol'šaja Sovetskaja Ènciklopedija*. 1st ed. M, 1935.

Poggioli, Renato. *The Poets of Russia, 1890–1930*. Cambridge, Mass., 1960.

Red'ko, A. *Literaturno-xudožestvennye iskanija v konce XIX-načale XX v.* L, 1924.

Rozanov, Ivan. *Russkie liriki.* M, 1929.

Sajanov, Vissarion. *Očerki po istorii russkij poèzii XX veka.* L, 1929.

Selivanoskij, A. *Očerki po istorii russkoj sovetskoj poèzii.* M, 1936.

Spasskij, Sergej. "Itogi futurizma," *Zarevo Zavodov,* no. 2 (1919).

Stepanov, N. "Poèzija buržuaznogo upadka." In *Istorija russkoj literatury,* Vol. X (M-L, 1954).

Šamurin, E. I. "Osnovnye tečenija v dorevoljucionnoj russkoj poèzii." *In* I. Ežov and E. Šamurin, *Russkaja poèzija XX veka* (M, 1925).

Šapirstejn-Lers, Ja. E. *Obščestvennyj smysl russkogo literaturnogo futurizma.* M, 1922.

Tschižewskij, D. *Anfänge des russischen Futurismus.* Wiesbaden, 1963.

———. "O poèzii futurizma," *Novyj Žurnal,* no. 73 (1963).

Tynjanov, Jurij. *Arxaisty i novatory.* L, 1929.

Vinokur, G. I. "Rečevaja praktika futuristov." In *Kul'tura jazyka* (M, 1932).

Volkov, A. A. *Russkaja literatura XX v.* M. Several editions.

Xardžiev, N., and V. Trenin. "Kommentarii," *Literaturnoe Nasledstvo,* II (1932).

REFERENCE WORKS

Beleckij, A. I., *et al. Novejšaja russkaja literatura.* Ivanovo-Voznesensk, 1927.

Brodskij, N. L., and N. P. Sidorov. *Ot simvolizma do 'Oktjabrja.'* M, 1924.

Koz'min, B. P. *Pisateli sovremennoj èpoxi.* M, 1928.

Literaturno-xudožestvennye al'manaxi i sborniki. Vols. I–III. M, 1957–1960.

Markov, Vladimir, ed. *Manifesty i programmy russkix futuristov.* Munich, 1967.

Muratova, K., ed. *Istorija russkoj literatury konca XIX–načala XX v. Bibliografičeskij spravočnik.* M-L, 1963.

Nikitina, E. *Russkaja literatura ot simvolizma do našix dnej.* M, 1926.

Polonskij, V. *Očerki literaturnogo dviženija revoljucionnoj èpoxi.* M-L, 1928.

Speranskij, V. D. *Istoriko-kritičeskie materialy po literature, Vypusk 3: Majakovskij, Futurizm* (M, 1925).

Vitman, A. M., *et al. Vosem' let russkoj xudožestvennoj literatury.* M-L, 1926.

Vladislavlev, I. *Literatura velikogo desjatiletija.* M-L, 1928.

———. *Russkie pisateli.* L, 1924.

ITALIAN FUTURISM AND MARINETTI

Aleramo, S. "Futurizm v Italii," *Russkaja Mysl'*, no. 12 (1913). Trans. from Italian.

Baudoin de Courtenay, I. A. "Galopom vpered," *Vestnik Znanija*, no. 5 (1914).

Burljuk, David, et al. "K priezdu Marinetti," *Nov'*, Feb. 5 (18), 1914, no. 19. See also other letters to the editor by futurists in the issues of January 26, 30, and February 15 of the same paper.

Buzzi, Paolo. "Pis'ma iz Italii," *Apollon*, no. 9 (1910), no. 5 (1911), nos. 1, 5 (1913).

Color and Rhyme (N.Y.), no. 55 (1964).

Čulkov, Georgij. "Marinetti," *Včera i segodnja*. M, 1916. Also in *Naši Sputniki* (M, 1922).

Čužoj. "Moskovskie otkliki, Šampanskogo butylka," *Reč'*, Jan. 30 (Feb. 12), 1914.

Ėjxengolc, M. "Marinetti," *Literaturnaja Ėnciklopedija*, VI (M, 1932).

Ėrenburg, I. "F.-T. Marinetti." In his *Poèty Francii* (Paris, 1914).

Gorlov, N. *Futurizm i revoljucija*. M, 1924.

Kul'bin, N. "Pis'mo v redakciju," *Reč'*, Jan. 30, 1914.

Kuzmin, M. "Pis'ma iz Italii: Futuristy," *Apollon*, no. 9 (1910).

Livšic, B. *Polutoraglazyj strelec*. L, 1933.

Lunačarskij, A. "Futuristy," *Kievskaja Mysl'*, May 17, 1913.

———. "Sverxskul'ptor i sverxpoèt," *Den'*, July 29, 1913.

"Marinetti in Russia," *Lacerba*, April 1, 1914.

Merežkovskij, D. "Ešče odin šag grjaduščego Xama," *Russkoe Slovo*, July 29, 1914. Also see his *Nevoennyj dnevnik* (P, 1917).

Mixal'či, D. "Futurizm v literature," *Bol'šaja Sovetskaja Ėnciklopedija* (1st ed.), LIX (M, 1935).

Osorgin, M. "Ital'janskij futurizm," *Vestnik Evropy*. no. 2 (1914).

Panda. "Futuristy," *Večer*, March 8, 1949.

Percov, V. "Marinetti—fašist i futurist," *Krasnaja Nov'*, no. 8 (1927).

Pervuxin, M. "Psevdofuturizm," *Sovremennyj Mir*, no. 3 (1914).

Potapova, Z. M. "Marinetti," *Kratkaja Literaturnaja Ėnciklopedija*, IV (M, 1967).

Rabov, R. "Futurizm: Novaja literaturnaja škola," *Vestnik literatury t-va Vol'f*, no. 5 (1909).

Rozenfel'd, I. "Intuitivizm i futurizm," *Maski*, no. 6 (1913–14).

Slonim, M. "Novaja ital'janskaja literatura." In *Literaturnyj al'manax "Grani,"* Vol. III (Berlin, 1923).

Sapošnikov, B. "Futurism i teatr," *Maski*, no. 7–8 (1912–13).

Šeršenevič, V. Preface to Marinetti, *Bitva u Tripoli* (M, 1915).
Tasteven, G. *Futurizm*. M, 1914.
Tugendxol'd, Ja. "Pis'mo iz Moskvy," *Apollon*, no. 3 (1914).
————. "Zapozdalyj futurizm," *Reč'*, no. 31 (Feb. 1 [14], 1914).
Xardžiev, N. "Turne kubo-futuristov 1913-1914 gg." In *Majakovskij: Materialy i issledovanija* (M, 1940).
See also individual issues of the newspapers that covered Marinetti's visit to Russia from January 26 to February 14, 1914: *Birževye Vedomosti; Den'; Golos Moskvy; Moskovskie Vedomosti; Nov'; Novoe Vremja; Peterburgskaja Gazeta; Peterburgskij Listok; Reč'; Russkie Vedomosti; Russkoe Slovo; Večernee Vremja; Večernie Izvestija;* and *Teatr i Iskusstvo.*

ITALIAN FUTURIST MANIFESTOS IN RUSSIAN TRANSLATION

Marinetti. *Manifesty ital'janskogo futurizma*. M, 1914.
————. *Futurizm*. P, 1914.
Sojuz molodeži, no. 2 (1912).
Sovremennyj Zapad, nos. 1, 3 (1922).
Tasteven, G. *Futurizm*. M, 1914.
Teatr i Iskusstvo, no. 5 (1914).

FUTURISM AND THE ARTS

Andersen, M. "Reakcionnoe iskusstvo," *Sovremennik*, no. 4 (1914).
Burljuk, D. "Filonov," *Color and Rhyme*, no. 55.
Color and Rhyme, nos. 43, 56.
Evreinov, N. *Original o portretistax*. M, 1922.
Glagol', S. "Vyroždenie ili vozroždenie," *Žatva*, no. 5 (1914).
Gray, Camilla. *The Great Experiment: Russian Art, 1863-1922*. London, 1962.
Jakobson, Roman. "Futurizm," *Iskusstvo*, no. 7 (Aug. 2, 1919).
Larionov, M., *et al.* "Počemu my raskrašivaemsja," *Argus* (Christmas issue, 1913).
Makovskij, S. " 'Novoe' iskusstvo i 'četvertoe' izmerenie," *Apollon*, no. 7 (1913).
Oslinyj xvost i Mišen'. M, 1913.
Radlov, N. *O futurizme*. P, 1923.
Red'ko, A. "Sredi ustremlenij k neponjatnomu i nepostižnomu," *Russkoe Bogatstvo*, no. 3 (1914).
————. "U podnožija afrikanskogo idola," *ibid.*, no. 7 (1913).
Sojuz molodeži (P), nos. 1, 2, 3 (1912-1913).

448

Ternovec, B. "Futurizm," *Bolšaja Sovetskaja Ènciklopedija* (1st ed.), LIX (M, 1935).

Vološin, M. *O Repine.* M, 1913.

Xardžiev, N. "Majakovskij i živopis'." In *Majakovskij: Materialy i issledovanija* (M, 1940).

INDEX